CONTEMPORARY ORGANIZATION DEVELOPMENT

CURRENT THINKING and APPLICATIONS

Edited by

D. D. Warrick, Editor

University of Colorado at Colorado Springs

Past National Chairperson,
OD Division of the Academy of Management

Sponsored by the

American Society for Training and Development

Scott, Foresman and Company

Glenview, Illinois   London, England

For my wife, Anna, and our new son, Ryan

Library of Congress Cataloging in Publication Data
Main entry under title:

Contemporary organization development.

Includes bibliographies and index.
1. Organizational change—Addresses, essays, lectures.
I. Warrick, D. D.   II. American Society for Training and Development
HD58.8.C655 1985   658.4′06   84-10700
ISBN 0-673-18032-8

The authors and publisher would like to thank all sources for the use of their material.
The credit lines for copyrighted materials appearing in this work appear below and are
continued on page 488, which is to be considered an extension of the copyright page.

2-11, Copyright © 1982 by Marvin R. Weisbord; (**3-4,** From *The Cat In the Hat* by Dr.
Seuss. Copyright © 1957 by Random House); **28-41,** Copyright © 1984 by Peter B. Vaill;
42-48, Copyright © 1984 by Leonard D. Goodstein; **49-56,** Copyright © 1984 by Glenn H.
Varney; **57-68,** Copyright © 1983 by Kurt Motamedi; **69-75,** Copyright © 1983 by
Thomas G. Cummings (**71, 73,** Illustrations appear courtesy of *Outlook*, no. 6, pp. 40–41,
a magazine for the international business community published by Booz Allen &
Hamilton, Inc.); **76-85,** Copyright © 1983 by Philip H. Mirvis; **86-97,** Copyright © 1984
by Virginia E. Schein; **98-113,** Copyright © 1984 by Robert T. Golembiewski (**106-7,**
From "Efficacy of Three Versions of One Burnout Measure: MBI as Total Score, Sub-
scale Scores, or Phases?" by Robert T. Golembiewski and Robert Munzenruder in *The
Journal of Health and Human Resources Administration,* vol. 4, no. 4, 1981, pp. 228–46);
114-22, Copyright © 1984 by Craig C. Lundberg; **123-37,** Copyright © 1982 by Phillip L.
Hunsaker; **138-51,** Copyright © 1984 by Alice G. Sargent (**144,** From *The Competent
Manager* by Richard E. Boyatzis. Copyright © 1982, John Wiley & Sons, Inc. Reprinted
by permission of John Wiley & Sons, Inc.; **149,** Adapted by permission of the publisher,
from *The Androgynous Manager,* by Alice G. Sargent, p. 42. Copyright © 1983, 1981 by
AMACOM, a division of American Management Associations, New York. All rights
reserved; **150,** Copyright © 1981 by Neale Clapp & Peter Block, Block Petrella
Associates); **152-65,** Copyright © 1984 by Ralph H. Kilmann; **166-79,** Copyright © 1984
by Gordon A. Walter & Stephen E. Marks; **180-94,** Copyright © 1984 by Stanley D.
Truskie (**186-89,** Illustrations from the Developmental Management Survey,

credit lines continue on page 488

Contributors

John Adams
Consultant

Ronald N. Ashkenas
Robert H. Schaffer & Associates

Robert R. Blake
Scientific Methods, Inc.

Richard E. Boyatzis
McBer and Company

Ronald J. Burke
York University

Susan Claire
Claire Communications

Lora Colflesh
TRW

Cary L. Cooper
University of Manchester,
Institute of Science and Technology

Thomas G. Cummings
University of Southern California

Eleanor Fisher-Quigley
FAA Executive School

Wendell L. French
University of Washington

Robert T. Golembiewski
University of Georgia and
University of Calgary

Leonard D. Goodstein
University Associates

Ricky W. Griffin
Texas A&M University

Joan Harkness
El Camino Hospital

Phillip L. Hunsaker
University of San Diego

Todd D. Jick
York University

Coeleen Kiebert
Sentient Systems, Inc.

Ralph H. Kilmann
University of Pittsburgh

Paul R. Lawrence
Harvard University

Gordon L. Lippitt
George Washington University

Craig C. Lundberg
University of Southern California

Newton Margulies
University of California, Irvine

Stephen E. Marks
University of British Columbia,
Vancouver

Lynda McDermott
Main Hurdman

Philip H. Mirvis
Boston University

Kurt Motamedi
Pepperdine University

Jane S. Mouton
Scientific Methods, Inc.

Joseph S. Murphy
CAM Management Consultants

William A. Pasmore
Case Western Reserve University

Thomas H. Patten, Jr.
Michigan State University

Jerry I. Porras
Stanford University

Alice Sargent
Consultant

Marshall Sashkin
University of Maryland

Virginia E. Schein
Bernard M. Baruch College,
City University of New York

Jane Schmithorst
Naval Aviation Executive Institute

Abraham Shani
California Polytechnic University,
San Luis Obispo

Mel R. Spehn
Organizational Effectiveness
Center and School,
Department of the Army

John T. Thompson
David Powell, Inc.

Paul D. Tolchinsky
Creative Work-Life Systems

Stanley D. Truskie
Management Science & Development

Peter B. Vaill
George Washington University

Glenn H. Varney
Bowling Green State University

Gordon A. Walter
University of British Columbia,
Vancouver

Marvin R. Weisbord
Block-Petrella-Weisbord

Joe Wexler
Geosource Inc.

Richard W. Woodman
Texas A&M University

Preface

Contemporary Organization Development: Current Thinking and Applications began as a project initiated by the Executive Committee of the OD Division of the American Society for Training and Development (ASTD). My goal was to compile a set of original papers from the leaders in the field of OD that provided OD students, practitioners, human resource professionals, and progressive managers with a cutting-edge awareness of what is happening in OD. The contributing authors exceeded my expectations and helped me produce a book that more than fulfilled my original goal and that I hope will make a valuable contribution to the field of OD.

In our turbulent environment—characterized by rapid change, new attitudes and values, increased competition, and concerns about productivity and quality of work life—OD has emerged as a relevant and hot topic as organizations are seeking new ways to remain vital and to manage change. In less than two decades OD has grown from an obscure field practiced by a handful of pioneers to a field that is considered to provide essential knowledge for human resource professionals. OD is becoming accepted as an important subject in management curricula. Progressive managers increasingly consider OD interventions and strategies to be important parts of their management expertise. Add to these changes the growth of OD on a worldwide basis and the continually expanding applications of OD, and one begins to gain a perspective of just how rapidly the field is growing and changing.

As a relatively new field, OD has already provided needed alternatives for developing healthy and effective organizations. It also provides a much needed systems approach to managing the human resource function and helps integrate behavioral-science knowledge and skills. However, while OD is enjoying a period of rapid growth, it is also going through a period of upheaval and reevaluation. Basic definitions and theories are being reexamined, and new ones developed. New applications are being explored. Research that substantiates or refutes OD theory and practices is being conducted. These rapid developments have made the timing right for reflecting on this dynamic, relevant-for-the-times field.

Contemporary Organization Development is divided into three parts. Part 1 examines OD theory, while Parts 2 and 3 explore OD applications and OD research respectively. The book takes a broad approach in order to allow for a wide divergence of opinions about OD. This choice reflects one of the current developments in OD—broader definitions and applications. Though OD traditionalists may question the inclusion of some of the topics, the book is intended to cover current applications of traditional OD approaches as well as stimulate new discussions and ideas about OD.

The distinguished contributors for this collection were encouraged to present the latest information about OD developments based on their personal experiences, observations, and scholarly research in the field. All of the contributors were encouraged to be creative and to take risks in expressing their ideas about the current state of OD so as to present a thorough discussion of the foundations of OD and the most controversial issues in the profession. The issues raised range from the very definition of OD itself to the future changes expected in the workplace in general and in the roles of women and minorities in particular.

The result is a collection that begins with a brief history of OD, explores the current topics in human management—including quality of work life, organizational stress, managerial and consultant competence, job redesign, productivity, quality circles, affirmative action, and team building—and finally identifies areas in OD that should be explored further in the future.

I hope that you will enjoy reading and reflecting on this book as much as I enjoyed putting it together. A pleasant surprise that occurred upon completing the book was the realization that it provides in-depth coverage of the most traditional OD topics as well as the latest developments. Should you like to share your observations on the book or ideas on OD, I would welcome your comments as we all try to keep up-to-date on current developments in organization development. Write to: Marketing Manager; Professional Publishing Group; Scott, Foresman and Company; 1900 East Lake Avenue; Glenview, IL 60025.

Acknowledgments

I would like to thank my wife, Anna, who played a major role in helping me put the book together. Anna is a marvel! She made her valuable contribution while also producing and managing our latest arrival, Ryan Matthew Warrick, who has brought considerable joy to our lives. In addition, I would like to thank my editor at Scott, Foresman, Craig Pugh. Craig is a thorough professional who was a delight to work with. Finally, I would also like to thank Richard Staron who, at Scott, Foresman, managed this book to completion.

DDW

Contents

Part 1 OD Theory   1

1   The Cat in the Hat Breaks Through:
Reflections on OD's Past, Present, and Future
Marvin R. Weisbord   2

2   The Emergence and Early History of Organization
Development with Reference to Influences upon
and Interactions Among Some of the Key Actors
Wendell L. French   12

3   OD as a Scientific Revolution
Peter B. Vaill   28

4   Values, Truth, and Organization Development
Leonard D. Goodstein   42

5   OD Professionals: The Route to Becoming a Professional
Glenn H. Varney   49

6   Transorganization Development:
Developing Relations Among Organizations
Kurt Motamedi   57

7   Designing Work for Productivity and Quality of Work Life
Thomas G. Cummings   69

8   OD vs. QWL
Philip H. Mirvis   76

9   Organizational Realities: The Politics of Change
        Virginia E. Schein   86

10 Enriching the Theory and Practice of Team Building:
        Instrumentation for Diagnosis and Design Alternatives
        Robert T. Golembiewski   98

11 Microinterventions for Team Development:
        Toward Their Appreciation and Use
        Craig C. Lundberg   114

12 Strategies for Organizational Change:
        Role of the Inside Change Agent
        Phillip L. Hunsaker   123

13 Competency Based Management as an OD Intervention
        Alice G. Sargent   138

14 Understanding Matrix Organization: Keeping the Dialectic
        Alive and Well
        Ralph H. Kilmann   152

15 The Third Wave of Experiential Learning
        Gordon A. Walter & Stephen E. Marks   166

16 Improving Organizational Performance Through
        Development Management
        Stanley D. Truskie   180

Part 2   OD Applications   195

17 Effective Use of Task Forces in the OD Process
        Gordon L. Lippitt   196

18 A Comprehensive Approach to Planning an OD/QWL Strategy
        William A. Pasmore   204

19 Involving Employees in Productivity and QWL Improvements:
        What OD Can Learn from the Manager's Perspective
        Todd D. Jick & Ronald N. Ashkenas   218

20 An Organizational Development Approach to the Planning and Implementation of New Technology
Newton Margulies & Lora Colflesh 231

21 Career and Life Planning Program Designs in Organizational Development
Thomas H. Patten, Jr. 253

22 Organization Development Approaches: Analysis and Application
Marshall Sashkin, Ronald J. Burke, Paul R. Lawrence, & William A. Pasmore 264

23 Organization Development Strategies for Effective Management of Cockpit Crises
Robert R. Blake & Jane S. Mouton 281

24 Improving the Health and Stress of Federal Workers
John D. Adams, Eleanor Fisher-Quigley, & Jane Schmithorst 289

25 Utilizing Task Redesign Strategies Within Organization Development Programs
Ricky W. Griffin & Richard W. Woodman 308

26 Job Analysis System: A Model and Technology for Human Resources and Organization Development
Lynda C. McDermott 320

27 Quality Circles: Productivity with an OD Perspective
Susan Claire & Joe Wexler 329

28 Executive Profiles: A Feedback System for Senior Executives
John T. Thompson 340

29 Affirmative Action: A Guide to Systems Change for Managers
Alice G. Sargent 350

30 Profitable Decision Making
Joseph S. Murphy 365

Part 3 OD Research   381

31 Stream Analysis: A Method for Decomposing Organization
Development Interventions
Jerry I. Porras, Joan Harkness, & Coeleen Kiebert   382

32 The Search for Consultant Competencies
Mel R. Spehn   402

33 Building on Competence: The Effective Use of Managerial Talent
Richard E. Boyatzis   414

34 Organization Inquiry: Towards a New Model
of the Action Research Process
Abraham Shani & William A. Pasmore   438

35 Coping with Organizational Stress
Cary L. Cooper   449

36 Measuring Program Implementation, Adoption, and Intermediate
Goal Attainment: Missing Links in OD Program Evaluations
Philip H. Mirvis   461

37 Expectation Effects: Implications for Organization
Development Interventions
Richard W. Woodman & Paul D. Tolchinsky   477

Index   489

Part One

OD Theory

1 The Cat in the Hat Breaks Through: Reflections on OD's Past, Present, and Future

Marvin R. Weisbord

ABSTRACT

This paper contains several thoughts I have been wanting to express for some time. Reading Frederick Taylor I found the right framework, the "Gresham's Law" of organizational life—that technological values tend to drive out social values in the workplace. OD practice evolved from the tension between democracy and science in the workplace. However, OD'ers are just as seducible as industrial engineers by technology's siren songs. I believe we can't resolve our dilemmas with fancier techniques and novel skills. To be a whole practice we need to reaffirm the values of the pioneers of action research, socio-technical systems, and survey feedback—who believed in more open systems and societies, and a democratic approach to work life. Social change is sweeping the world. We will have to rethink every form of work—just as Taylor and his disciples did—and the *way* we do it, as much as *what* we do, will be the measure of our success.

AUTHOR BACKGROUND

Marvin R. Weisbord has been an organization development consultant since 1969. He is the Senior Vice President with Block-Petrella-Weisbord, working mainly on the reorganization and redesign of work in large systems. Mr. Weisbord is a member of the NTL Institute and Certified Consultants International and has staffed many consultant training workshops in the United

Adapted from a keynote address, OD Network meeting, Lake Geneva, Wisconsin, October 5, 1982. From a work-in-progress, *Organization Development Consulting: Practice Theories in Action.* (The conference theme was "Breakthroughs," and the speaker was asked to discuss OD history and future prospects in this light.)

States and abroad. For six years he was an associate editor of the *Journal of Applied Behavioral Science,* and has written widely on the theory and practice of organization development, and is the author of *Organizational Diagnosis: A Workbook of Theory and Practice.*

A few years ago I was asked to participate in a Delphi study of OD's future, which included questions on what skills would be needed. I found my mind reeling when I learned that my colleagues and I had brainstormed 150 skills, finally boiling the list down to fifty "Ideal Core Skills" and thirty-four "Advanced Skills for Future OD Practitioners."[1] The final list included such "skills" as management policy and strategy, transorganization theory, job measurement, operations research, marketing, accounting, systems engineering, cultural anthropology, finance, and hypnosis. In case you're beginning to feel obsolete, there are also old friends like power, conflict, leadership, and active listening.

Whenever I come across one of these all-inclusive OD future scans, I think of a story I used to read my kids when all of us were a lot younger. It's Dr. Suess' wonder fable, *The Cat in the Hat Comes Back.* Let me give you a brief synopsis.

Two small children are left alone by their mother to shovel snow. They are visited by a mischievous cat in a high top hat, who enters the house uninvited, takes a bath, and leaves a "pink cat ring" in the tub. The kids order him to clean it up. No sweat, says the cat, grabbing their mother's best dress and swiping the spot away. Clean tub. Messy dress. Don't worry, says the cat: to takes spots off a dress you hit it against a wall. Deftly he transfers the spots to the wall. Next he demonstrates that shoes take spots off walls, rugs take spots off shoes, and that to take spots off rugs you need exactly the right bed. (This is called having an intervention for every contingency.)

Gleefully, he slaps the rug on "dad's bed." Suddenly, the cat looks crestfallen. Dad's bed, he admits, "is not the right kind." He needs *help* to clean this bed. He lifts his hat and reveals Little Cat A, who has under his hat B, who has under his hat C. They proceed to chase the spot all over the house, pursued by the frantic children. Finally, they chase the red stuff outside. Now the house is clean but the environment—oops, I mean the yard—is a mess.

The cats grow more determined. Each in turn removes a hat, revealing an alphabet of tinier and tinier cats. They attack the red snow spots with popguns, lawnmowers, rakes, shovels—spreading it further and wider until the whole yard becomes a red blob. The cat goes at last to his tiniest helper, Little Cat Z. This last is too small to see, but in his hat he has a substance called "Voom." Voom, we learn, "is so hard to get, you never saw anything like it I bet." He instructs Z (Theory Z?) to unleash the Voom.

The Voom goes VOOOOOMMMMM!

The red spots disappear in a swirling vortex. The yard is restored, better in fact because the walk has been neatly cleared from street to front door. "If you ever have spots now and then," says the cat magnanimously, "I will be very happy to come here again." The awestruck children, mouths open, watch silently as the cat walks away. The narrator says,

Now, don't ask me what Voom is,
I never will know.
But, boy! Let me tell you
It *does* clean up snow![2]

That, roughly speaking, is what much of our literature says is the definition of Organization Development. Whenever I read about some wonderful new OD technology, or about the 84 skills we're all going to need in the future (a proposition so preposterous I shudder at my own complicity in advancing it), I'm reminded of the Cat in the Hat. Which brings me to the theme of this essay. What I want to discuss here is a kind of "Gresham's Law" of organizational life—the way technological values tend to drive out social values in the workplace.

OD folks are not exempt from this law either. Our favorite conferences focus on new technologies, and you can go through a lot of case studies and symposiums at the OD Network, lapping up new ways to collect data, new techniques for unleashing the right side of the brain, and new strategies for holding hands with those whose hands hold the levers of power, without ever running into those few values which all of our magic methodologies were supposed in the first place to support. There is a tension everywhere between technology and democracy, between technical and social values. And the VOOM game, even if your racket is behavioral science, rather than the old-fashioned kind, is terribly seductive.

To make the point, I want to speculate about an aspect of OD that has excited me for nearly twenty years—the design of work and, more importantly, the processes by which we organize and reorganize it. Our successes and failures hinge largely, I think, on the redistribution of labor and rewards in organizations, for it is the division of labor and reward which influences the normative behavior we seek to change or preserve. I want to look at work redesign—past, present, and future. So climb into the time machine with me, and let's start this trip by leaping back to the turn of the century—no airplanes, no cars to speak of, no radio or TV, no Pac-Man, and certainly no OD.

We find ourselves well into the industrial revolution, and we are witnessing a major breakthrough in the performance of work. The setting is the factory, where our ancestors, at least some of ours, are busy remaking society with the tools of—quaint phrase now—"the machine age." The innovator's name is Frederick Taylor. He is creating the field of industrial engineering—harnessing science to productivity without reference to democracy, an American value which will be a long time influencing American industry. Taylor is systematically investigating the one best way, consistent with human capability, to do everything—from drilling holes to shoveling sand.

We don't talk much about Taylor in OD circles, except to strike terror into the hearts of small children and human resource managers. I became interested in him as a result of some work my company has been doing with Bethlehem Steel Corporation—where some of Taylor's early experiments, in the most effective way to load pig iron, were conducted starting about 1899.[3]

Few people are neutral about Taylor. He has been written about as an agent of the devil, hell-bent to turn workers into machines,[4] while Peter Drucker has argued that Taylor, among all his contemporaries, truly deserved the title "humanist."[5] From my own perspective, I think he held a number of assumptions and values widely shared in the OD world. Indeed, though we may be loathe to admit it, I imagine we inherited some of our cherished practices directly from him. Taylor believed, for example, that productivity is closely related to clear tasks and clear goals. He believed that the performance of work should be based on scientific principles derived from firsthand study of human nature and human motivation. He also believed in matching the person to the job—the more complex the task, the more skilled the person required.

He encouraged worker suggestions. He was opposed to dictatorial behavior. Taylor believed in letting knowledge, proof, and facts—not the authority or prejudices of the boss—determine the best way to do work.[6] In this he would be echoed a quarter century later by an early humanizer of work, the great teacher Mary Parker Follett, whose concept of the "law of the situation" would later influence many people in our field, notably Rensis Likert.[7]

Taylor, like many of us, saw worker restriction of output (employees deliberately holding back ideas, skills, and energy) as a consequence of poor management, not worker inferiority. He believed in having workers trained by experts thoroughly familiar with the job, rather than throwing them into the water to see whether they sink or swim. He advocated standardized tools and equipment to match human capability. Today we call that *ergonomics,* and it's an important factor in the electronic office. He believed in giving people feedback on their performance, a central tenet of quality circles and all systems of participative mangement.

Taylor believed, as do many of us, that labor strife was not inevitable—an extraordinary view in light of the violent, bitter, sometimes murderous relations between employers and employees eighty years ago. He argued that raising output and cutting costs would make possible higher wages, a view embodied in labor/management cooperation in many industries.

He thought the most important motivator was money, certainly true in the factories of his day, and still true for many people on the lower rungs of the economic ladder—a conclusion Abraham Maslow would applaud.

In short, Taylor sought humane and sensible antidotes to the degradation of work which, like smog and pollution, was an early by-product of the industrial revolution. He did not impose that revolution, with its machine pacing and assembly lines, any more than OD consultants are imposing the current one, with its banks of computer terminals and communications links.

We were not, as some romantics would have it, a society of innocent artisans before Taylor. We were a society of growing inequity, sweatshops, brutal working conditions; and he wanted, with all the tools of science and engineering then available, to do something about that. One of his contemporary champions was attorney Louis Brandeis, a social activist and later Supreme Court Justice, who coined the term *scientific management* to lend respectability to Taylor's work.

Taylor also had many ideas that don't stand up so well to modern scrutiny. He had an extremely narrow view of human capability. While his schemes always included a chance for workers to earn more money, he held firmly to the principle that management, not the workers, had to structure every task, based on systematic study by trained engineers—the people with the stopwatches. Worker suggestions, yes; problem solving, no. That was for experts only.

Taylor also advocated individual work. He opposed group tasks and group incentives. He broke jobs into their smallest feasible components, arguing that the greater the specialization, the shorter the learning time to achieve competence and skill. He had no concept of the power of interdependence, mutual problem solving, joint decision making. These matters would not become the subject of systematic research for many more decades.

We know enough now to realize that, even at his worst, Taylor was not all wrong. After all, it's we OD consultants who run around insisting that not *all* tasks require participation, that the fastest way to solve some problems is to find the expert. (*We* call that "using everybody's resources.") Of course, we also recognize the peculiar and unpredictable synergy among well-motivated workers. We know now that performance will never be a wholly rational process.

In retrospect, Taylor was a Paul Bunyan of the left brain, an apostle of closed-system methods before open systems were understood. He was right for his time, though, and he devised a powerful prescription for improving work. Peter Drucker credits Taylor with having as much influence on the modern world as Karl Marx and Sigmund Freud. Taylorism endures wherever repetitive work is performed.

Many of Taylor's descendents, of course, picked up on his technologies without internalizing his values. So Taylorism has become synonymous with speedups, employer insensitivity, and people turned into robots. I think it's more accurate to view Taylor as the true founder of the QWL movement—the first person in history to make a systematic attempt to improve both output and worklife in factories.

Now, let's leapfrog our time machine a half century, over the roaring twenties, the Great Depression, and the terrible war in which we endeavored to make not just the workplace but the whole world safe for democracy by using the tools of science. We are about to witness the birth of OD as a quasi-legitimate profession.

Our practice has been influenced by three streams of work which date from the 1940s and 1950s. One stream began after World War II in the coal mines of North West Durham, in the United Kingdom. There a group from Tavistock Institute, Eric Trist is one you probably know, began to investigate the connections between the division of labor, the equipment, and the social systems of coal miners, seeking an optimum balance that would produce the most coal and the most human satisfaction out of the same mine at the same time. They replaced

Taylor's closed-system work loop with a richer, more complete vision that went beyond economic need to the social functions of work. They came to call this approach "joint optimization"—the balancing of social and technical systems.[8]

A second stream flowed from the work of some visionary educational psychologists, led by the late Kurt Lewin. Starting in the 1930s, Lewin evolved a theory that when people participate in a study of their own behavior they are more likely to accept and act on the results. He named the method *action research*. In 1946 the state of Connecticut's Interracial Commission sponsored a conference built on this method. The question they were asking—we still are—is what sort of leadership is required to improve intergroup and race relations. They discovered, quite by accident, that people nearly always—in the words of my colleague Jim Maselko—attend "the same different meeting together." They found that group members had wholly different perceptions of training sessions from what staff had. You may say, "So what else is new?" I can only tell you that in the mid-1940s trading these perceptions—processing the meeting—provided a level of energy, excitement, and learning heretofore unavailable in more traditional seminars.[9] I'm describing, of course, the discovery of the T-group, which led to the founding of NTL Institute, and spawned a vast social technology of experiential learning.

Finally, we come to the invention of survey data feedback by Floyd Mann and others at the University of Michigan's Institute for Social Research in the 1950s.[10] This technique, coupled to the late Rensis Likert's prescription for high performance, which he called "System 4,"[11] provided us at once with a new measurement tool, an action research method, and a process for inducing dissonance into a whole social system, causing its members to want to change it.

If we add to these Chris Argyris's powerful theory of intervention—valid data, free choice, commitment to act[12]—which was an outgrowth of the T-growth movement, I think we have the major foundations of current OD practice.

Notice, however, how quickly, when we think about these breakthroughs, the first thing that's likely to pop into our minds is technology—how to do it. This way of thinking comes so naturally to me—so much am I a child of my time—that I must stop and remind myself that the people who created our field were driven by a passionate belief in open societies, and more rational and decent relationships across lines of color, class, nationality, hierarchy, and status. They saw their new social technologies as ways to implement this belief, to join science and democracy, task and process, productivity and participation in ways no one had ever done before.

How easy it is in the age of micro-chips to become so hung up on newness in the pursuit of "desired end states" and "ideal future scenarios" that we lose touch both with our human limitations and the source of our formidable power. That power lies in our values, not our methods, in the marriage of democracy and science, and not in science, behavioral or any other kind, alone.

While many organizations struggle toward greater openness and participation—Bethlehem Steel is only one of dozens we could name—the OD profession seems to me bogged down in a mire of conflicting theories, methods, endless "discoveries" of new aspects of the human condition, new variables to work on, and new techniques by which to work them. In that respect, we're not so different from Taylor's other descendents, the industrial engineers. We too risk cutting ourselves off from our roots—important values that nourish our practice. Neither personal growth on one hand, nor productivity improvement on the other, makes sense to me without the mediating values of more open systems and more self-governance in the workplace.

The world is changing around us, and we have been for some time, I think, caught up in a very grandiose VOOM game, imagining that, if only we can combine all 84 basic and advanced skills, we will be able, simply by lifting our hats, to clean up snow. That kind of thinking is the problem, not the solution.

Today we know a great deal more about social systems than Taylor did, and a great deal more about the care and feeding of the human psyche—the complex subject of motivation. At the same time, we and our clients face all over again every dilemma of work, the workplace, and job design that faced Taylor and his contemporaries in the heyday of the first industrial revolution a century ago.

More, we are facing these problems not just on the factory floor, but in staff conference rooms and executive suites, too. Of course, the problem is not specialization this time. We solved that one brilliantly. We have specialists for anything you can name. Now the problem is cooperation, integration, and wholeness. Figuring out how to live with specialization, recognizing that whatever expertise we have is quite useless unless others can access it, is *the* dilemma of working life in our time.

To appreciate this, let me accelerate our time machine just a little way into the future to get a look at where we're heading before coming back to where we are. John Naisbitt, who forecasts the future by describing what's happening now, spots 10 "megatrends" which are remaking our world.[13] I want to highlight a few which already are affecting OD.

First, the United States is changing over from an industrial to an information-based society. Only 13% of us work in factories now in the U.S., while 60% produce or process information. It's as if, in the single global economy toward which we're moving, the United States is becoming the data-processing department, and the Far East is taking over manufacturing. (Of course, we should expect some interdepartmental squabbles.)

For every "high-tech" development, says Naisbitt, we develop a "high-touch" response—the hospice movement, for example—in reaction to complex life-support machinery that can prolong life past the point worth living. Or, to take a more mundane example, the preference of many people who *could* work at home on computer terminals, for a central office where they can use the terminals *and* can see others face-to-face.

Organizations are decentralizing everywhere. Consumers demand more choice and workers more influence on the workplace. We are moving from hierarchies to networks. "The computer is smashing the Soviet pyramid," writes one business editor of this trend, "and the same thing is happening in the U.S. corporation. . . . the way people are managed in organizations will never be the same."[14]

Well it doesn't take a three-day lab in values clarification to see that a great deal of the workworld will move, is moving, in directions members of this profession have espoused for some time—toward decentralization, greater openness, more influence, freer expression, freer choice. "Democracy," Warren Bennis, one of our elder statespersons, wrote prophetically nearly twenty years ago, "becomes a functional necessity whenever a social system is competing for survival under conditions of chronic change."[15] Democratic values are never secure. They must be fought for over and over again. What is striking to me is that today, true to Bennis's prophecy, we are joined in the battle by the steel and auto industries and large corporations in many fields.

However, the road to good intentions, as my old friend Milton Mayer used to say, is paved with hell. We have a lot to learn about the linkage of democracy and technology in the workplace. Let us program our time machine for a soft landing in the here-and-now in Anywhere, U.S.A.

The office of the "future," we learn, has arrived already. The computer terminal, hooked up to a telephone, and interconnected to the photocopier, becomes the locus of much repetitive and potentially stressful work. While robots take over factories, we are left with perplexing questions about how to organize medical care, education, government services, software companies, research laboratories. We have many questions Taylor never asked and were he alive could not answer, though perhaps he would appreciate action research as an elegant way to answer them.

While new models abound (even, many claim, whole new paradigms), old ways of working are going to take a long time to unlearn. For Taylorism—at least its organizational partner, bureaucracy—has been carried far beyond the factory floor. In many places it persists as functional management that pits department against department, specialist against specialist, and adds layers of coordinators and assistants who fight to maintain control, pulled one way by the advance of knowledge, another by the changing whims of the customer.

Technical staff—in computers, maintenance, finance, engineering, personnel, planning, public relations, you name it, even organization development—have in many places become, sometimes willingly, sometimes unwittingly, a lot like Taylor's pig iron haulers, repeating the same techniques over and over again, having little influence on the overall course of events, knowing little about how what they do fits with what other people do, and even less about their organization's central purposes. Their biggest frustration is their inability to get other people to adapt their state-of-the-art solutions to old problems or new ones.

There's no end of work for an energetic organization developer. Creating flatter organizations is taking enormous human toll and taxing our ingenuity to the limit. Union workers, for example, are finding—once they start participating more fully in management—that work rules, job categories, incentive schemes fought for at a thousand bargaining tables make no sense anymore and will have to be revised. That is a very hard pill to swallow.

The trauma is worse for supervisors and middle managers. In more participative systems, there are fewer chances for status and advancement than there used to be. In business school, people learn how to rise to the top, and suddenly, we have fewer tops. In many industries we are facing a revision of manager expectations like nothing that has happened before. One company I know cut fourteen levels of management to seven overnight. They count on worker participation to take up the slack. As people at the bottom assume more responsibility, Taylor's managers and experts, the ones who used to make all the decisions, have a lot less direct control. There will be fewer managers, and they will have more to do. They won't be moving in nine months or a year to the next rung on the ladder. They may stay at the same level for years.

As we learn to manage all this, I believe we will make enormous contributions to the quality of worklife. Many people will find their work more interesting, more whole. Workers and managers will become more firmly connected to one another, more cognizant of their mutual stake in success and more equitably rewarded for their contributions. They will commit to purposes anchored more securely in customer need. Capable people will have jobs worthy of their talents, instead of middle-manager positions so dull and alienating that you can't blame them for chasing the next promotion.

However, with fewer upward career paths, we may have to think about managerial work the way we think about innovative factories. There, people are paid for the number of skills they acquire, not for what they happen to be doing today. A management career may consist of lateral movements—across functional specialties—instead of up the hierarchy. People will have to develop what my colleague Aubrey Cramer calls "horizontal ambition." The Japanese have something roughly akin to this and we will imitate them not because they are so successful, but because there are so few alternatives.

In the nonindustrial world we have hardly scratched the surface of potential new ways for working. The modern hospital is a hotbed of super-specialization which, even some doctors realize, will only be cured by more democracy, not more science. The need to link government more firmly to its customers—citizens and taxpayers—is enormous and growing.

Where does this leave OD? We have a tremendous lot to work on, and the only thing we bring to the party that the other specialties don't is a commitment to democratic processes for achieving desired results.

Do we wish to become one more narrow Taylor speciality, competing for attention among all the other specialties? Or will we establish a legitimate humane and sensible "third voice," supporting with our skills and ingenuity those clients who *know* that working *with* other people, face-to-face, is the only way to stop moving the mess from one place to another, the only way out of the VOOM game, the only way to make technology serve us instead of the other way around? Science begets more science; and science, we have learned, will never be enough. Our ability to *use* what we know for social good is strongly limited by our capability to trust others, which can only be developed by facing them.

My summary is brief. Our strength—the power of OD—will never be in knowing the answers, but only in showing people a practical way to find them. The antidote for technological excess is not more technique. It's more open systems, more participation, more democracy. Frederick Taylor had no way of knowing this. We do. It doesn't require eighty-four specialties to act on our knowledge. The basic OD skills, as Larry Porter pointed out recently, are few in number and easy to learn.[16] They are generalist skills. If we haven't learned them in two or three years of practice, going to more labs won't help. What we need most right now is an appreciation of our heritage and the courage of our convictions.

The dictionary definition of *breakthrough* is "a new, superior level of performance." The world of work is ready for a merger of technology and democracy.

My question is, are we?

Notes

1. Shepard, K. O., & Raia, A. P. "The OD Training Challenge." *Training and Development Journal* April 1981, pp. 90–96.
2. Seuss. *The Cat in The Hat Comes Back.* New York: Beginner Books, Inc., 1958.
3. Taylor, F. W. *Scientific Management.* New York: Harper & Brothers, 1947.
4. Braverman, H. *Labor and Monopoly Capital.* New York: Monthly Review Press, 1974.
5. Drucker, P. F. *Tasks, Responsibilities, Practices.* New York: Harper & Row, 1974.
6. Locke, E. A. "The Ideas of Frederick W. Taylor: An Evaluation." *Academy of Management Review* vol. 7, no. 1, 1982, pp. 14–24.
7. Likert, R. *New Patterns of Management.* New York: McGraw-Hill, 1961.
8. Trist, E. L.; Higgin, G. W.; Murray, H.; & Pollock, A. B. *Organizational Choice.* London: Tavistock Publications, 1963.
9. Marrow, A. J. "Events Leading to the Establishment of the National Training Laboratories." *Journal of Applied Behavioral Science* vol. 3, no. 2, 1967, pp. 144–50.
10. Mann, F. C. "Studying and Creating Change: A Means to Understanding Social Organization." In *Research in Industrial Relations,* 1957, Industrial Relations Research Association, Publication No. 17.
11. Likert, R. *The Human Organization.* New York: McGraw-Hill, 1967.
12. Argyris, C. *Intervention Theory and Method.* Reading, Mass.: Addison-Wesley, 1970.
13. Naisbitt, J. *Megatrends: Ten New Directions Transforming Our Lives.* New York: Warner Books, 1982.
14. Richman, T. "Peering Into Tomorrow." *INC.* October 1982.
15. Bennis, W. G. *Changing Organizations.* New York: McGraw-Hill, 1966.
16. Porter, L. "How Do I Think About What I Do and Why Do I Think That Way?" *OD Practitioner* vol. 14, no. 2, (September 1982) pp. 1–4.

2 The Emergence and Early History of Organization Development with Reference to Influences upon and Interactions Among Some of the Key Actors

Wendell L. French

ABSTRACT

Systematic organization development activities have at least three root stems: (1) application of laboratory training insights to organizations, (2) survey research and feedback methodology, and (3) action research. Paralleling these stems were Tavistock psychotherapeutic and consulting approaches. The key actors focused upon in this history interacted with each other and were influenced by experiences and concepts from many fields, including social and topological psychology, group dynamics, general semantics, systems theory, family group therapy, military psychiatry and psychology, psychodrama, philosophy, non-directive counseling, survey methodology, experimental and sociotechnical approaches, personnel and industrial relations, and general management.

AUTHOR BACKGROUND

Dr. Wendell French is Professor of Management and Organization at the Graduate School of Business Administration, University of Washington. He is a well-known author in the field of organization development and personnel management and has consulted with a wide variety of organizations in the United States and abroad. Professor French is a Fellow of the Academy of Management, is accredited in laboratory training and organization development by Certified Consultants International,

Adapted from Wendell L. French, "The Emergence and Early History of Organization Development with Reference to Influences upon and Interactions among Some of the Key Actors," *Group and Organization Studies,* Vol. 7, No. 3 (September 1982), pp. 261–78. Copyright © 1982 by Sage Publications, Inc. Reprinted by permission of Sage Publications, Inc.

is a licensed psychologist in the State of Washington, and has long been associated with the NTL Institute for Applied Behavioral Sciences. Professor French has served as personnel director in industry as well as Chairman of the Department of Management and Organization, and Associate Dean for Graduate Programs at the University of Washington Graduate School of Business Administration. His books include *The Personnel Management Process* and *Organization Development: Theory, Practice, and Research.*

Systematic organization development activities have a recent history, and, to use the analogy of a mangrove tree, have at least three important trunk stems. One trunk stem of OD consists of innovations in the application of laboratory training insights to complex organizations. A second major stem is survey research and feedback methodology. Both stems are intertwined with a third stem, the emergence of action research. Paralleling these stems, and to some extent linked, was the emergence of the Tavistock sociotechnical and socio-clinical approaches. The key actors focused upon in this account interacted with each other and were influenced by experiences and concepts from many fields, as we will see.

This account attempts to capture some—certainly not all—of the major highlights in the history of OD until about 1960 with a few references to events in the early and mid-1960s. A more exhaustive and lengthy history would focus on additional persons, institutions, and conceptual roots of that early period, and on a number of practitioners, theorists, and researchers whose seminal contributions were conspicuous from the 1960s through the early 1980s.

THE LABORATORY TRAINING STEM

The T-Group

One stem of OD, laboratory training, essentially unstructured small-group situations in which participants learn from their own interactions and the evolving dynamics of the group, began to develop about 1946 from various experiments in the use of discussion groups to achieve changes in behavior in back-home situations. In particular, an Inter-Group Relations workshop held at the State Teachers College in New Britain, Connecticut, in the summer of 1946 was important in the emergence of laboratory training. This workshop was sponsored by the Connecticut Interracial Commission and the Research Center for Group Dynamics, then at MIT.

The Research Center for Group Dynamics (RCGD) was founded in 1945 under the direction of Kurt Lewin, a prolific theorist, researcher, and practitioner in interpersonal, group, intergroup, and community relationships. Lewin had been recruited to MIT largely through the efforts of Douglas McGregor of the Sloan School of Management at MIT. Lewin's original staff included Marian Radke, Leon Festinger, Ronald Lippitt, and Dorwin Cartwright (Benne, Bradford, Bigg & Lippitt 1975, pp. 1–6; Marrow 1969, pp. 210–14). Lewin's field theory and his conceptualizing about group dynamics, change processes, and action research were of profound influence on the people who were associated with the various stems of OD.

The staff for the New Britain Workshop fo 1946 consisted of Kurt Lewin, Kenneth Benne, Leland Bradford, and Ronald Lippitt. Feedback at the end of each day to groups, and to group leaders and members about their individual and group behavior, stimulated great interest and appeared to produce more insight and learning than did lectures and seminars. From this experience emerged the National Training Laboratory in Group Development, which was organized by Benne, Bradford, and Lippitt (Lewin died in early 1947), and which held a three-week session during the summer of 1947 at the Gould Academy in Bethel, Maine. The work of that summer was to evolve into the National Training Laboratory, later called NTL Institute for Applied Behavioral Science, and into contemporary T-group training (Benne, et al, 1975, pp. 1–6; Marrow 1969, pp. 210–14). Out of the Bethel experiences and NTL grew a significant number of laboratory training centers sponsored by universities, such as the Western Training Laboratory sponsored by UCLA (Benne, et al, 1975, p. 6).

In addition to Lewin and his work, influences on Bradford, Lippitt, and Benne relative to the invention of the T-group and the subsequent emergence of OD included extensive experience with role playing and Moreno's psychodrama (Smith 1980, pp. 8–91). Further, Bradford and Benne had been influenced by John Dewey's philosophy of education, including concepts about learning and change and about the transactional nature of humans and our environment (Chin & Benne 1969, pp. 100–102). In addition, Benne had been influenced by the works of Mary Follett, an early management theorist, including her ideas about integrative solutions to problems in organizations (Chin & Benne 1969, p. 102).

As a footnote to the emergence of the T-group, the widespread use of flip-chart paper as a convenient way to record, retrieve, and display data in OD activities and in training sessions was invented by Ronald Lippitt and Lee Bradford during the 1946 New Britain sessions. As Lippitt reports:

> The blackboards were very inadequate, and we needed to preserve a lot of the material we produced. So I went down to the local newspaper and got a donation of the end of press runs. The paper was still on the rollers. We had a "cutting bee" of Lee, Ken, myself and several others to roll the sheets out and cut them into standard sizes that we could put up in quantity with masking tape on the blackboards and walls of the classrooms.[1]

Over the next decade, as trainers began to work with social systems of more permanency and complexity than T-groups, they began to experience considerable frustration in the transfer of laboratory behavioral skills and insights of individuals into the solution of problems in organizations. Personal skills learned in the "stranger" T-groups setting were very difficult to transfer to complex organizations. However, the training of "teams" from the same organization had emerged early at Bethel and undoubtedly was a link to the total organizational focus of Douglas McGregor, Herbert Shepard, and Robert Blake, and subsequently the focus of Richard Beckhard, Chris Argyris, Jack Gibb, Warren Bennis, and others.[2] All had been T-group trainers in NTL programs.

Douglas McGregor

Douglas McGregor, as a professor-consultant, working with Union Carbide, beginning about 1957, was one of the first behavioral scientists to begin to solve the transfer problem and to talk systematically about and to help implement the application of T-group skills to complex organizations (Beckhard, Burke & Steele 1967; Jones 1967). In collaboration with McGregor, John Paul Jones, who had come up through industrial relations at Union Carbide, and with the support of a corporate executive vice-president and director, Birny Mason, Jr. (later president of the corporation), established a small internal consulting group which in large part used behavioral science knowledge in assisting line managers and their subordinates in learning how to be more effective as groups. McGregor's ideas were a dominant force in this consulting group; other behavioral scientists who had had an influence on Jones's thinking were Rensis Likert and Mason Haire. Jones's organization was later called an "organization development group" (Burck 1965; McGregor 1967, pp. 106–10).[3]

Herbert Shepard

During the same year, 1957, Herbert Shepard, through introductions by Douglas McGregor, joined the employee relations department of Esso Standard Oil (now Exxon) as a research associate. Shepard was to have a major impact on the emergence of OD. While we will focus mainly on Shepard's work at Esso, it should also be noted that Shepard was later involved in community development activities and, in 1960, at the Case Institute of Technology, founded the first doctoral program devoted to training OD specialists.

Before joining Esso, Shepard had completed his doctorate at MIT and had stayed for a time as a faculty member in the Industrial Relations Section. Among influences on Shepard were Roethlisberger and Dixon's *Management and the Worker* (1939) and a biography of Clarence Hicks. As a consultant to Standard Oil, Hicks had helped develop participative approaches to personnel management and labor relations (French 1982, pp. 29–30). Shepard was also influenced by Farrell Toombs, who had been a counselor at the Hawthorne plant and had trained under Carl Rogers, a leading theorist and practitioner in nondirective counseling. In addition, Shepard had been heavily influenced by the writings of Kurt Lewin. NTL influence was also an important part of Shepard's background; he attended an NTL lab in 1950 and subsequently was a staff member in many of its programs.[4]

In 1958 and 1959 Shepard launched three experiments in organization development at major Esso refineries: Bayonne, Baton Rouge, and Bayway. At Bayonne an interview survey and diagnosis were made and discussed with top management, followed by a series of three-day laboratories for all members of management.

Buchanan and Shepard

Paul Buchanan, who had been using a somewhat similar approach in Republic Aviation, collaborated with Shepard at Bayonne and subsequently joined the Esso staff. Buchanan had previously been employed as a consulting psychologist by the Naval Ordinance Test Station at China Lake, California, where he had engaged the managers in a number of activities as early as 1952, including "retreats" in which they worked on interpersonal relations. (In 1961, Shepard was applying OD approaches to community development at China Lake, conducting one-week labs for cross-sections of the civilian and military populations toward the resolution of a number of community and intercommunity issues.)[5]

Blake and Shepard

At Baton Rouge, Robert Blake joined Shepard, and the two initiated a series of two-week laboratories attended by all members of "middle" management. At first an effort was made to combine the case method with the laboratory method, but the designs soon emphasized T-groups, organizational exercises, and lectures. One innovation in this training program was an emphasis on intergroup as well as interpersonal relations. Although working on interpersonal problems affecting work performance was clearly an organizational effort, between-group problem solving had even more organization development implications in that a broader and more complex segment of the organization was involved.

At Baton Rouge efforts to involve top management failed, and as a result follow-up resources for implementing organization development were not made available. By the time the Bayway program started, two fundamental OD lessons had been learned: the requirement for active involvement in and leadership of the program by top management, and the need for on-the-job application.

At Bayway there were two significant innovations. First, Shepard, Blake, and Murray Horwitz utilized the instrumented laboratory, which Blake and Jane Mouton had been developing in social psychology classes at the University of Texas and which they later developed into the Managerial Grid approach to organization development.[6] Second, at Bayway more resources were devoted to team development, consultation, intergroup conflict resolution, and so forth, than were devoted to laboratory training of "cousins," that is, organization members from different departments. As Robert Blake stated, "It was learning to *reject* T-group stranger-type labs that permitted OD to come into focus," and it was intergroup projects, in particular, that "triggered real OD."[7]

Robert Blake

As in the case of Shepard and others, influences on Robert Blake up to that point were important in the emergence of OD. While at Berea College majoring in psychology and philosophy (later M.A., University of Virginia; and Ph.D., University of Texas), Blake had been strongly influenced by the works of Korzybski and in general semantics and found that "seeing discrete things as representative of a continuous series was much more stimulating and rewarding than just seeing two things as 'opposites.'" This thinking contributed in later years to Blake's conceptualization of the Managerial Grid with Jane Mouton, and to their intergroup research on win-lose dynamics. This intergroup research and the subsequent design of their intergroup conflict management workshops were also heavily influenced by Muzafer Sherif's fundamental research on inter-group dynamics.[8] Mouton's influence on Blake's thinking and on the development of the Grid stemmed partly, in her words, "from my undergraduate work [at Texas] in pure mathematics and physics which emphasized the significance of measurement, experimental design, and a scientific approach to phenomena."[9] (Mouton later attained an M.A. from the University of Virginia and a Ph.D. from Texas.)

During World War II, Blake served in the Psychological Research Unit of the Army Air Force where he interacted with a large number of behavioral scientists, including sociologists. This contributed to his interest in "looking at the system rather the individuals within the system on an isolated one-by-one basis."[10] (This is one of probably many links between systems concepts or systems theory and OD.)

Another major influence on Blake had been the work of John Bowlby, a medical member of the Tavistock Clinic in London, who was working in family group therapy. Blake, after completing his Ph.D. work in clinical psychology, went to England for sixteen months in 1948–49 to study, observe, and to do research at Tavistock. As Blake states it,

> Bowlby had the clear notion that treating mental illness of an individual out of context was an . . . . ineffective way of aiding a person. . . . As a result, John was unprepared to see patients, particularly children, in isolation from their family settings. He would see the intact family: mother, father, siblings. . . . I am sure you can see from what I have said that if you substitute the word organization for family and substitute the concept of development for therapy, the natural next step in my mind was organization development.

Among others at Tavistock who influenced Blake were Wilfred Bion, Henry Ezriel, Eric Trist, and Elliott Jacques.[11]

After returning from Tavistock and taking an appointment at Harvard, Blake joined the staff for the summer NTL programs at Bethel. His first assignment was co-responsibility for a T-group with John R. P. French. Blake was a member of the Bethel staff from 1951 to 1957 and continued after that with NTL labs for managers at Harriman House, Harriman, New York. Among other influences on Blake were Moreno's action orientation to training through the use of psychodrama and sociodrama, and Tolman's notions of purposiveness in man.[12]

Richard Beckhard

Richard Beckhard, another major figure in the emergence and extension of the OD field, came from a career in the theatre. In his words:

> I came out of a whole different world—the theatre—and went to NTL in 1950 as a result of some discussions with Lee Bradford and Ron Lippitt. At that time they were interested in improving the effectiveness of the communications in large meetings and I became involved as head of the general sessions program. But I also got hooked on the whole movement. I made a career change and set up the meetings organization, "Conference Counselors." My first major contact was the staging of the 1950 White House conference on children and youth. . . . I was brought in to stage the large general sessions with six thousand people. . . . At the same time I joined the NTL summer staff. . . . My mentors in the field were Lee Bradford, in the early days, and Ron Lippitt and later, Ren Likert, and very particularly, Doug McGregor, who became both mentor, friend, father figure . . . and in the later years, brother. Doug and I began appearing on similar programs. One day coming back on the train from Cincinnati to Boston, Doug asked if I was interested in joining MIT. . . .

> In the period 1958–63, I had worked with him [McGregor] on two or three projects. He brought me to Union Carbide, where I replaced him in working with John Paul Jones, and later, George Murray and the group. We [also] worked together at . . . Pennsylvania Bell and . . . at General Mills.[13]

Beckhard worked with McGregor at General Mills (1959 to 1960) where McGregor was working with Dewey Balsch, vice president of personnel and industrial relations, in an attempt to facilitate "a total organizational culture change program which today might be called quality of work life or OD." Beckhard goes on to say that

> The issues that were being worked were relationships between workers and supervision; roles of supervision and management at various levels; participative management for real.[14]

Beckhard developed the first major nondegree training program in OD, NTL's Program for Specialists in Organizational Training and Development (PSOTD). The first session was an intensive four-week session held in the summer of 1967 at Bethel, Maine. Core staff members the first year were Beckhard as dean, Warner Burke, and Fritz Steele. Additional resource persons the first year were Herbert Shepard, Sheldon Davis, and Chris Argyris. Beckhard was also active in the development and conducting of NTL's middle and senior management conferences and president's labs.[15]

The Term *Organization Development*

It is not entirely clear who coined the term *organization development*, but it is likely that the term emerged more or less simultaneously in two or three places through the conceptualization of Robert Blake, Herbert Shepard, Jane Mouton, Douglas McGregor, and Richard Beckhard.[16] The phrase *development group* had earlier been used by Blake and Mouton in connection with human relations training at the University of Texas and appeared in their 1956 document which was distributed for use in the Baton Rouge experiment.[17] The same phrase appeared in a Mouton and Blake article first published in the journal *Group Psychotherapy* in 1957. (Mouton & Blake 1961, pp. 88–96.) The Baton Rouge T-groups run by Shepard and Blake were called *development groups*,[18] and this program of T-groups was called "organization development" to distinguish it from the complementary management development programs already underway.[19]

Referring to his consulting with McGregor at General Mills, Beckhard gives this account of the term emerging there:

> At that time we wanted to put a label on the program at General Mills. . . . We clearly didn't want to call it management development because it was total organization-wide, nor was it human relations training although there was a component of that in it. We didn't want to call it organization improvement because that's a static term, so we labelled the program "Organization Development," meaning system-wide change effort.[20]

The Role of Personnel and Industrial Relations Executives

It is of considerable significance that the emergence of organization development efforts in three of the first corporations to be extensively involved, Union Carbide, Esso, and General Mills, included personnel and industrial relations people seeing themselves in new roles. At Union Carbide, Jones, in industrial relations, now saw himself in the role of behavioral science consultant to other managers (Bruck 1965, p. 149). At Esso, the headquarters human relations research division began to view itself as an internal consulting group offering services to field managers rather than as a research group developing reports for top management (Kolb 1960).[21] At General Mills, the vice president of personnel and industrial relations saw his role as including leadership in conceptualizing and coordinating changes in the culture of the total organization.

THE SURVEY RESEARCH AND FEEDBACK STEM

Survey research and feedback, a specialized form of action research, constitutes the second major stem in the history of organization development.[22] The history of this stem, in particular, revolves around the techniques and approach developed by staff members at the Survey Research Center (SRC) of the University of Michigan over a period of years.

Rensis Likert

The SRC was founded in 1946 after Rensis Likert, director of the Division of Program Surveys of the Federal Bureau of Agricultural Economics, and other key members of the Division, moved to Michigan. Likert held a Ph.D. in psychology from Columbia, and his dissertation, *A Technique for the Measurement of Attitudes,* was the classic study in which the widely used five-point "Likert Scale" was developed. After a period of university teaching, Likert had been employed by the Life Insurance Agency Management Association where he conducted research on leadership, motivation, morale, and productivity. He had then moved to the U.S. Department of Agriculture, where his Division of Program Surveys furthered a more scientific approach to survey research in its work with various federal departments, including the Office of War Information (ISR Newsletter 1981, p. 6). After helping develop and direct the SRC, in 1948 Likert became the director of a new Institute for Social Research, which included both the SRC and the Research Center for Group Dynamics, the latter moving to Michigan from MIT after Lewin's death.

Floyd Mann, Rensis Likert, and Others

Part of the emergence of survey research and feedback was based on the refinements made by SRC staff members in survey methodology. Another part was the evolution of the feedback methodology. As related by Rensis Likert:

> In 1947, I was able to interest the Detroit Edison Company in a company-wide study of employee perceptions, behavior, reactions and attitudes which was conducted in 1948. Floyd Mann, who had joined the SRC staff in 1947, was the study director on the project. I provided general direction. Three persons from D.E.: Blair Swartz, Sylvanus Leahy and Robert Schwab with Mann and me worked on the problem of how the company could best use the data from the survey to bring improvement in management and performance. This led to the development and use of the survey-feedback method. Floyd particularly played a key role in this development. He found that when the survey data were reported to a manager (or supervisor) and he or she failed to discuss the results with subordinates and failed to plan with them what the manager and others should do to bring improvement, little change occurred. On the other hand, when the manager discussed the results with subordinates and planned with them what to do to bring improvement, substantial favorable changes occurred.[23]

Another aspect of the Detroit Edison Study was the process of feeding back data from an attitude survey to the participating departments in what Mann calls an "interlocking chain of conferences" (Mann 1961, p. 609). Additional insights are provided by Baumgartel, who participated in the project, and who drew the following conclusions from the Detroit Edison Study:

> The results of this experimental study lend support to the idea that an intensive, group discussion procedure for utilizing the results of an employee questionnaire survey can be an effective tool for introducing positive change in a business organization. It may be that the effectiveness of this method, in comparison to traditional training courses, is that it deals with the system of human relationships as a whole (superior and subordinate can change together) and it deals with each manager, supervisor, and employee in the context of his own job, his own job problems, and his own work relationships (Baumgartel 1959, pp. 2–6).

LINKS BETWEEN THE LABORATORY-TRAINING STEM AND THE SURVEY FEEDBACK STEM

Links between people who were later to be key figures in the laboratory-training stem of OD and people who were to be key figures in the survey feedback stem occurred as early as 1940 and continued over the years. These links were undoubtedly of significance in the evolution of both stems. Of particular interest are the links between Likert and Lewin and between Likert and key figures in the laboratory-training stem of OD. As Likert states it, "I met Lewin at the APA annual meeting at State College, Pa., I believe in 1940. When he came to Washington during the War, I saw him several times and got to know him and his family quite well."[24] In 1944 Likert arranged a dinner at which Douglas McGregor and Kurt Lewin explored the feasibility of a group dynamics center at MIT (Marrow 1969, p. 164).

Likert further refers to McGregor:

I met McGregor during the war and came to know him very well after Lewin had set up the RCGD at MIT. After the War, Doug became very interested in the research on leadership and organizations that we were doing in the Institute for Social Research. He visited us frequently and I saw him often at Antioch and at MIT after he returned.

Likert goes on to refer to the first NTL lab for managers which was held Arden House in 1956:

Douglas McGregor and I helped Lee Bradford launch it. . . . Staff members in the 1956 lab were: Beckhard, Benne, Bradford, Gordon Lippitt, Malott, Shepard and I. Argyris, Blake and McGregor joined the staff for the 1957 Arden House lab.[25]

Links between group dynamics and survey feedback people were extensive, of course, after the RCGD moved to Michigan with the encouragement of Rensis Likert and members of the SRC. Among the top people in the RCGD who moved to Michigan were Leon Festinger, Dorwin Cartwright, Ronald Lippitt, and John R. P. French, Jr. Cartwright, who was selected by the group to be the director of the RCGD, was particularly knowledgeable about survey research, since he had been on the staff of the Division of Program surveys with Rensis Likert and others during World War II.[26]

THE ACTION RESEARCH STEM

Participant action research underlies most of the interventions that have been invented in the evolution of OD.[27] Participant action research can be briefly described as a collaborative, client-consultant inquiry consisting of preliminary diagnosis, data gathering from the client group, data feedback to the client group, data exploration and action planning by the client group, and action. Participant action research is one of four versions of action research; the other three, as described by Chein, Cook, and Harding are "diagnostic," "empirical," and "experimental" (1948, pp. 43–50).

Kurt Lewin and Students

Kurt Lewin and his students conducted numerous action-research projects in the mid-1940s and early 1950s (Marrow 1964). An example of this orientation is the following statement by Lewin:

> To be effective, this fact-finding has to be linked with the action organization itself: it has to be part of a feedback system which links a reconnaissance branch of the organization with the branches which do the action (Lewin 1947, p. 150).

Lewin introduced a program of action research at the Harwood Manufacturing Corporation which he first visited in 1939. Alfred Marrow, a social psychologist, was an officer of the company and worked closely with Lewin and subsequent researchers from the research center for Group Dynamics. The studies that emerged focused on such areas as group standards, group decision making, and change processes. The classic study by Coch and French (1948) on resistance to change was one of the projects that emerged. The ongoing relationship between the RCGD and Harwood culminated in the comprehensive action-research OD effort that took place after Harwood acquired the Weldon Manufacturing Company in 1962 (Marrow, Bowers & Seashore 1967).

William Whyte and Edith Hamilton

William F. Whyte and Edith L. Hamilton used action research in their work with Chicago's Tremont Hotel in 1945 and 1946. They described their work as follows:

> What was the project? It was an action-research program for management. We developed a process for applying human relations research findings to the changing of organization behavior. The word process is important, for this was not a one-shot affair. The project involved a continuous gathering and analysis of human relations research data and the feeding of the findings into the organization in such a way as to change behavior (Whyte & Hamilton 1964, pp. 1–2).

John Collier and Others

John Collier, Commissioner of Indian Affairs from 1933 to 1945, like Lewin, found that action research was an important tool in the improving of race relations:

> We had in mind research impelled from central areas of needed action. And since action is by nature not only specialized but also integrative to more than the specialties, our needed research must be of the integrative sort. Again, since the findings of the research must be carried into effect by the administrator and the layman, and must be criticized by them through their experience, the administrator and the layman must themselves participate creatively in the research, impelled as it is from their own need (Collier 1945, pp. 275–76).

Among others who used and wrote about action research in its early history, as described by French and Bell (1978, pp. 88–100), were Corey, Shepard, Lippitt and Radke, Jaques, and Sofer. Stephen Corey was an advocate of action research to improve school practices (1953). Herbert Shepard, discussed above, described action research interventions in the oil refineries where he was a consultant (Shepard 1960, pp. 33–34). Ronald Lippitt and Marion Radke used action research in a community relations project (Lippitt & Radke 1946, pp. 167–76). Elliot Jaques used action research in his long-range work with a factory in England (Jaques 1952). Cyril Sofer used action research methods in three diverse organizations where he was a researcher-consultant (Sofer 1962). The work of these and other scholars and practitioners in the invention and utilization of action research was basic in the evolution of OD.

SOCIOTECHNICAL AND SOCIOCLINICAL PARALLELS

Somewhat parallel to the work of the RCGD, the SRC, and NTL was the work of the Tavistock Clinic in England. The clinic had been founded in 1920 as an out-patient facility to provide psychotherapy based on psychoanalytic theory and insights from the treatment of battle neurosis in World War I. A group focus emerged early in the work of Tavistock in the context of family therapy in which the child and the parent received treatment simultaneously (Dicks 1970, pp. 1, 32). The action-research mode also emerged at Tavistock in attempts to give practical help to families, organizations, and committees.

W. R. Bion, John Rickman, and Others

The staff of the Tavistock Clinic was extensively influenced by such innovations as World War II applications of social psychology to psychiatry, the work of W. R. Bion and John Rickman and others in group therapy, and Lewin's notions about the "social field" in which a problem was occurring, and by Lewin's theory and experience with action research. Bion, Rickman and others had been involved with the six-week "Northfield Experiment" at a military hospital near Birmingham during World War II, an experiment in which each soldier was required to join a group which both performed some task such as handicraft or map reading but discussed feelings, interpersonal relations, and administrative and managerial problems as well. Insights from this experiment were to carry over into Bion's theory of group behavior. (Dicks 1970, pp. 5, 7, 133, 140; DeBoard 1978, pp. 35–43).

Eric Trist

It is of significance that Tavistock's sociotechnical approach to restructuring work grew out of Eric Trist's visit to a coal mine and his insights as to the relevance of Lewin's work on group dynamics and Bion's work on leaderless groups to mining problems. Trist was also influenced by the systems concepts of von Bertalanffy and Andres Angyar (Sashkin 1980). Trist's subsequent experiments in work redesign and the use of semiautonomous work teams in coal mining were the forerunners of other work redesign experiments in various industries in Europe, India, and the United States. Thus, there is a clear historical link between the group dynamics field and sociotechnical approaches to assisting organizations.

Tavistock-U.S. Links

Tavistock leaders, including Trist and Bion, had frequent contact with Lewin, Likert, and others in the United States. One product of this collaboration was the decision to publish *Human Relations* as a joint publication between Tavistock and MIT's Research Center for Group Dynamics (Sashkin 1980). Of the Americans prominent in the emergence and evolution of the OD field—for example, Robert Blake, as we noted earlier, and Warren Bennis—twenty-eight studied at Tavistock.

SUMMARY

By the early 1960s, organization development had emerged largely from the applied behavioral sciences and had three major stems: the invention of the T-group and innovations in the application of laboratory training insights to complex organizations, the invention of survey feedback technology, and the emergence of action research. Parallel and linked to these stems was the emergence of the Tavistock sociotechnical and socioclinical approaches. The key figures focused on in this essay interacted with each other and across these stems, and were influenced by concepts and experiences from a wide variety of disciplines and settings. Among these disciplines and settings were clinical and social psychology, including field theory, family group therapy, military psychology and psychiatry, the theatre, general semantics, mathematics and physics, philosophy, psychodrama, nondirective counseling, survey methodology, experimental and action research, community development, systems theory, sociotechnical approaches, personnel and industrial relations, and general management.

Notes

1. Ronald Lippitt, correspondence with the author, November 23, 1981.
2. Ronald Lippitt, correspondence with the author, August 16, 1971. According to Lippitt, as early as 1945 Bradford and Lippitt were conducting "three-level training" at Freedman's Hospital in Washington, D.C., in an effort "to induce interdependent changes in all parts of the same system," and were using "intergroup task forces to work on the solution of specific problems identified across groups." Lippitt also reports that Leland Bradford very early was acting on a basic concept of "multiple entry," i.e., simultaneously training and working with several groups in the organization.
3. Rensis Likert, correspondence with the author, March 1, 1977. According to correspondence with Rensis Likert, discussions between McGregor and John Paul Jones occurred in the summer of 1957 when Jones attended one of the

annual seminars at Aspen, Colorado, organized by Hollis Peter of the Foundation for Research on Human Behavior and conducted by Douglas McGregor, Mason Haire, and Rensis Likert.

4. This paragraph is based on interviews with Herbert Shepard by the author, August 3, 1981.

5. Much of the historical account in the above two paragraphs and the following three paragraphs is based on correspondence and interviews with Herbert Shepard, with some information added from correspondence with Robert Blake. Shepard, correspondence with the author, March 1, 1971; July 18, 1971; interview with Herbert Shepard, August 3, 1981; Blake, correspondence with the author, March 8, April 12, and June 10, 1971. See also Porter (1976).

6. Blake and Shepard correspondence with the author. For further reference to Murray Horwitz and Paul Buchanan, as well as comments about the innovative contributions of Michael Blansfield, see Shepard et al. (1964, pp. 382–83). See also Sashkin (1978, pp. 401–407). Blake and Mouton credit Muzafer Sherif and Carolyn Sherif with important contributions to early intergroup experiments, and give credit to the contributions of Frank Cassens of Humble Oil and Refinery in the early phases of the Esso program. (Blake & Mouton 1962; 1976, pp. 332–36).

7. Robert Blake, correspondence with the author, March 8, 1981.

8. Robert Blake, correspondence with the author, November 12, 1981.

9. Jane Mouton, correspondence with the author, February 19, 1982.

10. Robert Blake, correspondence, November 12, 1981.

11. *Ibid.*

12. *Ibid.*

13. Richard Beckhard, correspondence with the author, December 17, 1981.

14. *Ibid.*

15. Based partly on Beckhard correspondence, December 17, 1981.

16. Interpretations of Shepard interview, August 3, 1981; Shepard correspondence, March 1, 1971; Blake correspondence, March 8, April 12, 1971; Richard Beckhard correspondence, December 17, 1981; and Porter (1974).

17. Blake, correspondence, April 12, 1971.

18. *Ibid.*

19. Interview with Herbert Shepard by the author, August 3, 1981.

20. Beckhard, correspondence, December 17, 1981.

21. The phrase *organization development* is used several times in this monograph based on a 1959 meeting about the Esso programs and written by Kolb, Shepard, Blake, and others (Kolb 1960).

22. This section is based largely on correspondence with Rensis Likert and partially on "The Career of Rensis Likert" (*ISR Newsletter*, 1971); *A Quarter Century of Social Research* (Institute for Social Research, 1971; and "Rensis Likert: A Final Tribute" (*ISR Newsletter* 1981).

23. Rensis Likert, correspondence with the author, March 1, 1977.

24. *Ibid.*

25. *Ibid.*

26. *Ibid.*

27. I am indebted to Cecil Bell for his research contribution to this section (French & Bell 1978, Chapter 8). See also Frohman, Sashkin, and Kavanagh (1976).

28. Warren Bennis address, Academy of Management, San Diego, California, August 3, 1981.

References

Baumgartel, Howard, Using Employee Questionnaire Results for Improving Organizations: The Survey (Feedback) Experiment. *Kansas Business Review* 12 (December 1959):2–6.

Beckhard, Richard; Burke, W. Warner; and Steele, Fred I. The Program for Specialists in Organization Training and Development. Mimeographed paper, NTL Institute for Applied Behavioral Science, December 1967, p. ii.

Benne, Kenneth D.; Bradford, Leland P.; Gibb, Jack R.; and Lippitt, Ronald O. (Eds.). *The Laboratory Method of Changing and Learning: Theory and Application.* Palo Alto, Calif.: Science and Behavior Books, 1975.

Blake, Robert R.; Shepard, Herbert; and Mouton, Jane S. *Managing Intergroup Conflict in Industry.* Houston, Tex.: Gulf Publishing, 1964.

Blake, Robert R.; and Mouton, Jane S. *Diary of an OD Man.* Houston, Tex.: Gulf Publishing, 1976.

Blake, Robert R.; and Mouton, Jane S. The Instrumented Training Laboratory, in Irving R. Weschler and Edgar M. Schein (Eds.), *Selected Readings Series Five: Issues in Training.* Washington, D.C., National Training Laboratories, 1962, pp. 61–85.

Burck, Gilbert. Union Carbide's Patient Schemers. *Fortune 72* (6), 1965, pp. 147–49.

Chein, Isadore; Cook, Stuart; and Harding, John. The Field of Action Research. *American Psychologist 3* (2), 1948, pp. 43–50.

Chin, Robert; and Benne, Kenneth D., General Strategies for Effecting Changes in Human Systems. Bennis, Warren G.; Benne, Kenneth D.; and Chin, Robert (Eds.). *The Planning of Change* 2d ed. New York: Holt, Rinehart & Winston, 1969.

Coch, Lester, and French, John R. P., Jr. Overcoming Resistance to Change. *Human Relations* 1, 1948, pp. 512–32.

Collier, John. United States Indian Administration as a Laboratory of Ethnic Relations. *Social Research 12*, (May 1945), pp. 275–276.

Corey, Stephen M. *Action Research to Improve School Practices.* New York: Teachers College, Columbia University, 1953.

DeBoard, Robert. *The Psychoanalysis of Organizations.* London: Tavistock Publications, 1978.

Dicks, H. V. *Fifty Years of the Tavistock Clinic.* London: Routledge & Kegan Paul, 1970.

French, Wendell L. *The Personnel Management Process* 5th ed. Boston: Houghton Mifflin, 1982.

French, Wendell L.; and Bell, Cecil H., Jr. *Organization Development: Behavioral Science Interventions for Organization Improvement* 2d ed. Englewood Cliffs, N.J.: Prentice-Hall, Inc., 1978.

Frohman, Mark A.; Sashkin, Marshall; and Kavanagh, Michael J.; Action Research as Applied to Organization Development. *Organization and Administrative Sciences* 7 (Spring/Summer 1976) pp. 129–42.

Institute for Social Research. *A Quarter Century of Social Research*, 1971.

Institute for Social Research. The Career of Rensis Likert. *ISR Newsletter* (Winter 1971).

Institute for Social Research. "Rensis Likert: A Final Tribute. *ISR Newsletter* (Winter 1981).

Jaques, Elliott. *The Changing Culture of the Factory.* New York: The Dryden Press, Inc., 1942.

Jones, John Paul. What's Wrong with Work? in *What's Wrong with Work?* New York: National Association of Manufacturers, 1967.

Kolb, Harry D. Introduction. *An Action Research Program for Organization Improvement*. Ann Arbor, Mich.: Foundation for Research on Human Behavior, 1960.

Lewin, Kurt. Frontiers in Human Relations II. Channels of Group Life; Social Planning and Action Research. *Human Relations 1* (2), 1947, pp. 143–53.

Lippitt, Ronald, and Radke, Marion. New Trends in the Investigation of Prejudice. *Annals of the American Academy of Political and Social Science. 24* (4) (March 1946) pp. 167–176.

Mann, Floyd C. "Studying and Creating Change" in Bennis, Warren; Benne, Kenneth; and Robert Chin. *The Planning of Change*. New York: Holt, Rinehart & Winston, 1961.

Marrow, Alfred J. Risks and Uncertainties in Action Research. *Journal of Social Issues, 20* (3), 1964, p. 17.

Marrow, Alfred J. *The Practical Theorist: The Life and Work of Kurt Lewin*. New York: Basic Books, 1969.

Marrow, Alfred J.; Bowers, David G., and Seashore, Stanley E.; *Management by Participation*. New York: Harper & Row, 1967.

McGregor, Douglas. *The Professional Manager*. New York: McGraw-Hill, 1967.

Mouton, Jane S.; & Blake, Robert R. University Training in Human Relations Skills in *Selected Readings Series Three: Forces in Learning*. Washington, D.C.: National Training Laboratories, 1961, 88–96. Reprinted from *Group Psychotherapy*, 1957, *10*, pp. 342–45.

Porter, Larry. "OD: Some Questions, Some Answers—An Interview with Beckhard and Shepard." *OD Practitioner*, 6 (Autumn 1974), p. 1.

Porter, Larry. A Conversation with Bob Tannenbaum. *OD Practitioner, 8* (October 1976), pp. 1–5ff.

Roethlisberger, F. J.; and Dickson, W. J.; *Management and the Worker*. Cambridge, Mass.: Harvard University Press, 1939.

Sashkin, Marshall. Interview with Eric Trist. *Group & Organization Studies. 5* (2), 1980, pp. 144–155.

Sashkin, Marshall. Interview with Robert R. Blake and Jane Srygley Mouton. *Group & Organization Studies. 3* (4), 1978, pp. 401–07.

Shepard, Herbert A. An Action Research Model. *An Action Research Program for Organization Improvement*. Ann Arbor: The Foundation for Research on Human Behavior, 1960.

Shepard, Herbert A. Exploration in Observant Participation, in Bradford, Leland; Gibb, Jack; & Benne, Kenneth, *T-Group Theory and Laboratory Method*. New York: John Wiley, 1964.

Smith, Peter B. (Ed.). *Small Groups and Personal Change*. London: Methuen & Co. Ltd., 1980.

Sofer, Cyril. *The Organization from Within*. Chicago: Quadrangle Books, 1962.

Whyte, William F., and Hamilton, Edith L. *Action Research for Management*. Homewood, Ill.: Irwin-Dorsey, 1964.

3 OD As a Scientific Revolution

Peter B. Vaill

ABSTRACT

This paper argues that in the philosophies and methods that OD has developed for introducing change into organizations lie important insights about the nature of inquiry into all kinds of human systems and situations. OD, almost without realizing it, has contributed to the resolution of what are in some cases century-long debates.

The paper uses as a foil for OD a formulation called the Expository Model of Science (ExpM), which is a personal version of traditional positivistic philosophies of science. The paper shows how OD cannot be true both to the ExpM and to its philosophy of change, how it has wisely and consistently opted for its own philosophy when faced with the choice, and how this is creating a revolution in social science. As results of an unfinished revolution, final forms can only be imagined. This paper, however, develops seven categories in which OD's contributions are of a seminal nature.

AUTHOR BACKGROUND

Peter B. Vaill is professor of human systems at George Washington University. He has published numerous articles on OD and has taken a special interest in the problems of epistemology and of scientific method which exist in the social sciences. He is also the creator of the theory of High Performing Systems, a series of studies now in progress for over a decade to discover the properties of human systems conducting themselves at high levels of excellence.

A few years ago, I undertook to describe the properties of scientific theory and research which I thought my colleagues in the applied behavioral sciences and I had inherited from the natural sciences. I called my list of properties the Expository Model of Science" (the ExpM). These properties I believed were getting in the way of the kind of disciplined inquiry I and others were trying to do, and were also getting in the way of the process of using the results of this inquiry to improve organizations and the lives of the people in them.

At the same time that I and many others[1] were developing our criticisms of the ExpM and its variations, the field of OD was energetically developing its philosophy and methods for introducing change into organizations. At the level of practice, OD was ignoring the ExpM or perhaps, to be a bit more exact, OD was ignoring the ExpM in favor of the work to be done whenever the norms of the ExpM conflicted with what was needed and appropriate in the change situation. And in addition to being a critic of the ExpM, I and many others were also active practitioners of OD methods and formulators of OD theories. This led to a kind of professional schizophrenia. One knew, at one and the same time, that some theory was perfect for the project in question and utterly "unrespectable" by the standards of the ExpM; that some data collection methodology was perfectly suited to some organizational situation, but that it was also probably seriously contaminated with "values" or "politics" and hence could make no claim to objective validity; that regardless of the ExpM's emphasis on carefully thought-out research design before beginning an inquiry, we knew that the kind of inquiry OD does is based on only the loosest front-end design, choosing instead to be as open and responsive as possible to the emergent data of the situation; and, finally, we knew that we couldn't prove that we were creating the changes we were trying to create, even though the ExpM insisted on persuasive and logically unassailable evidence to justify rejection of its null hypothesis.

At times the schizophrenia threatened to overwhelm us. The only intellectual grounding many of us had was in the ExpM, yet here was OD, its philosophy, and its objectives, inviting us to think very differently about what systematic inquiry and planned change are.

Now, after twenty years, it is beginning to appear that OD, hand in hand with other social change philosophies and methods, may be pointing to a rather new way of thinking about the social sciences—both their conduct and their value. In the currently fashionable language, OD is playing a central role in the "paradigm shift"[2] that has attracted so much speculation.

In this paper, I will attempt to describe what OD has taught me about science, both the old-style positivistic science and the new ideas and possibilities which are in ferment everywhere. OD, I will argue, is an engine of change not just at the level of people's relations to one another, but also at the level of theory and the nature of scientific inquiry.[3] OD is a scientific revolution in precisely the sense that Kuhn used the phrase.[4]

THE EXPOSITORY MODEL OF SCIENCE

Here are the relevant excerpts from my original attempt to describe the model of science which was provng to be impossible to practice in OD (with apologies for the all-male pronouns):

The fundamental thrust of the ExpM is indicated by its title: the function of science is to expose nature, its inner workings and its uses, to mankind. To expose and to explain—that is what science is for. . . . The ExpM has some . . . interesting characteristics which deserve attention. The following listing is incomplete but it is suggestive in any case:

1. The ExpM asks the investigator for his findings, not for his "understandings."
2. The ExpM values the cumulation of knowledge in the public domain of the science. It does not demand that learning cumulate within a given investigator.
3. The ExpM tends not to regard the scientific enterprise as an activity that is any more or less self-fulfilling for the scientist than any other activity. The value to the scientist of his own behavior is irrelevant in the ExpM.
4. The ExpM asks that the report of the investigator's procedure meet certain standards. It does not concern itself with the investigator's mood [i.e., with the meaning to the investigator of the inquiry and its findings].
5. "Methodology" in the ExpM is determined by the nature of the phenomenon in question, and the investigator's hypotheses about it. Methodology screens and controls the investigator's relation to the phenomena.
6. The needs and motives of the investigator need not be questioned in the ExpM since his methodology supposedly screens his data from contamination by his own values and biases as a person.
7. Over time, the ExpM tends to produce routines and subroutines which investigators are expected to follow. For many of the investigator's behaviors in the ExpM, there is "one best way" to do whatever it is he is trying to do.
8. Science in the ExpM is practiced by professionals—men who have passed successfully through a long period of training and testing. A working familiarity with the phenomena of the science is not an adequate credential by itself to support theory or research.
9. From the standpoint of a given investigator, the work of other scientists is useful in the ExpM insofar as it is verifiable independently by the investigator in question.
10. The ExpM does not hold the investigator responsible for the use made of his findings. In fact, such worries by an individual investigator are held to be dysfunctional to his research.
11. "Scientific progress" can be measured according to various criteria in the ExpM. However, these criteria have in common a relative lack of concern with the value of science to society. The fruits of the science are 'applied' to social problems, of course, but these applications are assumed to be valuable by the fact of their applicability [i.e., applicability per se is not a yardstick of scientific progress.]

. . . The main reason for all the exactitude demanded by the ExpM in methodology, verifiability, disinterested observation, etc., is to produce knowledge about the world of which we may be certain. The ExpM leads us to believe that we can . . . apply our social science findings to real-world situations. Yet when we try we find that the findings never quite fit the situation exactly, and usually they don't fit the new system at all. . . . [We] must then fall back on a process of reasoning by analogy and designing by hunch and intuition.[5]

It is possible to go back over these eleven assertions (some of which I might rephrase today) and show how one cannot do OD theory or practice while adhering to the assertion. But this is not the approach I have chosen to take in the remainder of this paper. Rather, I have chosen to ask, What kind of model of science is OD pointing *toward*? What kinds of new characteristics will this model have? The characteristics I discuss below are simply generalizations from the concrete working interpretations, solutions, and philosophies which OD people have invented in order to get on with their change projects. What I am seeking is a way of thinking about inquiry and about knowledge which grounds and justifies these efforts, and more importantly, which points the way beyond current efforts to deeper levels of understanding and appreciation of man in organization.

NEW GROUNDS FOR PLANNED INQUIRY AND CHANGE

Normative Character

Perhaps of all the aspects of the new model discussed in this paper, the normative character of planned inquiry and change is the one matter on which there would be the widest agreement. It is also the largest and most troublesome aberration of all in the ExpM. There simply can be no disinterested inquiry into human systems, and there certainly cannot be disinterested change, i.e., change which is objectively based on principles logically deduced from disinterested theory. The social sciences, OD has taught us, are interventionist even when they are not trying to be. One cannot study a human system without changing it, and since no two human systems are identical, the interventions are irreversible: we cannot know what the system would have been like or what would have been discovered there had the investigators chosen to collect data from different people than they did, or on different issues than they did, or with different methods than they used.

Human values pervade inquiry and change. Choice points abound. Feelings are generated by the issues in the system and by its unfolding character as the project proceeds. One cares about what one discovers there and about the effects one has there.

These remarks are commonplaces for an OD theorist or practitioner, anathema as they may be to the ExpM. It is not that OD teaches us to do *better* applied science by bringing values in than by leaving them out. Rather, what has been discovered is that one can't do science at *all* without values; they cannot be left out. "Disinterested inquiry" is not a meaningful ideal, but a meaningless caricature. Without "interest" planned inquiry and change do not have meaning.

The question, then, is not objectivity versus subjectivity, but one kind of subjectivity versus another kind. What *is* "good subjectivity?" The ExpM gives us no guidance on this question. Nevertheless, we may speculate from the experience of OD that "good subjectivity" balances the attainment of task objectives with the development of people; believes that liberation from all dogma is a valuable end; seeks to increase the degree of democracy and participation in all systems; understands that it is not always "right to be right"[6]; and shows that integration of interests to the extent possible is more valuable than differentiation of interests; that talking conflicts through is better than suppression or avoidance; and that consideration of the long run needs of a system is better than merely satisfying the most vocal interests in the short run.

Doubtless there are other characteristics of "good subjectivity," but these are sufficient to make the point: OD has taught us how to take caring action in human systems. If it has done nothing else in the past twenty-five years, this one contribution earns OD its place in intellectual and moral history.

Existential Apples . . . and Oranges

By letting itself be classed as an "applied" science (at best!) OD has obscured an important fact from itself: that it deals with heterogeneous phenomena, but still holds itself to the standard of trying to think about all these phenomena at once and trying in the change effort to manage all the systemic ripples and interrelations that occur. The fact that is thus obscured is that OD (and probably other "applied" sciences as well) are more honest and robust for confronting all this variability than their more pristine sisters who have retreated into a defined discipline with a defined domain of questions and a defined domain of methods by which these questions are may be addressed. OD is messy—again an observation that is a commonplace to OD people, and heresy in the ExpM.[7]

In a landmark formulation, Herbert Simon developed the concept of the "artificial system," that is, the system that is crafted by man for a purpose.[8] The point is that what science even *is* in an artificial system, a system designed to do something, may be different in significant ways from a science developed to study truly natural phenomena, that is, phenomena in which man's interests and objectives play no part.

OD is trying to do planned inquiry and change in systems that mix natural and artificial phenomena, which by Simon's definition makes such systems artificial overall. In some deep sense, OD does not know what the objects of its efforts really are. It has experienced the temptation to reduce one type to the other. There are assertions that human systems are "natural social systems"[9] although one does not hear these claims so frequently anymore except among the "living systems" theorists[10] and possibly the sociobiologists.[11] More common today are the efforts to redefine the phenomena as completely man-made and artificial, as with the groundswell of interest in politics in systems and in the powerful arguments made on behalf of the idea that all human systems are inventions of consciousness.[12]

One of the deep learnings of OD is that none of these models are adequate, that at the concrete level of real people doing real things, all models pale before the complexity of what is there. It is not the model one is changing, it is what is there, so one uses the model as what many years ago was called "a useful walkingstick to help along the way,"[13] not a panacea and definitely not something to be "proved" or "verified," as the ExpM would ask of the theory one employed. In this respect OD is not so much pointing the way to something new as it is keeping alive one of the deepest truths of epistemology: the word is not the thing; the map is not the territory.[14] OD keeps this flame burning by confronting territories whose strangeness and caprices elude all known models—which only means that every time you begin a project of planned inquiry and change you must be prepared to tailor your model to the exigencies of the situation you are dealing with.

Another way to say what OD has learned is that it has been forced to rethink what the salient elements of the client system are without unconsciously assuming that the only thing of interest there is the people. In order to introduce change effectively, one has to be interested in the whole system—the people and all the other things that are there. In order to understand such situations, OD has needed to learn to talk about all the elements of the situation at about the same level of abstraction, rather than the people at a low level and everything else at a high level. This has been a painful learning for OD. All through the 1960s OD tried to ignore technology and the business realities of the organization and the environment it existed in. But in the last ten years OD has become more and more comfortable with the fact that the whole system must be the object of change, and the *whole* system is a stew of people and things and factors, not a homogeneous and regular phenomenon at all.

Social Science—For Whom?

In the ExpM, inquiry is conducted for its own sake, out of the investigator's "disinterested fascination" with the phenomena and thirst to know more about them. In the eighteenth and nineteenth centuries, the investigator was frequently an amateur who either was independently wealthy or else earned money by some other set of activities entirely. It is important to say this because it meant that the investigator chose the questions to be addressed, the methods to be used, and the audience to whom the results were communicated under much simpler conditions than we face today.

Today, for all our science, there is a system of interested parties to any planned inquiry and change. The investigators themselves have career interests as well as change interests. Those who fund the effort have their purposes and frequently these are quite intense and partisan. The "user" or "client" also has responsibilities and "agendas" which the effort must fit into.

The ExpM would assume that meaningful inquiry cannot be conducted under these conditions, but OD knows differently. The process is more complex; the ways one can go wrong are more numerous and more tempting. But countless OD people know that one can still gaze at an organization, figure out what it needs to function better and be a more humane place, and then help it move in that direction. In particular, OD knows that all this can still be done with élan, that one can study human systems with a feeling of enjoyment and a sense of delight in discovery. Enjoyment in the practice of a methodology is an odd sounding idea. Somehow it does not seem quite right that one should take *pleasure* in a process of inquiry—but that is only a measure of how far down the alienated road the ExpM has taken us. OD knows that if one cannot have some fun looking into what is going on in an organization, one can hardly mount the energy that is needed to help it work better.

OD is routinely integrating the interests of the investigator, the user, the subject, and the charterer-funder of the effort. It has taught itself that in the long run, the enterprise of planned inquiry and change is more viable and valuable when all of these interests are integrated than when only one, the "disinterested needs" of the investigator, are elevated to a paramount position.

Who Was that System I Saw You with Last Night?

The broader issue growing out of the section above is how we are going to think of the setting within which we do planned inquiry and change. The ExpM teaches us to think of it in physical, structural terms mainly, that is, that all these parts are somehow "here" together, each having its own properties, and that they all together somehow have some "dynamics," that is that we perceive them as "moving" and "changing," within limits anyway. The ExpM lets the parts sort of gyrate, move around, do strange things, but the ExpM leads us to assume that the aggregate, our phenomenon, remains whole no matter how much the parts gyrate.

(The point is thrown into relief for me as I recall worrying about the integrity of the Washington Redskins football team in the fall of 1981. They lost their first five games under their new coach. The newspapers were filled daily with reports of the chaos that pervaded the team. I had this odd feeling: Is the team going to just fall apart? What if on some Sunday they are in such disarray that they can't take the field? Is there any provision for a franchise to just fold up in the middle of the season? etc. The Redskins confronted me with the tacit assumptions I was making of an underlying stable structure which would endure. My God, what if it doesn't, I found myself wondering.)

The ExpM relies on two complementary assumptions about the underlying, enduring reality of the phenomena it investigates. These are the *assumption of atomism,* and the *assumption of mechanism.*

The assumption of atomism says that when you are faced with a complex system you are justified in breaking it down into smaller more comprehensible parts than the entity-itself you are trying to understand. You can simplify your problem, no matter what it is, because it can be broken into pieces. Ultimately, you reach the fundamental building blocks, each homogeneous, unitary, and regular-unto-itself. Thus, says the ExpM, the anxiety one feels with a complex, gyrating whole will abate as one clarifies these atoms, these ultimate building blocks, for they will be safe and comprehendible in their homogenous, unitary, regularity.

The assumption of mechanism complements the assumption of atomism. In some deep, half-aware way, the ExpM knows that in breaking things down into component parts it is violating the integrity of the phenomenon. By itself, the assumption of atomism is a little bit scary. But the assumption of mechanism says, "Don't worry. No matter how far you go breaking things down, you will be able to add them back together. Their essential relationships are mechanical relationships, and therefore the whole is merely the summed action of each part on the other." And so the ExpM rests easy.

OD, however, knows differently. It knows that when people change they change not atomistically, but wholistically. The difference between Theory X and Theory Y is not a rearrangement of the atoms of attitude. To help a team develop, one does not work with one member at a time. The feelings one person has about another are neither linear nor cumulative nor easily separable. OD also realizes, I think, that we do not have good ways of transcending the silliness of the atomistic and mechanistic assumptions. There are increasing calls to get beyond these two assumptions, but there is a frustrating fuzziness to these summonings.[15]

In my view, OD understands the problem as well or better than any discipline, but it has not yet gotten beyond the strictures of atomistic/mechanistic thinking at the conceptual level. There is still too much talk about human behavior as if it obeyed the laws of physics: forces, dynamics, drives, dimensions, etc. The very concept of "change" itself is talked of as a physical phenomenon, for example, "movement," "momentum," "blockages," "resistances," etc. These modes were probably inherited primarily from Kurt Lewin with his famous "unfreezing" model and his concept of quasi-stationary equilibrium.[16]

The new sources of language which make breakthroughs by OD probable in the area of a new image of change include OD's investigations of the application of right brain activity in management, OD's long-time interest in helping organization members develop guiding images and metaphors to undergird change, and its general comfort with nonverbal modes of communication and interpretation. However, this work seems not yet to have jelled into a public and cumulative language system to replace the older atomistic and mechanistic modes. The one possible exception to this point is the "percept language" of John Weir and Joyce Weir, which hundreds of OD people have learned to use over the years. While percept language still uses the ordinary nouns and adjectives of physics-dominated social science language, by forcing the speaker to use a grammar which emphasizes the to-me-ness of all phenomena, the way is opened for new metaphors and images which may fuel the breakthrough I am talking about.[17]

Hopefully this process will occur before another set of trends makes it moot, namely, the increasing interest in metaphors and linguistic constructions from the field of computer programming and artificial intelligence. "Neuro-linguistic programming" is probably the best example of reliance on information theory and its application in computer technology for ways of talking about human behavior.

In summary, the general question of the identity of the entity we are trying to understand and change is central in OD. It has deep historical roots; it is intimately tied up with language; at bottom it involves a debate between those for whom human behavior is "nothing but———" (that is, the reductionists) and those for whom human behavior is *always* "more than———," and most OD people would be in this latter camp.

Back To Idiographics

The ExpM is primarily oriented toward the search for the general laws that govern the behavior of phenomena. Its great emphasis on precision, objectivity, representative samples, etc., derive from this interest. At the other extreme, in most people's minds I think, are artists who are preoccupied with particulars, with the minute inspection of individual "cases." OD and the other disciplines concerned with change bridge these two points of view in their practice. They make what use they can of law-like generalizations and abstractions, and make the contributions that they can to progress at this level. But OD also knows something that social sciences dominated by the ExpM do not know half so well, namely, that no scientific generality, no matter how comprehensive and buttressed by fact, can ever completely explain an individual case in all its concreteness and complexity. It is that individual case that OD is primarily concerned with. OD knows that a case is not "merely" an instance of the general law, and I think it also knows that in some profound way there can never be a deductive science of change for this same reason. The solution to the individual case will never be deducible from the general law, where by "solution" I mean what the manager or the consultant or the organization member should do in *this* situation.

Idiographics is the careful analysis of individual cases. One of the most refreshing things about OD is its creativity with methodology. Innovative ways of finding out what is going on in a system, many of which are too sloppy and unrigorous ever to be sanctioned by the ExpM, are one of OD's main trademarks. OD uses the unfortunate term *diagnosis* for what it is doing when it is inquiring into a system. But setting that aside, techniques such as survey feedback, diagonal slice sensing, metaphorical imaging, Beckhard's justly famous "confrontation meeting,"[18] Weisbord's "helpful mechanisms"[19] and many others are testimony to OD's fertility with methodology.[20]

Furthermore, new methods are arising constantly. Some OD people are experimenting with videotape and other electronic techniques for mapping organizational events. Others are rediscovering the importance of the history of organizations and of the situations they have gotten themselves into. Documentation of myths and rituals is another method that is becoming more and more well understood. All kinds of nonverbal methods have been created for helping organization members express their experience of the organization and what they and it need without having to put it all in linear-logical language.

It is ironic that the ExpM, with its great emphasis on refined method, cannot tolerate many of these techniques. The investigator is frequently involved by the technique in the life of the system. The data that many of these techniques yield is hardly "objective," but no less meaningful to organization members for that.

Nearly three decades ago, Maslow in a little-remembered essay forecast quite accurately what has happened.[21] The ExpM is "means-centered" through and through. The study that is not done "rigorously and correctly" is not worth doing. As a result, the science the ExpM does is sterile. OD, on the other hand, has its eye on the task, which is change. It is not means-centered; it is purpose-centered, and in its concern with purpose it has been enormously inventive with means and methods. Its purpose has been to create change among particular people, in particular systems, around particular issues. A further irony, therefore, is that OD has possibly moved us farther along the road of our ancient dream, the dream of a unified science of all things, than has the ExpM in its obsession with right method.

A further implication of OD's concern with particulars is that this is how ethics and morals are saved. It is at the level of individual dilemmas and choices that the relevance of morals and ethics is enlivened. Social science in the ExpM is concerned with the generalized value judgments of a generalized role incumbent in a generalized setting. OD people are concerned with helping real decision makers make real decisions. Not surprisingly the ExpM is able to ignore ethics and morals entirely or else deal with them casually and even glibly (for example, "The American businessman ought to ———") whereas OD cannot.

A final discovery OD has made with its interest in idiographics is that what is happening in a system and what should be happening are not as easily separated as the ExpM thinks. The faith of the ExpM is that we can separate "fact" and "value", what is from what ought to be, and that we can focus science on the former and exempt ourselves as scientists from responsibility for the latter. The methodologies mentioned above are both useful for learning about the system and for influencing it. In fact, OD *seeks* methods which have this dual quality—something that is dramatically apparent in a technique such as action research.[22] OD has learned something the man in the street would say is obvious, but which the ExpM still cannot see—that facts and values are inextricably intertwined. Neither has any meaning without the other. How the ExpM can cling to the distinction in the face of such decisive criticism is a puzzle.

Images of Humankind

OD has known for its entire existence that its image of humans is different from orthodox social science. Its image is more positive, more developmental, and concerned with human possibility, more forgiving of our "dark" side, more interested in our highest possibilities. OD has been accused constantly of being naive about human nature, of looking at the world through rose-colored spectacles, of being conflicted about power and about the unconscious. But through all this criticism OD has not wavered in its belief system.[23] It realizes that its belief system about man is one of its most distinctive attributes.

What is at issue is the tension between who we can see that the human being is and who we hope that he or she can be. Stated this way, it seems apparent to me that OD has a healthier posture on the question than any of the sciences deriving from the ExpM. It can see who men and women are in all the organizational issues that ExpM confronts. And it can see who we can be in the results of its efforts to improve communication, increase trust, strengthen a person's sense of self, and facilitate attention to the task. As on so many other matters, OD bridges the debates, in this case between realism and idealism, and does not permit the intellectual wrangles to displace its interest in change at the concrete level.

Another dimension of OD's work is to treat *both* investigator and subject as worthy of a positive image. Humans, for OD, are conscious, thinking, feeling, choosing beings; this includes both the person being investigated and the person doing the investigating. Planned inquiry and change in OD therefore hold out the possibility of an authentic, mature relationship between investigator and subject, whereas social sciences dominated by the ExpM have a great deal more difficulty achieving this condition. Much more commonly, allegiance to the ExpM leads to treating the subject or the investigator or both as relatively mindless beings, controlled by unconscious forces, constrained by principles and protocols, unable to experience the process as fully-functioning human beings. The extreme case is laboratory research in Skinnerian psychology. The subject is viewed very narrowly as an entity controlled by conditioned stimuli. The experimenter, too, must adhere to the ExpM's definition of "correct" behavior. As a result, the chances of true discovery are minimized. Instead, such an artificial situation can only verify what has already been guessed, and even here, the question is of what "verification" even can mean under such stilted conditions. Furthermore, certainly no "change" can be thought through and decided upon by either party. Beings in the grip of reflexes or genes or environmental conditioning cannot decide what is good for them and commit themselves to its pursuit.

Thus, OD's great interest in the nature of the consultant role, in the nature of the client, and in the relation between them becomes exactly the right thing to be concerned about. In effect, OD poses us with one of the most interesting questions in all social science: what is *collaborative* inquiry?[24]

THE SCIENCES OF DISCOVERY

A very important debate in the philosophy of science is over the role and relative importance of the so-called contexts of discovery and of verification.[25] The ExpM and its variations is much less interested in the context of discovery than it is in the context of verification. The ExpM is willing to let all kinds of black magic go on when science is trying to generate ideas about phenomena. What the ExpM insists on is that when science is trying to claim something or prove something—that is, the process of verification—it must adhere to very strict standards of logical analysis.

OD has always been much more interested in discovery than in verification, and what it has done, I believe, is raise this question again for all of social science: what, indeed, is it we are trying to "verify" when we attempt to convert our rich and diverse speculations and discoveries about man into unassailable laws?

OD and the other social sciences concerned with change have brought home an important truth about us and our society: the basic phenomena of social science are in a state of continuous creation. There are few if any other sciences that can make this statement—that one of the properties of the phenomena themselves is to create new facts and patterns hitherto unseen. To be in a state of continuous creation is a direct implication of Herbert Simon's realization that each of us, as a human being, is an artificial system.[26] We fill our teeth with silver, put on glasses, wear clothes, manage our diets, kill the bacteria that would infect us, control the light and temperature level, set out broken bones, craft our image, and choose our friends. Virtually no one in the civilized world is alive at all and is who he or she is without the interventions into the natural systems of the body and the environment which we take for granted. Thus, in a host of ways, the human being is in the process of creating a being—a society of beings, really, whose properties remain to be discovered, forever!

The search for general, regular laws governing human behavior make the assumption that for all practical purposes the human being as a phenomenon is finished, complete, not likely to change any further in any significant ways. OD, which has watched such movements as the T group, Quality of Working Life, participative management, matrix structures, civil rights, and MBO work their effects in organizations knows what unexpected new kinds of behavior emerge when human structures and processes are disturbed. Sometimes the new behaviors are charming and constructive, and sometimes they are demonic beyond belief. But no one who has paid close attention to the gyrations of organizations and the people in them over the last fifty years could believe that there are no forms of behavior left for us to invent.

To the extent that the ExpM cares only for the context of verification, it is irrelevant. OD people and others who are concerned with understanding and changing human society can proceed with their work without worrying about the norms of the ExpM. No matter how deeply into our cultural consciousness it has been ingrained that the ExpM is the real standard of truth, it is not. OD is one of the leading intellectual movements demonstrating this fact. OD's legacy is precisely this—to lead the social sciences out of their two-century-old trance before the ExpM.

SUMMARY

In this paper I have argued that OD, viewed both as a body of theory and a set of practices, has been showing for over twenty years that it is possible to engage in disciplined inquiry and initiate appropriate change in human systems without subscribing to the norms of the Expository Model of Science (ExpM). The ExpM derives from an idealization of the nature of physical and natural science. The social sciences have been inordinately fascinated with the ExpM. OD, almost alone, has half-consciously realized that the ExpM cannot guide planned inquiry and change. Instead, OD has intuitively developed a set of ideas about planned inquiry and change that constitutes a dramatic alternative to the ExpM. These new ideas do not yet constitute a unified paradigm. Yet is is possible, as this paper has shown, to identify some of the key properties of the new view. These properties include: (1) an integration of normative values and objective inquiry; (2) a willingness to confront rather than avoid the inherent heterogeneity of all human systems; (3) a new understanding of who the enterprise is for; (4) a new understanding of what the phenomena in question are; (5) a major reaffirmation of the importance of understanding individual cases, despite the ExpM's commitment to the verification of general laws; (6) a continuing stream of new ideas about human behavior; and (7) a radical reconceptualization of human phenomena as artificial, with the crucial corollary that they have the property of continuously creating themselves.

OD, by trying to be and do what it is trying to be and do, is creating a new science of human systems.

Notes

1. Good critiques of the positivism from which the ExpM draws many of its ideas may be found in Russell Ackoff, *Redesign the Future* (New York: Wiley, 1974); in A. H. Maslow, *Motivation and Personality* (New York: Harper and Row, 1954), especially Chapter 2 on "Problem-Centering vs. Means-Centering in Science"; in Marcello Truzzi, ed., *Verstehen: Subjective Understanding in the Social Sciences* (Reading, Mass: Addison-Wesley, 1974); and finally a devastating critique mounted by Jay D. White, "Public Policy Analysis: Reason, Method, and Praxis", unpublished doctoral dissertation, George Washington University, 1982.

2. Thomas Kuhn, *The Structure of Scientific Revolutions* (Chicago: Univ. of Chicago Press, 1970), 2d ed. See also, Gary Gutting, *Paradigms and Revolutions: Applications and Appraisals of Thomas Kuhn's Philosophy of Science* (Notre Dame, Ind: Univ. of Notre Dame Press, 1980).

3. The theory *is* the intervention say James Foltz, Jerry Harvey, and Joanne McLaughlin, "Organization Development: A Line Management Function."In John D. Adams, ed., *New Technologies in Organization Development* 2 (LaJolla, Calif.: University Associates, Inc., 1975) pp. 185–210. Also, "theory and principles" as a type of intervention are forecast to be rapidly increasing in popularity and effectiveness in R. Blake, and J. Mouton, *Consultation* (Reading, Mass: Addison-Wesley, 1976).

4. Kuhn, *op. cit.*, especially Ch. 10, "Revolutions as Changes of World View".

5. Peter B. Vaill, "The Expository Model of Science in Organization Design". In R. H. Kilmann, L. R. Phody, and D. P. Slevin, *The Management of Organization Design* (New York: North-Holland, 1976) vol. 1, pp. 78–79.

6. Warren H. Schmidt, "Is It Always Right to Be Right?" In Warren H. Schmidt, *Organizational Frontiers and Human Values* (Belmont, Calif.: Wadsworth Publishing Co., 1970).

7. Ackoff, *op. cit.*, proposes that a system of interrelated problems indeed be named a "mess," which would make OD unusually relevant to such situations! See p. 21.

8. Herbert Simon, *The Sciences of the Artificial* (Cambridge, Mass.: MIT Press, 1981), 2d ed.

9. A. R. Radcliffe-Brown, *A Natural Science of Society* (Glencoe, Ill.: The Free Press, 1957).

10. James Miller, *Living Systems* (New York: McGraw-Hill, 1978).

11. Edward A. Wilson, *On Human Nature* (Cambridge, Mass.: Harvard Univ. Press, 1978).

12. Peter L. Berger and Thomas Luckman, *The Social Construction of Reality* (New York: Doubleday Anchor Books, 1967).

13. Bernard Barber, *L. J. Henderson on the Social System* (Chicago: University of Chicago Press, 1970) p. 67.

14. S. I. Hayakawa, *Language in Thought and Action* (New York: Harcourt, Brace & World, 1964) pp. 30–31.

15. For example, Ackoff, *op. cit.*, p. 12.

16. Kurt Lewin, "Quasi-stationary Equilibria and the Problem of Perception." In Warren Bennis, Kenneth Benne, and Robert Chin, eds., *The Planning of Change* (New York: Holt, Rinehart, Winston, 1961) 1st ed. (only), pp. 235–37.

17. Richard A. Richards, "Percept Language: A Tool for SelfAwareness," unpublished manuscript, 23 pp., 1978.

18. Richard Beckhard, "The Confrontation Meeting," *Harvard Business Review*, 45:2 (March–April, 1967), pp. 149–55.

19. Marvin Weisbord, *Organizational Diagnosis*, Boston: Addison-Wesley, 1978.

20. Thomas Pattern, and Peter Vaill, "Organization Development," in Robert Craig, ed., *The Training and Development Handbook*, Madison, Wis.: American Society for Training & Development, Ch. 20, pp. 20-10 ff.

21. Maslow, *op. cit.*

22. William F. Whyte, Edith Lorentz, and Meredity Wiley, *Action Research for Management* (Homewood, Ill.: Irwin-Dorsey, 1961).

23. Robert Tannenbaum, and Sheldon Davis, "Values, Man, and Organizations." In Warren H. Schmidt, *op. cit.*, pp. 129–49.

24. William Torbert, "Why Has Educational Research been so Uneducational: The Case for a New Model of Social Science Based on Collaborative Inquiry," paper presented as part of a symposium, "Toward a Reconceptualization of Research and Method," American Psych. Association Annual Meetings, San Francisco, 1977. Lippitt's "multocular process" is also germane, see Gordon Lippitt, *Organization Renewal*, Prentice-Hall, 1982, pp. 226–27, 2d edition.

25. Barney Glaser, and Anselm Strauss, *The Discovery of Grounded Theory: Strategies for Qualitative Research* (New York: Aldine, 1967) pp. 10–18.

26. Simon, *op. cit.*

4 Values, Truth, and Organization Development

Leonard D. Goodstein

ABSTRACT

The importance of values in organization development is reviewed as are the changes in values in the contemporary American workplace. The principal values dilemma—freedom versus constraint—is examined as it affects the work of the OD consultant. There is a shifting need from organizations for support and constraint in order to increase productivity and quality. The research base of OD as an applied behavioral science is examined and there is strong support for obtaining increases in both productivity and quality without sacrificing OD's traditional humanistic values.

AUTHOR BACKGROUND

Leonard D. Goodstein is Chairman of the Board of University Associates, an international consulting, training, and publishing company. Dr. Goodstein completed his graduate work in psychology at Columbia University and has over thirty years of teaching at the University of Iowa, the University of Cincinnati and Arizona State University. He is a frequent contributor to the professional literature.

All professions are, in the final analysis, value based. The value of the traditional professions—law, medicine, dentistry, teaching, and so on—is reasonably clear-cut to the members of these professions and their respective consumer groups. The value of justice over injustice, life over death, comfort over pain, and knowledge over ignorance are but the most obvious of such respective professional values. The long historical development of these established professions provides a context for the resolution of these dilemmas, at least to some extent. Organization development, however, is a very new profession and lacks both the clarity of the value base and the historical context for resolving professional values conflicts. The intent of this paper is to provide both greater clarity of the values underlying organization development and a context for understanding and hopefully resolving values conflicts and dilemmas.

In the context of this discussion we shall rely upon Rokeach's (1973) definition of values and value systems.

> A *value* is an enduring belief that a specific mode of conduct or end-state of existence is personally or socially preferable to an opposite or converse mode of conduct or end-state of existence. A *value system* is an enduring organization of beliefs concerning preferable modes of conduct or end-states of existence along a continuum of relative importance. (p. 5)

A profession has a value system to the degree to which there is an obvious consensus among the members of that profession about the continuum of values it seeks to attain in its routine work, that is, what sorts of end-states or modes of conduct it regularly attempts to develop in its clients.

There has been early agreement (Bennis 1969) that organization development is a value-based process, but there has not been the same degree of consensus about the nature of the values. A review of the various definitions of organization development (Beckhard 1969; Burke 1982; Burke & Schmidt, 1971; French & Bell, 1978; Golembiewski 1972; Lippitt 1969; Schmuck 1976) does, however, suggest that there is some agreement as to the core values of organization development. What all of these definitions seem to have in common, at least from my reading of them, is an attempt to deal with the central value dilemma of interpersonal relationships, *freedom* versus *constraint*.

As long as I can live by myself (most easily on a deserted island), I can have complete freedom. Freedom to do what I want, when I want, and for as long as I want. But, as soon as I encounter another person, by choice or necessity my freedom is impacted by the freedom of the other person which must constrain me. I want to sleep when the other person wants to play, to eat when I am not hungry, or to have me take out the grabage when I do not wish to. Somehow we must resolve these differences if the relationship is to continue. Somehow we must constrain our freedom is the relationship is to "work." This tension between freedom and constraint exists in every relationship and is an unresolvable one. It can be managed but not resolved, and the tension is always a dynamic one. What worked today may not work tomorrow.

This same dialectic between freedom and constraint typifies the individual's relationship with more formal organizations as well. "As long as you work here you'll dress (talk, cut your hair, work) appropriately!" The choice is a rather clear one—constrain yourself or use your freedom to leave. Except in highly coercive organizations, such as the military or prisons, there is some range of acceptable behavior and the freedom to leave is a real one. But constraint is the cost of belonging.

The history of Western civilization since the beginning of the Industrial Revolution has been toward the surrender of more and more freedom to the ever-more constraining organization, especially the work organization. As Weisbord (1977) has noted previously, organization development has had as its primary purpose the redress of the balance toward more freedom for the individual. Indeed many OD consultants were organizational anarchists who counted as their successes those members of the client system who had been helped to drop out from the client system. How these consultants could justify their fees as being "helpful" to the organization or as helping the organization develop is quite another matter.

But times have changed. Where organization development values were once avant garde, the value discrepancy between organization development professionals and the rest of the society has become much smaller, if not nonexistent. The recent survey of work attitudes by the University of Michigan's Institute of Social Research (Rosow 1979) indicated five highly significant attitude changes on the part of the workers sampled:

1. Less unquestioned acceptance of authority, especially by young people
2. Reduced confidence in traditional institutions, such as schools, churches, and political structures
3. Less willingness to work for the sake of work
4. More expectation that work should be intrinsically challenging and rewarding
5. Higher expectations for participation in the decision-making process

These changes are clearly in the direction of greater freedom and less constraint for the individual and congruent with the value aspirations of organization development.

There is some fairly direct, empirical evidence to support this assertion. Goodstein (in press) contrasted the responses of a sample of line managers with those of a sample of OD practitioners on the Management Values Inventory (MVI) (Howe, Howe, & Mindell 1983). The MVI yields scores on five major value dimensions: (1) locus of control, (2) self-esteem, (3) tolerance of ambiguity, (4) social judgment, and (5) risk taking. The only significant differences were that the OD consultants were higher on tolerance of ambiguity, social judgment, and risk taking, suggesting that consultants are more comfortable with unstructured and ambiguous situations in the work environment, have higher social perceptiveness and social intelligence, and are more willing to make decisions with less data than are managers. The differences, although statistically significant, are small in absolute size and scarcely surprising in view of the nature of the OD enterprise. What is more important is that both the managers and the consultant patterns fit the profile of the contemporary manager previously outlined by Howe (1981), a profile congruent with the value changes reported above.

Another way of examining the freedom-constraint dilemma in OD is in terms of whether OD practitioners equally value organizational task accomplishment and human fulfillment. Friedlander and Brown (1974) suggest that, while both are explicitly part of the goal of an OD intervention, the client system that has engaged the consultant strongly, but subtly, presses for task accomplishment. They go on to warn that OD runs the risk of exploitation of people in the name of performance and profitability. In contrast to Weisbord who sees the tension between freedom and constraint as a positive source of energy for OD as a field, Friedlander and Brown are pessimistic about any rapprochement between what they see as inconsistent goals.

My personal view is that OD has been clearly on the freedom side of the dialectic for most of its existence and that it is now time for OD, as a science and a profession, to move the pendulum more to the constraint side of the dialectic. The reasons for the move are clearly apparent, at least to me. American industry is in trouble—productivity is down, quality is largely poor, and our entire economic system is being challenged from abroad. While the foreign challenge is friendly, the risk is no less severe. What seems apparent to me is that, without some help to remedy these problems, there may be little in the way of viable organizations to develop and OD as a discipline may join the roster of the unemployed. There is, however, one point that I wish to make quite clear—the activities of OD to support the task accomplishment of American business and industry does not represent a change in the basic values of OD, only a necessary balance in the never-ending dialectic between freedom and constraint. And, there is a strong foundation of research upon which we can base our interventions, one that neatly blends the traditional values of OD and the "truth" of research data.

TRUTH AND ORGANIZATION DEVELOPMENT

Increasing productivity and quality is not best accomplished by a return to the sweat shop conditions of the early Industrial Revolution nor by the adoption of nonhumanistic management strategies. The field research on industrial productivity and quality provides solid research support for the contention that such increases are most likely to be achieved and sustained when workers are involved in setting production goals, in directly assuring quality standards, and are directly rewarded for such activity. To the degree to which OD achieves its ambition to be an *applied behavioral science*, OD practitioners need to be aware of these data and use them when marketing and implementing their services.

To put it more simply, humanistic work environments and management strategies are those that are most likely to pay off in increased productivity and quality. Managers who are interested in achieving productivity and quality increases can be encouraged to use such humanistic strategies out of enlightened self-interest, which is probably more potent in producing change than any philosophically based value system.

A few concrete examples may be necessary to support the above position. Over thirty years ago Coch and French (1948) reported a field research study in which several groups of factory workers were given differential opportunities to participate in making choices about changes in the production processes in the factory. This classic study clearly demonstrated that the group of workers with the highest level of participation in decision making was most accepting of the changes in the manufacturing process and also showed remarkable increases in productivity. This relationship between participation in the decision-making process, acceptance of and commitment to the decision, and productivity has been replicated and extended consistently by additional studies.

Another line of evidence is found in the Scanlon System (Driscoll 1979) for improving productivity from the workforce. This system, developed in the 1930s by Joseph Scanlon of the Massachusetts Institute of Technology, involves three primary elements: (1) a monthly bonus paid to everyone in the organization regardless of level, based upon unit or total organizational productivity; (2) joint worker-management groups, a pivotal feature, which meet regularly to evaluate suggestions for innovations in the work process, product, or any other aspect of the business that might impact quality or productivity; and (3) a strong belief in participative management, especially in the concept that workers are capable of self-initiated efforts towards accomplishing organizational goals. What differentiates the Scanlon Plan from most other suggestion programs is that in the Scanlon Plan any gains in productivity are passed on to all employees in the form of bonuses. Thus the Scanlon Plan condones participative decision making and rewards for those behaviors.

A related development, of course, is the quality control circle, a unique part of Japanese management. This bit of social technology marries two concepts, participative decision making and quality control, in a small group context. The widespread use of quality circles in Japan produces ten times as many employee suggestions for changes in manufacturing processes as is the case in equivalent U.S. companies as well as a much higher rate of acceptance of the suggestions (Cole 1979). Similar positive effects are now being reported by those American firms who have introduced quality circles into their operations.

There is a major line of research on the critical role of contingent rewards upon behavior. While much of this work has been basic research, there is now emerging some clear-cut evidence on the importance of direct positive rewards on worker behavior. In perhaps the most famous such case, the Emery Air Freight Company used such contingent rewards to increase the utilization of its productive capacity from 45% to 90%, with a savings of over $2 million over a three-year period ("At Emery Air Freight" 1973). Similar positive consequences for utilizing contingent positive rewards are now reported elsewhere as well (Luthans & Kreitner 1976).

Without belaboring the point, it seems clear to me, and hopefully now to you, that productivity and quality are best increased by applying the same values to which OD has been committed, but to enhance organizational goals rather than individual goals. There is research evidence—very strong evidence indeed— that the reverse is true as well. Namely, harsh and indifferent management practices lead to low organizational effectiveness. Bowers (in press) reported on the reasons for the 11,000 air traffic controllers to go on strike, a strike which led to their being fired and barred from future federal employment. Over 6,000 current FAA employees and over 2,000 controllers who were fired were surveyed by a special form of the Survey of Organizations, a morale and climate measure. The findings show that morale was very poor at all levels of the organization and that there were no differences between those employees who were fired and those who remained on the job. The FAA managers endorsed an autocratic, no-questions-asked style of management while the controllers strongly rejected such a style. Inequitable treatment by supervisors and the controllers' perception of management as autocratic, rigid, punative, and uncaring led to the strike, not inadequate pay or benefits. Bowers concluded that a participative management approach would have prevented the strike and the adoption of such an approach is mandatory if future labor problems are to be avoided.

I believe that the score is in. The last four decades of research in real-world settings provide reasonably unequivocal evidence that participative management and rewards provide the only sure way to produce increases in industrial productivity and quality. Further, the data on the changes in the values of the workplace strongly suggest that it will be far easier to implement such programs than it has ever been in the past. The task for organization development as a profession is clear: to produce and market programs based upon the research findings that offer managers and workers opportunities to collaborate in increasing productivity and quality.

References

At Emery Air Freight Positive Reinforcement Boosts Performance. *Organizational Dynamics*, 1973, 2 (1), 41–50.

Beckhard, R. *Organization Development: Strategies and Models*. Reading, Mass.: Addison-Wesley, 1969.

Bennis, W. G. *Organization Development: Its Nature, Origins, and Prospects*. Reading, Mass.: Addison-Wesley, 1969.

Bowers, D. G. What Caused 11,000 Air Controllers to Quit Their Jobs? *Organizational Dynamics*, in press.

Burke, W. W. *Organization Development: Principles and Practices*. Boston, Mass.: Little, Brown, 1982.

Burke, W. W., & Schmidt, W. H. Primary Target for Change: The Manager or the Organization? In H. A. Hornstein *et al.* (Eds.), *Social Intervention: A Behavioral Science Approach*. New York: Free Press, 1971.

Coch, L., & French, J. R. P. Overcoming Resistance to Change. *Human Relations*, 1948, 1, 512–32.

Cole, R. E. *Work, Mobility, and Participation: A Comparative Study of American and Japanese Industry*. Berkeley: University of California Press, 1979.

Driscoll, J. W. Working Creatively with a Union: Lessons from the Scanlon Plan. *Organizational Dynamics*. 1979, 8 (1), 61–80.

French, W. L., & Bell, C. H., Jr. *Organization Development* (2d Ed.). Englewood Cliffs, N.J.: Prentice Hall, 1978.

Friedlander, F., & Brown, L. D. Organization Development. *Annual Review of Psychology*, 1974, 313–41.

Golembiewski, R. T. *Renewing Organizations*. Itasca, Ill.: Peacock, 1972.

Goodstein, L. D. Managers, Values, and Organization Development. *Group and Organization Studies*, in press.

Howe, R. J. *Building Profits Through Organizational Change*. New York: AMACOM, 1981.

Howe, R. J., Howe, M., & Mindell, M. *Management Values Inventory*. San Diego, Calif.: University Associates, 1983.

Lippitt, G. L. *Organization Renewal*. Englewood Cliffs, N. J.: Prentice Hall, 1969.

Luthans, F., & Kreitner, R. *Organizational Behavior Modification*. Glenview, Ill.: Scott, Foresman, 1975.

Rokeach, M. *The Nature of Human Values*. New York: Free Press, 1973.

Rosow, J. M. Organizational Issues in the 80's: Shifts in Work Force, Changing Values, New Patterns of Work. *OD Practitioner*, 1979, 11 (2), 1–7,14.

Schmuck, R. A. Process Consultation and Organization Development. Professional Psychology, 1976, 7, 626–31.

Weisbord, M. R. The Organization Development Contract. *OD Practitioner*, 1977, 9 (3), 1–8.

5 OD Professionals:
The Route to Becoming a Professional

Glenn H. Varney

ABSTRACT

Many issues and concerns are currently being expressed and debated in organization development. The question of professionalism is one of the most debated. Professionalism is achieved because practitioners are competent and perform in a professional manner. Becoming a professional means developing (1) a systematic educational process, (2) a common body of knowledge, (3) a certification procedure, (4) ethical standards, and (5) a professional association.

Foremost among these is the development of a competency base for OD practitioners. Based on a search of the literature, three competency areas emerge: (1) self and impact awareness; (2) conceptual, analytical, and research skills; and (3) organizational change and influence skills. Each area has a subset of specific skills.

For OD to become a profession, the field needs to develop an accepted and relatively uniform competency model to guide the essential development of OD practitioners.

AUTHOR BACKGROUND

Glenn H. Varney is president of Management Advisory Associates, Inc., a consulting organization dedicated to advising and guiding management in the use of applied behavioral science concepts and techniques for improving individual, group, and total organizational effectiveness. In addition to managing his consulting activities, Dr. Varney is also a professor of management in the College of Business Administration at Bowling Green State University and director of the International MBO Institute.

There is a variety of issues and concerns that can be argued and discussed relevant to the fledgling field of organization development. The concern that seems to override all others is the question of whether OD is or will ever be a profession in even the broadest definition of *profession*. It seems that we act and like to be referred to as professionals, however we pay little attention to what needs to be done to develop the field into a profession.

Issues such as OD ethics, lack of theory base, softness of technology, certification of practitioners, and so on all symbolize the struggle to "professionalize" the field. The focus needs to be sharpened; we first need to examine the skill and competency of the OD practitioner. OD is a profession to the extent that OD people act and perform like professionals.

This paper will examine OD as a profession with emphasis on the current status of OD practitioners. The underlying premise is that OD will become a profession to the extent that practitioners are competent and perform in a professional manner.

IS ORGANIZATION DEVELOPMENT A PROFESSION?

Like medical professionals, organization development specialists engage in the art of improving health and solving problems; however, they do so at the organizational rather than at the individual level. And, as in medicine, an incorrect diagnosis and the resulting prescription can have a devastating impact. The difference between the profession of medicine and the practice of organization development, at this state of OD's evolution, is basically the distinction between a professional and nonprofessional organization. Furthermore, when the "patient" is viewed as the entire organization of human beings (as opposed to a single individual in the case of medicine), a strong argument can be advanced for professionalizing organization development. Although organization development has not reached the professional status of, say, medicine, dentistry, veterinary medicine, or certified public accounting, it is emerging rapidly in the direction of a full-fledged profession.

Historical Perspective

Organization development mainly grew out of the academic disciplines of psychology and sociology, when applied behavioral scientists wanted to enter organizations to test their research concepts in real situations. Those initially looking for research sites were soon followed by others who approached the organization from the point of view of helping the client organization learn something about itself and helping it change.

As time went on, not-so-well-trained individuals were attracted to the rapidly emerging OD profession. Many of those who began to label themselves as OD consultants were from other academic fields or from personnel departments. The field had developed out of multidisciplinary philosophies, so varied backgrounds were encouraged. Readers need only look at the credentials of members in the various OD networks and OD-related organizations to see how easy it is still for almost anyone to enter this field.

The field has also resisted legal guidelines for defining what an OD professional is or does. The Certified Consultants International (CCI) maintains that statutory regulations such as licensing or certification by a state or national agency is inappropriate because of a lack of reliable and valid standards, because of a lack of knowledge about how to train OD professionals effectively, because methods for measuring a practitioner's competency do not exist, and because traditional means of disciplinary enforcement have not proven very effective (Pfeiffer 1976, p. 373). A fear of losing the excitement of discovering different and unique change theories and strategies may stop people from developing professional standards. Many think that both professionalism and the cutting edge of discovery cannot simultaneously exist, and, faced with a choice, would opt for innovation over standards.

The client organizations must also assume some of the responsibility for this dilemma, since many are looking for quick-change solutions to very complicated problems. Their own lack of understanding of organization theory makes them vulnerable to the organizational "change artist" who has developed a flashy picture of how organizations should work and three easy steps for success.

It is one thing to recognize the need for a developmental model for OD professionals, and quite another to design it. This is particularly a problem given the range of skills and knowledge required of an effective organization development professional. Peter Vaill (1971) aptly points out that the complexities in defining what OD is (and therefore what an OD professional does) arise from the fact that OD professional usually look at the entire organization as their province. This includes all the social and technical nooks and crannies of an organization. He states that, "the range of activities they may perform is huge; the variety of organizational circumstance in which they operate is enormous."

What is an OD Professional?

We have not systematically defined what an OD professional is or does. Edgar Huse notes that "although many authors have described the personal qualities of change agents, little empirical research has been done on OD practitioner's" (Huse 1975, p. 303). OD practitioners may describe their experiences, conjecture about what the traits of successful OD professionals are, and even define the appropriate styles to be used in varying situations. But there exists no detailed, empirically based analysis of the skills and competencies needed to succeed as an OD practitioner. The limited documentation on OD competencies consists largely of defining specific traits or talents and various rules of thumb for change agents (Shepard 1975). In the absence of empirically based data we must rely on the judgments and opinions of experienced practitioners as our starting point.

Huse, for example, identifies the following eight personal styles and philosophies as important characteristics for OD professionals: (1) ability to assess themselves accurately, (2) objectivity, (3) imagination, (4) flexibility, (5) honesty, (6) consistency, (7) trust, and (8) stable and secure self-image. Cotton and others identify neutrality, open-mindedness, and flexibility in processing information as the personal qualities necessary to practice OD successfully (Huse 1975, pp. 306–09).

Partin identifies the following seven skill areas as essential for a change agent: (1) assessment of personal motivation and relationships to change; (2) helping the changee become aware of the need for change and for the diagnostic process; (3) diagnosis by the changer and changee, in collaboration, concerning the situation, behavior, understanding, and feeling for deciding upon the problems; (4) involving others in the decision, planning and implementation of action; (5) carrying out the plan successfully and productively; (6) evaluation and assessment of the changee's progress, methods and working, and human relations; and (7) ensuring continuity, spread, maintenance, and transfer of information (1973 p. 20).

Margulies and Wallace suggest several aspects of the OD consultant's behavior important to successful OD practice. These include (1) facilitating the diagnosis of problems, (2) assisting the clear statement and communication of problems, (3) pointing out those things not seen or said by the client, (4) facilitating the formulation of change plans, (5) acting as an integrator, and (6) providing internal continuity (1973 p. 141).

Criteria for Professional Status

Several criteria must be met before a field such as organization development truly can be called a profession. These include:

1. A well-developed field of specialized knowledge supported by an extensive educational system, including an accrediting process. Educational facilities should be highly standardized in the way in which they educate professionals in the field.
2. A common body of knowledge supported by extensive literature and journal documentations.
3. A licensing procedure, usually by examination, with a renewal requirement after some specified period of time. This licensing or certification procedure should be designed to maintain a level of competency for all those attesting to be professionals in the field.
4. The establishment of professional standards and ethical guidelines by which all professionals would be guided. Variation from these standards should subject the individual to censorship or possible removal of license or certification.

5. The creation of professional association that should serve as an educational, ethical, and congregating body for professionals in the field.

OD PRACTITIONERS AND PROFESSIONALISM

If the issue of professionalism is centered on the competence of the practitioner then our focus should be on the development of the practitioner. A distillation of various perspectives of what an OD practitioner does and of the skills and competencies necessary suggests two types of definition for a competent OD professional. First, we can define such a person by identifying the traits or characteristics that he or she should possess and, second, by defining the activities he or she needs to know. Because the trait approach fails to predict successful behavior in other fields, I believe it cannot succeed in defining or distinguishing competent performances in OD.

The definition of activities and knowledge holds more promise. A distillation of the literature yields the following list:

1. *Self-Awareness and Personal Impact Awareness*—Ability to sense organizational needs and generate organizational and individual awareness of need for change.
2. *Conceptual, Analytical and Research Skills*—Ability to link scientific and organizational information; ability to research and diagnose problems within the organization; ability to evaluate with the client the results of the change process.
3. *Change and Influence Skills*—Stimulation of the organization to change; facilitating and assisting the organization to change; following up and providing continuity of direction.

DEVELOPMENT OF AN OD PROFESSIONAL

The three categories cited in the preceding section represent a starting point for defining the major developmental areas for an OD professional. We now can ask what content should each area cover, and how do we organize a learning sequence that provides a systematic acquisition of both knowledge and skills. We can organize the three areas as illustrated in Figure 5.1 which describes the three areas in relationship to the individual practitioner and the client organization involved.

Let us define the three areas in more detail.

1. *Self- and Impact Awareness*—The skills that appear to fall into the self- and impact awareness category are listed below.
   - *Self-Awareness*—Self-awareness refers to being aware of one's own set of values, beliefs, ideas, general emotional state, intellect and all those things that make up the total person, being aware of how these things

FIGURE 5.1   Individual Practitioner and Client Organization Relationship

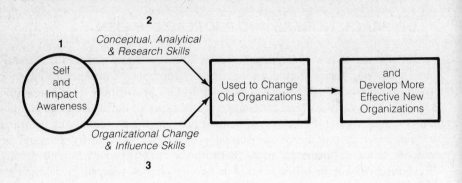

interact within the individual as well as how they are stimulated from outside a person.

- *Self-Awareness and Others*—This skill area has to do with the impact an individual has on others and being aware of the other person's reaction to you.
- *Other Awareness and Interpersonal Awareness*—This set of skills has to do with the awareness of transactions and associated consequences growing out of interpersonal relationships.
- *Personality Theory*—Being knowledgeable about personality models and how personality theories can be useful in understanding human behavior.
- *Group Theory*—Being knowledgeable of how groups of people work together and what group dynamics can contribute to OD practice.
- *Organizational Theory*—Organizational theory attempts to integrate various behavioral theories. The OD practitioner needs to develop an awareness of theoretical organizational constructs already developed.

2. *Conceptual, Analytical and Research Skills*—The general category of conceptual, analytical, and research skills involves the following basic skills and competencies.
   - *Theory Building*—OD practitioners need to be able to theorize about what's happening in organizations. Such theories help practitioners make predictions about the organization.
   - *Theoretical Mapping*—Assuming that the OD practitioner has knowledge about organization, group and personality theories, theoretical mapping simply takes that theory and applies it to the organization, describing the organization in terms of known theories.

■ *Concept Model Building*—This skill involves the ability to conceptualize and design mental as well as graphic models of what an organization is like and in particular ways in which the organization can be conceptualized differently from what it is today.

■ *System Analysis and Organizational Diagnosis*—As the title implies, this involves being able to analyze the interaction between systems such as the technical and social systems and being able to design methodologies and procedures for collecting information about the organization.

■ *Data Processing*—Here an OD practitioner needs to be able to assemble data which has been collected and apply statistical techniques to test hypotheses, thus assuring valid and meaningful information about the organization.

■ *Feedback and Presentation*—This skill has to do with the ability that a person has to develop approaches to feedback information to the organization.

3. *Organizational Change and Influence Skills*—Finally, the basic organizational change and influence skills are as follows.

■ *Change Strategy Design*—This skill involves the ability to design basic strategies for helping the organization change. This is to be differentiated from the actual use of specific interventions such as team-building, confrontation meetings, etc.

■ *Intervention Design*—In this skill area we are referring to the specific activities that an OD practitioner uses to help the organization learn about itself and about the impact of change. This includes the full spectrum of experience-based exercises.

■ *Persuasion/Power*—OD practitioners need to develop skills as well as be able to know how to use the power of a consultant, either internal or external, to help the organization or to influence the organization to change.

■ *Facilitation/Process Skills*—These skills are commonly thought of when one thinks about an OD practitioner. The ability to "help" the organization and to facilitate changes. This is commonly referred to as "process skills."

■ *Intervention Styles*—This is being aware of the different styles that can be used to interact with the organization and the adaptability of the OD practitioner to the particular needs of the organization.

■ *Teaching and Educative Skills*—These skills have to do with the ability to conduct stand-up teaching both cognitively or experientially.

Although we have no doubt left out some areas which may be important to the well-rounded development of an OD practitioner, we have tried to cover the most important areas.

OD may or may not become a profession in the same sense as psychology, sociology, medicine, and so forth. However, it has the potential of becoming a highly useful practice in organizations that have a high level of need for systematic change. Whether the field of OD survives may largely depend on the kinds of people who practice in the field and the ability they have to influence and successfully assist organizations in changing. What all this amounts to is that if you desire to practice in the field of organization development you need to be aware of the kind of skills and competencies that are required to succeed. Not only will you be doing yourself a favor, but you'll also be aiding your own organization or client organizations in the long run. I believe that organization development is here to stay whether it is conducted by people who call themselves organizational development practitioners or by some other professional field under some other label.

References

Huse, E. F. *Organization Development and Change.* St. Paul, Minn.: West, 1975.

Margulies, N., & Wallace, J. *Organization Change: Techniques and Application.* Glenview, Ill.: Scott Foresman, 1973.

Partin, J. J. *Current Perspectives in Organization Development.* Reading, Mass.: Addison-Wesley, 1973.

Pfeiffer, J. W. "Perspective." *Group and Organizational Studies.* 1976, 1 (4).

Vaill, P. B. "Practice of Organization Development." Position Paper. *Organization Development Section of the American Society for Training and Development,* Madison, Wisc.: 1971.

6 Transorganization Development: Developing Relations Among Organizations

Kurt Motamedi

ABSTRACT

Since its inception, the target of OD planned changed efforts has been individual organizations. This article proposes that the underlying "rugged organizational individualism" paradigm can be augmented. Transorganization development (TD) consists of planned change efforts which facilitate the development of relations among organizations. It can change transorganizational systems (TS) through identification, convention, organization, and evaluation processes. The article discusses the use of TD planned change processes among organizations in TS.

AUTHOR BACKGROUND

Kurt Motamedi (Ph.D., U.C.L.A.) is professor of management at the Graduate School of Business and Management, Pepperdine University, and visiting professor at the Graduate School of Management, University of California, Los Angeles. His areas of research, teaching, and practice include organization development, design, and strategy. He first began his study of trans-organization systems and development in 1975 during the "Anti-herbicide (dioxin) movement" in the Pacific Northwest forests. Kurt has conducted many symposiums and workshops on trans-organization development during the past five years. He has published numerous articles in national journals and is a consultant to organizations in the United States and abroad.

The author expresses his gratitude to earlier comments of Tom Cummings, U.S.C.

To survive and retain vitality, organizations must understand and deal with their external environment. In a turbulent environment, characterized by uneven change and complexity, organizations are more interdependent than in more simple and stable environments. Such interdependency is increasingly manifest in aggregates of organizations pursuing common or complementary purposes. The "rugged organizational individualism" paradigm is gradually being expanded to include organizations as members of transorganizational systems (TS). TS are multiorganizational forms and include consortiums, joint ventures, industries, stakeholder groups, political action committees, coalitions, community organizations, and other aggregate groupings of organizations. Although the organization development (OD) literature treats organizations as open systems, in practice it has neglected dynamic interactions among organizations. The literature has tended to focus on single organizations and their internal dynamics with OD strategies applied to organizational systems which have well-defined boundaries, formal hierarchies, and relatively stable structures and processes. TS typically do not have these bureaucratic features. It is an open question whether current forms of OD are appropriate for developing TS.

This article draws attention to transorganizational systems and develops a preliminary outline for a new field of planned change called *transorganizational development*. It includes a discussion of transorganizational systems (TS) and presents strategies for transorganizational development (TD). The aim is to increase the awareness of OD practitioners and researchers to this emerging field of planned change.

TRANSORGANIZATIONAL SYSTEMS

Transorganizational systems (TS) comprise organizations that have joined together, explicitly or implicitly, to accomplish common or complementary purposes. TS are embedded in a larger network of organizations (Aldrich & Whetten 1981) and constitute a level of analysis intermediate between single organizations and societal systems. TS members maintain their own individual goals and identities while pursuing collective goals either through formal structures or through informal relations and processes. They attempt to resolve problems that single organizations cannot solve alone.

There are abundant examples of TS in our society. Whenever the interests of a group of organizations are at stake, there is potential for emergence of TS. Governmental regulations, citizen concerns, economic policy changes, international trade modifications, technological development, and other similar changes frequently impact not one organization but groups of organizations. For example, gun control legislation affects the set of organizations comprised of gun collectors, manufacturers, suppliers, sellers, law enforcement agencies, and other related organizations.

TS are frequently created in response to internal or external changes. According to Boje (1982), TS members attempt to influence the direction or magnitude of change to their advantage. They may cooperate or compete with one another to promote, avoid, or resist change. For example, oil companies have often collaborated with one another to explore, produce, and distribute fossil fuel products, influence legislation, and control foreign policy. Their interactions represent a TS.

There are many different bases for forming TS, from interagency coordination in the public sector to industrial and organizational competition and cooperation. Although each TS is unique and requires careful study, at least two dimensions are helpful for categorizing TS. One dimension represents the extent of relatedness (intensity and frequency of interaction); the other represents the extent of coordination of TS members and activities. These provide information for understanding four types of TS as shown in Table 6.1 and Figure 6.1.

In *Type I* TS, relationships are direct and coordinated, typically through centralized distribution of resources, hierarchies of policies, or mandates. A central organizational body might emerge to regulate the direct interactions of members according to plans, established authority, set patterns of resource allocation (budgeting), and rules. For example, the National Collegiate Athletics Association (NCAA) regulates sports activities among member colleges, monitors their interactions during games, and determines many policies and rules to which member colleges must conform. When members deviate from those established procedures and rules, they are disciplined and all or part of their privileges of membership are removed.

Type II TS involve organizations that interrelate indirectly through intermediaries who coordinate their transactions. The Organization for Petroleum Exporting Countries (OPEC) is an example of this type of TS. Through a central representative body, activities of members are coordinated. The level of oil output, price, and members' monetary receipts are regulated. Countries in this case do not directly interact, but rely on intermediaries, such as shipping organizations and foreign oil companies, for information regarding production, schedules, and deliveries.

Historically, the Civil Aeronautics Board (CAB) has assumed the role of promoting air traffic and its safety. Among the many coordinating and regulating activities of the CAB are the enforcement of safety procedures, route scheduling,

TABLE 6.1   Typology of Transorganizational Systems (TS)

		Relatedness	
		High	Low
Coordination	High	Type I	Type II
	Low	Type III	Type IV

FIGURE 6.1 Four Types of Transorganizational Systems (TS)

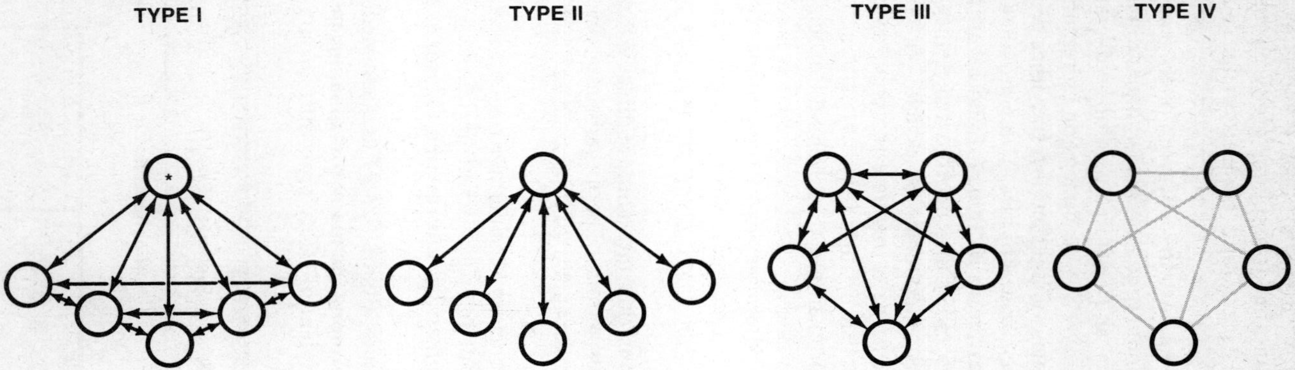

	TYPE I	TYPE II	TYPE III	TYPE IV
Coordination:	High (centralized)	High	Low	Low
Relatedness:	High	Low	High	Low
Example:	NCAA, NBA, NFL, etc.	OPEC, CAB, United Way, etc.	Interacting Organizations and Industries (Vertical) (e.g., personal computer industry)	Uncoordinated Freestanding Organizations and Industries in the General Environment

*The Coordinating Body

and pricing. Until a few years ago, airlines (TS members) relied on the coordinating agency (CAB) to assign and protect routes and fares. CAB reduced competition among TS members by partitioning the TS field according to geography, economics, quality, and quantity of service. Eventually, airlines joined forces, and through lobbying (a TS process), successfully limited the coordinating role of CAB. The planned transorganizational changes have resulted in an increase in direct competition among the airlines, that is new norms of behavior in the TS. (A number of airlines have been acquired by others, have found themselves in financial ruin, or have profited from this TS change.) Type II examples are prevalent in many regulated industries. The United Way is another example of Type II TS. It collects funds and resources in the environment, distributes them among TS member organizations, and monitors their operations and expenditures.

Type III TS have direct relationships, but are not highly coordinated. Relations among community action groups or private enterprises doing business with one another fall into this category. These organizations freely interact to achieve individualistic, but complementary purposes without established coordinating bodies. For example, in the personal computer (PC) TS, microcomputer manufacturing, consumers, and software producers interact directly to enhance members satisfaction. They attempt to manage change and maintain a dynamic equilibrium through mutual adjustment, trade, publications, education, and a host of vertical and horizontal transorganizational activities.

Type IV TS comprise loosely connected member relationships which are indirect and low in coordination. Many adjoining neighborhoods or cities in a given region may work toward mutual concerns, but seldom interact directly or coordinate their relationships. TS members may pursue common purposes implicitly, for example, safety and protection, and may not be highly aware of the other's concerns. Other examples of Type IV TS include the uncoordinated efforts of diverse numbers of independent organizations responding to a societal concern. In recent years, Type IV TS have loosely formed around such issues as nuclear power, nuclear arms race, pollution, civil rights, toxic waste, and abortion. In economics, the pure competitive environment in which each firm independently produces products (for independent consumers) can be construed as a Type IV TS.

The collective performance of any type of TS depends on a complex set of variables and processes. The type of TS is determined by two critical variables: the level of coordination and the directness of relations. The success of planned change efforts will depend on the selection of appropriate strategies and interventions in each TS type. In the following section, two approaches to planned change in TS are outlined and their uses discussed.

PLANNED CHANGE IN TS

Bennis et al. (1976) define planned change as a conscious, deliberate, and collaborative effort to improve the operations of human systems. OD is a dominant planned change strategy for improving operations in organizations. It is frequently directed at single organizations with developed purposes, structures, and processes which are often organized and bureaucratic. The application of OD strategy in TS is limited and is not appropriate to all four types of TS. The four types of TS described represent a continuum, ranging from tightly related and highly coordinated Type I, to loosely related and highly uncoordinated Type IV. The kinds of developmental issues facing TS can be expected to vary depending on the amount of coupling and coordination. The form of planned change necessary will vary accordingly. TS with tightly-coordinated relationships among member organizations, such as those found in Type I TS, resemble bureaucratic organizations. They are likely to exhibit many of the developmental problems faced by bureaucracies, such as rigid adherence to rules and procedures, overcommunication, and relationships. Given the resemblance between Type I TS and bureaucratic organizations, OD appears an appropriate form of planned change for developing those kinds of TS, particularly when the amount of coupling and coordinating of relationships among member organizations thwarts effective TS performances.

As relationships among TS members become more indirect or uncoordinated, such as those found in Types II, III, and IV TS, new kinds of developmental problems emerge. The change issues are typically quite different from those occurring in bureaucracies. They include such problems as lack of cohesion among member organizations, ambiguous directions and goals, and poor coordination of members' behaviors, and resources. Generally, the less a TS is organized, the greater are the possibilities of conflict among TS members and their inability to plan for the needed changes. The planned change problems faced in these types of TS are generally caused by underorganization, rather than overorganization, which typically plagues bureaucratic Type I TS. For example, without the help of influential TS coordinating bodies and tight coupling of membership, it would be difficult to engage a TS in the OD change effort. In these systems, there are neither influential coordinating bodies to sponsor OD efforts nor direct interactions among members. There is a lack of a shared sense of reality, awareness of problems and their solutions, and commitment to action.

Successful planned change in the under-organized TS requires an approach beyond OD. Transorganizational development is such an alternative strategy. It has the potential to bring about effective planned change in Types II, III, and IV TS.

TRANSORGANIZATIONAL DEVELOPMENT (TD)

Transorganizational Development (TD) is a planned change strategy with three purposes. First, TD is directed to improve collective performance of TS in the broader environment. Second, TD aims to increase TS members' satisfaction and goal fulfillment. Third, TD attempts to accomplish the previous two purposes through generation and utilization of relevant and valid knowledge and the involvement of professional practitioners. It comprises the application of planned change beyond single organizations. TD is not a straightforward extension of OD.

Entry into TS can occur in various ways and is not a central theme in TD. The change agent (person or organization) might be a TS member, an outside party contacted by a single, multiple, or collective of TS members. Regardless of the entry process, successful TD efforts often consist of four essential processes. They are identification, convention, organization, and evaluation (Table 6.2).

Identification

The first step in TD involves the identification of both existing and potential members who have a desire to join or an interest in influencing TS outcomes. It helps partition the collective from the environment and determine membership identity and boundaries. In under-organized systems with ambiguous purposes, the criteria for membership is frequently vague. As a result, the identification process might be subjective and arbitrary. Care must be taken not to exclude potentially relevant members. Williams (1980) suggests including peripheral

TABLE 6.2 Elements of Transorganizational Development

Phases	Purpose	Processes
1. Identification	Partition TS membership from the environment	■ Identify existing and potential members ■ Determine and map relationships ■ Assess ideologies, goals, and aspirations ■ Analyze strategies and actions ■ Verify abilities, resourcefulness, significant contributions, and threats ■ Classify TS membership in relevant groupings
2. Convention	Develop commitment to solving TS problems	■ Create opportunities for members to interact ■ Share ideas, information ■ Assess present needs, future desired outcomes and methods of change ■ Surface assumptions regarding problems and solutions ■ Reach concensus on major decisions
3. Organization	Design mechanisms to accomplish desired ends	■ Jointly optimize TS members' needs, TS task and environmental requirements ■ Allow freedom for TS members to pursue own goals while implementing effectively TS purposes
4. Evaluation	Monitor and assess TD change and take corrective action	■ Collect data preferably on pre, post, and on-going change ■ Analyze the data ■ Feedback the data to relevant TS members ■ Jointly diagnose problems and take corrective actions ■ Recycle all or part of TD process when necessary

members, although there may be costs. The cost is the increased size of the membership and increased confusion at the early stages of TD.

There are a number of tasks that gain importance during TD identification. TS members' relationships are determined and mapped; their ideologies, goals, aspirations, strategies, and actions determined; and their abilities, resourcefulness, significant contributions and threats, and informal influence verified. These activities help identify and classify TS membership in accordance with similarity and diversity of goals, ideologies, abilities, intensity of relations, coordinating roles, and other factors.

Convention

Once identification is completed, relevant TS participants convene. The convention process creates an opportunity for members to interact, share concerns, reach consensus on the nature of problems, and formulate strategies to resolve or deal with problems. The primary purpose is to enable members to share ideas and information regarding (1) the current state of needs, potential opportunities, and threats, (2) the future desired outcomes, and (3) methods for bringing about change. The change is aimed at reducing the discrepancies between the present state of affairs and future desired states. Members motivation to interact is an important concern in the convention process. Motivation to interact derives from actual and perceived levels of common purpose, commitment to share concerns and problem solving, dependency on resources, or external mandate. TD change agents can alleviate some of the motivational barriers by increasing the awareness of the membership of their needs and potential benefits of TD outcomes.

There are a number of practical convention problems that require attention of TD change agents. First, the identity and role of the organization (or organizations) that initiates the convention process will have impact on the outcome. Gricar (1981) has pointed out the problem of legitimacy, credibility, and authority that often faces the convenor. Convenors are sometimes drawn from institutions of higher learning and research to maximize neutrality, objectivity, and expertise. The convenor, in the face of strong differences and adversities among TS members, is frequently pressured to take sides. To reduce the extreme polarization of conventions by members, Van de Ven (1976) suggests that organizations be represented by individuals who relate with other TS members. Organizational boundary spanners (Miles 1980) might be such representative individuals.

Second, the size of convention is another issue of concern. Williams (1980) proposes that thirty to thirty-five members is a sufficient size to represent the range of interest of most any search conference. The convention must attempt to represent proportionately equal representation of TS organizations. The aim is to reach a balance between size and fair representation.

Third, the outcome of the convention process is much influenced by kinds of interventions used and their impact on the unique needs of TS members. The convention design must facilitate surfacing of TS members needs, assumptions, and solutions. Ends and means are discussed. A successful convention process will result in commitment of members to explicit TS goals and outcomes in view of the broader environment and enlightened self-interest. Care must be taken to minimize undesirable side effects. Unnecessary confusion, unproductive behavior, and domination of the process by a few members should be minimized. The impact of the convention design on members' contributions must be seriously considered. Neither a rigid design nor a loose and unfocused design is helpful. Efforts must be made to develop a balanced design that enhances members' contributions and the effective outcome.

A successful convention outcome is a requisite to facilitate the organization of efforts. Once the required and desired TS outcomes are determined, the TD change efforts focus on the design and structure of TS activities and tasks to be accomplished.

Organization

The organization phase involves the development of strategy, planning of actions, design of relationships, and determination of procedures and protocols. It is comprised of structuring (McCann 1982) and developing mechanisms and processes that both enhance and regulate members' performances. It directs TS members' efforts to accomplish desired ends.

The process of organizing deserves special attention. In order to increase acceptance of change efforts and member commitment, TS members should participate in the TD organization process. Trist (1976) has discussed the need for designs that are based on socio-ecological principles. They encourage diffusion of power, shared problem solving, and involvement in implementation. It is important to tailor the design and implementation to "jointly optimize" TS members' needs and TS task environment requirements. Survey feedback of implementation and design data among TS organizations (Taber 1979) have been helpful in the development of effectiveness of TS organizations. It is desirable to develop designs that allow members to pursue individualistic goals while contributing effectively to TS collective purposes. Care must be taken to encourage diversity and innovation while dealing with dysfunctional dynamics. Organic designs tend to prevent TS over-organization and bureaucratization and increase the effective performance. To prevent and eliminate undesirable consequences, TD change and TS outcomes need to be periodically evaluated. Effective evaluation will identify present and future potential problems and possible solutions.

Evaluation

The purpose of the evaluation process is to monitor and assess the impact of TD change and to make timely corrections to minimize unintended dysfunctional consequences. The process might include data collection before, after, and frequently during the TD change effort. Three sets of TS variables deserve attention:

1. The environmental receptivity of TS outcomes determines the level of TS collective performance and its desirability in the environment.
2. Members' need fulfillment is a measure of the internal effectiveness of TS.
3. The availability of input resources from the environment indicates TS resource dependencies and control of the environment.

Results of the analysis are used in further diagnosis, identification, convention, reorganization, and TD change. In cases in which TD efforts have been successful, choices are to disband and terminate TD efforts or continue to deal with other present or future problems. Given the loosely coupled nature of many TS, the TD evaluation can be helpful to identify important emerging issues and concerns, take appropriate corrective actions, and avert or reduce the possibilities of future difficulties. The evaluation of the end results provides an additional opportunity to recycle the TD processes for another round of improvements.

Planned change efforts in TS require approaches that extend beyond traditional OD. Aspects of OD can be applied successfully to the bureaucratic Type I TS. The loosely coupled and uncoordinated Types II, III, and IV TS can be benefited by application of TD (see Figure 6.2). As TS move closer to Type IV, there is a greater need for application of TD. Each of the above four phases of TD requires different skills and competencies. Effective TD practitioners are aware of dynamics of each phase and possess the appropriate skills to meet the challenge.

FIGURE 6.2 TS Typology and the Appropriate Application of OD and TD Planned Change Strategy

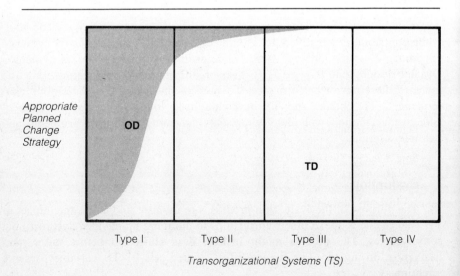

Transorganizational Systems (TS)

SUMMARY

Knowledge of transorganizational systems and their design and development is critical to sustaining organizational effectiveness. In complex and changing environments, the institutional infrastructure consists of many interdependent organizations that are embedded in transorganizational systems (TS). Two dimensions, the extent of coordination and directedness of relations, can be used to classify TS. The classification is helpful in selecting planned change strategies. The strategies consist of OD and transorganizational development (TD). The former is more applicable to TS types that are tightly related and coordinated, the latter to other types. OD has a long tradition of application, while TD is in its infancy and requires considerable conceptual and practical development.

To be effective, TD change agents must be skillful in identifying, convening, organizing, and evaluating TS. They must design and develop large systems and be responsive to change-related issues across a broad range of variables. TD extends beyond current OD to include competencies in (1) the "macro" organizational field involving organization theory and design, interorganization theory, and environmental analysis; (2) policy sciences and strategic planning; and (3) affiliated "macro" fields including economics, sociology, marketing, political behavior, social movements, social ecology, research methods, and the like. These requirements help prepare the TD practitioner to respond appropriately to the needs of TS and their change.

TD can make a significant contribution to the design and development of needed TS in our society. It can contribute to the development of relations among organizations, interfacing diverse groups of organizations for the effective pursuit of common or complementary purposes. In a rapidly changing and diverse society such as ours, TD has many opportunities for making important institutional contributions. TD needs further conceptual and practical refinement to fulfill its current potential. This article is an attempt in that direction.

Bibliography

Aldrich, Howard and David A. Whetten, "Organization—Sets, Action Sets, and Networks. Making the Most of Simplicity," In P. Nystrom and W. Starbuck (Eds.) *Handbook of Organizational Design,* I (London: Oxford University Press, 1981), 385–408.

Bennis, Warren; Kenneth Benne; Robert Chin, and Kenneth Corey, *The Planning of Change* (New York: Holt, Rinehart & Winston, 1976).

Boje, David, "Towards a Theory and Praxis of Transorganizational Development: Stakeholder Networks and Their Habitats," Working paper, 79–86. Behavioral and Organizational Science Study Center, Graduate School of Management, University of California, Los Angeles, February, 1982.

Gricar, Barbara, "Fostering Collaboration Among Organizations," In H. Meltzer and W. Nord (Eds.) *Making Organizations Human and Productive* (New York: John Wiley & Sons, 1981) 38–49.

McCann, Joseph, "Social Problem Solving," unpublished paper. University of Florida, Gainesville, 1982.

Miles, Robert, *Macro-Organization Behavior* (Glenview, Illinois: Scott, Foresman and Co., 1980).

Taber, Thomas Walsh, Jeffrey; & Cooke, Robert, "Developing a Community-Based Program for Reducing the Social Impact of a Plant Closing." *Journal of Applied Behavioral Science,* 1979, (15) 133–55.

Trist, Eric, "A Concept of Organizational Ecology," Invited address to Department of Psychology, University of Melbourne, Melbourne, Australia, July, 1976.

Van de Ven, Andrew, "On the Nature, Formation and Maintenance of Relations Among Organizations," *Academy of Management Review,* 1976, (4) 24–36.

Williams, Trevor, "The Search Conference in Active Adaptive Planning," *The Journal of Applied Behavioural Science,* 1980, (16) 470–83.

7 Designing Work for Productivity and Quality of Work Life

Thomas G. Cummings

ABSTRACT

This paper presents two critical contingencies affecting work-design success: the technological demands of the production process and the social/psychological needs of employees. Different kinds of work design are shown to be effective under different technological and employee-needs conditions, and it is argued that in most work situations, compromises will have to be made between designing work to optimize technological rationality and designing work to optimize employee satisfactions.

AUTHOR BACKGROUND

Thomas G. Cummings is associate professor of organizational behavior at the Graduate School of Business Administration, University of California. He received B.S. and M.B.A. degrees from Cornell University, and his Ph.D. in socio-technical systems from the University of California at Los Angeles. Dr. Cummings was previously on the faculty at Case-Western Reserve University. He has authored five books: *Job Satisfaction and Productivity; Management of Work; Improving Productivity and the Quality of Work Life; Systems Theory for Organization Development;* and *Labor Relations: A Multi-Dimensional Perspective.* Dr. Cummings has also written numerous scholarly articles, and given several invited papers at national and international conferences. He is associate editor of the *Journal of Occupational Behavior,* and past chairman of the Organization Development Division of the Academy of Management.
   Dr. Cummings's major research and consulting interests include designing work systems and organizations, planned

organization change, and occupational stress. He has conducted
several large-scale union and management projects for improving
productivity and quality of worklife, and has been consultant for
a variety of private and public-sector organizations in the United
States, Europe, and Mexico.

The past decade has witnessed a growing and, at times, evangelical call for improving productivity and the quality of work life (QWL). Clearly, the future will see more and more organizations seeking to design work with these objectives in mind. Almost as numerous will be the published reports, workshops, and experts offering how-to advice on the topic. Much of this information will be general and theoretical. If it is to be applied in a specific corporate setting and satisfy specific corporate needs, then corporate planners will need to know precisely what the key success factors in work design are. Cull through all the data, models, and empirical studies and you'll find that there are at least two critical contingencies affecting work-design success: the technological demands of the production process and the social/psychological needs of employees.[1]

TECHNOLOGICAL CONTINGENCIES

From a technological perspective, there are two facets of the production process that are critical in making work-design choices (see Figure 7.1). The first, *technical interdependence*, involves the extent to which a company's technology requires a high level of employee cooperation to achieve a productive outcome. In general, the degree of required cooperation determines whether work should be designed for the individual or for work groups. When technical interdependence is low and there is little need for worker cooperation—for example, in field sales, keypunching, and telephone installation—work can be designed for individual jobs. On the other hand, when technical interdependence is high and employees must cooperate—in such processes as coal mining, oil refining, and assembly lines—work must be designed for groups that comprise employees performing interdependent tasks.

The second technological dimension involves *technical uncertainty*, as measured by the amount of information employees must process in order to produce a product or service. In general, the amount of input demanded by the technology determines whether the work design should be geared to external mechanisms of control, that is worker self-regulation. When the amount of technical input is small and little information has to be processed by employees, as in assembly work and repetitive jobs, work can be reprogrammed and designed for external forms of control. On the other hand, when the technology requires employees to process considerable information in their work, as happens in research, professional services, and maintenance tasks, work must be designed for a high level of employee decision making and self-control.

OPTIMIZING TECHNOLOGY

Figure 7.1 shows how these two technological dimensions, interdependence and uncertainty, combine to form four different work situations. Quadrant 1 includes areas where technological interdependence and uncertainty are both low; given these conditions, work can be designed for individual jobs with external mechanisms of control. These "traditional jobs" are preprogrammed or routine tasks offering little latitude for employee discretion, task variety, or feedback.

On the other hand, when task interdependence is high but uncertainty is low, as in the second quadrant, work should be designed for groups and should include external forms of control. These work designs would include "traditional work groups" such as those found on assembly lines, where worker interaction is scheduled and lower levels of individual discretion, task variety, and feedback are necessary.

In quadrant 3, representing low technical interdependence but high un-certainty, work should be designed for individual jobs with internal forms of control. These "enriched jobs," such as those in the skilled trades, allow high levels of employee autonomy and task variety, and employee feedback is important.

The final set of technical conditions is shown in quadrant 4. One example of a quadrant-4 situation would be a team operating the control room of an auto-mated production process. Here, technical interdependence and uncertainty are

---

FIGURE 7.1 Work Designs Optimizing Technology

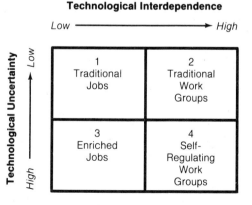

Courtesy of *Outlook* (no. 8, p. 40)

both high, and require work-group designs with internal control. Referred to as *self-regulating work groups*, quadrant-4 teams engage in relatively distinct group tasks and team members have the necessary skills, discretion, and information to control their interactions around those tasks.

These four work designs are intended to satisfy specific technical demands concerned with interdependence and the need for input. When work designs do not match these technological requirements, unintended but serious consequences may result. One common problem is overdesigned work, which results in a more complex and costly design that is technically necessary. For example, some organizations attempt to enrich jobs of low technical uncertainty. But enriched jobs and self-regulating groups require lengthier and more sophisticated employee selection and training, higher wage rates, more complex and socially oriented managerial skills, and longer-term implementation than traditional designs, and such an investment may be so costly as to weaken the company's competitive position.

The reverse problem arises when work is underdesigned for the company's technology, as when traditional work designs are applied to conditions that demand high levels of technical input (see quadrants 3 and 4). Here, poor performance results from the inability of the work force to adjust rapidly and effectively to technical problems. Thus, from a technological perspective, the consequence of mismatching the work design to the technology is either a design that is more sophisticated and costly than necessary, or a design that does not make the most of the technology.

HUMAN-NEED CONTINGENCIES

The second major contingency that affects work-design success are the employees' needs, both social and psychological. The first need involves people's desire for significant social relationships. These *social needs* determine whether work should be designed for individual jobs or work groups. Generally, the stronger the employees' social needs, the more group oriented their work should be.

The second need is related to people's desires for personal accomplishment, for learning, and for developing themselves. These *growth needs* dictate whether work should be designed to allow for low or high levels of complexity and challenge. In general, the stronger an employee's growth needs, the more complex and challenging that employee's work should be.

OPTIMIZING HUMAN NEEDS

Like the technological dimensions, the two kinds of human needs can be combined and optimized through different kinds of work designs, as shown in Figure 7.2. When an employee needs a relatively low level of social interaction, but strong direction (quadrant 1), traditional jobs are most appropriate. Here again, the term refers to highly routine, repetitive tasks. For people who are quadrant-2 types, who have a strong need for social interaction, but less of a

FIGURE 7.2 Work Designs Optimizing Human Needs

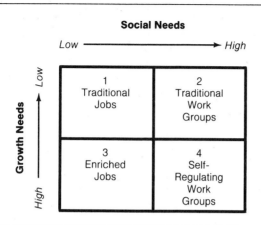

Courtesy of *Outlook* (no. 6, p. 40)

need for growth, traditional work groups that allow for more interaction are most productive. Here the tasks these groups perform need not require a high level of discretion, variety, or challenge. Quadrant 3 represents those employees who have relatively weak social needs, but strong growth needs; their work should be designed as individual jobs offering greater complexity and challenge. These enriched jobs should afford high levels of employee discretion, task variety, and feedback. When people's social and growth needs are both relatively strong (quadrant 4), the most effective work design is self-regulating work groups, which offer opportunities for significant social interaction around complex and challenging tasks.

If employees' social and growth needs are accommodated through work design, high levels of motivation and satisfaction and low levels of absenteeism and turnover can be expected,[2] assuming, of course, that wages, benefits, and other factors are perceived as satisfactory. When work designs do not match employee needs, and employees are unable to find satisfaction through work performance, they will search for other behaviors or jobs to fulfill their needs. For example, people with relatively weak social needs often withdraw from interaction when placed in work groups; such behavior can hinder the cooperation necessary for interdependent tasks. Conversely, employees with strong social needs tend to seek social relationships when working on individual jobs; this can lead to the creation of informal work groups that detract from individual job performance. Employees who have less need for growth can experience stress and frustration when confronted with highly complex and challenging work designs, while people with strong growth needs tend to feel alienated and bored with routine tasks. In both cases, the usual results are dissatisfaction, withdrawal from work, and other forms of counterproductive behavior.

OPTIMIZING BOTH TECHNOLOGY
AND HUMAN NEEDS

So far, the technological and social/psychological contingencies affecting work-design outcomes have been discussed separately, as if work were designed to maximize either technical rationality or human-need fulfillment. However, if high productivity and QWL are to result, work must satisfy both technical and human requirements. Yet, as Figures 7.1 and 7.2 suggest, joint optimization is likely to occur only in very limited circumstances. For example, when the technological dimensions of production processes shown in Figure 7.1 are compatible with the social and psychological needs of employees shown in Figure 7.2, the respective work designs combine readily and can satisfy both. However, when technology and people are incompatible—when you have, for example, quadrant 1 technical conditions, but quadrant 4 employee needs,—joint optimization is difficult, if not impossible. Unfortunately, such mismatches prevail in most organizations, but a number of options are available to management for resolving the problem. On one hand, technology and/or people can be changed to bring them more into line with each other; on the other hand, the two can be left unchanged and compromise work designs can be created. In most such compromises, either human resources or technology will be favored, depending on the company "culture."

COMPONENT CHANGES

Traditionally, most work designers have taken the second approach—leaving the people and the technology unchanged—and have developed compromise work designs in accordance with company policy. Sociotechnical systems design has shown, however, that technology and people can often be modified or juggled, so that work can be designed to satisfy both.[3] For example, technological interdependence can be reduced through the expedient placement of buffer stocks and inventories, breaking long assembly lines into smaller, more discrete units. Conversely, technical interdependence can be increased by reducing the physical or temporal distance between sequential stages of production. Technological uncertainty can be reduced by standardizing and programming as many tasks as possible; it can be increased by allowing employees more discretion over work-related matters.

Modifying employees' social/psychological needs is more complex. One promising approach is to match new or existing workers with available work designs. For example, organizations can assess employees' social/psychological needs through standard instruments that have been developed for that purpose; this information can then be used to counsel employees and help them find jobs compatible with their needs. Similarly, employees can be allowed to volunteer for specific work designs; such a self-selection process seems to increase the chance of a productive match. Both examples typically require high levels of trust and cooperation between managers and workers, and a shared commitment to designing work for high performance and greater QWL.

COMPROMISE WORK DESIGNS

The second strategy for accommodating both technical and human requirements is to create compromise work designs that leave the technology and the people unchanged and only partially fulfill the demands of either. A key issue in choosing a compromise work design is the extent to which one kind of contingency will be maximized at the expense of the other. For example, when capital costs are high relative to labor costs, organizations typically tailor the work design to the technology and relegate employees' needs to a less important role. Whatever social costs are incurred—such as employee dissatisfaction, absenteeism, and turnover—they are considered minor relative to the benefits of maximizing technical rationality. On the other hand, organizations may choose to invest in employee motivation and satisfaction at the risk of short-changing their technology. Here, for example, increased motivation and satisfaction may be judged to be worth the expense of providing complexity and challenge to employees who have a strong need for growth.

These examples show either end of a range of compromises based on different weightings of technical and human demands. Whether you choose a strategy that is based on compromise work designs, or a strategy that directly matches technology and people, your success in improving productivity will depend on a thorough assessment of these factors and of the cost/benefit tradeoffs between them.

Notes

1. See Thomas G. Cummings and Edmond S. Molloy, *Improving Productivity and the Quality of Work Life.* New York: Praeger Publishers, 1977.
2. J. Richard Hackman and Greg R. Oldham, *Work Redesign.* Reading, Mass.: Addison-Wesley, 1980.
3. See Thomas G. Cummings and Suresh Srivastva, *Management of Work: A Socio-Technical Systems Approach.* San Diego: University Associates, 1977.

8 OD vs. QWL

Philip H. Mirvis

ABSTRACT

This article looks at differences between contemporary organization development (OD) and quality of work life (QWL) change programs and looks toward their integration in the management of change in the future. It looks first at definitional distinctions and calls them inaccurate, wrongheaded, and unholy and then turns to differences observed in philosophy and practice. These center on the morality of means and ends, on orientations toward clients, and on the conduct of practitioners. Only dedication to development in the field and quality in the delivery of service can reconcile them.

AUTHOR BACKGROUND

Philip H. Mirvis is associate professor of behavioral science, Boston University, and is interested in the study of organizational change efforts. He is the co-editor with Stanley Seashore, Edward Lawler, and Cortland Cammann of *Assessing Organization Change,* and the co-editor with David Berg of *Failures in Organization Development and Change.* His recent research and consultation is addressed to corporate acquisitions and mergers.

This article is adapted from a speech delivered to the National Academy of Management. The speech followed presentations by Michael Beer, of the Harvard Business School and formerly director of OD at Corning Glass, and Ted Mills, director of the American Center for Quality of Work Life.

In the beginning, God created the heaven and the earth. And the earth was without form and void, and darkness was upon the face of the deep. And the spirit of God moved upon the face of the waters. And God said, let there be OD, and there was OD.

My candle burns at both ends. It will not last the night. But ah my foes, and oh my friends, I've had a quality work life.

It seems we are always grasping for definitions. Definitions classify our world, making it less formidable, more manageable. They inform and guide us and, particularly when we try something new, they enable us to communicate about what we are doing. In the emerging practice of managing organization change, there have been many attempts to define approaches and distinguish between them. Mike Beer, in the *Handbook of Industrial and Organizational Psychology*, defines the approach called organization development (OD) as a set of technologies, including process consultation, team building, and the like, while Ted Mills, in a document prepared for General Motors, distinguishes quality of work life (QWL) programs as a competing approach, for he says quite emphatically that they are not process consultation, team building, and so on.[1,2] Are these approaches different? And is one superior to the other as each of these definers implies?

They are different. The difference, however, is not found in definition, but in history, orientation, and purpose. Indeed most who study organization change and nearly all who practice it find such definitions muddled and, at times, fanciful. I believe this is because we cannot precisely define the processes of change. What is more, to attempt to do so, and to label one approach to managing these processes as superior can be wrongheaded, unholy, or worse: it can be at the expense of developing organizations and providing quality of work life to their members. I know. I've tried to define these approaches.

I recently spoke at a seminar at the University of Michigan, and began my talk by handing out a sheet of paper that had a list of OD definitions, one by Bennis, one by Beckhard, one by French and Bell, and then used the overhead projector and put my own definition on the screen.[3,4,5] After the seminar, I received a report from one of the attendees, a man named Frank Smith from the Tennessee Valley Authority, an organization sponsoring a quality of work life program in which he was a leader. His report began, "The subject of this seminar was organizational development, or OD. What is OD?" Well, to tell you the truth, we never did get around to any precise definition. Smith continued:

I suppose that is one thing I've learned about this type of activity as opposed to engineering, things are not always precisely defined. For instance, do you know a definition of quality of work life? This lack of definition bothered me for a long time, but I think that at the school I began to appreciate the logic. In dealing with human behavior, where things are not very precise anyhow, perhaps it is better to give things only broad general meanings. This gives us the flexibility to tailor the particular term to achieve the specific purpose we want from it. In other words, we decide what we want to do right here with OD or QWL, or whatever.

Behind Smith's statement, I believe, is the problem with definitions. They can inform and guide, but they, and we, can be misused; so let me speak to my objections to definitions. First of all, I said it is wrongheaded to define OD. Why? Because the phenomenon itself defies precise definition. Marvin Weisbord, a prominent OD consultant, defines it as a secular religion.[6] It has its priests, its rituals, its followers, its moral dogma, and like all religions, its truth is not found in words, but in belief and action. We know that God made light the first day and that Edna St. Vincent Millay's candle gave such a lovely light. For those who follow the faith of OD, or the faith of QWL, then precise definitions are impossible. Instead, definitions must be prophetic and poetic—metaphors for a way of life.

However, certainly the scientist in us must scoff at poetic and prophetic definitions. After all, can't scientists define light? Well, no they can't, as a matter of fact. They can't decide whether it's energy, matter, neither or both. Well, how about Webster? Webster offers fourteen definitions of light, and the fifteenth is "that by which something as a cigar may be lighted."

Precise definitions do serve a function. They make the management of change seem more rational, more like a science. They leave us with a feeling of mastery, in the belief that change is predictable, that we have events under control. Yet when we move away from their abstraction and into the processes of change, we find they are both rational and emotional. And when we undertake change efforts, we find ourselves both in and out of control. By describing OD and QWL change efforts in the precise language of scientific discourse, we neglect their nonrational, noncontrollable elements. We make them seem straightforward and fool ourselves into believing they are easy and manageable. We deny they are risky and fun. That misrepresents the process of change and makes our definitions incomplete and misleading.

Webster does not mislead because definitions convey multiple meanings and these are ordered historically, on the basis of dated citation and semantic development. And scientists limit their attentions solely to essential realms, leaving religion and the arts to communicate the meaning of existential experience. It is thus wrongheaded to draw precise definitional distinctions between OD and QWL, for in their definition we become ahistorical and neglect the meaning of these activities. Worse still, we trivialize them.

Is it better to give these approaches to change broad, general meanings so that the terms might be tailored to specific purposes as Frank Smith recommends? No, for today countless management practices are labelled under the rubric of OD and QWL with scant attention given to what or whose purposes are served. Broad definitions are not only innocuous and irrelevant, they are unholy. Whereas OD is a secular religion to some, politics is a secular religion to others, and our broad, general definitions of management practices have become part and parcel of the political process. Look, for example, to the politics of working America in the U.S. government in the late 1960s. Were we to have a National Commission for Productivity *or* for Quality of Work Life? Behind these semantics was a struggle between government agencies and institutional forces with one camp advancing industrial democracy, and the other interested in output from employees. The compromise was a National Commission for Productivity *and* Quality of Work Life. But this term did not define the commission's joint mission; instead it was a cover under which competing interests concealed their distinctive political pursuits.

We needn't look only at government to see the politicization of definitions— it is also at work in private enterprise. There is a book popular among educators that includes a chapter by Ted Mills in which he refers to Fromm's distinction between the ethic of having and the ethic of being.[7] QWL, he states, is very much in keeping with the ethic of being. It's a spiritual way of life, an evolution of natural forces into a pattern of social change. Yet in a *Harvard Business Review* article, he notes QWL has been accepted as a tool for improving return on investment.[8] This sounds suspiciously like the ethic of having with its emphasis on an economic way of life and welding "natural" forces to the interests of corporate chieftains. Clearly this gives consultants, trainers, and managers the flexibility to tailor the term to fit their purposes. Thus it becomes a marketing device to appeal to the varied interests of clients and those who serve them. It conceals their political differences from one another, and, ultimately, it conceals their political differences from themselves.

Lest we look only at government and the private sectors, look also at academe: Walt Westley has noted how we define QWL to serve our own purposes.[9] Sociologists define it in sociological terms, psychologists in psychological terms, engineers in engineering terms, and fill their journals bickering with one another over what quality of work life "really" means. Clay Alderfer and David Berg, writing about the profession and the practitioner, note that such terms serve more than purely academic debate.[10] After academicians arrive at very precise definitions of their concepts and measure them, they attempt to beat practitioners over the head with their findings and expose them as frauds! Here, again innocuous definitions put to political purpose. They fill the journals, maintaining divisions between scholars. And lest anyone outside the academe pay attention to them, they will note that academics discredit not only one another, but always and especially the practitioners.

As we enjoin the discussion over quality of work life and organization development over the next few years, as we will, I urge that we not worry about our definitions, that we not debate them, that we not bicker over them. Whatever definitions we arrive at will be wrong. They will be used, and we will be used in the process. And unintentionally or intentionally, we may do damage to the spirit of organizational development and quality of work life itself.

Well, then, what are scholars to do? And how will practitioners communicate about their activities to peers and superiors? What I am suggesting is that we change the way we think about and undertake change programs. In an earlier time, myths served the functions that definitions do today. And today's science-based practices were seen as instrumental and expressive rituals. History records differences in these myths and practices, of course; of interest is not only what they accomplished for the society, but what they meant to people—how they ordered existence and made life fulfilling. Here history shows impressive commonality.

Such commonality is also evident in looking at OD and QWL. Both are based on the marriage of scientific and humanistic world views and both incorporate communal, collaborative rituals. Their myths and rituals serve the same functions that myths and rituals always have: they preserve the social order and maintain the social position of leaders, nobles, and priests. The rewards they offer to working people are sought and available in our enlightened and affluent times.

Still, despite an essential commonality in myth, ritual, and purpose, there are differences in orientation and enactment between these two approaches to managing change that are rooted in their histories and evident in contemporary practice. As definitions misrepresent these differences and are politicized and exploited, scholars need to "go native" to understand them. This means putting away disciplinary blinders, throwing off preconceived notions, and getting involved. In turn, practitioners need to stand back from their activities and consider openly and freely what they do and what it means to people. This is the real contribution of Ted Mills and Mike Beer. While I'm not fond of their definitions, I have learned a great deal about OD and QWL from them. This learning follows from their candid descriptions of their own change efforts and their poetic and prophetic thinking about OD and QWL, which is not represented in their definitions.

Let me elaborate on two of the key differences noted by Beer and Mills: the ways those who practice OD and QWL conceive of their means and ends and of the larger purpose of their endeavors. First, Beer stated that OD efforts are intended to improve both business *and* human results in organizations—as though the two are separable. This follows, in part, from the historical development of OD with its emphasis on small group "process" rather than "products" and continues today with the separation of OD from economic functions in many organizations. By contrast, Mills noted that many proponents of QWL trace their roots to the European sociotechnical school with its emphasis on joint optimization of human and technical processes in production. In its American form this implies the collaboration of labor and management in achieving this joint social and economic function. Thus, for QWL, business and human results are inseparable.

Second, Beer emphasized that the "technologies" of OD, and their application through a diagnostic and prescriptive model, aim to improve the integration of the individual and the organization. Mills criticized this as a "cookbook" approach. But this criticism transcends preferences over cuisine, for to many proponents of QWL, the OD problem-solving methodology ignores larger political and societal forces. Hans van Beinum of the Ontario Quality of Working Life Centre has stated that work life is at the conjunction of three social systems: individual, organizational, and societal.[11] Thus efforts to improve it will necessarily involve all three. QWL, then, is equally concerned with the integration of the individual and the organization into the larger society. Hence it is perhaps best viewed not solely as an approach, but as a movement.

These differences and distinctions, however, are drawn from observations about current practice and, in my view, will not endure. Research on human resource management, including my own work with Barry Macy and Edward Lawler on the financial impact of employee attitudes and behaviors, has documented the link between human and economic processes and products in organizations.[12, 13] Research of organizations as "systems", including my own work with David Berg and Don Michael on sources of failure in organization change, has documented the impact of personal and societal forces on even the best-conceived change efforts.[14] Thus, as we enter an era of accountability, I would expect to see change agents of all stripes become increasingly conscientious and skilled in achieving socially and economically beneficial results. Similarly, I would expect to see them become increasingly sophisticated and savvy in taking account of systemic forces and foibles in planning and implementing programs.

There is, of course, always a lag between research and practice and some risk that the uninformed tail may wag the dog. But competitive pressures from Japan, Inc., which takes behavioral science research very seriously, and from firms practicing what *Business Week* hailed as the "new industrial relations" in the society, which draws from the work of Mayo, McGregor, Kilert, Argyris, and many others, means that practice will be catching up fast and that the dog will be shaking all over. My view is that these research findings and their practical import for organizations here and abroad are so damned obvious that they will inevitably shape both OD and QWL activities and dissolve the distinctions Beer and Mills have observed. That is to say more broadly that the larger forces of history will make these current distinctions moot. One small vehicle may be cross-fertilization between scholars and practitioners of OD and QWL. History shows that such co-mingling between groups produces common myth and ritual synthesized from distinct ones. That is not to say that the passage of time alone will cause such distinctiveness to blur. There are other aspects of OD and QWL, deeply rooted in psyche and tradition, that may resist mingling and this, in the end, could foredoom them both to faddishness and irrelevance to future needs. Let me consider these next.

One notable value difference between proponents of OD and QWL is the "morality" of their means and ends. What are the ends of organization development? Definers say effectiveness and health. What is a developed organization? Scholars say it is adaptive, productive, and galumphing. People can't seem to relate to those terms. They don't have any real internal meaning. But when Edward Lawler and I issued an audit of quality of work life in Graphic Controls Corporation we could count the number of women and minorities employed by and promoted in the organization thus attesting to its equal employment practices.[15] We could count those injured on the job thus evaluating its commitment to safe working conditions. We could ask employees whether they enjoyed their jobs, their bosses, and themselves at work. And we could report this in the firm's annual report such that employees could say, "Yes, this is what work is like in our company"; stockholders could say, "Yes, it is important for us to know how our company is doing in this area"; and both could say emphatically, "The quality of work life in the company is an integral part of its financial health." For them, these ends were more understandable and more meaningful than indicators of adaptiveness and galumphing. Why?

It may be only that there are no personalized criteria of a developed organization. We can measure the height and weight of developed people, of course, and the productivity and profits of a developed organization, but we cannot capture their essence. Quality, as Zen motorcyclists know, is an inner experience, as is work, as is life. Thus I have spoken of the need to represent these experiences through art—stories, paintings, pictures—as these appeal to the senses, much more so than abstract indicators of organization effectiveness.[16] But the measures Ed and I reported in Graphic Control's annual report were not "arty" and were not "inner essences"; they were measures of everyday existence and behavior. Their appeal, I believe, goes beyond the metaphysics of measurement to their resonance with our moral compass. Criteria of QWL represent broadly shared standards of what is right and wrong about the quality of work and life. One real difference between OD and QWL, then, is the values of their ends to people. QWL has a moral component about the rights of working people and the responsibilities of employers to honor and respect them.

What is the morality of OD as a secular religion? In the years gone by, Tannenbaum and Davis articulated its value base, Argyris stressed its relation to personal development and learning, and Bennis and Likert underscored its implication for societal change.[17, 18, 19] But as I meet OD specialists at seminars at the University of Michigan, I find these values have passed into abstraction, and as I visit organizations I find they have disappeared from pragmatic practice. OD proponents scarcely talk about employee rights and employer responsibilities. It's as though they have no quality in their own work lives. QWL proponents say again and again what they seek is simple human dignity at work. From this, they believe, will follow adaptability, productivity, and maybe even galumphing. Their lesson is that faith in people and commitment to moral organization produces "quality" and "development." It's a lesson OD must relearn.

Another look at the morality of OD and QWL, however, reveals a paradox, for if OD has no "soul" in its ends, there is considerable soul and some practical guides to living embedded in its means. The "cookbook" Mills discredited is, in fact, an educational menu, with elaborate ingredients, and recipes that call for preparation in an atmosphere of free choice, personal commitment, and collaborative inquiry. Moreover, OD professionals, as Walton notes, have standards of ethical conduct and procedures for certification far more demanding than those of professional chefs.[20] Finally, they set their table with training, serve with process consultation, and clear with an eye to revising the menu on the basis of the diner's content. By contrast, the menu of QWL is sparse, the methodology inelaborate, the standards of conduct lax, and the procedures for certification absent. More to the point, there is no soul in its means. Calls for collaboration between labor and management scarcely mention the joy of working together, and procedures for joint optimization give no explicit recognition to the human emotions and feelings involved in learning. So if OD can learn from QWL of the morality of ends, then QWL can learn from OD of the morality of means.

There is some evidence that these lessons will be learned. Dutch Landon, Director of Organization Development at General Motors, recently worked with managers and employees at Buick to draft an employee's "bill of rights" and in a subsequent speech suggested that "industrial democracy" in General Motors and throughout American industry was "inevitable." Mike Brower, Director of the Massachusetts Quality of Work Life Center, recently worked with managers and employees at Malden Mills to introduce training, process consultation, and evaluation in their QWL program. With such cross-fertilization it may be that we will see more souled OD and QWL programs and practitioners in the future. Maybe—for this integration of value and orientation also depends upon clients who will support it and practitioners who will deliver it. Let me turn my attention next to the clients and practitioners of OD and QWL.

Who is OD for? People who want it. OD practitioners are very explicit about offering their services to clients in need. Theirs is an organization-wide change strategy based upon support from the "top." Often this implies considerable front-end investment in the development of internal resources or in the top-down implementation of a change program. Who is QWL for? From all appearances, some who want it and some who do not. I have seen in the past year more slick brochures lauding the aims of QWL than in the past ten years of mailings from OD people. But that may have to do more with marketing trends and my professional affiliations than the inherent slickness of OD and QWL themselves. More telling, I think, are the numbers of QWL efforts that are begun as "demonstration projects." Ostensibly such projects are begun as pilot efforts in order to "learn" from them. The real intent, I believe, is to demonstrate for proponents that it "works" and for antagonists that it "does not."

Bob Cole, a sociologist who has studied workplace changes in the U.S., Sweden, and Japan notes there is a singular interest in measuring the impact of QWL efforts in this country.[21] Partly this may be attributable to the numbers of underemployed academics in the U.S. who are eager to ply their trade. But it may also be attributable to the fact that U.S. managers and union personnel are uncomfortable with collaborative undertakings and have to "test" them. The inevitable consequence is the politicization of measurement as the results of QWL programs are twisted and turned to twist and turn out "right."[22]

OD and QWL clients can learn something about commitment from one another. I believe QWL clients can learn from those who sponsor OD of the importance of organization-wide support and the heartfelt commitment of the "powers that be." In turn, OD clients can learn from those who sponsor QWL efforts that that commitment must come not only from management, but also from employees and their representatives in unions. In that context measurement is no longer a report card, but an aid to learning.

This brings me to the final distinction between OD and QWL. OD practitioners, by training, value, and orientation conceive of themselves as *helpers* who are there to help the client *learn* and *learn to learn*. They stand apart from organizational dynamics and facilitate, educate, and train. They mirror organizational conflicts and act as catalysts in the creation of change. By contrast, QWL practitioners are *organizers* who are there to help the client *move* and to *move to move*. They immerse themselves in organizational dynamics and jockey, gamble, and horse-trade. They "absorb" organizational conflicts and lead in the creation of change.

These differences in style go beyond machismo in manner to the roots of professional socialization. Many OD practitioners came from the helping professions and many QWL proponents come from consulting or labor organizing traditions. And each is well prepared for their client situations. But as client's expectations and orientations change, so shall those of change agents. Warren Bennis has long criticized OD practitioners for ignoring power politics in development efforts. QWL practitioners have shown how these forces can be productively managed and even changed. But QWL practitioners can be criticized for losing the human touch in their efforts. In this regard, OD experts have shown the way. It should be remembered that history's preeminent change agents—Jesus, Marx, and Ghandi—were both politicians *and* helpers.

In sum, these, I believe, are the meaningful differences between OD and QWL—not in definition, but in value and orientation—differences in means, differences in ends, differences in clients, and differences in the way they are put into practice. I also believe that these differences will not be bridged by research or eroded by changed in the context of professional practice. What is needed is reform within the profession—a dedication to *development* in the field and to *quality* in the delivery of professional services. This will lead to a reconciliation of means and ends and of the interests of clients and practitioners toward an integrated standard of practice. Today we have split into two camps, argued definitions, called each other names, and discredited ourselves, clients, and, as always, practitioners. A pox on both the QWL and OD houses. I would propose instead that as scholars and practitioners we seek to look for common ground and reconcile differences in the spirit of development. In the process we will develop, and our views of development and quality of work life will be enlarged and in turn change the way we develop.

This is the essence of Frank Smith's concluding message to his personnel:

> One thing mentioned early in the seminar was that behavioral philosophies come and go. I asked one of the visiting professors if he thought OD was a fad. He said perhaps some of its aspects were not permanent, and that the name might not survive. But he thought that maximizing human resources was here to stay. I don't know about you, but I share that view. We no longer have a society made up of the educated rich and the uneducated poor who can be easily exploited. That day has long past. I know that here in TVA we have sharp, intelligent people, with capabilities far beyond the use they are being put to on the job. I believe that people want to use those capabilities and to make the best possible contribution they can in their work. This thinking is a common thread to QWL, and to OD, and that is why I am committed to them both. (*Personal correspondence*)

Notes

1. Beer, M. The Technology of Organization Development in M. Dunnette (Ed.) *Handbook of Industrial and Organizational Psychology*. Chicago: Rand-McNally, 1976.
2. Mills, Ted. *Quality of Work Life: "What's in a Name?"* General Motors Corp., 1978.

3. Bennis, W. *Organization Development: Nature, Origins, and Prospects.* Reading, Mass.: Addison-Wesley, 1969.

4. Beckhard, R. *Organization Development: Strategies and Models.* Reading, Mass.: Addison-Wesley, 1969.

5. French, W. L., and C. H. Bell. *Organization Development.* Englewood Cliffs, N. J.: Prentice-Hall, 1973.

6. Weisbord, M. How Do You Know It Works If You Don't Know What It Is? *OD Practitioner*, 9, 3, 1977, 1–8.

7. Mills, Ted. Work as a Learning Experience. *Relating Work and Education.* San Francisco: Jossey-Bass, 1977.

8. Mills, Ted. Human Resources—Why the New Concern? *Harvard Business Review.* March–April 1975: 120–34.

9. Westley, W. Problems and Solutions in the Quality of Work Life. *Human Relations.* 32, 2, 1978, 113–23.

10. Alderfer, C. P., & D. N. Berg. Organization Development: The Profession and the Practitioner in P. H. Mirvis, and D. N. Berg (Eds.) *Failures in Organization Development and Change.* New York: Wiley Interscience, 1977.

11. van Beinum, H. *On the Strategic Importance of Quality of Work Life.* Paper presented to the 5th International Personnel Conference. Montreal, CA., 1975.

12. Mirvis, P. H., & B. A. Macy. Accounting for the Costs and Benefits of Human Resource Development Programs: An Interdisciplinary Approach. *Organizations, Accounting, and Society.* 1976, 1, 179–94.

13. Mirvis, P. H., & E. E. Lawler. Measuring the Financial Impact of Employee Attitudes. *Journal of Applied Psychology.* 1977, 62, 1–8.

14. Michael, D. N., & P. H. Mirvis. Changing, Erring and Learning. In P. Mirvis and D. Berg (Eds.) *Failures in Organization Development and Change: Cases and Essays for Learning.* New York: Wiley, Interscience, 1977.

15. Lawler, E. E.; P. H. Mirvis; W. Clarkson; & L. Randall. Measuring the Quality of Work Life How GRAPHIC CONTROLS Assesses the Human Side of the Corporation. *Management Review.* October 1981, pp. 54–63.

16. Mirvis, P. H. The Art of Assessing the Quality of Work Life. In E. Lawler, D. Nadler, and C. Cammann (Eds.) *Organizational Assessment: Perspectives on the Measurement of Organization Behavior and the Quality of Work Life.* New York: Wiley Interscience, 1980.

17. Tannenbaum, R., & S. Davis. Values, Man and Organization. *Industrial Management Review*, 10, 2, 1969, 67–83.

18. Argyris, C. *Management and Organization Development.* New York: McGraw-Hill, 1971.

19. Likert, R. L. *New Patterns of Management.* New York: McGraw-Hill, 1961.

20. Walton, R. E. The Ethics of Organization Development. In G. Bermant, H. Kelman, and D. Warwick (Eds.) *The Ethics of Social Intervention.* Washington: Hemisphere, 1978.

21. Cole, R. *Work, Mobility and Participation.* Berkeley: University of California Press, 1979.

22. Mirvis, P. H., & D. N. Berg. Failures in Organization Development and Change. In P. Mirvis and D. Berg (Eds.) *Failures in Organization Development and Change: Cases and Essays for Learning.* New York: Wiley Interscience, 1977.

9 Organizational Realities: The Politics of Change

Virginia E. Schein

ABSTRACT

Viewing organizations as political environments, the development of power bases and the use of political strategies are necessary for effective implementation of change programs in organizations. Major power bases include expertise, informational, political access, assessed stature, staff support, traditional and credibility/mobility. Since power alone is insufficient unless one uses it astutely, strategies for implementation are also presented. Drawn from executive interviews, these strategies include presenting a nonthreatening image; diffusing opposition and bringing out conflict; aligning with a powerful other; and developing liaison, among others. The role of deception and its differential operation in static and dynamic systems are also discussed.

AUTHOR BACKGROUND

Dr. Virginia E. Schein is associate professor psychology, The Bernard M. Baruch College of the City University of New York. Formerly she was associate professor of management, The Wharton School, University of Pennsylvania, and director of personnel research for Metropolitan Life Insurance Company. An active consultant to business and industry and author of over twenty scientific publications, she is listed in the American and World editions of *Who's Who of Women*. Dr. Schein received her Ph.D. in industrial-organizational psychology from New York University.

One reality of organizational life consists of rational behaviors involving planning, organizing, directing, and controlling. Underlying these activities is another set of organizational behaviors revolving around gaining and keeping power. Power struggles, alliance formation, strategic maneuvering and cutthroat actions may be as endemic to organizational life as planning, organizing, directing, and controlling.

Machiavelli (1513; 1964), in giving advice to his Prince, spoke openly of the importance of being political—that the illusion of being honest, compassionate, and generous was important to gaining and maintaining power, yet so, too, was the realistic necessity of breaking one's word, being cruel, and being parsimonious. Be a lion and a fox was his counsel.

Although this advice was directed at those interested in the takeover of principalities, a cursory look at behavior within organizations suggests that Machiavelli is still with us and still doling out advice. His ghostly hand would seem to be behind memorandums that distort or omit information; meetings held to decide what has already been decided; coalitions formed covertly to block a decision; rewards promised but never given out, and so on.

If organizations are viewed as political environments in which the acquisition of power is the key ingredient, then the similarity in tactics and strategies between managers and princes should not seem strange at all. It is only when we view organizations as rationally structured systems, built on a division of labor, separation of function, hierarchical flow of communications, and formal authority, and operated by individuals working toward the corporate objectives, that political behaviors appear dysfunctional, appear to be behaviors that muddy the waters and prevent the work of the organization from getting done.

The view presented here is that the latter description is an illusion and that the reality of the way organizations do function is far more similar to a political arena, with individual managers jockeying within it for power and influence. Within this political arena, the effective change agent needs to develop a power-oriented approach to achieving organizational-change objectives.

THE POLITICS OF CHANGE

The politics of change refers to the use of or the need for power acquisition behaviors in order to implement new ideas or approaches in an organization. Viewing organizations as political environments, any proposed change program will threaten the current power distribution. According to Pettigrew,

> others may see their interests threatened by the change, and needs for security or the maintenance of power may provide the impetus for resistance. In all these ways new political action is released and ultimately the existing distribution of power is endangered. (1975a, p. 192)

Given this possibility redistribution of organizational power, many high-quality and seemingly beneficial change attempts can be thwarted by political strategies employed by organizational members who seek to maintain their own power or eliminate the power of the change agent. Systematic change programs that impact a variety of organizational levels often fall prey to the political strategies designed to block the change effort. Supervisors, middle managers, and other staff groups perceiving the new program as a threat to their power can employ a variety of tactics, both overt and covert. For example, middle managers can stall and de-energize in order to avoid loss of their power. The staff department can block by use of its expertise. A supervisor can align with a powerful person in upper management or with a key subordinate in order to maintain the current distribution of power. Given the political nature of organizations, such counterstrategies and resistance should always be expected. They are offensive and defensive strategies designed to acquire and maintain the power necessary to function and to achieve one's objectives within the organization. Counterstrategies are a natural and expected component of any proposed change program.

The dual components of the change agent's job—content development and implementation responsibility—are not always recognized, especially by internal staff specialists.

The content aspect of the job refers to the specific technical aspects of programs and proposals. For the most part, given a reasonable amount of expertise in the area, one's credibility and qualifications with regard to the technical components are rarely questioned. On the other hand, there is limited legitimate power for the implementation aspects of the job. Successful implementation of a particular project or proposal requires the development of power bases, usually above and beyond that of technical competence, and the use of strategies in order to successfully implement one's project.

Unfortunately, the implementation aspect is often not fully understood by many professionals. A qualified specialist very often undertakes a project, develops a high-quality proposal, and assumes that since the project meets the highest technical and professional standards that the bulk of his or her work is completed. To the extent that such specialists neglect the implementation aspects of their projects, however, they will usually find that their proposals or projects will remain in their own or someone else's desk drawer.

To counter natural resistance to change and its concomitant redistribution of power, and to successfully implement one's ideas, one needs to develop both power bases and the skill in strategically using the resources one has developed. The two key components of the politics of change and implementation are power bases and power strategies.

POWER BASES

Power bases are those resources available to an individual that give the individual the ability to convince another to go along with his or her innovative ideas. Few power bases are given—that is, few come with the job. Most need to be developed by the individual and continually maintained else they be eroded by others seeking to expand their own power and influence.

Among the power bases available to internal and external consultants are expertise (French & Raven 1959; Pettigrew 1975a); informational (Pettigrew 1975a; Raven 1965); political access and assessed stature (Pettigrew 1975a); staff support; tradition; and credibility/mobility.

Expertise

A major power base for any professional is that of expertise. Such expertise, acquired through prior education or on-the-job experience can be a strong base for influencing others.

Moreover this base can be expanded through careful assessment of the needs of the organization and development of expertise that meets those needs. For example, in the United States, personnel departments have been gaining power and influence due to their ability to cope with a major external force—the government. Over the last ten years, a whole host of governmental regulations affecting the organization's personnel, such as equal employment opportunity, occupational health and safety, and privacy, among others, required major policy changes. In response to this need, personnel specialists have acquired expertise in these areas and with this expanded power base, they have increased their influence in organizations.

While expertise is a useful power base, two aspects must be noted. First, attempts to exert influence outside of one's areas of expertise can be ineffective and reduce positive perceptions of one's actual expertise. Second, overuse of one's expertise—for example, the use of jargon particular to the area of expertise and too much technical information—can diminish the influence and impact of this base.

Information Power

Related to the base of expertise is that of information power. Internal and external consultants have access to a variety of functional groups, and as such can acquire information from all of them and be the central source of information. External liaisons, such as colleagues outside of the organization, can also provide information sources not available to anyone in the organization. Given this access to and control over information, one can influence others by (1) having more information than the other party, (2) withholding portions of the information, or (3) distorting the information one transmits.

Political Access

Political access refers to the ability to call upon informed networks of relationships within the organization. The development of an informal network of relationships provides the consultant with information as to what's happening and is a means of influencing other individuals. Members of this network can also be used to influence operating heads who might not otherwise listen to a staff specialist or outside professional.

Assessed Stature

Assessed stature is "the process of developing positive feelings in the perceptions of relevant others" (Pettigrew 1975b, p. 200), and is usually developed out of one's base of expertise. By initially having a run of successes, one develops these positive feelings and from there on, becomes known as a winner. Political timing with regard to the use of assessed stature is important. Given that assessed stature can ebb and flow within an organization, it is imperative that influence attempts be made only when assessed stature is high, and avoided when assessed stature is low.

Staff Support

A fifth power base, for internal consultants, is that of support within one's own staff group. Such support is not difficult to achieve since staff people often develop strong bonds among themselves in order to fortify themselves against negative outcomes and rejection of their ideas. Despite the use of power tactics and strategies outside of one's unit, the head of such a unit can best maintain staff support by being open and honest with his own subordinates. In a way, the unit head becomes a kind of military leader, commanding loyalty and support from his troops. As long as the troops can trust him, they will continue to work hard on the technical aspects of the proposal and aid the unit head in developing strategies and tactics to achieve his outcomes. In addition, staff members who are loyal to the project can also develop their own liaisons with individuals at their own levels in other similar units in order to further increase the amount of information that flows into their work unit.

Tradition

By virtue of long service or affiliation with an organization, individuals can acquire unique organizational knowledge and use it to influence others. Defensive strategies usually accompany the power base of tradition. For example, telling a new entrant that "this organization is a house of cards" can deter the implementation of his new idea.

Credibility/Mobility

Unlike line and operating personnel, internal consultants are more likely to have outside professional groups from whom they receive recognition and support. This outside support base and the building up of professional credibility gives the specialist far more leeway and freedom within the organization. If all else fails, the internal consultant can always leave his or her particular job and get an equal if not better job in another organization. Hence, this mobility factor provides the internal consultant with certain amounts of freedom of expression not available to other individuals within the organization.

POWER STRATEGIES

Power alone is insufficient unless one uses it astutely. Strategic maneuvers based on the resources available are vital to successful implementation. The selection of a particular strategy, the means by which influence is attempted, is a function of four factors: one's own power bases; the power bases of others; situational awareness (that is, what are appropriate organizational behaviors); and personal awareness (what strategies work well for a particular person). Given the situational specificity of strategy selection, there are no "ten best strategies." However, one can build up a repertoire of strategies from which to choose. What follows, then, are illustrations of strategies for implementing change. Among other sources, they have been taken from 146 situational descriptions of uses of power gleaned from interviews with 73 executives, discussions with internal and external consultants, and the author's own management and consulting experiences.

Present A Nonthreatening Image

When attempting to introduce innovative programs it is often important to be perceived as being conservative and essentially nonthreatening to ongoing organizational activities (Kelley 1976). Related to this, the innovator should learn the repertoire of acceptable arguments and cast his or her change proposals within these terms. For example, one consultant, in seeking to get a new policy adopted, strategically identified all the decision makers who might influence its adoption, ascertained their motives, and coached the policy in terms they might accept. For the vice president interested in better accountability, the accountability aspect of the policy was highlighted. The point is not to distort information, but to make arguments related to the client's interests, not just one's own interests and needs.

Diffuse Opposition and Bring Out Conflict

Rather than stifle opposition, it can often be diffused through an open discussion of ideas. One hospital director, in attempting to introduce a major new program, strategically blocked all resistance by expressing openness to new ideas and inviting suggestions and criticism. As noted by Kelley (1976), the conflicts that do develop should be dealt with, again by engaging the opposition in legitimate discussion, answering objections, allaying fears with facts, and keeping the innovation within the safe and familiar parameters of the organizational value systems.

Finally, an open discussion beforehand can spotlight any die-hard resistors. Their units can be more carefully monitored during implementation, thereby reducing their opportunity for undercover resistance tactics designed to thwart the change effort.

Align with a Powerful Other

Gaining top management approval is another way of acquiring power within an organization; however, it may provide only a minimal power base from which to operate. More effective alliances are those with operating or line managers directly impacted by change approaches. Such alliances are more difficult, however, since alliances with operating managers need to be based on the consultant's demonstration of expertise in his field of operations and often are developed and nurtured through informal contacts and relationships.

One manager of a new organization development unit successfully used this approach to get his department off the ground. At a management conference, he made friends with the head of a claims processing department about to introduce a new computer system. After much informal discussion, the department head decided that the organization development group could facilitate this changeover and allowed him to "experiment" with his unit. The successful introduction of the system, coupled with the department head's credibility with the "old guard" of the organization, prompted numerous requests for the organization development unit's services, producing an increase in their staff size and budget.

Develop Liaisons

Pettigrew (1975b) outlines three linkage mechanisms for internal consulting units: location, planned liaisons, and satellites. A unit should be positioned so as to increase informal interaction patterns. An isolated unit can limit the opportunity for the specialist as well as his staff members to mingle with other employees and form informal liaisons with them. In addition, an overly isolated unit can develop an aura around it of mystery. While such mystery may on one hand be a useful power base, on the other hand, it can seriously limit the number of individuals who will attempt contact with that group. To the extent that people in the organization are unsure what "that group does," they are less likely to form interactions with them. Developing planned liaisons requires each staff member to have an assigned contact in a line department and be responsible for meeting with that person on a weekly or monthly basis. And finally, on an even more formal level, develop satellite units in important client areas, whereby individuals with particular staff expertise report both to the head of the staff unit and to the line officer.

Tradeoff

The ability to introduce change programs, especially unique or untried ones, may hinge on the amount of assessed stature one has accrued. Such assessed stature as a power base can be enhanced by first attending to projects or programs designed to meet the client's needs, as did one inexperienced management consultant who first solved a small but annoying problem for a project leader before presenting his own ideas to the department. The resultant increase in assessed stature can then be used to implement programs more clearly in line with one's own objectives. As noted by Pettigrew (1975a), credit can be built up by attending to projects which relate to the client's role needs. This credit can then be cashed in on projects the specialist has a particular interest in.

Strike While the Iron's Hot

Another strategy is to quickly follow up a successful program with a request for approval to implement a somewhat less popular or less well understood program. For example, a research manager submitted a request for approval to do research on job-skills matching immediately after his successful implementation of flexible working hours. While the new proposal was not well understood, due to its highly technical nature, the success of the flexible working hours prompted the response, "Well, if Research thinks it is a good idea, it must be. Look how well flexible working hours turned out."

Research

The use of research projects is an effective influence strategy, especially in emotionally charged areas such as enhancing the status of women and minorities in organizations (Schein 1974). In these areas, decrying the biases underlying current organizational policies, pointing out stereotyped attitudes, or proposing radical change programs can be met with resistance. In turn, the consultant's credibility and power is lessened through the organization's perception of him or her an an interloper or rabble-rouser. On the other hand, the role of researcher can provide the individual with a legitimate power base from which to speak—and be heard—regarding such issues. The research endeavor itself is a useful means by which the consultant gains credibility and expert power in a difficult situation.

Use a Neutral Cover

Experimental investigations are usually viewed as nonthreatening and have a neutral image. With a base of expertise, an effective strategy is to first implement a small experimental study and then, if successful, build on this expanded power base in order to promote broader organizational change. Such initial success, especially if the results are reasonably well documented and objective, can give one sufficient expertise power to overcome the expected power tactics from other organizational levels as one expands the program throughout the organization. For example, the research manager introduced flexible hours on an experimental basis and then used the positive results to counter the wide spread resistance within the organization.

Another neutral cover strategy is to link up with an already approved and noncontroversial company-wide program. For example, one internal OD consultant asked to assist with the implementation of a merit compensation program. Under the guise of such implementation, he managed to introduce various programs designed to improve supervisory-subordinate relationships—programs he would have been unable to implement on his own.

Inch Along

At times, it may be more effective to accept a client's immediate needs, within professional standards, and inch along toward more expansive aims, rather than maintain an all-or-nothing stance. For example, one consultant found his client interested in instituting an employee attitude survey, but resistant to a full-scale survey feedback process. After gaining the client's approval for publication of the survey findings to all employees, he strategically involved the client and his senior executives in all aspects of the process. Management fears and resistance were gradually allayed, resulting in a full feedback process and active employee-management participation in implementation of changes.

Withdraw

As the number of groups claiming some degree of organization development expertise increases, internal and external consultants can find themselves in competition with these groups for heading up change programs. In such competition, one unusual strategy is to openly and abruptly withdraw from the competition. Using this tactic, one internal consulting group found that their assessed stature increased and their expertise remained unchallenged. More importantly, the group's underlying long-shot strategy—that the other unit was not capable of succeeding—proved correct and they were then requested by the client to complete the project, thereby increasing the unit's status and its power.

THE ROLE OF DECEPTION

Both the development of power bases and the use of strategies and tactics are vital components of any job involving innovation and change. Resistance to changing the status quo is to be expected and change agents should be equipped to deal with such resistance. Within this viewpoint, a final factor deserves consideration—that of the role of deception (Schein 1979). Despite the need for implementation strategies, very often these behaviors must be kept undercover and not discussed. And, in other instances, when these strategies and tactics do not seem necessary, there nonetheless appears to be a great deal of politics and concomitant deceptive behaviors.

To understand the role of deception and its differential usages requires an examination of two types of power-related behaviors and two types of organizational climates. First, not all strategies and tactics are for work-related reasons. Personal intents also exist and correspond to power-related behaviors designed to promote the self-oriented objectives of the individual and are unrelated to organizational concerns (Schein 1977). Examples of such personal intents include career advancement, status, money, recognition, and job survival. While such intents are not directly related to organizational functioning, their influence must be considered in any discussion of power and political behaviors in organizations.

The relationship between deception and personal power acquisition behaviors comes out of the very nature of these behaviors, as they are designed to achieve personal, not work-related outcomes. Clearly if you are seeking power for your own personal aggrandizement you are more likely to be covert with regard to your means and desired outcomes.

The second distinction to be made is between two types of organizational climates. As an explanatory concept, organizations are dichotomized here into either dynamic or static systems (Cyert & March 1964). Dynamic systems are those operating in a highly competitive environment, which requires rapid and nonroutine decision making on the part of its members and a high level of productive energy and work outcomes in order to deal effectively in this environment. Static systems, on the other hand, are those operating in a reasonably stable environment requiring rather routine functioning and the maintenance of day-to-day activities in order to continue to operate effectively. The record industry and the container industry reflect the difference between dynamic and static systems.

Given this distinction, it is proposed that the ratio of personal to work-related intents and concomitant power acquisition behaviors is in favor of personal power acquisition behaviors in static systems, where the reverse is true in dynamic systems. In essence, vigorous competition in the environment will prevent managers from manipulating their activities in order to achieve their own personal ends and require more work-related behavior; whereas the absence of such competitive conditions permits managers to pursue their own goals without obvious disruption of the system.

Deception Within Static Systems

Returning now to personal intents, while such covert intents and means of achieving personal outcomes—such as status and promotion—might at first glance seem dysfunctional within organizations, these behaviors within static systems might actually be quite functional. More than likely in low competitive environments, even high-level managerial jobs are somewhat routine, thereby prompting the need for excitement through political warfare. As parts of this warfare, deception and intrigue add interest to the otherwise routine and even keel environment in which they were operating.

The functional aspects of personal power acquisition behaviors are important to consider. Within organizations characterized by a stagnant, tenure-based promotion system, tactics designed to take over another subunit may, if successful, provide satisfaction during the long intervals between organization rewards. Similarly, in a boring or routine job this kind of political warfare serves to rev up the system and, hence, energize what would be an otherwise static job and environment. As reward mechanisms and energizers, they may be far more functional than dysfunctional.

Furthermore, this political warfare, by revving up the system, fosters, at the organizational level, the illusion that it is an active system, one filled with excitement and competition. The reality of an ongoing and perhaps boring system never has to be faced. This organizational deception, the illusion of excitement and activity, keeps members involved in the organization and provides rewards not ordinarily forthcoming in a stagnant and routine system.

Deception within Dynamic Systems

Within dynamic systems, the ratio of personal to work-related behaviors is in favor of the latter. Yet even work-related power acquisition behaviors tend to have an air of deception about them. They are not openly discussed, rarely acknowledged, and certainly never read about in management texts, or taught in business schools. What seems to be occurring in these dynamic systems is an organizationally based deception as to how one operates effectively in the system. Within a competitive, turbulent, everchanging environment, a functionally based structure, characterized by a chain of command, functional specialization, written communication, use of formal authority, and so on, can be obstructive to effective functioning. Fast action and rapid decision making may require circumventing the formal systems so as to deal effectively with environmental demands. Hence, behaviors designed to develop power outside of one's formal authority to operate effectively—behaviors such as the development of influential contacts, trading favors, coalition formations, and so on—become useful strategies for effective work performance. Mintzberg (1973) has documented the existence of these managerial behaviors, and descriptive studies by Strauss (1962) and Izraeli (1975), among others, have suggested the need to exhibit these behaviors in order to operate effectively.

These work-related power acquisition behaviors need not be deceptive. Yet they become so to the extent that the organization deludes itself as to the way things really get done. To the extent that the organization maintains the illusion that the formalistic structure is sufficient to meet the demands of the work and the environment, it denies the reality of the way managers function within it, and hence fosters the deceptiveness of these behaviors. Furthermore, to the extent that organizations reward successful members—acknowledging their outcomes but not acknowledging their means of achieving these outcomes—such reward systems perpetuate and foster deceptive strategies and tactics. And finally, management theorists and organizational behaviorists who speak only of rational behaviors help perpetuate this myth. By not legitimatizing the role of strategies and tactics, as noted by Robbins (1977), they reinforce the perceived need on the part of managers to be covert about the actions they take. Hence, within dynamic systems it is an organizational deception about the way people in it function that produces deceptive behaviors on the part of its members.

ORGANIZATIONAL REALITIES

Consideration of the politics of change forces the consultant to confront the realities of organizational life. Power bases and strategies on the one hand, and deception on the other are far removed from the direct task of problem diagnosis and solution development. And in the evolution of a successful professional, perhaps they should be. Quality ideas and approaches, developed out of sound professional training, are the foundations for helping organizations. Strategic implementation of shoddy approaches helps no one, except perhaps the short-term career goals of the consultant. But failure to develop and sharpen strategic and tactical implementation skills, once the professional foundation is strong, and swim in the sometimes murky waters of organizational realities, is harmful as well. The organization is robbed of insights, ideas, and new approaches that can change its course and improve the quality of the working life of the people within them.

It is imperative that organization development professionals understand the operation of power and politics in organizations. To deny the reality or importance of these behaviors is to deny the reality of the way organizations really function. The innovator or implementator of new ideas and approaches needs to develop power bases and learn strategic behavior if he is to be successful in his endeavor. The politics of change are a vital component of the job.

References

Cyert, R. M., & March, J. G., *A Behavioral Theory of the Firm*. Englewood Cliffs, N.J.: Prentice Hall, 1964.

French, J. R. P., & Raven, B., "The Bases of Social Power," In D. Cartwright (ed.), *Studies in Social Power*. Ann Arbor: University of Michigan, Institute for Social Research, 1959, pp. 150–67.

Izraeli, D. N., "The Middle Manager and the Tactics of Power Expansion: A Case Study," *Sloan Management Review*, 1975, vol. 16. pp. 57–70.

Kelley, G., "Seducing the Elites: The Politics of Decision Making and Innovation in Organizational Networks," *Academy of Management Review*, July 1976: pp. 66–74.

Machiavelli, N., *The Prince*. (T. G. Geigin, ed.) New York: Appleton-Century-Crafts, 1964. (Written 1512–1513).

Mintzberg, H., *The Nature of Managerial Work*. New York: Harper and Row, 1973.

Pettigrew, A. M., "Towards a Political Theory of Organization Intervention," *Human Relations,* vol. 28 (1975a): pp. 191–208.

Pettigrew, A. M., "Strategic Aspects of the Management of Specialist Activity," *Personnel Review*, vol. 4 (1975b): pp. 5–13.

Raven, B. H., "Social Influence and Power," In I. D. Stein and M. Fishbein (eds.), *Current Studies in Social Power*. New York: Holt Rinehart and Winston, 1965, pp. 371–82.

Robbins, S. P., "Reconciling Management Theory with Management Practice," *Business Horizons*, vol. 20 (1977): pp. 38–47.

Schein, V. E., "Research as an Influence Strategy," *Personnel Psychology,* vol. 27 (1974): pp. 443–45.

Schein, V. E., "Individual Power and Political Behaviors in Organizations: An Inadequately Explored Reality," *Academy of Management Review*, vol. 2 (1977): pp. 64–72.

Schein, V. E., "Examining an Illusion: The Role of Deceptive Behaviors in Organizations," *Human Relations*, vol. 32 (1979): pp. 287–95.

Strauss, G., "The Tactics of Lateral Relationships: The Purchasing Agent," *Administrative Science Quarterly,* vol. 7 (1962): pp. 161–86.

10 Enriching the Theory and Practice of Team Building: Instrumentation for Diagnosis and Design Alternatives

Robert T. Golembiewski

ABSTRACT

This paper contributes to an encouraging trend: the improvement in the efficacy of team-building designs via the increasingly precise specification. The success rates of applications seem substantial in the cases of single work teams where, by hypothesis, intervenors can make on-the-spot adaptations to variable environmental textures. The record for large-batch applications of a standard team-building design seems less attractive, consistently, where *the* standard design could be diversely compatible with conditions in specific work groups.

The present focus deals with two contributors to enhanced diagnosis prior to a choice of team-building designs: a crisis of agreement vs. a crisis of conflict, and degree of burn-out. Useful ways of estimating the two sets of conditions are introduced, and their implications for design variants are discussed.

AUTHOR BACKGROUND

Robert T. Golembiewski is a research professor at the University of Georgia, and a distinguished visiting scholar at the University of Calgary. He has authored or edited forty-three books, and published approximately about one hundred eighty articles and cast studies. He received his doctorate from Yale, and is a past winner of the Douglas McGregor Memorial Award for Excellence in Applications of the Behavioral Sciences.

Some readers of the OD literature may have recently spotted an apparent anomaly. On the one hand, individual applications of team-building designs seem to be increasingly popular and appear to have the expected effects, on balance.[1,2,3] On the other hand, applications of common teambuilding designs to large numbers of work units in the same organization have fared more poorly.[4]

Hence experience with team building can be fairly characterized as Janus-faced. Most observers reflect sunny and optimistic visage. Thus De Meuse and Liebowitz (1981) review thirty-six separate applications and, despite concern about the casual methodology of many of the studies, they see a robust and burgeoning theory-cum-technology. Other observers—for example, Harris and Porras, 1978; Porras and Wilkins, 1980—are dour after surveying their attempts at mass team building. Things just did not turn out as predicted. Perhaps too much was expected of a brief design, went the overall evaluation of one of the efforts.[5] The other effort motivated far greater concern: the authors interpreted their results as possibly undercutting the basic role of effective socioemotional processes, which in turn could undermine OD's credibility among potential users. Porras and Wilkins conclude:

> Several key measures of performance showed . . . significant improvement. . . . Yet, measures of organizational processes indicated a deterioration of the internal dynamics of the system. This was clearly . . . unexpected . . . . Other alternatives must be sought or OD will be viewed as irrelevant to large-system change.[6]

TOWARD PROFITING FROM THE APPARENT ANOMALY

This essay is not deterred by the apparent anomaly—quite the opposite, in fact. This essay seeks to encompass both anomalous positions in a direct way that will elaborate the theory underlying team building and also enrich its practice. Specifically the two reactions sketched above will be said to reflect the impact of two seldom-diagnosed conditions in team-building settings:

- the underlying character of the conflict or tension in the subsystem, which can be highlighted by distinguishing conditions of agreement vs. disagreement in small groups
- the degree of psychological burnout experienced by members of the team

Generally, then, the argument below will follow a direct line. Individual team-building applications do not have to encompass the degree of variation in these two features characteristic of mass team-building ventures. Skillful intervenors working with single teams, goes this line of argument, can adjust to incongruencies between their basic design and specific context for intervention. A design useful for some teams in a mass design, in contrast, is likely to be beside the point or even counterproductive for other teams in the batch. If the standard confrontational design is utilized[7,8,9], for example, there is some probability that it will be inappropriate to some or even many units in the batch. Subsequent analysis will develop this critical point.

Hence enhanced diagnostic power is the goal here. Available work provides instrumentation for such diagnosis, fortunately, and it also suggests the character of appropriate designs. That is an attractive combination, and deserves to be exploited quite generally.

CONDITIONS OF DISAGREEMENT VS. AGREEMENT

Attention to disagreement vs. agreement as a central condition in a group has a substantial history, in various forms, from Janis (1972) to Harvey (1977) and to Dyer (1977). Harvey's is perhaps the most arresting formulation, which he began expressing as "the Abilene Paradox" and subsequently refined into a comparison of a "crisis of agreement" with a "crisis of disagreement." Exhibit 10.1 generates the fuller sense of the critical distinction.[10]

The thrust of the differences in Exhibit 10.1 seems direct. Basically, concern about membership seems to dominate in agreement—given that prestige of membership can derive from the "best and brightest" view characteristic of the Kennedy administration,[11] or from the desire for continued membership rooted in suspicion and fear, as seems to have been the case with Nixon appointees who believe there was no other way they could attract similar power or salary.[12] Testing for actual agreement would risk membership, in both cases, and hence the test tends to go forfeit. In disagreement, the primal concern is one of unsatisfactory inclusion, which typically gets reflected in we/they modes.

Appropriate interventions in the two systems will differ profoundly. In disagreement, a legitimate process for exploring differences is needed, and that need can be easily satisfied by various confrontational and interaction-oriented designs.[13] In agreement, membership must be safeguarded. This is a more delicate and chancy matter.

Although the distinction has been in the common realm for a period, and in attractive formulations, the distinction gets reflected in diagnosis and design only in rare cases.[14] And more's the pity, for solid guides for both diagnosis and design are available.

Exhibit 10.2, following Harvey,[15] provides a clear guide for diagnosis. It lists a set of questions for interviews with all members of a work unit before a specific team-building design is decided upon. Exhibit 10.2 is more limited than, for example, a paper-and-pencil diagnostic instrument that might be applied to very large populations, later to be machine scored. But the exhibit provides considerable aid even as it is deficient in this important particular.

Prescription of a specific team-building design for disagreement seems to pose no great problems, at least as a first approximation. The usual confrontation designs should work well. Simple interview feedback designs could do the job, for example.[16]

My personal preference is for designs building around three-dimensional images, which have been widely used and reported on.[17, 18, 19] They tend to "work" for several reasons, with two reasons being perhaps primary. First, such designs inherently provide a procedure for gathering data, which rests on specific values

EXHIBIT 10.1 A Contrast of Two Types of Crises

Crisis of Agreement	Crises of Disagreement
Underlying behavioral processes	Underlying behavioral processes
1. Organization members experience pain from some specific collective problem(s), with feelings about impotence or incompetence deriving from the failure to resolve or manage the problem(s) somehow.	1. Organization members may or may not experience pain from some specific collective problem(s), but such problem(s) do exist although consciousness-raising about them may be required.
2. Members share the same private concept or problem(s) facing their organization, and individually recognize the same or similar underlying explanations or causes of the problem(s), if any are acknowledged.	2. Members do not share the same private concept of problem(s) facing their organization, and individually have very different underlying explanations or causes of the problem(s), if any are acknowledged.
3. As individuals, many or all organization members have similar and compatible preferences for coping with the problem(s).	3. As individuals, many or all organization members have different and incompatible preferences for coping with the problem(s).
4. As individuals, many or all organization members see the same or similar solution as appropriate for resolving or managing the problem(s).	4. As individuals many or all organization members see different or incompatible solutions as appropriate for resolving or managing the problem(s).
5. In public settings, organization members consistently do not communicate accurately to one another—about their preferences, beliefs, knowledge of causes and consequences of organization problems—and hence mutually create a false or misleading collective reality. ■ In the longer run, the probable result is a low-energy system—careful, perhaps polite, and very conscious of roles and jurisdictions. ■ In some highly prestigious groups, the facade may emphasize potency and a high energy level.	5. In public settings, therefore, organization members may deal with one another in two basic ways: ■ probably in a minority of cases, to risk open conflict, hostility, etc., attendant to the expression of disagreements ■ probable in most cases, to avoid the risk of acrimony (as by agreeing not to disagree openly on certain issues) but at the expense of suppressing real issues and conflict. The openly conflictful organizations probably will be high-energy systems, with substantial but perhaps incompatible personal commitment and involvement, great but perhaps fruitless expenditures of effort, and so on. The suppressing organization probably will be characterized by low levels of energy, commitment, and involvement.
6. Given a false or misleading collective reality, on definite balance, collective decisions get made that reflect neither member preferences nor their real views of reality, with the results more than likely being counterproductive both for individual and organization goals.	6. The probability seems high that both adaptations—if for different reasons—will lead to a false or misleading collective reality, over time. Openly conflictful organizations may develop polarizations that inhibit or preclude members from communicating accurately with one another. Suppressing organizations may create the same effect by defining certain subjects as off limits.
7. Greater member pain is likely, and a sense of both individual and collective incompetence and impotence probably will grow.	
8. The cycle is set to repeat itself, probably with greater speed and intensity as well as with a lessened probability of corrective action.	

EXHIBIT 10.2   Some Questions for Diagnostic Interviews and Guidelines for Using Them

---

Differentiate Agreement from Disagreement

A. Diagnostic questions
1. In general, how are things going in the organization?
2. What in particular is going well?
3. What are some specific organization problems that need to be solved?
4. What actions do you think need to be taken to solve them?
5. What problem-solving actions have you and others attempted, and what were the outcomes?
6. If you have not taken action, what prevents your taking action to solve them?

B. Diagnostic guidelines
1. If answers to question 1 are consistently positive, the organization presumably experiences neither conflict of disagreement nor conflict of agreement. Only reporting back to confirm the health of the organization is necessary.
2. If answers to questions 1 through 4 consistently differ, the organization may be presumed to be in a conflict of disagreement. A design like the confrontation design would be appropriate.
3. A crisis of agreement may be presumed when:
   ■ Pain and conflict get emphasized in responses to questions 1 through 3.
   ■ Agreement about organization problems surfaces on questions 3.
   ■ Agreement about probable solutions exists on question 4.
   ■ Much rationalization about why what should be done cannot be done gets expressed in responses to questions 5 and 6.
   ■ Evidence is presented about actions actually taken, especially in response to question 5, that are contrary to what respondents believe should be done.

---

and empirical theory fragments. This provides the "legitimate process" that Exhibit 10.1 sees as central in a condition or crisis of disagreement. Second, 3-D designs seem to quickly liberate energies, which by hypothesis were used earlier to repress conflict. Such energy release can be exhilarating and, in combination with the newly legitimatized process for problem analysis, can induce a very tangible sense of movement or progress in what was a blocked and frustrating situation. This release of energy often comes as a tangible "whoosh," once it is no longer needed for suppressing conflict or avoiding unsatisfactory inclusion. Crudely, one guesses that the cost/benefit ratio is very favorable in conditions of disagreement. If the design works, new data and membership become available. If the design fails, one is not very much worse off.

As for prescribing a basic design for a condition or crisis of agreement, greater tentativeness is appropriate. It seems clear that confrontational designs have significant drawbacks in such cases. Indeed, they may be generally counterproductive. Recall that continued membership is postulated as central in conditions of agreement. Hence a confrontational design might well avoid *the* critical issue, while also raising very troubling questions for those preoccupied with membership:

■ What is there about us as a group that led us to publicly suppress what we in fact largely agreed about?
■ How can we be confident that we will not again fall into a condition or crisis of agreement again?

We can be less certain about what designs will work, given a diagnosed crisis of agreement, for little research or experience has been accumulated. However, Harvey seems to point a useful way of approach in Exhibit 10.3.[20] Read between the lines a little, and his basic thrusts seem clear. The design's multiple checks imply care to establish that only broadly held materials get admitted to analysis. Pretty clearly, this re-checking process no doubt seeks to reduce the probability that anyone's membership is threatened, even as it seeks to provide some guarantee that not just another crisis of agreement is being developed.

The careful character of Exhibit 10.3 contrasts markedly with the wham-bang quality of many confrontational designs. For example, boss reports a threatened fistfight in one of the latter designs.[21] There is too much to be lost in the ideal conflict of agreement for such precipitous acting out; and even an impactful learning design could generate very mixed results. Crudely, again, the cost/benefit ratio seems relatively balanced in a crisis of agreement. Hence the careful character of Exhibit 10.3.

Conclusions should not be rushed beyond the reasonable suggestions of Harvey, but the argument thus far does suggest a range of other designs that are indicated and some that are contraindicated for the conditions of agreement and disagreement. Some such provisional assignments seem reasonable:

Conditions of Disagreement

- interaction-centered team building[22]
- T-Groups with intact work groups
- specific goals to quick confrontation such as those used in some organizations: "tell your boss what's wrong with him or her"
- Third-party interventions and other conflict-oriented designs[23]

Conditions of Agreement

- task-centered teambuilding[24]
- role negotiation[25]
- designs that focus on a task or product: for example, skill building[26] or developing a management credo or statement of mission-and-role.

In a rough sense, the designs in the left column emphasize differentiation and, although this will often lead to integration, their basic character could pose

---

EXHIBIT 10.3 Sketch of an Intervention for a Condition of Agreement

1. Sort the interview data into the basic themes of agreement.
2. Themes get reported back in a public session in ways that use respondents' own words as much as possible, but that protect anonymity.
3. All those interviewed then write a collective summary of all of the data supporting each theme of agreement, decide on the action implications of the themes, and plan specific actions.
4. Summarize the theory of agreement sketched in Exhibit 10.2 to reinforce understanding of why and how members were inhibited from sharing agreements with each other.
5. Individual organization members are coached, in private, about actions they might take in light of agreements shared with their colleagues.

definite threats to membership in the group. This constitutes no basic problem for a condition of disagreement, where *the* key issue is unsatisfactory inclusion with which, obviously, even extended differentiation is consistent. The designs in the left column focus *ab initio* on a common product, and hence will be less upsetting where *the* issue is continuing membership.

Some designs seem to be more or less equally applicable to the two conditions. Survey/feedback and interview/feedback designs permit flexibility. Why? Possible reasons include a subtle relocation of responsibility for what gets said and how, and perhaps also the possibility of disavowing any and all feedback by the external intervenor if membership seems threatened. In one such application, for example, an executive team was not willing to deal with a critical situation until they heard the results of interviews, which feedback had this tenor: "11 of 13 of you agreed about X, 12 of 13 about Y, and all of you agree about Z." Such a report could not threaten group membership very much, patently. Three-dimensional images developed *in groups* also may have a broad application, in that the focus is the development of a set of consensual images to present to others. This does not threaten individual membership. Indeed, the design properties were intended to heighten group cohesiveness in generating a common and defensible product.[27]

More broadly, this line of thought also supports a reasonable conclusion. Consider the work which supports the "greater effectiveness" of, for example, survey/feedback as compared to laboratory training or T-grouping.[28] Common interpretations conclude that some designs are "better" than others. The present line of thought encourages a more restricted interpretation. When you cannot differentiate targets for interventions, some designs like survey/feedback may be safer in that they can apply to both conditons of disagreement and agreement. Other designs may be more target specific. The moral of the research is not that some designs are "better" than others. On the contrary, the highlighted need involves diagnosing more specifically the conditions to which various designs are more or less applicable.

DIFFERENCES IN PSYCHOLOGICAL BURNOUT

Newly accumulating evidence also suggests that team-building diagnosis and designs, especially when masses of teams are involved, need to be sensitive to one major characteristic of participants as individuals and in the aggregate—their degree of psychological burnout. This emphasis on individuals complements the earlier emphasis on the character of their relationships. Broadly, burnout has a central conceptual status as "a syndrome of inappropriate attitudes towards clients and towards self, often associated with uncomfortable physical and emotional symptoms."[29] In addition to reduced productivity, burnout's dreary inventory of effects includes "job turnover, absenteeism, and low morale (as well as) various self-reported indices of personal distress, including mental exhaustion, insomnia, increased use of alcohol and drugs, and marital and family problems."[30]

Major progress has been made toward the development of a paper-and-pencil measure of burnout (e.g., Maslach & Jackson 1981), but it is not yet clear how best to aggregate the items of the Maslach Burnout Inventory, or MBI. Three alternative ways have been tested, using as a basic referent twenty-two target variables thought to tap important aspects of the worksite. The variables and predictions about them can be introduced in three categories:

1. **Job Descriptive Index, or JDI,** which measures satisfaction with five facets of work and also provides a total satisfaction score (Smith *et al.* 1969). As burnout increases, one expects reduced satisfaction on all JDI measures with the possible exception of JDI Pay. The host organization's pay policies are considered superior, generally, and satisfaction with them consequently might not differ among those experiencing various degrees of burnout, estimated in this case by aggregating all MBI items into a total score.
2. **Job Diagnostic Survey, or JDS,** which measures satisfaction with ten facets of the job.[31] As burnout increases, with the possible exception of JDS Compensation, one expects reduced satisfaction on all JDS facets.
3. **Assorted scales** that, with one exception, should decrease as burnout increases. The Job Tension Scale[32] should reflect a direct relationship with burnout. These other scales should deteriorate as burnout increases:
   - Trust in supervisor[33]
   - Trust in fellow employees
   - Job involvement[34]
   - Willingness to disagree with supervisor[35]
   - Participation in decisions re work[36]

Tests of the three ways of aggregating MBI items may be summarized briefly. First, as Table 10.1 shows, the MBI total score correlates quite regularly with a number of variables describing important aspects of the worksite. That puts it mildly, in fact. All twenty-two of the correlations are in the expected directions: twenty-one of them attain the .05 level and the significant correlations account for a substantial 13% of the total variance, with several accounting for as much as a quarter of the total variance in specific target variables.

Second, as Table 10.1 also shows, the three component MBI subscales have marked patterns of association with the twenty-two target variables. Thus the level of association is lower, on the average, than for the total score. Moreover, the subscales differ substantially in their association with the target variables. Specifically, on the average, the subscales singly account for the following percentages of variance:

- Emotional exhaustion accounts for 12%, with subscale items tapping the degrees to which respondents feel inadequate in coping with strain in their lives, to which they are at "the end of the rope" in psychological and emotional terms.

TABLE 10.1   Correlations Between Total and Subscale MBI Scores and 22 Scales (Correlations with MBI Items, Aggregated as Total Score or Three Sub-scale Scores)

	Alpha	Total Score
1. JDI scales: satisfaction with		
Work	.80	−.51*
Supervision	.83	−.37*
Co-workers	.86	−.24*
Promotion	.90	−.28*
Pay	.92	−.15*
Total JDI	.73	−.49*
2. JDS scales: satisfaction with		
Experienced meaningfulness of work	.78	−.39*
Experienced responsibility for work	.66	−.19*
Knowledge of results	.71	−.26*
Work in general	.75	−.51*
Work motivation	.58	−.26*
Growth	.84	−.51*
Job security	.84	−.33*
Compensation	.86	−.13*
Co-workers	.67	−.36*
Supervision	.90	−.34*
3. Selected scales		
Trust in supervisors	.83	−.43*
Trust in fellow employees	.78	−.36*
Job involvement	.77	−.45*
Willingness to disagree with supervisor	.70	−.12
Job-related tension	.81	.40*
Participation	.76	−.31*

*Indicates a correlation coefficient statistically significant at .05 level.

From Robert T. Golembiewski and Robert Munzenruder, "Efficacy of Three Versions of One Burnout Measure : MBI as Total Score, Sub-scale Scores, or Phases?", *Journal of Health and Human Resources Administration,* vol. 4, no. 4, 1981, pp. 228–46.

- Personal accomplishment accounts for 8%, and subscale items here relate to feelings about the effectiveness of performance on a meaningful and worthwhile job.
- Depersonalization accounts for 4% of the variance, with its items referring to the degree to which humans and relationships with them are considered to be objects or things.

Third, the MBI items can also be used to generate a set of burnout phases or stages. By dichotomizing one population of respondents at the median for each subscale, and by assuming that depersonalization characterizes the least-

Depersonalization	Personal Accomplishment (Reversed)	Emotional Exhaustion
−.26*	−.34*	−.49*
−.21*	−.20*	−.37*
−.16*	−.25*	−.29*
−.12	−.16*	−.29*
−.01	−.07	−.19*
−.25*	−.33*	−.45*
−.20*	−.30*	−.31*
−.12*	−.26*	−.05
−.23*	−.12	−.20*
−.26*	−.33*	−.50*
−.13*	−.32*	−.08
−.17*	−.32*	−.32*
−.19*	−.20*	−.26*
−.03	−.02	−.15*
−.18*	−.33*	−.24*
−.18*	−.17	−.33*
−.23*	−.29*	−.39*
−.27*	−.24*	−.26*
−.25*	−.42*	−.33*
−.02	−.25*	−.02
.23*	.13*	.42*
−.08	−.34*	−.25*

virulent phases of burnout while emotional exhaustion impacts the latter phases, eight phases or stages were distinguished, as shown in Table 10.2.

The complex tests of the burnout phases cannot be summarized here in any detail, but briefly the results are quite encouraging. Two kinds of evidence suggest the point. First, the phases isolate nonrandom variation on almost all of the target variables described above, almost all of the time, in all of the several tests run thus far. On the average, eighteen or nineteen of the twenty variables on which significant variation was expected generate F-ratios that surpass the .05 level. Second, paired comparisons establish the robustness as well as regularity of the differences in target variables isolated by the phases. Depending upon the

TABLE 10.2 MBI-Generated Phases of Burnout

	I	*II*	*III*	*IV*	*V*	*VI*	*VII*	*VIII*
Depersonalization	Lo	Hi	Lo	Hi	Lo	Hi	Lo	Hi
Personal accomplishment (reversed)	Lo	Lo	Hi	Hi	Lo	Lo	Hi	Hi
Emotional Exhaustion	Lo	Lo	Lo	Lo	Hi	Hi	Hi	Hi
N =	53	26	36	27	26	37	26	50

specific phase formulation tested, 30% to 50% of the paired comparisons of differences on the target variables attain statistical significance. Details are available in several sources.[37]

Especially in its phase formulation, burnout seems to have significant implications for team-building designs, particularly in mass populations. For teams with all or many members in Phases I through IV, for example, standard confrontational designs should suffice. In those phases, individuals score high on depersonalization, and interaction designs should be helpful in arresting or reversing such a trend. Here new stimulation would generally be effective: individuals would receive heightened feedback and disclosure concerning the effects of their response to others as objects, and, ideally, individuals also would come to feel the rewards of greater acceptance and liking that typically follow as a consequence of responding to individuals as persons.

For more advanced burnout phases, however—Phases V through VIII—interaction-oriented designs seem awkward, even counterproductive. Here individuals already have a surfeit of negative stimuli, and may even possess a response set that encourages them to perceive neutral or even positive stimuli in negative terms. Here, the additional stimulation characteristic of interaction-centered designs might result in overstimulation, a bombardment that could reach nonhelpful or even hurtful proportions. Looked at from another perspective, cases of advanced burnout might be particularly responsive to policy and structural amelioration—as in reductions in role overload, the greater clarification of roles, and so on. The evidence is far from conclusive on the point, but some experience in day-care centers supports the present position. There, staff with high burnout responded positively to various restructuring efforts—for example, rescheduling the children's day to ease the demands on the adult staff.[38]

AN IN-PROCESS SUMMARY

Let us bring these preliminary considerations to several suggestive, if tentative, conclusions. First, there seems ample reason for intervenors to broaden their perspectives to include two classes of differentia—agreement vs. disagreement and degree of burnout—when considering a team-building design. This will be particularly apt counsel in mass team-building designs, which are seen more and more and may indeed constitute one of the immediate future's major challenges to OD credibility. For a while, very few examples could be found in the literature.[39] But more recently, their incidence has increased substantially as has their tendency to generate mixed or unexpected results.[40,41] By hypothesis, these surprises are provisionally attributed to the common imposition of a standard design on mass team-building populations. As the number of teams increases, more likely is the appearance of variant conditions to which the usual confrontational designs adapt poorly. With single units or small numbers of them, in contrast, alert intervenors will be able to adapt even standard designs to the specific texture and flow of individual teams. Here the success rates are substantial, even formidable.[42] For example, I have reported success rates in changing specific group variables via a standard design that approximate 80%.[43]

This notion should not astound. Even brief consideration—which can be reinforced by sophisticated research[44]—strongly suggests little reason to consider all work units as essentially homogeneous. Hence the lower success rates of standard team-building designs in large populations of formal work units.

Second, convenient approaches exist for testing for agreement vs. disagreement, as well as for burnout. The paper-and-pencil instrument developed by Maslach—her Burnout Inventory, or MBI—is particularly appropriate for large populations. Harvey's guidelines for interviews also can be applied to large batches of work units. Clearly, additional effort will be required. But even brief interviews with members of teams-to-be-built seem useful. Moreover, OD's credibility depends on increasing effectiveness in making desired/predicted things happen. So convenience cannot be a determinative criterion even as it remains a compelling and often attractive one.

Third, albeit provisionally, the evidence implies the need for OD intervenors to keep a 2 × 2 grid in mind as they diagnose team-building populations. See Exhibit 10.4, which supports a brief sketch of dominant properties of the four grid quadrants:

- I is likely to be a high-energy condition, at least initially. Thus the condition of disagreement should induce some frustration, which can be motivating for at least a time, and may indeed erupt into open conflict. In addition, low levels of burnout imply few energies bound up in symptomology and its consequences.
- II will probably be characterized by a reduced but still substantial energy level. The positive appeal of membership should generate substantial flows of energy, discounted to a meaningful degree by the prevailing condition of agreement. The low burnout implies no great drain on the basic energy level.

  Designs like Harvey's should be appropriate here. Confrontation designs could threaten membership, and thus might seriously reduce the energy available for isolating and solving problems. Note, however, that designs like Harvey's are slow-moving compared to confrontation designs

EXHIBIT 10.4   A Provisional Grid for Team-Building Diagnoses

		Prevailing Condition or Crisis	
		Agreement	*Disagreement*
Proportion of Work Unit Members in Advanced Phases of Burnout	*Low*	I	II
	High	IV	III

and imply a substantial energy drain, without the potential for the quick and great leaps forward that are characteristic of confrontation designs.

■ III seems a more difficult change-target than I or II. The energy level will probably be low, but with dual potential for substantial increases.

A two-phase design may be appropriate. Structure- or policy-oriented designs could be used to arrest or reverse burnout. Standard confrontational designs then might be applied. Such efforts seem likely to reinforce one another: any increases in energy due to amelioration of burnout could be applied to the condition of disagreement, and the possible bursts of energy from progress there could in turn reduce burnout.

■ IV seems the chanciest condition, especially if feelings of low self-esteem or self-worth characterize team members. In such a case, their attachment to membership might be desperate, and hence their willingness to threaten it might be exceedingly low. A two-stage design again seems indicated as in III, but the prognosis seems less favorable. The key question is whether prior amelioration of burnout can make available sufficient energies to support the chancy test of the threat to membership associated with change under the condition of agreement.

These general musings rest unevenly on theory and practice, especially in the case of psychological burnout. But the usefulness of the distinctions no doubt will have analogs in the experience of many intervenors, and that is certainly true in my case. Consider one example from approximately 10 years ago, which came as something of a shock after a number of early successes with a three-dimensional image design,[45] which basically proposes that participating pairs of work units develop three lists for sharing in response to these questions:

■ How do we see our work team?
■ How do we see the other work team?
■ How do we believe the other work team sees us?

This clearly represents a confrontation design, which intends a mutually empathic escalation based upon (if for different reasons) both successes and failures in describing selves as others see them. The "successes" would enhance self-esteem and in effect build bridges between the two work units. The "failures" also would be there for both groups to see, with knowledge being gained and with reward and reinforcement consequently characterizing the learning environment.

Matters turned out differently in one case, radically so. The two groups were basically right-on in their mutual perceptions, as Exhibit 10.5 illustrates using only one of the three cross-comparisons possible via the sharing of 3-D images. Group A was essentially the top-level operating committee, and the larger group B was composed of the directors who were the first-reports of OD members. After much prodding, the two groups separately developed images that were more or less unanimous expressions of previously private materials. The result? General silence and apathy, after considerable effort at analysis of what happened and why. One participant reported,

> It surprised me that pretty much everyone saw matters as I did. It was not our style to talk about such things. My reaction was despair. All of us saw things as awful, I learned, and we did nothing. I felt communally flaccid afterward; I always had felt individually impotent. We huddled together in our common nakedness, more fearful than ever of acting.

In retrospect, diagnosis was lacking in this case. I would now see the situation as a condition of agreement, reinforced by advanced burnout. In the terms of Exhibit 10.4, this illustrates a Quadrant IV case to which was disingenuously applied a Quadrant I design. The common and consensual disclosure did not release energies, but bound them more tightly to preserving the increasingly tenuous membership. Even that strained comfort was soon forfeited when corporate made wholesale personnel changes.

EXHIBIT 10.5 Partial Products of 3-Dimensional Image Design

How Team B Sees Team A	How Team A Believes Team B Sees Them
■ Not communicative enough ■ Floundering indecisive	■ Divergent group ■ Lack of evidence of authority and decisiveness
■ Defensive, unreceptive ■ Too involved in day-to-day operations and decisions ■ Cautious	■ Spend much time on *non*-key issues ■ Poor catalysts
■ Under tight Corporation control; i.e., restricted and at a competitive disadvantage for corporate resources	■ Lack of communicating a sense of direction and purpose ■ Nice Guys!!? (i.e., not competent)
	■ Too much resistance rather than encouragement

References

1. Dyer, W. G., *Team Building*. Reading, Mass.: Addison-Wesley, 1977.
2. De Meuse, K. P., & Liebowitz, S. J., "An Empirical Analysis of Team-Building Research," *Group and Organization Studies,* 1981, vol. 6, pp. 357–78.
3. Golembiewski, R. T.; Proehl, C. W., Jr.; & Sink, D., "Success of OD Applications in the Public Sector: Toting-up the Score for A Decade, More or Less," *Public Administration Review,* 1981, vol. 41, pp. 679–82.
4. Harris, R. T., & Porras, J. I., "The Consequences of Large System Change in Practice: An Empirical Assessment," *Proceedings '78,* 1978, Annual Meeting, Academy of Management.
5. Porras, J., & Wilkins, A., "Organization Development In a Large System: An Empirical Assessment," *Journal of Applied Behavioral Science,* 1981, vol. 16, pp. 506–34.
6. *Ibid.,* esp. pp. 531–32.
7. Dyer, *Team Building*.
8. Golembiewski, R. T., & Kiepper, A., "MARTA; Toward An Effective, Open, Giant," *Public Administration Review,* 1976, vol. 36, pp. 46–60.
9. Boss, W., "It Doesn't Matter if You Win or Lose, Unless You're Losing," *Journal of Applied Behavioral Science,* 1979, vol. 15, pp. 198–220.
10. Golembiewski, R. T., *Approaches to Planned Change*. New York: Marcel Dekker, 1979, Part 2, pp. 151–58.
11. Janis, I. *Groupthink*. Boston: Little, Brown, 1972.
12. Raven, B. "The Nixon Group," *Journal of Social Issues,* 1974, vol. 30, pp. 304–20.
13. Golembiewski, R. T., *Approaches to Planned Change*. New York: Marcel Dekker, 1979, Part 1, Chapter 6.
14. Dyer, *Team Building*.
15. Harvey, J. B., "Consulting During Crisis of Agreement." In W. W. Burke (Ed.), *Current Issues and Strategies in Organization Development*. New York: Human Sciences Press, 1977.
16. Fordyce, J. K., & Weil, R. *Managing with People*. Reading, Mass.: Addison-Wesley, 1971.
17. Golembiewski, R. T., & Blumberg, A., "Confrontation as a Training Design in Complex Organizations: Attitudinal Changes in a Diversified Population of Managers," *Journal of Applied Behavioral Science,* 1967, vol. 3, pp. 524–47.
18. Golembiewski, et al., pp. 46–60.
19. Boss, pp 198–220.
20. Harvey, "Consulting During Crisis of Agreement."
21. Boss, pp. 198–220.
22. Dyer, *Team Building*.
23. Filley, Alan. *Interpersonal Conflict Resolution*. Glenview, Illinois: Scott, Foresman, 1975.
24. Dyer, *Team Building*.
25. Harrison, R. "Role Negotiation." In W. W. Burke and H. Hornstein (Ed.), The Social Technology of Organization Development, Washington, D.C.: NTL Learning Resources, 1977.
26. Golembiewski, pp. 151–58.
27. Golembiewski & Blumberg, pp. 524–47.
28. Bowers, D. G., & Huasser, D. L., "Work Group Types and Intervention Effects in Organizational Development," *Administrative Science Quarterly,* 1977, vol. 27, pp. 76–94.

29. Kahn, R. L., "Job Burnout: Prevention and Remedies," *Public Welfare,* 1978, vol. 16, pp. 61–63.
30. Maslach, C., & Jackson, S. E., "The Measurement of Experienced Burnout," *Journal of Occupational Behaviour,* 1981, vol. 2, pp. 99–113.
31. Hackman, J. R., & Oldham, G. R. *Work Redesign.* Reading, Mass.: Addison-Wesley, 1981.
32. Kahn, pp. 61–63.
33. Roberts, K., & O'Reilly, C. A., III, "Failures in Upward Communication in Organizations: Three Possible Culprits," *Academy of Management Journal,* 1974, vol. 17, pp. 205–15.
34. White, J. K., & Ruh, R. H., "Effects on Personal Values on the Relationships Between Participation and Job Attitudes," *Administrative Science Quarterly,* 1973, vol. 18, pp. 506–14.
35. Patchen, M. *Some Questionnaire Measures of Employee Motivation and Morale.* Monograph no. 41. Ann Arbor, Mich.: Survey Research Center, 1965.
36. White & Ruh, pp. 506–14.
37. Golembiewski, R. T., & Munzenrider, R., "Efficacy of Three Versions of One Burn-out Measure: MBI as Total Score, Sub-scale Scores, or Phases?", *Journal of Health and Human Resources Administration,* 1981, vol. 4, pp. 228–46.
38. Pines, A., & Maslach, C., "Combatting Staff Burn-out In A Day-Care Center: A Case Study," *Child Care Quarterly,* 1980, vol. 9, pp. 5–16.
39. Golembiewski, R. T. *Public Administration as A Developing Discipline,* vol. 2. New York: Marcel Dekker, 1978.
40. Harris & Porras, "The Consequences of Large System Change in Practice."
41. Porras & Wilkins, pp. 506–34.
42. De Meuse & Liebowitz, pp. 357–78.
43. Golembiewski, pp. 151–58.
44. Bowers, pp. 76–94.
45. Golembiewski & Blumberg, pp. 524–47.

11 Microinterventions for Team Development Toward Their Appreciation and Use

Craig C. Lundberg

ABSTRACT

As team development became the foci of much OD strategy and practice, team-focused interventions proliferated. Most, however, are time consuming, fairly complex, well structured, and assume a prior diagnosis. This paper argues for the use, legitimization, and further development of more brief and simple interventions. Minimal interventions are characterized and examples are given. Several advantages are noted, e.g., the short real time requirements, the high diagnostic utility, the minor need for member readiness, the high participative quality, and the perception of being more under member control.

AUTHOR BACKGROUND

Craig C. Lundberg, Ph.D., Cornell University, is a professor of management and organization in the School of Business Administration at the University of Southern California. Active in several professional associations, including ASTD and the Academy of Management, he is currently the editor of *Exchange*.

While there exists at present a large and useful set of approaches for team development, they tend to be portrayed as linked intervention sequences that take time and focus on the end of improving team effectiveness. This essay attempts to draw attention to interventions that are short and simple and may even stand alone as well as contribute to the enhancement of team practice: microinterventions.

It is now widely recognized and accepted that teams are a major as well as crucial vehicle for accomplishing much of the significant work of modern organizations. This recognition has prompted the elaboration of team training and development—there is now a large toolkit of developmental approaches and interventions. Team development has in fact now become central to much of organizational development strategy and practice. Changes of an improvement nature are the prime focus of team development and most team improvement events are composed of a series of interventions.

In the pages that follow, attention is drawn to micro team development interventions, that is, those relatively simple and brief interventions used with teams. A case is argued that such microinterventions can be congruent with organization development (OD) values and are often organizationally functional and interventionally appropriate. This essay will first briefly review the history of team building and development, list major team interventions and their commonalities, and critique the state of our team intervention craft. (*Team development* and *team building* tend to be used interchangeably in the literature and will be considered synonymously here.) Second, it will provide some examples of micro team interventions in action as the basis for characterizing them. Finally, it will suggest some interventionist rules of thumb for the effective use of micro team development interventions.

TEAM DEVELOPMENT: ORIGINS, HISTORY AND CRITIQUE

The origins of what we now think of as team development tactics probably go back to the so-called human relations movement (Margulies & Raia 1978). Early spokesmen such as Roethlisberger, Whyte, and Leighton and the next generation of proponents such as McGregor, Argyris, and Bennis drew attention to the social side of enterprise, emphasizing individual and group processes and consequences, as well as more participative management philosophies and practices. At approximately the same time, laboratory education with its T-Group methodology, was transferred into industry. Quickly the focus of group training efforts shifted to natural work groups and their communications and decision-making processes. By the 1960s and 1970s team-building activities began to flourish with more and more of these devoted to management teams. OD's planned, system-wide change orientation no doubt fueled this movement as did the increasing complexity of managerial work which necessitated the increasing use of teams of managers (Patten 1981).

Where is team development today? Beyond simple enhancements of team performance, team development techniques now are regularly used to aid newly formed teams, project teams, and other temporary groups, to bring new members onto established teams, and a wide variety of other purposes, for example, Plovnick, Fry and Rubin (1975) and Beckhard (1972). There is an elaboration of technique that parallels the ever widening applications. There is also considerable literature available at this time on both practice and research. Team development currently has a decidedly multiple focus, including the processes, content, and structures of teams, inter-team relations, and teams as agents of organizational renewal and change. Team development has clearly become central to many of the conceptions of what OD is and how it works (for example, French & Bell 1978; Golembiewski 1972; Patten 1981; and Lippitt 1982). One is tempted to argue that the contemporary emphasis on team development reflects the resurgence of interest in action research as a central OD strategy in addition to linear, planned, educative change.

As was noted above, there exists a large array of team development interventions and a growing literature. There are now books devoted exclusively to it, for example, Dyer 1977 and Patten 1981. While this is not the place to describe major team development approaches, a listing makes the point:

1. family group diagnostic meeting (e.g., Fordyce & Weil 1971, French & Bell 1978, Huse 1975),
2. family group team-building meeting, also called core group and action group (e.g., Fordyce & Weil 1971, Golembiewski 1967, Huse 1975, Beckhard 1972),
3. process consultation (e.g., Schein 1969),
4. structured sensitivity training (e.g., Kelly 1973),
5. team training T-Groups (e.g., Margulies & Raia 1968, Argyris 1964),
6. role analysis technique (e.g., Dayal & Thomas 1968),
7. management responsibility guide (e.g., Melcher 1967),
8. job expectation technique (e.g., Huse & Barebo 1976),
9. role negotiation (e.g., Harrison 1972),
10. grid team development (Blake & Mouton 1968),
11. gestalt techniques (e.g., Herman & Korenich 1977).

What do these major team development approaches share in common? They seem to reflect six commonalities:

- Most require considerable real time, in the form of a few days all at once, or as multiple separate days.
- They are well structured in the sense that either there is a set of several interventional steps to be performed in a given sequence or clear parameters are stipulated.
- They presume or require that some initial, minimal conditions of openness and candor exist in the team.
- Most assume that some diagnosis exists which calls for a change intervention.
- They are change oriented, that is, they have predetermined goals to work towards.
- They are recommended as best being guided by a third party or consultant.

Let us now turn to a critique of contemporary team development. Of note is that the critical literature on team development is very limited (for very useful exceptions see Lewis 1975, and Woodman and Sherwood 1980). The structure of team interventions may be overly linear—not only in the sequencing of steps, but in the more fundamental sense of assuming that diagnosis precedes change. Experienced facilitators, however, know that diagnostic activities can be and often are change interventions. Most team interventions are not explicit about the team's tasks, work technologies or organizational context, and hence appear to be naive about these fundamental factors as well as matters of organizational status and politics. For example, the literature referred to above seldom differentiates between teams as organizational units and teams defined by the task interdependency of members. Given the extent of the literature, it is surprising that no typology of team development interventions has yet been created beyond Beer's (1976). In fairness, however, a number of dimensions potentially useful for such a typology have been mentioned or alluded to, for example, teams that share time and space versus those that are geographically separated; interventions that facilitate the management of conflict; interventions that focus on personal work style versus those that focus on emotional reactions to team events. There is almost no effort made to conceptually link team development to either the rich literature on group development in social psychology and sociology, or to major changes in organizational culture, managing strategic change or change in public and third-sector systems. While the institutionalization or reinforcement of change is broadly discussed as a vital component in the OD process, team development interventions seldom explicitly incorporate it. Dyer (1977, pp. 63–64) is the exception. Many team interventions may easily lead to or even promote behaviors inconsistent with basic OD values, for example, dependency on and/or control by third parties, incongruency with organizational culture, the generation of invalid information (Argyris 1970), and so forth.

There are four prevalent situations that the well-known team development approaches do not address. One can be called Band-Aid team consultation, the situation where team development is clearly tangential, but where a bit of such work is functional for the teams' work. A second is where team development is desired, but where near-crisis conditions exist or where there is very little time available. A third is where a very conservative, traditional management exists, anything like OD is unthinkable, and team development, even if needed, meets resistance. Last, there is the situation where a manager and perhaps his or her team desires an exploratory consultation and there is only sketchy, secondhand information available about the team's problems, functioning, real readiness, and so on. These four situations as well as some of the critique above, have resulted in skilled team development interventionists creatively ad-libbing, adapting and innovating in their practice. One form of these endeavors is what was previously termed micro team interventions and it is to these we now turn.

EXAMPLES OF MINIMAL TEAM DEVELOPMENT INTERVENTIONS

To provide a clinical feel for minimal team interventions, four brief descriptive "cases" from a variety of organizations are offered below. The first involves a Ranger District of the U.S. Forest Service.

An external consultant was asked to work with a management team with which he was unfamiliar and whose members he had no opportunity to meet or talk with before the scheduled weekend. He had, however, assured himself that the team was reasonably motivated for the off-site event and he enlisted as an associate another team manager with OD skills from another region of the Forest Service. The first session began with the consultant attempting to be self-disclosing about who he was. He then invited any and all inquiries about himself and responded candidly. He then stated that, while the team members had gotten acquainted with him, he had not learned much about them. He suggested an activity where team members would voluntarily take turns being silent, while the others would voluntarily offer comment about their silent associate, which would let the consultant "learn about that person in ways that might enhance our weekend together." The team of ten proceeded to do this, starting slowly but soon doing it fully without consultant involvement. Three sorts of information were elicited in this activity: information about tasks and responsibilities; information about the focal person's work history, relationships and extra-work activities; and, information about how the informant perceived the focal person doing his job and some of the consequences for others. Everyone took part. This activity took nearly three hours. The agenda building for the remainder of the weekend went swiftly and was very much enhanced by the third sort of information elicited in the activity.

The second case takes place in a midwestern truck manufacturing firm and involves an internal consultant, the manager of the production division, and his departmental managers.

The staff consultant was just beginning to work with the team. She determined that the team members were at a point where getting a listing of their expectations for future meetings would be useful, but also believed that team members tended to be too judgmental of one another and tended to wander from any agenda. The consultant asked about these two hunches and the team quickly confirmed them. A "nominal group technique" variation was suggested as a way of getting out the expectational data, as well as experiencing a device that might help structure the generation of information. Individuals were asked to write a list of their expectations of the team for themselves as persons and another list for their positions. The team manager and two members then consolidated individual anonymous lists while the others had a break. The consolidated lists were not too long (reflecting a lot of overlap of individual lists) so the consultant suggested the manager lead a team discussion prioritizing the items of the two lists. After this was done, a team member suggested subgrouping as a means of generating ways of better meeting the high priority items. This also happened, followed by a total team discussion. The resulting discussion led the team to action planning on how members would have to behave in the future. The actions just noted took approximately three hours and post-meeting response form indicated a higher than usual degree of satisfaction.

A major California social welfare agency is the site of the third case.

A professional in applied behavorial science was making a social visit to a manager friend at the latter's work site. The manager invited the professional to observe a regular staff meeting. The manager half-jokingly suggested that the professional might be able to give him tips on running the meeting better. At the outset of the meeting, the manager introduced his friend, passed out a conventional meeting agenda, and then publicly repeated his hope that his friend would provide "some feedback that would make our meetings more effective." The professional, noting what to him appeared to be a widespread hopefulness around the table, spoke up and suggested two activities for the group before they began their work for the meeting. One was for everyone individually to get in touch with their level of energy or enthusiasm for today's meeting and to compare it with their typical level. Several people immediately closed their eyes or looked down, apparently following the professional's suggestion. Most others, noting this, joined in. In a few minutes, most people were once again focusing their attention on the guest. The visitor had glanced at the group's agenda and then suggested that the group might find it useful to redo the agenda—to divide it into informational and decision items, to put someone's name by each item so that that person would guide that part of the agenda, and that the final agenda item be a short, voluntary, descriptive discussion of what had happened during the meeting. The manager's smile seemed to initiate one person's suggestions for agenda item division, followed by an active completion of the visitor's suggestions. The activities noted above took about fifteen minutes. The meeting then went on with the visitor offering no further word. The new last agenda item was hardly descriptive, rather the discussion was full of minor suggestions for how to build agendas, conduct future meetings and requests for help, as well as expressions that this meeting was one of their best. Later that afternoon, the manager expressed his amazement that restructuring the agenda had brought in silent members, tended to keep the group from drifting and allowed him to take good notes for a change.

The last case to be offered took place in a stable, older printing equipment business in the northeast.

The consultant was working with a small department of long service technical specialists whose manager had hired him to provide "any help you can that will get us to pull together a little better. Most of us have been here so long we probably aren't very conscious of how we work with one another." The initial session had been devoted to outlining a conventional diagnostic team meeting series. The consultant had made a presentation of the purposes, benefits, and limitations, as well as the process of such a series and had led a discussion by the team. His impression of that initial session was that it was rather perfunctory. The discussion was not hostile or resistant, but little energy was apparent. The departmental personnel seemed "locked-into" some long established patterns of relating. At the beginning of the second session, the consultant felt both perplexed and uncertain. He believed that the series would be minimally effective unless the members gave it more energy. The consultant also began to doubt that he had a very good "feel" for departmental relationships and norms. As a consequence of his reflections, the consultant began the second session by inviting the members of the department to go outside onto the lawn. Once outside, he asked if they would cluster themselves into small groups around highly interrelated jobs. After some shuffling, several clusters of five to seven persons began to form. The consultant asked each group to sit around a picnic table. He then said they were to take turns being "it," who was to be silent while his or her coworkers told "it," *only* about his or her strengths. The activities of physical clustering and strength bombardment took just a little over an hour. Following these activities, the department reassembled to discuss and formulate some general change goals for the department. This discussion went quite smoothly.

MICRO TEAM DEVELOPMENT INTERVENTIONS CHARACTERIZED

Quite obviously the four brief cases just sketched only begin to illustrate the range and type of micro team interventions. They do serve, however, as the basis for a first, somewhat tentative, characterization of the more obvious features of minimal team development interventions and their use.

Given the critique of major team building interventions, which stated that the group dynamics and group development literature was woefully underused, let us begin by suggesting how the interventions illustrated above may reflect some of our basic knowledge. The acquaintancing intervention with the forest ranger's team acknowledges the consultant as a new, if temporary, member and the need to deal with the inclusion issue as well as the oft-noted stage of group development usually termed *forming* or *solidarity,* which precedes structuring and task phases. The nominal group variation intervention used with the trucking managers reflects a couple of well-established findings of social psychology, namely, that clarifying expectations contributes to role performance and that public discussion, with its interactional sequencing, reduces the amount and variety of member contribution. The intervention in the social agency staff meeting where the agenda was differentiated and personal responsibility for parts of it established, contributed to members' needs for a psychological structure (which frees energies), reducing anxiety by reducing uncertainty. The two interventions in the printing equipment firm, physical clustering and strength bombardment, utilized the potency of behavior and the visual compared to simple auditory impact and the energizing impact of positive reinforcement, respectively. Space prohibits an exhaustive analysis, but enough has been noted to indicate the apparent success of these minimal interventions.

What seem to be the distinguishing features of micro team interventions? Some features are rather obvious, others are less so. Nevertheless, the following six appear to characterize minimal team interventions:

- They do not require much real time—a few hours at the outside and not more than one session.
- They have as their focus only a part of the teamwork process, or only a part of any of the major team interventions—they are relatively simple and their foci seem to have an ad hoc quality and may or may not appear to fit into a logical sequence of steps.
- They all seem to have the generation of information as a primary function regardless of their apparent purpose—their diagnostic utility is high.
- They may or may not be initiated by a third party or consultant—more importantly they are probably perceived as being largely under the control of participants.
- They tend to be highly participative and reflect current team needs.
- They do not require a high state of team readiness—although member motivation no doubt helps.

CONCLUDING COMMENT

Micro team development interventions as characterized in this article would seem to be useful additions to any manager's repertoire, as well as to the OD professional. The examination of these interventions suggests several general points for the team interventionist:

- The "commonalities" of all team interventions need to be more actively questioned than in the past. Since most were simply expedient inventions, there is nothing authoritative about them. This questioning may lead to a less slavish adherence to their structure and, perhaps, thereby promote a more situationally appropriate application and a greater willingness to experimentally adapt, or modify, known interventions.
- We need to accept that briefer and simpler interventions are potentially as valuable as are the better known more elaborate ones.
- We need to invent and better utilize those interventions which truly encourage participants to generate valid information and which foster free choices.
- We need to design team interventions, macro and micro, that explicitly reflect our conceptual understanding of team dynamics and development.
- We need to utilize microinterventions when they fit the situation and have some theoretical basis, trusting that they will be functional to the natural development of a team, even when some emcompassing plan is not obviously being supported.
- We need to follow up on our interventions, especially on minimal ones, to assess their utility—by consciously noting, and where feasible, scientifically measuring, their impacts and sharing our experiences with our colleagues.

References

Argyris, Chris, "T-Groups for Organizational Effectiveness," *Harvard Business Review,* vol. 42, no. 2, 1964, pp. 60–74.

Argyris, Chris, *Intervention Theory and Method.* Reading, Mass.: Addison-Wesley Publishing, 1970.

Beckhard, Richard, "Optimizing Team-Building Efforts," *Journal of Contemporary Business,* vol. 1, no. 3, 1972, pp. 22–32.

Beer, Michael, "The Technology of Organization Development," in M.D. Dunnette (ed.) *Handbook of Industrial and Organizational Psychology,* Chicago: Rand McNally, 1976.

Blake, Robert, & Jane Mouton, *Corporate Excellence through Grid Organization Development.* Houston: Gulf Publishing 1968.

Dayal, I., & J. M. Thomas, "Operation KPE: Developing a New Organization," *Journal of Applied Behavioral Science,* vol. 4, 1968, pp. 473–506.

Dyer, William, *Team Building: Issues and Alternatives.* Reading, Mass.: Addison-Wesley Publishing, 1977.

Fordyce, Jack, & R. Weil, *Managing With People*. Reading, Mass.: Addison-Wesley Publishing, 1971.

French, Wendell, & C. H. Bell, *Organization Development*. Second Edition, Englewood Cliffs: Prentice-Hall, 1978.

Golembiewski, Robert, "The 'Laboratory Approach' to Organizational Change: Schema of a Method," *Public Administration Review,* vol. 27, no. 2, 1967, pp. 211–21.

Golembiewski, Robert, *Renewing Organizations: The Laboratory Approach to Planned Change*. Ithaca, Ill.: F.E. Peacock, 1972.

Harrison, Roger, "When Power Conflicts Trigger Team Spirit," *European Business,* Spring, 1972, pp. 27–65.

Herman, Stanley, & M. Korenich, *Authentic Management*. Reading, Mass.: Addison-Wesley Publishing, 1977.

Huse, Edgar, *Organization Development and Change*. New York: West Publishing, 1975.

Kelly, Joe, "Organizational Development Through Structured Sensitivity Training," *Management International Review,* vol. 13, no. 4–5, 1973, pp. 83–96.

Lewis, John W., "Management Team Development: Will it work for You?" *Personnel,* July/August, 1975.

Lippit, Gordon, *Organizational Renewal*. Englewood Cliffs: Prentice-Hall, 1982.

Margulies, Newton, & A. P. Raia, "People in Organizations: A Case For Team Training," *Training and Development Journal,* August 1968.

Margulies, Newton, & A. P. Raia, *Conceptual Foundations of Organizational Development*. New York: McGraw-Hill, 1978.

Melcher, Robert D., *Roles and Relationships: Clarifying the Manager's Job*. New York: American Management Association, 1967.

Patten, Thomas H., *Organizational Development Through Teambuilding*. New York: John Wiley and Sons, 1981.

Plovnick, M. S.; R. E. Fry; & I. Rubin, "New Developments in OD Technology: Programmed Team Development," *Training and Development Journal,* vol. 29, no. 4, 1975, pp. 19–27.

Schein, Edgar, *Process Consultation*. Reading, Mass.: Addison-Wesley Publishing, 1969.

Woodman, Richard W., & John J. Sherwood, "The Role of Team Development in Organizational Effectiveness: A Critical Review," *Psychological Bulletin,* vol. 88, no. 1, 1980, pp. 166–86.

12 Strategies for Organizational Change: Role of the Inside Change Agent

Phillip L. Hunsaker

ABSTRACT

This paper describes the role of an inside change agent
and strategies for enhancing the success of change efforts.
It discusses advantages and disadvantages of internal positioning, principles for enhancing influence, role differentiation,
considerations in choosing change strategies, and a range of
interpersonal strategies for bringing about organizational
change.

AUTHOR BACKGROUND

Dr. Phillip L. Hunsaker is a consultant, seminar leader, speaker,
author, teacher, and researcher in the areas of management
and organizational development. He has authored over eighty
publications including numerous articles in academic and
professional journals, and the books: *The Art of Managing
People* (Prentice-Hall); and *You Can Make It Happen: A Guide
to Personal and Organizational Change* (Addison-Wesley).
He is also a professor of management at the University of
San Diego.

Portions of this paper were originally presented at the Twenty-Third Annual Western
Academy of Management Meeting, Colorado Springs, Colorado, April 1–3, 1982.

When individuals are faced with a conflict of values between their personal lives and the organizations in which they work, it is not always possible or preferable to change the personal aspects of the situation. In such cases, the optimal course may be one of changing the organization to make it more compatible with one's personal needs. The following guidelines present a format for becoming an inside change agent.

When you plan to invest effort in making your organization more compatible with your values, it is important to perceive it as a social reality within which individuals make decisions. This shift in personal frame of reference changes our perspective of organizations from a *fixed given*, which we can only respond to, to an *agreed-upon social invention*, which members of the organization have created for themselves and now take for granted. Since individuals not only create the organization, but "are" the organization, we can change the organization by changing the perceptions, awareness, and values of those who make it up.

ROLE OF AN INSIDE CHANGE AGENT

Ronald Havelock of the University of Michigan Institute of Social Research has combined in the experience of researchers and practicing change agents in an analysis of over one thousand studies of innovation and the process of change, Havelock's findings concerning the relative advantages of being an "insider" or "outsider" appear to be a good place to start in considering your role as an "inside" change agent.

Advantages and Disadvantages of the "Inside" Change Agent

"Outside" change agents possess several advantages, such as being independent and having an objective, new perspective. They also have several disadvantages, however, such as being a stranger, lacking "inside" understanding, and not being able to identify adequately with the problems. As insiders, we are intimately involved with the well-being of our organization, as well as ourselves, which gives us a different motivation than monetary compensation for initiating change processes. Some of the advantages of being an inside change agent are:

- You know the system: where the power is, who the opinion leaders are, where the strategic leverage points are.
- You understand and speak the language of the organization: the special ways members refer to things; the tone and style of discussing things.
- You understand the norms: the commonly held beliefs, attitudes, and behaviors; you probably follow and behave in accordance with them.
- You identify with the organization's needs and aspirations: if the organization prospers, this will also probably help you; you have a personal incentive for helping.

■ You are a familiar figure: what you are trying to do is understandable as "member" behavior; you don't represent the threat of an unfamiliar outside force.

As an insider, you also have the following *disadvantages*:

■ You may lack an "objective" perspective: because of your involvement and history with the organization, you may be biased or not be able to see the organization as a whole system.
■ You may not have the special knowledge or skill required: since consulting is not your primary vocation you may not have had enough training to be a true expert in the change situation.
■ You may not have an adequate power base: unless you are at the top of the organization your plans may be confronted by superiors or competing peers.
■ You may be hindered by past images: you may have to live down past failures or the hostility generated by past successes.
■ You may not have independence of movement required to be effective: the obligations of your job may severely limit the time and energy that you can invest in a change agent role.
■ It may be difficult to redefine your on-going relationships with other members of the organization: when taking on the change agent role you must be able to change the expectations that your associates have about how you will behave and how they will relate to you.

In order to capitalize on the advantages and avoid the disadvantages of being an inside change agent, many experienced professionals have suggested that insiders work together with outsiders as a team. Such a team would provide the insider with "expert" legitimacy for his efforts along with real expertise, an objective perspective, and moral support. If you do not have the advantage of outside support and are not in a position of power and authority within your organization, it is, nevertheless, possible to be effective in bringing about change.

Ten Principles of Being a Successful Inside Change Agent

These principles should be kept in mind in all change situations and are prerequisites to any specific change technique. These ten principles are as follows:

1. To bring about desired changes, it is first necessary to truly *know yourself*. We must be aware of our needs, values, and objectives in order to be able to determine what it is that we need to be happy in our organization.
2. For change strategies to be effective, we must truly *understand the organization*. Knowledge of values, norms, key people, subsystems, cliques and alliances is prerequisite for assessing the situation and

planning realistic change efforts. Your personal knowledge can be supplemented through contacts with "political" colleagues.

3. In order to make informed decisions, we must *keep lines of communication open*. One of the most devastating blockages to change efforts occurs when we cut off communication with our adversaries. This can cause affirmation of negative stereotypes without the possibility of new disconfirming information that could shed new light on the situation.

4. It is important to *determine how others feel* about the situation and whether they agree with your desires. If no one else agreed with your assessment of the situation, maybe another self-assessment is called for. On the other hand, if you can identify potential allies who share your desires, they can contribute to an effective team effort with a higher probability of success.

5. The situation should be *analyzed from the many points of view* of all parties involved. Assessing the perceptions of a proposed change from adversaries' points of view may reveal how they would have overlooked an important point that would change their minds. It might, on the other hand, demonstrate something that convinces you to alter your own position.

6. A *thorough understanding* of all dimensions of the proposed change is a prerequisite. The innovator must be "the expert" in the change to maintain his own credibility, and to aid others in understanding what he is trying to bring about. This knowledge should include all strengths, weaknesses, evaluations, and possible objections.

7. Successful changes are not usually accomplished without *continued effort*. The innovator must be persistent and continually make inroads whenever opportunities present themselves. Giving up before you even start leads to very predictable negative results.

8. A sense of *timing* is just as important as the strategy employed. Waiting for the opportune moment, as opposed to reacting spontaneously, can make a key difference in the success of a change effort.

9. *Sharing credit* with others can also be vital in creating enthusiasm about a desired change. People support and feel committed to ideas they feel part of.

10. *Avoiding win-lose strategies* and seeking changes where everybody wins can avoid standoffs where everyone loses what they want directly or indirectly through hard feelings.

How to Define Your Role as an Inside Change Agent

Regardless of your formal job title or position, there are four primary ways in which a person can act as a change agent. These roles have been defined by Ronald Havelock (1973) as:

■ *Catalyst*—The catalyst role is needed to overcome existing inertia and start the organization members working on their serious problems. The catalyst's primary role is to make personal dissatisfaction known and by upsetting the status quo, catalysts energize the problem-solving process.

- *Solution Giver*—As a solution giver you have a chance to apply your ideas about what the organizational change should be. In order to have your suggestions accepted, however, you must know when and how to offer them, and how others in the organization can adapt them to their needs.
- *Process Helper*—This is a critical role concerning the "how to" or process of change. It involves the activities of showing organization members how to (1) recognize and define their needs, (2) diagnose problems and set objectives, (3) acquire relevant resources, (4) select or create solutions, (5) adapt and carry out solutions, and (6) evaluate solutions.
- *Resource Linker*—A person in this role brings people and other resources together so that they can be applied to the problem. Resources include not only people with necessary skills and knowledge, but also financial and political backing.

In defining your own role, you should keep in mind that all of them are necessary and that you may be able to fill more than one of them yourself. The roles are not mutually exclusive. Also, it is possible for you to be effective in these change roles regardless of whether you are "line" or "staff," or working from above or below.

Tips for Being Successful in Each of the Change Agent Roles

All four change agent roles are important and partly interrelated. The overall task of any change agent is to establish and build a relationship with the organization members he or she wants to help with a change, work with them collaboratively in a problem-solving process, and leave them with the ability to solve similar problems effectively themselves in the future.

How to be an effective catalyst. A catalyst is the initial change advocate who stresses the need for change to further the interests of the organization or disadvantaged subgroups and individuals. Catalysts are often deeply committed and emotionally involved in the change effort because they personally feel injured, or they identify with some subgroup which they feel is being exploited. To maximize their effectiveness as an emotionally involved change advocate, catalysts need to make certain that they:

1. Think reasonably about steps that need to be followed to win support for their cause and to reduce resistance to the changes they desire.
2. Try to see the situation from the point of view of the existing organizational leadership.

3. Promote a feeling of common identity and purpose in those supporting the change effort.
4. Form alliances with others who can take on other types of change roles, such as process helper and linker.
5. Have a sense of timing. Catalysts need to assess the support for change and judge the most opportune moment for bringing it about.

How to be an effective solution giver.   Most of us have, at one time or another, thought that we had a better solution to an organizational problem than the one adopted. Whether we were effective in being a "solution giver," however, depended on how well we communicated our solution to others. As solution givers, we need to concentrate on the following check points:

1. Find out the real needs of the organization before you decide it needs the solution you have in mind.
2. Adapt innovations so that they are maximally beneficial to all members of the organization.
3. Have more than one solution to offer and be adaptable.
4. Ensure those affected by the change continued assistance beyond the point of adoption.
5. Help organization decision makers be good judges of solutions so they can decide for themselves what is best for all.
6. Build an open and authentic relationship with others in the organization by knowledge sharing and helping.
7. Become a resource linker to aid the organization in implementing the solution.

How to be an effective resource linker.   A resource linker is one who matches resources of one person or group with needs of another. Persons with skills in communicating and relationship building are important change agents in this role. To be most effective resource linkers should:

1. Listen to what the organizational leadership has to say about their problem and what they have done in trying to solve it. A resource linker must understand "where the organization is at" before he can successfully match its needs with the right kind of resource, at the right time, in the right way.
2. Establish two-way communication between resources and the organizations.
3. Show organizational leadership resources they have within themselves and among their own group, as well as outside resources.
4. Continue to build additional networks after the initial problem is resolved. Each new resource link established adds to the organization's capacity to work collaboratively on problems.

How to be an effective process helper. The helping process is needed from the very beginning stages of establishing a relationship and diagnosing the problem, through the acquisition of relevant resources, choosing a solution, gaining acceptance, and stabilizing the change. Three things necessary to building and maintaining an effective process helper relationship are defining your relationship with the organization, successfully managing your initial encounters with the target group, and accurately assessing your relationship.

Define your relationship with the organization. In order to accomplish this, it is necessary to first determine the nature of the group you are going to work with directly. Once this is done, formal and "informal" key people (opinion leaders) should be identified to help you understand the norms, values, and beliefs of the target group and the strictness of these characteristics.

After you have assessed the situation, you can then determine whether opinion leaders, formal authorities, or representatives of major factions or others will be best to work with regarding their credibility, respectability, or public relations ability and compatibility with you.

Next, a determination needs to be made of other groups to which the target group is related. This may be the larger organization or the community surrounding an organization. Again, norms, values, objectives, and the degree of influence it represents for the target group need to be identified. In addition, it is also important to find out the relative potency of different influentials, such as pressure groups, in the larger environment and how to approach these influentials.

Successfully manage initial encounters with the target group. How those in the target group see you and feel about you initially will determine whether you will be able to proceed with the change process at all.

The change agent must start the relationship by establishing high trust and friendliness. A start in this direction can be made with simple things like a smile, firm handshake, warm greeting, straight look to the eye, or using first names. You should also try to be a familiar person by using the appropriate dress, speech, and bearing, and identifying some common interests.

In order to establish the image that you can be helpful you should find the earliest opportunity to do something for the client that will be perceived as such by him. Only a token is usually necessary, such as providing a useful piece of information, a book, or a technique. Finally, you must show the client that you are a good listener, that you are interested, and that you care. This can be communicated by asking for clarifications, nodding, paraphrasing, and other verbal and nonverbal techniques.

Accurately assess your relationship. Ronald Havelock (1973) has identified nine characteristics of a change agent-client relationship that comprise an ideal. Although they do not cover everything, they may serve as a yardstick against which we can measure our own circumstances. They include the following conditions:

■ *Reciprocity*—Both the change agent and target group should be able to give and take, transfer information both ways, and mutually appreciate the problem.

■ *Openness*—Both should be willing and ready to receive new inputs from each other.

■ *Realistic Expectations*—Reasonably realistic expectations should be set from the start so that the change effort will not be plagued by undue disillusionment.

■ *Expectations of Reward*—The change agent must be seen as providing a valuable resource which can solve problems and significantly improve the situation.

■ *Structure*—Definitions of roles, working procedures, and expected outcomes are necessary to provide a sufficient structural basis for successful interactions.

■ *Equal Power*—Under most circumstances, lasting effectiveness and commitment can best be brought about where neither party has the power to compel the other to change.

■ *Minimum Threat*—Because the idea of change is threatening to most of us, everything possible should be done to minimize the perception of threat.

■ *Confrontation of Differences*—A relationship that allows the honest confrontation and talking through of differences may be stormy at times, but it will also be healthy and strong when the going gets rough.

■ *Involvement of All Relative Parties*—As noted earlier, the change agent must relate to influential others in the community. They should at least know that you are there, why you are there, and approve of your being there.

A change relationship can be an exciting and rewarding experience for everyone involved, but it can also degenerate into a meaningless exercise which only produces frustration and disappointment. Some examples of "danger signals" are given below.

If the organization lacks the ability to assemble resources, communicate, or elicit concern from key members, or if it seems to possess excessive rigidity and tendencies to externalize conflicts and see issues only in black-and-white terms, these conditions may signal innate incapacity to change.

Even if these degenerative organizational conditions do not exist, you as a change agent may have done everything right and still be greeted with hostility or indifference. Negative responses to a well-managed initial encounter effort signal that the future is not very bright. If you are greeted in an overly enthusiastic manner, on the other hand, the organizational leadership may only want to use you as a pawn. This is a common type of exploitation where the change agent is supported only to serve special interests in an internal power struggle. A change agent may in rare instances be able to turn this type of situation to an advantage, but in general it should be avoided.

CONSIDERATIONS IN CHOOSING A CHANGE STRATEGY

It is important for anyone desiring to bring about a change to develop strategies to fit his or her own unique characteristics and circumstances. The strategies discussed in the following sections may provide useful ideas, but it is your own experience, level of competence, and overall objectives that are most important in developing a game plan. Some general considerations, which should always be a part of your strategy building, are listed below.

Personal Skill and Style

A change agent should have a realistic understanding of his or her own skills and best styles. Stick to techniques you know are applicable and are competent to administer. When picking an appropriate strategy mix, also be aware of the resources you and the organization have access to for making them work. These include internal, external, human, material, informational, and motivational resources.

Type of Relationship

Political and economic tensions must also be considered in picking a strategy. If you are considered an expert and people have confidence in you, the number and types of tactics which will be acceptable are greater than if you are considered a peer or novice.

Special Characteristics of the Organization

One of your first steps as a change agent is to make a thorough assessment of the organization to understand its weaknesses, strengths, ideologies, structural characteristics, and other special features. These considerations should then be carefully weighed to determine appropriate strategies. Specific situational factors such as time, place, and circumstance, can provide restraints and guides to appropriate strategies.

Characteristics of the Strategy

The strategy must also be analyzed in relationship to the organization to determine whether it is compatible with organization ideologies, how much adaptation will be required to make it fit this situation, the probability of its success, how long before results are apparent, how much can hope to be accomplished, how much effort must be put into it by whom and for how long.

Feasibility

Three primary considerations in evaluating competing strategies are: benefit, practicability, and diffusibility. How much good would it do if it worked? Will it really work, especially in this particular organization? Will it be accepted by members of the organization? By asking these questions it is often possible to reduce the number of possible approaches to one or two.

Implementation

When you start planning how to implement the particular strategy, or strategy mix, you have decided upon, the relevance of the above criteria will become immediately apparent. If you do not possess sufficient skill, have not established an appropriate relationship, or have failed to consider a value conflict between the organization and strategy characteristics, the infeasibility of your proposed strategy will be clear when you try to implement it.

INTERPERSONAL STRATEGIES FOR ORGANIZATION CHANGE

The strategies presented in this section refer to behavioral skills you can apply personally to bring about changes in others' behaviors and attitudes. Some of the reasons for presenting these interpersonal techniques are to raise your awareness of different approaches, and to increase your personal control over situations through the ways you communicate and utilize your own human resources and those of others around you.

These strategies obviously represent an incomplete list. They are basics, however, and may provide the insights to give you that extra personal power to effectively bring about the changes you desire. They may also stimulate other ideas and alternatives that are unique to your situation and personality style. Some of the interpersonal change strategies you may want to consider are summarized below. For more thorough explanations of these and similar strategies, you may wish to consult the references by Byrd (1974), Culbert (1974), Havelock (1973), and Langer and Dweck (1973) listed at the end of this paper.

Directed Thinking

Directed thinking means clearly specifying what it is you hope to accomplish in an interpersonal situation and systematically considering all factors that may influence achieving it. Spontaneity is often good for building strong interpersonal relationships, but it can also hurt people. When we hurt or insult others without thinking, it often is very difficult to undo the damage, and sometimes the damage is irreparable.

There is an abundance of information available in any interpersonal situation to help guide your behavior in a directed way. The following questions can help you select and organize information in a meaningful way: How has this person or group reacted to similar situations? What approaches worked in the past? Which ones did not? How does this person or group feel about me? How can I influence this impression? How does this person or group feel about the change being proposed? What is their point of view? Why? What are the most effective ways of communicating the change ideas? What unique considerations are relevant to this person or group in this situation?

Disclaimers

The context in which we are interacting has a great deal of influence on others' reactions. If the target person, or target group, feels that you will personally benefit from the change you are suggesting, they may feel that they are being manipulated for your personal gain, or that you are unduly biased. To counter this atittude, you need to "disclaim" their feeling that you are promoting the change just for your personal benefit. If you will benefit from the change, you need to own up to this, but convince the target group that it is also a good thing for them regardless of your situation. Then they can listen to what you have to say without constantly being on guard to detect what they expect to be your own hidden agenda.

If the situation you are trying to change is one in which you are obviously very emotionally involved, your credibility may be reduced even if you make a disclaimer. This may sometimes help in these circumstances to present a more balanced account of the situation including positive and negative sides of the proposed change and the strategies you are suggesting. This approach is more apt to lead others to believe that you have done a thorough investigation regardless of your emotional concerns.

Authentic Feedback

Authentic feedback consists of nonevaluative interpretation of how a person's or group's behavior affects you. It can often lead to the target person's or target group's increased understanding of problems their own behavior creates. Such self-diagnosis can decrease resistance to change when the personal need for it is demonstrated and accepted.

Sometimes leveling is done in emotional and evaluative manners. This type of confrontation is often risky, but sometimes necessary to get feelings out and open the door to suppressed organizational problems.

Initial Agreement

Agreeing with a person or group at the beginning of our change effort is important to ensure that you are not turned off immediately. Showing that you have something in common serves to favorably dispose the target group to both yourself and your proposal. If you contradict yourself later on, or propose contrary approaches, members of the target group are more apt to be open to you and your ideas if they believe that you are similar to them.

Inoculation

If you are fairly certain that there are members of the target group, or other influential people, who will later attempt to refute your position, it is a good idea to try and inoculate key decision makers against arguments which may change their minds. This can often be done by sharing possible counterarguments with the target group during your presentation and demonstrating their fallacies. This technique tends to build resistance to opposition who may later voice such objections.

Limited Choice

People like to feel that they have some power over what happens to them, but when they are faced with an unlimited number of alternatives to choose from it is very difficult to make a decision. The strategy of providing a limited choice maximizes your chances of having the target group accept a change proposal you favor because it lets the people make a choice, but only from alternatives acceptable to you. The key is to phrase your questions as if a given event will take place and the target group is to choose how or when. When a person is confronted with a limited choice of alternatives and asked to choose from them, most often he will do so, and only rarely will he question initial assumptions or raise additional alternatives.

Obligating in Advance

The advantages and disadvantages of a commitment become more prominent at different times. The advantages are more clear when the action is to take place in the future. As the event becomes more immediate, however, the disadvantages become more eminent. Since most people feel compelled to meet their obligations, it is to your advantage to gain commitment to participate in a change effort well in advance of its planned occurrence. If participants feel that they have made a prior obligation, it will be more difficult to back out when the anxieties associated with the approach of the event occur.

Positive Expectation

Indicating to a person that you expect that he or she will be a valuable participant in a change effort can often act as a self-fulfilling prophecy, that is, the person will behave in a way to fulfill your expectations in order to prove himself worthy of your high regard. Successful utilization of this approach also decreases begrudging participation because people feel that they are important and are doing something valuable for you, which they are.

Compliments

Trying to get someone to change through criticism has negative consequences even if the strategy is successful. People usually take criticism as a slap in the face and react defensively and with hostility towards its source. Phrase your criticism in positive terms and frost it with preceding compliments. For example, a line manager could say to a staff group leader, "We like your work very much. If you people would take a little more interest in personally relating these ideas with ours, we could probably make even better use of them."

Indirect Comparisons

Another way to suggest ways of improving without bringing out defenses is to use indirect comparisons. With this technique, corrective information is given in terms of another person or group in a similar situation. It is important, of course, that the target group is aware that it is behaving in the same fashion for this tactic to be effective. The awareness of present, indirect comparisons allows target groups to evaluate the suggestions without losing face and becoming defensive.

Holding Out

Holding out is a blocking strategy sometimes representing all that a change agent performing a catalyst's role can muster. It is a method of preventing a decision or calling attention to a negative program that needs your approval or participation to be successful. Failing to cooperate or go along with a decision or plan of action is dangerous and unpleasant, but in some situations the risk and abuse is necessary to get your point across.

Going Around Superiors

You may find yourself in a situation where your superior in the organization simply will not agree to consider a change that you feel is vitally necessary for the organization. Under such conditions, you may feel that your only alternative is to go over your superior's head to gain support for the desired change. This is a dangerous maneuver because it will violate the trust of your supervisor and make you vulnerable to any sanctions he or she is able to apply. If you have applied the ten principles for being a successful inside change agent presented earlier in this paper and you still want to proceed, you will have a fairly good chance of being successful.

Threatening Resignation

This is your ultimate weapon. If you are a valuable employee, your opposition will listen to you when you lay your job on the line. Obviously, this is an extremely dangerous strategy, and the warnings administered with respect to going around superiors should be doubled or tripled in this case. Never call wolf with this strategy.

Media Dissemination

Disseminating your ideas and proposals to others in the organization through newspapers, memos, or bulletin announcements, is a relatively risk-free strategy which may be effective in gaining support of opinion leaders or other influential organizational members. It is a good approach to raise awareness concerning a problem situation and start people thinking of ideas to improve it. The same thing can be done on a smaller scale through word of mouth.

Support Groups

Support groups consist of organization members who share a common concern for changing some aspect of the organization. They are important for testing ideas, expressing empathy, and supporting one another under heavy opposition. Such group meetings can produce increased awareness about the nature and consequences of a purposed change and provide us with a better perspective on how to gain more control over our organizational life.

Gatekeeping

Gatekeeping refers to a process-helper role where you facilitate the communication process so that everyone concerned has an equal chance to participate and be heard. Through a simple comment as, "What do some of the rest of you think?" it may be possible to decrease the influence of some of your more assertive opponents and solicit important information from those who support you and the desired change.

SUMMARY

Being aware of the advantages and disadvantages of internal positioning provides the foundation for the internal change agent to build an effective action plan for change congruent with the specifics of the organizational situation being confronted. Basic principles have been described to help define the specific type of role the internal change agent should engage in, and how the chances for success can be increased.

It is also important to develop specific change strategies that fit the change agent's unique characteristics and circumstances. Then interpersonal strategies for influencing others can be utilized to increase personal control over situations through the ways you communicate and utilize your human resources.

Suggested Readings

Hunsaker, Phillip L. and Alessandra, Anthony J., *The Art of Managing People*, Englewood Cliffs, N.J.: Prentice-Hall, Inc., 1980.

Huse, Edgar, *Organization Development and Change*. New York: West Publishing Company, 1975.

References

Byrd, Richard E., *A Guide to Personal Risk Taking*. New York: Amacom, 1974.

Culbert, Samuel A., *The Organization Trap and How to Get Out of It*. New York: Basic Books, Inc., 1974.

Havelock, Ronald G., *The Change Agent's Guide to Innovation in Education.* Englewood Cliffs, N.J.: Educational Technology Publications, 1973.

Langer, Ellen J. and Dweck, Carol S., *Personal Politics: The Psychology of Making It.* Englewood Cliffs, N.J.: Prentice Hall, 1973.

Sperry, Len, Michelson, Douglas J., and Hunsaker, Phillip L., *You Can Make It Happen: A Guide to Self-Actualization and Organizational Change.* Reading, MA.: Addison-Wesley, 1977.

13 Competency Based Management as an OD Intervention

Alice G. Sargent

ABSTRACT

The current theory of situational management, while important, does not provide managers with models and practices necessary to manage better. To learn how to manage more effectively, we need to upgrade the quality of management education and management systems. Technology creates problems of its own and no longer provides sufficient solutions. Other countries that produce higher quality products with fewer layers of management and a more stable workforce understand some aspects of management that we need to learn. Failure in American corporations to pay adequate attention to human values has led to isolation, alienation, and low productivity. Management needs to build models of manageral effectiveness. This article describes two competency models—one of which, the androgynous manager, attempts to be responsive to what the future manager will be like—and shows how integrated human resource development systems can use the competency model to link training, development, and performance appraisal. Finally, this article suggests how an organization can involve line managers in building a competency model.

AUTHOR BACKGROUND

Alice G. Sargent is an organization consultant living in Washington, D.C., serving as a consultant and trainer to E.I. Dupont de Nemours, Federal Executive Institute, Australian Institute of Mangement, Agency for International Development, and NTL Institute. Previous clients include the General

Accounting Office, Overseas Private Investment Corporation, Federal Energy Regulatory Commission, U.S. Department of Commerce, Celanese Corporation, Procter & Gamble, CIGNA Corporation, and The National Cancer Institute. She is an adjunct faculty member in the Key Executive Program at The American University School of Government and Public Administration and at the University of Southern California Washington Public Affairs Center. She was formerly Director of the MBA Program at Trinity College. She is the author of *Beyond Sex Roles* and *The Androgynous Manager,* and co-editor of *The NTL Manager's Handbook.* She is on the Board of the Organizational Development Network and has been named in *Who's Who in the East, Who's Who in American Women,* and *Outstanding Young Women of America.*

In the 1980s the challenge to American organizations is to learn how to manage more effectively. The current theory of situational management, while important and useful, does not provide managers with models and practices necessary to manage better. Organizations must upgrade the quality of management education and management systems to meet the complex problems of the decade—problems for which technology no longer provides sufficient solutions and, furthermore, creates vast problems of its own.

A key to managing better is learning to value human resources as we have valued technology in the past. Other countries produce higher quality products with fewer layers of management and a more stable workforce. While the Japanese have a better long-range financial base on which to build, they also foster human values of intimacy, subtlety, and trust in dealing with organizational problems. That these values receive so little attention in American organizations, whether corporations, government or educational institutions, has led to isolation, alienation, and low productivity in the workplace.

As a step towards dealing with these issues, management needs to build models of managerial effectiveness at supervisory, middle and executive levels; a curriculum to develop managers as practitioners based on these models; and systematic methods for assessment, career development, and performance appraisal that reinforce the models.

What are the signs that our current managerial process is not working? We have serious productivity problems and breakdowns in supervisor-subordinate communication. Many of our organizations are not renewing, healthy places to live eight to ten hours a day. Instead, they are stressful and lead either to rustout or burnout. Our organizations do not help many people feel efficacious or empowered, particularly middle managers. Numerous managers report they lack a common vision around which to mobilize their people.

MANAGEMENT ISSUES FOR THE 1980s

To examine the issues of managerial effectiveness, we need to know what is in store for managers in the 1980s, what are the issues facing the manager of the future? These include great changes in the nature of work and changes in the composition of the workforce.

The workforce is no longer primarily a homogeneous, white male population. Women and minorities have brought different values and skills to management from those of white males. Women tend to be more spontaneous, emotional, expressive, and concerned with human interaction. By contrast, the prevailing management style emphasizes an analytical, rational approach that focuses on systems and tasks. There are also differences in the value orientations of black managers with respect to concern for employees. Black managers show a greater concern for employees than do white managers and place a higher value on both emotions and on trust. White managers tend to value change, risk, and rationality more.

Management has the opportunity to respond to diversity, to nurture differences and to learn from new workers to build a multicultural work environment. Or management can continue to attempt to "mainstream" the new workforce by socializing it into present patterns, thereby losing the unique skills women and minorities possess. All of these changes raise issues that concern management in the 1980s. As a result of interviewing managers in both the public and private sector, I have developed a list of contemporary management issues, which are outlined in Figure 13.1.

VALUE SHIFTS IN THE 1980s

Underlying the great changes in management is an even larger trend in the 1980s that can best be characterized as a value dilemma or value shift. Daniel Yankelovich talks most articulately about changes in values in *New Rules*. Yankelovich (1981) suggests that we may adopt a new ethic of commitment in the 1980s following a decade in which people focused on themselves and their own needs. Yankelovich says we are now "stepping off Maslow's escalator." Many of us grew up with values that taught us to act out of guilt and responsibility. Then psychologist Abraham Maslow said self-actualization was the pinnacle of the individual's hierarchy of needs. Self-denial was replaced by self-actualization during the 1970s. Yet Yankelovich argues that the human self cannot be wholly autonomous, solitary, contained, and "self-created." Many people are now searching seriously for something more to believe in, a workable vision around which to coalesce. We know that we need a balance between concern for self and others; what remains is to articulate an agenda which operationalizes our concern for others. Figure 13.2 is an attempt to begin to define areas of value conflicts and to suggest some of the new directions in which we are headed.

FIGURE 13.1   Management Issues for the 1980s

1. Transition from the Industrial Age to the Age of Communication: How to manage knowledge workers
2. Era of increasing complexity and frequency of change: High uncertainty, lack of control, and everyone has a piece of the pie
3. Need for future-oriented responses: Shift from tactical, short-range to strategic, long-range management
4. Decrease in hierarchical, authority-oriented managerial forms to more participative structures: Productivity increased through people, team effectiveness, and networking
5. Growth of a highly diverse workforce: Need to respond to diversity and nurture differences
6. Environmental uncertainty; everything is changing
   - Economics
   - Education
   - Medicine
   - Auditing
7. Leadership that builds goals and a shared vision:
   - Security
   - Equity
   - Participation
   - Individuation
   - Employees
   - Consumers
   - Experimentation
   - Quality
8. Labor-management partnerships characterized by trust
9. Customer-oriented/consumer-oriented styles
10. Increased methods for rewards & recognition: Cafeteria benefits
11. Need for managers to deal constructively with stress & stay healthy:
    - Autonomy
    - Resonance
    - Tone
    - Perspective
12. Need to build organizational climates that foster:
    - Autonomy
    - Colleagueship
    - Entrepreneurship
13. Transition from national to global market

Theorists have defined management as a concern for people and for task, and concern for productivity and morale, which requires both supportive and directive behaviors. Managers need the ability to deal effectively with an organization's administrative, technical, and social systems; to plan for short- , middle- , and long-term goals; to solve problems; to develop employees; and to get desired results. Management accomplishes tasks through people, through relationships between executive and manager, manager and subordinates, and manager and peers.

Yet business schools and public administration programs have not taught applied management skills. An MBA is primarily a business degree; it requires only nine hours of management education. As Sterling Livingston, President of

FIGURE 13.2   Value Shifts in the 1980s

Traditions	New Directions
1. Role models/authority	
■ Heroes and heroines	■ Interdependence
■ Lone Ranger & Cinderella	■ M*A*S*H
2. Role of government	
■ Centralized	■ Decentralized with mediating structures
3. Families	
■ One career	■ Two career
■ Stationary	■ Mobile
4. Management	
■ Hierarchical	■ Participative management teams
■ Concern for task	■ Concern for task, people, customers,
■ Traditional competencies	quality, technology
■ Public vs. private	■ High performance
	■ Public/private partnership
5. Health	
■ Sickness/discharge	■ Wellness/organizational fitness
6. Security	
■ Bureaucratic/institutional	■ Personal responsibility
responsibility	■ Communities, networks, personal support
	systems
7. Materialism	
■ More & big is better	■ Quality
■ Flashiness	■ Respect for scarcity
	■ Reliability
8. Morality	
■ Private	■ Public
9. Ethnicity	
■ Majority vs. minority	■ Pluralism
	■ Multicultural

Sterling Institute, has said, "business schools teach how to problem-solve—not problem-find; how to work with money, but not with people" (Livingston 1982). The new applied management skills must meet the criteria of relevance, application, and results. A competency model for managers would provide business schools, public administration programs, and organizations with a model for developing practitioners.

Studies by Mintzberg (1974) and others show that managers spend a great deal of time interacting rather than solving problems in a more idealized, rational, objective manner. Managers spend 50% to 80% of their time communicating and nearly 70% of that time may be in meetings. Only 10% of their time is communicating with supervisors and 40% to 50% with subordinates; the remainder is with people outside the chain of command. To be effective, managers need entrepreneurial skills and interpersonal skills. In addition, organizational structures are shifting to require team effectiveness and skills in building consensus, rather than top-down authority.

Involvement and team effectiveness are crucial to building a more effective workplace. With interdependence a key factor in how people are organized for work, being a competent team leader and team member is a core skill. More and more matrix organizations have formed: teams (now including lawyers, accountants, and health-care specialists), quality circles, temporary task groups, project management, and program management. These forms or organizing require more collaborative and interdependent behaviors and less competitive, self-oriented behaviors. In the Katz model in Figure 13.3, the three areas of competence are technical, human and conceptual.

A more sophisticated model, shown in Figure 13.4, has been developed by McBer and Company for the Department of State and the Masters in Management Degree offered by the American Management Association. While this is one of the strongest models available, it is still simply building a management vocabulary. McBer's model does not supply behavioral descriptions. It does not describe something observable, but still relies on inferential language.

The model developed by Warner Burke at Columbia University, in conjunction with NASA, offers more behavioral descriptions of managerial behavior. Instead of competencies, the NASA model describes twenty-four management practices (Figure 13.5).

The McBer model introduces the notion of leadership, which we must reintroduce into the field of management in this decade for leadership and management as functions have become too separate from each other. Leaders need to learn how to manage, to know what issues are involved in implementing their rhetoric. Managers need to learn how to lead, how to build a common

FIGURE 13.3 Type of Skill Needed

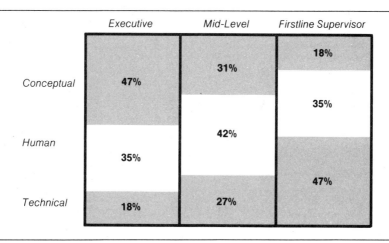

Concepts based on Robert Katz, "Skills of an Effective Administrator, *Harvard Business Review* (September–October 1974): 90–102.

FIGURE 13.4   Managerial Competencies

Competency: The characteristic of a person that underlies or results in effective performance.

I. Knowledge competencies—
   - Specific knowledge base

II. Emotional maturity
   - Self control
   - Spontaneity
   - Perceptual objectivity
   - Accurate self perception
   - Stamina & physical energy
   - Adaptability

III. Entrepreneurial abilities
   - Efficiency orientation
   - Productivity—goal setting & planning
   - Proactivity—problem-solving & information seeking skills
   - Concern for unique achievement
   - Task efficiency

IV. Intellectual abilities
   - Logical thought—perceive cause/effect relationships—inductive thinking
   - Diagnostic use of concepts—deductive thinking
   - Memory
   - Conceptual ability
   - Political judgment

V. Interpersonal abilities
   - Social sensitivity
   - Self presentation
   - Counseling skills
   - Expressed concern with impact
   - Compliance producing skills
   - Alliance building skills
   - Language skills
   - Non-verbal sensitivity
   - Respect for others
   - Effective as team member

VI. Leadership skills
   - Presence
   - Persuasive speaking
   - Positive bias
   - Negotiating skills
   - Takes initiative
   - Management of groups—team building skills

Source: Richard Boyatzis, President McBer & Co., Boston, MA

---

vision around which people can coalesce. Leadership is an influence process; in one commonly accepted definition it is interpersonal influence central with respect to the group goal. In Peter Senge's (1980) words, leadership requires the following:

1. Expression of a common vision that people need and want;
2. Communication and alignment around that vision;

3. Staying the course—renewing commitment to the vision; and
4. A structure to implement the vision that builds in frequent feedback.

METHODOLOGY FOR BUILDING A COMPETENCY MODEL: FROM CRITICAL INCIDENTS TO ORGANIZATION DEVELOPMENT

There is a variety of possible methodologies for developing a model of competency based management. They range from research to action research to an organization development model. The following is a summary in outline form of the various models to date.

1. *Critical Incident Method* (utilized by Richard Boyatzis and McBer)
   A. Identify high performers
   B. Interviewer probes them for behaviors
      Interviewer question: Think of a project you have managed—that had a beginning, middle and end; one project that was a winner; one project that didn't go so well.
   C. Do a content analysis of behaviors
2. *Subordinate Ratings* (utilized by Richard Boyatzis and McBer and Warner Burke and NASA)
   A. Identify high performers
      Establish criteria
   B. Subordinates rates these managers on numerous competencies and practices; analyze statistically to determine which practices are more closely identified with superior performers.
3. *Multilevel data*—boss, subordinate, self (utilized by Warner Burke, Columbia University for the NASA competencies)
   A. Bosses interviewed
   B. The managers for study are interviewed using critical incident method
   C. Subordinates rate managers on practices in questionnaire that is derived from interviews with bosses and managers.

Final set of practices comes from being identified by three levels or at least from two of the three.
Rate practices associated with successful management from all three.
Interview questions for bosses: What are the dimensions of management practice that are the most salient to you when you do your evaluation?

4. *Organization Development*
   A. Set up a task force to oversee competency development
   B. Utilize line managers to develop the model; possibly at an off-site engage managers in defining managerial effectiveness

FIGURE 13.5   NASA Senior Executive Program—Management Practice

Managing Tasks	Influence Management	Team Management
Structuring 1. You emphasize getting the work of the organization accomplished. 2. You have the technical knowledge required for your position. *Managing resources* 3. You are concerned about controlling project/operating costs. 4. You are able to accure, through negotiation and influence, the resources required to accomplish a project. 5. You are effective in the establishment of priorities, i.e., determining where limited resources and staff effort will be used. 6. You understand and make effective use of the budget process.	*Managing up* 7. If you feel your employees are right you definitely go to bat for them with your supervisor. 8. You are sensitive to and usually act in support of your supervisor's interests. 9. You have the ability to present bad news in a strategic way. 10. You establish good relationships with upper level executives. *Managing external relations* 11. You resolve conflicts with contractors/outside agencies in a collaborative manner. 12. You appropriately involve other managers and centers in your planning process.	*Building the team* 13. You select well-qualified and capable people for the job to be done. 14. When making assignments, you try to make the best use of your employees' skills and abilities. *Maintaining the team* 15. In work group meetings you make sure that there is a frank and open exchange of ideas. 16. You emphasize a team approach in accomplishing work. 17. You face up to and attempt to resolve/work out conflicts constructively between those who directly report to you. *Promoting involvement* 18. You communicate in a frank and open manner. 19. Your goals, objectives, and responsibilities are clearly defined and shared with your employees. 20. You solicit appropriate information from your employees—facts, opinions, and concerns about their work.

Source: NASA/Warner Burke, Teachers College, Columbia University

C. Through a series of iterations of the models developed by these groups, test them out in training programs at staff meetings throughout the organization. The goal is as much ownership and validation as it is a particular product.

As more and more organizations elect to use competency models, we have available more and more road maps. Nonetheless, the process is equally as important as the product if managers are going to experience ownership and validation for the competency model. My preference is to ask managers at different levels in organizations to design their own model, in the language of their own culture. To accomplish this, managers must make explicit that which

Managing People	Flexibility	Leadership
Managing personal relations	*Adapting Approach*	*Projecting self*
21. You build supportive relationships with your employees, rather than remaining distant and impersonal.	29. You modify your management style or practices so that different situations can be handled in the most effective manner.	35. You perceive yourself as a leader based on your employees' observations of your actions and statements.
22. You establish trust and mutual respect in relating with your employees.	30. You admit when you have made a mistake.	*Providing clarity*
23. You take a personal interest in your employees.	*Soliciting reactions*	36. Your employees get clear-cut decisions from you.
	31. You give your employees an opportunity to openly express their disagreement or to voice objections to your proposed actions/ decisions.	37. You establish organizational work group goals.
Managing group relations		38. Accomplishing high quality work within established time limits is important to you.
24. You emphasize cooperation as opposed to competitiveness among your employees.		
25. You understand other people's point of view.	32. You are open to and will listen to your employees' suggestions as to how you might improve your performance.	*Perceiving issues*
26. You pay close attention and seek to understand your employees when you are talking to them.		39. You demonstrate awareness of unspoken and significant issues (hidden agenda) in your relationships with others.
Managing performance problems	*Encouraging innovation*	40. You have an ability to anticipate controversial issues and political questions and deal with them effectively.
27. Your employees can be completely open with you in telling you about their mistakes.	33. You encourage your employees to submit new ideas and suggestions for improvement.	
28. You face up to and take appropriate action regarding poor performance on the part of those who report to you.	34. You usually give your employees full credit for their ideas.	

is implicit. The competencies exist in each organization's culture.* They can be extracted from promotion discussions or rankings of managers which in some organizations is called a totem pole.

There is a variety of questions that can be asked of managers to stimulate their thinking about effectiveness. Think of the last time someone called you about a recommendation to hire or promote someone into a management job.

---

*Such organizations as Citibank in its "Managing People" program, AT&T in its Assessment Centers, the Department of the Navy training program, the State Department, and the Overseas Private Investment Corporation in their performance appraisal system, utilize competency models.

■ How did you describe the person?
■ How did you differentiate her or him from the other candidates?
■ What skills did you value most highly?
■ Describe her or his effectiveness in the following areas: leadership; conducting meetings; level of awareness of impact on others; managing conflict; managing people; and planning.

AN ANDROGYNOUS APPROACH TO MANAGEMENT

A critical point in developing a model for effectiveness is not to have it status-quo oriented, but instead to also consider characteristics of the future manager. Organizations have rewarded new managers for adopting a rational, analytical, problem-solving style, and for giving up emotional and idiosyncratic behavior. We see this in the new workforce where in an effort to mainstream women and minorities, they are often encouraged to give up their natural styles for problem solving and dealing with people in exchange for the more rational, analytical approach. Hence women, black, Hispanic, Asian, and Native American managers are all expected to become carbon copies of white males, the models for success in organizations.

White men have paid a very high price for success. Until recently, their sacrifice was less obvious. More and more now, men find that the hard-driving organizational style creates too much stress, fosters dysfunctional competition, and inhibits close friendships. Men have had the strain of always being strong, never wrong. This style yields basically activity-oriented relationships, but not expressive, intimate friendships. It produces excessive emotional dependency by men on their wives who may, at this point in their lives, be preoccupied with their own identity; and it sometimes keeps men separate from their children.

A survey of American business executives by Fernando Bartolome, a Harvard Business School professor, found that most men seldom allow themselves to feel dependence or to admit such feelings when they do experience them (Bartolome 1972). The executives regarded such feelings as a sign of weakness. In addition, most men acknowledged that they usually limited their expressions of tenderness to family members, especially young children. Men said that they often avoided displays of tenderness even with children, and especially boys, for fear of smothering them or making them dependent.

In a 1979 survey by *Playboy Magazine*, American men ranked eleven basic values in the following order or importance: health, family life, love, friends, sex, respect from others, religion, peace of mind, work, education, and money. Yet, if one compiled a behavioral instead of an attitudinal index, it would probably show that these men spend most of their time on work, television, sports, and perhaps education. The men's belief in the importance of family life is not supported by their behavior. Slightly less than half said they were "very satisfied" with their sex lives. Many men obviously do not make developing intimate relationship a priority.

These concerns for organizational and individual well-being suggest the following factors that one must incorporate into a new definition of competence:

- Management has not been sufficiently concerned with people and relationships.
- Women and minorities who enter the workforce with interpersonal skills are being socialized into the dominant style of rational, analytical problem solvers, and relinquishing some of their relationship-oriented style.
- Men are dissatisfied with the dominant style because it produces great stress and inhibits intimacy.

This new model, which would blend so-called masculine and feminine behaviors, could be called androgynous management. John Naisbitt, author of *Megatrends* refers to androgyny as the eleventh megatrend (Naisbitt 1982). An androgynous manager can employ behaviors and capacities ascribed to both sexes: namely the more instrumental behaviors, which have been regarded as masculine, plus the more expressive behaviors, which have been regarded as feminine. For example, men would not give up the concern for power, but would learn to balance it with a concern for people. This change would mean broadening their range of responses in the areas of affiliation, trust, openness, intuition, and the expression of feelings. Women would not abandon their concern for relationships; they would supplement it with an increased focus on outcomes and self-expression. They would depersonalize some situations thereby utilizing more instrumental behavior. Sharing their competence more with other women would reduce their competition. Women generally need to increase their behavioral repertoire for managing conflict and dealing with power.

Figure 13.6 displays a competency model for an androgynous manager that includes effective masculine and feminine behaviors. This model is only a first step in developing competencies, since it does not utilize only behavioral descriptors and some of the terms are not observable. Further work is certainly necessary.

One can also categorize the androgynous blend of behavior as instrumental and expressive behaviors (Figure 13.7). Instrumental behaviors to date have

---

FIGURE 13.6 The Androgynous Manager

Masculine	*Neutral*	*Feminine*
■ Instrumental behavior	■ Command of basic facts	■ Expressive behavior
■ Direct achievement style	■ Balanced learning habits	■ Vicarious achievement style
■ Compliance producing skills	■ Continuing sensitivity to political events	■ Alliance producing skills
■ Negotiating/Competing	■ Quick thinking	■ Accommodating/ Mediating
■ Proactive style	■ Creativity	■ Reactive style
■ Analytical/problem solving, & decisionmaking skills	■ Social skills	■ Self knowledge
■ Visible impact on others		■ Nonverbal sensitivity

been highly valued in the marketplace and expressive behaviors in the home-place. If organizations are going to improve productivity significantly and become healthier places to work, then a critical step is the development of trust, starting with manager/subordinate relationships. Such a move requires a blend of androgynous behaviors in the workplace as well.

Instrumental behavior deals with ideas and tasks; expressive behavior deals with people and feelings. These behaviors are clear to us in our close relation-ships at home. If a couple engages in too much instrumental behavior, the relationship becomes stale, routine—not renewing. Instrumental discussions begin with questions like: "Have you paid the insurance?" "Where shall we go Saturday night?" "Who is going to take the car to the mechanic?" If communi-cation is all instrumental, it lacks spontaneity and self-disclosure, the precious expressive behavior: "How did it go today?" "How did you feel about my being late?" "I want to spend some time alone with you."

The same holds true for parent/child communication. Instrumental ques-tions include: "When are you going to clean up your room?" "Is your homework done?" "Did you brush your teeth?" "Did you feed the cat?" "Expressive ques-tions or statements might include: "How are you feeling about school?" "What would you like to do this weekend?" "I missed you while I was away in New York."

Supervisor-subordinate relationships also grow stale when they remain only in the instrumental mode. "Is the assignment done?" "When are you going to take care of ———." More open-ended communication, such as "How are things going?" "Where do you want to be five years from now?" "I wish we could get through with this project and on to something more interesting" also matter. The absence of expressive behavior produces brief, ineffective, stilted perfor-mance-appraisal sessions and frustrating staff meetings where what is said ten minutes after the meeting outside the room is much more meaningful than anything said in the meeting room.

FIGURE 13.7 Managerial Behavior

	Instrumental	Expressive
Purpose:	Problem-solving, avoid failure, achieve success	Self-expression, be acknowledged
Exchange:	Service, commodities, information, data	Empathy, feelings
Based on:	Data	Self-disclosure
Needs:	Control, power	Let it be, here & now
Time:	Future oriented, planning	Flexible, less predictable
Structure:	Predictable, certain	Ambiguous
Avoid at all cost:	Surprise	Boredom

Source: Neale Clapp & Peter Block, Block Petrella Weisbord, Designed Learning Associates

Men fear that androgynous behavior will diminish their strength because of years of socialization that taught them to develop cool, rational, stay-in-charge behavior. The opportunity to rely less on objectivity and rationality opens up the whole world of feelings, making contact, building close relationships, relaxing, and having more fun. This threatens some men who have used physical and political power to define themselves and to bend the world to their wills. Sometimes the exercise of such power is necessary and appropriate. But organizations and individuals suffer when managers use power in lieu of other more appropriate tools such as persuasion, negotiation, concern for others, or cooperation.

For women, androgyny opens up the opportunity to be competent and have boundaries as well as to maintain close relationships. Women and minorities bring many strengths to management that should not be wasted.

Transition is the major trend in organizations for the 1980s. We are involved in a shift in values, searching for new role models, learning new technologies and seeking new forms of organizing to deal effectively with the enormous changes that are part of our lives. Our best hope for meeting this challenge successfully involves making explicit the issues of competencies and value differences inherent in models of managerial, individual, and organizational effectiveness so that we can continue to debate and to learn.

References

Bartolome, Fernando, "Executives as Human Beings," *Harvard Business Review*, (November/December 1972) pp. 62–69.

Bartolome, Fernando and Evans, Paul. *Must Success Cost So Much?* New York: Basic Books, 1980.

Boyatzis, Richard E., *The Competent Manager*. New York: John Wiley & Sons, 1982.

Davis, George and Watson, Glegg, *Black Life In Corporate America: Swimming in the Mainstream*. New York: Doubleday, 1982.

Katz, Robert. "Skills of an Affect Administrator," *Harvard Business Review,* vol. 52, (September-October, 1974), pp. 90–102.

Livingston, J. Sterling, *New Trends in Applied Management Development*, Paper presented at ASTD National Conference, San Antonio, Texas, May 1982.

Mintzberg, Henry. *The Nature of Managerial Work*. New York: Harper & Row, 1974.

Naisbitt, John. *Megatrends*. New York: Warner Books, 1982.

Peters, Thomas J., and Waterman, Robert H. *In Search of Excellence*. New York: Harper & Row, 1982.

Sargent, Alice. *The Androgynous Manager*. New York: AMACOM, 1981.

Senge, Peter M. "Systems Dynamics and Leadership," presented at IEEE 1980 International Conference on Cybernetics and Society, Cambridge, Massachusetts, October 1980.

Yankelovich, Daniel. *New Rules*. New York: Random House, 1981.

14 Understanding Matrix Organization: Keeping the Dialectic Alive and Well

Ralph H. Kilmann

ABSTRACT

Implementing a matrix structure is seen as a revolutionary rather than an evolutionary undertaking, requiring a rapidly different culture and reward system than exists in most organizations. Unless all those involved in the matrix understand the concept of the Hegelian dialectic and implement the type of culture and behavior supportive of the dialectic, the organization will experience the costs of matrix without the benefits. This paper suggests some of the concepts from the philosophy of science and the behavioral sciences that will help provide the understanding for making a matrix organization effective.

AUTHOR BACKGROUND

Ralph H. Hilmann is a professor of business administration and the coordinator of the Organizational Studies Group at the Graduate School of Business, University of Pittsburgh. He received his B.S. and M.S. degrees in industrial administration from Carnegie-Mellon University in 1970 and a Ph.D. in Management from the University of California at Los Angeles in 1972. He is president of Organizational Design Consultants, Inc., a Pittsburgh-based firm specializing in structural and cultural changes.

Several articles and books have appeared in the past two decades that examine the rather new type of organizational form generally referred to as *matrix* (see Knight 1976 for a review of the literature). Most of these discussions treat matrix as an evolutionary progression for organizations facing more complex and dynamic environments (Kingdom 1973; Kolodny 1979). Matrix is seen at the high end of a continuous scale of coordination devices for managing increased complexity (Galbraith 1977). Organizations are supposed to opt for matrix as the last alternative way of managing after all other methods have been tried, but no longer are effective (Davis & Lawrence 1977). To illustrate the relation of matrix to traditional organization designs, Galbraith (1971) positions matrix at the midpoint on a continuum between pure functional and pure project organization; matrix representing the in-between case where functional and project authority are shared on an equal basis.

My own experience in working with organizations adopting a matrix structure suggests that the change is more revolutionary than evolutionary, requiring a radically different way of managing resources and not just a next step in coordinating complexity. Matrix can be viewed more appropriately as being on a totally different scale or continuum than other traditional structures. It is, I think, a lack of awareness of what a change to matrix really entails that often leads organizations to a major confrontation of management style and culture. Only by understanding what the *essence* of matrix organization requires of the organization will organizations make well-informed choices of this form of structure, recognizing the additional changes in culture and management systems that need to take place in order for matrix to prosper.

This paper presents matrix as an example of the Hegelian Inquiring System (HIS)— a way of approaching information, decisions, and problems very different than the Lockean Inquiring System (LIS), which seems to be emersed in most of our contemporary organizations. These inquiring systems require a completely different kind of logic, frame of reference, and social system in order to approach different types of problems (Churchman 1971). The main argument is that if matrix is approached as simply another type of Lockean Inquiring System (on a continuum of management choices) then the benefits of matrix will not be realized. It is moving from the Lockean to the Hegelian system that brings out the need for the qualitatively different type of organization needed to address a qualitatively different type of problem (Mitroff & Kilmann, 1978).

SIMPLE VS. COMPLEX ORGANIZATIONAL PROBLEMS

A simple problem (decision or task) can be defined as being solvable by the expertise and information of one person. That is, one person can possess all the information and wisdom to address the problem. In contrast, a complex problem, by definition, cannot be addressed or solved effectively by one person, since one person cannot possibly have all the information, expertise, and knowledge to manage the problem. This follows from the limited cognitive capabilities of individuals referred to as "bounded rationality" (Simon 1957). Only for simple problems involving a few variables within a well-defined and narrow area of expertise can one individual be capable of developing the right answer or a best answer (which cannot be improved upon by utilizing additional individuals, the latter become redundant).

Organizations are divided into subunits also because of the cognitive as well as physical and social limitations of individuals (Barnard 1938). Each subunit is responsible for a small part of the whole as a way of decomposing a complex problem into a simple problem. When traditional organization design is done well, each subunit contains the necessary information, skills, and knowledge to address its responsibilities (its part of the whole) efficiently and effectively. In this sense, a single subunit (analogous to one individual) is addressing a simple organizational problem (analogous to a simple problem for one individual).

Functional organization breaks down the complex problem the organization is addressing into such functional subunits as marketing, finance, manufacturing, engineering, and so on. Project organization breaks down the whole problem into specific product or project groups. The latter may seem more complex within each group since all the functional areas are represented. However, since each individual is oriented to one objective—the product— each project group as a whole still has the requisite information and expertise to solve the "problem." Besides, product divisions are often subdivided further into functional areas even if each of these is contributing to one product only.

Matrix organization violates the concept of a single subunit containing all the relevant inputs to solve its assigned problem. Matrix purposely places individuals in one business team containing different areas of expertise and information, but the business team does not have all the necessary inputs. Some of the inputs to solve any particular problem have to come from the overlapping functional organization, via the members of the business team interacting and receiving guidelines and information, and so on, from their respective functional managers. Thus, one member on a matrix team will go back to his or her marketing manager (his or her functional boss) to discuss an issue and take a position, while another member on the matrix team will go back to his or her finance manager (his or her functional boss) to develop a different perspective on the problem in question, and so on. Thus, during the matrix team meetings managed by a matrix manager (or business-team manager), the information and expertise is not complete, but is necessarily and purposely incomplete.

Furthermore, because of the dual reporting relationship of the matrix-team members, there is a perpetual state of conflict in the system (Butler 1973). Team members must comply with their business-team manager and, at the same time, are expected to follow the guidelines and objectives of their functional-area manager. Since these two types of bosses reflect different objectives, members often feel "pulled apart" and unable to attain each set of objectives simultaneously. As will be seen shortly, the actual reward system is a key factor in determining whether the allegiance of the team members is toward either boss or if it supports the two bosses equally. Only the latter would bring about the benefits of the matrix organization.

Defining Matrix Organization

Matrix has been defined numerous ways in the literature, and many other terms have been used to describe overlapping responsibilities and dual membership in two or more organizational subunits. Gibson et al. (1973) report that terms such as grid structure, multidimensional structure, global matrix, program management, and project management have been used interchangeably with matrix organization. Davis and Lawrence (1977), providing the most comprehensive discussion on matrix to date, define the term by the existence of the two-boss model—where some people are simultaneously reporting to two superiors, one in the functional organization and one in the matrix (business) team.

It seems that the prime characteristic of the matrix is to maintain a constant *dialectic* (a particular form of conflict, to be defined shortly) between two or more competing objectives in the organization (as represented by two or more formally structured subunits). Further, the dialectic is managed *within* an additional designed team or subunit with representatives from the relevant subunits in the organization. Thus, a matrix can be said to exist if there is a strong difference in goal orientation between say marketing and operations, and in order to manage this conflict, a third unit is established as a "business team." The latter's objective is to keep the tension between marketing and operations alive and well so that the conflict can be managed constructively for the benefit of the organization. In this case, the members in the business team would be representatives from the marketing and operations departments in the organization and would be reporting not only to their functional-area managers, but to a formally designated business-team manager as well.

Defining the matrix in this way excludes a number of organizational forms that have been used interchangeably with matrix, as mentioned above. For example, if the purpose of project management is to assemble a team of representatives from different subunits, but the effort is to develop a new product without an ongoing mix of competing objectives and orientations, then I would not view this as matrix. Besides, while the project is in operation, members would be reporting to one boss entirely (their project manager) and would not be subject to the authority of their functional-area managers until the team disbanded upon completion of the project. Similarly, if any "two-boss" arrangement resulted in a team that had a goal orientation in one direction (rather than in two or more competing, *equal* directions), I would not refer to the system as matrix.

In essence, this definition involving two bosses *and* an ongoing dialectic helps distinguish organizational forms that previously have been lumped together. I also believe that this distinction will help get at the essential character of matrix organization that is the most difficult to manage precisely because its character is opposed in a fundamental way to the typical style and culture of most contemporary organizations.

INQUIRING SYSTEMS FOR PROBLEM SOLVING

Churchman (1971) presents a variety of approaches and methods for "knowing" derived from the philosophy of science. Each approach assumes certain things about the nature of problems as well as the mechanism (guarantor) to assure that the correct solution to the problem has been achieved. For current purposes it is sufficient to distinguish two such "knowing" systems or inquiring systems: the Lockean IS and the Hegelian IS.

The Lockean Inquiring System

The Lockean IS generally assumes the existence of *simple* problems where a group of experts can uncover the true solution via agreement and consensus. For example, if a group of experts were given some problem to solve or asked to state some opinion or prediction, the one that they could agree upon would represent the best position. In other words, if a group were asked to state why they believe in the worth of a particular solution, the approach would be considered Lockean if the members responded, "because we *agree* that this is the best solution."

The Lockean IS can be shown as a normal distribution where the ends or extreme positions are eliminated simply because agreement and consensus cannot be reached on these "minority" views. However, support for the middle of the distribution can be achieved since the majority of experts holds that view. Thus the Lockean IS tends to gravitate toward the mean (average) and stay away from the end-points of any distribution. An example of the Lockean IS is the Delphi approach to planning where the deviants on any opinion or prediction are asked to revise their judgments when these differ from the majority views. Another example is the method of scoring a diving competition in the Olympics where the high and low judgments by experts are thrown out and the remainder are averaged to derive the "true" performance of a person on a particular dive.

The Hegelian Inquiring System

The Hegelian IS, also known as the Hegelian Dialectic, portrays a very different approach to knowing truth and "the best solution" to any problem. First, the Hegelian system assumes that problems are *complex* and therefore any one person is not likely to have all the information and expertise to solve it. Rather, each person with a different area of expertise might be able to address, at best, only a piece of the whole problem. By this approach, truth is not in the majority but more likely resides in minority viewpoints as appropriately combined or synthesized. The synthesis of expert views is developed by debating the extreme, opposite opinions instead of eliminating these "end-point" positions as in the case of the Lockean IS. Therefore, the Hegelian IS can be represented as a normal distinction that de-emphasizes or even rejects the middle of the distribution and concentrates on the tails (end-points) of the distribution.

Truth for the Hegelian IS is through the dialectic debate. Experts representing the extreme opposite positions are expected to debate their viewpoints. During these debates, underlying assumptions are exposed and challenged, and thereby each extreme position is scrutinized and dissected. It is through these debates that the "truth" is expected to emerge for any complex problem. If a group of experts were asked why the proposed solution was the best, their approach would be considered Hegelian if their response were, "Because we debated the extreme viewpoints to understand their underlying assumptions." But the final position need not be any of the positions that were debated. It is the debate that enhances understanding so that the best solution among all alternatives can be made or some synthesis derived. Furthermore, the dialectic is not the same as the straw-man approach where one alternative is set up as the devil's advocate only to be disarmed so that the original position is chosen. In the Hegelian IS, each extreme position is for real and equal; the debate, therefore, is intense and balanced, not one-sided.

The Lockean IS vs. The Hegelian IS

It should be apparent that these two inquiring systems are quite different, almost opposite to one another as diagrammed in Figure 14.1. Here the relevant portion of each system is portrayed on a normal distribution of opinions or proposed solutions, as discussed above. This diagram also suggests how both

FIGURE 14.1 Two Inquiring Systems: Lockean and Hegelian

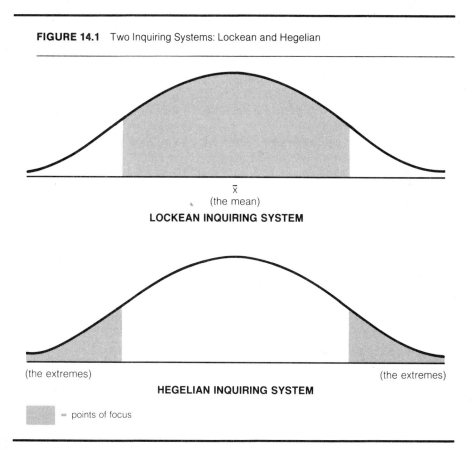

$\bar{x}$
(the mean)
LOCKEAN INQUIRING SYSTEM

(the extremes)   (the extremes)
HEGELIAN INQUIRING SYSTEM

= points of focus

inquiring systems together present the full picture. In essence, each one presupposes the other and has to deal with the other in some form. For example, before the Lockean IS suppresses disagreement and extreme positions, it has to recognize them. Consensus and agreement may be the final outcome, but surely some debate would have taken place along the way. The Lockean system does not like to acknowledge this and tends to minimize conflict as such. On the other hand, the Hegelian IS has to achieve some agreement or consensus regarding which extreme opinions to debate, for how long, and which synthesis will represent the choice of the experts. The Hegelian approach, in its emphasis of differences, tends to suppress or make light of the role that consensus plays in its process.

The difference between the two, therefore, is a critical matter of emphasis. They both come to agreement on a final solution, but the Hegelian IS first explicitly creates debates, conflict, and divergence before it moves toward an agreed synthesis (emphasizing the former over the latter). The Lockean IS tries to converge directly to the final choice by ignoring and downplaying the differences along the way. Figure 14.2 diagrams these two inquiring systems as each initiates, processes, and then resolves some problem situation.

As mentioned early, the Lockean IS is expected to be suited better for simple problems—where *one* area of expertise can be applied to solve the problem. If several experts agree, then the chosen solution must be correct. The majority is expected to hold the modal wisdom and the minority is assumed to be off-base. The Hegelian IS is most appropriate for complex problems, where different areas of expertise can all contribute to developing a synthesized solution. Different positions thus represent different areas of expertise and world views that must be debated and then combined. The majority in a group of varying expertise is not expected to hold common wisdom in solving the problem because they all have different backgrounds and perspectives. In fact, any majority view would be suspect and would be regarded as common *ignorance* on the problem. The Hegelian IS gives special attention to the minority areas of expertise before any sort of agreement is reached.

THE ESSENCE OF MATRIX

To understand the differences between the Lockean and Hegelian IS is to understand the essential differences between a functional or product organization and a matrix organization. A single-boss arrangement that is built around a well-defined, single objective is best suited to the Lockean IS. Not surprisingly, most organizations would be viewed as Lockean in that methods of gaining agreement and reaching consensus are paramount priorities. Similarity of values, goals, and motives in selecting and training individuals for organizational responsibilities are widespread. Further, tales abound of how deviates are treated in organizations where there is tremendous pressure toward uniformity of opinion. "Don't rock the boat" and "Getting everyone on board" are just some examples of the efforts at guaranteeing agreement and consensus. Conflict is viewed as painful,

FIGURE 14.2   Diverging and Converging Aspects of Lockean and Hegelian Inquiring Systems

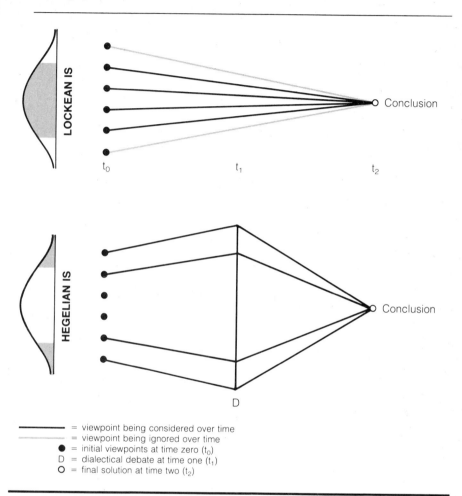

= viewpoint being considered over time
= viewpoint being ignored over time
● = initial viewpoints at time zero (t_0)
D = dialectical debate at time one (t_1)
O = final solution at time two (t_2)

unnecessary, and blocking goal achievement. If the problem is rather simple and straightforward (because the organization has been designed into a structure that has taken a complex problem and subdivided into simple parts via departmentalization), then the Lockean IS is appropriate. Perhaps not much is lost by suppressing conflict since the majority view within any department or functional area probably is correct most of the time (especially among experts in the same field).

The matrix organization, however, is meant to address a very complex problem. At a minimum, it attempts to manage conflicting goals, keeping a variety of technical concerns as an explicit part in all decision making along with a product orientation. That several representatives from different functional areas are all on the same team and are expected to contribute different areas of expertise highlights the complex problem that matrix seeks to manage. It would be a waste of time, energy, and resources for the organization to design a complex team (different areas of expertise and functional divisions) to solve a simple problem (requiring a narrow or single range of expertise). The very point of the matrix is to approach a complex problem in a way that cannot be accomplished within the typical organization structure designed for simple problems (Argyris 1967).

This perspective suggests why going from a functional or product organization to a matrix organization is so difficult. It is moving from a Lockean to a Hegelian IS—a revolutionary change, not just a change along a continuum of complexity as other authors have suggested. And while the two inquiring systems presuppose one another, there are some fundamental differences with regard to the value of conflict and how to assure that conflicts will be brought out in the open, debated, and resolved. This is the major challenge to designing a matrix organization. Specifically, what does it take to create a Hegelian IS in an organizational culture that historically is based on the Lockean IS?

Culture and Systems to Support Matrix

Perhaps one of the most difficult "variables" to manage in an organization is its culture. By culture is meant the collection of norms, values, beliefs and attitudes concerning what behavior is appropriate and acceptable in the organization. Culture develops over time as members learn what behavior and views are really rewarded regardless of what the formal statements of purpose and reward systems may indicate. This culture is passed on from generation to generation as new employees are socialized and learn the unwritten rules. Even if all the members who created the "initial" culture have left the organization, the culture survives and often becomes an untested assumption that is considered a given (Baker 1980).

The Lockean IS that seems to be engraved in most of our contemporary organizations is very much supported by a particular organizational culture, one that encourages the suppression of conflict and disagreement, among other things. People learn that to confront their superiors and to confront the customary ways of reaching decisions, is simply inappropriate. Further, the reward system, as utilized by those persons in positions of formal authority, tends to support the culture if it is used to reward these who help generate consensus and agreement, and to punish those who foster conflict and disagreement. Generally, given human nature, once a person has been "burned" many times for taking independent stands on central issues to the organization, he or she will either leave the organization, be treated as a deviant and trouble maker, or be co-opted as a like-minded member of the organization. Rarely, in a Lockean organizational culture, would a person of views that conflict with key organizational issues be rewarded and encouraged to continue his or her confrontation of established practices and viewpoints.

But this is exactly what the Hegelian IS and an effective matrix organization requires. In order to bring conflict out into the open so that real, intense debates can take place over key organizational issues, the culture and reward systems must support such behavior and attitudes. Superiors have to feel suspicious if too much agreement is reached too early in any important decision process. Certainly, at the early stages of debate, conflict and exteme positions of "minority" members (those having unique and highly specialized knowledge) must be signaled out and must be allowed to be expressed. Here people would be rewarded for differences and not coming to agreements at the outset. In fact, in the extreme case, a member would lose rewards (or be punished) if he or she continually sought agreement and consensus and did not engage in conflicts and debates when complex issues were being explored.

MAKING MATRIX WORK

Four major steps can be proposed for helping an organization move from a Lockean to a Hegelian IS. It should be emphasized that such a move is appropriate only in these cases where a matrix arrangement is considered essential in order to manage some complex-problem situation. There is little gained by taking a simple problem and managing it as if it were complex. Consequently, only when the organization has found that various Lockean approaches are no longer adequate would a matrix organization be chosen. This is consistent with the findings of Davis and Lawrence (1977) that matrix should be used only if all other methods have failed.

The first step is to *educate* all members who would be involved in a matrix (business) team including their functional managers and the business-team manager. In most cases it would be necessary to include the next higher level of management in the educational program: the president or vice-presidents of the whole division, for example. The latter may be critical to include since these persons have to understand *why* the culture and other supporting management systems must be altered.

Briefly, the educational input would entail a two- or three-day workshop where the basic concepts of matrix are introduced and the differences between the Lockean and Hegelian IS are explored in depth. Various case analyses of successful and unsuccessful attempts at introducing matrix would be examined to derive the principles and guidelines for *successful* matrix management. Material on conflict management, leadership styles, personal vs. positional power, personality types, organization culture, reward systems, and so on, would be presented and discussed also. As suggested above, it is not enough for the business-team members themselves to receive this education; the next higher levels of managers who have some control over the culture and management systems must take part (in either the same or a separate workshop). Ironically, in order for matrix to work, an educational input *and* a Lockean agreement on the need and character of the Hegelian IS is essential for the latter to be applied successfully. The relevant organizational members have to agree to disagree when the various dialectics are put in motion at the workshop.

The second step in moving to matrix is to outline the current culture of the organization and contrast it to the type of culture necessary to support the matrix organization. In a second workshop setting (time away from day-to-day pressures so that longer-term issues can be reflected upon and explored), those to be involved in the matrix are asked to generate individually a list of current *norms* of behavior in the organization. By norms is meant the written or especially the unwritten expectations of what makes a good, solid organizational citizen. What behaviors and expressed attitudes are rewarded and encouraged, and which are punished or frowned upon? (See Silverzweig and Allen 1976 for a similar approach.)

It does take a little time to get members thinking about norms (because these are usually covert and taken for granted), but with a little encouragement and several illustrations, most people recognize what is being asked. Sometimes it is best to do this sort of "exercise" among peers rather than including both superiors and subordinates in the same room. The latter might stifle the listing of the true norms if the culture in the organization does not encourage making norms explicit in front of one's superiors. Thus, this step in the process assumes that with the proper guidance (generally by an outside, organizational development consultant), the present culture of the organization will not prevent an investigation and explication of the culture. If this turns out to be a false assumption, then it is unlikely that the present culture can be changed to one supportive of a matrix. Under these circumstances, the process should be terminated and other efforts at "culture management" might be considered.

Once each individual has listed the present norms of behavior, he or she is asked to generate a second listing, this time expressing the necessary norms for a matrix culture. When each individual has completed this task, all the lists are displayed and an effort is make to summarize and synthesize the various norms into a more parsimonious list of current vs. matrix culture. A skilled consultant would illustrate and guide the members to debate some of their differences (as in a Hegelian dialectic) before consensus is reached on the two sets of norms. Such a consultant also would suggest in what manner the two sets of norms represent the type of dialectic that will be experienced continually by the matrix team members as they cross the boundaries of their business team and interact with the functional organization.

The third step requires that a plan be developed to create the matrix culture (norms for behaviors and attitudes) for that part of the organization that will be designed as a matrix. It is recognized that most of the organization (for better or worse) will retain the current culture. However, can the relevant persons and parties: (1) appreciate the need for a separate matrix culture where necessary, (2) allow it to develop, and (3) actively encourage and support its development? Too often an organization's members assume that one culture is for all and do not allow for differences. Here it must be argued that, analogous to the concept of differentiation and integration advanced by Lawrence and Lorsch (1967), if two "parts" of the organization address different types of problems requiring different types of organizational behavior, then each part should have a different culture supportive of the desired behavior patterns. It then takes skilled managers to "integrate" or even work across these different cultures.

Developing a plan to create the appropriate matrix culture entails examining the current reward systems. First, what changes can be made for the business-team members so that they would be rewarded for promoting and managing conflict effectively? Perhaps as part of a regular review and performance appraisal (every few weeks or months) assessments would be made regarding each member's contribution to airing differences, challenging underlying assumptions, debating positions and perspectives, and so on, in order to foster a better understanding of a complex situation. This type of assessment might be easier said than done, but the intention has to start with the formal, explicit acknowledgment of the need and value for these behaviors (and attitudes). Naturally, one has to distinguish constructive conflict and dialectics from destructive, blocking, and spiteful behavior. Further, a member's contribution to the Hegelian IS can be assessed via the member's attitude toward furthering a productive climate (vs. a defensive climate) for other team members. Thus, specific behaviors and general attitudes toward a matrix mission should be articulated and codified in a formal statement of policy and assessment method.

Another possibility, one that I have found to be very successful, is for the members themselves to outline the necessary behaviors and attitudes for their matrix culture and for them to define specifically, in their own words, what the new set of norms will be. Then the members of the matrix team, with the support of the business-team manager, share responsibility for monitoring and enforcing the stated norms. In this way, the members themselves determine when a norm is being violated and they then institute a procedure to correct the violation. Since these norms are theirs (as in participative management), one can expect more ownership and commitment to follow and enforce the new norms. In essence, the power of the group is utilized to design and implement the new culture of the matrix, rather than trying to rely on a one-by-one individual understanding of the new culture and reward system.

It is imperative, however, that the new system is understood and accepted by the functional-area managers and by the next highest level of managers (for example, the vice-presidents and president of the division). Otherwise, these individuals might inadvertently undermine the matrix culture by applying the old culture during performance reviews, during informal assessments, and as guides to all types of decision making and action taking.

This brings us to the fourth and last step in switching from a Lockean to a Hegelian Inquiring System. It is essential that the balance of power between the business-team manager and the functional-area managers be *equal* (Davis & Lawrence 1977). Typically, as a functional organization takes on a matrix concept, the vested authority remains with the former even if team members are "told" to give equal weight to their new team managers. In addition, if performance reviews are done primarily by the functional-area managers with little input from the business-team manager, then members clearly can see where their rewards come from. Even separate performance reviews by each member's two bosses is not enough when the functional organization has the historical advantage, culture, and the clout behind it.

The only viable solution is to have performance reviews conducted by both bosses *simultaneously*—each member meets with his functional-area manager and the business-team manager in one meeting. But for this method to work, the two bosses must be sure to communicate their *joint* assessments and must support one another's perspective and appraisal, equally. In one sense, the functional manager might emphasize the Lockean aspects of the member's performance while the team manager would evaluate the member's Hegelian contributions. At the end of the formal review, the member should feel that each perspective is equally important and that he or she will strive to develop the appropriate balance in subsequent behaviors and attitudes. Such a dual-performance evaluation, if conducted properly, would help assure that the matrix concept will work.

CONCLUSIONS

My experience in working with matrix organizations is what highlighted this distinction of a Lockean vs. a Hegelian IS applied to alternative structural forms. At the same time, it became apparent to me that the culture of the organization represents a special variable to manage in any major change effort. It seems appropriate to expand briefly on these themes in the conclusion of this paper.

Perhaps one might consider why the Hegelian IS is likely to be more and more relevant to our contemporary organizations and the organizations in the future. If, as a society, we are facing more complex problems that cannot be decomposed easily into simple, well-structured problems, then it seems reasonable to conclude that more of our organization structures need to shift from a Lockean to a Hegelian IS. Matrix represents one way in which the latter can be operationalized, but there may be a number of other Hegelian forms as well. The use of a dual hierarchy in a hospital organization, one hierarchy of doctors and the other one of administrators, would be one example. Having the CEO role assigned to a *team* of managers rather than to one person as is the tradition, would be another example. The ability of these various forms to foster a Hegelian IS needs further theoretical attention and empirical research.

"Culture management" is another by-product of the current paper's focus on understanding the essence of matrix organization. Taking the orgnaization's culture as a given or only concentrating on describing and measuring it, is quite different than purposely trying to change it. In any OD program where a major shift in organizational behavior is desired (through process and structural change), it is virtually impossible not to run up against the history, tradition, and power of the organization's culture. You can't see it or touch it, but it is there nevertheless, and since you can't go through it or around it, the culture will often prevail. I am suggesting that *altering* the culture is another option and that intervention methods be devised to do just that. Certainly this is a main part of the four steps to a Hegelian IS, as discussed in this paper.

In sum, if social scientists, including organizational development practitioners, could develop technologies to (1) move organizations from Lockean to Hegelian IS where appropriate, and (2) alter the organization's culture to support such a movement, I predict that the success rate of major organizational changes will increase dramatically. Thus, managing complex problems with the right inquiring system and culture can be viewed as a hallmark of applied social sciences. It may well be our bottom-line of what *can* be changed and what *should* be changed.

References

Argyris, C. "Today's Problems with Tomorrow's Organizations," *The Journal of Management Studies,* vol. 4, no. 1 (1967), 31–35.

Baker, E. L. "Managing Organizational Culture," *Management Review,* vol. 69, no. 7 (1980), 8–13.

Barnard, C. I. *The Functions of the Executive* (Cambridge, Mass.: Harvard University Press, 1938).

Butler, A. "Project Management: A Study in Organizational Conflict," *Academy of Management Journal,* vol. 16, no. 1 (1973), 84–101.

Churchman, C. W. *The Design of Inquiring Systems* (New York: Basic Books, 1971).

Davis, S. M., & P. R. Lawrence. *Matrix* (Reading, Mass.: Addison-Wesley, 1977).

Galbraith, J. "Matrix Organization Design," *Business Horizons,* vol. 14, no. 1 (1971), 29–40.

Galbraith, J. *Organization Design* (Reading, Mass.: Addison-Wesley, 1977).

Gibson, J. L., J. M. Ivancevich, & J. H. Donnelly, Jr. *Organizations: Structure, Processes, Behavior* (Dallas: Business Publications, 1973).

Kingdom, D. R. *Matrix Organization* (London: Tavistock, 1973).

Knight, K. "Matrix Organization: A Review," *The Journal of Management Studies,* vol. 15, no. 3 (1976), 111–30.

Kolodny, H. F. "Evolution to a Matrix Organization," *Academy of Management Review,* vol. 4, no. 4 (1979), 543–54.

Lawrence, P. R., & J. W. Lorsch. *Organization and Environment* (Homewood, Ill.: Dorsey-Irwin, 1967).

Mitroff, I. I., & R. H. Kilmann. "On Integrating Behavioral and Philosophical Systems: Toward a Unified Theory of Problem Solving," in R. A. Jones (Ed.), *Research in Sociology of Knowledge, Sciences and Art* vol. 1 (Greenwich, Conn.: JAI, 1978), 207–36.

Silverzweig, S., & R. F. Allen. "Changing the Corporate Culture," *Sloan Management Review,* vol. 17, no. 3 (1976), 33–49.

Simon, H. A. *Administrative Behavior* (New York: Free Press, 1957).

15 The Third Wave of Experiential Learning

Gordon A. Walter
Stephen E. Marks

ABSTRACT

Three distinguishable thrusts in the advancement of the experiential approach to learning have occurred since World War II. This paper describes and discusses these three waves using a typology of learning comprised of education, training, professional development, personal growth, and therapy. The first wave arose in the 1940s and was mostly concerned with the discovery of and philosophizing about the experiential approach and its divergence from the traditional approach to learning.

The second wave arose in the 1960s and differed from the first in its accessibility to many more people and its emphasis on more personally oriented topics like emotions. Basic experiential ideas were proliferated and elaborated during the second wave; the technology was demonstrated to be effective and a wide variety of participants and leaders became involved.

The third wave, which rose in the 1970s and is now gaining dominance, has an accountability theme and extends the applications of the second wave to more specific groups. The central objective and aspiration of third-wave experiential learning is professional development, achieved by providing people with the knowledge and capacities they need to perform complex tasks more effectively.

AUTHOR BACKGROUND

Gordon A. Walter received his Ph.D. in human behavior in organizations from the University of California, Berkeley, in 1971. He currently serves as associate professor of organizational behavior and industrial relations and the chairperson of the Industrial Relations Management Division at the University of British Columbia, Vancouver.

Stephen E. Marks is an associate professor of counseling psychology at The University of British Columbia, Vancouver. He received his Ph.D. in counseling psychology, personnel, and industrial management from the University of Oregon in 1969. Dr. Marks served as the president of the British Columbia Psychological Association from 1974 to 1975.

The roots of experiential learning extend to Freud [1, 2, 3] and James [4] although they are perhaps most directly connected to John Dewey [5]. In *Experience and Education,* Dewey called for a change in the approach to learning and advocated divergence from what was then and is still called the traditional teaching method. The traditional approach emphasized the centrality and authority of the teacher and the submission and passivity of the students in the learning process. The objective was the assimilation of information directed by a knowledgeable teacher who would use coercion if necessary to keep students in line.

In contrast, Dewey advocated creating experiences that were developmental, stimulating, and rewarding. Not surprisingly, a psychological perspective on individuals and the way they cope with their environment became central to the experiential approach. The recent popularity of the experiential approach tends to obscure the fact that even in the late 1940s and early 1950s, very clear articulations of the characteristics of experiential learning existed. For example, Nathaniel Cantor in *The Teaching—Learning Process* [6] presented nine conditions for modern learning which would be difficult to improve upon today when defining experiential learning.

1. The pupil learns only what he is interested in learning.
2. It is important that the pupil share in the development and management of the curriculum.
3. Learning is integral: genuine learning is not an additive experience, but a remaking of experience.
4. Learning depends on wanting to learn.
5. An individual learns best when he is free to create his own responses in a situation.
6. Learning depends on not knowing the answers.
7. Every pupil learns in his own way.
8. Learning is largely an emotional experience.
9. To learn is to change.

[6, pp. 286–312]

The basic philosophy underlying experiential learning was well established before 1940, but it is only within the last twenty years that the philosophy has been put into practice on a broad scale. It is the purpose of this paper to describe the three waves of experiential learning that have occurred since World War II and categorize and analyze them using a typological model of learning.

TYPES OF LEARNING EXPERIENCES

In *Experiential Learning and Change,* Walter and Marks [7] classified experiential learning into five fundamental types and describe these in terms of the goals of the experience. For example, should a course on computers inform people about market conditions and the variety of equipment available, teach them how to operate a piece of equipment, improve their programming skills, or help them develop the ability to design computer systems to meet specific organizational needs? Or maybe the activities are intended to help the participants become more aware of their feelings or assist them in resolving some personal problem. The intent of the learning experience will influence the choice of objectives and the manner in which these objectives are pursued. The types of learning experience are education, training, professional development, personal growth, and therapy. The types of learning experiences represent ways of addressing certain topics or objectives and should not be confused with activities that are associated with specific settings or individuals. For example, teachers in schools are responsible for education, but that in no way implies that education is the only type of learning experience occurring in the schools. Similarly, trainers in organizations are responsible for the training function that probably encompasses education, training, and professional development. Also the term *leader* is used here to signify the person conducting a learning experience and is interchangeable with teacher, trainer, or facilitator (Table 15.1).

TABLE 15.1   Types of Learning and Emphasis on Related Objectives

	Change Objectives			
Types	*Cognitive*	*Affective*	*Psychomotor*	*Integration*
Education	5	2	1	2
Training	2	2	5	2
Professional development	4	4	3	3
Personal growth	4	5	4	4
Therapy	4	5	5	5

Key: 1 Low
2 Moderate to Low
3 Moderate
4 Moderate to High
5 High

The objectives define the expected outcome of the learning experience. They fall into three general domains:

cognitive, affective, and psychomotor (Bloom, 1956; CSC/Pacific, Inc., 1972a, 1972b, 1972c; Krathwohl, Bloom, & Masia, 1964; Ringness, 1975) [8, 9, 10, 11, 12, 13]. The cognitive domain consists first of activities related to remembering and recalling information or knowledge, and, second, of skills and abilities such as problem solving related to working with that knowledge. A taxonomy of objectives for the cognitive domain proposed by Bloom (1956) [8] includes the following general categories: knowledge, comprehension, application, analysis, synthesis, and evaluation. The affective domain contains objectives that are concerned with feelings and emotions. A taxonomy of objectives for the affective domain developed by Krathwohl, Bloom, and Masia (1964) [12] has the following categories: receiving, responding, valuing, organization, and characterization by a value or value complex. Objectives in the psychomotor domain focus on movement and perceptual motor behaviors such as language skills. A schema for classifying objectives in the psychomotor domain emphasizes perception, set, guided response, mechanism, and overt response (Simpson, 1972, p. 50–55) [14]. [*7, p. 238*]

We can now discuss the five types of learning in terms of objectives. First and most simply, the goals in education are almost entirely cognitive since the intent is for participants to acquire information. If affective material is considered, it is not addressed in an intense manner. Classical training has been defined as a process to assist people in developing or acquiring specific psychomotor or physical capacities or skills. Training, for example, typically involves teaching someone how to use a word processor, how to run a lathe, how to sort, or how to do inspections. Training was a very clearly understood function in business in the 1930s. However, one of the problems for the field of experiential learning is that the descriptive and respectable term *training* has been used to describe a variety of learning experiences which involved little real training in the traditional sense of the term.

The third type of learning, professional development, is something much broader than training or education. It involves cognitive, affective, and psychomotor change plus some integration of learning in these areas. It encompasses acquiring skills that are broader and less physical in nature than are addressed in training. For example, leadership is a professional capacity. A person cannot be taught how to run a lathe effectively in three hours, yet it is astounding that some experiential leaders seem to *think they can* teach a person to be a leader in *less* than three hours! Professional development refers to the assimilation of broad sets of capacities that are integrated into complex tasks such as group leadership, counseling, and supervision. It is much more ambiguous, complex, and ambitious than training or education. Much of what organizational experiential leaders do is education under the name of training that aspires to be professional development. It is not surprising that the participants can become confused or cynical when "it doesn't work in the real world!"

The next type of learning experience—personal growth—involves many things including becoming a better person, becoming a bigger person, or getting more out of life. It can be called existentialism, self-actualization, and autonomy needs satisfaction. It involves a large affective component; that is, learning how to deal with emotions, perceptions, and reactions to perceptions. The integration of these awarenesses with cognitive as well as behavioral capacities is also involved and requires time and a talented leader to be achieved. Personal growth is laudable, but much more difficult to pursue constructively in an organizational setting.

The last type of learning experience is therapy. Therapy involves not only deep affective and behavioral change, but also correlative cognitive change, and has a very strong emphasis on integration of the changes. In the last decade, many people involved with personal growth have failed to distinguish the difference between personal growth and therapy. In some cases leaders did not distinguish between increasing an individual's awareness of feelings and dealing constructively with neurosis.

It is very difficult and perhaps rarely desirable to pursue one pure type of learning during a given activity. For example, most interpersonal "skills" courses are not exclusively skills oriented. They are a combination of professional development, personal growth, and education, but generally comprise almost no classically defined training. The development of awareness rather than a new skill is the primary purpose here, and generally this is a realistic aspiration. It might be best in such instances to call the experience primarily education rather than training so that unrealistic expectations and confusion are avoided.

With this brief overview of learning experiences and their component objectives, the task of discussing the three post-World War II waves of experiential learning can now be considered.

THE THREE WAVES OF EXPERIENTIAL LEARNING

Alvin Toffler's [15] wave metaphor is useful in describing the evolution of experiential learning over the last thirty-five years. For this discussion, each of our three waves is characterized by a set of qualities that captures the essence of the style and substance of leading practitioners and spokespersons of the day. These in turn are related to the prevailing mood in society at that time. The three waves metaphor provides a provocative way of viewing how the field of experiential learning has changed and serves as a model for leaders to use in self-analysis as to the nature of their experiences. Readers, hopefully, will also be able to check which of the three waves has passed through their organization and whether it is the best choice for the organizational/social/cultural context within which they function.

The first of the three waves was predominant from the mid 1940s to the 1960s. The theme was one of discovery and description and was characterized by people like Kurt Lewin [16, 17], Edgar Schein and Warren Bennis [18], Leland Bradford, Jack Gibb, and Ken Benne [19], and Norman Maier [20]. The spirit of this style of experiential learning was curiosity and inquiry; everything was possible. Open the door; listen, look, imagine; it is all there for you; and so on.

The second wave seems to have started in the mid 1960s and peaked in the mid to late 1970s. The theme for the second wave is proliferation and elaboration. Gerard Egan [21, 22] and William Schutz [23, 24] with their encounter groups and sensitivity training are illustrative of one aspect of this wave. Personal growth, education, and training were aggressively pursued and advocates of experiential learning such as Pfeiffer and Jones of University Associates [25, 26, 27] made many of the first wave experiences available to a much wider audience.

The third wave began rising in the mid 1970s. The theme here is segmentation and specification. This wave is characterized by the design of learning activities to achieve a specific purpose for a particular group. Assertiveness training for women in their thirties and in managerial positions is an example of the application of this segmentation. In contrast to the other periods, no single individual or group can be clearly identified as representative of third wave experiential learning. This fact is one important indication of the success of the proliferation achieved by the second wave. The expansion and growing importance of the American Society for Training and Development is partially a direct manifestation of third wave training needs in modern organizations. It is also significant that many members of ASTD creatively contribute to training and development in their organizations rather than merely relying on prepackaged learning experiences as was more dominant in the second wave. Segmentation and the need for highly skilled applications go hand in hand.

First Wave: Discovery and Description

The social environment in the period of the first wave was one of peace, stability, and security, Thus the themes of open exploration and analysis were natural. The leaders in the first wave emphasized analytical insight, scientific clarification, and philosophical presentation as an approach to learning and as an attitude about life. Gibb [28] communicates that spirit particularly well today and did so when the first wave had just begun to rise. The spirit is one of anything being possible; "let us look at it, let us dream."

There really are two schools of thought in the first wave: National Training Laboratories (NTL) of Bethel, Maine, on the one hand and non-NTL on the other. It was at NTL that Kurt Lewin conducted his original L (learning) groups, which were self-analytic in nature and composed of social scientists. T-groups were an out-growth of L-groups in which group dynamics and interpersonal relations were analyzed by lay participants under the guidance of a social scientist leader. What NTL did was take the L-group spirit, philosophy, and style and start making it available to nonsocial scientists, people who just wanted to learn about group dynamics and did not have ongoing collegial relationships with each other. The central goal of those L-groups and even of the original T-groups was education. They were almost exclusively cognitively focussed and in no way were quasitherapeutic experiences.

There was also a non-NTL component. Some people associated with this school included N. R. F. Maier [20], George Homans [29], Frederick Bales [30], and others who tended to be involved with role playing and problem solving. Further, Jacob Moreno [31] and Carl Rogers [32] focused on psychotherapeutic applications and contributed technique and philosophy to this period.

The style of first wave experiences emphasized exploration and experimentation—thinking through issues and events together. Most of the original non-NTL experiences and problems were experiments that social scientists had created to explore social dynamics with student subjects. Students found participating in experiments educational and stimulating, and the professors of this period started using them as education enhancers as well as research vehicles. The applications in those days were broad and included business, government, and even the family. There was a search for universal answers. But the population of participants who were exposed to the techniques was quite restricted. Social scientists and their graduate students, executives, and small numbers of clients were the primary participants. The influence mode of the leaders was primarily intellectual. They tried to stimulate intellectual insights with experiments or group experiences. It was assumed that people would aggregate their learning. It was also assumed that generalizing the learning would occur as would transfer to back-home situations.

Leaders tended to be education oriented because of their science values. The spirit that pervaded their conduct was one of zeal for discovery. Scholarly research and analysis were refined skills they brought to the learning situation. They were adept at replicating social conditions. There were a mere eighteen Fellows who were central to the original NTL and thus the in-group, elite, nature of this half of the first wave is easy to imagine. Figure 15.1 shows a bar chart illustrating the relative pursuit of types of learning for the two schools.

NTL is seen to be very strongly professional-development oriented and also to have a strong education component. The non-NTL school was much more oriented toward training, and much more focused on specific skills. There is little emphasis on personal growth or therapy in either school of the first wave except of course for Moreno and Rogers, who were experimenting with new therapeutic forms. These influences are dramatically reflected in the second wave.

Second Wave: Proliferation and Elaboration

The second wave is typified by the terms *proliferation* and *elaboration* and started in the mid-1960s. At this time, our culture was starting to change. There was a breakdown of the conformity of the 1950s and, at the same time, an opening-up to new possibilities. It was a time of intense energy. Great enthusiasm for finding applications swept the field. There was a sense that one should be able to improve life and make organizations more effective. The field of organization development was only one application to originate in this period.

Two schools of thought existed in the second wave also, those interested in personal growth and therapy and those focused on education, training, and professional development. The growth school is typified by such diverse people as Golembiewski and Blumberg [33], Egan [21, 22], Schutz [23, 24], Gunther [34, 35], Perls [36, 37], and Berne [38, 39]. The education and training school comprised many members of NTL, trainers working in organizations and associated with the American Society for Training and Development and the American Management Association, and educators in a wide variety of fields such as organizational behavior, psychology, and counseling.

FIGURE 15.1 Relative Pursuit of Types of Learning for Schools During Each Wave

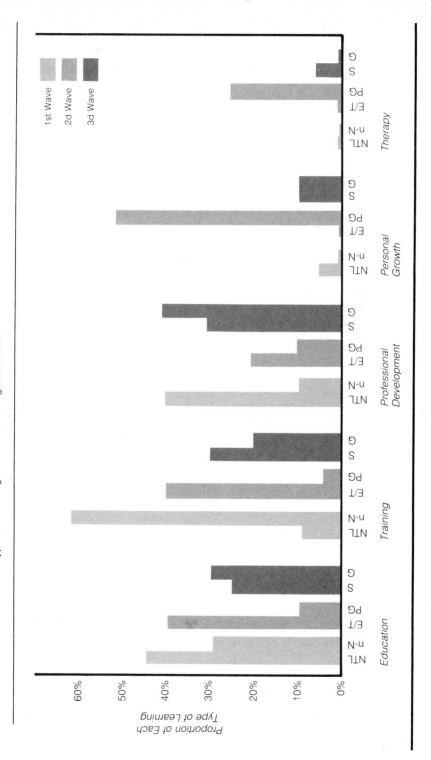

The methods of the second wave included sensitivity training and encounter for the growth-oriented people; and exercises, cases, and simulations for those more concerned with education and training. The University Associates publications reflect the interests of both schools although they were focused primarily on the needs of the latter. The University Associates organization probably made the single most significant contribution to the latter second wave school since it made the technology of experiential learning, in the form of materials and guidelines for using them, available to anyone who was interested.

Consequently, accessibility to experiential learning dramatically expanded. Varieties of encounter groups and other personal growth experiences as well as a range of activities that were education, training, or professional development in focus became available to middle managers, supervisors, church groups, volunteer organizations, and interest groups. Access to these was no longer restricted to elite managers or behavioral scientists. Initially, effective participant self-selection came along with the increased accessibility. The advertising, the enthusiasm, the way people were inducted into situations seemed to get the excitement seekers into exciting experiences. People went into encounter because somebody else was turned-on to encounter and gave them a sense of the process. There was such a variety of experiences available that the majority of interested people found the approach, leader, and location that best met their needs. However, as time passed, this voluntary self-selection process, which is so important in personal growth experiences, became somewhat compromised when training and development managers who were turned-on to encounter or some other procedure that was in vogue were in a position to require involvement from line managers.

The focus of the learning experience in the second wave is on the learner—that is, the person—in contrast to the first wave where the focus was on the task. First wave leaders asked, What's going on in this group? How do we solve that problem? What do we do with this simulation? How do we move this information around? But the second wave leaders, especially of the growth school, asked participants to tune in to themselves or to other people rather than to the activity. Aggregation of learning was still assumed; transfer of learning was still assumed. If one got a brilliant insight during a Gestalt session, it was assumed that one's life would be transformed. If one suddenly realized that one had been rude to people for the last thirty-seven years and it came though like a bolt of lightening on a dark night, one changed! One would immediately become "nicer" according to the advocates of some techniques.

However, second wave personal growth experiences suffered from several more serious problems. First, the labels that were used to describe the experience lacked clarity and were at times misleading. For example, sensitivity training was personal growth, not training. In addition, although the label "T-group" did not change, the nature of the experience did. While first wave T-groups emphasized education, training, and professional development, many second wave "T- groups" were really personal growth experiences that even included a therapeutic component. Second, of course, were the excesses of some marathon encounter experiences that went far beyond many people's standards of acceptability. Finally, the growth movement inadvertently provided a public forum for untrained leaders to dispense therapy essentially to a group of ideological converts. The consequences were group casualties and the loss of opportunities for experiential learning to be used for legitimate organizational purposes because the entire field had gained a bad reputation from the actions of a faction within the personal growth school [40, 41].

Second wave leader characteristics were different from those in the first wave. With the increased emphasis on personal growth, second wave leaders with these interests needed to have therapeutic skills for working with people. Unfortunately, this condition often was not met. The proliferation of materials and cookbook guidelines created the illusion, even for the educationally focused leaders, that conducting a learning experience required little more than following the directions and having the materials on hand! Consequently, the phenomenon of group casualties became an increasingly important issue and research demonstrated a relationship between leaders and casualty rates [40, 41]. Whereas the first wave was always characterized by a small group of highly trained leaders and small numbers of carefully selected participants, the second wave eventually had a large number of leaders, many of whom were untrained or marginally trained, at best, in conducting learning experiences and large numbers of highly diverse participants. One of the drawbacks of proliferation was that leader competence became a pivotal problem to the entire field.

Returning to Figure 15.1, it is possible to differentiate clearly between the two second wave schools in terms of the types of learning experiences they pursued and then reflect on some of the differences between the first and second waves. The names selected for the two schools clearly reflect their respective emphases; the education/training school emphasized these types of learning while the growth school focused on personal growth and even therapy. Professional development is pursued somewhat by both schools, but is much more central to the education/training school.

The major differences between the first and second waves is the extent to which they address different types of learning. Personal growth and therapy are virtually absent from the first wave, but are central in the second wave growth school. One sees similarities between an emphasis on education and training in the first wave non-NTL school and the second wave education/training school, but second wave education/training is a little more ambitious in terms of professional development. Finally, in general, the second wave activities were much more concrete than those of the first wave because of the availability of increasingly tested and standardized materials and procedures.

Third Wave: Segmentation and Specification

The theme of the third wave of experiential learning is segmentation and specification. Here the techniques are not really new, but they are more refined and their use is focused on specific needs. The environment surrounding the third wave is turbulent, with social fragmentation, disillusionment, and confusion. Consequently, the problems associated with first wave idealism and second wave self-indulgence are less prevalent. Instead there is an emphasis on account-ability and responsibility which is demonstrated through efforts to make tighter and more legitimately science-based predictions about the outcomes of the applications of specific techniques and to understand at a deeper level the broad processes involved. In the second wave heyday, a leader might use ten interesting exercises over a three-day workshop and thus keep the participants entertained. In the third wave, however, in a time of cutbacks, training departments must show their contribution to the bottom line. To have such impact, leaders need increased skill and depth of understanding. In essence, third wave leaders must display increased professionalism.

Again, two major schools are identifiable in the third wave. Both are con-cerned with carefully selecting participants and clearly articulating goals and objectives. The resulting focused programs are more likely to yield measurable results. In the third wave, outcomes are paramount! These two third wave schools comprise people who are oriented toward specifics and toward general-ization. The specifics school encompasses a wide range of practitioners who use experiential learning techniques to address specific issues for specific popula-tions. Examples range from assertiveness training for black women, to life plan-ning workshops for chief executive officers and their spouses, to negotiation training for bankers who manage portfolios of over twenty million dollars. Team building, a popular technique in organizational development, also has this specific quality since it focuses on problems of a given work group. The specificity of this school provides homogeneous learning groups and promotes accurate self-selection.

The generalist school is highly concerned with understanding how experien-tial learning processes work and with articulating the principles underlying the successful use of the approach. Example contributors are Kolb [42], Torbert [43], and Walter and Marks [7]. In *Experiential Learning and Change,* Walter and Marks provide broad conceptualizations of the field of experiential learning. Themes that emerge from the generalist school are a need to understand how and why particular methods work, how to use methods constructively in a coherent and integrated fashion, and to document the impact of the procedures. These and many other works signal a coming-of-age of the field of experiential learning and argue that a truly comprehensiove behavioral science base is central to the success of the experiential approach. The time has passed for simplistic theories, ideologies, or gurus.

Figure 15.1 provides a summary of the types of learning in each of the schools. The specialists have slightly more emphasis on training and the general-ists more emphasis on education and professional development. The generalists, however, are also concerned with specification—the specification that comes from rich and detailed behavioral science research. Both third wave schools emphasize professional development much more than preceding waves, with the exception of the first wave NTL approach. Both third wave schools, however, in contrast to this first wave school, also emphasize training rather than strictly cognitively focused education.

Leader characteristics emphasized in the third wave are task expertise, facil-itation, and flexibility. Paradoxically, any third wave leader, regardless of school, requires both specialist and generalist skills. Increasingly, leaders need not only to understand the tasks performed by the people they are training, but also to have a knowledge of designing and conducting a learning experience that permits participants to link the task information to the experience. Thus leaders must be able to develop suitable new materials as necessary. This is in contrast to the many learning experiences that were taken directly "from the book" in the second wave. In terms of facilitation, the third wave finds leaders going to groups of learners, rather than vice versa, and making a concerted effort in the learning experience to simulate task reality accurately. The focus is more of a person-task *balance* in contrast to the person focus of the second wave and the task focus of the first wave. Flexibility is reflected in the need for leaders to have a broad range of skills, be able to adapt to the situation they are confronted by, and not be overly committed to or stuck on one of the five types of learning. The demand for skill and professionalism of experiential leaders has dramatically increased in the third wave.

SUMMARY

The three waves illustrated in Figure 15.1 comprise different constellations of types of learning experiences. The ambitious pursuit of professional development is salient in the third wave. Leaders who can learn how to deliver true professional development effectively will have long, successful, and rewarding careers. We noted above that, in the past, training was often assumed to be professional development, education was often called training, and personal growth and therapy appeared in the most unexpected places! One should hope that this era will witness more accurate labeling of activities and a reduction in unrealistic claims of effectiveness. The trend towards accountability is a healthy one for the field. The types and objectives presented in Table 15.1 will assist leaders in clarifying their perceptions about what it is they are currently doing, and in deciding how best to spend time working with others. The present climate offers the challenge of designing relevant, cost-effective programs that provide learning experiences for individuals that are both more ambitious and reality-based than what occurred in the past. We strongly believe that third wave experiential learning can meet the challenge.

Notes

1. Freud, S., *The Ego and the Id.* London: Institute for Psychoanalysis and Hogarth Press, 1925.
2. Freud, S., *Civilization and Its Discontents.* New York: Norton, 1927.
3. Freud, S., *New Introductory Lectures in Psychoanalysis.* Sprott, trans. New York: Norton, 1933.
4. James, W., *The Principles of Psychology.* New York: Holt, 1890.
5. Dewey, J., *Experience and Education.* New York: Collier Books, 1938.
6. Cantor, N., *The Teaching-Learning Process.* New York: Holt, Rinehart, and Winston, 1953.

7. Walter, G. A., and Marks, S. E., *Experiential Learning and Change: Theory, Design, and Practice.* New York: Wiley-Interscience, 1981.
8. Bloom, B. S. (Ed.), *Taxonomy of Educational Objectives.* New York: McKay, 1956.
9. CSC/Pacific, Inc., *The Affective Domain.* Washington, D.C.: Gryphon House, 1972.
10. CSC/Pacific, Inc., *The Cognitive Domain.* Washington, D.C.: Gryphon House, 1972.
11. CSC/Pacific, Inc., *The Psychomotor Domain.* Washington, D.C.: Gryphon House, 1972.
12. Krathwohl, D. R.; Bloom, B. S.; & Masia, B. B., *Taxonomy of Educational Objectives: The Classification of Educational Goals. Handbook II: Affective Domain.* New York: McKay, 1964.
13. Ringness, T. A., *The Affective Domain in Education.* Boston: Little, Brown, 1975.
14. Simpson, E. J., "The Classification of Education Objectives in the Psychomotor Domain." In CSC/Pacific (Ed.), *The Psychomotor Domain.* Washington, D.C.: Gryphon House, 1972.
15. Tofler, A., *The Third Wave.* New York: Bantam Books, 1981.
16. Lewin, K., *A Dynamic Theory of Personality.* New York: McGraw-Hill, 1935.
17. Lewin, K., *Field Theory in Social Science.* New York: Harper & Row, 1951.
18. Schein, E. H., and Bennis, W. G., *Personal and Organizational Change Through Group Methods.* New York: Wiley, 1965.
19. Bradford, L. P.; Gibb, J. R.; & Benne, K. D. (Eds.), *T-Group Theory and Laboratory Method: Innovation in Re-education.* New York: Wiley, 1964.
20. Maier, N. R.; Solem, A. R.; & Maier, A. A., *Supervisory and Executive Development: A Manual for Role Playing.* New York: Wiley, 1957.
21. Egan, G., *Encounter: Group Processes for Interpersonal Growth.* Belmont, Calif.: Brooks/Cole, 1970.
22. Egan, G., *Encounter Groups: Basic Readings.* Belmont, Calif.: Brooks/Cole, 1971.
23. Schutz, W. C., *Joy—Expanding Human Awareness.* New York: Grove, 1967.
24. Schutz, W. C., *Elements of Encounter.* Big Sur, Calif.: Joy Press, 1973.
25. Jones, J. E.; & Pfeiffer, J. W. (Eds), *The Annual Handbook for Group Facilitators,* (4 vols). Iowa City: University Associates, 1973, 1975, 1977, 1979, 1981.
26. Pfeiffer, J. W.; & Jones, J. E. (Eds.), *The Annual Handbook for Group Facilitators,* (5 vols). Iowa City: University Associates, 1972, 1974, 1976, 1978, 1980.
27. Pfeiffer, J. W.; & Jones, J. E. (Eds.), *A Handbook of Structural Experiences for Human Relations Training,* 6 vols. La Jolla, Calif.: University Associates, 1969, 1970, 1971, 1973, 1975.
28. Gibb, J. R., "TORI Theory and Practice." In J. W. Pfeiffer and J. E. Jones (Eds.), *The 1972 Annual Handbook for Group Facilitators.* Iowa City: University Associates, 1972, 157–62.
29. Homans, G., *The Human Group.* New York: Harcourt Brace, 1950.
30. Bales, R. F., *Personality and Interpersonal Behavior.* New York: Holt, Rinehart & Winston, 1970.
31. Moreno, J. L., *Psychodrama, Vol. 1.* New York: Beacon House, 1946.
32. Rogers, C. R., *Client Centered Therapy.* Boston: Houghton Mifflin, 1951.

33. Golembiewski, R. T.; & Blumberg, A., *Sensitivity Training and the Laboratory Approach.* Itasca, Ill.: Peacock, 1970.
34. Gunther, B., *Sense Relaxation.* New York: Macmillan, 1968.
35. Gunther, B., *What To Do Till the Messiah Comes.* New York: Macmillan, 1971.
36. Perls, F., *Ego, Hunger and Aggression.* New York: Random House, 1969.
37. Perls, F., *Gestalt Therapy Verbatim.* Lafayette, Calif.: Real People Press, 1969.
38. Berne, E., *Games People Play.* New York: Ballentine Books, 1964.
39. Berne, E., *What Do You Say After You Say Hello?* Beverly Hills, Calif.: Grove, 1972.
40. Liberman, M. A.; Yalom, I. D.; & Miles, M. B., *Encounter Groups: First Facts.* New York: Basic Books, 1972.
41. Yalom, I. D.; & Liberman, M. A., "A Study of Encounter Group Casualties," *Archives of General Psychiatry,* 1971, 25, pp. 16–30.
42. Kolb, D. A.; & Fry, R., "Toward an Applied Theory of Experiential Learning." In C. Cooper (Ed.), *Theories of Group Process.* London: Wiley International, 1975.
43. Torbert, W. R., *Learning from Experience—Toward Consciousness.* New York: Columbia University Press, 1972.

16 Improving Organizational Performance Through Developmental Management

Stanley D. Truskie

ABSTRACT

Management development and organization development are conceptualized as two separate but complementary processes. Management development tends to focus on improving individual management performance by introducing skills, information, and experiences to management personnel through a variety of developmental processes. Organization development tends to focus on improving the health and effectiveness of the organization through the implementation of strategies designed to improve organizational conditions and processes. While the notion of combining the two is not new, implementable models supporting the underlying logic of this approach are in short supply to those interested in developing an integrated approach to management development and organization development. This paper presents major limitations of conventional management development practices within organizations and suggests a model for combining management development with organization development strategies for improved results in organization performance.

AUTHOR BACKGROUND

Stanley D. Truskie has extensive experience as a consultant to many large private and public corporations. He has held executive level positions within the academic setting and in the utility and transportation industries. Dr. Truskie has written extensively in the area of management and organization development, is a member of several professional groups, and was recently elected to *Who's Who In the East.*

Developmental management, at first glance, may very well be confused with *management development,* a term quite familiar to those involved in the field of management and organization development. The term, however, is used to describe an approach designed to effect change within an organization utilizing management development and organization development strategies. The net effect is significant impact on improving organization performance, which makes developmental management a superior choice over conventional management development strategies. This article is intended to discuss current management development practices; their limitations in impacting organizations; and how these limitations can be overcome by combining management/organization development strategies.

CURRENT STATE OF AFFAIRS

Most theorists and practitioners involved in management education and training generally agree that the purpose of management development is to improve the skills and abilities of managers by engaging them in a prescribed process of learning and experiential activities. Processes designed to achieve this purpose include a wide variety of activities. Most activities typically include various combinations of coaching, programmed instruction, rotational assignments, executive seminars, and in-house training programs. The effectiveness of these activities in terms of their ability to improve management performance is often questioned due to the lack of empirical findings substantiating long-term behavioral change. The most well known work citing this lack of documented evidence is that of Cambell and others.[1]

In spite of this lack of evidence, almost every moderately large organization sponsors managerial and supervisory training of one kind or another. In many cases its a matter of keeping up with the Joneses—if other organizations are conducting formalized management development activities, then it must be a worthy pursuit.

The problem most organizations face in sponsoring management development activities is the lack of a superordinate goal that provides direction in the selection, design, and implementation of appropriate strategies. The lack of a goal is related to the general state of confusion that presently exists within the field of management theory and science.

Scholars engaged in research and writing about management have created what Harold Koontz refers to as a "management theory jungle."[2] His extensive research in this area has uncovered *eleven* major schools of thought or approaches to management theory and science currently being espoused by leading management scientists. Two of his conclusions relate to the problem organizations face in establishing clear goals for their management development activities: (1) there is still no clear notion of the scientific underpinnings of managing, and (2) there is still no clear definition of what is meant by a competent manager.

Given this state of affairs, it is not surprising to observe organizations struggling to establish direction, purpose, and strategies for their management development efforts. The residual effect of this struggle is a general pattern of developmental efforts that can be characteristically described as follows:

- Many organizations have either no policies or goals guiding their management development efforts, or the policies and goals adopted are ambiguous.
- Implemented management development programs are often ill-founded and poorly designed. Many programs are based on the perceived needs rather than on identified needs of the managers and their respective organizations.
- Due to their design, most development efforts have low impact on the organization. For example, top managers attend executive programs, middle managers attend local seminars, and supervisors attend in-house programs. These fragmented and sporadic approaches result in minimal improvement in the organization as a system.
- The entire management development efforts of most organizations are often a concoction of experiential and educational programs that appear to resemble a collage rather than an organized approach to management development.

IMPLEMENTING DEVELOPMENTAL MANAGEMENT

Developmental management is an approach designed to overcome the limitations of conventional management development practices. It is an approach that links basic theory about behavior in organizations with practical technologies for change, which include instructional and organization development strategies. The action plan for implementing developmental management follows:

- Redirect the primary goal of management development to focus on improving organization performance rather than on attempting to develop "ideal" managers;
- Assess organizational needs in two areas: (1) determine the training needs of the managers; and (2) determine the change needs of the organization.
- Develop and implement change strategies that will meet these needs and will also impact the entire organization.
- Establish plans to provide reinforcement and evaluation of results.

Figure 16.1 summarizes the concept of developmental management described above.

Redirect Management Development Goal

Focusing on improving the performance of an organization rather than on developing "ideal" managers is essentially what developmental management is all about. Since research has revealed that there is still no clear notion of the

FIGURE 16.1 The Developmental Management Process

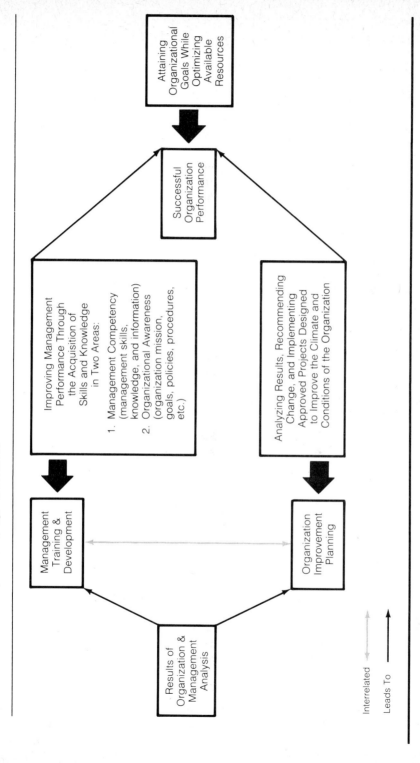

Attaining Organizational Goals While Optimizing Available Resources

Successful Organization Performance

Improving Management Performance Through the Acquisition of Skills and Knowledge in Two Areas:

1. Management Competency (management skills, knowledge, and information)
2. Organizational Awareness (organization mission, goals, policies, procedures, etc.)

Analyzing Results, Recommending Change, and Implementing Approved Projects Designed to Improve the Climate and Conditions of the Organization

Management Training & Development

Organization Improvement Planning

Results of Organization & Management Analysis

Interrelated

Leads To

scientific underpinnings of managing, and since no clear definition of a competent manager exists, the logical choice for a worthy and attainable management development goal is the improvement of organization performance.

Organization performance is essentially the degree to which a particular organization attains its goals and objectives in relation to the degree to which it optimizes its resources in attaining those goals and objectives. On a two-dimensional grid, an organization with a high performance rating would be high in goal attainment and high in optimizing its available resources.

Establishing the improvement of organization performance as the primary goal of management development aids in accomplishing the following:

- It forces the organization to identify critical management skills and abilities which are central to the fulfillment of its mission and goals.
- It eliminates the confusion associated with attempts to describe and develop the "ideal" manager, consequently it eliminates much of the meaninglessness and directionless efforts associated with many management development programs.
- It reinforces the fact that organization performance and management performance are interdependent and interrelated.

Assess Organizational Needs

The purpose of developmental management is to improve organization performance, therefore the present level of organization performance must first be assessed. After this is accomplished, the desired level of performance is determined, and then, the means or strategies for moving the organization to the desired level are determined.

There are essentially two major areas that are explored in assessing the performance improvement needs of an organization. One area relates to the training needs of the management personnel and the other relates to the change needs of the organization. The requirement to concurrently assess management training needs and organizational change needs is based on a fundamental behavioral principle that most conventional management development strategies overlook: Significant, long-term behavioral change of individuals (or managers in this case) cannot be effected unless the context within which they function is also changed. In other words, training efforts alone cannot improve deficiencies in policies and procedures, or other organizational problems that may be adversely affecting the performance of an organization. The misconception that management training alone can significantly improve organization performance is undoubtedly the reason management training programs produce disappointing results within organizations.

Assess management training needs.   Assessing the training needs of managers within an organization requires answers to two questions:

- What do they do as managers?
- What knowledge, information, and skills do they need to effectively perform those identified duties and responsibilities?

There has been considerable controversy recently concerning what managers really do within organizations. The classical or tradition functional description of planning, organizing, staffing, controlling, and evaluating has come under attack, most notably by Mintzberg.[3] He classifies such managerial functions as "folklore," claiming that managers act out a set of roles that defy being described in the usual functional terms. He concludes that managers act out the set of ten roles under the three major categories of interpersonal roles, informational roles, and decision roles.

Whether they are referred to as roles, functions, or activities, it is important to identify what managers do within the organization. The method suggested here is to develop a combination of surveying and structured interviewing to determine what managers actually do; and further, to determine the skills, knowledge, and information they need in order to perform those activities more effectively.

Two areas in which managers need to develop include management competency and organizational awareness. Management competency includes knowledge, information, and skills in the practice of managing. Specific examples would be coaching subordinates, disciplining subordinates, conducting performance appraisals, planning objectives, and effectively utilizing time. The identification of which management competencies should be improved upon again depends upon what the managers actually do in performing their jobs. This information can be obtained through a survey administered to the management population, an example of which is illustrated in Figure 16.2.

Note that the survey in Figure 16.2 identifies areas of responsibility that may or may not be important to the managers' jobs. Managers have an opportunity to indicate the job importance of each area, and they have an opportunity to indicate their need for training in each responsibility area. Last, and of equal importance, they have an opportunity to indicate the functional area in which the training is needed, that is, planning, doing or implementing, coordinating, directing or controlling, and/or evaluating. Managers at various levels within an organization function differently in various responsibility areas and this is reflected in the survey format included in Figure 16.2.

The organizational awareness of a manager is just as important as his or her management competency. Organizational awareness refers to the manager's grasp of organizationally related information. It has to do with a body of knowledge and information relating to the mission, goals, policies, procedures, and operations of the organization. A specific example of this competency area is the equal employment opportunity policy of the organization. If such a policy exists within an organization, the importance of managers understanding the nature, scope, and details of the policy is critical if the policy is to be uniformly and consistently applied. The presentation of this type of topic is seldom present in most conventional management development programs.

FIGURE 16.2   A Sample Of Items Assessing Management Training Needs

Responsibility Area	Not Important	Some Importance	Great Importance
1. New ideas	_____	_____	_____
2. Work improvements	_____	_____	_____
3. Work assignments	_____	_____	_____
4. Department/unit goals and objectives	_____	_____	_____
5. Organization goals and objectives	_____	_____	_____
6. Written policies	_____	_____	_____
7. Written procedures	_____	_____	_____
8. Problem solving-decision making	_____	_____	_____
9. Personnel selection or hiring	_____	_____	_____
10. Performance appraisals	_____	_____	_____

Source: Development Management Survey © 1981 Management Science and Development

The method suggested for obtaining managers' training needs in this area is the structured interview approach. Heads of functional units within the organization are interviewed for the purpose of determining what information from their respective areas should be included as topical areas in the instructional program. The head of the personnel department may, for example, recommend the inclusion of the topic on equal employment opportunity because he or she has observed weaknesses in administration of the program at all levels of management. Another example is the head of the finance department who may recommend a session on capital expenditure analysis for higher levels of management due to the inability of these managers to accurately calculate a return on capital.

The information and data collected from surveying and structured interviewing provide direction for the selection of topics that should be included in the instructional portion of the program. But, as mentioned earlier, training alone will not significantly impact an organization. An assessment is also required to determine the organizational change needs.

Assess organizational change needs.   Assessing the change needs of the organization should be done while assessing the training needs of the managers within the organization. There are two major areas that require probing: (1) an assessment of organizational climate, and (2) an organizational rating assessment. Information for these two areas should be supplied by managers at all levels since they have the most thorough and complete knowledge of the conditions that exist within the organization. The method recommended for obtaining information in these two areas is through survey administration.

	Planning	Doing or Implementing	Coordinating	Directing or Controlling	Evaluating
			I Need More Training In:		
1.	———	———	———	———	———
2.	———	———	———	———	———
3.	———	———	———	———	———
4.	———	———	———	———	———
5.	———	———	———	———	———
6.	———	———	———	———	———
7.	———	———	———	———	———
8.	———	———	———	———	———
9.	———	———	———	———	———
10.	———	———	———	———	———

Organizational Climate Appraisal. There is a body of knowledge, based on substantial research, that strongly suggests that organizations interested in improving their performance ought to be concerned about eight major areas or dimensions.[4] They are as follows:

- *Goal Clarification*—The extent to which the organization explicitly states and effectively communicates organization goals within the context of its stated mission.
- *Management Style*—The extent to which the organization utilizes its human resources in managing the organization.
- *Performance Emphasis*—The emphasis the organization places on defining, measuring, and rewarding high individual performance.
- *Human Resource Maintenance*—The degree of concern the organization maintains for employee personal well-being.
- *Motivational Conditions*—The degree to which the design and nature of the tasks to be performed is psychologically satisfying and rewarding.
- *Internal Cooperation*—The degree to which the organization fosters efficient and cooperative efforts within and between its units or departments.
- *Decision-Making Process*—The degree to which decisions are made at appropriate levels within the organization utilizing pertinent information in a logical and timely manner.
- *Compensation and Benefits*—The degree to which compensation and benefits are perceived as being commensurate with job responsibilities, and competitive with other organizations.

FIGURE 16.3   Items Composing the Goal Clarification Scale from the Survey

Item Number	Item
7	To what extent are people who work here aware of the organization's annual goals and objectives?
10	To what extent do unit or department goals and objectives relate to the organization's goals and objectives?
18	To what extent are people who work here truly committed to attaining the goals and objectives of this organization?
30	To what extent are the goals of this organization clearly communicated to all who work here?
38	To what extent do the people who work here really know the mission or purpose of this organization?
46	To what extent are established goals of this organization clearly stated?

Note: Responses are made on a five-point Likert Scale

Source © 1981 Management Science and Development

The eight dimensions described here collectively combine to form the climate of the organization. Organizational climate is both the ethos and the context within which activities are planned, executed, and evaluated. An organization's ability to carry out these activities effectively and efficiently is determined to a large extent by its ability to establish and maintain a healthy organizational climate.

To assess organizational climate, the formulation of survey items should be structured to measure an organization in each of the eight areas. The items should be in the form of questions and should yield the data and information that reflect managers' perception of how the organization rates in each dimension. It is important here to emphasize perception because, even though formalized strategies, structures, policies, and procedures may exist within an organization, it is the managers' perception of how well the organization is functioning in each of the eight areas, not how well it appears to be functioning according to formalized policies and procedures.

Each of the eight climate dimensions is represented by a number of related items which are included in the survey. Consequently, it is the collection of certain items that enter into the formulation of each climate dimension. An example of the items that constitute the dimension of "Goal Clarification" is illustrated in Figure 16.3.

Organizational Rating. An assessment of climate may indicate a need to effect change in one or more of the eight dimensions being measured. There may, however, be specific problems that are adversely affecting the performance of an organization but have not been uncovered by the organizational climate assessment. For this reason an effort should be made to identify such problems. As in the organizational climate assessment, survey items should be formulated to gain managers' ratings of the organization in specific areas. Examples of the kinds of items included in this section are illustrated in Figure 16.4.

FIGURE 16.4   A Sample Of Items Assessing Organizational Conditions
From The Survey

Item Number	Item
1	Job security within the organization
2	Employees trust of top management
3	Quality of supervisory and management personnel
4	The organization's ability to maintain a low level of absenteeism
5	The organization's ability to retain employees
6	Employee's pride of the organization
7	The enthusiasm of the people who work here

Note: Responses are made on a five-point rating scale ranging from excellent to poor
Source: © 1981 Management Science and Development

In concluding this section relating to the assessment of management training needs and organizational change needs, it is important to note two principles that should be considered when applying the approach outlined here. One principle is that all levels of management should be included in the assessment. Assessing just one or two levels of management may not yield the breadth and depth of information required to uncover performance weaknesses within the organization. The other principle deals with interpretation of the results gained from surveying and interviewing. It must be remembered that this assessment approach probes the organization like a physician probes the patient during a physical examination. The results or the evidence of an existing problem is an indication of something which may require further investigation before specific action is taken. Post-assessment strategies are included in the next section.

Implementing Change Strategies

The surveying and interviewing activities will provide direction for the implementation of change strategies in two areas. One area is the required learning that must be provided through an instructional setting. The other area is planned organizational change, which must be provided through some type of organization development process.

Instructional program planning.   The instructional program is an integral part of development management. It provides the knowledge, information, and skills that the managers need in order to help improve organizational performance. Based on the assessed training needs of the managers, a commonly designed in-house management development program should be pursued. This strategy permits the organization to develop an instructionally based program that can be presented to all managers throughout the organization. Although the program is commonly designed in terms of format and presentation, it should include topics that vary according to the needs of managers attending from various management levels with the organization.

FIGURE 16.5   Topics Of An In-House Management Instructional Program Of A Transportation Company

Topic of Session	Level of Management Attending				
	Top	4th	3rd	2nd	1st
1. Definition & nature of management	■	■	■		
2. The management planning process	■	■	■		
3. Financial management	■	■			
4. Conducting performance appraisal interviews	■	■	■		
5. Chief executive's review session	■				
6. Senior management exchange session		■	■	■	■
7. Styles of management leadership	■	■	■	■	■
8. Elements of interpersonal communications	■	■	■	■	■
9. The motivation of behavior	■	■	■	■	■
10. Fair employment practices	■	■	■	■	■
11. Conducting productive meetings	■	■	■		
12. Time management	■	■	■		
13. Problem solving and decision making	■	■	■	■	■
14. Counseling the marginal performer				■	■
15. The human side of management				■	■
16. The manager's job				■	■
17. Effective job instruction					■
18. Conducting formal briefings				■	■
19. Understanding the labor agreements			■	■	■
20. Conducting an investigation			■	■	■

Note: 1. Topics were selected based on the results of the assessed needs of the organization and its managers
2. The instructional staff consisted primarily of senior managers and staff within the organization.

Individuals presenting the program should include those from within the organization. Senior managers and staff are valuable resources in presenting management material that is relevant to the developmental needs of the managers and the organization. Their presence as presenters also indicates their commitment to implementing program content. An example of the topics included in an instructional program designed for a transportation company is included in Figure 16.5.

The concept of presenting instructional programs in-house is a key ingredient in the process of impacting the organization. The underlying principle of this approach is to communicate to managers the management principles and practices of the organization. It provides a method of articulating the important tenets of the organization including its mission, its goals, its operating procedures, its philosophy of management, and the various management skills and abilities it expects its managers to develop. No person or program outside the organization can communicate this comprehensive message with more effectiveness, and more impact, than the senior management group within the organization.

Organizational improvement planning. As mentioned earlier, the mere implementation of an instructional program—regardless of quality, intensity, and duration—cannot be expected to produce significant improvement in organization performance. Some type of organization development strategy must accompany the instructional component of the process if significant change within the organization is to occur.

Organizational improvement planning is an integral part of developmental management. It is a method of involving managers, at all levels, in the process of identifying root causes of organizational problems and recommending actions to improve existing conditions. The process is facilitated by the establishment of a number of task groups representing all levels of management within the organizations.

The task groups have the responsibility of recommending to top management, through a linking fashion, actions that should be taken to improve the organizational conditions that exist. The task groups' efforts are aided by input received from all managers who participate in the development management process. Here is how it works:

As managers go through the instructional program, they are given an opportunity at some point during the program to review and discuss the results of the organizational assessment. Through small group discussions and brainstorming, root causes of organizational conditions are identified and recommended corrective actions are submitted. The recorded information of these groups is then passed along to the task group formation for further consideration.

The task groups meet regularly to discuss the recommendations made by managers who participate in the instructional program. The task groups, in turn, formalize recommendations and pass them through the linking formation to top management for implementation. Each level of the task group formation has the authority to approve, modify, or reject submitted recommendations. Ultimately, the top management group responds in the same manner. The flow of the entire developmental management process is illustrated in Figure 16.6.

The organizational improvement planning process provides three major benefits that do not exist in conventional management development programs. One benefit is obvious. It is the opportunity to identify and change organizational conditions that may be impeding effective organization performance. The second benefit is that managers gain the feeling of teamwork and cooperation in the process of attempting to improve the performance of the organization. And the third benefit is that managers gain skills, information, and knowledge in the process of organizational improvement planning, an important part of the management function.

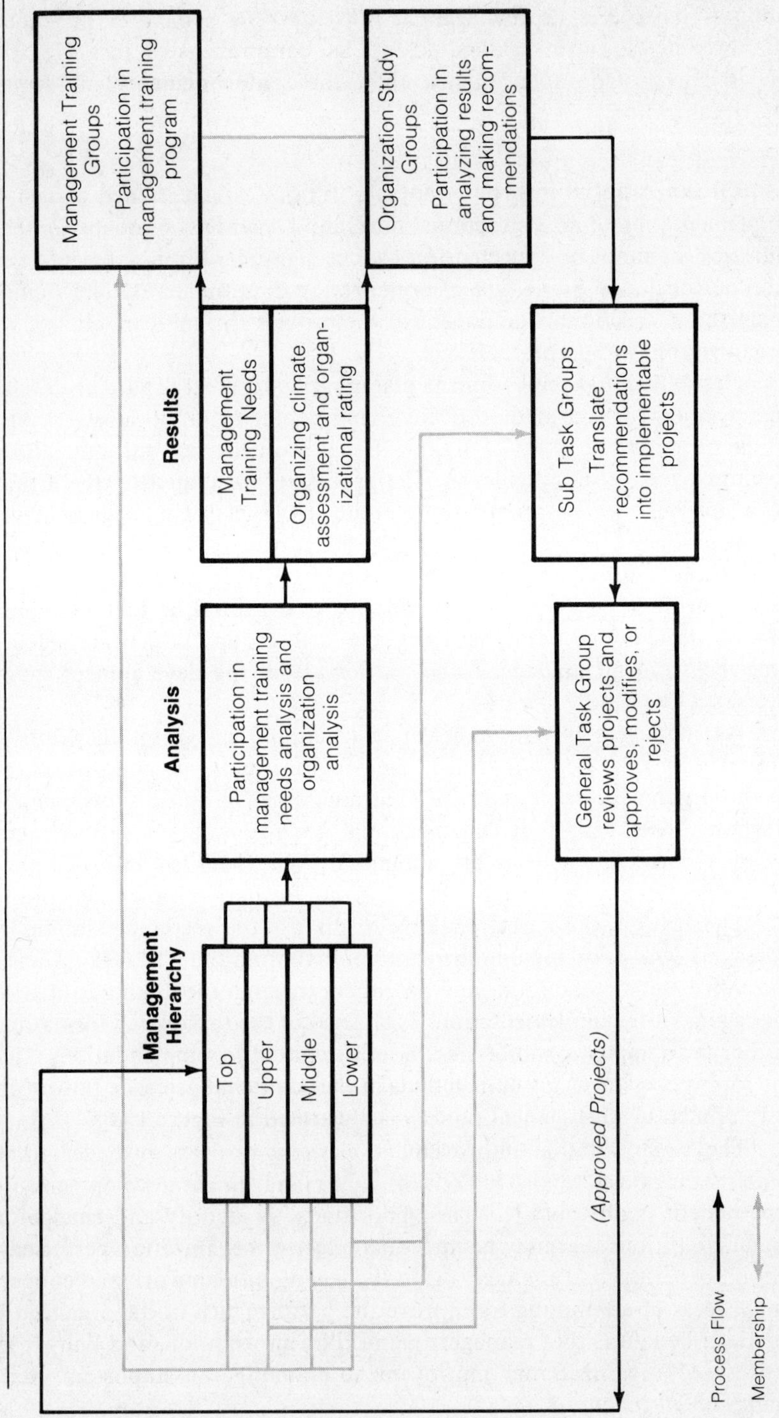

FIGURE 16.6   Management Involvement in the Developmental Management Process

Process Flow ———▶

Membership ◀——▶

Evaluating and Following Up

The evaluation and follow-up of this process is as important as the change strategies used during the process. Evaluation is required to determine what changes occurred within the organization as a result of the instructional and organizational improvement planning strategies. Follow-up is important to determine what additional strategies are required to sustain high organization performance.

One method that can be used to evaluate the process impact on the organization is to utilize the same survey and interviewing techniques used during the assessment stage. This reassessment conducted periodically over a given period of time can gauge the effectiveness of the developmental process. Other evaluative procedures can be utilized to determine the behavioral impact of the instructional program such as pre-post testing, participants' evaluations of the program, and participants' job performance following their participation in the instructional program.

These evaluation procedures can also be utilized to determine what additional instructional strategies should be pursued and what organizational changes should be considered in order to strive for improved organization performance. In other words, the process should be continuous if long-term results are to be expected.

SUMMARY

In summary, developmental management is a process designed to improve the performance of an organization. It combines management development and organization development strategies for the purpose of impacting an organization for positive results. It must be noted, however, that certain conditions must be present if the process is to be successful. They are as follows:

- The complete process must have the commitment and support of the chief executive.
- The design of the instructional program must be based on the measured needs of the managers and the organization.
- The instructional staff should include in-house staff and managers.
- All managers, at all levels, must participate in the process.
- The organizational planning process must be part of the overall process.

The net effect of combining management development and organization development strategies, if the above conditions are met, makes developmental management a superior choice over conventional management development strategies.

Suggested Readings

Gordon, G. G., & Goldberg, B. E., "Is There a Climate for Success?", *Management Review* by AMACOM, May, 1977, pp. 37–44.

Guion, R. M., "A Note on Organizational Climate," *Organizational Behavior and Human Performance,* 1973, vol. 9, pp. 120–25.

James, L. R., & Jones, A. P., "Organizational Climate: A Review of Theory and Research," *Psychological Bulletin,* 1974, vol. 81, pp. 1096–112.

Lawler, E. E., Hall, D. T., & Oldham, G. R., "Organizational Climate: Relationship to Organizational Structure, Process, and Performance," *Organizational Behavior and Human Performance,* 1974, vol. 10, pp. 139–55.

Litwin, G., & Stringer, R., *Motivation and Organizational Climate,* Cambridge, Mass.: Harvard University Press, 1968.

Payne, R. L., & Pheysey, D. C., "G. G. Stern's Organizational Climate Index: A Reconceptualization And Application To Business Organizations," *Organizational Behavior and Human Performance,* 1971, vol. 6, pp. 77–98.

References

1. Campbell, J. P., Dunnette, M. D., Lawler, E. E., & Weick, K. E., *Managerial Behavior, Performance and Effectiveness.* New York: McGraw Hill, 1970.

2. Koontz, H., "The Management Theory Jungle Revisited," *Academy of Management Review,* 1975, vol. 5, No. 2, pp. 175–87.

3. Mintzberg, H., "The Manager's Job" Folklore and Fact," *Harvard Business Review,* 1975, vol. 53, No. 4, pp. 49–61.

4. See the list of suggested readings.

Part Two

OD Application

17 Effective Use of Task Forces in the OD Process

Gordon L. Lippitt

ABSTRACT

The reasons for the use of OD task forces are articulated with their eight characteristics. The author presents five phases of OD to which the task force should give leadership. Suggestions for organizing the task force are presented with the roles of the group chairman, process observer, group recorder, and resource specialist. Some criteria of an effective task force and the ways for team building of that group are also presented.

AUTHOR BACKGROUND

Dr. Gordon L. Lippitt is professor of behavioral science in the School of Government and Business Administration, The George Washington University; a charter member of the International Association of Applied Social Scientists, Inc.; and a diplomate of the American Board of Professional Psychology. He serves as president of Project Associates, Inc., chairman of the boards of Organizational Renewal, Inc.; International Institute for the Study of Systems Renewal, Glenwood Manor Farms, Inc.; and the International Consultants Foundation. He has published over three hundred articles, pamphlets, and books in the field of human behavior, leadership and organizational effectiveness. He is the author of *Optimizing Human Resources* and *Organizational Renewal,* coauthor of *Consulting Process in Action,* and coeditor of *Management Development and Training Handbook, Helping Across Cultures,* and *Systems Thinking.*

It has been my experience in thirty years of OD work that the success of an OD effort and process will be enhanced with the formulation of a task force to oversee the multiple OD initiatives throughout the total system. The reasons for such a task force are multiple:

- Better internal coordination
- Better managerial surveillance
- Better versatility and utilization of varied resources
- Better morale—more involvement
- Better focus on results
- Better utilization of talent, both technical and managerial
- Better relations within the organization
- More effective follow-through OD
- More effective evaluation and recycling of continuous initiatives

In this age of organizational complexities the use of an OD task force is another manifestation of matrix management. As in project management, some of the characteristics of an OD task force are as follows:

- *Problem orientation*—A task force is used to initiate, coordinate, and solve complex, identifiable problems in the organization. It is used to accomplish a solution within stated objectives for improving the effectiveness of the organization.
- *Multidisciplinary focus*—Effective OD problem solving demands inputs of several disciplinary specialists. Task forces should be composed of a range of expertise and serve as a vehicle for integrating the inputs of diverse specialists.
- *Systems perspective*—An OD task force must be cognizant of the internal workings of the organization as well as the larger organizational environment of the system.
- *Horizontal/vertical organizational relationships*— OD task force work is a process that must often operate both vertically and horizontally within the organization. It often violates classical, chain-of-command principles. There is often a greater potential for flexible, free-form problem solving in OD efforts.
- *Finite duration*—Task forces are established and maintained only until the OD process is applied and integrated into the operating mode of the organization. Once the objectives have been achieved, the task force should be disbanded.
- *Change oriented*—Task forces must be flexible. Environments change, political influences change, budgets change, even the scope of problems change, so the task force is focused on change.
- *Innovation in the organization*—Complex OD processes often require one-of-a-kind organizational efforts. Innovative organizational methods supported by the task force will help managers capitalize on the strengths in the functional organization while simultaneously overcoming deficiencies inherent in many functional organizations.

■ *Responsibility identification*—OD task forces will employ a deductive approach in breaking the objectives down into manageable components. Points of commitment can then be assigned for accomplishing a system of responsibility and accountability for each phase and activity in the OD process.

While there is no correct size for an OD task force, I have found that between nine and twelve seems to be the right size. In one large organization we had an overall OD task force for the total organization and eight subtask forces built around the organization with issues that were derived from the data collection phase. It should be noted that the office of the CEO should be represented on the overall task force to lend credibility and follow through implications.

TASK FORCE RESPONSIBILITIES

In a general way an OD task force will have responsibility for overseeing five phases of the OD process:

Phase I: Define mission, goals, and objectives
Phase II: Data collection and analysis
Phase III: Plan activities and processes
Phase IV: Implement and schedule
Phase V: Review and evaluate progress

These five phases are presented in sequence in Table 17.1. It might be relevant to elaborate about the first step of defining the OD mission, goals, and objectives. These are the early responsibilities of the OD task force.[1]

Mission Statements (Key Objectives): By their nature mission statements are broader, more encompassing statements than goals and objectives, and are therefore described in general language. Mission statements are likely to be set effectively when they are a statement of the fundamental commitments that an organization or unit are organized to achieve, answering these key questions:

■ *Why* are we in existence?
■ *What* is it that we aim to achieve in the way of products and services?
■ *Who* are our clients?
■ *Where* are our clients located and in what area are we focusing our efforts?

Goals (Critical Objectives): These derive directly from the mission statements, constructed as described above, and consist of statements of the most important overall, continuing results that must be accomplished in major categories of work, to achieve what has been written in the mission statements. The task of the goal statement, therefore, is to answer this question:

TABLE 17.1 OD Task Force Management

	Process	Time	Cost	Performance	Resources
I.	Define objectives	Completion date	Total budget	Specifications	People, materials, technology
II.	Data collection and analysis	Duration	Cost estimates	Identify kinds of desired data	Use of interviews, observation, surveys, audits and written resources
III.	Plan activities and processes	Duration	Activity cost estimates	Define milestones	Define availability
IV.	Implement and schedule	Trade-offs with operations	Trade-offs with operations	Trade-offs with operations	Allocation
V.	Review and evaluate progress	Planned vs. actual	Actual vs. budget	Measurement of progress	Planned vs. actual

■ *How* are we to achieve our mission?

Objectives (Specific Objectives): This is a statement of a measurable result to be accomplished within a stated time period. The statement should specify both the *desired result* and the *work* needed to achieve that result. A preferred format for a specific objective is: "To (the work to be done) so that (the result to be achieved)."

In Phase II the task force will determine what data collection needs to be planned and methods for data collection. Obviously, involvement throughout the system would take place to implement observations, surveys, interviews, etc., which would be analyzed and fed back so that "natural" work units could plan action and implement activities (Phase III).

The task force would help implement and schedule training and problem solving events utilizing internal and external resources (Phase IV). The task force would also develop ways to evaluate the progress toward the OD mission and be ready to report same to the total system as well as to management.

ORGANIZING THE OD TASK FORCE

The OD task force should see itself as a demonstration of a cooperative, problem-solving group that takes full advantage of resources both within and outside the group, and seeks consensus regarding the solution of a problem rather than a decision by a majority vote.

To help a task force fulfill its task there will be related to it a team of four persons.

The Task Force Chairperson

This person should think of himself or herself as the chairperson of the team. The function generally will be to help the task force define and select the problems related to its work, to see that all points of view are expressed, to help keep the discussion of the group on the subject, to clarify and summarize from time to time the progress of the group toward its objectives, and to help maintain an atmosphere in which the greatest cooperation and production can be achieved.

The Group Facilitator (Process Observer)

This person is a special resource person to help the group use its own power to improve its functioning by making appropriate observations, as needed, to facilitate the task force problem solving. Such a function is a resource to stimulate the task force group to examine the content and process of its own functioning. The facilitator/observer can help the leader and group members be more aware of the group processes that can contribute to its teamwork.

The Recorder/Reporter

This person's functions are to get down the chief points of content which the group produces. This includes the major problems or issues identified by the task force, the pros and cons indicated, the major agreements reached by the group, the decisions made, and the recommendations agreed upon. The recorder will have the task of seeing that the group's thinking is available for reporting to the management of the organization. It will also help "fix" the action assignments and dates for following up the task force decisions.

The Resource Person

Actually in a task force group every member is a resource person. The suggestions below, therefore, are offered to those who, as designated "resource persons," have prepared themselves more carefully in advance as potential contributors to the discussion in specific areas of OD concern such as finance, HRD, information technology, and so on.

Kenneth Benne states in brief that the duties of the resource person are to furnish the group with facts and points of view which contribute to the deliberations. He makes the following suggestions:

1. The primary duty of the resource person is to contribute facts and points of view of the discussion when it is evident that these are not likely to be contributed by others. This, of course, does not apply to the "every member" resource person but only to those who are experts or who have made special preparation.

2. The views stated by a resource person should be stated as contributions to the discussion rather than as personal opinions of the resource person about which there should be no debate.

3. The resource person should be careful not to reflect discredit upon the contribution of any member of the group, or make light of a statement made by another member of the group.

4. The resource person should, in general, "not speak until they are spoken to." That is, they should answer questions of fact directed to them by members of the group or referred by the group leader and should break this rule only when the person is confident that their contribution will improve the discussion.

It follows from this brief statement that the task force has some responsibility in using the resource person properly. The resource person should be called upon frequently for facts or expert opinion (not necessarily arising from their own first-hand experiences, since most people's expertness comes largely from the experience of others).[2]

HELPING TASK FORCES BE EFFECTIVE

So much has been written about developing the teamwork of groups. Let me summarize some of the characteristics of a *productive* task force:[3]

- All members are working together toward common goals which are well understood and accepted.
- The values and goals of the group are a satisfactory integration and expression of the relevant values and needs of its members. Clear assignments are made and accepted.
- Team leader adheres to a supportive and cooperative versus competitive relationship among members. Mutual help is characteristic.
- Frequently the group will examine and discuss how it is functioning.
- High participation in discussion.
- Discussion remains pertinent to task of group.
- Communication takes place.
- Members listen to one another, do not topic jump and are free in expressing feelings and ideas.
- People are involved and interested and the atmosphere is informal and relaxed.
- The group is comfortable with conflict and carefully examines and resolves it.
- Criticism is constructive in remaining obstacles to getting job done.

In a similar fashion let me make some generalizations on unproductive task forces:

- Members are *unclear* of their's and other's *goals* and priorities and what the overall goals of the team are;

- There is unnecessary duplication of effort;
- Some *things* just don't get done, they seem to *"fall between the cracks"*;
- Group *members* seem to be *pulling* in different directions;
- Team productivity is *low*;
- *Decisions* are not *followed up* as well as they could be;
- *Meetings* are *ineffective,* dull, and get off the subject;
- *Communications* are *blocked,* messages are not received—some people don't know what is happening;
- Communications primarily up and down, little laterally;
- People are very careful about what they say;
- *Members* of the team are *frequently in conflict* and conflict is suppressed;
- Group *morale* is *low,* people are grumbling;
- *All goals* are *not being met* or the process of setting and accomplishing them could be smoother or better.

It is observed that an OD task force should receive some training and team building preparation for this important role and function.

In such a group they are constantly dealing with four main problems: the problem of identity, the problem of power and influence, the problem of goals and needs, and the problem of acceptance and intimacy.

Problem of identity.   Questions each person in a task group seeks to answer are Who am I in this group? What kinds of resources do I have that will be useful? What roles will I play or be called upon to play? How will this group affect the way I see myself?

Problem of power and influence.   Members are concerned with who will have the power and influence; how much others will exert influence; how much others can be influenced.

Problem of goals and needs.   "What are the needs of others in the group?" and "Will any of my needs be met?" are questions constantly asked by both the leader and members. In many groups little information is available to answer these questions because members are unaware of their needs or are unwilling to share their concerns and feelings.

Problem of acceptance and intimacy.   A group often confronts persons with the issue of their needs, difficulties, hopes, and feelings of adequacy and inadequacy in forming close, trusting, and intimate relationships with other persons. For some persons, to be alone is very threatening; while to others, to be close is more difficult. The problem of achieving appropriate levels of intimacy is often worked out covertly as the group works on its task.

Members of groups will exhibit many different kinds of emotional behavior as they struggle to cope with the four problems listed above.

SUMMARY

As an OD task force works, a number of characteristics indicate its effectiveness. Among the most important are these:

- Ability to integrate organization, group, and individual goals.
- Different members perform appropriate leadership functions as needed.
- Balance of communication between content and feeling—and freedom to communicate both.
- Tolerance for a wide range of individual behavior.
- Adequate cohesion for efficient functioning.
- Appropriate decision-making procedures—with minority viewpoints being considered—and a growing awareness of consensus.
- Flexible group procedures adapted to accomplish the task.
- Ways of examining group operation, with members giving and receiving frank reactions to individual behavior.
- Appropriate use of the resources available to the group both inside and outside the organization.

Such a task force will be a powerful synergetic force to initiate and implement OD activities and processes. While it will not guarantee success, it is an effective methodology for enhancing the accomplishment of OD objectives.

Notes

1. *Task Force Notebook,* (Washington, D.C.: World Bank, 1982).
2. Kenneth Benne, NTL Institute Take Home Packet, 1981.
3. Ideas based on Douglas McGregor, *The Human Side of Enterprise* (New York: McGraw-Hill, 1960); Rensis Likert, *New Patterns of Management* (New York: McGraw-Hill, 1961); Gordon Lippitt, *Organizational Renewal* (Englewood Cliffs, New Jersey: Prentice-Hall, 1982).

18 A Comprehensive Approach to Planning an OD/QWL Strategy

William A. Pasmore

ABSTRACT

This paper addresses current issues observed in the implementation of quality work life programs and argues for a reintegration of quality of work life and organization development techniques. It is posited that organizations have the potential to be societal value shapers through quality of work life programs, providing that QWL efforts are undertaken in systematic, collaborative ways. The paper describes the development of an action research system to support QWL implementation and also outlines a model for introducing sociotechnical systems change using a variety of other organization development techniques in addition to standard analytic methods.

AUTHOR BACKGROUND

William A. Pasmore is associate professor of organizational behavior at the Weatherhead School of Management, Case Western Reserve University. As an educator, he has taught courses in work design, organizational behavior, organizational theory, and organizational development. As a certified consultant, he has contributed to the sociotechnical design and organization development of both industrial and nonindustrial firms. His research has appeared in a number of journals, including *Human Relations, Administrative Science Quarterly,* and *The Journal of Applied Behavioral Science.* He is coauthor of *Sociotechnical Systems: A Sourcebook.* Dr. Pasmore is a graduate of Purdue University, where he received both his B.S. in industrial management and his Ph.D. in administrative sciences.

The topic addressed in this paper is the need to integrate quality of work life efforts into larger and more systematic organization development programs that reflect the complexity that characterizes our institutions today. I shall argue that the *separation* of QWL and OD programs in the past has impaired the efficacy and durability of QWL programs and further detached them from the mainstream economic considerations of most firms. To counter this trend, I will provide my own views on how OD and QWL should become more intertwined by talking about some of the assumptions that underlie QWL programs and sharing a model for intervention that I have developed based on my own experiences and the observations of others. I will conclude that an effective OD/QWL program must emphasize the relationships between labor and management and between the organization and its environment simultaneously, that careful attention must be paid to the *process* used to plan and implement the QWL program rather than to the specific targets or techniques that characterize the program. I shall argue that OD/QWL programs must be systemic in nature, impacting the technology, structure, and reward systems used by the organization in accomplishing its purpose, and, to make this possible, I will argue that managers need to approach QWL/OD programs with an *investment* mentality rather than as a quick-fix strategy and with full recognition of their role in shaping the future values of our society regarding work itself.

To frame this discussion, I need to first define briefly what I mean by QWL and OD, and then state some of the assumptions upon which I have based my arguments. *Quality of work life* has been defined by various authors in different ways; and as far as I know, there is no agreed-upon definition of what the term means or even the dimensions along which it should be measured. Borrowing primarily from the definitions provided by Maccoby and Walton (1975), I shall use the term *quality of work life program* to refer to any activity undertaken by an organization for the expressed purpose of improving one or more of the following conditions that affect an employee's experience with an organization:

- Security
- Equity
- Individual choice
- Participation in decisions
- Safety and health
- Opportunities to use and develop human capacities
- Meaningful work
- Control over work time or place
- Protection from arbitrary or unfair treatment
- Opportunities to satisfy social needs

I should note that while it is difficult to get scholars to agree on what dimensions make up the quality of work life, it is even more difficult to determine when the actions of an organization that affect one or more of these dimensions constitute a quality of work life program. I do not want to settle this controversy here by providing either an all-encompassing definition or a fool-proof checklist that can be used to size up QWL programs; I simply want to note that the term *quality of work life* is fuzzy at best, and that some organizations without programs probably do more to improve it in the normal course of doing business than others which engage in elaborate and costly efforts.

The term *organization development* has been with us longer than QWL, and so we have even a larger number of definitions to choose from in trying to describe what we mean when we talk about an organization development program. The definitions provided by Bennis (1969), Beckhard (1969), French and Bell (1973), and others characterize OD as a collaborative, educational, *planned* change strategy intended to alter the beliefs, values, attitudes, structures, and processes of organizations so they can better adapt to new technologies, changes in society, and environmental uncertainty. In practice, the field of OD is not neatly defined at all, and consists of a jumble of *techniques* designed to bring about improved interpersonal or intergroup relationships or a better *fit* between the needs of people and the tasks they perform.

Incidentally, before my bias begins to show through if it hasn't already, let me state it clearly. My own training in engineering, management, and the behavioral sciences as well as my subsequent experience with organizations has led me to believe that undertaking *either* a QWL *or* OD program just for the sake of "doing something for the workers" is a mistake. We do not live in a world of unlimited resources, and we cannot expect organizations to survive if they squander the resources they have on programs with no clear objectives or reasonably assured outcomes. As I said, *effective* programs aimed at improving the quality of work life must do so in the context of realities with institutions, as open systems in a free market economy.

I believe strongly that organizations *must* address themselves to the quality of work life of their employees if they wish to be successful in coping with the demands employees will place upon them in even the next one or two decades, but I also believe that they cannot do so in ways that threaten the ability of the organization to respond to the other demands of its environment.

To go even further, let me state some of the beliefs underlying some QWL programs which I do *not* agree with. First, I do *not* believe that increased organizational effectiveness can be achieved by increasing employee motivation. Organizational effectiveness hinges on a plethora of variables in any given situation, and the impact of increasing employee motivation from three to five on a seven-point scale is probably nil compared to the impact of changes in variables such as technology, market strategy, organizational structure, or vertical or horizontal integration. To lay the problem of organizational effectiveness at the feet of our workers makes no more sense than blaming schoolchildren for the declining quality of our educational systems. This is not to say that employees cannot, under the right circumstances, contribute significantly to improving the effectiveness of organizations: when employees purchased the Chicago and Northwestern railroad in 1972, it was nearly bankrupt; through their efforts, it has become one of the most profitable lines in the Midwest and each investment of $500 they made then is now worth over $400,000. One could argue that it was increased employee motivation that brought about this remarkable metamorphisis; but in reality, changes in many systems were required to make the transition possible.

I likewise do *not* believe that we can define an organizational structure or program that can *consistently* guarantee that a high quality of work life will be provided for employees regardless of unforeseen circumstances we will face in the future. Solutions are static, and even those that seem to work well today will be untenable in light of tomorrow's realities. In fact, even our definitions of what *constitutes* a high quality of work life must change to correspond with the concerns and expectations that each new generation of workers bring with them to the workplace. At the turn of the century, a sixty-hour work week would have been considered a significant improvement in the quality of work life by most employees; ten years from now, the question could easily revolve around whether some employees should have to report to their organizations to work at all, as computers and information systems make it possible for more work to be done by individuals at home. In short, we cannot promise employees that if they go along with our programs now, they will necessarily be better off at some time in the future.

I also do *not* believe that the answers to our quest to find ways to improve QWL and organizational effectiveness lie in studying the Japanese and trying to borrow from their culture the solutions to our problems. Their solutions work *because* of the culture and context of relationships in which they are applied; when we try to apply their solutions in the absence of that context, they are at best hollow testimonials to the way we would like things to be.

I have said that workers are not solely or even primarily accountable for organizational effectiveness; at the same time, I believe that organizational effectiveness in many instances is also beyond the control of managers. I do *not* believe that most managers make choices that significantly impact either the quality of workers' lives or organizational effectiveness. The vast majority of managers are far removed from organizational and technological design choices that create systems within which *they* are as much the victims as are workers. Managers are trapped by existing conditions into remedial roles vis-à-vis workers in which the question they must ask is *not* How can we be effective? but How can I get more out of these people and this technology? These remedial actions by managers evoke delinquent responses from employees, so that energy which *could* be directed toward organizational improvement is quickly consumed in pursuing the forever unattainable goal of maintaining the status quo. Seen in this light, some QWL programs are no more a cure for organizational ills than a dose of cod liver oil, and frequently even less pleasant for managers to swallow. From the perspective of a large number of first-line supervisors whom I have spoken with, this is one area in which the side effects of the cure may be worse than the disease. Given the realities of production deadlines and quality standards, who has time to devote to QWL? Even if time is devoted to QWL, what can realistically be changed? Why raise the expectations of my workers to levels where they cannot possibly be met? So we should not lay the responsibility for QWL at the feet of the shop-floor supervisor either, as is commonly done.

Finally, let me deal with the belief that QWL programs are undertaken out of a sense of social responsibility and moral commitment on the part of a few enlightened managers who hold positions of such power that they can imbue others throughout the organization with these same values and sense of obligation to society. Certainly, there are those managers who recognize that in today's world, organizations *are* the primary instruments that can be used to shape values and bring about social change. One need only watch the evening news and listen carefully to what is being said to discern that automakers dictate foreign policy; that oil companies decide to which uses our natural resources should be put; that utilities decide where and how nuclear waste should be disposed of; that commercial establishments create products they think consumers and then proceed to tell us why we need them and even why we should prefer one brand over another. The undeniable truth is that for most us, organizations determine to a large extent our identities, where and how we should live our lives, and what we can reasonably expect to be the significance of the time we have spent on this planet. Organizations provide the relative yardstick by which each of us gauges our personal success, and by which others assess our abilities, intellect, and worth.

Therefore, when we speak of changing the relationship between labor and management through a quality of work life program, are we not talking about a radical effort to bring about significant and repercussive changes in the very fabric of our society? The answer to my own question, at least in most cases I fear, is a resounding *no*. Managers I have spoken with would deny that they are the master planners and architects of our society and its values, and if one examines some of the programs that have been undertaken under the guise of QWL, one might be inclined to agree. Many programs are either piecemeal, isolated, broad brush, low impact, low budget, inconsequential, or blatantly manipulative.

To understand the recent groundswell in QWL activities, one must look beyond the fulfillment of social responsibilities to other motives. We find, behind the words, well-intentioned efforts to protect the most basic of all the quality of work life dimensions—namely, job security through the continued success of the organization. Managers may not have fully comprehended their responsibility in influencing the values we have about work, but they do at least understand that people, like machines, function more reliably with some investment in periodic maintenance. QWL programs, as they currently exist in many instances, can be thought of as periodic maintenance programs for people that are undertaken to ensure that human resources perform their roles in the organization more dependably. My own review of 134 work restructuring efforts is revealing in that the most frequently measured variable in these efforts was *productivity,* while the variables on which success was most likely to be achieved were attitudes and quality (Pasmore et al. 1981). Few studies discussed the need to fit the organization to new work values, and none provided any indication of results on this dimension. The focus of QWL programs, quite simply, has been on making money. At the same time, the result of most QWL programs is to leave employees more satisfied, but not necessarily more productive.

In reviewing some assumptions underlying QWL programs which I regard as unfounded I have revealed something of what I *do* believe to be true of QWL programs and the manager and organizations that undertake them.

First, I *do* believe that organizations are societal value shapers and that the goal of pursuing QWL improvements by organizations is a legitimate and worthy one. The values and beliefs that accompany concerns about the quality of work life are in concert with changes in our society and the need of organizations to better utilize their human reosurces in responding to challenges presented by virtually every segment of their environment.

Secondly, I believe that most quality of work life programs are ineffectual or at least do not reach their potential because they are viewed as ways to appease workers or increase organizational effectiveness through improved employee satisfaction and motivation. I believe that the quality of work life experienced by an employee is the *result* of a coming together of a variety of systems and forces that impact the health and viability of the organization at large. In this way, I see QWL as a *dependent* variable rather than an independent variable that can be manipulated directly by managers or behavioral scientists.

Finally, I believe that improving the quality of work life is not something that you do *for* workers, but something that you do *with* workers. Because we cannot unilaterally define for another individual what for him or her should constitute a high quality of working life, we must allow others to be intimately involved in creating the conditions that *they* consider important. This involvement brings with it the added benefit of commitment to the program and the organization, which may do more to improve the state of organizational health in and of itself than any specific action taken as a result of the program. The outcomes of QWL programs cannot be mandated, and any attempt to do so will undoubtedly short-circuit both the program and the willingness of employees to engage in efforts of a similar nature in the future. Let me review each of these assumptions in greater detail. That QWL programs are in tune with forces at work to change our society is evident when one considers the trends displayed in Figure 18.1.

That QWL programs need to be more systemic in nature is something I discovered in my own research comparing the effects of QWL/OD interventions on organizational outcomes. The programs consisted of survey feedback, job redesign, and sociotechnical systems interventions in a single organization. Through time series analysis, I was able to conclude that all of the programs left employees more satisfied than before the programs were undertaken, but that only the sociotechnical system (STS) intervention impacted organizational productivity and costs. The STS intervention was more successful because it addressed the technology used to produce the goods manufactured by the firm, as well as reward, supervision, and information systems (Pasmore & King 1978). My own review and those of others have consistently shown that sociotechnical system interventions outperform other OD interventions in producing bottomline results because they recognize the impact of technology on productivity and

---

FIGURE 18.1   Forces Affecting the Future of Organizations

---

1. Productivity is beginning to decline
2. International competition is becoming more severe
3. Cost of U.S. products is high and rising compared to foreign sources
4. Technology is becoming increasingly sophisticated
5. Younger workers are better educated, more dissatisfied than older counterparts
6. Strikes are increasing in frequency
7. Turnover is increasing
8. Absenteeism is increasing
9. Managers are receiving better education
10. Trend toward greater leisure time
11. Women are achieving equality in the workplace
12. Increase in dual income families
13. Labor shortages are forecast by 2010
14. More work is being done at home
15. Relative income is increasing
16. Changing careers is becoming increasingly acceptable
17. Electronics are improving mental capabilities
18. Robots are forecast to eliminate many jobs

QWL and view the organization as an open system in which the relationship between people and technology must be jointly optimized in ways that allow the organization to deal effectively with its environment (Friedlander & Brown 1974; Srivastva et al. 1974). QWL programs that do not focus on the technology used by an organization to produce its goods or services will provide short-term gains in employee satisfaction that will erode under the constant pressure to make existing systems somehow respond to new circumstances foisted on them by their changing environments. To understand this more fully, it should be recognized that technology has impacts on organizational functioning at a number of levels, as shown in Figure 18.2.

Figure 18.2 indicates that technology directly affects productivity, the motions and places workers will engage in and be located at, and the behaviors that are required of them. With specialization, some will manage while others operate the technology: thus, second-order effects will be observed in terms of organizational roles, relationships, contracts with the organization, and attitudes toward it. The technology also specifies to a large extent who will be hired according to the skills needed to operate it; the structure of the organization; and, over the long run, the adaptability, learning potential, and self-concepts of organizational members. Finally, as organizations develop similar patterns, exchange information, and influence their environment, the initial technological choices they make may influence societal and interorganizational relations.

Furthermore, it should be recognized that technology is not the only system that constrains the degree of freedom available for organizational experimentation and change. Similar analyses could be performed regarding organizational structure, reward systems, and information systems. To have *truly* significant effects that guarantee the *long-range* viability of a QWL program, the effort should eventually address all of these systems. The efforts that we point to as

FIGURE 18.2 Impact of Technology on Behavior

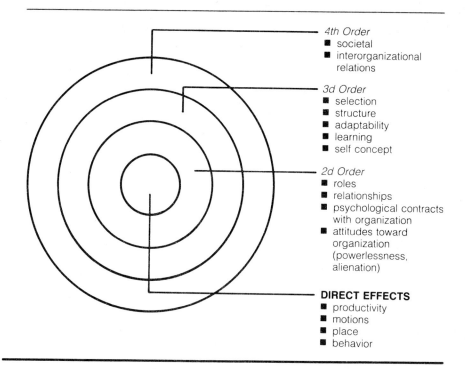

4th Order
- societal
- interorganizational relations

3d Order
- selection
- structure
- adaptability
- learning
- self concept

2d Order
- roles
- relationships
- psychological contracts with organization
- attitudes toward organization (powerlessness, alienation)

DIRECT EFFECTS
- productivity
- motions
- place
- behavior

examples of outstanding QWL projects have attempted to do this: Topeka, Jamestown, Shell UK, and Volvo are the names of some projects that come immediately to mind. Even in these efforts, we see that the failure to address a critical system can cause some regression in the results attained. For example Walton (1977) has noted that workers at Topeka have become increasingly dissatisfied with the corporation's refusal to set up some sort of profit-sharing plan so that they can participate in the gains they have helped achieve. In considering a larger number of efforts, I have become aware of the following list of roadblocks in various attempts at work restructuring (Figure 18.3).

The intent of sharing this list is not to discourage the undertaking of QWL projects, but to underscore the fact that programs must be systemic in nature if these roadblocks are to be avoided or dealt with successfully. It should also be clear that dealing with these roadblocks requires a great deal of commitment from *all* those involved in the effort; asking people to dedicate this amount of energy *solely* in order to improve the quality of working life requires either a great deal or courage or naiveté; trying the program to achieve organizational effectiveness if not survival seems both more appealing and more sensible.

Finally, my belief that QWL programs must be collaborative in nature stems again from a combination of theory and experience. I think Miles' (1965) article on human relations versus human resources makes the point most clearly

---

FIGURE 18.3 Some Reported Roadblocks in Work Restructuring Efforts

---

1. Insufficient technological change to achieve the joint optimization of the social and technical systems
2. Pressures for uniformity
3. Employee resistance due to lack of early involvement
4. Lack of hierarchical support
5. Loss in internal leadership skills
6. Pressure from competitors to maintain/improve productivity/quality
7. Technical problems
8. Collective bargaining dynamics
9. Unfavorable ratio of psychological costs to benefits for employees
10. Isolation, loss of support due to failure to diffuse original effort to other parts of the organization
11. Shifts in the demand for the firm's products
12. Insufficient training for employees and supervisors for new roles
13. Insufficient understanding of work restructuring theory on the part of management
14. Lack of necessary change in related support functions
15. Absence of review and adjustment mechanisms

---

that programs intended to simply improve employee relations fail to tap into the creativity and resources employees can bring to bear in helping to solve organizational problems. McGregor's (1960) Theory X and Y and Likert's (1961) System 1 and System 4 say essentially the same thing. Sociotechnical system approaches recognize this, too, in designing work for employees that calls upon them to utilize a wider range of their abilities and take on more responsibilities than is usually the case in traditionally designed systems. All of these views hold that people are more than parts of machines, and that they have more to contribute to an organization with their heads than with their hands, when given the opportunity to do so. Yet we continue to observe top-down attempts to legislate for employees how motivated they should be and how good the quality of their work life is whether they recognize it or not.

One company I worked with experienced a rather unique and devastating problem having to do with injuries to employees. For some unknown reason, a large number of employees working for this manufacturing concern were afflicted with injuries to their wrists, elbows, and shoulders, which in a few cases were severely debilitating. Over a period of several years, managers of the organization sought to identify the cause of the problem in order to rectify the situation. None of their investigations directly involved employees, and unfortunately, not only were the answers not forthcoming, but each effort to understand the problem seemed to make things worse. Managers tried to assure employees that there were no logical reasons for the problem to exist; but employees continued to report to the infirmary despite managements' contentions.

Our approach in dealing with this problem was to fully involve employees in the study of it through a representative group of employees who worked closely with us in designing interviews and a survey to be used in collecting data from the rest of the workforce. What we eventually found was that poor materials were making it impossible for people to meet their production quotas, but that because of their loyalty and dedication to the company, people pressured themselves to meet their quotas anyway. This pressure, combined with the intricate hand movements required to make the product resulted in the original few cases; these outbreaks caused stress and fear on the part of the other employees who felt they might also be affected. This lowered productivity and brought more pressure from supervisors to meet quotas and production deadlines. The problem spiraled until over three-fourths of the work force had been affected.

When this data was shared with management, pilot programs were undertaken in which employees took the lead role in redesigning their work and even setting their own quotas. These programs did not affect the majority of the workforce, however. Consequently, to this day, I believe strongly that the disappearance of the problem had more to do with the willingness of management to involve employees in the study and change of the situation than anything else we did.

I have since become involved in another project examining the feasibility of introducing sociotechnical analysis and change to the U.S. Army. The research is taking place at a computer facility located in Heidelberg, West Germany. There, too, I have utilized employees as resources in shaping and implementing the proposed changes. From that experience, I have developed a model which I feel clearly indicates the need to integrate efforts at improving quality of work life with almost every other kind of OD activity. The model is specific to sociotechnical systems change, but should be more broadly applicable to QWL Programs in general since at its core is the creation of an action research system which provides a *structure* for full collaboration in the analysis and change of an organization.

The action research system consists of three parties: a *steering committee,* composed of the top-level decision makers in the organization who have the authority to grant permission for undertaking the program and implementing whatever changes come out of it; a *core group,* consisting of representatives from all levels and parts of the organization, but heavily weighted to represent employees; and the *consulting-research team,* which provides facilitation, general direction, and expertise based on other efforts and knowledge.

The functions of the core group include:

- Acting as a representative body of the organization
- Acting as a liaison between the ARS and others in the organization
- Acting as a counterweight to formal organizational leadership
- Taking part in the research process
- Serving as a change agent in the organization

Specific core group tasks include:

- Describing social system
- Identifying problems in social system
- Generating questions to be asked
- Participating in analysis of technical system

- Generating recommendations for change
- Reacting to recommendations from consultants or scientists
- Communicating continuously with others in organization

The action-research system consists of three parties in order to help preserve a healthy system of checks and balances throughout the program. Much like our own government, these three parties must work together collaboratively if the task of understanding the organization before fixing it is to be accomplished. For example, the relationship between the steering committee and core group remains balanced because the consultant is present to make certain that neither group dominates the other. Similarly, the steering committee oversees the efforts of the core group and consultant so that changes which are eventually recommended fit with organizational goals and interests. The core group, as a member of this action-research system, provides data, reactions, and ideas both in response to and separately from the consultant and steering committee's direction. It is at the same time an advocate of employee rights and managerial decisions; it should both lead and be led; and it should strive for improvement in the organization while not overlooking what is good about the organization as it currently operates. Above all, the action research system is created to facilitate learning about the organization so that the core group has the responsibility to educate others and itself be educated. In the end, change based on the shared knowledge of the three parties will be superior to any that just one of two of the parties alone would recommend.

To reach the point where this system can function effectively, a good deal of groundwork needs to be laid, and this is where QWL efforts can benefit greatly through a reunion with OD. The model outlined in Figure 18.4 borrows from the work of Emery and Trist (1978) and Cummings (1977) in pointing out some of the skills, analyses, actions, and issues the OD/QWL practitioner might wish to keep in mind while conducting a sociotechnical system intervention in an organization.

Of course, the success of a program like the one outlined in Figure 18.4 depends heavily upon support from management, and thus we have come full circle. If QWL programs are to be effective, they must be both collaborative and systemic in nature, as emphasized here. If managers are looking for a quick fix for organizational ills, then QWL programs are likely to be mandated from the top down with minimum employee involvement and touch upon only the most visible problem areas that can be addressed within the confines of the current design of the system. I contend strongly that managers need to approach QWL programs with the same investment mentality they use in making capital purchases, and that they should recognize that the process of changing values about work and the social processes of the organization requires an effort at least comparable in size to that involving a major replacement of technology. If that means that fewer efforts are undertaken, perhaps that is better than undertaking a larger number of programs, many of which are predestined for failure. In my way of thinking, the way to get the most out of a QWL program is to invest enough in it that it pays for itself through measurable increases in organizational

FIGURE 18.4 Program Model

I. Skills needed to facilitate sociotechnical system interventions
  A. Organization development (effectiveness) skills
  B. Training-educating skills
  C. Systems conceptualization skills
  D. Research skills
  E. Communication skills
  F. Engineering skills
  G. The importance of linking up with others
II. The intervention model
  A. Entry/scouting
    1. The genesis of sociotechnical system change
    2. The importance of early involvement by consultant
    3. The need for top level support
    4. Identifying the pressure for change
    5. The need for stable commitment
    6. The need for commitment from lower levels
    7. Previous history of organization effectiveness efforts
    8. Time and resource availability
    9. Internal consultants and liaison roles
    10. Defining the scope of intervention
    11. Organizational scanning
      ■ Goals
      ■ Layout
      ■ Processes
      ■ Services
      ■ Structure
      ■ Composition
      ■ History
      ■ Management style
      ■ Employee attitudes
    12. Making the decision to proceed
  B. Contracting
    1. The importance of establishing an action research system
    2. Clarifying expectations
    3. Contracting points
      ■ Compensation
      ■ Contract review and change
      ■ Procedures to be used in decision making regarding the project and contract changes
      ■ Data confidentiality
      ■ Time and resources available
      ■ Role of the consultant
      ■ Role of the decision makers
      ■ Philosophy of intervention
    4. Defining the client steering committee
    5. Sanctioning experiments
    6. Clarifying expectations across levels
    7. Plans for diffusion
  C. The creation of core groups
    1. Membership
    2. Selection processes
    3. Size
    4. Replacement mechanisms
  D. Educating the client
    1. STS theory
    2. History of STS interventions
    3. Steps in the STS change process

    4. Agreement regarding decision making
    5. Timeframe for project
    6. Potential roadblocks to change
    7. Roles
E. Open Systems planning
    1. Real future
    2. Ideal future
    3. Variance between real/ideal
    4. Pressures for change
    5. Identifying targets/opportunities for change
F. Core group development
    1. Identifying resources available
    2. Appreciating differences
    3. Problem solving techniques
    4. Developing a shared knowledge of the organization
    5. Team building
    6. Reviewing roles, functions and structures
    7. Decision making rules
    8. Outside involvement in core group activities
    9. Process consultation skills
    10. Group learning aids
    11. Tasks and functions
G. Clarifying the relationship between the core group and steering committee
    1. Action research perspective
    2. Co-inquiry
    3. Planning for feedback/information exchange
H. Developing analytical methods and instruments
    1. Interviews
    2. Surveys
    3. Task/technology assessment
I. Analyzing the social system
    1. Confidentiality
    2. Data collection
    3. Data preparation
    4. Data feedback
J. Analyzing the technical system
    1. Selecting resources to assist in technical analysis
    2. Using the guide to task analysis
    3. The variance control matrix and table
    4. Generating immediate hypotheses for redesign
K. Analyzing supply and user systems
    1. Using the systems model as a guide to analysis
    2. Obtaining information about supply and user systems
    3. Preparing the results
    4. Feedback of results
L. Generating alternatives for joint optimization
    1. Education in goals for joint optimization
    2. The importance of compatibility
    3. The importance of adaptability, redundancy, multifunctionalism
    4. The importance of collaboration between consultant and organization
    5. Visiting other sites
    6. Idea generation and review
M. Experimental implementation
    1. Conditions of experimentation
      ■ Commitments
      ■ Time frame
      ■ Plans for evaluation
    2. Feedback of results
N. Stabilizing results
    1. On-going review and adjustment
    2. Handling turnover of key personnel

III. Diffusion of results
    A. The importance of diffusion
    B. Keeping track of what happens
    C. Developing diffusion processes

---

effectiveness. Cosmetic treatments are expensive, and particularly penny wise and pound foolish when a larger and more thoughtful investment can create the potential for developing a new set of social values about work which will continue to benefit all concerned.

References

Beckhard, R. *Organization Development: Strategies and Models.* (Reading, Mass.: Addison-Wesley, 1969).

Bennis, W. *Organization Development: Its Nature, Origins, and Prospects.* (Reading, Mass.: Addison-Wesley, 1969).

Cummings, T., & Srivastva, S. *The Management of Work.* (Kent, Ohio: Kent State University, 1977).

Emery, F., & Trist, E. "Analytical Model for Sociotechnical Systems." In W. Pasmore and J. Sherwood (eds.) *Sociotechnical Systems: A Sourcebook.* (San Diego: University Associates, 1978).

French, W., & Bell, C. *Organization Development.* (Englewood Cliffs, New Jersey: Prentice-Hall, 1973).

Friedlander, F., & Brown, L.D. "Organization Development." *Annual Review of Psychology,* 1974.

Likert, R. *New Patterns of Management.* (New York: McGraw-Hill, 1961).

Maccoby, M. "Changing Work, The Bolivar Project." In *Working Papers for a New Society* vol. 5, no. 3 (Summer 1975).

McGregor, D. *The Human Side of Enterprise.* (New York: McGraw-Hill, 1960).

Miles, R. "Human Relations or Human Resources?" *Harvard Business Review.* (July–August 1965).

Pasmore, W., & King, D. "Understanding Organizational Change: A Comparative Study of Multifaceted Interventions." *Journal of Applied Behavioral Science* (1978).

Pasmore, W.; Francis, C.; Shani, R.; & Haldeman, J. Sociotechnical Systems: A Review and Appraisal. Cleveland, Ohio: Case Western Reserve University, 1981. Unpublished.

Srivastva, S.; Cummings, T.; Salipante, P.; Notz, W.; & Bigelow, T. *Job Satisfaction and Productivity.* Cleveland, Ohio: Case Western Reserve University, 1974.

Walton, R. "Work Innovations at Topeka After Six Years." *Journal of Applied Behavioral Science,* 13, 1977, pp. 422–33.

19 Involving Employees in Productivity and QWL Improvements: What OD Can Learn From the Manager's Perspective

Todd D. Jick
Ronald N. Ashkenas

ABSTRACT

This article focuses on how OD practitioners can help managers institute employee involvement processes more effectively in order to improve quality of work life and productivity. Several cases are used to identify some of the common pitfalls which cause employee involvement strategies to miss their mark, such as the expectation of dramatic changes, the use of standardized "packages," the creation of confusing new structures, and the absence of productivity goals.

    Successful interventions are then described as a basis for proposed guidelines, based on the manager's perspective, that may increase managers' chances of success. The authors argue that, among other things, OD professionals should help managers integrate the program into existing structures, processes and preoccupations, and to create early bottom-line results. By achieving some early modest success with those managers and supervisors who are most ready to involve their people more fully, an expanding pattern of involvement can be developed.

AUTHOR BACKGROUND

Todd D. Jick is associate professor of organizational behavior and industrial relations at York University in the Faculty of Administrative Studies. In addition, as a part-time associate of Robert H. Schaffer & Associates, he has worked with a number of large companies in the introduction of employee involvement programs and processes.

Ronald N. Ashkenas is a partner in the management consulting firm, Robert H. Shaffer & Associates (Stamford, Connecticut, and Montreal, Canada). He received his doctorate in organizational behavior from Case Western University. His articles on organizational change and improvement and QWL have appeared in the *Harvard Business Review* and other management journals.

I would like to make this department a model of employee participation for the plant.

–A manufacturing manager

I've read about quality circles and some of the other things the Japanese are doing—and I think we can make them work here.

–A plant superintendent

I think it's time we got the hourly people's ideas about how to run this area.

–A bank operations manager

Comments such as those above have become almost commonplace for managers in many organizations today. In the past few years there has been an unprecedented explosion of popular, practitioner, and academic interest in new work designs, quality circles, and other interventions that aim, in broadest terms, toward involving both hourly and salaried workers in improving productivity and the quality of work life (for example, Walton 1979, Glaser 1980, and Robin 1981). Dozens of productivity and quality of work life centers have sprung up around the country; the International Association of Quality Circles has thousands of members; leading business journals, including the ASTD journal, have carried cover stories on the subject; and a recent Toronto conference on QWL in the 1980s drew over 1500 managers, labor leaders, practitioners, and academics from around the world. What was once a series of largely academic experiments, conducted in relative obscurity in places like Tarrytown, and Topeka, has become a popular movement.

Perhaps the most important and exciting consequence of this phenomenon is that middle managers and first-line supervisors are now attempting to introduce employee investment mechanisms into their own organizations—often at their own initiative. Their interest stems from multiple concerns; for example, their inability to achieve better bottom-line results in the face of stiff new competition, their awareness of deteriorating work place relationships, and their frustration with daily hassles of supervising dissatisfied employees.

Unfortunately, most managers with these concerns do not have the benefit of the generous resources and long-term expert help of the earlier pioneering efforts in employee involvement. Nor are they protected from the day-to-day demands for continued output. Moreover, while many of the well-known experiments have taken place in green-field sites (Lawler 1978), most managers work in ongoing enterprises that face formidable existing constraints such as wage scales, plant design, local customs, and territorial parochialism. (Jick 1981) As a result, despite some impressive successes in grass-roots employee involvement efforts, there has also been much floundering, many false starts, and all too many dashed expectations (Walton 1975; 1979).

It is clear, however, on the basis of considerable research, that under certain conditions employee involvement is more likely to be successful than under others. Nadler, Hanlon, and Lawler (1980) found that three factors were most critical in shaping the success of a QWL project: the competence of the labor-management committee, a supportive organizational climate, and the presence of a skilled external consultant. Guest (1979) listed twelve principles of an effective project, including the prescribed roles of union and management, the need for flexibility in the project design, and the importance of participation by middle and first-line supervisors. Others have developed similar lists (Glaser 1980; Walton 1977, 1979; Cummings, Malloy, & Glen 1975). Yet in reviewing these, few extensively address the role of middle and lower managers (with the exception of Walton and Schlesinger 1979, and Westley 1981) and few assume that managers are initially motivated to experiment. More importantly, it is rare for all of these preconditions to exist in any one site. Thus, if managers are encouraged to wait for these conditions to occur before experimenting, then few innovations will actually take place.

Our paper will focus on how motivated managers, with minimal assistance from OD professionals, can effectively institute employee involvement processes—no matter the existing conditions—and have a good chance to experience, quickly, some modest and reinforcing success. Using several cases we observed in a consulting capacity, we will describe some of the pitfalls that can occur in the headlong rush toward involving employees. And we will suggest some guidelines by which OD practitioners can help managers avoid these pitfalls based upon interventions in two of the cases described.

CASE OBSERVATIONS: SOME COMMON PITFALLS IN EMPLOYEE INVOLVEMENT

Following are three cases (presented pseudonymously) observed by the authors in which employee involvement failed to achieve the desired results. These cases exemplify some of the common pitfalls that can ensnare well-meaning managers who genuinely want to create a new spirit of collaboration and achievement with their work force.

Case 1: File Fast Office Products

In the late 1960s and early 1970s, the File Fast Office Products Company grew into a multi-billion dollar corporation, largely on the success of several innovative products. After this period of rapid growth, it developed numerous staff and administrative structures to control the sprawling organization. By the late 1970s, new competitors had aggressively entered the field, and File Fast needed to respond. But the excessive staff and administrative structure was choking off productivity. Management realized that a fresh approach was needed. After trying several programs, including some new worker incentives, managers in a production division of File Fast implemented an ambitious QWL program. Based on the approach of a consultant in this field, the program created an intricate committee structure throughout the division. Representatives from every management and worker level, as well as the union, were represented. There was extensive training of facilitators for the small worker/supervision teams. After two years, at considerable cost—both in hard dollars and in lost time—there was good participation, but minimal bottom-line results.

Case 2: RAMCO Machine Shop

In 1978, RAMCO, a small one-hundred-person machine shop, was acquired by a large corporation. A major expansion—leading to a doubling of the facility—began immediately. The corporate manager responsible for this facility realized that the expansion could disrupt the existing work force—as could the introduction of a new management team. In order to minimize the disruptions, he introduced a QWL program into RAMCO's shop. He based his program on prior reading and consultation with his human resources staff. He hoped that this experiment would provide a model for how other shops in the corporation could be managed.

The initial moves at RAMCO were as follows: Time clocks were removed and workers were put on salary. Then a new "people-oriented" plant manager was brought in to work with the existing, traditional managers and foremen. He conducted meetings with RAMCO's employees and told them that RAMCO was going to become "the best place to work in the city."

After six months, the corporate manager was dismayed to learn that the QWL program was creating employee dissatisfaction instead of good will. The workers who were now on salary felt obligated to come to work—even if they wanted to take off. The traditional foremen didn't seem to have any rational way of saying whether people should be paid for days off or not. So their decisions were often arbitrary. And the hiring of new people for RAMCO's expansion was creating disparities in the salary structure.

Case 3: TUF-RUB Molded Rubber Products

In 1978, TUF-RUB, a medium-sized plant that manufactured molded rubber products, experienced a period of increased demand. But as volume increased, quality went down. Having heard about quality circles, management decided that a circle program might be the answer. With the approval of the union, employees throughout the plant were asked to volunteer. Many of them responded and a number of circles were started. Unfortunately, many ideas that the circle members recommended involved changes that people who had not volunteered for the circles were asked to implement. Since they did not understand them, they usually did not occur. In addition, despite the participative mode of TUF-RUB's circles, foremen were still supervising their own lines in much the same way as before. The result was that after six months of quality circles there was little change in quality.

What happened in these cases, as well as in dozens of other disappointments that we have seen or read about?* Our analysis suggests that well-meaning managers fell into five common traps:

The "program" was seen as a magic variable.   In almost all of the "failure" cases we have seen, managers expect, perhaps unconsciously, that by introducing an involvement program, results, satisfaction, and the whole organizational culture will exhibit dramatic shifts. Yet rarely, if ever, will one variable cause that kind of change. More modest expectations are called for, as well as the realization that other managerial actions may be needed at the same time. For example, in Case 2, a variety of management action steps were needed to manage the rapid expansion of the work force (for example, a restructuring of wage scales, creation of new job classifications, clarification of seniority rules, and so on). Over-reliance on the QWL program was one factor that caused management to neglect some of these.

The involvement programs were standardized or mechanized.   The second pitfall that often occurs is standardization, what Walton (1979) calls the promotion of particular techniques. In all three of the cases cited above, programs and methods (such as QWL committees, the all-salaried work force, and quality circles) were taken from other situations and applied without much tailoring. This seems a pervasive problem. As the market for employee involvement programs increasingly outstrips the capacity of knowledgeable and experienced professionals to provide service, newly minted consultants have filled the gap with standardized, mechanized programs. However, since each organization is unique and each situation is different and changing, these packaged approaches with standard blueprints and manuals rarely work uniformly well in all situations (Mills 1978).

Involvement programs superceded, substituted for, or confused existing management structures and processes.   A third common pitfall is that employee involvement programs often are overlaid on existing management structures and processes rather than integrated with them (e.g., Kanter & Stein 1980). Consequently, existing apart from the normal way the organization is managed, they often create confusion or inefficiency.

This pitfall was most clearly demonstrated in Case 1. In that organization, existing bureaucratic structures (such as approval forms, resource committees,

*Unfortunately, similar unsuccessful cases from which one could draw important learnings are rarely reported. Nor has there been enough written about why successful experiences often "don't take" in other parts of the organization (Walton 1975; Berg, Freedman, & Freeman 1978; Jick 1981). Such learnings in the general field of organizational change and development can be found in a thoughtful collection edited by Mirvis and Berg (1978).

TABLE 19.1   Common Pitfalls in Employee Involvement Programs and How to Avoid Them

Pitfalls	Guidelines for Overcoming the Pitfalls
1. "Program" seen as a variable	Create early, modest success
2. Standardized or mechanized approach	Tailor and expand the process, flexibly
3. Program overlaid on existing management structures and processes	Integrate involvement processes into existing management practices
4. Emphasis on reformation of managers	Build on readiness—not resistance
5. Program exclusively focused on "people-orientation"	Start with managers' bottom-line preoccupations

and staff studies) were already making it difficult for managers to take effective action. In fact, this was a precipitating factor that caused management to launch a productivity improvement effort. Yet the program itself spawned a completely separate, parallel organization, which left many managers even more bewildered and frustrated about how to "make something happen."

The emphasis was on reformation of middle managers and first-line supervisors versus starting with their readiness.   The fourth common pitfall that plagues many involvement efforts is the tendency to reform middle managers and supervisors. In all three of the cases cited here, top management and/or consultants began by telling the working level of management that they had to change their traditional ways of dealing with people and achieving performance results—without getting their views, or involving them in planning. They did what Kanter and Stein (1980) describe as a model of how-not-to-do-it: "the top of the organization tells the middle [what] to do for the bottom." Unfortunately, such an approach is all too common, usually manifest by a great deal of early training and help from outside "experts." In this way, right from the beginning working managers are made to feel as though they are inadequate and have to "become better," rather than being helped to feel that they are successful and can build upon their success.

The involvement program had too much of a human resources focus versus a balance between human resources and productivity.   The final pitfall illustrated in these cases is that involvement programs often are seen as being people-oriented alone instead of having the dual goal of increasing productivity *and* changing the atmosphere and climate of the organization. Walton (1979) observed that one reason several innovative work systems were ineffective was that management was too heavily influenced by QWL considerations at the beginning. For example, in Case 2 a new manager was brought in primarily because he was "people-oriented"—quite apart from his ability to take an organization in transition and manage it in a way that achieved improved results. Similarly, in Case 3 the emphasis was on participation in quality circles versus the demand for improved quality results *through* participation in the circles.

SUMMARY

The tendency to fall into these five traps, or pitfalls, is understandable. It is part of our national character to seek a quick fix to complicated problems (Trap 1). Today managers are reaching for the employee-involvement fix. In response, overburdened and under-experienced human resources consultants and staff are giving them increasingly standardized programs (Trap 2). Often these programs are "dropped" into organizations—regardless of whether the working managers can absorb them, and without sufficiently helping these managers to plan and control them. Consequently, too often the programs are not integrated with ongoing management processes (Trap 3). At the same time, these programs create a great deal of threat and anxiety among middle and lower managers who are being asked to fundamentally change the way they work (Trap 4). The compounded result is that in many cases much of the involvement effort goes toward human relations activity, and the productivity focus is lost in the shuffle (Trap 5).

But improvements in QWL and productivity through employee involvement strategies need not be doomed to faddism. It would be a tragedy to lose the opportunity that the enthusiasm and interest of many managers represent. Thus how can OD professionals help managers avoid the pitfalls identified above? How can employee involvement efforts be designed in a more realistic, achievable way?

Guidelines for Success: From Means Back to Ends

Naturally, there is no magic answer to the questions posed above. Yet it is possible for OD practitioners to facilitate managers' success. To do so, there is a need to go back to the basic principle of employee involvement—that workers have much to contribute and can enrich themselves and the organization if encouraged to do so. Then this principle needs to be integrated into the existing readiness, reality, skills, capacity, preoccupations, and management processes of organizations. The key word here is *integrate*. "Involvement" cannot be overlaid on already existing complex organizations. It must be integrated into the ongoing here-and-now of the organization, step by step. In such a way, employees can begin to have greater influence. But, they have a slightly different influence in every situation. Two illustrations of how this occurred in the cases cited earlier may be helpful here:

What happened in Case 2, the RAMCO machine shop.   While on the one hand management and supervisors were feeling confusion and pressure about quality of work life, on the other hand they were also being pressured to hire a new work force for an expanded operation. And, since skilled machine tool workers are at a premium, they were having difficulty. This preoccupation with hiring provided a low-risk opportunity to introduce the management team to quality of work life. Essentially, they were asked the question How can the work force be helpful in hiring other employees? The eventual answer was a modest one: The managers agreed to circulate to the work force the draft of a recruitment advertisement that was to appear in local newspapers. Much to the managers' surprise, employees who were asked had very good suggestions about how to improve the advertisement—and make it more appealing to people who lived in the community. As a result, the ad was modified, and began to show some different results.

From this modest beginning, a series of discrete projects was organized, each one based on a bottom-line preoccupation of management, with the aim of finding ways that the work force could help management accomplish a needed bottom-line goal. Over the course of six to eight months, employees contributed to reducing an inspection backlog, reorganizing steel inventory, setting standards for attendance, screening applicants, orienting new employees, and other projects. Eventually employee-management committees were established to work on matters of safety, recreation, and training on the many new machines that were coming into the plant. After a year, a new atmosphere had been created. And the plant even began to show a profit—despite original projections that it would take at least two years to get into the black.

What happened in Case 3, TUF-RUB Rubber Products. In this case, six months of quality circles had not produced any different results. But management firmly believed that better results were possible—if the quality circle program could be tailored to the unique needs of their organization. As a result, they decided to try an experiment. They chose one line where there was a particular quality problem. They asked everyone that worked on that line, including the foremen, to be part of a unique quality circle. The foremen were given some help as how to be the leaders of that circle. Then the circle focused on one kind of defect in that line. The people made all sorts of suggestions, and the foremen put those suggestions together into a written work plan. Within a month results had been achieved. That line then began to work on other kinds of defects. Over the course of six months this process was expanded to other lines. Many thousands of dollars in quality savings were achieved—and employees were proud that they had contributed.

Guidelines to Avoid Common Pitfalls

What can OD learn from cases like these and other success stories such as those in Figure 19.1? It seems that there are a number of implementation principles or guidelines that may be useful in avoiding the pitfalls—and actualizing the promise—of employee involvement. They include starting with managers' bottom-line preoccupations, building on readiness, creating early success, building involvement processes into existing management structures, and flexibility.

Start with managers' bottom-line preoccupations. The starting point for the cases described above was the managers' bottom-line preoccupations. In the first case it was a preoccupation with hiring. In the second, it was a preoccupation with quality. The question that was asked of these managers was not

---

FIGURE 19.1 Involving Employees and Supervisors: Illustrative Cases of a Bottom-line Approach

---

1. *Insurance claims processing: error reduction and productivity improvement.* The manager of a medical insurance claims processing department increased productivity 30% within six months and reduced error rates and processing time. This was accomplished by implementing employee ideas for changing work flow, for having examiners check their own work, and for tracking work group performance. Also, by delegating responsibility for implementing ideas, supervisors had more free time for planning and control purposes.

2. *Computer manufacturer billing department: productivity improvement.* A computer manufacturer plagued by cash shortages set out to speed the billing process. OD consultants helped billing department supervisor/employee teams to change a few critical procedures, to develop better control measures, and to set sharp priorities. After one month, the teams reduced the backlog by 42% and increased productivity by 25%. Overtime and turnover decreased as well.

3. *Chemical plant maintenance: service and productivity improvement.* Maintenance workers in a chemical plant offered dozens of ideas to improve service and reduce the costs of maintaining a major, complex production unit. OD consultants helped their managers translate those ideas into action with the help of their workers. Waste was reduced. On-time performance was upgraded. In the first six months, over $300,000 was saved, with greater savings projected beyond.

4. *Chemical plant operations: productivity improvement.* Despite many efforts to improve productivity, one production department of a large chemical plant remained dissatisfied with its performance. Meetings were held with hourly workers in Operations, Maintenance, the Laboratory, and other appropriate groups to present a clear picture of the business challenge and to solicit ideas for improvement. Employees then collaborated with supervisors to create work plans and implement projects. Within four months, onstream time rose from 75% to 92%. Onstream efficiency rose from 97% to 106%. Production rose from 90% of capacity to 108% of capacity. The Packaging Department produced 125% of their goal. And lab turnaround time consistently met the target of three hours.

5. *Hospital emergency room: patient service and quality of work life improvement.* The emergency room at a major urban hospital was plagued by long delays, patient complaints, and friction between nursing and medical staff. An OD consultant helped to create a steering team comprised of physicians and nurses, and to develop a series of conferences with all doctors, nurses, and support personnel, in order to generate ideas for improving service and morale. Implementation of these ideas resulted in reduced waiting time; the virtual elimination of written patient complaints; an ongoing MD/RN Steering Group that collaborates on further improvements, including the design of new facilities; and an increased nursing role in patient assessment.

6. *Textile manufacturer: sales productivity improvement.* In response to a decline in sales, lack of motivation of sales people, and considerable uncertainty about the business future of the company, consultants helped the sales manager of a textile manufacturer to identify measures for evaluating salesmen and to involve them in training efforts to upgrade their sales skills. The sales manager set goals for the sales people and then split them into groups of 3 or 4 individuals. These groups met once every two weeks to talk about sales approaches and different ways of meeting their individual goals. Each salesman improved at least 15% on performance measures such as overall sales, dollars per call, and the ratio of calls to sales "hits."

Authors' Note: These cases have been excerpted from the RHS&A files with the assistance of Charles S. Baum.

"how do we get the quality of work life program implemented," but "how do we get the better bottom-line results that you are seeking through the help and participation of your employees?" Thus, the focus was kept on the results that the working level of management needed to achieve. The involvement program was not presented as an additional distraction that would prevent them from giving full attention to achieving these results. Rather, it was presented as a means that they might use to achieve the results.

Since quality circles, quality of work life, and employee involvement are often regarded as human resource development activities, this emphasis on bottom-line results may sound foreign. In fact, many proponents of human resource development activities of this sort have argued that too strong an emphasis on bottom-line results can be detrimental to achieving attitudinal and motivational changes. Why then the focus on results?

The answer is that the working level of management—which has ultimate responsibility for the successful implementation of change efforts—is always feeling the pressure to produce bottom-line results. In the long run, their success is not judged by the number of quality circles that they have going. Rather, success is judged by the degree to which their quality has improved. In fact, Walton and Schlesinger (1979) found that supervisor participation can be increased by emphasizing the accomplishment of key tasks *through* the vehicle of employee involvement.

This is not to say that the attitudinal, motivational, and work climate results are not important. Indeed they are. However, in the absence of bottom-line results, the subjective or soft results are hard to sell. More importantly, the soft results will often be cancelled out if bottom-line results are not produced because, after a period of time with no bottom-line results, managers are subjected to pressures that often force them to revert to more traditional authoritarian patterns. And thus the gains that have been won fade away.

In addition, there is increasing evidence that hourly employees themselves want to see bottom-line results from their efforts. A recent study by researchers at the University of Southern California found that the greatest frustration of quality circle participants was their inability to see bottom-line results quickly. They, too, want to experience tangible, measurable success.

Build on readiness—not resistance. In both of the cases described above, involvement principles were implemented through the path of least resistance, rather than trying to force people to change.

For example, in the machine shop there was little initial readiness to involve hourly people in any of the expansion planning. Foremen especially saw it as an abrogation of their authority. Passing around a draft advertisement to employees was a long way from a QWL effort. But it was all that management was ready to do at that point. In the molded rubber products plant not all the foremen were willing to begin working in a new, more collaborative way. One of the reasons why one line was chosen over others was that the foremen there were more ready. So management decided to start with those foremen rather than force all the foremen to work differently.

Create early success. With the initial focus on modest, bottom-line products—based on readiness—it was possible in these cases to produce a short-term success. Thus, unlike many typical involvement efforts, no one was asked to wait for the big long-term payoff or to accept, on faith, that "involvement" was worthwhile. Rather, managers were asked to try a very modest, nonthreatening innovation and see if it worked. And as soon as they saw that it paid off, it gave them more confidence to take the next steps.

The key here is early success. For involvement efforts to really become a fundamental part of an organization's culture, middle managers and supervisors need a positive experience. They need to know, with the confidence born of personal success, that involving their people will actually help them achieve their bottom-line goals—and does not have to be difficult, demeaning of their authority, or uncomfortable. They need to know that involvement can be easy—and that it can be managed at a pace that they set. But this kind of experience must come quickly, for initial impressions—especially if they are negative—will set the tone for the future. Kanter and Stein (1981) found, for example, that early successes of individual managers served as invaluable building blocks and role models for others to follow. Schaffer (1981) also reported that short-term success projects at Bell Canada and Atlas Steels gave managers the confidence to sustain major improvement efforts.

Build involvement processes into existing management structures and processes. An additional learning from these cases is that at least initially, involvement processes need to be adapted into existing management structures, processes and lines of authority—rather than vice versa. There are a number of reasons for this. First, the creation of new management structures adds one more level of complexity and confusion to an involvement effort. For example, if a foreman needs to take an employee-generated improvement idea through a series of steering committees in order to get approvals, rather than just take it to his or her boss, he or she may be less inclined to follow through. Second, creating new or modified management structure takes time. Thus, after six months of an involvement effort, the only results might be a network of new committees.

Finally, and perhaps most importantly, the creation of parallel involvement structures gives working managers the message, perhaps unintentionally, that employee involvement is not their responsibility—that it is being managed by "those committees," or staff groups, and so on. For example, the initial quality circle experiences at Tuf-Rub were disappointing partially because the foremen let the "facilitators" take the lead. Only later, when the foremen themselves took charge of getting improvement ideas from their people—and getting results from them—did the character of the situation begin to change.

Recent experience in the Bell system lends further support for building employee involvement into the management process. As described by Kanter and Stein (1980), QWL programs at Bell are part of standard operating procedures.

Expand the process as you go along—flexibly. In all of the successful cases we have seen, there was no prearranged plan as to how the involvement effort was going to look eventually. Based on each small success, another slightly more ambitious success was constructed. The readiness of the people who were involved and the urgency of the various bottom-line goals were the guides—not a standard theory or model of how things ought to work. This principle is well supported by observations of other cases by Walton (1979), Guest (1979), and Mills (1978). However, while often preached, this message is not always practiced. As Marcus (1983) notes:

> In spite of explicit statements by socio-technical systems proponents that autonomous work groups are not appropriate to all settings . . . it is not clear that a consultant could follow the recommended . . . methodology and arrive at anything *other* than . . . autonomous work groups.

CONCLUSION

We have identified some factors which cause employee involvement strategies to miss their mark. Using several cases as illustrations, we have developed some pragmatic guidelines—based on managers' common preoccupations, capacities, and readiness—that OD practitioners can apply to heighten chances for success. These guidelines, moreover, seem consistent with parallel learnings from employee involvement efforts reported in the literature.

There is no doubt that employee involvement is an essential ingredient in the success of QWL and productivity improvement projects. But it is an ingredient (among many other managerial tools) that must be managed effectively. Perhaps the critical question, as identified by Robin (1981), is whether involvement will be sought as a goal in and of itself *or* as a means of improving workers' satisfaction and productivity. This paper has demonstrated that the latter approach is most effective for OD practitioners who are actively interested in helping managers achieve a better motivated, well-utilized work force.

References

Berg, I., M. Freedman, & M. Freeman, *Management Work Reform: A Limited Engagement,* New York: The Free Press, 1978.

Cummings, T.G., E. Malloy, & R. Glen, "Intervention Strategies for Improving Productivity and the Quality of Work Life," *Organizational Dynamics,* 4, 1, 1975, 52–68.

Glaser, E., "Productivity Gains Through Worklife Improvement," *Personnel* (January–February 1980): 71–77.

Guest, R., "Quality of Working Life—Learning from Tarrytown," *Harvard Business Review* (July–August 1979): 76–87.

Jick, T., "Managers and Quality of Worklife: A Clash of Values?" in *Management Under Different Value Systems,* G. Dlugos and K. Weirmair (eds.), New York: Gruyter Publisher, 1981, 359–427.

Kanter, R. and B. Stein, "The Egalitarian Revolution," *Bell Telephone Magazine,* 1981, vol. 59, no. 4, 14–19.

Lawler, E., "The New Plant Revolution," *Organizational Dynamics* (Winter 1978).

Marcus, L. "Socio-Technical Systems: Concepts and Applications" in *Scientists, Engineers and Organizations,* T. Connolly (ed.), Monterey, California: Brooks/ Cole, 1983.

Mills, T., "What Is Quality of Working Life?" Address to International Center for Management Research and Study, Montreal, 1978.

Mirvis, P., & D. Berg, *Failures in Organizational Development,* New York: John Wiley, 1978.

Nadler, D., M. Hanlon & E. Lawler, "Factors Influencing the Success of Labor-Management Quality of Work Life Projects," *Journal of Occupational Behavior,* vol. 1, 1980.

Robin, J., "Concepts and Programs for Change," *Labour Canada* (February 1981): 21.

Schaffer, R., "Make Success the Building Block," *Management Review* (August 1981), vol. 70, no. 8.

Walton, R., "The Diffusion of New Work Structures: Explaining Why Success Didn't Take," *Organizational Dynamics* (Winter 1975): 3–22.

Walton, R., "Successful Strategies for Diffusing Work Innovations," *Journal of Contemporary Business* (Spring 1977): 1–22.

Walton, R., "Work Innovations in the United States," *Harvard Business Review* (July–August 1979): 88–98.

Walton, R., & L. Schlesinger, "Do Supervisors Thrive in Participation Work Systems," *Organizational Dynamics* (Winter 1979): 25–38.

Westley, W., "QWL: The Role of the Supervisor," *Labour Canada* (February 1981).

20 An Organizational Development Approach to the Planning and Implementation of New Technology

Newton Margulies
Lora Colflesh

ABSTRACT

This paper is an illustration of how two basic models, the socio-technical systems model and the life-cycle planning model, can be used to guide and direct the implementation of technological change. The contribution of this approach to the practical formulation of change strategies is that it supplements existing change theory, which focuses much more on processes of change rather than on the implementation of substantive change. Furthermore, the project described herein is an example of the prevalent and pressing need to develop specific methods to perform quality analysis of the technical, human, and managerial components of an organizational system. Because there is a lack of such methods, the field of organizational development still comprises abstract strategies that do not fully meet the requirements of pragmatic and expedient organizational needs or of techniques that are distinct from any model of change.

The application of this approach, to a significant degree, still is consonant with basic principles of implementing change. That is, the importance of ongoing communication, involvement, and careful planning cannot be overemphasized. Regardless of the level of complexity, the speed, or the breadth of the change, recognizing the reality of human resistance and the management responsibility for effectively coping with this resistance is paramount.

AUTHOR BACKGROUND

Newton Margulies, Ph.D., is currently professor of organizational behavior in the Graduate School of Administration, University of California, Irvine. He received a B.S. in engineering from Brooklyn Polytechnic Institute, a M.S. in industrial management from MIT, and a Ph.D. in behavioral science from UCLA. He has been on the faculty of the Division of Organizational Sciences, Case Institute of Technology, and in the Department of Management, University of Miami. Dr. Margulies has had an opportunity to consult in the area of organizational development and team building with a variety of organizations including TRW Systems Group, Department of Water Resources—State of California, Northrop Corporation, and the National Emergency Medical System. He has written and lectured extensively in the field of organizational behavior and is coauthor of *Organizational Development: Values, Processes, and Technology, Organizational Change: Techniques and Applications, Conceptual Foundations of Organizational Development, Organizational Development for Health Care Organizations,* and *Managing Organizational Change and Development.*

Lora Colflesh is currently manager, human resources for TRW's Energy Products Group. In this position she is responsible for the full range of human resources activities including employment, compensation, benefits, and employee and organizational development. Prior to her position with TRW, Ms. Colflesh was employed by Northrop Corporation. She began her tenure there as Corporate Coordinator of Management Development and Training. She was subsequently promoted to Program Manager Human Factors where she was responsible for a wide range of technology transfer projects. Her major areas of emphasis in these projects included organizational development, strategic implementation planning (management and manufacturing computer systems) and work team development. Ms. Colflesh completed a B.A. in English/psychology in 1976 and a M.S. in organizational development in 1982.

This paper was adapted from an article that appeared in the *Training and Development Journal,* vol. 36, (December 1982): 6–30.

Continued concerns over decreasing productivity growth in industry has encouraged, out of necessity, interest in developing and implementing sophisticated technology in the manufacturing sector.

Reports (e.g., *Business Week,* August 3, 1981; *Special Report: Automation*) and predictions indicate that the current growth rate of productivity may have already reached a level of significant concern. The balance-of-trade position has steadily declined since 1971 as high-technology products, once a major export of this country, have become a major import from foreign countries. Those competitors, including Japan and West Germany, are moving ahead of the United States by making maximum use of new manufacturing technology. A 1976 report from the U.S. Comptroller General (ICAM Program Prospectus, 1979) indicted U.S. industry for ignoring a situation that contributes to productivity deterioration. What may have been ignored in 1976 is a key concern for industry today. A major emphasis on increasing productivity is taking the form of developing and implementing computer technology formats, to be used in almost every stage of the manufacturing process.

Computer-aided design and manufacturing (CAD/CAM) is causing sweeping and radical changes in many facets of organizational life. Those changes often include modifications of the physical plant, automation of functions in the design and production processes, restructuring of the organization, development of new styles of management, and creation of new and different jobs.

Given these very real impacts on the organization, it is clear that careful planning and analysis must take place before implementing new technology. Planning considerations must include the design of the technology itself as well as the modification of the existing human system. The approach presented in this article uses the Sociotechnical Systems concept (Trist & Bamforth 1951; Rice 1958) and a generic systems planning model as a guiding perspective in the implementation of any new technology. The strength of this approach is its ability to integrate changes in people and technology during periods of rapid technological change. Designing and implementing new technology, while simultaneously considering the human component, makes the sociotechnical approach an effective and practical management technique, where major technological change is an issue as illustrated in the following information and case study.

BACKGROUND

Over the past three years, the Integrated Computer-Aided Manufacturing (ICAM) Research and Development team of a large aerospace organization has been designing cam systems and studying the impact of technological transitions, including impacts on the human system. A thorough review of existing research,* entitled *Review of Empirical and Conceptual Literature on Implementation of Computer Technology,* confirmed the team's early experience with system design and implementation, which indicated that rapid technological change can best be accomplished with careful and systematic implementation planning. The empirical literature, while not conclusive by any means, indicates that careful planning

*This research review was supported by U.S. Air Force IMC-MM System Design Contract (F336615-78-5088, August 1980).

for human system modifications during the transitional phases of a technological change is more likely to result in successful implementation of sophisticated computer-aided manufacturing systems.

These conclusions tend to support the approach to techological change that is described as a sociotechnical systems approach. The potency and strength of the sociotechnical systems concept lies in its ability to proceed with organizational change in both a planned and experimental manner. As a guiding model, it is comprehensive, manageable, and pragmatic for introducing technological transitions in the course of achieving organizational goals.

THE SOCIOTECHNICAL SYSTEMS CONCEPT

The concept of sociotechnical systems emerged from studies and consulting work by the Tavistock Institute in England.

> The essence of the emerging interventions [was] to try to develop a better fit between the technology, structure, and social interaction of the workplace so as to enhance desired organizational outcomes. (French, Bell, & Zawacki 1978)

Generally, the Tavistock work and later studies by E. Thorsrud, S. Myers, T. Mills, and others (French, Bell, Zawacki 1978) used the sociotechnical concept as a basis for organization development projects in autonomous work group design, job enrichment, and job enlargement. Many of these early studies involved social changes in work arrangements more so than changes in technology; changes in the technological aspects of sociotechnical organizations were fewer and had less profound results, perhaps because changes to some existing factories and machines were too costly and actually unnecessary for task completion (Katz & Kahn 1978). Realizing the expense and difficulty of modifying existing plants, particularly those with large machinery, the sociotechnical approach was applied to the design of new plants. The best known of these new plant designs, considering both technology and psychosocial aspects of the organizations, are the Saab-Scania and Volvo plants in Sweden.

Sociotechnical systems simply refers to the notion that organizations are more than task systems, or structural entities, or human systems. They are, in fact, a composite of task (technical) subsystem factors, human processes, and management subsystems.

To further elaborate, the sociotechnical system view of organizations may be conceived of as comprising three interrelated subsystems: (1) technological subsystem, (2) human subsystem, and (3) management subsystem. These subsystems are briefly defined in the following way:

- *Technological Subsystem*—includes the technology itself, work flow, information flow, job roles, job relationships, task configurations, relationships, policies, procedures, and job feedback.
- *Human Subsystem*—includes organization climate, level of motivation, communication, level of commitment, participation, cooperation, satisfaction with work environment, willingness to accept change, work group

factors, human resources development, and satisfaction with compensation, company policies, and procedures.

■ *Management Subsystem*—includes management technologies and structure used to control and direct technology and people.

Figure 20.1 shows the interface among the subgroups (Margulies & Raia 1978).

Management's role and responsibility, and perhaps it most difficult task, is to dynamically manage the interface between the technological and human subsystems. This interface, when managed properly, provides the appropriate compatibility or fit between the two subsystems. Understanding both the technical and human subsystems through appropriate assessment is essential to managing this fit, even during times of static conditions. When a technological change is imminent, concern with the fit becomes imperative because of the high probability that changes create a "misfit" between the two systems. Traditionally, organizations have not balanced their concerns for technological and human subsystem change. The result has been misfit, which has the apparent consequences of lowered morale, decreased productivity, lower quality of work, increased conflict and even sabotage, waste, job stress and duplication of efforts. The final result for many organizations has been increased costs of technological implementation and, often, underutilization or failure of the new technology.

From case studies reported in the literature, emerging patterns suggested some reasons for the failure of new computer-aided systems which were being introduced into a variety of industries and organizations. Common themes were:

■ Poor and untimely communication about the new technology to the organization, and little or poor education about the system's use for the person required to interact with the system on a daily basis.
■ Low or nonexistent "user participation" in decisions about the system that affected them, particularly how the user's job role and duties would

---

FIGURE 20.1   Socio-Technical System Model

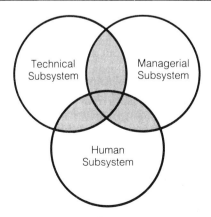

be affected, and lack of employee participation in the organization itself prior to the implementation of the new system.

- Natural resistance and uncertainty about changes in the *status quo*.
- A system designer's notion that people are flexible and adaptable to any new system, even one designed with the intent of minimizing human involvement and responsibility.
- Lack of clear commitment from senior management, and lack of clarity about senior management's position on the wisdom of implementing a particular system, that is, specifically how this system will improve our organization and justification of the overall investment.

In addition to these trends, our own studies seem to indicate that blue collar production employees were less resistant to technological change than were supervisors and managers. When managers perceived a change in the political/ power structure of their organization, their resistance increased, particularly if that shift meant a loss of control, information, or procedures to the system designers or computer department.

The sociotechnical systems perspective, then, provides a guiding model that is comprehensive, manageable, and pragmatic, for introducing technological transitions in the course of achieving organizational goals. The ability to design technological innovation, while at the same time maintaining an awareness of the human component, affords the sociotechnical systems approach an opportunity to be rooted in the science of organizational behavior, as well as in the pragmatism of practicing management.

THE SOCIOTECHNICAL SYSTEMS APPROACH

Some theories of organization emphasize the principle of "technological determinism." As such, these theories view the goal of improving the organization as the more efficient use of human resources. In this sense, change in technology may be needed to affect human performance in an enduring manner. Although the environment cannot be ignored, the sociotechnical systems perspective studies the relationship between the social and technical systems, considering the internal and external forces that act upon it.

Sociotechnical systems theory provides the guidance and direction for the diagnosis and implementation of required change, and takes into account the complex relationship between people, tasks, management, and technology. The theory has evolved a set of fairly reasonable and recognizable propositions which specify the following:

1. The design of an organization must fit its goals, and take into account the technology, the human system, and the processes of management.
2. Employees directly affected by organizational change must be actively consulted in the design and implementation of new task systems and new managerial structure.

3. Subsystems must be designed around specific recognizable tasks, and support systems (human factors) must be congruent with technological design.

4. Effective use of the new technology must include the development of a high quality of life.

Using Sociotechnical Systems Model

The sociotechnical systems model provides an approach for undertaking organizational diagnosis and change. In this sense, data about an organization's technology, structure, personnel, and management practices can be collected, organized, and utilized for the purpose of showing the current status of the organization, and as a basis for designing organizational change. Typically, the data/diagnostic process involves the following steps:

- General information in both the sociotechnical subsystems is collected and organized.
- Specific information about the technology and the processes of production is utilized to best understand the required changes that will occur in the technical system for the purpose of improving efficiency.
- Specific information about the human system and the quality of working life is generated to identify the needs to be met in light of proposed changes in technology.
- Information about the organizational environment is viewed to predict the necessary organizational changes required for efficiency in the future.

This diagnosis involves assessment of the current status of the organization, as well as clear and specific statements about required future changes for the organization. With this information and organizational diagnosis, a plan for introducing and implementing sociotechnical systems change can be developed. The plan involves clear statements of the purpose and direction of the change process and identification of specific events that will facilitate the implementation of change within the several subsystems of the sociotechnical system.

The use of the sociotechnical systems model has been applied in a variety of blue collar, production-oriented organizations. This approach has been relatively successful in helping to implement technological change, and in understanding the dynamics of the change process. It is clear that, with production-oriented blue collar populations, the role of the first several levels of supervision is significant in the success of this approach.

In our own efforts we began with a simplified version of the sociotechnical model (Figure 20.2). The managerial subsystem is initially held in abeyance with the initial thrust considering the technical and human subsystems. In a subsequent phase, the managerial subsystem must be considered as a significant target of change likely to be impacted by technological modifications. The approach described herein is sequential; first, efforts are designed to implement new technology while considering appropriate human subsystem modifications,

FIGURE 20.2   Simplified Version of Socio-Technical System Model

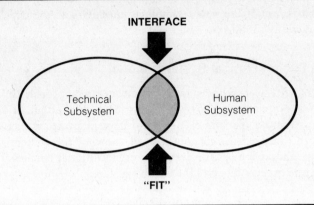

and second, appropriate changes are made in the managerial/organizational subsystem. Obviously, the process is an iterative one, in which "fine tuning" each of the subsystems is ongoing, to reach and maintain system compatibility or "fit."

DEVELOPING AN INTEGRATED PLANNING APPROACH

Our recent experience in working with several ICAM projects has helped develop a reasonable and logical approach to the implementation of new technology. It included an approach that combined the processes of technological change with assessment and modification of human support systems comprising the total sociotechnical system of the factory.

From our empirical review already cited, it seemed clear that the following factors contribute to "successful" implementation of computer technology:

- *Communication and Education*—In most cases where technological implementation was judged to be effective, special attention was paid to communicating with prospective users prior to the actual introduction of the technology. Education in new concepts, new job roles, and ways to manage the change was also provided.
- *User Participation*—Active participation by organizational members is important. Opportunities to interface with users concerning potential problems in the change implementation can be extremely useful. More important, creating a climate for accurate and ongoing participation during the change process results in valuable information about the usefulness and required improvements in the computer technology.
- *Dealing With Uncertainty and Resistance*—Supervisor skills in managing the change effort is a valuable ingredient in "successful" implementation.

Often, supervisors and managers are not trained to cope with natural resistance to new technology. Training in communication, dealing with uncertainty, understanding human behavior, evaluating performance standards, and so on, can enhance the possibility of success.

■ *Awareness of Organizational Dynamics*—Very often, technological change requires new organizational and management styles. For example, there are occasions when new technology may stimulate the need for new structure, new occupational roles, and new management approaches.

THE SYSTEMS DEVELOPMENT PLANNING MODEL

In addition to the sociotechnical systems model, we developed and utilized a generic systems development planning model, developed around the ICAM eight-step product life cycle (Figure 20.3). This serves to integrate system planning and implementation.

The generalized and generic steps to integrated transitional planning may be characterized as follows: initial scanning, analysis of the human system, development of the integrated plan, and proposals for change.

Initial Scanning

The objectives of this step are (1) to identify the major characteristics of the organization and the production system, and (2) to determine projected problems to be addressed by the technical experts in the design and formulation of the new technology which will have an impact on human factors. This will include understanding the following characteristics:

■ General geographical layout of the production system
■ Existing organizational structure and main groupings within it
■ Projected inputs of the system and output
■ The major transforming processes to take place within technical system
■ Other relevant technical information, e.g., the nature of raw material, the equipment and critical interfaces

Analysis of the Human System

The objective of this step is to identify the current major characteristics of the existing human system. This would include the nature of the work population, the set of complex task relationships required to complete tasks, the set of attitudes predominant to this group, and perceptions of the organizational climate. By structuring the analysis carefully, it is possible to draw sufficient and relevant information to begin the necessary design of the human system in light of proposed changes in the technology. The following substeps are the minimum necessary:

FIGURE 20.3   Systems Development Planning Model

LIFE CYCLE PLANNING
Technology and Human Factors

	Review			Review			Review		Review
Technology Program Life Cycle	1	2	3	4	5	6	7	8	
Sequence of Technological Change Events	Needs Analysis	Requirement Definition	Preliminary Design	Detail Design	Construct Verification and Test	Integration Validation and Test	Implementation and Use	Maintenance and Support	
H/F Program Life Cycle	1	2				3		4	
Sequence of Human Factor Change Process	Design Method for H/F Assessment Assess current human system	Develop model and plan required for new human system				Develop plan for human system development Implementation of human factors plan		Evaluation and Recommend Adjust to human system	
	Phase I Preliminary work to insure implementation of new technology	Phase II Predictive modeling of new technical system and appropriate new human system			Phase III Implementation and demonstration (use)			Phase IV Evaluation		

- Identification of workers' roles in the new production system and description of activities associated with these roles.
- Identification of the new skills required of supervisory personnel and specification of developmental plans.

Recognition and assessment of an organization's need for any new system or change is always the first step in a problem-solving process; for example, dry system development life cycle begins with needs analysis. This beginning point is also necessary in understanding human factors issues for any project. Some form of needs analysis is necessary, to both capture a picture of organization attitudes and climate at specific points in time, and also to identify problem areas which may be compounded by a new technological implementation.

The organization assessment focuses on (1) those areas most affected by a major change in the organization, (2) satisfaction with communication and information, (3) perceptions about job security, (4) career development opportunities, and (5) attitudes toward changes in their organization.

Development of the Integrated Plan

This step is designed to identify both the technical and human factor issues that must be considered in the total and successful implementation of the new technology; an integrated plan which considers both the modification of the technical system and the human system can then be developed. This step has two substeps: (1) development of a specific integrated plan which takes into account both technical and human system changes, and (2) development of generalized policy or practices to facilitate and support the new production system. These might include methods of promotion and compensation, information about career development and establishment of technical and supervisory long-term training programs.

Proposals for Change

The purpose of this step is to carefully consider the viability of the integrated plan, and to develop necessary action steps to ensure successful implementation. These might include the following steps: (1) the development of a coordinating plan to ensure the involvement and communication of specific steps in the plan to the relevant parties, and (2) establishment of a user group to help predict problems and issues in the implementation of the plan.

CASE ILLUSTRATION: USING THE CONCEPTUAL MODELS

The following description is a step-by-step illustration of how the sociotechnical systems and systems development planning models can guide technological implementation. A specific, detailed plan for implementation can be developed only after the careful analysis of survey data, information interviews, synthesis of literature research, and careful coordination with technological planning and development have been performed. We have developed a generic six-step implementation plan that provides the guidance for a specific plan. This six-step process follows closely the integrated systems development planning model (Figure 20.3). The process is represented in Figure 20.4.

Step 1: New Technical System Design

The first step for implementation planning represents the conceptualization and initial definition of requirements for a new technology. This specific case example was concerned with the development of a shop floor scheduling and control system. Once the initial concept and design have been created, manufacturing management must develop the commitment and resources for implementing such a system.

Step 2: New Human System Design

The design for the assessment of human factors included two major activities: (1) review of current empirical literature to learn more about the impact of technological change on a specific work group and possible models that may have been used for past implementations, and (2) developing a profile of the existing human system through an organization assessment survey, and interviews of the work group. Additionally, information was compiled from organization source including such data as turnover rates, grievances, absenteeism, and other similar dimensions.

The synthesis of all this information provides an empirical basis for developing the human systems profile as it exists prior to the change. When viewed in terms of forthcoming technological and structural changes in the organization, preliminary predictions and design for the "required" human system can be established. The intent is to fit the new human system to the requirements of the new technology and new structures.

Step 3: Human System Change Plan

Several iterations are usually necessary to understand what modifications in the human system are required for compatibility with the new technical changes. Discussions with working-level employees, managers, and supervisors are helpful in determining necessary changes. A thorough understanding of research findings will also assist in these determinations.

In this case, five major areas stood out. They were participation, education/ orientation, supervisory development, human resources information, and technical training. Clear indications for change in these areas was supported in both the literature review for this project, and the survey and interview assessments. Specific plans to begin to change the human system are developed in this step. This may include training, increased discussion with the work force about the change, providing of additional information about the organization itself, and

FIGURE 20.4 Integrated Planning and Implementation

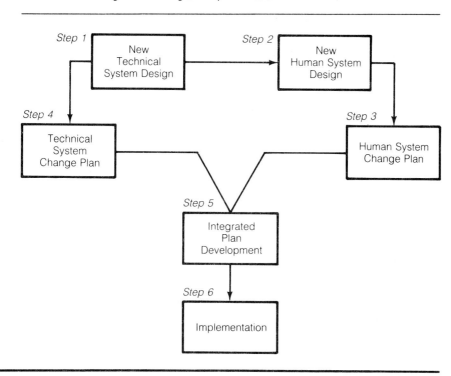

certainly increased participation of the work force with decisions which will affect their working environment, roles, and tasks.

The proper sequencing of these events is imperative. Initial schedules are developed in this step; however, final sequence plans are made in coordination with technical change events.

This change plan will be unique for each application, and requires flexibility in its implementation to deal with the dynamically changing environment.

Step 4: New Technical System Change Plan

Developing a change plan for the new technical system requires a thorough understanding of that new system and the process required to install and implement it. Consideration of facilities modification, computer installation, interfaces with existing systems, technical training and user interface with the new system are necessary before the plan is established (Figure 20.5).

The sequence of these events is important, and will determine a smooth or troubled transition period. Again, a preliminary schedule is developed in this step, with the final schedule developed in concert with human system change plans.

FIGURE 20.5   Evaluation Measures

1. Technical system (case example)
   Number production orders
   Production order throughout
   Time required to locate orders
   Time required to move orders
   Users utilization of the system
2. Other indicators
   Turnover rate
   Absenteeism
   Tardiness
   Accidents
   Grievances
3. Human system
   Personal Involvement with job and company
   Increased satisfaction with:
   ■ Communication
   ■ Career and development opportunities
   ■ Supervision
   ■ Performance feedback
   ■ Pay and promotion equity
   ■ Attitudes toward work environment changes

Step 5: Development of the Integrated Plan

Integrating the required human system change plans with the design for technological implementation is a complex process which requires a systematic team approach. This team approach provides the necessary technical and human factor expertise, which produces a truly integrated plan. A more detailed description of our team approach is discussed at the end of this section. It is in this step that all needed change events, technical, and human factors are scheduled in detail, paying particular attention to realistic time estimates for each event.

One very important process that originates in the very first phases of an implementation plan, is a multiple-level coordination design. This concept calls for participation at multiple levels of organization management to help with design and implementation. In this particular case, three levels of management participated: project review team, project management team, and project operations team.

Project Review Team.   This team is made up of the senior managers of manufacturing and senior project consultants, with occasional vice presidential input. This Project Review Team meets at least quarterly to update reports of the project's progress, and to guide the overall project design. Costs, time, and all resource allocations are approved by this team.

Project Management Team.   This team consists of managers directly responsible for project sites and interfacing departments. This group receives updates on project progress monthly and reviews the events that will impact their supervisors, work force, and operation. Their recommendations are encouraged and to date have served to enhance the implementation process.

Project Operations Team. This team is made up of all supervisors involved and key shop floor employees who are responsible for day-to-day shop floor operations. This group is involved, both as a group and at times individually, on an ongoing basis. They assist with the communication process to the rest of the shop employees, and contribute implementation and system design details to assure that any new system will indeed provide assistance with their daily work and management, in a timely and reasonable format.

Step 6: Implementation of Plan

Following the development of an integrated plan, the implementation phase begins. Initially, planning for the two subsystems proceeded somewhat independently. The establishment of one integrated implementation plan is a tedious and complex process. During this process, all of the required commitments, resources, and key interfaces are developed, which are necessary to ensure the successful implementation of the new technology and the accompanying change in the human system. What remains is the flexible management of the plan, ongoing assessments of the dynamics of the organization in transition, and periodic adjustment to the plan as needed.

THE APPROACH TO PLANNING AND IMPLEMENTATION

Our approach to technological implementation planning is fairly explicit. The sociotechnical framework and the system development planning model that guides our analysis and planning requires several specialists with specific areas of expertise. The skills in manufacturing management, technology, technical systems analysis and design, organizational change and human factors are rarely found in one person. Our intention has been to build a design and implementation team made up of individuals with the various skills necessary for analysis, technical design, and human system assessment, planning, and implementation in the manufacturing area. The team approach requires a close working relationship; therefore, time for interaction, joint planning and mutual problem solving has been explicitly allocated.

Thus far, our team approach has created an environment of mutual and cross learning, effective coordination of manufacturing management, technological change plans, and human factors modification. The effort appears to be a more integrated and comprehensive process than one in which each expert proceeded independently, or if the implementation were left in the hands of a single individual.

In the former case, the parties often impede one another, schedules often conflict, and the "clients" are often left confused and irritated with uncoordinated events and dissonant communications. In the latter case, it is a fallacious assumption that one individual can develop the sophistication and the range of required skills necessary to implement a complex new technology. If there is a single person with a general understanding of the technology and the process of implementation, that person is best utilized in providing a leadership and management function—primarily in the formation and management of an implementation team, and providing the primary interface with the "client system."

Generally, our orientation to the process of implementation was based on the growing empirical knowledge (beginning with the classic Harwood Manufacturing study in 1947) that effective implementation of change occurs when those directly affected by the change are involved in early discussions of the change and its potential impact. Therefore, the ICAM implementation team proceeded to meet and inform the manufacturing management and the shop floor operators about the project and new technology. Many of these discussions were informal in nature, and were intended to build a working relationship with the "client," and to remove as much uncertainty about the project as is possible in early stages of its development.

The implementation plan itself formally identified specific steps (throughout the duration of the project) intended to maintain a partnership between the ICAM team and the clients during the implementation process.

Our experience thus far is that this approach reduced resistance to the technological change, provided the team with important information from the "clients," and utilized client resources in the implementation of this new technology.

Evaluation

Throughout the design and implementation period it is important to monitor and evaluate the process of developing an integrated plan and its implementation. This was accomplished by using a survey methodology specifically designed for this project, and supplemented by detailed interviews with operators and supervisors, to help assess the effectiveness of this process and the success of the implementation plan. Additionally, objective technical and human resource information will contribute to the evaluation (see Figure 20.5).

KEY LESSONS TO DATE

In the course of this article, the more important techniques for implementing planned and deliberate technical and human system change have been examined. Based on those techniques and the research experience gathered in the case study presented here, certain key lessons for successful implementation have surfaced.

Internal Resources Development

Successful change programs must rely upon informed and motivated persons within the organization if the results are to be maintained. Although the outside consultant is often useful in the preliminary stages of analysis designing the program and executing the initial efforts of organizational change, that consultant cannot sustain the organization's efforts over time. The maintenance of change falls on the internal resource persons within the organization. Those internal resources do not develop by magic; the persons must be trained, developed, and given the same managerial legitimacy as other respected and valued members of the organization.

Senior Level Management Commitment

Organizational change is more likely to meet with success when key management persons initiate and support the change process. Planned technical change must have the support and understanding of management and key personnel if it is to proceed smoothly and produce enduring effects. While there may be exceptions, planned change without support of key management is generally at a great advantage. Basically, there is no substitute for the positive boost that an informed and sophisticated management can provide.

Cooperation From Diverse Groups

As in any system of an organization, there must be cooperation from diverse groups and individuals. The cooperation must come from all levels of the organizational structure, since a technology system change will affect everyone, from president to production worker. Therefore, an appreciation for a new technology system must be cultivated among all members of the organization, to ensure their cooperation and, ultimately, the success of the system.

Technological Change Management in a Dynamic Environment

Technological change is a vital, creative, and energizing force, and its management must possess the same qualities. There are no magical panaceas in organizational change techniques. Choosing the right techniques is essentially a management decision problem where one must match the technique to the need, the situation, the constraints, and the objectives. Each technique has a certain range of effectiveness; what is successful for some purposes is irrelevant, perhaps even destructive, for others.

The application of change techniques requires informed managerial choice; it is clear that the effectiveness of any technique depends on the quality of analysis that precedes its selection. As with any decision, faulty and incomplete prior analysis will result in poor decisions and, ultimately, in ineffective action.

Management must also be concerned with means versus ends in the application of new technology. The techniques of implementation are *not* ends in themselves. They *are* means toward reaching clearly defined organizational change goals. Sometimes managers, as well as consultants and organization members, become so intrigued by the personal development and interpersonal interaction represented in the techniques of change that they forget their original purpose.

Dynamic management must monitor such techniques continually to make sure they remain in the service of the organizational objectives and do not become ends in themselves.

Importance of Identifying Key Individuals

In the planning and implementation stages, it is important to identify key individuals in the organization. While the importance of management commitment has been mentioned, it is equally important to solicit the support of key production systems and technical specialists. By finding a specialist who is well respected by his or her co-workers and subordinates and gaining his or her support, the idea of change can filter down through the organization in a positive way.

Importance of Participation and Ownership of Change

Organization change is best accomplished when persons likely to be affected by the change are brought into the process at its beginning. Change threatens many persons; while some can adapt to nearly anything, most persons could not handle arriving at work in the morning and discovering a whole new technology and structure.

For the most part, sudden and unexpected change creates and intensifies resistance to it. Involving persons early in the change process not only acclimates them to the idea of change, but permits them to take a hand in those changes that will affect their jobs, relationships, and personal satisfactions.

Necessity of Being Open and Honest About Change

Given the feeling of threat and paranoia brought on by technological change, honest and open dealings with change plans are imperative. We have found that timely communication with all those involved in the change, including managers and employees, will reduce a good deal of the natural resistance to change.

ORGANIZATIONAL DEVELOPMENT AND TECHNOLOGICAL CHANGE

The preceding presentation has attempted to demonstrate how two basic models, the sociotechnical systems model and the life-cycle planning model, can be used to guide and direct the implementation of technological change. The contribution of this approach to the practical formulation of change strategies is that it supplements existing change theory that focuses on the processes of change. Furthermore, the project described herein does provide an example of the need to develop specific methods to perform quality analysis for the purpose of understanding the complex technical, human, and managerial components of an organizational system.

Because the field of organizational development seems to lack specific methodology that can assist in these analytical activities, the field remains for the most part either abstract or descriptive with regard to theory and somewhat mechanical with regard to the pragmatic methods for concrete technological change.

Conceptual Considerations

This project clearly highlights the rapid expansion and utilization of sophisticated technology in our society. This phenomenon is by no means a short-run occurrence, but in fact is likely to continue at increasing rates indefinitely. There has been a number of different perspectives on rapid technological change, some more conceptual and others more popular. For example, Alvin Toffler's book *The Third Wave* is one such treatment that predicts ongoing and rapid technological impacts on our society. The field of organizational development, while purporting to facilitate change in organizations, has for the most part concentrated on change in organizational processes within an existing organizational framework. While some of these attempts may in fact involve some structural interventions, generally speaking, organizational development has continued to emphasize the importance of change in the human subsystem of an organization. It is clear to us that a viable and challenging direction for the field involves the design and facilitation of new technological implementation.

In this regard the OD field must also become more intimately involved with the key strategic directions for the organization and with creative solutions to major organizational design issues in the context of technological determinism. What this simply means is that new technology can often be viewed as a given and the challenge for organizational development is to create major organizational contextual changes that are compatible with the new technology, and at the same time continue to respect and appreciate human resources. Our approach does not ignore the basic values of OD, it simply recognizes the systems perspective.

With regard to the specific models utilized in this case, the sociotechnical systems approach has generally been used to assist in the re-design of work at the operational level of the organization. Additionally, much of the literature surrounding the sociotechnical systems concept is descriptive in nature. For example, the Pasmore and Sherwood (1978) work, which presents a variety of perspectives by different authors associated with the sociotech movement, is excellent in providing descriptive material and explanations of the theoretical and conceptual foundation for this approach. However, there is very little specific methodology presented to assist operationally in the utilization of this approach.

Moreover, while specific techniques appear to be lacking, we found the use of this model extremely beneficial as a guide for technological change when the planning for such change is done at the upper levels of the organization. This interesting use of the sociotechnical systems model coupled with the life-cycle planning model becomes a unique and comprehensive perspective that can permit methodical and logical step-by-step planning and implementation of new technology. To be sure, some education of management with regard to these models and their use was necessary.

One rather intriguing complexity surrounding the process of change that does not seem to be addressed in the theoretical literature is that change phenomena encompasses both the rapidity of what is to be changed and the very real sluggishness of change advocated by the character of the organization. On the one hand, we identify an extremely rapid proliferation of new technology and on the other we experience a natural organizational resistance to new organizational configurations. A very good example is the rather well established notion that organizational development involves specific targets of change as well as changes in the underlying culture of the organization. What we have found is that the specific technological changes can occur rather quickly while the cultural elements seem to have an inertia that often requires a rather slow incremental change. Thus, the intriguing dilemma that we found ourselves in is trying to manage rapid change on the one hand and pursue incremental culture change on the other.

Indeed, one of the major difficulties experienced in this case study has been the continued management of this critical dilemma. Organizational development as a field has argued for some time that organizational change must involve change in the organizational culture. The theoretical and methodological clarity that can facilitate slow and deliberate culture change in light of rapid technological change is not yet well developed in the field of OD. This avenue offers important potential if the field is to continue its vitality and its critical role in the implementation of new technology.

Professional Considerations

In the context of this case study, and assuming that there will be a continuation of the need for technological implementation, it is likely that the professional directions for the field may require the following:

1. Organizational development professionals must insist on greater emphasis in understanding and diagnosing the technological context of organizations. What this suggests is that much more attention must be given to understanding the technological subsystem and the role and importance of technology in the behavior of the organization. The field's emphasis on the human element in the organization will only have continued importance if this work is pursued within the technological contextual environment of the organization. Without this connection, OD continues

to be an interesting but perhaps less vital resource for managers.

2. It also seems clear, based on this one case, that OD professionals in the future must develop a systems perspective. While this point may seem redundant, it is in fact not the case at all. The field has emphasized for some years sociotechnical systems, organizational systems, and systems of change, and yet there has been very little emphasis in the training of OD professionals that focuses on the development of "systems thinking." Some recent work, especially Marilyn Ferguson's *The Aquarian Conspiracy* and Fritjof Capra's *The Turning Point,* emphasize more and more the holistic nature of organizations, societies, and the processes of change. Much of the field of organizational development has been adequately descriptive in this regard and yet its methodology is still linear, short run, and specialistic.

3. In complex organizational environments the need for organizational development professionals to develop a greater cognitive understanding of the interaction of environmental forces and their impact on organizational behavior is of central importance. The ability of organizational development specialists to develop models that help understand the complex forces that affect their efforts toward change will indeed be a necessary and critical skill in the future.

The experience presented above has reemphasized the need for organizational development to insist on ongoing evaluation of the change strategies employed for technological implementation. While managers are often less interested in evaluation of efforts in planning and implementing technological change, insistence must and should come from the organizational development specialists. It is imperative in the planning for new technological implementation that an action-evaluation component be carefully and thoughtfully considered. The field will continue to develop new theoretical foundations appropriate for a dynamic changing environment, and will also continue to develop new methods for implementing complex organizational change. To do this, however, requires some empirical basis derived from the succession and failures of change strategies.

There is no doubt that organizational environments are becoming more and more complex and as such, there will be a continuing need for professionals in organizational change and development. While managers are likely to become better informed consumers of OD, the field is nevertheless a professional specialty. The role of organizational development professionals in the context of this paper will remain to assist organizations in the design of technological change plans and to act as key integrators between technologists and human resource specialists.

Overall, central involvement in an organization's strategic plans and the requirements for change in the context of these directions provides a rich and fertile ground for continued application and continued development of organizational development methodology.

Bibliography

Capra, F. *The Turning Point.* New York: Simon and Schuster, 1982.

Emery, F. E., & Trist, E. L. "The Causal Texture of Organizational Environments", *Human Relations.* 1965, 18, p. 21–31.

Ferguson, M. *The Aquarian Conspiracy.* Boston: Houghton Mifflin Company, 1980.

French, W. L., Bell, C. H., & Zawacki, R. A. *Organization Development: Theory, Practice, and Research.* Plano, Texas: Business Publications, Inc., 1978.

Katz, D., & Kahn, R. L. *The Social Psychology of Organizations.* 2d ed., New York: John Wiley & Sons, 1978.

Margulies, N., & Raia, A. P. *Conceptual Foundations of Organizational Development.* New York: McGraw-Hill, 1978.

Margulies, N., & Raia, A. P. eds. *Organizational Development: Values, Process and Technology.* New York: McGraw-Hill, 1972.

Pasmore, W. A., & Sherwood, J. J. *Sociotechnical Systems: A Sourcebook.* San Diego: University Associates, Inc., 1978.

Rice, A. K. *Productivity and Social Organization: The Ahmedabad Experiment—Technical Innovation, Work Organization, and Management.* London: Tavistock Publications Ltd., 1958.

Thompson, J. D. *Organizations in Action.* New York: McGraw-Hill, 1967.

Trist, E. L., & Bamforth, K. W. "Some Social and Psychological Consequences of the Long Wall Method of Coal Getting." In *Human Relations,* vol. 4 (January 1951): 3–38. Reprinted in R. E. Mankin, Russell E. Ames, Jr., and Milton A. Grodsky (eds.), Classics in *Industrial and Organizational Psychology,* Oak Park, Ill.: Moore Publishing Company, 1980, pp. 316–44.

Woodward, J. *Industrial Organization: Theory and Practice.* London: Oxford University Press, 1965.

Zwerman, W. L. *New Perspectives on Organization Theory.* Westport, Conn.: Greenwood Publishing Co., 1970.

21 Career and Life Planning Program Designs in Organizational Development

Thomas H. Patten, Jr.

ABSTRACT

Career and life planning (C/LP) designs have been used for years by organizations for their managerial and professional employees. We do not know how many people annually have a C/LP experience. Probably invented by Herbert Shepard, C/LP has become a vehicle elaborated upon by many others for exploring new perspectives from which to view one's past experience, current life, and possible future alternatives. A two-day workshop on C/LP designed by the author and described in detail provides an illustration of a well-considered C/LP offering that has had favorable feedback. However, questions are raised about the evaluation of such workshops and the paucity of published information available. For example, the OD community knows little about the results of C/LP programs, what the participants gain or lose, or what the sponsoring business or agency gains or loses. The author concludes by speculating on how to fulfill these lacunae and their implications.

AUTHOR BACKGROUND

Thomas H. Patten, Jr., is a professor in the School of Labor and Industrial Relations, Michigan State University, where he has served for sixteen years. He was chairman of the OD Division of the ASTD in 1972 and is the author of eight books and seventy-five articles. His latest book on OD is *Organizational Development Through Teambuilding,* which reviews the design, content, and evaluation of ten years of sustained intervention in one super-large organizational system.

On every side of us we see people entering careers, changing lines of work, and job jumping, switching professions at midlife, enduring the so-called managerial menopause, retiring early (or retiring later based upon one's preference), and expressing the blue-collar blues, white-collar wails, and executive blahs as a reaction to the quality of work life in America. We also see such social trends as concession bargaining and pay cuts, the emergence of the steel-collar worker in an environment of robotics and high technology, and continuation of efforts—maybe less conscientiously policed than in the past—aimed at equal employment opportunity, affirmative action, career planning, and the upward organizational mobility of women and minority group members. The careers picture is a confusing and turbulent one filled with contradictions and quite variable in different sectors of the economy and different regions in the nation. Yet there is no doubt that the career management of human resources is a dynamic field and one that is going to increase in importance in the years ahead. In fact, I would venture the opinion that career and life planning programs will become a type of micro-MBO (self-management-by-objectives) that is analogous to macro-MBO (organizational-management-by-objectives) in the next decade. Therefore, I strongly believe that training, human resource management, and organizational development specialists need to know how career and life planning (henceforth C/LP) program designs can be utilized to solve some of the organization's problems in dealing with career issues.

C/LP programs have been utilized for many years by companies and government agencies for their managerial and professional employees; by school districts for their employees; by community colleges on an openenrollment basis for people interested in self-development; and by churches and not-for-profit organizations for their clergy, members, or associated personnel.

I do not know how many organizations offer C/LP programs in a typical year or how many people participate in the various offerings made available. Based upon a pure guess, my hunch is that in a typical nonrecession year probably fifty- to one-hundred thousand people in America have some kind of C/LP program experience of a duration of one to three hours (on the low side) to two days (on the high side). I wish I could verify this estimate and target more effectively where C/LP programs are flourishing, but that task is beyond me at present.

In this article I do the following: review the main literature on C/LP, calling the reader's attention to the wealth of excellent sources for program design and utilization available today; share a design that I have used successfully with military and civilian managers in several large systems as well as with graduate students; provide a critique of C/LP programs which should prove helpful to human resource development and OD practitioners; and draw a few conclusions.

Although I do not highlight them, I would like to acknowledge that mini-C/LP efforts that are sometimes included as one- to three-hour modules at the end of lengthy training and OD interventions designed for other purposes are important and well known to me. Such mini-C/LP efforts often partake of some facets of the designs I discuss in this article; and I do favor them when adequately integrated with other relevant content. Last, I provide little coverage of the use of C/LP content for training the trainer who aspires to be a C/LP workshop facilitator, primarily because such a task transcends what can be done in a short article. Similarly, I avoid in-depth treatment of how C/LP content can be used in college-level, graduate-level, or MBA-focused courses. However, I believe that C/LP content can and should be properly packaged for training trainers and for use in the curricula of institutions of higher learning, as well as for practicing managers.

PROGRAM CONCEPTS AND RESOURCES

I believe Herbert A. Shepard is the progenitor of career and life planning workshops in OD, although the annals of OD history are not entirely clear. On the other hand, Shepard's explanation of the conceptual underpinning of life planning is very lucid and provocative and probably has strongly influenced everyone who has followed in his footsteps.[1] However, it should be noted that Shepard stresses *life* planning of which careers are but one part, separable in theory, but hardly separable in fact. People who have written about C/LP since Shepard have put equal or more emphasis on career planning than Shepard has.

Shepard has pointed out that only the future is manageable. The past can be re-interpreted. It cannot be managed. Life planning is thus conceptualized by Shepard as planning "life worth living" as perceived by the individual and brings to mind rejoicing in life, resonance, autonomy, and the search for ways to attain peak experiences. Life planning becomes essentially an invitation to explore new perspectives from which to view past experience, one's current life, and future alternatives. Life planning should help a person live life more fully, but this does not imply protection from pain or an entirely euphoric experience. Life planning thus has several aspects: arousal of motivation, freeing of imagination, generation of data about oneself, identification of themes in the data, formulation of purpose, and the development of action plans.[2]

Shepard has also set forth the various self-confrontation exercises that have become well known tools for use in C/LP workshops. These include "draw your life line," "write your obituary," "share newspaper clippings," the review of highs and lows on one's life, the inventorying of one's strengths and weaknesses, and personal goal setting.

I find that Ford and Lippitt have done an excellent job in providing a format for personal goal setting that builds upon Shepard's ideas.[3] The format provides text material as well as exercises and allows a focus on family-related goals as well as life and career goals. I especially find "Appendix B: Life Planning Sponsored by Organizations" in their book a useful tool bridging life and career planning concerns.

Weiler has written a book on career and life planning that provides extensive textual material, numerous exercises, and a transactional analysis orientation.[4] I find the Weiler book to be more strongly oriented to career planning per se than the Ford and Lippitt book and to culminate in concrete steps in marketing oneself in the job market.

Hagberg and Leider share their format for a life and career-renewal process in yet another carefully prepared C/LP book.[5] Similar to the books by Ford and Lippitt and Weiler, they (Hagberg & Leider) permit the reader, on a step-by-step basis, to find out what he or she wants out of life and career and then to expand and explore the options. Their theme caters to "inventurers," a special breed of person who takes charge and creates challenges to get himself or herself moving. There is a wealth of useful experiential material in this book.

Consistent with the above volumes is another by Kirn and Kirn, which has gone through a number of editions.[6] Their self-instructional volume seems to very thorough and to incorporate a number of exercises based upon the behavioral science writing of Joseph Luft, Frederick Herzberg, Abraham Maslow, Elizabeth Kubler-Ross, and others. Kirn and Kirn, in a way, hark back to Shepard in an emphasis on life planning rather than career planning. Their book also contains a wealth of useful exercises.

The above resources in no way exhaust the options available from the recent literature. We seem to be living at a time when C/LP designs are proliferating. The same can be said about the literature on careers in general. It is thus worth stating a few thoughts about the careers literature because it can be consulted by the human resource development and OD specialist in tailor-making a C/LP program for a particular company or agency.

I have found Bolles' work useful in designing C/LP programs because he has given explicit attention to the design of C/LP programs in the broader context of career management—organizational and personal.[7] Walker has probably done the best job to date in explaining the nuts and bolts of organizational career planning systems.[8] He makes a number of fundamental points including the key thought that in a free society career planning is ultimately an individual responsibility—if a person feels blocked in one organization and sincerely desires career progress he or she should job jump to get it. We cannot rely on everyone being "given" a career by the employer; the person who seeks a meaningful career and development may have to bite the bullet, take a risk, or job jump to get it. It seems to me that sometimes we forget this fundamental tenet whenever we think that career planning is merely an organization's playing chess and checkers with people.

Hall has provided a very readable text on career-development and career-management.[9] While the book may appear to be overly basic to the specialist in the field who has gotten his or her hands dirty in live organizations, there is no doubt that the book is sensible and clear for the novice. The same can be said about Jelinek's book of readings.[10] It is a very basic book of readings, but a good place to begin in getting up to speed in the field. The cases in her book could be easily adapted for use in train-the-trainer efforts in developing C/LP program facilitators.

Finally, there is a pragmatic literature (much of it in paperback) that I have found informative and instructive. For example, Buskirk's book provides a great deal of personal information on career management and career changing that makes sense and is eminently discussable in any group where careers are the central topic of concern.[11] Sheehy's work is especially notable and provocative.

Her *Passages: Predictable Crises of Adult Life* was on the best-seller list for many months several years ago and probably caused many Americans—female and male—to take a look at themselves and what they believed about career and life planning.[12]

I might also mention books in the genre of that represented by the Allen text.[13] She has addressed herself to career planning for people at the high school age level. The book can be placed in the literature of guidance, counseling, and pupil personnel work. She has set forth a great deal of pragmatic information in addition to a framework to which the young person can relate in taking the very first steps in career and life planning.

In the above summary of the literature I have failed to mention Kellogg's work, which I personally admire and would recommend be read prior to examining any of the literature I have briefly discussed.[14] Her book is now more than a decade old, but the insights it contains about career management should be especially useful to anyone contemplating engagement in a C/LP program or workshop.

A TWO-DAY C/LP PROGRAM DESIGN

Having examined concepts and the literature, I think it would be useful next to share a design I have used in C/LP workshops. I am not suggesting that this design is universally applicable because I do not believe it is. However, I feel it is well tested and has been reported as useful and energizing by people who have experienced it in a workshop setting. The design uses some of the early concepts set forth by Shepard as well as some new ideas on value clarification,[15] which I find managers need badly because they often appear to me at mid-career as ships lost at sea. Value clarification exercises enable managers to get back to a consideration of their moral and ethical anchorages, which, on reflection, most find useful and growthful. Organizational management has a tendency to cause managers to cut their moorings and drift on the sea of the work culture in which they find themselves. Once such managers are given a chance to recognize they are drifting rather than pro-actively planning, the realization that they are afloat and allowing themselves to be buffeted by apparently uncontrollable currents and waves has a tonic effect. In a word, it causes them to feel more autonomous and in charge of their destinies.

Figures 21.1 and 21.2 display the content and format that I use together with the time frame. I ask the participants in the C/LP workshop to use the aforementioned Ford and Lippitt workbook and, in fact, build the workshop around its constituent parts. I think the format should be self-explanatory in at least a general way based upon the information provided in Figures 21.1 and 21.2.

I also provide a notebook of background readings and require all the participants to read two articles by Harvey.[16] In one of these, "Organizations as Phrog Farms", I find that a vehicle and vocabulary is provided that enables managers to talk about their employment and employer without feeling disloyal,

---

FIGURE 21.1   Seminar/Workshop Content-First Day

8:30- 9:30	Presentation on overall concepts of career and life planning
9:30-10:00	Life awareness exercises
10:00-10:15	Coffee
10:15-10:30	Theory input on life stages and discussion
10:30-11:45	Theory input on value clarification concepts and value clarification exercises
11:45-12:45	Lunch
12:45- 1:45	Continuation of value clarification exercises
1:45- 2:45	Theory input on planning one's life as a manager, supervisor, or professional person—"micro-MBO for macro-MBO"
2:45- 3:00	Coffee/Coke
3:00- 4:15	Lifeline exercises

Tonight or tomorrow before we meet read "Organizations as Phrog Farms," which we will discuss tomorrow morning, and the "Abilene Paradox," which we will discuss tomorrow afternoon.

The other reading in the notebook can be done whenever you have the inclination. You will find it of value depending upon where you see yourself in terms of career and life planning.

---

insubordinate, or unjustifiably critical. The lightness in approach and verisimilitude of the "Phrog Farm" to many contemporary work organizations enables managers to move openly into a spirited discussion of how they feel about being managers in their present organizations.

The "Abilene Paradox" causes managers to wonder if they are masters of their career fates in their present organizations or like passive travelers in an unairconditioned automobile who participate in a long ride from Coleman, Texas, to Abilene on a typically hot summer Texas day when none of the riders really wanted to make the broiling, dusty trip to Abilene yet really voiced no opposition to it. Many managers find themselves regularly driving to a metaphorical Abilene every day in their work lives—perhaps many times a day!—and would like to take charge and change matters, but do not do so.

I believe Harvey's two articles allow the workshop facilitator to intervene in the C/LP workshop's participants' life spaces and open discussion on topics in organizational development that should not be ignored. As I previously noted, life planning and career planning are virtually inseparable except for analytical purposes. The micro-MBO of the person and macro-MBO of the employing organization are bridged when the Phrog Farm and Abilene Paradox issues are dissected and debriefed in detail.

CRITIQUE OF C/LP PROGRAMS

What are the results of C/LP programs? What does the participant gain or lose? What does the sponsoring business or agency gain or lose? I have never seen any research that provides answers to these important but basic questions.

FIGURE 21.2 Seminar/Workshop Content-Second Day

8:30– 9:30	Discussion: Are Organizations Phrog Farms? and completion of Lifeline exercises
9:30– 9:45	Coffee
9:45–11:45	Exercise on life inventory and planning for the future; and debriefing of the exercises
11:45–12:45	Lunch
12:45– 2:45	Exercise on making a career decision and building commitment to it
2:45– 3:00	Coffee/Coke
3:00– 3:30	Debriefing of career decision exercise, emphasizing one's taking control over his life and career development
3:30– 4:00	Discussion: What Can Be Done About the Abilene Paradox?
4:00– 4:15	Formal seminar/workshop evaluation
End of program

However, I have some thoughts on these matters based upon my experience and that of others, which may partly answer our main queries.

First, the person who attends a C/LP program with the attitude that it is merely another training event probably is shocked at the level of intimacy aimed at in these sessions and may be quite unprepared for the degree of self-revelation involved. Such persons may either get in the spirit of the event and see where it takes them or simply go through the motions, learning little, feeling perhaps the event is too personally intrusive.

Persons who are *sent* to C/LP programs demonstrate all the possible reactions of people who are sent to any training or OD event: they may be resistant, passive, passive-aggressive, or potentially interestable in the event. However, most generally, sent participants need to have their "sentness" addressed at some point before they can get into the spirit of the event. Depending upon their working through of why they were sent, they may become effective and contributing participants—indeed often heavy contributors to everyone's growth.

In my experience the right people for an adult C/LP program are industrial or agency managers and employees who are at a critical juncture in their careers and lives. They possess readiness. Examples of such persons are legion. A person in his or her early thirties who has job-jumped a bit and still feels the grass is greener in a different organization (but is not as convinced of this likelihood as before he job-jumped once or twice) is a good C/LP candidate. A middle-aged manager or military officer contemplating retirement or a new career in the same field but in a different institutional domain or in a different field entirely may obtain a degree of closure in a C/LP program that energizes him or her to act. Almost any person who is open to reflecting on himself or herself and where he or she is at in social space (life) will find a C/LP program that is well designed and conducted by a competent workshop leader as growthful and a useful basis for embarkation on new ventures or creative risk-taking in the future. When twelve to sixteen of the right people meet in a C/LP workshop—and only a few of the participants are sent—the foundation for impacting one's career and life plans is laid and may move to fruition, sometimes with very dramatic results, almost like a "Eureka!" experience.

Put another way, the potential for individual gain is rather high for the right mix of participants. The potential for loss in a well conducted C/LP workshop is miniscule. A few participants may grouse about the lost time from the office to attend a C/LP program, but these are likely to be people who feel work pressures acutely and generally dislike any interventions that separate them from their work. Included in this group would be workaholics who if they could ever be unblocked might gain a great deal from a well-conducted C/LP workshop.

I have a generalized vague feeling that I would like to share about participants in C/LP program workshops. People who know how to deal with (or can learn how to deal with) the following maxim gain the most from workshop participation: "if life hands you a lemon, make lemonade." They realize that even the happiest life and career pattern is likely to have rocks, shoals, detours, and tragedy at some point. Some people experience a plethora of the tragic whereas others have fewer problems and no calamities. The sensitive, insightful, and proactive person is likely to see problems as challenges and blockages as occasions for thinking through options and alternatives. These persons are not prone to see themselves as victimized, unjustly treated, and as pawns moved about by powerful forces beyond their control. To be sure, they are sufficiently realistic to identify parameters in life and in jobs in organizations; but they seem to know how to work within them so that perceived sources of satisfaction and joy are tapped. They feel relatively less deprived than others and can bounce back.

On the other hand, other personalities lack resiliency and feel relatively impotent in their ability to engage in career and life planning. For them the important consideration is not the planning per se, but the plan. They do not seem to realize that C/LP is a planning process that at its best culminates in gingerly taking some concrete first steps and must be flexible because the steps may falter. The person may need to reassess the planning quickly after obtaining data and then act again. However, the person who seeks a plan when given a lemon by life may not realize the *planning* needs to be re-examined because the *plan* is not leading where expected. The sour lemon can be used growthfully and beneficially if one is willing to venture forth and experiment.

Turning to what the sponsoring company or agency might gain or lose, I believe it must face the fact that a C/LP experience may be the precipitating cause for a manager's quitting his or her job. I doubt if the C/LP workshop does more than help a disgruntled or vaguely uneasy person obtain a perspective on what is bothering him or her in the life-space or career-domain. But the workshop may be the straw that breaks the camel's back; and the result may be that a valuable employee quits employment. Stated differently, the employer may have stimulated an action that is in opposition to his perceived economic interest. Yet may not the employee have quit anyhow—and the only real issue is one of sooner or later? In my opinion, the wise employer does not become angry or vindictive when a valuable employee or manager quits, especially if the event takes place some time after C/LP workshop participation. The issue should not be reduced to loyalty and disloyalty. The proper employment policy covering these situations is one that allows the employee to bow out gracefully and leaves the door open for the employee's return should he or she have a change of heart and there be a suitable vacancy available at the time of reapplication for employment. After all, the prodigal son story of the Bible suggests the value of making it possible to return to the fold. And a C/LP graduate who quits to seek the personally developmental is hardly prodigal! Waste in the utilization of human resources is found more often in organizations where people are blocked by picayune bureaucratic rules and mindless attitudes about loyalty rather than by people who experiment, experience, and may change their minds about where the green grass really is. In fact, returning employees may approach the job once again with vigor and imagination, turning in a performance better than ever before.

As for the quitters who never return, the wise employer can take the gracious view that a contribution has been made to the better allocation of human resources and careers in America. Who knows, perhaps that same employer will obtain a newcomer to the firm who quit somewhere else and seeks challenge and an opportunity to contribute in the subject employer's firm or agency! C/LP programs coupled with enlightened re-employment policies are probably better for America than such costly and mal-allocative devices as golden handcuffs and golden parachutes.

In the broadest perspective, C/LP programs are consonant with many of the values and social trends in contemporary America. Their intent is not naive and altruistic. They do recognize the changing demographics in America: people are living longer, they want more from jobs than money, they expect equal opportunity for development, and they will job jump until either they find the career opportunity they want or are prohibited from changing jobs because the spouse refuses, the low-interest mortgage becomes an anchor, or off-job life-style advantages outweigh the value of changing job sites. If this reasoning is valid, it should be obvious that C/LP programs have an assured place in organizational development efforts in the 1980s and 1990s.

CONCLUSION

Looking at OD from the standpoint of a person who was in the field before it was a field, as absurd as that statement may seem, I see broadly the 1950s and 1960s as the sensitivity/encounter group era and the 1970s as the managerial grid, teambuilding, TA, assertiveness training, and EST era. That last statement is perhaps a gross oversimplification because many other concepts, techniques, and programs came into being, were tried and tested, and put in perspective in those decades. C/LP probably goes back to at least twenty years and is not new or likely to preempt the field for the remainder of this century. Yet as I look ahead in OD and read the periodic volumes that attempt to provide an evaluation of where we have been in OD and what lies ahead, [17] I think I see the broad trends by decade which I have already labelled.

The years ahead of us are likely to require us to consider more carefully the career fates of people in large-scale and other organizations, especially if equal employment opportunity and affirmative action programs are re-emphasized again. As a result, I believe that C/LP program designs *should* and *will* get more attention than in the past.

Also, many organizations are heavily investing in people today, and C/LP is becoming a natural focus of attention for organizational effectiveness. For those organizations where a major cost of being in business is governed by human contentment in a career, OD efforts that include C/LP programs would seem to be essential now and for the future.

Notes

1. Shepard, Herbert A. "Life Planning," in Kenneth D. Benne *et al,* eds., *The Laboratory Method of Changing and Learning: Theory and Application,* (Palo Alto: Science and Behavior Books, 1975), pp. 240–51.
2. Shepard, pp. 240–51.
3. Ford, George A., & Gordon L. Lippitt., *Planning Your Future: A Workbook for Personal Goal Setting* (rev. ed.), (San Diego: University Associates, 1976).
4. Weiler, Nicholas W., *Reality and Career Planning: A Guide For Personal Growth,* (Reading: Addison-Wesley, 1977).
5. Hagberg, Janet, & Richard Leider, *The Inventurers: Excursions in Life and Career Renewal,* (Reading: Addison-Wesley, 1978).
6. Kirn, Arthur G., & Marie O'Donahoe Kirn, *Life Work Planning,* (4th ed.), (New York: McGraw-Hill, 1978).
7. Bolles, Richard Nelson, *What Color Is Your Parachute?* (Berkeley: Ten Speed Press, 1977), see especially pp. 83–107.
8. Walker, James L. "Personal and Career Planning," in Dale Yoder and Herbert G. Heneman, Jr., eds., *ASPA Handbook of Personnel and Industrial Relations, Training and Development,* (Washington: Bureau of National Affairs, 1977, vol. 5), pp. 5-57–5-74.
9. Hall, Douglas T., *Careers in Organizations,* (Pacific Palisades: Goodyear, 1976).
10. Jelinek, Mariann, ed., *Career Management for the Individual and the Organization,* (Chicago: St. Clair Press, 1978). Another excellent book of readings is: Marilyn A. Morgan, ed., *Managing Career Development* (New York: Van Nostrand, 1980).
11. Buskirk, Richard H., *Your Career: How to Plan It, Manage It, Change It,* (New York: New American Library, 1976).
12. Sheehy, Gail, *Passages: Predictable Crises of Adult Life,* (New York: Bantam Book, 1977).
13. Allen, Roberta., *Planning Your Career,* (Chicago: American School, 1980).
14. Kellogg, Marion S., *Career Management,* (New York: American Management Associations, 1972).
15. Kirshenbaum, Howard, *Advanced Value Clarification,* (La Jolla: University Associates, 1977) and Smith, Maury, *A Practical Guide to Value Clarification,* (La Jolla: University Associates, 1977).

16. Harvey, Jerry B., "Organizations as Phrog Farms," *Organizational Dynamics,* vol. 5, no. 4, Spring 1977, pp. 15–23; and Harvey, Jerry B., "The Abilene Paradox: The Management of Agreement," *Organizational Dynamics,* (Summer 1974) vol. 3, no. 1, pp. 63–80.

17. Burke, W. Warner, ed., *Contemporary Organization Development: Conceptual Orientations and Interventions,* (Washington: NTL Institute for Applied Behavioral Science, 1972); Adams, John D., ed., *Theory and Method in Organization Development,* (Arlington: NTL Institute for Applied Behavioral Science, 1974); Burke, W. Warner, ed., *Current Issues and Strategies in Organization Development,* (New York: Human Sciences Press, 1977); Burke, W. Warner, ed., *The Cutting Edge: Current Theory and Practice on Organization Development,* (La Jolla: University Associates, 1978); and Burke, W. Warner, & Leonard D. Goodstein, eds., *Trends and Issues in OD: Current Theory and Practice,* (San Diego: University Associates, 1980).

22 Organization Development Approaches: Analysis and Application

Marshall Sashkin
Ronald J. Burke
Paul R. Lawrence
William A. Pasmore

ABSTRACT

There are perhaps two dozen identifiably distinct approaches to OD. Of these there are eight to twelve that are commonly recognized as major OD approaches. Huse (1980), for example, identifies and reviews twelve such approaches. We briefly describe in this paper ten major OD approaches. We then review in more detail three of these approaches, arguing that these are especially important approaches that have been underused. After exploring some of the possible reasons for the failure to widely use these OD approaches, we discuss some of the diffusion ideas that were generated in a symposium discussion held as part of the Academy of Management national meetings in August of 1982. We conclude that this report itself is directed at fulfilling some of the suggestions (specifically, suggestions that clear descriptive presentations of the OD approaches be made available to managers and practitioners) but that serious and major new efforts are required if real diffusion progress is to be made.

AUTHOR BACKGROUND

Marshall Sashkin is a professor of industrial and organizational psychology at the University of Maryland, University College, College Park, Maryland. Dr. Sashkin earned his degree in organizational psychology at the University of Michigan and has taught at several universities including the State University of New York, the University of Michigan, and Wayne State University. The author or coauthor of five books including *A Manager's Guide to Participative Management, Assessing Performance Appraisal,* and *Organization Behavior in Action,* Dr. Sashkin was for five years associate editor of the *Annual Handbook for Group Facilitators.* He has published numerous papers in scholarly journals and is currently editor of the quarterly journal *Group and Organization Studies.* Dr. Sashkin's work covers a wide range of topics including group dynamics, leadership, group problem solving, human relations training, and organization development and change. His most recent work has been in the area of performance management and appraisal. Dr. Sashkin consults to a variety of organizations, government as well as private, on management and performance systems.

Ronald J. Burke is a professor of organizational behavior and industrial relations at York University in Toronto. His research interests include occupational stress, the work-family interface, aging and managerial performance, and career-development processes in organizations. Dr. Burke has received numerous research grants and has published in many academic and professional journals. He has researched extensively in group problem-solving process and on performance appraisal. His awards include listings in *American Men and Women of Science, Who's Who in Education,* and *International Biographies.* He received his doctorate from the University of Michigan.

Paul R. Lawrence is Wallace Brett Donham Professor of Organizational Behavior in the Graduate School of Business Administration at Harvard University. He received his M.B.A. and D.C.S. degrees from Harvard and his A.B. from Albion College. A member of the American Sociological Association, Applied Anthropology Society, and a fellow of the National Training Laboratories, Dr. Lawrence has written numerous articles and books on organization behavior. He has given special attention to organizational change. He is the coauthor (with Jay Lorsch) of *Organization and Environment,* the book in which the contingency theory was first developed.

William A. Pasmore is an associate professor of organizational behavior in the School of Management at Case Western Reserve University, Cleveland, Ohio. He received his Ph.D. from Purdue University in administrative sciences in 1976. He has acted as a consultant for both production and health-care organizations in addition to teaching and writing about work redesign and organizational behavior. His interests include the extension of work-redesign principles to health-care organizations and studying the impact of work configurations on the physical and mental health of employees. He is co-author (with John J. Sherwood) of *SocioTechnical Systems* (University Associates), a comprehensive sourcebook on the Socio-Technical Systems approach to organizational change.

Ten approaches to organization development (OD) are listed in Table 22.1. Each approach is categorized according to the extent to which it is "structured" in terms of a standard set of application steps, and according to the primary problem areas the approach is intended to deal with. The approaches in Table 22.1 are certainly not exhaustive of all OD approaches in use today. These are, however, the most widely used and best known approaches, and we believe that they represent a sound basic foundation for OD practice.

It is interesting that eight of the ten approaches center on just one of the four primary areas for organizational change identified by Leavitt (1965): human behavior. Only contingency theory and the sociotechnical systems approach to OD are at all concerned directly with organizational structure, technology, or job design. This is one reason we feel these two OD approaches are especially important. Another reason is that they, along with the third-party consultation OD approach, seem to center on some of the most crucial content issues of our time: managing the fit between human needs and technological realities (sociotechnical systems), adapting the organization to fit its environment while maintaining effective internal operations (contingency theory), and managing interpersonal and intergroup conflict effectively (third-party consultation). For these reasons we will review each of these approaches in somewhat greater depth.

THIRD-PARTY CONSULTATION

This is an approach typically associated with Richard Walton (1969) although others (e.g., Blake, Shepard, and Mouton 1965) have written about it. Walton and his colleagues have done extensive research for a number of years on organizational conflict processes (Dutton & Walton 1966; Walton & Dutton 1969; Walton, Dutton & Cafferty 1969). The third-party consultation approach represents the practical application of this research to the confrontation of interpersonal and intergroup conflict.

Walton has developed a comprehensive theoretical framework for understanding conflict in organizations (Walton & McKersie 1965). The key variable is the type of process by which conflicts are typically handled. Two basic processes have been identified. In an *integrative* process, the parties confront

TABLE 22.1   Ten Common Organization Development Approaches

Approach	Structure	Problem Focus
I. Laboratory method Clients learn more effective behaviors by examining their own experiences in real and in "artificial" situations (Bradford, Gibb, & Benne, 1964).	Low	Any behavioral process problems, typically on an individual and interpersonal level
II. Survey feedback Data gathered through questionnaire surveys is analyzed, summarized and "fed back" to work teams for problem-focused discussions, at all hierarchical levels (Mann, 1957).	Moderate	Any organizational problems; group focus is common.
III. Action research Problem-focused research conducted by clients and OD consultants collaboratively (Frohman, Sashkin, & Kavanagh, 1976).	Low/ Moderate	Any organizational problems
IV. Process consultation Consultant directs interventions to help clients deal with interpersonal behavioral process problems (Schein, 1969).	Low	Interpersonal behavior, but may extend to the small group
V. Third party consultation Consultant analyzes conflict processes and with client collaboration designs interventions to move the conflict process from a distributive to an integrative dynamic (Walton, 1969).	Low/ Moderate	Interpersonal and intergroup conflict
VI. Contingency theory Consultant analyzes organizational differentiation and integrations, checking the organization/environment fit and use of integrative mechanisms; patterns of differentiation may be altered and new integrative mechanisms added as needed (Lawrence & Lorsch, 1969, a,b).	Moderate	Organizational structure and coordination patterns; primarily intergroup concerns but extends to organization/environment relations.
VII. SocioTechnical systems Analysis of "fit" between social and technical systems; redesign of work structures using autonomous groups trained to control their own work processes (Trist, 1969; Pasmore & Sherwood, 1978).	Low/ Moderate	Organizational structure using self-controlled work groups

Approach	Structure	Problem Focus
VIII. Grid organization development Client system managers learn more effective leadership style, move through a six-phase sequence of OD activities that focus on successively higher organizational levels (Blake & Mouton, 1969).	High	Leadership style, primarily individual and interpersonal behavior, but involving large subsystems as clients proceed through the six "phases".
IX. Management by objectives Supervisor-subordinate goal setting is carried out at all organizational levels, beginning at the top of the organization, such that lower-level goals are consistent with all higher level goals; client system members are trained in the goal setting process (Beck & Hillmar, 1972).	Moderate/ High	Goal setting, primarily interpersonal, but designed to impact on the entire organization when the OD approach is properly implemented
X. Survey-guided development Data gathered by means of a standardized questionnaire survey is analyzed, summarized, and fed back to work groups at all organizational levels for problem centered discussion, after all managers are trained in the concepts of group-centered leadership (System 4) (Bowers & Franklin, 1977).	High	Leadership style & organizational climate, primarily at group level 3 but extending to the entire organization in terms of overall climate, when the OD approach is implemented as planned.

the conflicts as problems to be jointly resolved. This involves a high level of interaction between the conflicting parties as well as positive feeling toward one another.

This high level of interaction, characterized by positive sentiments (Homans 1950) supports and reinforces the joint problem-solving process. A *distributive* process works in just the opposite way. The parties automatically assume a win-lose position when conflicts arise. They work to "win" for their side and "defeat" the opponents. They may call for a third party to render judgment and decide who will win, but when the stakes are high, the fight can be lengthy and vicious. The parties keep to their own group, have as little to do with each other as possible, and often dislike the others. The lack of contact and negative feelings serve to reinforce the win-lose conflict dynamic.

Walton's diagnostic model of interpersonal conflict (1969) has four basic elements: (1) the conflict issues; (2) the circumstances that precipitate manifest conflict; (3) the conflict-relevant acts of the principals; and (4) the various consequences of the conflict. Four approaches to conflict management are therefore possible. First, one can prevent ignition of the conflict interchange by controlling the circumstances that precipitate manifest conflict. Second, one can constrain the form of the conflict by controlling the conflict-relevant acts of the principals. Third, one can help the parties cope differently with the consequences of the conflict. Finally, one can eliminate or resolve the conflict issues.

Walton proposes that third parties can serve at least seven functions in surfacing interpersonal or intergroup conflict:

- Ensuring mutual positive motivation
- Balancing the situational power of the two principals
- Synchronizing their confrontation efforts
- Pacing of the differentiation and integration phases of the dialogue
- Creating conditions favoring openness in dialogue (norms, reassurances, skills)
- Developing reliable communicative signs
- Maintaining optimum tension in the system (moderate stress)

Third-party interventions and tactical choices open to the interventionist typically include

- Conducting some preliminary interviewing to identify motivation, issues, and skill levels, among other things.
- Structuring the context for the confrontation to increase the probability of a successful session. This includes attention to such things as the:
  Neutrality of turf
  Formality of the setting
  Timeboundedness of the encounter
  Composition of the meeting
- Intervening in ways that facilitate the dialogue process:
  Refereeing the interaction process
  Initiating agenda
  Restating the issues and the principal's views
  Eliciting reactions and offering observations
  Diagnosing the conflict
  Prescribing discussion methods
  Diagnosing conditions causing poor dialogue
  Counseling interventions (advice on time, suggestions about realistic expectations of progress)
- Planning for future dialogue, so that the start that has been made can be maintained, fostered and developed.

Walton's (1969) OD approach is oriented toward the development of an integrative process for dealing with conflicts. It can be very difficult to move from the distributive process toward an integrative process. This is especially true when the distributive process has been used for a long time, and the negative feelings are very strong. The distributive process serves to perpetuate itself, often with conflicts that are primarily emotional in nature, rather than having real substance. A certain degree of conflict is inevitable in organizations because of limited resources and the competition that ensues. However, a long history of conflicts handled via a distributive process can lead to further conflicts that are based not on such problems of substance, but merely on the parties' dislike for one another. These emotional conflicts are especially hard to deal with, and often a substantive conflict cannot be resolved because of the emotional conflict that accompanies it.

A great deal of skill seems required on the part of the third-party consultant. The consultant must scout the situation, making neutrality very clear to the parties involved. Only then can the consultant get valid information. Confidentiality must be emphasized because only then will the clients trust the consultant enough to open up and uncover the details of a conflict episode as well as the roots of the conflict process. To these process skills the third-party consultant must add content skills—a thorough awareness of the nature of organizational conflict and of conflict dynamics. This places a double burden on the OD consultant who must not only have extensive process skills, but must also be a content expert with respect to conflict.

CONTINGENCY THEORY

This approach, developed by Lawrence and Lorsch (1969a, 1969b), states that the most appropriate structural arrangement is determined on the basis of certain environmental characteristics, especially "uncertainty." Uncertainty refers to the stability or instability of environmental conditions, such as technological change or market competition. Thus, whether a firm should adhere to a traditional structure or use one or more of the newer structural innovations (such as project teams or coordinating departments) will depend on the nature of the environment that the organization finds itself in. When an environment is very uncertain the organization usually develops new, specialized units to cope with the specific types of uncertainty in the environment. The more specialized, or differentiated, that organizational units are, the more difficult it is to provide adequate coordination among the units or, in Lawrence and Lorsch's terms, "integration."

All organizations require a high degree of integration. Organizations, however, that are more differentiated will require more sophisticated integrative mechanisms. These mechanisms may be specific structures, such as temporary task-force teams, or may primarily involve new processes, such as a liaison process between two units that must coordinate effectively. The integrative efforts must match the level of differentiation. That is, integrative efforts must be neither too little nor too great.

There are six primary integrative mechanisms. The first three—written communication, the formal hierarchy, and informal contacts—are normally used in all organizations. The remaining three are more sophisticated mechanisms and are used only as needed in order to effectively integrate under varying degrees of increased differentiation. These three mechanisms, identified by Lawrence and Lorsch, are formal liaison roles, temporary integrating teams, and permanent integrating departments or units.

To this point it may seem that contingency theory is directed solely at structural factors in the organization. This however is not true. All three of the more sophisticated integrative mechanisms require a great deal of attention to organizational processes if they are to be implemented effectively. This is especially true of formal liaison roles and temporary integrative teams. Moreover, effective integration is only possible when an integrative dynamic exists, as defined by Walton and his colleagues (e.g., see Walton, Dutton, & Fitch 1966). When such a dynamic exists, conflict is dealt with through problem solving, that is, "confrontation." In various studies of real organizations Lawrence and Lorsch (1969a) found that only the problem-solving approach is consistently associated with effective resolution of conflicts among differentiated units. Thus, contingency theory, while focused on organizational structures, does pay attention to behavioral processes as well.

In terms of OD applications one can derive three specific questions from contingency theory. First, one must ask whether the structure of the organization fits the environmental demands. To do this, of course, one must assess environmental uncertainty. It should then be possible to determine whether an organization is overly differentiated or is not differentiated enough. The second question is whether the integrative mechanisms being used are adequate to provide integration under the level of differentiation that exists. Again, one must determine whether more sophisticated mechanisms are needed or whether the mechanisms now being used result in overkill. The third and final question has to do with the type of inter-unit dynamic that exists along the integrative-distributive dimension. The nature of this dynamic will determine the way in which conflicts are typically dealt with in the organization.

Although the three questions imply a clear sequence of activities—starting with identifying the nature of the environment and ending by examining the nature of conflict dynamics within the organization—specific action steps are not identified (Lawrence & Lorsch 1969b). Thus, it is not clear exactly how to go about answering each of the three questions. Measurement for diagnosis is quite important for this OD approach, but the measurements developed by Lawrence and Lorsch (1969a) are crude at best, and have been attacked by some (Tosi, Aldeg, & Storey 1973) as being deficient on methodological grounds, making the change agent's task all the more difficult.

Despite the problems we have just identified, contingency theory remains a promising OD approach. This is because it is one of the very few OD approaches that deals explicitly with both structure and behavioral processes and because it is the only OD approach that is concerned with the organization as a whole in interaction with its environment.

SOCIOTECHNICAL SYSTEMS

This approach was developed by researchers at England's Tavistock Institute (Trist & Bamforth 1951; Emery 1959; Rice 1958) following the Second World War. In an effort to understand different productivity levels achieved by various coal mining operations, the researchers discovered that organizational structures formed around the same "core" technology could account for the differences observed in technical and human outcomes. This conclusion led to a theory that proposed that organizations consist of both a social (or human) system and a technological system, and that the "fit" (or lack of fit) between these two systems determines the overall effectiveness of the organization. As the theory would indicate, the sociotechnical systems approach is primarily a theory of organizational design (or redesign); it is unique however, in that it incorporates both industrial engineering and behavioral science concepts in the diagnosis of organizational problems. Moreover, it is a contingency approach, in that the organization is viewed as an open system that must be designed with respect to its environment, thereby calling for each design to take into account the salient features of the environment rather than advocating a single solution for all organizations.

In terms of the social system the STS OD approach centers on the development of small groups that can operate relatively independently or semi-autonomously. This often requires modification with respect to both the technology of the organization and the structure of the organization. A typical pattern is the use of an "intensive" technology (Thompson 1967) within each autonomous group. This means that group members are multi-skilled and involved in highly interdependent team work. Intergroup operations are designed in terms of a pooled technology, that is, each group makes its own relatively independent contribution to the organization. Alternatively, groups may depend on one another in an assembly-line sequence ("long link" technology) with buffers (of inventory, for example) set up between adjacent groups. Such changes obviously require major changes at the organizational level, in terms of both structure of the organization and the forms of technology used, although the STS approach impacts most directly upon small groups.

In order for the small autonomous groups to operate effectively using an intensive technology, they are trained in a variety of technical approaches to dealing with operating problems. These methods include various traditional quality control techniques, centered on methods of variance analysis and control. What this means is that groups learn how to identify important variations in the inputs they receive—that is, in the materials that they must perform work on—as well as in their own task activities. They identify the sources of these variations and make sure that the variations are not outside limits of tolerance. If variations are outside the acceptable limits, groups then proceed to attempt to solve the problems by identifying the reason for the unacceptable variation and correcting it. Thus, the STS OD approach involves technical changes on the small group level, as well as technological change on the organizational level.

The original concepts were successfully put to the test by Rice in his work in the Indian textile mills of Ahmedabad (Rice 1958). Since then, much work has been done both in Europe and the U.S. to extend the sociotechnical systems approach to a wide variety of industries. Some thirty years after the ground-breaking research of Trist and his colleagues in the British coal mining industry, several reviews have concluded that sociotechnical systems approaches are among the most effective methods of planned organizational change (Friedlander & Brown 1974; Srivastva et al. 1975; Pasmore et al. 1982). Accounts of over one hundred experiments have appeared in the literature (Taylor 1977) with many more being kept secret by organizations that believe their work in this area provides them with a competitive edge.

The STS approach has not been without problems. One widely known and initially successful STS OD effort (Walton 1972) conducted in a pet food plant in Topeka, Kansas, eventually failed (Walton 1975). The approach was not accepted at the corporate level or by top management in other plants. This pattern of initial success followed by eventual failure of the STS OD change has been relatively common, occurring in a number of Scandinavian STS OD efforts as well as in American attempts. Still another problem is the confusion between the STS OD approach and the approach to change commonly called "quality of work life." Quality of work life or QWL efforts have become so diverse that the label has little specific meaning. The result is that the STS approach has become confused with a variety of specific OD interventions and may have lost some of its identity as a clear and specific approach to organization development.

As can be seen from our discussion, although the concepts involved in the STS OD approach are essentially simple, the complete theory and the details of its application are rather complicated. Although the measurement methods involved in implementing the STS OD approach may be quite sophisticated, especially variance analysis techniques, there is little attention to diagnostic measurement in this OD approach, that is, the assumption is that any organization ought to be redesigned according to the STS approach. In fact, the STS OD approach seems to be more effective when used to organize new plants rather than as an approach to improve existing organizations. This may be because existing organizations have their own history of problems, most of which are not directly addressed by the STS OD approach.

The sociotechnical systems OD approach is one of the most sophisticated organization development approaches. It normally involves a large-scale effort and commitment on the part of the organization involved, as well as requiring considerable skill on the part of the OD consultant. At this point, it is safe to conclude, given the preponderance of evidence, that the sociotechnical systems approach has had a significant impact on ideas about what it takes to design organizations for both machines and people in ways that result in higher productivity and satisfaction. It also seems clear that the current level of success achieved by sociotechnical systems designers will lead to further application of the approach (Pasmore et al. 1982). Nevertheless, the complexity of the theory and analytic techniques used (Herbst 1974) as well as political, social, and economic roadblocks (Pasmore 1982) continue to restrict the spread of socio-technical systems OD. Fortunately, more information is becoming available about the approach itself and its application that should help to counteract these difficulties.

APPLICATION

Of the ten approaches briefly reviewed in Table 22.1, we selected the three just described for a more in-depth review, due to their special relevance to current organizational problems. One might, then, think that these three would be the most widely used OD approaches. This is not true. The most widely used approaches are the final three in Table 22.1. These highly structured "programmed" approaches typically focus on specific concerns such as leadership practices, goal setting, and group problem solving. In contrast, with the possible exception of the sociotechnical systems approach, the three we just detailed have probably had the *least* widespread use of any of the ten approaches listed in Table 22.1.

We should note that all three critical approaches are widely recognized and are seen by many as basic to OD theory and practice. Thus, on a conceptual level these approaches have had considerable impact; they have also deeply affected OD practice. For example, third-party consultation OD introduced the concepts of conflict episodes and of integrative versus distributive conflict processes existing between or among organizational units. Contingency theory OD has led to the general recognition of the importance of the environment for choosing an appropriate organizational structure, as well as identifying a variety of basic devices and procedures for improving interunit coordination. Sociotechnical systems OD has made commonplace the basic insight that the social and technical subsystems of an organization must "fit" one with the other, and has also served as a vehicle for the infrequent (but important) attempts to implement sophisticated tools such as variance analysis and the frequent efforts to implement "quality of worklife" (QWL) programs.

Our point remains, however: none of the three approaches has become widely used as specific applications of what Burke and Hornstein (1972) call the "social technology of organization development." Why has there been no widespread "diffusion" of these approaches throughout the field of OD? We suggest two primary reasons. The first centers on certain distinguishing characteristics of widely used OD approaches: they are clearly structured, often in step-by-step fashion, with little mystery or uncertainty as to what actions the OD practitioner must engage in at any particular time. Moreover, they focus on fairly well-defined issues or problems. In contrast, our three underused approaches are characterized by lack of clearcut step-wise action plans and, in the case of contingency theory and STS, complex or unclear central themes.

A second reason goes deeper behind the rational factors just cited. This concerns the sources of support that change approaches draw upon. Chin and Benne (1969) identified three such primary factors. The first involves rational argument and evidence; Chin and Benne call this the "rational-empirical" sup-port base for change. It relies on the assumption that a clear and logical argu-ment, coupled with empirical evidence as to the potential benefits of change, will lead people (and organiztions) to implement and support changes that are in their own self-interest. Chin and Benne (1969) note that while there is truth to this assumption, we often credit the rational-empirical approach with much more strength than it really has.

Another commonly recognized basis of support for change is *power*. Mao Tse-tung put it most concisely when he said, "Power comes from the barrel of a gun." Most OD practitioners overtly shy away from such values, although many will recommend the use of "legitimate" authority (such as executive management support) to bolster OD efforts.

The final support base for change discussed by Chin and Benne grows out of group norms. When members of a group openly agree to some change in the way people "ought to" behave, this provides a very powerful support for the change. This has been demonstrated repeatedly in a wide range of research and application reports, beginning with the classic work of Kurt Lewin (1947) in changing housewive's food buying behaviors. "Normative-reeducative" support for change, as Chin and Benne call it, is perhaps the most powerful of all the support bases, and is integral to most of the early approaches, especially approaches II, III, and IV in Table 22.1. Apparently a normative-reeducative support base can even make up for weaknesses in terms of the rational-empirical support base (such as an unclear structure or focus to the OD approach).

Returning to our three critical OD approaches, we can see that only the rational-empirical support base for change has been used as a consistent element in the spread of these approaches. That is, the approaches are covered in most OD tests, classes, and training activities and have thus become part of the formal "rational" knowledge base of organization development. As a result, as students, especially MBA students, move into upper level managerial positions they may be more open to the use of these OD approaches. And, students in more specialized OD practitioner programs may "seed" these approaches in their consulting work.

Unfortunately, these are long-range prospects. When we think of today's managers in upper-level positions, it is clear that it is rare for such individuals to have any meaningful rational-empirical understanding of the three critical OD approaches. The OD practitioner may indeed have a clear understanding of these approaches, but may not be equipped to effectively communicate this understanding to managers.

When we look at the three critical OD approaches in terms of the more powerful normative-reeducative support base, it appears that none of them make effective use of this support for change, in the context of the actual implemen-tation of the approaches in OD. (The sociotechnical systems OD approach may be something of an exception; groups are typically involved as a basic aspect of STS implementation programs, and a normative-reeducative support base is thus created. The effective use of this base to further the OD effort is another matter.)

It may not distress one that the power-coercive support base is unused. It should, however, be of great concern that the OD approaches that seem most important for organizations in our society remain underutilized, in terms of direct applications if not in conceptual influence on practice. One remedy would involve efforts to develop the normative-reeducative support base in terms of each of these approaches. One might also speculate on how to strengthen the rational-empirical base. A variety of approaches toward these aims would be desirable, and we now turn to a brief report of one attempt to generate such approaches.

PROMOTING APPLICATION

In order to promote the application of the three critical approaches, a symposium was organized to review the problem and the above explanation, and to generate ideas for increasing use of third-party consultation, contingency theory, and sociotechnical systems in OD practice.* The authors of this report served as presentors and discussion leaders. After brief presentations of the three OD approaches and of the problem of diffusion, there was a general discussion involving about thirty persons (in addition to the presentors). Table 22.2 lists the ideas brought up, in abbreviated form.

We have tried to categorize the fifteen suggestions in Table 22.2 in terms of the support base for change that each one draws on. The first two ideas clearly rely on power as their support base for change. The next five are just as clear in their reliance on rational-empirical support for change. (Suggestion 3 was noted earlier as one that is probably being used.) Suggestions 8 and 9 may be somewhat more sophisticated, but still seem to draw on the rational-empirical base.

The next three ideas, 10–12, (mentioned earlier as having some degree of use), combine the rational-empirical base with a much more sophisticated strategy for diffusion, based on a simple, but workable, marketing model for diffusing knowledge or innovations (for example, see Havelock 1969 or Sashkin et al. 1973). Suggestions 13 and 14 are based on diffusion models, in the former case on the opinion leader model of social interaction and diffusion (e.g., Menzel & Katz, 1955–56) and in the latter case on the sort of "linkage" model proposed by Havelock (1968). The final idea *might* involve the application of normative-reeducative support for change in terms of OD practitioner training.

At the time of the discussion, a brainstorming approach was used to generate as many ideas as possible. Ideas were explored only very briefly; for the most part, such exploration was limited to extending or adding to the suggestion rather than involving any in-depth focus. Reviewing the ideas in the process of preparing this report, the authors were struck most by the lack of suggestions that made use of the normative-reeducative basis for change. We were, however, consoled by two facts: the appearance of several rational-empirical based suggestions that involve developing clear structures for these OD approaches (for

---

*The symposium was held as part of the annual national meeting of the Academy of Management, in New York City, on August 13, 1982.

TABLE 22.2   Diffusion Suggestions

1. Legislate "human organization maintenance," as Lawler suggests, and develop clear application strategies for maintaining the human organization.
2. Design actions at the top of the organization. Develop support for the OD approaches at the level of the board of directors.
3. Make these OD models clearer to students; build them into MBA programs, so that managers will have clear conceptual models of OD as well as awareness of good OD practice.
4. Raise consciousness among managers about OD approaches. This can be done by writing in their "language" and by identifying costs and benefits.
5. Build "application structures" by providing clearcut sets of steps for implementing various OD approaches, so that they are not mysterious and can be applied by persons with only a basic level of OD competency.
6. Develop discrepancy motivation among managers, by "fostering discontent." This can be done by making OD success highly visible and making sure that knowledge of the success is as widespread as possible among managers. Then develop and disseminate simple diagnostic tools that a manager can use to see where he/she stands.
7. Identify OD strategies that apply to specific organizations, that are geared to certain organizational contingencies.
8. Look for organizations in crisis and offer the OD approaches as potential treatments.
9. Identify managerial resistances to OD approaches, trace the sources.
10. Train OD practitioners in specific OD approaches, so that they can effectively implement them, much as one trains agricultural agents and gives them working knowledge of new agricultural innovations.
11. "Seed" the large consulting firms with well-trained students.
12. Develop a sophisticated mass marketing design, including films and campaigns (as used in agricultural change) focusing on the needs of managers.
13. Seek out "leading edge" organizations, that can give commitment to applying these OD approaches.
14. Develop a distribution system, for distributing OD knowledge. Such a system may be created from scratch or may be coopted using some existing infrastructure.
15. Provide improved process skill training for OD practitioners.

example, suggestions 3–5), and the presence of several ideas that incorporate elements from the literature on diffusion of knowledge and innovation (for example, numbers 10–14).

Many of the ideas make good sense. If applied to the three critical OD approaches, they would provide added support for their use. Still, there would seem to be even greater benefit obtained by somehow making use of the normative-reeducative support base.

We believe that it is possible to increase rational-empirical support, as well as "designing" normative-reeducative support into the three critical approaches. In the case of third-party consultation, this would involve re-focusing on intergroup (rather than interpersonal) conflicts and involving intact work groups in the OD process to a much greater extent. Further, the model needs to be redeveloped in terms of generic steps or sequences of actions, and a simplified description would also help.

With respect to contingency theory OD, the role of work groups and project teams could be enhanced throughout the OD process. This would build in the normative-reeducative support. Again, a clear set of steps or activities is needed to improve the rational-empirical support base.

Finally, we have noted that the emphasis on the use of work groups in implementing the sociotechnical systems OD approach has been its strength. What is greatly lacking is an easy-to-understand description of the approach, along with a typical sequence of activities. The provision of these would add rational-empirical support to existing normative-reeducative support for change.

CONCLUSION

In this report we identified and briefly described a set of basic approaches to OD. We argued that three of these seem to us to be of special importance, due to their relevance to major social issues of our time. We noted, however, that while the three "critical" OD approaches have all had substantial impact on how organization development is studied and carried out, none has had equivalent impact in the sense of direct application in OD efforts. We suggested that this may be due to emphasis on rational-empirical support for change and inadequate focus on the development of normative-reeducative support. The most directly applied of the three OD approaches, sociotechnical systems OD, may owe this fact to the incorporation of a group change—normative-reeducative—aspect as a standard element.

To generate ideas for increasing the use of the three critical approaches a symposium was designed and conducted. The arguments detailed here were presented and a group discussion ensued, resulting in a set of specific suggestions. Most of these ideas centered on developing more or stronger rational-empirical support bases; some even focused on using the power-coercive base. None overtly and clearly involved new normative-reeducative elements.

It may be that the development of a social "infrastructure" is a precondition for creating such new normative-reeducative devices. That is, some continuing group may be needed to develop and disseminate normative support bases for OD involving any of the three critical approaches. One possible movement in this direction is an ongoing informal contact among the primary professional OD groups—the OD Network, the OD Division of the Academy of Management, and the OD Division of the ASTD, along with several smaller OD-related organizations. Several of the most promising ideas for generating wider use of the three critical approaches seem to require some organized entity that could normatively validate such diffusion efforts and serve as a means for spreading knowledge.

References

Beck, A. C., Jr., & Hillmar, E. D. *A practical approach to organization development through MBO.* Reading, MA: Addison-Wesley, 1972.

Blake, R. R., & Mouton, J. S. *Achieving corporate excellence through grid organization development.* Reading, MA: Addison-Wesley, 1969.

Blake, R. R., Shepard, H. A., & Mouton, J. S. *Managing intergroup conflict in industry.* Houston: Gulf, 1965.

Bowers, D. G., & Franklin, J. L., *Survey-guided development I: Data-based organizational change.* San Diego, CA: University Associates, 1977.

Bradford, L. P., Gibb, J. R., & Benne, K. D. *T-group theory and laboratory method.* New York: Wiley, 1964.

Burke, W. W., & Hornstein, H. A. (Eds.) *The social technology of organization development.* San Diego, CA: University Associates, 1972.

Chin, R., & Benne, K. D. General strategies for effecting change in human systems. In W. G. Bennis, K. D. Benne, & R. Chin (Eds.), *The planning of change.* (2nd ed.) New York: Holt, Rinehart & Winston, 1969.

Dutton, J. M., & Walton, R. E. Interdepartmental conflict and cooperation: Two contrasting studies. *Human Organization,* 1966, *25,* 207–221.

Emery, F. Characteristics of Socio-Technical Systems. Doc. No. 527, Tavistock Institute of Human Relations, 1959.

Friedlander, F. and Brown, L. D. Organization development. *Annual Review of Psychology,* 1974, *25,* 313–41.

Frohman, M. A., Sashkin, M., & Kavanagh, M. J. Action-research as an organization development approach. *Organization and Administrative Sciences,* 1976, *7* (1–2), 129–42.

Havelock, R. G. Dissemination and translation roles. In T. L. Eidell & J. M. Kitchell (Eds.), *Knowledge production and utilization in educational administration.* Eugene, Ore.: University Council for Educational Administration, and Center for Advanced Study of Educational Administration, University of Oregon, 1968.

Havelock, R. G., with Guskin, A. E., Frohman, M. A., Havelock, M., Hill, M., & Huber, J. *Planning for innovation.* Ann Arbor, Mich.: University of Michigan, Institute for Social Research, 1969.

Herbst, P. G. *Sociotechnical design.* London: Tavistock, 1974.

Homans, G. *The human group.* New York: Harcourt, Brace, 1950.

Huse, E. F. *Organization development and change* (2d ed.) St. Paul, MN: West, 1980.

Lawrence, P. R., & Lorsch, J. W. *Organization and environment.* Homewood, IL: Irwin, 1969a.

Lawrence, P. R., & Lorsch, J. W. *Developing organizations: Diagnosis and action.* Reading, MA: Addison-Wesley, 1969b.

Leavitt, H. J. Applied organizational change in industry: Structural, technological, and humanistic approaches. In J. G. March (Ed.), *Handbook of organizations.* Chicago: Rand-McNally, 1965.

Lewin, K. Group decision and social change. In T. M. Newcomb and E. L. Hartley (Eds.), *Readings in social psychology,* New York: Holt, Rinehart and Winston, 1947.

Mann, F. C. Studying and creating change: A means to understanding social organization. In C. M. Arensberg et al. (Eds.), *Research in industrial human relations.* New York: Harper, 1957. (Industrial Relations Research Association, Publication Number 17.)

Menzel, H. & Katz, E. Social relations and innovation in the medical profession: The epidemiology of a new drug. *Public Opinion Quarterly,* 1955–1956, *19,* 337–52.

Pasmore, W. A. Overcoming the roadblocks in work restructuring. *Organizational Dynamics,* 1982, *10,* (4), 54–67.

Pasmore, W. A., Francis, C., Haldeman, J. & Shani, A. Sociotechnical systems: A North American reflection on empirical studies of the seventies. *Human Relations,* 1982, *35.*

Pasmore, W. A., & Sherwood, J. J. *Sociotechnical systems: A sourcebook.* San Diego, CA: University Associates, 1978.

Rice, A. K. *Productivity and social organization: The Ahmedabad experiment.* London: Tavistock, 1958.

Sashkin, M., Morris, W. C., & Horst, L. A comparison of social and organizational change models: Information flow and data use processes. *Psychological Review,* 1973, *80,* 510–26.

Schein, E. H. *Process consultation.* Reading, MA: Addison-Wesley, 1969.

Srivastva, S., Salipante, P., Cummings, T., Notz, W., Bigelow, J. & Waters, J. *Job Satisfaction and Productivity.* Department of Organizational Behavior, Case Western Reserve University, Cleveland, Ohio, 1975.

Taylor, J. Experiments in work system design: Economic and human results. *Personnel Review,* 1977, *6.*

Thompson, J. D. *Organizations in action.* New York: McGraw-Hill, 1967.

Tosi, H., Aldeg, R. & Storey, R. On the measurement of the environment: An assessment of the Lawrence and Lorsch environmental uncertainty subscale. *Administrative Science Quarterly,* 1973, *18,* 27–36.

Trist, E. L. On socio-technical systems. In W. G. Bennis, K. D. Benne, & R. Chin (Eds.), *The planning of change.* (2d ed.) New York: Holt, Rinehart & Winston, 1969.

Trist, E. L., & Bamforth, K. Some social and psychological consequences of the longwall method of coal-getting. *Human Relations,* 1951, *4,* 1–38.

Walton, R. E. *Interpersonal peacemaking: Confrontations and third-party consultation.* Reading, MA: Addison-Wesley, 1969.

Walton, R. E. How to counter alienation in the plant. *Harvard Business Review,* 1972, *50*(6), 70–81.

Walton, R. E. The diffusion of new work structures: Explaining why success didn't take. *Organizational Dynamics,* 1975, *3*(3), 3–22.

Walton, R. E., & Dutton, J. M. The management of interdepartmental conflict: A model and review. *Administrative Science Quarterly,* 1969, *14,* 73–84.

Walton, R. E., Dutton, J. M., & Fitch, H. G. A study of conflict in the process, structure, and attitudes of lateral relationships. In A. M. Rubenstein and C. J. Haberstroh (Eds.), *Some theories of organization.* (rev. ed.) Homewood, IL: Irwin, 1966.

Walton, R. E., & McKersie, R. B. *Interpersonal interdependency: A behavioral theory of labor negotiations.* New York: McGraw-Hill, 1965.

23 Organization Development Strategies for Effective Management of Cockpit Crises

Robert R. Blake
Jane S. Mouton

ABSTRACT

This paper presents an OD effort designed to improve managerial performance in the airliner cockpit. Specific application of organization development strategies to the problem of air safety is described in detail. Through this systematic approach, crew members who equate strong leadership with quick, decisive, unilateral action come to understand the importance of leadership that taps all available resources and brings them to bear on finding and implementing optimal solutions to flight-related problems. Practical application of the theory and principles of participation during simulated flight situations allows crew members to personally experience the benefits of effective cockpit teamwork. Results reported here illustrate that OD can shift managerial attitudes, values, and behaviors in ways that maximize human potential.

AUTHOR BACKGROUNDS

Robert R. Blake is chairman of Scientific Methods, Inc., in Austin, Texas, and formerly a professor in the Department of Psychology at the University of Texas. He was a Fulbright scholar, studying in Great Britain; has a B.A. from Berea College; and M.S. from The University of Virgina; and a Ph.D. from The University of Texas.

Jane S. Mouton is president of Scientific Methods, Inc., and formerly an assistant professor in the Department of Psychology at The University of Texas. She holds a B.S. Ed. from Florida State University, and a Ph.D. from The University of Texas.

The Captain and other officers in the cockpit of the modern jet constitute an organization charged with responsibility for conducting each flight safely to its destination. Effective team action is critical to meeting this important objective, especially when an emergency or crisis arises.

> I was the first officer on a flight into Chicago O'Hare. The Captain was flying, we were on approach and moving along about 250 knots. Approach Control told us to slow to 180 knots. I acknowledged and waited for the Captain to slow down. When he failed to respond, I repeated "Approach said slow to 180." His comment was, "You just look out the damn window." Approach Control called again, "Why haven't you slowed yet . . . . You almost hit another aircraft."

The paraphrased example above[1] and recent episodes such as Air Florida's 14th Street Bridge crash in Washington or Pan Am's New Orleans catastrophe suggests that more is involved in airline safety than communication between the plane and tower, instrument malfunctioning, bad weather, or crew member competence. While these may be important contributing factors, the "ultimate cause" of many air disasters may be most directly related to the exercise of cockpit leadership and captain/crew decision making.

The National Aeronautics and Space Administration (NASA), in researching and evaluating air safety, points to the "human factor" as a most frequent cause of disastrous and near disastrous incidents.[2] In a landmark airline industry study and conference held in San Francisco in 1979, NASA officials reported the conclusions of airline safety studies completed up to that time. By way of paraphrase, they indicated that:

> Too many crashes and near misses occur in circumstances where the "ultimate cause" cannot be traced to air-to-ground communications, equipment failure, lack of technical competence or a time factor. In too many cases, it has been demonstrated that adequate technical resources for solving the problem *were available* in the cockpit, but were not mobilized effectively.

Is it possible to apply behavioral science principles in analyzing and developing leadership skills that contribute to effective resource utilization in the airliner cockpit? A recent experiment suggests an affirmative answer. In fact, important organization development strategies are now being applied to cockpit management through application of a sound, team-based approach.

This is a report of our involvement in an organization development project designed to provide a solution to the airline industry's "human factor" problem. Recognizing the importance of effective leadership and decision making to successful routine flight operations, as well as resolution of crises and emergency situations, a major airline contracted with Scientific Methods, Inc., for study and analysis of cockpit dynamics. On the basis of our study and research, it was possible to isolate and identify the strengths and weaknesses of various management styles and to determine their effectiveness in mobilizing the cockpit's human resources. This joint effort is detailed here, along with a description of the significant conclusions reached, and the training and development strategies that are being implemented, as a result.

SORTING OUT THE CRISIS MANAGEMENT PROBLEM

Despite improved technology and increased automation, piloting today's aircraft is a complex and complicated activity requiring both aviation proficiency and managerial expertise. For the most part, airline industry training and development efforts of the past focused on the technical rather than human aspects of flight safety. Systematic development of cockpit leadership skills, though critically needed, has historically been regarded as secondary in importance.

Recognizing this pressing problem, one airline was willing to invest both time and resources in finding a creative, innovative solution. Seven airline officers were placed on temporary duty with our organization. We designated seven key personnel to complete a joint task force which had major responsibility for this priority effort. The task force worked for eighteen months, initially meeting together for a week at a time, then returning to their home bases. During later phases of the project, much of the work was completed individually or in pairs.

At the beginning of our work, the flying personnel made a major point with regard to the exercise of captain authority. They emphasized the importance of captain decisiveness. Without decisiveness, uncertainty is communicated; divergent, uncoordinated, individually centered actions are more likely to be taken by other crew members; and conditions for insubordination may be created. Their primary concern was that captain authority in the cockpit should be strengthened so that conditions favorable to insubordination are not created.

Once these ground rules were clearly established, our challenge was to apply the theory and principles of participation and teamwork to the cockpit environment. Though the captain is ultimately responsible for the mission, each crew member's involvement and commitment are critical to a safely conducted flight. A team approach in the cockpit ensures that the crew's best resources are brought to bear on both routine flight operations and emergency or crisis situations. When seen from an organization development perspective, strong leadership is the ability to mobilize available resources.

Traditional perceptions regarding strong leadership may imply greater independence than is characteristic of team-oriented, participative management. Cockpit effectiveness is more than each crew member knowing and executing his or her own responsibilities, more or less independently, in accordance with standard operating procedure. A truly effective cockpit requires the interdependent, coordinated, collaborative pursuit of superordinate goals and agreed upon standards of excellence.

BEHAVIORAL SCIENCES ANALYSIS OF LEADERSHIP UNDER CRISIS

Our second step was a systematic analysis of alternative ways of exercising captain authority. The basic grid structure was used to identify various captain authority options, that is, 9,1, 1,9, 1,1, 5,5 and 9,9. This framework, which we will discuss in detail later, provides a basis for evaluating the strengths and limitations of each of the five primary leadership styles, not only for routine flying circumstances but also for managing emergencies.

Next, we isolated five of the most important considerations in effective cockpit leadership. These elements of cockpit management are prerequisites for crew member teamwork and maximum resource utilization. One of these teamwork requirements involves a heightened standard for continuous *inquiry* by all crew members into the flight's operating status. When inquiry is practiced in the cockpit, increased understanding, greater vigilance, and deeper awareness of the flight's development results. Proactive monitoring of the technical environment of the airplane and its instruments becomes a shared responsibility. Inquiry is at its peak when crew members are alert to the existence of discrepancies between conditions as programmed and actual conditions. Inquiry helps ensure that crew member input will be pertinent and valid if an emergency arises.

Another critical element in effective teamwork under crisis conditions is *advocacy*. Advocacy means that all crew members are open and direct in forwarding information and expressing convictions, reservations, doubts, and misgivings until the captain makes a final decision.

Conflict is the third important element identified during our study. By focusing on *what* is right, rather than *who* is right in conflict situations, win-lose arguments that polarize crew members can be avoided. If conflict surfaces and is explored and resolved, it can provide a foundation for mutual trust and respect, deeper analysis, better problem definition and improved solutions.

The fourth identified element of effective cockpit leadership is *critique*. Critique describes a process of preplanning, ongoing feedback and post-mortem evaluation that enhances a crew's potential for learning from their experiences. Mistakes of the past do not have to be repeated when a thorough examination and analysis reveals their causes and suggests future alternatives.

Finally, the element of *decision making* emerged as critically important to leadership effectiveness. Many cockpit decisions are so complex and consequential that broad-based input is essential to high quality solutions. Crew members' participation in cockpit decision making impacts not only the quality of an eventual decision, but increases crew member commitment and support as well.

ORGANIZATION DEVELOPMENT THEORY INTERVENTION

To increase cockpit effectiveness, it is necessary to deal with the cockpit trio (captain and first and second officers) as an organization led by the captain and governed by established norms, practices and procedures. The new norms of (1) reponse to input, (2) more thorough inquiry, and (3) advocacy need to be brought into use for maximum use of crew resources. The next step of our project involved designing a training seminar based on these new insights in which captains test their own natural inclinations regarding the use of authority against a sound model. Two prototype seminars, each attended by twenty-four captains, were undertaken to evaluate the seminar content and design. Participants read *The Cockpit Grid* text, as prework.[3] This text, written with participation and involvement from the task force, applies grid theory to cockpit leadership with special emphasis placed on leadership effectiveness in managing crisis situations. Prior to seminar attendance, each captain completes a number of self-assessment instruments that reveal his personal assumptions about exercising captain authority within the cockpit. This three-and-a-half-day seminar allows captains to experience the following design, which is becoming the standard airline industry approach for strengthening teamwork in the cockpit.

The seminar begins with participant teams working on measurable activities designed to strengthen their cognitive understanding of grid theories and principles as they apply to cockpit management. For the initial task, each team member has information that is not known to the others. Members must explore and develop the skills of inquiry and advocacy in order to complete the task successfully. The activity also tests the participants' abilities to effectively work together in mobilizing knowledge essential for reaching valid decisions. This is a realistic methodology because the content of the tasks reflects the need for taking advantage of input prior to decision making. When synergy is experienced, the importance of inquiry, advocacy, and input to managing a cockpit becomes self-evident.

In subsequent tasks, participants experience a variety of activities designed to strengthen application of the theories introduced previously. Role-played simulation of cockpit situations provides experience in solving real flying problems, for example, technical difficulties with equipment or weather, contradictory instrument information, or conflicting or alternative approaches to a problem.

In another exercise, captains work in six-member teams to discuss and reach mutual agreement on sound cockpit leadership. The task is to rank the five basic grid alternatives for effectiveness for seven critical elements of cockpit coordination. For this exercise, the five basic elements are expanded to include *captain authority* and *training and development*. The first element is related to valid problem definition; another deals with creating a spirit of inquiry rather than taking data at face value; a third relates to the resolution of conflict among crew members; a fourth is concerned with utilizing critique to promote an attitude of continuous learning. The fifth deals with strengthening advocacy whenever a crew member has a conviction. In the sixth, captains explore how training and development can best be used to upgrade crew performance. The seventh area of exploration relates to the exercise of the captain's authority in directing and coordinating crew effort in non-crisis as well as crisis situations.

As an example, the seventh item, Captain's authority, is reproduced in Table 23.1.

When rankings of each of the five grid styles are combined for the seven leadership elements, the highest ranking any grid style can receive is 35 and the lowest, is 7. The data shown in Table 23.2 reflects the rankings compiled from 36 different seminars attended by approximately 780 commercial airline Captains.

TABLE 23.1   The Exercise of Captain's Authority Under Different Leadership Styles

---

Leadership style: Rank from most effective style (5) to least effective style (1)

A. _____   The Captain seeks to establish a warm and friendly atmosphere in the cockpit. This minimizes the need to exercise authority. Agreements come in an easy way since there is cohesion among crew members.

B. _____   The Captain exercises authority so as to maintain a balance between the needs for effective performance and the desires of other crew members. He retains responsibility for ultimate decisions but understands that it is important to take the views of others into account.

C. _____   The Captain makes effective use of authority by directing the effort in such a manner as to maximize crew involvement and participation. In this way he gains the use of all available resources toward the objective of excellence. When time is a critical factor he does not hesitate to decide or choose a course of action.

D. _____   The Captain rarely exercises authority; as for the most part the flight operates itself. Other crew members offer relevant information if necessary.

E. _____   The Captain feels accountable only to himself. Since the responsibility is his, he expects his decisions to be accepted as final. He asks for information from the other crew members only when necessary.

Source: Blake, R. R., and Mouton, J. S. Command/Leadership/Resource Management Seminar Materials. Austin, Texas: Scientific Methods, Inc., 1981.

The average score given by captains to the 9,9 alternative demonstrates that they see this leadership orientation as the most effective way of exercising captain authority in mobilizing human resources. Expressed in percentages, the 9,9 style is the first choice of 99.7% of the captains, a result which is statistically significant far beyond the .001 level of confidence for an X^2 test of significance.

A final segment of the seminar involves Captains in giving and receiving feedback and critique of one another's professional effectiveness as leaders of the cockpit organization. Through the feedback process, Captains assist one another in seeing opportunities for improving personal and team effectiveness in flying situations.

A key to solving the "human" problem in airline safety is the transfer of these skills back to the cockpit. Transferability is enhanced by use of the 727/747/767 simulators to study teamwork effectivness and evaluate captain proficiency in applying sound leadership. Once all three crew members have attended the Cockpit Grid seminar, real lifelike crises are programmed into the simulator for a team-building experience. This approach allows the cockpit organization to gain experience in exercising effective crisis management before the occurrence of a flight malfunction at 33,000 feet.

In terms of actual flying experience, crew members have had much lower mistake rates on flights with FAA inspectors than they did before the program was started a year ago, according to Robert S. Crump, United Air Lines Vice President for Flight Standards and Training.[4]

TABLE 23.2 Effectiveness Scores by Leadership Style in Three-Man Air Crews

Leadership style	9,9	9,1	5,5	1,9	1,1
Keyed alternatives in Table 23.1	E	D	B	A	C
Average score	34.9	20.4	23.4	17.5	8.8

SUMMARY AND IMPLICATIONS

Conclusions from this research and training project have significant implications for individual and organization development. A small group, such as the two or three member crew of the modern airline, is an organization development unit. Together the captain and other officers exercise ultimate responsibility for proficient and safe flying performance. Their task is to mobilize and make maximum use of all *resources*: technical and human. An organization development theory-based intervention can strengthen leadership effectiveness and increase crew member inquiry and advocacy as ways of mobilizing all human resources.

Another important conclusion is that conventional views regarding the unilateral exercise of power and authority under crisis conditions needs reexamination. More than a thousand airline captains have evaluated the options for exercising leadership and have concluded that the 9,9 approach is the most effective, especially under crisis conditions. Strengthening inquiry and advocacy by all crew members is recognized as critical to the captain's exercise of 9,9-oriented authority.

The findings reported here suggest similar conclusions as to the exercise of authority in corporate decision making, even under crisis conditions. Crises in the air arise when something unanticipated or not readily explainable occurs. In business, industry, and government, unexpected, inexplicable situations are a frequent occurrence. Unless these situations are dealt with effectively, their consequences can be equally disastrous. Routine, recurring problems that are allowed to fester until they assume crisis proportions can have the same disruptive effect.

Managers at every level, in every organization, make important decisions under difficult and trying conditions. The consequences of poor decisions are individually and organizationally costly. Effective leadership and good teamwork results in better utilization of human resources and improved management of organizational crises. Cooperation and participation among managerial team members results in higher quality decisions to which those involved are committed, and earn for the manager increased respect from his or her superiors, colleagues, and subordinates.

References

1. Foushee, H. Clayton. "The Role of Communications, Socio-Psychological, and Personality Factors in the Maintenance of Crew Coordination." *Aviation, Space and Environmental Medicine.* In press.
2. Cooper, George E., White, Maurice D., and Lauber, John K. (Eds.). *Resource Management on the Flight Deck.* Moffett Field, California: National Aeronautics and Space Administration, 1980.
3. Blake, Robert R., Mouton, Jane S., and Command/Leadership/Resource Management Steering Committee and Working Groups—United. *Cockpit Resource Management.* Denver, Colorado: Cockpit Resource Management, 1982.
4. Feaver, Douglas B., "Pilots in Retraining Learn to Handle Crises, and Themselves . . . While Pointing to the Cockpit After a Crash, Asking 'Why?,'" The Washington Post, Sunday, September 12, 1982.

24 Improving the Health and Stress Management of Federal Workers

John D. Adams
Eleanor Fischer-Quigley
Jane Schmithorst

ABSTRACT

This study describes a stress management training design and reviews its use in three different federal agencies. In each case, a comprehensive set of stress- and health-related questionnaires (including a pre-post measure) is completed prior to training. Six months following the training, the pre-post measure is repeated. Differences in stress management and life-style habits are compared. Length of training program is found to be a major factor generating sustained improvements in stress management and life-style habits.

AUTHOR BACKGROUND

John Adams, Ph.D., is an independent consultant with an international practice in organization development, serving a variety of clients including hospitals, R&D centers, public utilities, industry, government agencies, and schools. He also is an adjunct faculty member at two universities. Prior to becoming a full-time consultant, Dr. Adams was Director of Professional Development for the National Training Laboratories and a visiting professor at the University of Leeds (England). He is a member of the National Training Laboratory and is on the board of directors of the International Association of Applied Social

This paper was presented at the Wellness in the Workplace Conference, May 1982, in Pittsburgh, Pennsylvania.

Scientists. He also belongs to th American Psychological Association, the Association for Humanistic Psychology, and the Organization Development Network. Dr. Adams has written numerous books and articles on stress, transitions, organization development, and professional development. His most recent book is entitled *Understanding and Managing Stress.*

Eleanor Fischer-Quigley is a mid-level management training project manager for the Internal Revenue Service in Washington, D.C. where she manages activities of task forces designing human relations, stress management, and ADP training, supervises computerization of program administration, makes presentations, conducts classes and research, and secures resources for highly visible training efforts. She has a master's in public administration from The George Washington University.

Jane Schmithorst is employed by the Department of the Navy as an associate with the Naval Aviation Executive Institute, part of the Naval Air Systems Command. She has formerly worked with the National Institutes of Health and the Food and Drug Administration, as well as the Procter and Gamble Company. She holds a bachelor's in economics from Purdue University and a master's in business administration from The George Washington University. She is currently pursuing doctoral studies in public administration at the University of Southern California's Washington Public Affairs Center.

While precise figures may never be available, it is now well established that the costs, both in direct payments and in lost productivity, of stress related problems are staggering. Over half of the premature deaths (before age 65) in the U.S. are due to heart disease; and over half of the risks associated with developing heart disease are due to life style-habits, which include how one manages stress.[1] Dr. E. M. Gherman estimates that 132 million workdays per year are lost in this country due to heart disease; that treatment costs for heart disease average $40,000 per incident; and that the recruiting cost alone for replacing organizational members felled by heart disease is at least $700 million per year.[2] Similar statistics could be cited for other stress-related causes of lost productivity, for example, cancer, ulcers, and accidents. An employee assistance counselor in one federal agency recently estimated that a "troubled" employee loses an average of 25% of her or his productive capacity and that a high percentage of federal employees could be considered to be troubled. Stress and burnout clearly are very costly, and an understanding of what might be done to reduce their impact is urgently needed.

These kinds of estimates are alarming to a growing number of executives across the spectrum of federal agencies. Their concerns, coupled with both the concerns of and the methodologies available to training program specialists, has led to the development of a number of educational programs intended to educate agency employees about what stress is, where it comes from, what it can do, and how to reduce its impact.

This paper reviews the experience to date of three federal agencies that have made use, in slightly different formats, of one widely successful approach to helping managers understand what stress and burnout are all about and what they can do to protect themselves from experiencing burnout due to excessive, poorly managed stress. The agencies and programs involved in this study include educational programs offered by the Executive and Management Development Branch of the National Institutes of Health, the Department of the Navy (an R and D group and the Naval Aviation Executive Institute of the Naval Air Systems Command), and the Internal Revenue Service. While the programs offered have ranged from three hours to four residential days, all have involved extensive prework diagnosis of stress and other health risk levels and all have involved a post-training followup assessment of personal changes relevant to managing stress and preventing burnout. In addition, all of the programs have been based on the same model of how stress operates and the same overall framework for developing a personal stress management plan.

This paper describes the needs analyses used in these agencies that led to the decision to offer stress management education programs. The model used and the design of the programs are described in some detail. Summaries are provided of the workshop evaluations and of the impact of the workshops on individual participants. Finally, implications for stress reduction and burnout prevention in federal agencies are discussed.

TRAINING NEEDS ANALYSIS

The three agencies became involved in stress management education programs through three different routes. There is a common element in their experience—the presence of an employee development specialist with personal interest and commitment to stress management education.

Beginning in 1977, the staff of the Naval Aviation Executive Institute (NAEI), in consultation with their Advisory Council and Executive Board, identified the need for stress management education. The need was supported by NAEI's discussions with nongovernmental educational and industrial organizations. In 1979, an early version of a stress management program was offered. In 1980, the current program was implemented when an employee development specialist with experience in and commitment to stress education was hired. A critical element in NAEI's stress education efforts is the presence of top-level managers with personal commitments to and interests in the program. Their support is most instrumental.

In 1976, at the National Institutes of Health (NIH), "Coping with Managerial Stress" was one of fourteen topics on a training needs survey sent to all NIH employees at level GS 13 and above. Approximately 800 employees responded to the survey. This 1976 survey, coupled with a second in 1978, received very positive responses, but the actual results are no longer available. The training specialist involved in both surveys had become aware of the potential for stress education through his own personal experiences. The inclusion of the course offering on the survey was the result of his experience, skill, and knowledge, coupled with a budding interest in the topic among the institute's managers. "Coping with Managerial Stress' was listed among the top needs by the survey respondents.

At the Internal Revenue Service, a detailed task analysis was initiated in 1980 to determine mid-level management training needs. Both mid- and top-level managers were asked about tasks mid-level managers are expected to perform. The written data were subsequently checked and corroborated by assembled groups of managers. The need for stress education was not a significant outcome of this task analysis. However, the written responses from the mid-level managers contained a "thread" of comments about their need for better stress management. This thread was less discernible in their superiors' responses. However, in responding to open-ended questions about recurring problems on the job, the need for stress education was more forcefully articulated. In IRS data processing centers, 28% of the responding mid-level managers identified stress or burnout as a problem and 37% of their bosses did as well. Among a segment of IRS district office managers, 60% of the mid-level managers identified stress as a problem, but only 6% of their managers did.

Analysis of the IRS data indicated that the respondents did not perceive the management of stress (either their own or their subordinates') to be a central task; but many perceived it as a significant problem. As in the previously described situations at NAEI and NIH, the employee development specialist responsible for mid-level training had a personal interest in stress management education. Based on the written data, an agreement was reached to experiment on a small scale within an already existing mid-level management development training program.

In the data gathering methods described above, different approaches yielded similar results—a willingness to commit resources to initiate stress management education programs. We recommend that a program have a data gathering component as a part of its foundation so that the hoped for results can be clearly stated and measured. Finally, as training budgets tighten, data bases will become more crucial in setting up programs where none exist and in maintaining them where they do exist.

DESIGN

All of the programs were designed to educate employees about what stress is, where it comes from, what it can do, and how to reduce its impact. The major segments of the program cover the understanding of stress, the importance of holistic living, creating and using support networks, managing work-related stress, and personal planning.[3]

The model used in the programs describing how stress operates is presented in Figure 24.1. As shown, there are both work and nonwork sources of stress and either of these can be in the form of acute episodes or chronic conditions. As individuals get a clear sense of the kinds of stress they are exposed to, they can deal more directly with those stressors. The interaction of these four types of stress with the mediators (including both situational givens and individual stress management skills) influences the amount of strain resulting, both physically and psychologically. The outcomes of too much stress and inadequate stress management include adverse effects on health, work effectiveness (productivity), and personal satisfaction and growth (morale).

Individual stress management techniques must focus on three levels of response: (1) removing or avoiding unnecessary stressors, (2) coping effectively with necessary stressors, and (3) building health via life-style management to buffer the long-term impacts of stress. Participants spend time before and during the program diagnosing their current levels of stress and identifying specific personal and organizational causes of stress. Once those causes that cannot be alleviated are determined, the emphasis shifts to understanding how stress affects the individual and to exploring coping mechanisms for the short run as well as longer term life management planning. The philosophical basis for the program is that each individual must take active responsibility for her or his own life situation.

All three programs include an extensive prework diagnosis of stress and a post-training followup assessment of individual changes relevant to managing stress and preventing burnout. This diagnostic package consists of two comprehensive questionnaires.

The first questionnaire provides an extensive, computer-analyzed assessment of the respondent's current and projected health risks based on physiological measures such as blood pressure, weight, and cholesterol level; mental health indicators such as self-satisfaction and social support; and health-related behaviors such as diet, exercise, smoking, and alcohol consumption. Participants receive individualized analyses of their current health risks as well as data on how they compare with others of the same age, race, and gender. Analysis of risk and information about steps an individual can take to lower risk levels are based on the premise that there are four major categories of risks to health: biological, environmental, quality of health-care services received, and personal life-style choices. A study conducted by the Center for Disease Control in Atlanta has determined that in seven of the ten leading causes of premature death and serious illness, more than half of the risk factors are life-style related (see Figure 24.2). The summary report includes suggestions for controlling these controllable risks through making healthful choices about diet, weight, smoking, alcohol, exercise, driving habits, type A behavior, blood pressure and cholesterol management, social support, stress coping, and work hazards.

The second questionnaire examines levels of stress and strain, and includes a section on exercise and nutrition habits. Also included is a section covering work outcomes and stress managment and life-style habits recommended as being health promoting. This last section is sent to participants a second time six

FIGURE 24.1   The Experience of Stress

Stressors

	On the Job	Off the Job
Events	Type I	Type II
Conditions	Type III	Type IV

Stress Mediators

- Personal characteristics and background
- Quality and amount of support
- Organizational factors
- Self management
- Creation and use of support systems
- Organizational improvement

Strain

Physiological and Psychological Strain Examples

- Hypertension
- Elevated cholesterol
- Elevated heart rate
- Depression
- Insomnia
- Irritability

Outcomes

- Work effectiveness
- Health
- Satisfaction and growth

months after their program to assess its impact on their life-style behaviors and attitudes. This same before/after questionnaire (see Table 24.1 below) also was used for a group of people who filled out the questionnaires only and did not participate in any additional training and with a group of people who did not fill out either questionnaire or participate in any form of health promotion or stress management training (control group). These two groups provide an additional basis of comparison for the relative impact of the stress management training programs being offered by these three federal agencies.

FIGURE 24.2   Health and Risk

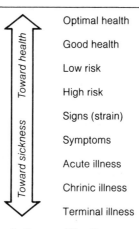

Risk: A term for the odds that something will or will not happen. It is based on the statistical concept of probability.

A person who is, for example, a heavy smoker or is overweight is said to have high risk characteristics and has a heightened risk of dying from a heart attack. No one knows for sure whether that person *will* die from a heart attack; but it is known that people who have these high risk characteristics *do* die from heart attacks at a higher rate than people who don't smoke or have normal weight.

A statement about risk is not a prediction about you as an *individual.* Statements of risk are about the likelihood of an event like death occurring in a group of people with a certain set of characteristics.

Toward health

Optimal health

Good health

Low risk

High risk

Signs (strain)

Symptoms

Acute illness

Chrinic illness

Terminal illness

Toward sickness

Estimated Percent Contribution to Cause of Death

10 Leading Causes of Death	*Life-style*	*Environment*	*Health Care Services*	*Biological*
1. Heart diseases	54	9	12	25
2. Cancers	37	24	10	29
3. Motor vehicle accidents	69	18	12	1
4. Other accidents	51	31	14	4
5. Stroke	50	22	7	21
6. Homicide	63	35	0	2
7. Suicide	60	35	3	2
8. Cirrhosis	70	9	3	18
9. Influenza/Pneumonia	23	20	18	39
10. Diabetes	34	0	6	60
All 10 Combined	51	19	10	20

Source: Center for Disease Control, Atlanta (1978)

During each training program, time is spent reviewing participants' results from the questionnaires and discussing the significance of these results for each participant. A thorough understanding of the importance of good nutrition and regular vigorous exercise is emphasized, and relaxation and meditation techniques are practiced. The concept of support networks is explored through analysis of participants' current support networks and areas for improvement.

In addressing organizational stress, participants look at elements in their work environments as well as their own personal fits with the positions they hold. In a recent study, Kolbasa and Maddi (Pines 1980)[4] found that people who felt they were in control of their work environment, felt challenged by their work, and felt committed to the importance of their work withstood higher levels of stress better than those who felt little control, challenge, or commitment. Using a person-environment fit instrument, participants diagnose their satisfaction with the elements of their current jobs in relation to what they would prefer in an ideal job. Small groups then review those factors identified as most stressful in the agency and discuss skills and practices necessary to: remove unnecessary stressors; respond effectively to unavoidable stressors; and provide long-term health protection against the effects of stress.

The final session of the programs asks participants to review what they have learned about stress and its management to develop individualized plans of action. For each of the major blocks of the program, participants review their learnings and analyze for themselves what things they need to start and stop doing; the factors that will help and hinder their change efforts; and the kinds of support they will draw on in making changes.

The programs have varied in length from a three-hour session embedded in a three-week-long management development workshop (IRS) to a four-day residential seminar (NAEI). Other formats have included three-day seminars given at NIH's on-site training facility and a half day session at the Naval Ships Research and Development Center to provide interpretation and analysis of the questionnaire process. The three-hour IRS session was lengthened after the first offering to a one-and-a-half day session and then to a two-day session at the suggestion of participants to allow for more involvement with the subject.

While the programs have generally covered the same material and followed similar formats, the residential program (NAEI) permitted the development of a total environment for practicing stress management techniques during the week. One of the unique features of this program was a highly nutritious, low fat and cholestrol diet planned by the seminar staff. A yoga instructor presented a half-day session on basic yoga techniques and many participants attended followup practice sessions throughout the week. In addition, guest speakers presented evening sessions on fitness and environmental stress. Overall, longer programs allow for greater depth of coverage and the use of more resources in working through the basic model.

PROGRAM EVALUATIONS

At the conclusion of each program, participants' reactions are solicited relative to the content and delivery of the seminar, their opinions of the usefulness of each topic, how well the program met its objectives, and whether or not they would recommend the program to their colleagues. While differing somewhat in format and language, the evaluation forms used in each program are similar.

The general objectives announced at the beginning of each program are the ability to

- understand the normal physical and psychological reactions to stess;
- diagnose sources of stress in both work and nonwork situations;

- describe present health risks;
- develop a framework for understanding practical approaches to stress management from both individual and organizational perspectives.
- develop personal strategies for coping with stress and protecting health.

On a scale of 1 to 5 (5 meaning clear achievement of the stated objectives) responses averaged 4.5 for participants in the three day on-site program. The shorter programs (three-hour, one and a half days, two days) that were a part of the ongoing management development program averaged a 4.4 response. A numerical rating of objectives was not included in the evaluation of the four-day residential program.

Participants also were asked to list the most important things they had learned as a result of the workshops. Nutrition, holistic health concepts, relaxation techniques, overview of stress management, importance of self responsibility, and the impact of self-controlled life-style factors have been most consistently mentioned.

The four-day residential program evaluation asks for participants' opinions as to how the workshop benefits the organization. Participants indicated their beliefs that attention to health is necessary for high productivity and morale, for reductions in waste, and that it contributes to a more effective workforce. Participants stated that the workshop demonstrated a "corporate concern" for employees, and that the benefits would also be carried over to their families. All indicated they had benefitted personally from their participation and many indicated that they had already begun making changes and correcting bad habits. Every participant in the IRS workshops agreed that the material was relevant to the public sector managerial situation.

Participants rated the residential seminar as either outstanding or very good (vs. adequate or poor); numerically averaging 4.5 on a scale of 1 to 5 (5 indicating excellent). The group unanimously indicated they would recommend the program to their colleagues.

Most participants in the three-day nonresidential program felt the length was appropriate. The participants in the three-hour program recommended lengthening the session and positioning it other than as the last event of the management development program. With only one exception, the four-day residential program participants felt the workshop length was adequate.

The seminar leaders have been uniformly highly rated by participants; many made special note of their knowledge and abilities to answer questions from the audience as well as their abilities to make the content both useful and interesting.

In all except the four-day residential program, the evaluations were distributed at the end of the workshop and completed before the participants left the training site. In the four-day residential program, the evaluation programs were mailed to the participants three weeks after the seminar. The participants' evaluation responses were thoughtful for all of the programs; however, a few key questions about the workshop's usefulness to the individual and the organization in the delayed evaluation elicited especially useful information.

MEASURING CHANGE IN THE INDIVIDUAL

As we pointed out, a major feature of each of the workshops was the feedback of the summary analyses of the questionnaires each of the participants filled out about a month before their training session. All participants fill out the following questionnaires:

Acute Stressors
1. Change events on the job
2. Change events away from work

Chronic Stressors
3. Conditions on the job
4. Conditions away from work
5. Strain response
6. Nutrition assessment
7. Exercise assessment

In addition, participants in all but the NIH programs also were asked to complete the "Personal Health Questionnaire," the analysis of which provides an extensive review of the individual's present health risks in comparison with others of the same age, race and gender.[5]

Included with these questionnaires is a 29- (24- at NIH) item questionnaire (see Table 24.1) that asks participants to assess their work effectiveness, morale, and present life-style and stress-management habits. The items on this questionnaire are all addressed in the workshops. This "before" questionnaire is retained and is matched with participants' responses to it a second time, about six months after their training experience, to determine whether they are making personal changes as a result of their workshop experiences. In addition to the before and after comparisons for each of the workshops offered, there is also a control group (no questionnaires or training) and a group who completed the diagnostic process, but did not attend any training in conjunction with that process.

The before and after data from the workshops being discussed in this paper are presented below. While a total of eight training programs are reviewed and compared to both a control group and a questionnaire-only group, only six of these groups are included in most of the analysis because of some differences in the before-after questionnaire used in one of the agencies. The data clearly indicate that many participants do make significant positive life-style and stress management changes during the six months following their training experiences. It is likely that six months is too short a time to really measure the impact of the prework process and the workshop experience. This period was chosen, however, because the response rate on the after questionnaire declines with increasing time.

Participants are asked to rate themselves on a seven-point scale (1 = rarely or never; 7 = always) regarding how often each of the statements on the before-after questionnaire (Table 24.1) presently are true for them. Lower total scores indicate lower stress awareness and poorer life-style and stress-management

TABLE 24.1 Before-After Impact Measure

1. I meet or beat my work deadlines.	22. I am supported adequately at work.
2. I do at least as much work as is expected of me.	23. I am aware of the primary sources of my stress.
3. The quality of my work is at least as high as is expected of me.	24. I take responsibility for removing as many of these stressors as I can.
4. Overall, I am satisfied with my present job.	25. I am aware of the possible consequences to me of poor stress management.
5. I am learning and growing in my present job.	26. My stress management skills are adequate.
6. I have a sense of fulfillment and accomplishment at the end of the day.	27.* I am responsible for my life situation.
7.* I wear seatbelts.	28.* I am satisfied with my life style.
8. I use tobacco. (Scale reversed)	29.* I am supported by my spiritual/ religious beliefs.
9. My use of alcohol is moderate (0–2 drinks per day average).	30. In your own words, how would you describe the impact of the Health, Stress and Your Life Style program on your life style and your responses to stress?
10. I maintain my recommended weight.	
11. I eat three balanced meals per day.	
12. I eat breakfast every day.	
13. I get sufficient restful sleep each night.	
14. I have a regular (3 or more times a week) vigorous exercise routine.	
15.* I have a daily stretching exercise (e.g., yoga) routine.	
16. I feel responsible for my well being.	
17. I am assertive about my needs and preferences.	
18. I am striving to become more knowledgeable about myself.	
19. I engage in a daily relaxation routine (e.g., rest, meditation, prayer, solo walks, etc.)	
20. I use my time well.	
21. I have a sufficient number of close friends.	

*Not included on NIH before-after questionnaires.

habits. Higher scores indicate higher stress awareness and better life-style and stress management habits. When an individual's total score on the after questionnaire is 10 or more points higher than her or his score on the before questionnaire, we consider that the person has made a "significant" overall improvement. Conversely, if an individual's after score is 10 or more points lower than her or his score on the before questionnaire, we consider that the person has made a "significant" overall decline (see Table 24.2). Further, differences of two or more points between the before and after responses to a specific item on the questionnaire are considered to represent a significant change with respect to that item (see Table 24.3).

While this mode of detecting life-style and stress-management changes is far from ideal, it is to date the only way we are able to do it given limited budgets

TABLE 24.2   Significant Overall Changes

	Group Size	Number (%) Showing Significant Overall Improvement	Number (%) Showing Significant Overall Decline
Control	47	3(6)	12(26)
Questionnaires only	37	12(32)	2(5)
Agency A-1	11	4(36)	0(0)
Agency A-2	8	3(38)	0(0)
Agency B-1	19	11(58)	2(11)
Agency B-2	16	13(81)	0(0)
Agency C-1	7	3(43)	0(0)
Agency C-2	15	9(60)	1(7)
Agency C-3	16	11(69)	1(6)
Agency C-4	16	9(56)	1(6)
Training Group Totals	108	63(58)	5(5)

and the fact that the participants involved live and work in all parts of the United States. We are confident, however, that this method is providing us with a clear indication that many participants are making significant personal changes as a result of the training efforts. It certainly is a major step beyond the followup scrutiny afforded to most management training programs.

Overall, the results presented in Table 24.2 indicate that a sizable proportion of the participants are making positive changes in their life-styles and stress management habits. As can be seen, members of the control group made more significant negative changes than positive. The membership of the group which completed the prework questionnaire process only, but did not attend related workshops, made a fair number of positive overall changes. The members of the eight training groups made the greatest positive changes and, in general, the fewest negative changes. Combining all groups, 58% of the participants showed significant overall improvement, while only 5% showed significant overall decline.

Analyzing the before-after questionnaire on an item-by-item basis indicates the nature of the specific changes being made by the population of this study. Table 24.3 provides before and after averages for each group and Table 24.4 summarizes the item-by-item analysis.

As can be seen in Table 24.3, both the questionnaire-only group and the training groups made overall improvements during the six-month period. The *average* improvement for agencies B-1, B-2, C-2, C-3, and C-4 are significant. As can be seen from the third column, the average improvements for those who did improve also are, for the most part, significant; and the average decline, for

TABLE 24.3 Group Averages

	Before Score	After Score	Improve	Decline	Spec. # Items Improve	Spec. # Items Decline
Control Group	152.4	149.0	5.19	9.7	1.4	2.8
Questionnaires only	149.1	156.8	12.8	5.4	3.5	1.4
Training Groups						
Agency A-1 3 day onsite	82.0	90.7	9.6 (n=10)	0.0 (n=0)	2.4	0.4
Agency A-2 3 day onsite	89.5	97.9	11.8 (n=6)	2.0 (n=2)	2.8	0.2
Agency B-1 1/2 day onsite	118.7	148.0	20.4 (n=14)	5.8 (n=5)	5.5	1.0
Agency B-2 4 day resid.	129.4	153.4	28.2 (n=14)	5.5 (n=2)	8.4	1.2
Agency C-1 1/2 day mgt. dev.	132.9	140.7	12.6 (n=5)	4.0 (n=2)	4.9	0.9
Agency C-2 1-1/2 day mgt. dev.	133.7	145.1	18.6 (n=11)	8.5 (n=4)	5.7	2.1
Agency C-3 2 day mgt. dev.	134.3	148.1	15.6 (n=15)	13.0 (n=1)	5.1	1.8
Agency C-4 2 day mgt. dev.	132.4	143.8	15.2 (n=13)	7.5 (n=2)	5.3	1.6
Agencies B and C overall	132.9	147.2	19.2 (n=72)	6.9 (n=16)	5.9	1.4

those who declined, insignificant. The final two columns of Table 24.3 indicate the average number of significant (change of 2 or more) improvements and declines per participant in specific items. With the exception of the control group, it should be noted that the number of specific improvements greatly outnumber the number of specific declines in each group. Agencies A-1 and A-2 are not included in calculating the group averages in Table 24.3 because of differences in the before-after questionnaire used.

The individual items on the before-after questionnaire are listed in Table 24.4, which summarizes the number of significant specific item changes. The items on which significant improvements and declines were made most frequently are drawn from Table 24.4 and presented below. The number of participants making significant changes on each item is given in parentheses.

Improvements
- Adequacy of stress management skills (48)
- Regular relaxation practice (37)

TABLE 24.4   Summary of Before-After Changes by Item

| | Number of Changes of 2 or Greater | | | | | |
| Questionnaire Item | Control Group (n=47) | | Questionnaire Only (n=37) | | Training Program Totals (n=108) | |
	IMP	DEC	IMP	DEC	IMP	DEC
1. Meet or beat work deadlines	2	3	3	3	8	4
2. Work as much as expected	1	1	0	1	6	7
3. Work as well as expected	1	1	2	1	4	1
4. Overall job satisfaction	1	6	5	2	15	12
5. Learning and growing on the job	2	10	5	2	21	12
6. Sense of fulfill-ment and accomplishment	0	7	2	1	22	9
7. Wear seatbelts*	4	2	4	1	12	3
8. Use tobacco	1	1	0	0	7	2
9. Moderate use of alcohol	5	5	7	3	13	13
10. Maintain recom-mended weight	3	8	7	3	27	3
11. Three balanced meals daily	1	4	9	0	26	4
12. Breakfast every day	2	6	5	1	19	5
13. Sufficient sleep	1	7	5	5	22	3
14. Regular vigor-ous exercise	5	8	9	3	34	6
15. Regular stretch-ing exercise*	6	10	3	5	21	4
16. Responsible for own well-being	1	1	3	1	16	3
17. Behave assertively	3	5	4	2	13	1
18. Striving for self knowledge	0	0	1	1	25	3
19. Regular relax-ation practice	4	11	8	3	37	8
20. Use time well	0	4	2	0	15	3
21. Sufficient close friends	6	2	5	1	21	4
22. Supported ade-quately at work	3	8	2	2	14	13

23. Aware of primary sources of stress	2	1	4	1	23	2
24. Self responsible for stress removal	3	3	4	2	24	4
25. Aware of consequences of poor stress mgt.	1	2	5	0	34	0
26. Adequacy of stress management skills	2	4	12	0	48	2
27. Responsible for life situation*	0	3	1	3	15	2
28. Satisfaction with life style*	2	4	6	1	15	1
29. Supported by spiritual/ religious beliefs*	4	3	7	3	19	1
Totals	66	130	130	51	575	135
Average No. Changes/Partic.	1.4	2.8	3.5	1.4	5.3	1.2

*Items not included for Agency A

- Regular vigorous exercise (34)
- Aware of consequences of poor stress management (34)
- Maintain recommended weight (27)
- Eat three balanced meals daily (26)
- Striving for self-knowledge (25)

Declines
- Moderate alcohol use (13)
- Adequately supported at work (13)
- Overall job satisfaction (12)
- Learning and growing on the job (12)

As can be seen, those items on which improvement occurred most frequently represent basic habits necessary for protecting and building health. With the exception of alcohol use, the items on which decline occurred most frequently are job related. These findings are similar to the findings of other before and after studies conducted by the senior author.[6, 7] While the apparent increase in reported alcohol use by 13 of the 108 participants in the training programs is of concern, the declines in job factors is of even more concern.

Our conclusion is that stress education helps make people more aware of, and thus somewhat less satisfied with, the stressful nature of their everyday work environments. Upon returning from the training program, many people attempt to do things to reduce their on-the-job stress and meet with resistance from others in the workplace—thereby reducing the level of support they are experiencing on the job.

On the positive side, participants who most need to make improvements seem to be the ones making the improvements. While this does not show up in the tables presented in this paper, those with the lowest before scores in the six groups from agencies B and C make a disproportionate amount of the positive changes. For example, 36 of the 45 people whose before scores are below the overall group average (132.9; see Table 24.3) made overall improvements of 10 or more on the after questionnaire. Further, this same group (the lower half on the before questionnaire) made 66% of the total specific-item changes.

While the number of before-after comparisons available to us at this time is relatively low, all of the indications are that the stress management education programs are having a durable, significant, positive effect on a large number of the participants. Sixty-eight percent of the responding participants have made significant *overall* changes and each participant has made an average of 5.3 significant specific-item changes. The fact that the specific improvements are relatively widely spread across the twenty-nine items on the before-after questionnaire suggests that participants learn to identify what their own specific needs for improvement are and that they are acting to make those improvements subsequent to the workshops.

IMPLICATIONS FOR TRAINING AND DEVELOPMENT STAFFS

A decision to initiate a stress management education program has implications for training staffs in two of their roles: first, on their role as deliverers of the training program and, second, on their role as catalysts for organizational improvement.

As trainers, a commitment to stress-management education requires attention to the content and the process by which the product will be delivered. A clear articulation of the intended results of the program is mandatory. The length of the classroom component of the program is another appropriate topic for the employee development specialist to explore. The advice of the stress consultant, the objectives of the program, and a sense of the "politics" of the situation are key to a good decision.

At one of the agencies, a conscious decision was made to pilot a four-hour program. The consultant and the employee development specialist both felt the time to be inadequate. However, it was felt that a modest initial effort had the highest likelihood of long-run success. Fourteen of the twenty-four students in this first class made a strong case in their written evaluations for a substantial increase in time. The second program offered by the agency was expanded to a day and a half. Still, eight of the twenty-four participants perceived the time as insufficient. The next two programs offered by the agency were extended to two full days, and feedback from the participants indicates that this is probably the correct length for the program to accomplish its objectives. An initial implementation of a two day program probably would not have been feasible, but data coming from the participants and training staff about the length of the program, based on their experiences with it, seems to have resulted in agreement for a substantial investment of time.

In all agencies, the employee development specialists directly involved have had personal commitment to stress management education. In all cases, this specialist has attended one or more of the workshops as a participant. At one agency, the emergence of the importance of the stress management education program has prompted the entire training and development division to undertake stress management training for itself to better equip all of its staff to respond to stress-related problems throughout the agency.

The methodology and process of the program ties into program costs. One agency assumed there would be more marketability for the program if a portion of the program was self-instructional. This is because the agency operates on the clearly stated and practiced proposition that self-instruction works and that it is more cost effective than classroom training. The other element in the agency's planning was the possibility of cuts to the program. Having a self-instructional component that could stand alone if need be would permit partial cuts. Since the same agency is placing considerable stock in increased self-awareness as a valid function of stress-management education, a reduced program could still accomplish substantial portions of the objectives.

Another area of interest to the deliverer of training is that of the criteria for selecting a stress management education consultant. As described above, all three of the agencies have decided that an expert in the field of stress management education is best suited for the instructor assignment. Since many consultants are offering such training these days, each agency must learn to make meaningful distinctions between candidates.

One of the agencies has developed criteria for selecting a stress-management education consultant. The criteria include the following factors:

1. Advanced degrees
2. Prior teaching experience
3. Consultation experience
4. Management experience
5. University/academic association
6. Publications/articles written
7. Instructor as role model

Each factor is rated on a sliding scale, with particular emphasis on the stress education experience, relevance of degrees and consulting experience, and so on. The instructor-as-role-model factor seeks to address the extent to which the consultant demonstrates, through personal life-style habits (smoking, drinking, nutrition, exercise, and so on) behaviors that will serve as positive models to her or his class members. Of course, once a minimally acceptable score on these factors is attained, cost becomes a significant factor in the selection of the stress-management education consultant.

There are additional questions the employee development specialist should consider. Among them are whether the program should be residential. The costs and benefits of a residential experience need to be addressed. The packaging of the results of stress management education efforts and the sharing of those results with others is another topic worthy of consideration.

There are many additional ways in which a human resource development staff can influence an organization and its individual members to lead healthier and more productive lives through alleviating some of the causes and expensive results of burnout. One important way is to provide stress management courses as described in this paper. Others include providing career development counseling and assistance to employees, supporting positive health practices in the agency, and proposing changes in management practices to support more humanistic values that recognize the needs of individuals to improve and protect their health and productivity.

Career development efforts can take many forms. Managers need to be taught the symptoms of burnout so they can recognize individuals who may need assistance. HRD personnel can provide career development tools and personality/skills inventories to employees so they can analyze what specific elements they are looking for in terms of job fulfillment. Some organizations have recognized the value of rotational assignments to provide new challenges to employees, but these often are perceived as a luxury and a disruption to the normal flow of work. Federal agencies need to develop a scheme for permitting employees who have reached their maximum level of performance in one occupation to transfer to new, more challenging lines of work without losing pay or status.

In addition to providing a range of educational seminars, agencies can support the health of employees through ongoing awareness programs like articles in agency publications, periodic short presentations by professionals in related health fields, and provisions for health screening and monitoring of basic functions such as blood pressure, respiratory functions, treadmill testing, and blood chemistry. Exercise programs with employee recreation associations can be reinforced and expanded, perhaps by adding a part time professional to coach and monitor progress. Food service can be improved by including more whole grains and fresh fruits and vegetables to the offerings while cutting back on fried, sugary, and processed foods. Fresh fruits, juices, and herbal teas can be made available for "coffee breaks." Employee assistance programs (including stress management counseling and smoking cessation programs) can be provided and designed to be nonthreatening to potential participants.

With the help of HRD professionals, managers can examine organizational practices to determine if they themselves are unnecessary causes of stress and strain. Organizational norms that discourage vacations and relaxation need to be recognized for their long-term negative effects. Periods of overwork should be followed by periods with lighter loads. The recognition of individuals' needs of flexibility in work hours can alleviate much underlying strain caused by family schedules, transportation problems, and individual physiological rhythms. While many agencies have instituted flextime, there are some that have not yet realized the need for it. HRD staffs can study problems and make recommendations for improvements concerning the physical environment of the work area, which is a frequent source of unnecessary stress caused by overcrowding, noise, and so on.

Changes caused by new policies, procedures and administrations; major reorganizations; job transfers; and the like are facts of life in most federal agencies and represent potential stimulators of ill health and job dissatisfaction. Managers can improve work effectiveness and employee satisfaction (and probably employee health) during times of transition by early and ongoing communication with their people regarding necessary changes. Following necessary changes, processes can be implemented to facilitate adjustment to them. Daily sources of ongoing stress in most agencies include work load, role ambiguity, conflicts, absence of planning and anticipation, and crisis management. Many of these are normative, unwritten rules in nature and do not arise from policies or management proclamations. They are, rather, generated by nonconscious agreements by organizational members and can be changed only through work-unit meetings in which individuals identify those habits or norms that are negative or stressful and decide together which to change and how to change them.

In most cases, HRD staffs are the part of the organization most enlightened about stress, its causes, and the results of not attending to it. It is, therefore, their responsibility to educate others in the agency, especially top managers, about the problem, and make specific recommendations for handling it. In most agencies, there undoubtedly are key people scattered throughout the organization who are already committed to the ways of thinking and behaving suggested by this paper. Identifying and networking with these people often helps considerably in establishing a momentum for change.

Notes

1. Bernstein, J. E. *Personal health profile.* Washington, D.C. General Health, Inc., 1980. p. 4.
2. Gherman, E. M. *Stress and the bottom line.* New York. AMACOM, 1981.
3. For a more detailed description of the design and materials used in these programs, see Adams, J. *Understanding and managing stress.* San Diego. University Associates, 1980.
4. Pines, M. "Psychological hardiness: the role of challenge in health." *Psychology Today.* Dec. 1980. pp. 34–44.
5. Bernstein, p. 4.
6. Adams, J. "Health, stress and the manager's life style." *Group and organization studies.* Sept., 1981. 6(3). pp. 291–301.
7. Adams, J. "Planning for comprehensive stress management." In Marshall, J. and Cooper, C. L. *Coping with stress at work.* Aldershot, U.K. Gower, 1981.

25 Utilizing Task Redesign Strategies Within Organization Development Programs

Ricky W. Griffin
Richard W. Woodman

ABSTRACT

Task redesign is becoming increasingly prevalent as a strategy for organization development. The technique, however, has suffered from an overgeneralization in applying specific task redesign strategies and a corresponding lack of appreciation for the necessity to tailor task redesign alternatives and implementation attempts to their unique organizational contexts. This paper summarizes a detailed nine-step program for more rigorously diagnosing and installing task redesign changes in organizations.

AUTHOR BACKGROUNDS

Ricky W. Griffin is an assistant professor of management at Texas A & M University. He received his MBA and Ph.D. from the University of Houston. Recent articles on task design and leadership by Professor Griffin have appeared in the *Academy of Management Journal* and the *Academy of Management Review*. In addition, he has published one book entitled *Task Design*.

Richard W. Woodman received a B.S. in industrial engineering and a MBA from Oklahoma State University, and a Ph.D. in organizational behavior from Purdue University. His work experience includes service as vice-president of a savings and loan association. Dr. Woodman's research and consulting focuses on organizational diagnosis, team development, and evaluation of OD programs.

This paper was presented at the National American Institute Decision Sciences (AIDS) Convention in Boston (November 1982).

Organization development encompasses a wide variety of methods and techniques that are used to manage organizational change in such a way as to move the system toward greater effectiveness. The actual boundaries of OD, however, are often difficult to discern.[1] Contemporary writers have often subsumed many markedly different improvement efforts under the label of organization development.[2] Whether we should regard any specific intervention or change effort as OD depends, in large measure, on (1) *how* it is conducted, and (2) the ultimate *objectives* of the effort. For example, a job enrichment program is less compatible with OD to the extent that the job changes are designed by staff or outside experts and imposed from above with no participation from those whose jobs are affected.[3] Job enrichment is more compatible with OD to the extent that a collaborative effort, which includes the jobholders, is undertaken to ascertain needed improvements and to design changes that meet both social and technical requirements of the system.

Our intention in this paper is to suggest practical ways to incorporate task redesign strategies such as job enrichment within the context of a comprehensive organization development program. Our position is that many work design changes in organizations are increasingly congruent with OD values and concepts. There appears to be a heightened concern on the part of OD practitioners and researchers with group and organizational effectiveness. While certain interpersonal variables (such as openness and trust) are likely to remain key targets of change in OD programs, they are increasingly likely to be viewed as instrumental goals rather than as ends in themselves. An effective OD program may result in technical and structural changes as well as in changes in organizational and group processes.[4]

TASK REDESIGN

Task redesign, as used in this paper, represents a deliberate, planned restructuring of the way work is performed in order to increase workers' motivation, involvement, and efficiency. As an organizational change strategy, task redesign represents a whole family of specific techniques including work simplification, job rotation, job enlargement, job enrichment, the redesign of salient task characteristics, and even overlaps some aspects of sociotechnical approaches to work restructuring. Under certain circumstances, each of these techniques can be effective in improving work performance in the organization. The literature contains many reports of favorable results stemming from job design programs.[5] One of the most impressive records in this regard was compiled at AT&T, where 17 of 18 controlled job design studies had positive results.[6] It is also true, however, that the literature contains many examples of failed redesign programs.[7] Redesign efforts have often ignored individual differences, technological differences, task differences, contextual differences, and so on. In other words, the approach has suffered from an overgeneralization in applying specific job redesign strategies and a corresponding lack of appreciation for the necessity to refine approaches to more optimally fit the situation and personalities involved. Nevertheless, the tremendous body of theory, research, and practice in this area has produced one of our more powerful and popular organizational change methodologies.

AN IMPLEMENTATION FRAMEWORK FOR TASK REDESIGN

Most organization development programs follow, either explicitly or implicitly, an action research sequence. This sequence consists of gathering information about the current state of the system, making this information widely available to those who must take responsibility for change, and planning improvement actions based upon an accurate, valid diagnosis of organizational problems. Getting from learning about the organization and its problems to actually doing something about them is always difficult in any improvement effort. Certainly, the redesign of work is no different. How can the manager, consultant, staff specialist, or whoever actually implement a task redesign intervention? The basic implementation framework proposed here suggests that a well-developed integrative approach to task redesign will follow nine important steps, which are essentially congruent with the action research model. These steps are summarized in Table 25.1.

Recognizing the Need for Change

As in other planned change sequences, the first step in the overall process of task redesign should be the recognition that some form of change is necessary. It is not likely, for example, that a manager will simply decide one day that some task design changes are needed. Rather, some work-related factor or set of factors will typically serve as a stimulus for this recognition. Several potential stim-

---

TABLE 25.1 An Integrative Framework for Implementing Task Redesign in Organizations

Step 1: Recognition of a need for change
Step 2: Selection of task redesign as a potential intervention
Step 3: Diagnosis of the work system and context
- Diagnosis of existing jobs
- Diagnosis of existing workforce
- Diagnosis of technology
- Diagnosis of organization design
- Diagnosis of leader behaviors
- Diagnosis of group and social processes
Step 4: Cost/Benefit analysis of proposed changes
Step 5: Go/No-go design
Step 6: Establishing the strategy for redesign
Step 7: Implementing the task changes
Step 8: Implementing any supplemental changes
Step 9: Evaluation of the task redesign effort

---

uli may be identified. Absenteeism and turnover may increase, productivity may begin to decline, and/or there may be more grievances filed. Supervisors may begin to hear more worker comments and/or complaints about the work being performed, or they may become aware of decreases in employee effort. An organization that competes for the same employees may make significant and positive changes that increase the attractiveness of its jobs. The organization may be forced to make changes because of changes in the nature of the work-force. Another cause of change might be a technological breakthrough that necessitates the introduction of new work methods. A final reason for changes may be a general concern for the quality of work life in the organization. Granted, the organization may expect to receive some benefits in return for a better quality of work life for its employees (that is, avoiding unionization, increasing motivation and/or performance, and so on). Overall, however, the manager may simply decide that the work environment needs to be changed in order to develop a better work experience for employees.

Selection of the Intervention

After the manager has recognized that some sort of change is needed, he or she must then determine the appropriate intervention. For some change situations, task redesign may be the "most logical" intervention. Further, in some situations, task redesign may be only one of several "equally" reasonable interventions (for example, if motivational problems have arisen, task redesign will be one of many potential solutions). Finally, some problems will clearly call for interventions other than task redesign. In summary, then, the manager's expertise, experience, and insight will be crucial at this stage of the process. He or she must assess the situation, bringing to bear all relevant information, and determine the most appropriate intervention strategy.

Diagnosis of the Work System and Context

If the manager decides that task redesign is the most appropriate strategy, the next step will be an in-depth diagnosis of the work system and work context. The crucial questions to be answered at this stage are: (1) will task redesign mesh with the existing work system and context and (2) will the existing work system and context constrain or facilitate task redesign?

Diagnosis of existing jobs. As a preliminary step, an assessment should be made of jobs within the organization as they are currently designed. Several strategies for this diagnosis could be developed. First, employees may be asked to complete a questionnaire designed to measure perceived task characteristics. Instruments such as the Job Diagnostic Survey might be appropriate.[8] A second technique for diagnosing jobs would involve the manager, perhaps with the assistance of other managers and/or supervisors, developing the assessment from personal observation and experience. A final task diagnostic tool would focus on a committee composed of the manager(s) and representatives from the labor force.

Diagnosis of existing workforce.   Diagnosing existing jobs is probably the most important phase of this process; however, diagnosing existing employees is also very important. Specifically, the manager tries to determine how motivated and satisfied they want to be, and what task elements are most likely to bring about this improvement. The assessment would also involve determining the extent to which relevant skills are currently being used, the extent to which they should be used, and appropriate task elements for facilitating an improved match.

Diagnosis of technology.   Technology is the conversion processes utilized by an organization in the transformation of inputs into outputs; as such, it may constrain or facilitate task redesign efforts. If the primary inputs into the conversion process are material in nature, task redesign efforts may be more difficult (that is, technology may be a constraint due to investments in machinery and equipment). At the other extreme, information inputs may result in an easier task redesign effort (that is, technology may facilitate the intervention). Finally, if human and/or monetary inputs dominate, task redesign efforts may have an intermediate level of difficulty. This diagnosis may be relatively simple or extremely complex in nature. For example, the larger the *number* of technologies utilized by the organization, the more difficult will be the diagnosis. By drawing upon the knowledge of relevant experts, however, the manager should be able to derive useful information about how the organization's technology will mesh with a task redesign intervention.

Diagnosis of organizational design.   Having assessed the organization's technology, the next step in the process should be a diagnosis of the organization's design. If the focus of the task redesign intervention will be on operating employees, then implications from the perspective of organization design will be relatively minor. If, however, the focus is managerial roles, organization design becomes more critical. Relevant spans of control, for example, might require modification. Desirable aspects of the formalization dimension may be eliminated by redesigning tasks. An especially significant consideration could be the task autonomy-decentralization link. If the proposed change is to increase managerial autonomy, for example, top management must recognize in advance that power and control will be channeled downward in the organization. That is, management must be willing to allow at least a certain amount of decentralization. The Mintzberg framework would also be very useful for diagnostic purposes.[9] A full-scale redesign program, for example, might involve actually changing the structural configuration of the organization, say from a divisionalized form to an adhocracy.

Diagnosis of leader behavior.   Analysis of leader behavior processes in the organization may be of extreme importance. On the one hand, the cooperation of supervisors may be crucial to the success of the task redesign intervention. At the same time, however, supervisors may have the greatest potential to impede the intervention. At least three different aspects of leader behavior that can facilitate task redesign efforts can be identified. First, supervisors can be a primary source of information in other diagnostic assessments of existing tasks, employees, technology, organization design, and group processes. Second, supervisors will probably be very actively involved in the actual task changes to be made. Finally, they will also be important for clarifying roles and providing additional training after the task redesign intervention.

A primary reason that supervisors may be problematic, however, is that the task changes may involve taking away part of their own job-related activities, power, and control in order to provide more autonomy for subordinates whose jobs are being redesigned. For example, a study by Lawler, Hackman, and Kaufman[10] indicated that supervisors whose jobs were "narrowed" so that subordinates could have more things to do reacted quite negatively. What could a disenchanted supervisor do to disrupt a task redesign intervention? Just in terms of the three positive roles described earlier, the supervisor could, in varying degrees, provide incomplete or inaccurate information during other diagnostic assessment, be less than totally committed to implementing the changes, and/or fail to provide relevant training after the change. He or she could also grow frustrated and develop an antagonistic attitude toward employees.

The diagnosis of leader behavior, then, should be done with utmost care. The most logical technique for handling the diagnosis would be to conduct one or more informal discussions with the supervisors to be affected by the change. The manager might also draw upon his or her own personal observations and insights. Finally, individual meetings might also be appropriate for supervisors who may be particularly opposed to or supportive of the intervention.

Diagnosis of group and social processes. A remaining contextual element—group and social processes—also warrants careful diagnosis. This is particularly true if the task redesign intervention is to include the development of autonomous work gorups or similar group-focused characteristics. The manager should attempt to ascertain the degree of cohesiveness that exists among the workers whose jobs are going to be changed, the level of relevant norms, and the nature of existing and potential role dynamics. The manager should also investigate the extent to which task changes might disturb existing norm patterns in a negative way. For example, existing norms might facilitate a great deal of interpersonal cooperation and assistance. Elements of the task changes, however, might be expected to increase competition and thereby decrease cooperation. Finally, assessment of role dynamics might indicate expected levels of role ambiguity, conflict, and/or overload that could arise either temporarily or permanently after the intervention and also suggest ways to overcome or at least minimize their disruptive consequences.

With the completion of the diagnosis, the manager must then assess potential costs and benefits of the impending change.

Cost/Benefit Analysis of Proposed Changes

The exact nature of the cost/benefit analysis will vary between organizations. Moreover, the specific costs and benefits may be different for each organization. The starting point in the analysis should be the specification of the goals of the intervention. The expectations of the organization should not be too excessive; the goals should be realistic and feasible. The firm should also recognize the costs it will incur in achieving these goals. A list of possible costs and benefits of a task redesign intervention is presented in Table 25.2.

A number of direct and quantifiable costs may arise. First, the intervention may require the purchase of new technology (for example, new machinery). It is likely that the organization will also incur some down time (for example, employees being unable to perform their tasks) during the transition between existing and redesigned tasks. Finally, wage increases may be necessary due to increased task importance. Several indirect or nonquantifiable costs will also likely follow the change. For example, workers will probably experience a certain degree of role ambiguity, conflict, and/or overload due to their initial lack of familiarity with new task-related procedures. Second, some employees may become alienated because of a preference for the original task, suspicion of management's motives, and so forth. In either case, turnover may result. Finally, several unexpected costs may arise. In a general sense, potential snags and delays may interrupt the intervention, prolong down-time, and so on. Unplanned supplemental changes may also be necessary. Contiguous organizational units may be affected in unexpected ways, thereby necessitating other organization design changes. Finally, unplanned morale problems with supervisors may arise.

On the positive side, the organization will likely also expect to reap some benefits from the task redesign intervention. A direct, quantifiable benefit that may accrue to the organization could be enhanced productivity due to improvements and refinements in the work system. Several nonquantifiable benefits may also be gained, including employee satisfaction, employee motivation, improved quality of work life, and/or improved group performance norms. Finally, some unexpected benefits may also arise. The improved employee motivation described

---

TABLE 25.2 Possible Costs and Benefits of a Task Redesign Intervention

Costs	Benefits
1. Direct/Quantifiable ■ Purchase of new technology ■ Down-time ■ Increased wages	1. Direct/Quantifiable ■ Enhanced performance via improvements in the work system
2. Indirect/Nonquantifiable ■ Short-term role ambiguity, conflict, and/or overload following change ■ Alienation of some employees who oppose change	2. Indirect/Nonquantifiable ■ Improved employee satisfaction ■ Improved employee motivation ■ Improved quality of work life ■ Improved group performance norms
3. Potential/Unexpected ■ Unplanned snags and delays ■ Unplanned supplemental changes ■ Unplanned changes in organizational design ■ Unplanned morale problems with supervisors	3. Potential/Unexpected ■ Enhanced performance via improvements in employee effort ■ Improved employee commitment

above may result in performance increases. Improved commitment may also follow the intervention.

The Go/No-Go Decision

At this point, the manager should be in a position to make a decision about whether to proceed with the task redesign intervention ("go") or to consider other alternatives ("no go"). The diagnosis of existing jobs, employees, technology, organization design, leader behavior, and group and social processes will give the manager insights into how these organizational factors may constrain and/or facilitate task design alternatives. The analysis will then provide additional information relative to the viability of task redesign.

Unfortunately, the results of the diagnoses and cost/benefit analyses will generally *not* provide information in a form amenable to quantitative analysis. This stems from the nonquantifiable nature of many of the expected costs (for example, alienation or unexpected snags) and benefits (for example, improved employee satisfaction, motivation, and quality of work life) which may relate to the change. Therefore, the manager must place greater reliance on his or her own intuition and expert opinion, must be willing to gamble "hard" expenses in the form of new technology, downtime and so forth in exchange for "soft" benefits such as improved quality of work life, and expect to wait for perhaps an extended period of time before these benefits offset the initial costs.

Development of the Implementation Strategy

The implementation strategy will consist of four basic components or steps. First, the manager must make decisions regarding *who* will plan the task redesign implementation. The decision regarding the appropriate degree of participation will probably be a function of the extent to which subordinates have needed information, the extent to which employees can be trusted to make substantive contributions, and the values of the managers involved. In any event, some form of group effort will likely be appropriate. If management decides to minimize participation, the planning group should consist of several managers. If participation is utilized, then members of the target employee group should be made formal group members.

Once the group has been formed, it will undertake the second phase of planning: outlining the actual job changes to be made. Information from the earlier diagnosis and the cost/benefit analysis will be useful at this point. In most cases, the planned changes should be detailed in writing and supplemented with projections of positive task changes, expected outcome changes (that is, new standards of productivity), and approximate costs of the changes.

As part of this effort, decisions must be made regarding whether to use individual- or group-based task changes. Hackman and Oldham[11] suggest that autonomous work groups should be created only when this alternative offers significant advantages over individually-based tasks. The rationale for this suggestion is based on the following points: (1) group designs involve not only the design of tasks, but also the design of teams, (2) group decisions will involve more complex interpersonal relationships, and (3) group decisions may dictate more extreme changes in other organizational components such as the reward system.

Once the redesign intervention has been mapped out, the planning group should then outline a time frame for implementing the changes. This time frame should allow for job-specific planning, purchasing new equipment, installing the task changes, integrating the new system with contiguous units, working out the "bugs," and, finally, returning to normal operations. An ideal technique for this step would be PERT.

Implementation

In theory, if proper diagnostic activities, cost/benefit analyses, and implementation strategies have been utilized, then the actual implementation of the task changes should go quite smoothly. Of course, as most managers know, theory and practice seldom mesh precisely. We can say very little here about implementation, because the exact mechanics of a task redesign intervention will be unique for each situation. We can, however, offer one very important observation for the manager: expect unexpected difficulties to arise.

Regardless of how complete the diagnosis or how well-developed the strategy, in all likelihood some unforeseen circumstance or problem will appear. This should not be perceived as a significant argument against the use of task redesign or any other change intervention, for that matter), of course, because to expect any change involving individuals to be 100% predictable would be quite unrealistic.

Supplements to the Intervention

The task redesign intervention may also dictate supplemental changes in other organizational processes in order to achieve a better integration. Hopefully, these supplements will have been identified and planned during the development of the intervention strategy. One area of supplemental changes may relate to the contextual elements of task design. New work-flow technological processes may be appropriate. Changes in the organization's design may be required. Supplements directed at leader behavior and/or group and social processes may also be needed. Other supplemental changes may be needed in areas such as selection criteria, the reward system, appropriate performance appraisal methods, the organization's work schedules, and so forth.

Evaluation of the Intervention

The final step in our integrative implementation framework is an evaluation of the effectiveness of the intervention. Recall that in step 4 (the cost/benefit analysis), desired outcomes were specified. At this point, it is worthwhile to ascertain whether the outcomes have actually been achieved. Unfortunately, this is one aspect of organizational change that is neglected by many managers. The evaluation framework we will suggest for minimal levels of scientific rigor is the pre-test/post-test control group design.[12]

It is important to measure task perceptions, because in some instances employees have not perceived changes that management has supposedly introduced. Outcomes should obviously be measured in order to assess the degree of change. The importance of collecting data from a comparison group is based on the fact that changes could occur as a result of other, uncontrolled factors. A final point relates to the timing of the measures after the change. Research has shown that employee perceptions and reactions to a task change may not become apparent for an extended period of time. As a general guideline, measures should be taken approximately three to four months after the change and again after one year.

CONCLUDING COMMENTS

In order to maximize the motivating potential of jobs, there must be a complex fit among the individual, the job, and the organizational structure/climate.[13] Organization development programs can play an important role in discovering and designing this fit. Indeed, the redesign of jobs is often an important part of a comprehensive OD program that arises naturally out of the diagnostic and action-planning process. The design of work represents an area where the evolution of ideas and practice is becoming increasingly compatible with OD principles and precepts. Managers are probably becoming more and more aware of crucial task design issues. Whether this awareness gets translated into practice, of course, remains to be seen. There are indications, however, that a variety of factors may stimulate more attention to appropriate task design in organizational settings.

First of all, changes in the physical task environment are occurring at an accelerated pace. Many firms now offer modular work stations for secretarial and clerical employees. For employees who work while sitting down, Norwegian designers have developed a new style of desk chair called the Balans chair. By forcing weight onto the individual's knees, the chair decreases back-strain and facilitates improved breathing. Even for operating employees, new physical breakthroughs are available. For example, an inventor has recently patented a revolutionary improvement in a centuries-old tool, the hammer. By placing two slight curves, or bends, in the handle of the hammer, elbow strain is reduced, the need for a tight grip is eliminated, and striking accuracy improves.

Another catalyst for change may be more employee involvement in company ownership. Federal legislation, for example, may require organizations to give employees a bigger voice in management. Stock ownership programs are already fairly common. Romac Industries in Seattle currently allows employees to vote on pay raises for all other employees. It follows that as employees gain more and more control over these kinds of decisions, they may well decide they also want some control over their work activities.

A continuing concern for quality of work life should also serve to increase managerial interest in task design processes. Regardless of the physical surroundings and other considerations, the fact remains that the job the individual performs is the most critical contact point the person has with the organization. Hence, almost by definition, any attempt to improve the employee's work-related experiences must, of necessity, include changes in the task the employee performs. In the years ahead, many innovative and enlightened approaches to designing work for organizational members will likely be attempted. Regardless of the degree or extent of automation, or work improvement, we are still likely to need human beings to work on our assembly lines, to make our clothing, to sweep our floors, and to do many of the routine but necessary tasks our society created. Hopefully, organizations and managers will initiate, maintain, and/or increase their efforts at making work more dignified, personally rewarding, and individually fulfilling. All of us stand to gain.

Suggested Readings

The concepts addressed in this paper are explained in more detail in Ricky W. Griffin , *Task Design—An Integrative Approach,* Glenview, Ill.: Scott, Foresman, 1982.

Other useful books pertaining to task design include Ramon J. Aldag and Arthur P. Brief, *Task Design and Employee Motivation,* Glenview, Ill.: Scott, Foresman, 1979, and J. Richard Hackman and Greg R. Oldham, *Work Redesign,* Reading, Mass.: Addison-Wesley, 1980.

Notes

1. Kahn, R. L., "Organizational Development: Some Problems and Proposals," *Journal of Applied Behavioral Science,* 1974, vol. 10, pp. 485–502, and Strauss, G., "Organizational Development." In R. Dubin (Editors), *Handbook of Work, Organization, and Society.* Chicago: Rand, McNally, 1976, pp. 617–85.
2. Huse. E. F., *Organizational Development and Change.* 2d ed. St. Paul: West, 1980.
3. Herzberg, F., & Zautra, A., "Orthodox Job Enrichment: Measuring True Quality in Job Satisfaction," *Personnel,* 1976, vol. 53, pp. 54–68.
4. Woodman, R. W., & Muse, W. V., "Organization Development in the Profit Sector: Lessons Learned," In J.O. Hammons (Ed.), *Organization Development in the Community College.* San Francisco: Jossey-Bass, 1982.
5. Davis, Louis E., & Cherns, Albert B. (Eds.), *The Quality of Working Life* (Vols. I & II). New York: The Free Press, 1975, and Davis, L. E., and Taylor, J. C. (Eds.), *Design of Jobs,* 2d ed. Santa Monica, California: Goodyear, 1979.
6. Ford, R., "Job Enrichment Lessons from AT & T," *Harvard Business Review,* 1973, vol. 51, pp. 96–106.
7. Lawler, E. E., Hackman, J. R., & Kaufman, S., "Effects of Job Redesign: A Field Experiment," *Journal of Applied Social Psychology,* 1973, vol. 3, pp. 49–62.
8. Hackman, J. R., & Oldham, G. R., "Development of the Job Diagnostic Survey," *Journal of Applied Psychology,* 1975, vol. 60, pp. 159–70.

 9. Mintzberg, H., *The Structuring of Organizations,* Englewood Cliffs, N.J.: Prentice-Hall, 1979.

10. Lawler, E. E., Hackman, J. R., & Kaufman, S., "Effects of Job Redesign: A Field Experiment," *Journal of Applied Social Psychology,* 1973, vol. 3, pp. 49–62.

11. Hackman, J. R., & Oldham, G. R., *Work Redesign.* Reading, Mass.: Addison-Wesley Publishing Company, 1980.

12. Campbell, D. T., & Stanley, J. C., *Experimental and Quasi-Experimental Designs for Research.* Chicago: Rand McNally, 1963.

13. Porter, L. W., Lawler, E. E., III, & Hackman, J. R., *Behavior in Organizations,* New York: McGraw-Hill, 1975.

26 Job Analysis System: A Model and Technology for Human Resources and Organization Development

Lynda C. McDermott

ABSTRACT

American business leaders must find new ways for their organizations to respond to the changing economic, technological, sociological "third wave" conditions they are now facing during this last quarter of the twentieth century. And OD practitioners, if they intend to take a vital role in the management of these changes, need to explore and adopt new models and technologies that are oriented to the strategic needs and changing nature of organizations.

Job analysis, a methodology used primarily by personnel specialists in the past, can provide a diagnostic tool and database for OD practitioners to use in creating new organization structures and systems. Working together with managers and other staff specialists they can use an OD-oriented job analysis system to increase productivity, create challenging work, and generally improve their contribution to the management of organizational change.

AUTHOR BACKGROUND

Lynda C. McDermott is director of Human Resources Consulting Services for Main Hurdman, a major international accounting and consulting firm headquartered in New York City. She directs a consulting staff that provides services to clients in such areas as organization and human resources planning, executive recruiting and compensation, management training and development, team building and survey feedback. She is formerly director of ASTD's Organization Development Division and serves on ASTD's National Board of Directors.

American industry is faced with a crisis in the workplace. Competition is threatening to close down entire industries; businesses are challenged with the need for improving productivity and the quality of products and services; automation is rapidly spreading from the shop floor to the office, bringing radical changes in how work is done and in the skills required to do it; and many workers are demanding more satisfying work, rewards in relationship to performance, and participation in decisions affecting their work. (Figure 26.1 outlines in more detail the myriad of other changes impacting organizations today.) As this turmoil continues, there is an even greater need and challenge, than in the past, for OD practitioners* to assist American business leaders in creatively managing work and the people of their organizations.

Throughout the century the science of management has been concerned with providing rational technologies and systems to organizations for improving the management of major business functions such as finance, production, administration, quality control, and sales. And for several decades, behavioral scientists have attempted to provide managers with tools for more effectively managing their organizations' potentially most valuable resource—people. However, these tools have not always appeared to be as relevant or systematically designed as other management systems.

The influence of behavioral scientists has been primarily through programs initiated by personnel specialists or organization development practitioners. Personnel specialists are concerned with improving pay, meeting government regulations requirements, and conducting training programs. OD practitioners gen-

---

FIGURE 26.1 Environmental Changes Affecting Organizations

1. Technological
   - Information systems
   - Service function
   - Automation
2. Economic
   - High inflation
   - Declining productivity growth
   - Shift to service sector, white-collar job
   - Low innovation/investment
3. Social
   - Aging work force
   - Increased minorities
   - Highly educated workers
   - Increasing worker demands: participation, recognition, challenge
4. Political
   - Power of internal groups
   - Reduced power in compliance & political markets
   - Government regulations
   - Cuts in public spending

---

*Because of the overlapping definitions and nature of their work, for the purpose of this paper, the title *OD practitioners* will be used generically to refer to both organization development and human resources development specialists.

erally focus on activities such as improving communications and team work. These programs are often delivered from different parts of the organization, appear disjointed, and are not generally viewed as directly contributing to an organization's increased productivity or profitability.

Regardless of the *real* short- or long-term value of OD practitioners' contribution to the development of human resources and organizational effectiveness, their relative lack of stature and power in organizations has generally impeded their ability to truly influence how organizations manage their valuable people resources. This low-level status has primarily been caused by OD practitioners' inability to quantify the value of their contributions to the organization in terms of hard dollars, their own resistance to evaluation, and their lack of understanding or comfort with profit and loss analyses. It is no wonder that in tough economic times OD practitioners, who are seen as working at the fringes of organizations, do not immediately come to mind as valuable resources to help managers with the "real" work of the organization.

But, considering today's current business climate, perhaps the stage is finally set for making dramatic changes that will offer OD practitioners increased opportunities to join forces with specialists in finance, systems, and engineering to help managers view work and their resources differently.

JOB ANALYSIS: AN "OLD" TOOL—A NEW SYSTEM

Job analysis, an "old" tool used by personnel specialists, but applied in a new, and more quantitative and systematic manner, can provide a cost-effective model and technology for developing a totally integrated system for managing the people and their work. Job analysis, when implemented as an OD-oriented system, can be used to diagnose opportunities for improving:

- an organization's structure
- work processes
- staffing procedures
- training programs
- compensation programs
- other management and human resources systems

It provides a data-based technology that can integrate the skills and perspectives of OD practitioners, industrial engineers, and cost accountants, each of whom tend to view work and people in very different ways. Through a job analysis system, these specialists work with managers to develop more effective and competitively strong organizations that can also respond to individual needs for a better quality of work life.

The overall purpose of a job analysis system is to systematically and objectively gather and analyze information about the major work tasks and processes of an organization. It also identifies the knowledge, skills, and abilities required to competently perform tasks. Through such a system, jobs are viewed as temporary groupings of tasks that can be redesigned to better achieve the organization's mission with greater efficiency. The output of such an analysis also provides information for analyzing the cost of work, altering compensation ranges, defining career paths, and analyzing training requirements.

Hackman and Oldham point out in their book *Work Redesign*[1] that "there are literally millions of people in tens of thousands of organizations who are neither giving as much to their work as they might, nor getting as much from it as they need." A job analysis system provides information that can be used to redesign jobs that are more challenging and require a full range of an individual's knowledge, skills, and abilities.

This new way of viewing work is referred to by Alvin Toffler in his book *Third Wave.* He suggests that during the "second wave" of industrial management, jobs were perceived as fixed entities. During the technology-driven "third wave," however, jobs should be viewed as "changing collections of tasks which can be altered, shaped, managed and specifically created to achieve economic and social goals."[2]

Job analysis is not a new technique. The process of reviewing a job's tasks and responsibilities has been used for years to support job evaluation and salary administration. Using this more traditional approach, a job is defined and analyzed according to criteria that are complex or not specifically job related. These imprecise criteria are scaled and then related to external market salary values in order to establish salary ranges for job categories.

Occasionally, a job description, which can be an output of job analysis, is used to establish recruiting criteria. Rarely though are such job analysis outputs used for productivity improvement, personnel cost control, or job redesign.

The technology of job analysis is also subject to criticism because of its lack of objectivity and its vagueness. Often the actual job content and job requirements are defined by job analysts, usually without primary input provided by people doing the job. Because of its limited and traditional uses, job analysis has rarely been used by OD practitioners.

However, applying a job analysis system using an integrated team of managers and OD personnel and accounting or engineering specialists offers a unique approach for using an *old* tool to solve *new* problems. Through it use, such a team can offer significant savings in salary expenditures and improved productivity. This bottom-line orientation offers OD practitioners an approach for joining forces with more traditional (and accepted) business function specialists and an opportunity to be seen as more useful in today's organizations.

THE JOB ANALYSIS PROCESS

The "new" and more OD-oriented approach to job analysis is systematic and process-oriented. It provides a model for looking beyond individual tasks and jobs to the larger organizational context. It requires a framework for collecting and organizing information into a form that is understandable, particularly to managers who will make decisions based on their understanding.

The job analysis process contains steps that can be summarized as follows: strategic organization analysis, organization review, job analysis, job and organization redesign, and management and human resources development.

Strategic organization analysis. With senior management, the overall mission and strategic plans of the organization are reviewed or defined based on current and planned external and internal environmental considerations (for example, economy, technology, new products, and new markets).

Organization review. The current organization structure is reviewed, vis-a-vis the organization's planned mission including organization charts, major functions, job descriptions, and staffing levels. The purpose of this step is to identify variances between mission and functions, and to target areas for further job analysis.

Job analysis. Each job is analyzed in terms of:

- its 4 to 8 (maximum) tasks
- the time allocated to each task
- the relationship and importance of the task to the organization's mission
- its degree of job satisfaction, skill variety, autonomy, decision-making authority, and task feedback—conducted using Hackman's (1980) Job Diagnostic Survey
- productivity, service, and quality inefficiencies or roadblocks
- The knowledge, skill, and ability requirements to perform each task, as it is currently defined. (*Note:* Traits, education, prior experience are not considered relevant in this job analysis system.) This step is conducted using information provided by people currently doing the jobs with verification by direct supervisors. (Where more than one person performs a job, the more competent performers are interviewed.)

Job and organization redesign. Based on the mission, strategic plans, and defined functional requirements, major job tasks are redefined and grouped for greater efficiency, job challenge, and appropriate groupings tasks. Job descriptions and organization charts are developed during this redesign phase.

Management and human resources systems development. It is likely that opportunities for altering work processes, or developing new and more integrated management and human resources systems will be identified in the four steps above. During this fifth step those processes and system are prioritized and implementation plans are developed.

One of the major weaknesses of traditional job analysis techniques is the inability to store, process, and retrieve timely and accurate information. Through the use of a job analysis system, a job database can be maintained which includes such information as:

- Each job's relationship to all other jobs in the organization in terms of:
    the tasks which are performed
    time allocation percentages
    the knowledge, skill, and abilities required to perform each task, subdivided into entry level and competent performance level requirements
- Each job's salary mid-point and salary costs per task
- Equal Employment Opportunity and Fair Labor Standards Act categories
- Job responsibilities for similar jobs external to the organization and their associated salary mid-points
- Task and job performance measurements and standards
- Job profile information (summary data)

This job analysis database can be created manually or automated on a computer system mainframe, a time-sharing system, or on the increasingly popular microcomputers. If computerized, the job database can be easily stored and updated at minimal cost. The specialist or line manager can then use the data to answer what-if questions for job redesign, career pathing, compensation planning, human resources planning, and so forth.

The database can be merged with traditional employee data bases (Human Resources Informations Systems) which are concerned primarily with individuals' experience and education histories, work performance, and skills data for such purposes as:

- Identifying applicant pools for job openings
- Planning future human resources requirements, etc.
- Identifying individual career paths
- Developing training needs requirements and budgets

Additional applications of the job analysis system are listed in Figure 26.2.

Throughout the process, job analysis information is used to answer such questions as:

- What *are* the major tasks performed in the organization?
- How do these tasks support the organization's strategic plans and objectives?
- How are these tasks organized into jobs and functional units?
- What are the knowledge, skill, and ability requirements necessary to perform each task?
- Are some high organizational level (and highly paid) jobs currently designed to include tasks that require lower-level knowledge, skill, and ability requirements?
- What differentiates entry-level requirements vs. training requirements?
- What are the highest training budget priorities?

FIGURE 26.2   Job Analysis Applications

- Job and organization redesign
- Human resources planning
- Identification of knowledge, skills and abilities (KSA) competency
- Job descriptions
- Job selection criteria
- Training needs assessment
- Job evaluation and compensation planning
- Job and individual performance measurement system
- Productivity improvement
- Career pathing and planning
- Cost of work (task) analysis
- Cost of management and supervisory time
- Fair labor standards act exemption
- Performance appraisal systems
- Equal employment opportunity compliance
- Flextime/job sharing
- Job posting
- Supervisory training

- Are we paying individuals for the high level of knowledge, skills, and abilities they bring to the organization, but giving them jobs with lower-level tasks?
- How should jobs and the organization structure be redesigned to group tasks in such a way as to maximize efficiency and quality, and provide challenging work?
- Are we hiring the right people for jobs, both now and for the future?
- What are the staffing levels required to perform the jobs in the redesigned structure?

In addition to these specific applications, a job analysis system increases managers' and their employees' awareness about the organization and processes of their work. It provides a common language for them to use with OD practitioners or systems and methods specialists as they search for ways to improve productivity, control costs, and enrich jobs.

MAINTAINING AN OD PERSPECTIVE

If a job analysis system is to be viewed as an OD intervention then it should be applied in a manner consistent with the definition and values of OD. It should be part of what Beckhard describes as "a total system, planned change effort designed to improve the organization's effectiveness."[3]

Successful OD efforts are not designed as isolated programs, but are viewed and shaped in accordance with a broader organizational and external environmental context. They are also intended to be educative and developmental for managers, staff, and employees so they can continue the effort after initial design and implementation.

While job analysis provides information for productivity improvement and job redesign, this information and the various functions it affects need to be constantly monitored to assure integration and consistency. For example, if jobs are redesigned, then selection criteria probably need to be revised as well as compensation plans. As an organization's strategic plans, financial status, or technology changes, the job analysis system's diagnostic mechanisms and applications should also change.

If a job analysis system is to truly succeed, it should be designed and implemented as a collaborative process among management, staff, employees, and external consultants, as required. Traditionally, when it has been used primarily for job evaluation and compensation purposes, it has been viewed as a staff program, conducted by "job analyst experts." The output of job analysis was generally not intended for use by managers or other functional specialists.

The design of an effective job analysis system from an OD perspective would include such elements as:

- Top management support and involvement
- Objectives for the system and its uses
- Mutual definitions of job tasks and knowledge, skill and ability requirements by job incumbents and supervisors
- Analysis and redesign of jobs, selection criteria, compensation programs, etc., using a team approach of managers, employees, staff specialists, and consultants
- Ongoing assessment of other organization systems and processes affecting or affected by the job analysis system and its outputs.
- Training of managers, employees and staff in the methodologies and capabilities of the system.
- Ongoing evaluation of the job analysis process and achievement of its objectives.
- Development of information systems to provide current and relevant data from the system.

SUMMARY

Although applicable across industries, a job analysis system is particularly well-suited for organizations that are:

- experiencing changes in mission or technology
- labor intensive, for example, service and government
- shifting to more white-collar jobs

- seeking to improve productivity or control personnel costs
- experiencing high rates of turnover or absenteeism

While job analysis is obviously appropriate for nonexempt or clerical jobs, it can and should be used to analyze jobs in the middle of the organization—where jobs often are not consciously designed, but evolve. Peter Drucker notes that in service-oriented and white-collar staff jobs, functions often evolve to support line operations, sometimes with little thought given as to whether the functions should continue to be performed.[4] He also notes that as technology moves into white collar areas it is inevitable that these jobs will change.

The time is now right for OD practitioners to take a proactive and more bottom-line oriented role in assisting with the management of these organizational changes. Their value to managers has been their ability to view organizations from a systems and process-oriented perspective. With a job analysis system they are able to expand that orientation and work with other business specialists to create more productive and effective organizations.

Notes

1. Hackman, J. Richard, & Greg R. Oldham. *Work Redesign.* Reading, Mass.: Addison-Wesley Publishing Company, 1980.
2. Toffler, Alvin. *Third Wave.* New York: William Morrow and Company, Inc., 1980.
3. Beckhard, Richard. *Organization Development: Strategies and Models.* Reading, Mass.: Addison-Wesley Publishing Company, 1969.
4. Drucker, Peter. "Getting Control of Corporate Staff Work," *Wall Street Journal,* April 28, 1982.

27 Quality Circles: Productivity with an OD Perspective

Susan Claire
Joe Wexler

ABSTRACT

When groups of employees meet regularly as quality circles to identify and solve problems, they save the company money and improve productivity. They also threaten middle management security and traditional power structures, the most common causes of quality circle "failure" in the U.S. Other causes of quality circle failure include poor communication during the program start-up, improper training, and improper implementation.

The case history that follows describes an OD approach to quality circles in a geographically dispersed manufacturing and service organization that avoided most of these problems and provides a model for successul implementation of employee participation systems. The case outlines specific design criteria and results from the first two years of implementing quality circles.

Like any major change in managerial style, employee participation programs such as quality circles require careful preparation of the organization and sponsorship by "operations" or line management, if they are to succeed. While quality circles per se may be a fad, productivity improvement through employee involvement in various formats will continue to evolve as an important management tool.

AUTHOR BACKGROUND

Susan Claire designs and conducts training and productivity improvement programs for clients throughout the U.S. An experienced line and staff manager with an M.B.A. from Pepperdine

University, Claire has served as a national speaker and facilitator for ASTD. She specialized in communication and stress management skills for the technical professional. Her company, Claire Communications, is based in Santa Cruz, California.

Joe Wexler is manager of organization development for Geosource, Inc., a natural resource product and service company with over ten thousand people in forty countries. He previously worked for the Center for Creative Leadership in Greensboro, North Carolina. Wexler received his B.A. in psychology from Long Island University and his M.S. in organization/industrial psychology from the University of Tennessee.

As OD consultants, our job is to manage change by helping clients gather data about problems, evaluate options, and make commitments to action. Ideally, we are training our client organizations to handle these functions effectively on their own. It seems particularly appropriate, then, to look at the installation of quality circles from an OD perspective.

Quality circles (QCs) are usually, but not always, defined as follows:

A group of 5 to 10 employees from one area of a company who volunteer to meet on a regular basis (usually one hour a week) during working hours to identify problems affecting quality in their work area, and to suggest solutions to those problems.

QCs have proven to be effective not only in actually solving problems, saving money, and increasing productivity, but also in involving employees in the process of managing change in the organization. The deceptively simple process has a powerful impact in moving the managerial style of the organization toward more participation and an upward flow of communication. Generally, senior management of companies in the U.S. tends to see only the benefits of the end result, while underestimating the preparation needed to avoid resistance to such changes at all levels.

This article will present a case history of the successful installation of a quality circles system with an OD approach. In describing the installation of the system, we will present a review of the primary causes for failure of QCs in America, and the training design considerations that allowed us to avoid them. Finally we will discuss what we have found to be the substantial benefits of an OD approach to QCs.

BACKGROUND

Geosource, a multi-national organization headquartered in Houston, Texas, provides high technology products and services to the petroleum industry worldwide. The company employs ten thousand people in forty countries.

In 1979, Geosource began the process of formal employee involvement programs with a climate survey system designed to identify the perceived areas of concern within the organization. Employees in each division completed an 80-item survey, covering the following eight categories:

1. Supervision
2. Organizational effectiveness
3. Compensation
4. Benefits

5. Working conditions
6. Management support
7. Personal involvement
8. Workforce stability

The computer-generated feedback on the level of satisfaction with each item is then used in an interactive employee meeting to clarify specific problems and develop suggestions for solutions. These are, in turn, converted into goals for completion by specific managers, with reports on progress to the full employee group.

Part of the survey reflects the managerial style of the division, ranging from a negative, dictatorial style to a participative style, and including passive, authoritative, benevolent authoritative, consultative, and participative styles of management. This information is helpful in predicting current readiness for more intensive employee involvement programs such as quality circles.

In 1980, publicity stories on the successful use of QCs in the U.S. were appearing frequently in the business and popular media, and several Geosource manufacturing divisions began to express an interest in the QC process. Following a preliminary review of existing quality circles materials, the Geosource OD Department contracted with Organizational Development Systems, Inc., a Houston-based consulting firm, to assist in developing a custom QC implementation system.

WHY CIRCLES FAIL

The first step in this development process was to examine causes for failure of QCs in the United States. The most frequent causes were: inadequate preparation of middle management, destructive actions by management, hostile organizational climate, poor communications at the start, lack of union support, improper training, improper implementation, slow management decisions and implementation, and lack of feedback on results.

Inadequate preparation of middle management. While senior management is pleased with the measurable improvement in productivity and circle members are thrilled with the chance to improve their jobs, middle managers and supervisors frequently feel threatened by the new system. Not only does it solve problems which they considered their area of responsibility, but it seems to interfere with their first priority—production. Most of all, it creates expectations for involvement and participation on the part of their employees that they have no idea how to handle. They see no benefits to themselves from the new system; it only gives them additional headaches. As a result, the middle manager will consciously or unconsciously sabotage the circles' effectiveness to prove they can't work.

Destructive actions by management.   Frequently, without thinking, circles can be destroyed by such simple acts as:

- Transferring several members to another shift
- Cancelling meetings "temporarily" to meet a big production crunch or special heavy workload
- Pulling members out of training to handle a "more important" problem
- Promising special meetings and storage space for the circles and then delaying completion of the space for months due to other priorities
- Booking a "more important" meeting or series of meetings in the circles' meeting room
- Delaying in providing data that the circle needs

These actions often unintentionally send the message to employees that no matter what management *says* about supporting the circles, in reality management is helping them fail. This kind of double message can leave morale in worse shape than if no intervention had been tried to at all.

Hostile organizational climate.   When employee/management relations have turned into a combat zone, management may try to use QC as a quick fix. Unfortunately, both employees and managers in this environment will sabotage the circles to prove the other side is wrong. Some other interventions are required before quality circles have a chance to be successful.

Poor communications at the start.   Too often, a hasty training program for a few people is the only notification the employee group has the initiation of quality circles in the organization. The only information they have is by rumor, and what they don't understand, they fear. Therefore, they don't volunteer for circles and they ridicule those who do. The program dies for lack of employee support.

Lack of union support.   Frequently, management isn't honest with itself about the real status of the relationship with the union, preferring to cast a rosy glow on the subject. Although the great majority of unions are supporting QCs as a way of increasing employee input to their jobs, a few local union stewards have been known to literally walk in and close down the meetings because they haven't been informed. If the QCs are being used in any way as part of a strategy to decertify the union, the union will see to it that the circles die.

Improper training.   When circles receive *too little* training, they feel like they are being set up to fail by management. When they get *too much* it is usually overengineered, focusing on arcane techniques that are rarely needed or used. This usually leads to training that is *too long;* the members get discouraged after months without real progress on their work problems. Training for QCs can also focus on the *wrong skills:* too much focus on solving problems as an individual and not enough on how to improve the problem solving synergy of the group. Most QC training currently available does not prepare members or leaders with any group process skills at all. The result is the death of circles due to personality conflicts and unclear expectations.

Training can also help circles fail due to the *wrong format.* Developed by technical specialists without the knowledge of adult learning techniques, most QC training is delivered in the traditional lecture and slide or tape format, and bored participants' retention rates on the new learning are frequently quite low. In addition,

> The traditional Quality Circles training program discriminates against the member. The facilitator receives five days of training, the leader receives three days of training, but the members receive only eight hours of training. This training is accomplished by using the transference method, wherby a Quality Circle consultant trains the facilitator, the facilitator trains the leaders, and the leaders train the members.*

By the time the member receives the training, it is watered down, both because the leader barely understands the concepts himself, and because he or she is not skilled in conducting training.

Improper implementation.   Circles are plagued by hosts of problems during implementation which seem unique to each location. For example:

■ One company prepared members of a new circle by conducting one "group survival" exercise, and then asked them to meet on their own time at lunch. The group was soon discouraged because they didn't know how to produce results, and resentful that their lunch hour was imposed on. (The practice of not paying for meeting time can result in instant union certification for nonunion organizations, meeting time being considered a "concerted activity.")

■ A facilitator was asked to continue full-time responsibilities on another job and conduct quality circles "in her spare time."

■ An autocratic supervisor, invited to be a circle leader, continued to be just as autocratic in the circle.

■ A circle that was given no limits to their field of inquiry, decided to change pay and benefit policies (a subject outside the scope of Quality Circles that endangered union negotiations).

Slow management decisions and implementation.   Employee's greatest fear coming into the circles is that they will do all this work defining problems and suggesting solutions, and management will ignore or not implement the

*Olson, Major R., and Reed, Sergeant First Class Thomas W. "Circle Quality—Members Remembered." Paper presented at the International Association of Quality Circles Meeting in St. Louis, March 1982. Copies available from the Organizational Effectiveness Center and School, Fort Ord, California 93941.

ideas. They are afraid this is just another management fad and that management doesn't really intend to do anything about the problems.

Management feeds this fear when, due to the press of other business, they delay in listening to circle presentations, or in getting back to the circle on a decision. In some cases, management actually did implement the suggestion, but didn't tell the circle or give credit to the circle in front of the rest of the organization.

Such a lack of communication obviously gives fuel to the skeptics who spread the word that quality circles is just another management trick that doesn't yield any results for the employees.

Lack of feedback on results.   When no one knows what the actual results were on solutions proposed by quality circles, everyone gets discouraged.

- The circle members have no feedback on whether their work makes any difference, or is doing any good.
- The employee group as a whole doesn't have information on the progress of the circles, and assumes that they have dissolved.
- Management begins to feel that circle meetings may be a waste of time.
- Without adequate follow-up and communication, the Circles die a natural death.

A successful QC system is easy to operate and a normal part of the work process, so management tends to overestimate the simplicity of getting it started: buy a training package, add water, and voila—instant quality circles! Unfortunately, as indicated by the listing above, the great majority of quality circles' failure are caused not by the operation of the circle, but the lack of adequate preparation and support.

NEXT STEP: DESIGN FOR SUCCESSFUL QCs

The outline of the QC implementation system that follows reflects a deliberate effort to avoid the most common causes of failure for QC programs.

Management Overview

Senior management needs to have a clear understanding of what commitment to quality circles can mean before a decision to implement is made. Objectives, benefits, and areas of concern are outlined in a special meeting with the consultants and questions are answered. If the decision is made to proceed, management signs a service agreement with the corporate OD department, which includes the commitment to timely decisions, and the provision of feedback to the whole organization.

Organization Readiness

If no climate survey has already been conducted, a readiness report is developed to spot any potential problem areas, and special preparation needs.

Middle Manager and Supervisor Training

At this point, supervisors and middle managers are oriented to participative management concepts. The importance of this step can't be overstated: The support of middle management is critical to the success of the QC process. Managers and supervisors are trained in participative techniques, including listening skills. In some cases, this process alone can increase productivity without going on to the formal structure of the QC process. However, if QCs are to be installed, managers and supervisors receive an overview of what to expect, how they will be expected to cooperate, and what benefits are in the system for them. Frequently, managers are made responsible for the success of "their" circles.

Steering Committee Formation

In addition, all operating and staff departments who can affect the success of the circles are represented on a QC steering committee. This group plans and directs the introduction and operation of the circles, including:

- Defining the scope of inquiry; what circles will and will not look into
- Informing the organization on the initiation and progress of the circles
- Selecting a full-time facilitator and pilot circle members from volunteers
- Defining procedures for circles. For example, a solution that will cost below a certain dollar value may be implemented directly. Above that amount, a presentation is made to the steering committee for approval.

The quality of members selected for this committee is critical, since they must have authority to approve capital expenditures, and are responsible for the success of quality circles in the organization.

Facilitator Selection, Assessment, and Training

It is generally preferable to identify a Facilitator candidate who already has experience and credibility within the organization. The Facilitator, as coordinator of the program, serves as a link between Management and the Circle, and is a major source of support and assistance to QCs in the early stages of implementation. Each Facilitator candidate is assessed for their current skill levels in the variety of competencies needed in this job, and then individually coached and trained to prepare them for the role.

Inform Potential Circle Members

The first responsibility of the new facilitator is to conduct an active PR campaign for the QC program to provide information to potential circle members. Bulletin boards, company newsletters, and special meetings have all been successfully utilized to publicize the program and provide a clear explanation of its concepts and structure. Good PR is critical, because participation is voluntary. Sometimes the decision to implement initial circles in a particular department is made as a result of the number of volunteers from a particular area of the company.

Training the Circle Leaders

Six hours of leader training provides initial quality circle orientation to selected group leaders. In preparation for that role, leader training provides the skills necessary for successfully selecting circle members, organizing and running a circle meeting. An agenda is provided for the first three sessions. Leader training provides the support needed in the critical organizational stages of the program.

First Three Circle Meetings

Between the leader training and the group training, members receive information on how the QCs will operate, and begin generating a list of problems they would like to solve. Those problems are used as "real world" illustrations during the group training. By using real problems, the issue of delayed start-up is avoided, and members quickly see the result of their efforts.

Leaders and Members Trained in GrouP.S.

Group Problem Solving (GrouP.S.) is probably one of the key factors in the success of this approach. During twenty hours of training, usually conducted in half days over a five-day period, the circle learns to deal with both the content they will need to know and the process of making the group work. Although additional polishing will be needed, they work from start to finish on a real problem from their work environment, using each QC skill area, including those listed below:

- Working effectively in a group
- Problem identification and clear problem statement
- Priority setting
- Information gathering and reducing defensive responses
- Problem solving: cause identification, solution generation and selection, utilizing a new, simplified QC model
- Presentations and persuasion
- Tracking results

During this time, the circles build a feeling of teamwork by sharing the fun and challenge of working together in an adult learning environment, and have professional facilitation available at the early stage of group formation to help with both process and content problems, if necessary.

An abbreviated version of GrouP.S. training is also used at Geosource for other employee involvement programs, such as short-term problem-solving task forces called productivity improvement teams.

Implementation and Presentations

As the circles have started generating solutions to problems, over 50% of the changes are implemented through normal supervisory channels, or on a one-to-one basis between employee groups. However, the opportunity to present their suggestions and receive recognition directly from senior management in the steering committee meetings is an important motivator in the QC process.

From the very beginning, the circles are aware that it is their job to speak the language of management in terms of the costs and benefits of any suggestion. Presentation training in the GrouP.S. includes both "idea selling" skills for overcoming natural resistance to change, and techniques for effectively presenting data. In turn, management makes a commitment during the training to respond to *every* QC suggestion within a specific time frame, with either a "yes-when" or "no-why" answer.

Tracking Results of Group Problem Solving

QC experts generally caution against expecting any measurable bottom-line results before the third year of implementation. At Geosource, however, with a total of 70 circles and PIT Teams in six locations, projected savings to date exceed $960,000. At the two locations where circles were started more than one year ago, pre- and post-survey feedback now exists. Since circle implementation, significant increase has occurred in employee perception of both management support and organizational effectiveness. Improvements were generally felt in supervision and personal involvement as well. Survey results and projected savings have encouraged the continued expansion of circle activities at Geosource.

BENEFITS OF THE OD APPROACH TO QC

The benefits of this design are obvious when compared with the causes of failure for circles in the U.S.

Adequate Preparation of Middle Management

The training in participative techniques pays off not only in ensuring the circles' success, but also in more effective day-to-day operations.

Clear Expectations of Senior Management

The management overview, consultant coaching, and, most of all, line responsibility for the success of circles operations, have reduced the frequency of thoughtlessly destructive actions by managers by clarifying what actions senior management must and must not take to help circles succeed.

Research Into Current Organizational Climate

The readiness report helps ensure that the current organizational climate is ready to support quality circles, or if other actions are necessary.

Employee Commitment Checked

Until the employee group understands the process and benefits of the QC system and volunteers in sufficient numbers, no circles are started. Employee commitment must be checked before proceeding.

Union Commitment Confirmed

If unions are already represented in the organization, a representative usually sits on the QC steering committee. The union commitment must be confirmed before start-up.

Proper Training

Ideally, circles receive the *right amount* of training focusing on the *right skills* in the *best format*. These include:

- Getting a "head start" on solving the first problem during training; application of problem solving techniques to real problems rather than abstract cases allows members to see immediate results of their efforts and the QC process.
- This "real problem" approach also makes use of the best of adult learning techniques, including simulation, role practice, and discussion.
- The practical group problem-solving model (GrouP.S.) emphasizes the reality that circles are dealing with, rather than wasting time on unnecessary busywork.
- Focus on group rather than individual problem solving; circles are formed during training and successful group interaction skills are treated as integral aspects of the QC process.
- Training is conducted by a qualified professional (either the facilitator or an in-house trainer) and is reinforced at circle meetings by facilitator assistance as needed.

Proper Implementation

By making the best decisions during the preparation phase, the steering committee reduces the potential for problems and ensures proper implementation.

Speedy Management Decisions

Emphasis on presentation to management and an action/implementation management response reduces frustrations of insufficient communication between management and circles. Effective presentation skills increase the likelihood of a good idea being understood and accepted by management.

Continuing Feedback

Continuing feedback to circles, management and all employees is essential for success. At least one installation is using a large bulletin board in the cafeteria area to keep all employees informed by pictures and graphs of what each circle is currently working on, and their successes to date. Facilitators maintain records of projected versus actual improvements in productivity. Managers are appraised, in part, by the success of "their" circles.

CONCLUSION

The success of the OD approach to quality circles implementation at Geosource has led us to several concluding thoughts on the participative management philosophy and specifically quality circles.

First, as they are now sweeping the country and dominating the literature, quality circles may well be a passing management fad. However, the underlying structure of an effective QC program—group problem solving by those closest to the problem—is not a fad. The process works. In the case presented here, its success is evident in both bottom-line dollar savings and an improved organizational climate.

Second, the group problem solving system described here is practical and flexible enough for application in a variety of settings. However, it can't be taken as a package and used to fit every situation. We feel a consulting approach which makes adaptations to fit the environment is a critical factor in the success of any QC program.

Finally, the question arises: Given the apparent logic of an OD approach to QC implementation, why is OD just now getting on the bandwagon of what is seen as an operations-sponsored program? Our answer is twofold: In the past, OD concepts of participation have been seen as idealistic and nice to have, but certainly not as essential to operations. Over the past ten years, QCs have proven their bottom-line value to the company, and that is the primary reason they are thriving.

When employee participation is seen as an operations (rather than consultant) sponsored program, the managers become the real change agents and will help ensure the success of a new managerial style. The result satisfies both management and employees, and strengthens the organization.

Executive Profiles:
A Feedback System for Senior Executives

John T. Thompson

ABSTRACT

This paper describes a third-party, feedback system used by an internal OD consulting group in a Fortune 500 corporation. The hypothesis that derives this continuing action research effort is based on observations that it is rare for high-level executives to fail for their lack of technical skills or professional background. Typically, the higher one ascends in an organization, the less the opportunity for objective feedback from relevant others. The executive profile is based on the need to provide high-level executives with discrepancy feedback on their relationship with other executives. Without knowing of possible discrepancies between one's own perception of the organization, the job, and one's performance, alternate approaches are not likely to be pursued. Descriptions of each of the systems, including instrumentation, analytical procedures, and consultant guidelines are included. The system has proven to be a constructive supplement to the feedback that executives need for effective performance and development.

AUTHOR BACKGROUND

An experienced consultant to senior executives, John T. Thompson is a Vice President of David Powell, Inc., an executive placement firm in Menlo Park, California. Previously, he served as corporate director of Human Resources Development for Atari, Inc., in Santa Clara, California, and as corporate director of organization development for The Williams Companies in Tulsa

This paper is adapted from a presentation the author made at the national conference of the American Society for Training and Development in San Antonio, Texas in May 1982.

where he successfully implemented the Executive Profiles process. Thompson has served on the board of directors of the American Society for Training and Development and has been recognized by ASTD as a top practitioner in OD with both the *OD Practitioner* and *Torch Award* recognitions. He is also widely published in many professional journals.

Having consulted for some twelve years in large organizations, I have observed that it is rare for high-level executives to fail for lack of technical skills or professional backgrounds. Many of us have no doubt heard the phrase "he or she was technically competent, but———" in describing the particular reasons an officer has left a corporation. While much has been written about the reasons for executive failure and success, there is a paucity of proven methodologies that can meet the real needs of senior executives for constructive feedback.

Given these observations, this paper will describe a successful intervention process, the Personal Assessment Development System (PADS), that is currently being used in a Fortune 500 corporation.* The process is based on the hypothesis that the higher one ascends in an organizational structure, the less the opportunity for objective feedback from superiors, peers, and subordinates. By virtue of the fact that higher assignment levels tend to amplify a senior executive's lack of awareness of his or her conflict with other senior executives, the intervention process discussed here has unusual flexibility to meet an executive's possible discrepancies of perception. Such a process has been successful in reducing the probability of collision courses between executives and the organization when the discrepancies of perception include incongruities involving the political environment, behavioral characteristics in interpersonal relationships, and the organization's goals.

As with most effective interventions, PADS is based on the need to provide high-level executives with objective third-party feedback on their relationships with other executives. Descriptions of each phase in the system, including the data-gathering instruments, analytical procedures, feedback processes and consultant guidelines, are included in the remainder of this paper.

THE PROCESS

Before describing each of the key phases of the process, it is appropriate to briefly describe the consulting environment. The corporate environment can be characterized as one of rapid growth primarily through acquisition. Rapid

*I am indebted to two professional colleagues, Fred Droege and Gary Richetto, who were insightful enough to recognize the need for PADS, and who initially developed and implemented the PADS process.

growth has been a key factor in the acceptance of PADS by senior management since this expansion resulted in major managerial transitions. The OD staff group of five professionals consistently focused on high impact interventions, rather than pursuing a strategy of "light many fires." The strategy for excellence can best be described by the following sports analogy: It is more important to pursue a record of 10 and 0 rather than be 20 and 7. Therefore, to ensure high-level impact, the group accepted projects requested from the officer level—thus ensuring commitment to these projects.

The complete PADS process is shown in Figure 28.1. The initial introduction of the system was made by the chairman and chief executive officer through a cover letter to each company officer. The cover letter stressed that the initial participation in the system was totally voluntary and that the system was designed for the personal growth of each company officer. His only request was for cooperation from all executives if asked to contribute to the PADS profile of a fellow executive. Over twenty profiles of company officers have been conducted during the last five years.

Once the six phases of the process have been described, I will note some of the major learnings from using PADS. Because of its perceived success, I believe the system can be incorporated into any large organization which has high level support for a consultation group and the willingness of senior management to take part in a personal feedback procedure.

Phase 1: Executive Orientation

The process begins once a company officer has volunteered to become a focal executive. Two members of the OD group conduct an initial briefing covering topics including system rationale, the ground rules of confidentiality and anonymity, and guidelines for a professional relationship. As a gestalt-oriented practitioner knows, "unless contact is made with the client, nothing else will happen." Therefore, the relationship-building portion of this briefing is critical for the process.

After explaining what the focal executive can expect during the process (typically five to six weeks), the consulting team distributes five or six written instruments to be completed prior to the focal executive interview. The instruments have varied based on the situation and the executive's expressed needs. However, the team has selected these instruments on a regular basis—Schutz's FIRO-B, Kolb's Learning Styles Inventory, the Strength Development Inventory, a team effectiveness instrument, a values clarification instrument, a leadership style instrument, and sixty semantic differential scales for measuring the focal executive's self-image in terms of evaluative, potency, and activity dimensions.

Phase 2: Focal Interview/Selection of Key Contribution Group

A key component of the system is a 26-page interview guide, which is an extensive protocol that consists of questions and space for notetaking by the consultant team. Focal interviews using the guide usually take two to three hours.

FIGURE 28.1 Personal Assessment and Development System

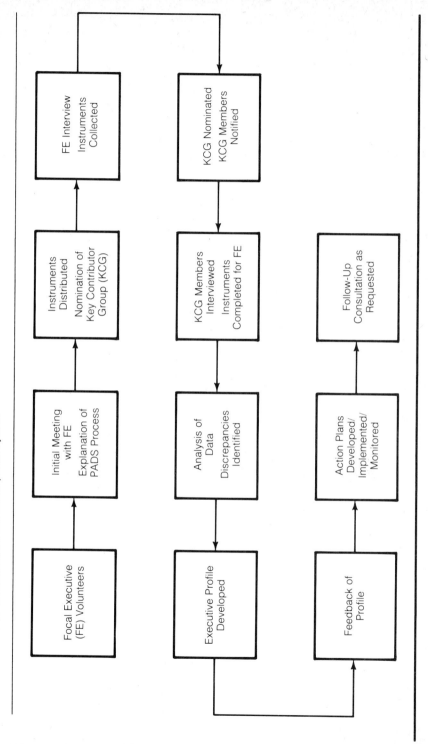

Before beginning the focal interview, we explain to the focal executive that the earlier written instruments will be used for one portion of the feedback and several of those instruments will be completed by members of the key contributor group (KCG). In addition, the KCG is established. The role of the KCG is to provide anonymous feedback along the same dimensions requested in the interview protocol. In selecting the KCG, the team recommends that the focal executives include immediate supervisors, immediate subordinates, peers reporting in the same structure, and any relevant others whose relationship is considered key to the executive's effectiveness. The size of the KCG typically ranges from ten to twelve executives.

The focal executive's interview is based on the interview guide. The interview guide focuses on five areas and uses a structure that moves from general, less sensitive issues to more personal and highly sensitive issues. These five areas include the focal executive's views toward:

- the company
- position held within the company
- performance within that position
- personal attributes and liabilities
- personal motives, wants and needs

As mentioned earlier, the interview with the focal executive is conducted by the consultant team. Decisions are made in advance on who will cover each section of the interview guide and who will have primary responsibility for notetaking during each section of the interview. Such a process allows for both consultants to be actively involved in the interview while allowing for detailed notes to be collected. Although one of the consultants is primarily responsible for notetaking, the team's experience has shown that it is often this consultant who identifies fruitful additional areas to probe during the interview process. In order to provide a more detailed description of the interview protocol, each of the subject areas—the company; the position; the performance; personal characteristics; and motives, wants, and needs—will briefly be described (see Figure 28.2).

The company. The interview begins by soliciting the focal executive's view toward the company in both broad and philosophical terms. The interview begins with the question, "What is the company?" in order to have the executive focus on the company's major efforts, the company's work climate, philosophical model, and other professional considerations regarding the company. The next question asked is, "What is the company becoming?" This question is used to determine which trends are reversible and which are irreversible. The executive is asked further to contribute views on what the company should become. These responses frequently focus on what the company's strategy should be in terms of product and market scope.

The focal executive is then asked to comment on the structure of the company in terms of the present and the future. Furthermore, the executive is

FIGURE 28.2 The Executive Profile Interview Content

1. *The company.* Questions pertaining to the corporation in terms of:
   - Philosophy
   - Organization
   - Direction
   - Strengths and weaknesses
2. *The position.* Perceptions on:
   - Parameters
   - Restrictions
   - Clients
   - Demands
3. *Performance.* Questions focusing on:
   - Strengths and weaknesses via a report card
   - Wins and losses
   - Good decisions/bad decisions
   - Things not done/to be done
4. *Attributes and liabilities.*
   - Behavioral traits in daily performance
   - Tendencies, mannerisms, habits, work methods
5. *Motives, needs, wants.* Questions on the "whys" of performance
   - Emotional needs
   - Motive drives
   - Career aspirations

probed for comments on the changes that are necessary for the company to move into the future.

The position. In the second area of the interview guide, the team asks the executive to mentally step back and focus on the role demands of the position. While this is difficult to do, this section provides data for the necessary comparison with the next section, job performance. In order to establish the demands from the position, the team begins by inquiring, "What services or products must come out of this position?" and "In what order of importance?" Next, the executive is asked to identify the primary clients of the position.

The executive also has an opportunity to comment on the output of the position that is not necessary, or conversely, "What should the position provide that it does not currently provide?" In addition to the outputs from the position, the team advises the executive to focus on the balance of inputs that are required for the job and the existence of barriers that impede these inputs. Finally, the team asks the executive to focus on strengths and weaknesses of the work group, including methods, equipment, and personnel.

The performance. After the executive has completed the questions on "the position," the executive is asked to evaluate his or her current performance. We begin this section by asking the executive to report on major contributions. Next, we suggest a "report card" be established by identifying the criteria for excellence in the job and then to evaluate on the criteria identified. The criteria chosen for evaluation represent data that is just as valuable for the profile as the executive's personal evaluation.

Personal characteristics.   After completing "the performance" area, we begin by soliciting information on personal characteristics, including strengths and weaknesses in relationship to superiors, peers, and subordinates. Further, we have the executive report on qualities that are most admired in subordinates, peers, and superiors.

Again, this information is very useful for comparative purposes with previous responses made during this section of the interview. In an attempt to more closely compare specific responses, we recommend the executive predict the responses the KCG will use in describing their strengths and weaknesses.

Motives, wants, and needs.   The fifth area of the interview represents the most sensitive questions. Up to this point, we have hopefully built a strong rapport and trusting relationship with the executive. Answers to questions in this section of the interview are frequently followed by long and somewhat involved answers. We begin this section by questioning, "Which work experiences are most emotionally rewarding to you?" The executive is also probed to identify any job-related fears and what parts of that job represent the least satisfying experiences.

In order to bring attention to career concerns, we ask the question, "What position do you see yourself promotable to within the next two years or so?" After identifying such a position, we urge the executive to comment on what he or she could contribute most in the future position. Finally, we have the executive focus on long-range career potential.

In the last section of questions, the executive is requested to identify a personal definition of success and to comment on whether that success has been achieved, and if not, whether that success can be attained in the future. In addition, we begin to focus on more philosophical issues, such as "What do you want out of life?" After reflecting on the answer to this question, we follow up with questions that ask the executive to estimate the probability for achievement of life goals, and what doubts and fears exist in the pursuit of life goals. Next, the executive is requested to reflect on behavioral changes made in the past five years. The interview is concluded by asking what the executive would like to know from the KCG. This open-ended question allows us to better tailor our questions for the KCG interviews.

At this point, we end the interview by thanking the executive for participation in this lengthy data-collection procedure. In addition, we answer any further questions about the PADS process and give the executive an indication of when we will have the feedback session.

Phase 3: Key Contributor Group—Data Gathering

All members of the KCG receive a similar orientation to the PADS system and its rationale in our initial contact with them. We spend considerable time with an explanation of our ground rules involving confidentiality and anonymity. Given this orientation, several of the written instruments used with the focal executive (the sixty semantic differential scales and the team effectiveness instrument) are provided. The KCG interview is then conducted. The interview follows a very similar format to that of the focal executive. The team uses each section of the interview guide except the area of "Motives, wants, and needs" in order to avoid the need of the KCG member to attribute motives to the focal executive. Our objective in all of the interviews is to obtain data that will allow for a discrepancy analysis once the interviews are completed.

Phase 4: Discrepancy Analysis

This phase of the PADS system is based on a research method known as "discrepancy evaluation." This method avoids arbitrary standards of good or bad, right or wrong. It allows for the recording of perceptions and the identification and analysis of discrepancies among them. At this point, our consultant team conducts the analysis of both the interview data and the written instruments. As much as is professionally possible, the analysis remains value-free by focusing on observed discrepancies between the focal executive's view of each of the five areas of the interview versus the perceptions of the KCG along these same variables.

Experience has shown that we must use professional judgment in identifying the data that is to be fed back to the focal executive. Most frequently, we report on discrepancies or consensus items that are held by a majority of the KCG. At times, however, a significant minority viewpoint of a superior or key peer will be fed back. Our entire purpose during the feedback portion of the process is to have the focal executive view the data and its meaning and *not* who contributed what part of the data. Because we have often found a need to report a "minority viewpoint," we now discuss our use of professional judgment about these viewpoints with the focal executive during our initial orientation.

Phase 5: Feedback of Profile Results

When scheduling the feedback session with the focal executive, we ask the executive to set aside at least four hours. First, we share the instrumented data by providing the focal executive with insight into discrepancies between views of self and organization versus those of the KCG. During this discussion, we provide relevant statistical analyses to make the data as meaningful as possible. In addition, we frequently reference supporting or nonsupporting interview data, which tends to give more reality to the instrumented data.

After we have explained the instrumented results, we share the interview data by providing the focal executive with a blank copy of the interview guide. Instead of providing the focal executive with a long written report, we focus more on a process consultation approach which allows us, page-by-page, to summarize the responses, and compare and contrast these with those provided by the KCG. We have found that this method provides for maximum personal growth by giving the focal executive an opportunity to judge and record those discrepancies of most personal interest and importance.

Since this phase of the process oftentimes includes a considerable volume of personal and sensitive data, we discuss the need for a follow-up interview with the focal executive after a period of personal reflection. Although many executives want to problem solve immediately, we have found that this incubation period provides for balance and a more reality-based approach to action planning.

Phase 6: Action Planning

After this incubation period, we schedule another meeting with the focal executive to develop action plans and set appropriate priorities for dealing with any discrepancies in the data. Of course, this step is optional, based on whether the executive decides to make any choices on the data. It is at this point in the process that we have frequently been asked to work with the executive on other projects relevant to the data. Such projects have included transition meetings, team-building sessions, goal-setting sessions, and one-on-one problem-solving. These requests allow us to maintain an important contact with our client in the months ahead. Some of these plans have included the desire to repeat the PADS process after a period of approximately twelve months.

CONSULTANT GUIDELINES

As with any OD intervention, guidelines for confidentiality and anonymity must be followed in order to maintain the integrity of the intervention. We have found the following guidelines to be useful in maintaining the integrity of the PADS process.

First, we maintain all written files on each profile in a safety deposit box. We choose to maintain these files in a bank vault in order to provide the needed security for such highly sensitive information. In addition, we do not leave the focal executive's file with the executive. Here again, for security reasons we would prefer to make the file available to the executive when requested instead of leaving our comprehensive files with the client. Further, we have established that data relative to any focal executive will not be shared with *anyone* other than the focal executive unless expressed written permission is granted by the focal executive in the presence of a member of the consulting team.

For example, this means that if a senior officer requested profile information about a junior officer, the data would not be made available unless the junior officer agreed. Even in this example, we have the confounding effect of the political sensitivities of refusing to make profile results available to a superior. For this reason, we would advise against this request unless it would appear to be in the best interests of the individual and the organization. The reality of the situation is that we have never been asked by any executive to violate these system guidelines.

In addition, we brief the focal executive on our expectations and requirements that contributions from the KCG (on subjects relative to the corporation's operations and future plans) not be shared with outsiders. Further, we ask that any notes on these subjects be surrendered to the Office of Organization Development should the focal executive leave the employment of the company.

As a practical matter, we never accept a request from a superior that a subordinate officer with serious performance difficulties be involved in the PADS process. In such cases where a decision to terminate an officer has already been made in the mind of an executive, we recommend that a profile not be initiated. Our belief is that such profiles would create the perception that those individuals involved in the PADS process are "on their way out" if a profile is completed just before they "leave." For this reason and others already explained, the PADS system is intended to be a developmental process and not a remedial process.

CONSULTANT OBSERVATIONS

The PADS process has provided me with an excellent opportunity to grow in the use of consultation skills such as contracting, interviewing, and process consultation. In addition, it has provided me with a unique opportunity to gain additional insight into complexities of reporting relationships and political considerations at the most senior levels in the organization. It has also provided me with opportunities for mutual learning with my clients. Needless to say, it is a very rewarding experience to find opportunities where both you and your client can grow concurrently. The successful use of this system has allowed me to build a solid base of client contacts throughout the corporation and, in many cases, has provided me with entry into other high-impact projects in the corporation.

Although the PADS process has the "downside" of requiring a professional sense of audience with what can be very sensitive data, I have found a countervailing "upside" that the resultant compilation of norms and corporate values provides me with an excellent basis for further organizational diagnosis.

The data collected from the profiles has provided me with a database which allows for observations of changes in the corporation. I believe this to be very important information for the internal consultant as one tries to assist the organization in managing and planning change.

My final observation is one of the apparent paradox that results from viewing the PADS process identified in Figure 28.1 as a complex set of steps and procedures. In essence, any successful OD intervention should collect data about the client, assist the client in making informed, free choices about the data, and assist the client in implementing a choice. Ultimately, the complex set of steps described here meet these simple requirements.

SUMMARY

In summary, we have found that the system has met the executive's need to take stock of his or her role in a rapidly changing environment. On the group level, the intervention has provided a common socialization and value-sharing result. On the organizational level, the system has assisted the senior officers address and problem-solve gaps in perceptions that affect high-level organizational requirements.

29 Affirmative Action: A Guide to Systems Change for Managers

Alice G. Sargent

ABSTRACT

Organizations currently take a piecemeal approach to affirmative action. An integrated affirmative action effort across all organizational planning and management systems would include the following components: appointing a top management task force, conducting a climate survey, designing an effective recruiting and hiring program, assessing the effectiveness of management systems, providing training programs that include women and minorities, promoting supervisory relationships to carry out human resource management functions, assessing upward-mobility programs, providing alternative work schedules, encouraging network building among women and minorities, establishing a spouse involvement program, and creating affirmative action teams.

AUTHOR BACKGROUND

Alice G. Sargent is an organization consultant living in Washington, D.C., serving as a consultant and trainer to E.I. Dupont de Nemours, Federal Executive Institute, Australian Institute of Management, Agency for International Development, and NTL Institute. Previous clients include the General Accounting Office, Overseas Private Investment Corporation, Federal Energy Regulatory Commission, U.S. Department of Commerce, Celanese Corporation, Procter & Gamble, CIGNA Corporation, and The National Cancer Institute, among others. She is an adjunct faculty member in the Key Executive Program at The American University School of Government and Public Administration and at the University of Southern California Washington Public Affairs Center. She was formerly director of the MBA program at Trinity College. She is the author of *Beyond Sex Roles, The Androgynous Manager,* and coeditor of *The NTL Manager's Handbook,* NTL Institute. She is on the board of the Organizational Development Network and has been named to *Who's Who in the East, Who's Who in American Women,* and *Outstanding Young Women of America.*

Organizations currently take a piecemeal approach to affirmative action. A more effective approach would be to integrate affirmative action across all organizational planning and management systems. Affirmative action can succeed only if management links it to the following: human resources management, which deals with having the right people at the right place at the right time; an effective performance management system, which includes both career development and appraisal; and the quality of work life, which concerns managing diversity and developing a multicultural work environment. Another approach, characterized by Juanita Kreps, former Secretary of Commerce, calls for "the second bottom line to be corporate social responsibility." The first line is profit; the second is a concern for such social factors as the effective use of human and environmental resources. At their roots, these approaches seek to generate awareness and change processes that have systematically failed to utilize fully our most important resource—people.

Affirmative action is a management problem, and as such proves the effectiveness or lack of it of most management practices with the organization. It spotlights the extent to which organizations regard managing human resources as a priority. It raises intense interdepartmental issues and evokes turf protection where there is not highly effective collaboration. Hence, affirmative action programs work best carried out by a top management task force working in conjunction with an EEO staff person. Without the management group the staff person can only attempt to influence, cajole, threaten, and beg to persuade managers to do their part.

Affirmative action covers all personnel management functions including hiring, recruitment, training, firing, and awards. Organizations need to assess management practices in all of these areas in order to remove discriminatory practices. As Diane Herrmann Clark, the Director of Office of Equal Opportunity Programs at the Department of the Treasury, says:

> It is critical each year to analyze and target priorities and to focus resources. We are talking about changes in management practices which will take years. Each year we work at moving toward parity. One year the priority may be shortening the time frame from the current two to three years it may take to process discrimination complaints in the federal government. The next year, it may be emphasizing awareness training for managers and information on sexual harassment.

The following issues are central to developing a total system affirmative action program:

- To what extent does the organization now value managing human resources?
- What is the present organizational culture for women, minorities, and white males? What would improve the climate for the employees and the organization?
- What sort of management resources does the organization need to make affirmative action work in the areas of recruiting, hiring, training, mentoring, monitoring the progress of women and minorities, and increasing the effectiveness of supervisors?

To deal with these questions, organizations need a total systems change model for affirmative action. The following approach was developed by me over a four-year period at a large manufacturing company, and segments of it have been used in government agencies and several other corporations (see Figure 29.1).

THE MODEL FOR TOTAL SYSTEMS CHANGE

Appoint top management task force.   The optimum situation occurs when the organization appoints a top management task force to set goals and objectives for affirmative action, to develop a plan, and to ensure enforcement. This team needs data on employee utilization; a work force analysis by gender, race, and job classification to determine status of women and minorities; an availability study for each job group; statistical information on selection, training programs attended, and promotion.

Conduct climate survey.   Conduct a climate survey to collect data on the quality of work life for women and minorities. Use group sensing sessions to collect data so that group discussions occur in both homogeneous and heterogeneous groups.

Design effective recruiting and hiring.   Design an effective recruiting and hiring program that uses women and minority recruiters. Identify areas of underutilization and analyze barriers.

Assess management systems.   Assess management systems for their effectiveness in the affirmative action effort, particularly the performance appraisal process that should monitor Equal Employment Opportunity and the career development system.

Provide training.   Provide training programs to include women and minority managers. Offer supervisor/women managers pairs training, supervisor/minority manager pairs training, and supervisor/secretary workshops. Mandate

FIGURE 29.1   Steps in a Total Systems Affirmative Action Program

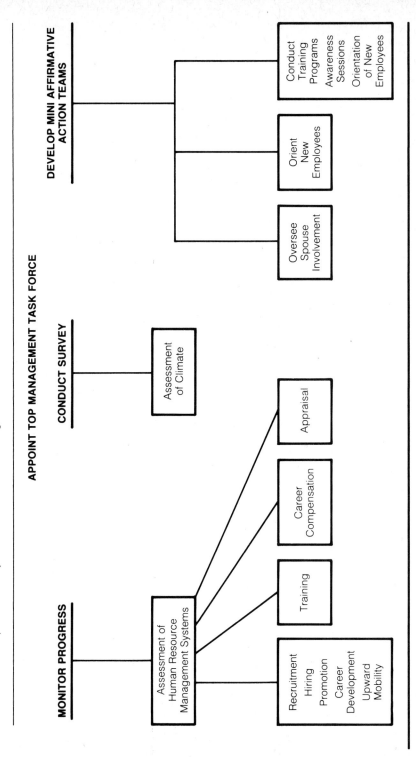

team building for teams that include women and minorities. Conduct awareness sessions on racism, sexism, and antidiscrimination. Include training modules in ongoing management education programs.

Promote supervisory relationships.   Promote supervisory relationships that carry out such human resource management functions as managerial coaching, career development, performance management and development of high-potential, but poor-performing, employees.

Assess upward mobility programs.   Assess upward-mobility programs to evaluate the effectiveness of placement and targeting for jobs.

Provide alternative schedules.   Provide alternative work schedules, for example, flex-time, job sharing, part-time work, and child care.

Encourage networks.   Encourage network building among women and minorities, such as minority managers' work groups.

Involve spouses.   Establish a spouse involvement program to explain affirmative action and deal with such issues as health benefits, financial planning, and men and women working and traveling together.

Create affirmative action teams.   Create affirmative action teams to identify problems and carry out programs.

Top Management Task Force

The task force needs a key decision maker to assure organizational commitment to affirmative action efforts. Neither personnel nor the Equal Employment Opportunity Office should direct the task force, but should serve as staff to it. The task force's goals are basically to change the climate, structures, policies, practices, and interpersonal relationships within the organization to eliminate discrimination and to build a multicultural work environment.

Affirmative action task forces commonly begin by team building off-site. For several days team members work with external resources to increase awareness of the issues and to build a better understanding among themselves. In one instance, an all-male task force recognized that they could not commit themselves to the effort until they discovered their own reasons for joining the affirmative action group. These men were asked to list ten ways affirmative action would benefit them. For several, the only obvious answer was that helping promote women and minorities was one measure of managerial effectiveness on their performance appraisal. Several managers wanted to understand the issues because women in their families were deeply involved in consciousness-raising groups or were returning to work or to school. No one could suggest more than two reasons.

A reading list helped task force members learn about issues and particularly to identify male sex-role expectations. Some men in manufacturing doubted that women could perform the required physical work. There was a lingering concern that women had less strength and energy. Therefore, task force members talked about the implications of sex-linked characteristics such as the physiological effects of testosterone and estrogen. The men felt that physical education programs and sex-role stereotypes in the educational system helped perpetuate the physical differences between the sexes. The most compelling logic was that the bona fide occupational requirement for lifting in most states ranges from 35 to 50 pounds; women routinely lift children or grocery bags that exceed 35 pounds.

The task force developed an action plan that established affirmative action goals for the next several years. The goals included data collection on the climate for women and minorities; recruitment, with women helping recruit for the first time; hiring objectives, and an upward-mobility program that considered educational backgrounds other than engineering. The task force also planned training, supervisor-secretary workshops, family awareness groups in the plant, work groups for women managers and mini-affirmative action teams composed of male-female pairs and minority-white pairs for each manufacturing module that comprised approximately seventy-five employees.

Climate Survey

A team of women and men should interview white male and female managers and minority women and men individually and in groups to identify the factors that contribute to an effective or ineffective work climate for women and minorities. A paper and pencil questionnaire is not nearly as helpful; it may only measure the level of awareness rather than the nature of the climate.

Recruitment Programs

The central need in the recruitment of women and minorities is the identification of new networks and new contact persons. Networks exist in all areas that can lead organizations to minority persons and to women. Institutional mechanisms are lacking, however, to draw on these resources and to radically shift old hiring patterns. In addition, organizations must build credible relationships with women and minority faculty in universities so that they will refer their students. These approaches suggest the depth and significance of the concept of affirmative action. It frequently requires a sizeable change in organizational attitudes and practices. If business continues to be done the way it has been, it will not yield new patterns. Taking affirmative action means a major restructuring.

Assess Management Systems: Performance Appraisal

Performance appraisal is the critical management system for effecting the changes sought in an affirmative action effort. If organizations do not evaluate and reward or punish managers for their behavior in implementing affirmative action, the system will lack accountability. Therefore, each manager must have a management by objectives plan that emphasizes clear performance criteria for hiring, developing, promoting, and supervising women and minorities. As Craig Schneier, Ph.D., professor of personnel and organizational behavior at the University of Maryland, has said, "In order to implement an effective affirmative action program a manager's effort must be anchored to the reward system. The evaluation tool for this performance appraisal system makes explicit the degree to which the manager's behavior is responsive to the affirmative action plan."

Training Programs

Many white managers have had a great deal of contact with women or minority professionals. Awareness workshops that address such issues as dealing with differences, issues of style versus competence, dependency, control, and sexuality can be quite useful. Furthermore, coalitions or support systems between women and minorities can increase their awareness, skill, and effectiveness in communicating their feelings.

People in organizations are only beginning to learn to *work* with a heterogeneous population; there has been very little integration at all in social life. The first step towards collaborative behavior across racial and sex differences is awareness. Differences in style, dress, language patterns, topics of conversation, and laughter are not understood. Just this lack of familiarity simply has served to keep people apart.

ISSUES TO BE COVERED IN AWARENESS WORKSHOPS

Competence

Since competent men and women may not have the same styles, it is important to be able to differentiate between style and competence. Significant gender differences occur in verbal and nonverbal behavior, namely in the areas of touch, interpersonal space, gaze, and body movement (Mayo & Henley 1981). All of these elements have power and warmth dimensions to them, but are interpreted differently when displayed by women and men. It is well documented that women are more skillful than men at decoding nonverbal cues. Therefore, since women are more partner-oriented, their responses are more likely to be affected by nonverbal behavior than those of men. Eileen Morley (1975) at the Harvard Business School has pointed out that women tend to feel/think and men to think/feel. In other words, a woman who is asked what she is thinking may report her feelings; a man asked what he is feeling may report his thoughts.

In a world dominated by male values, managers need to be able to recognize competent behavior in different styles.

Dependency

Under present practices of socialization, dependency typically is encouraged in girls and discouraged with boys. This has led to what has been labelled the "Cinderella Complex" in women and "learned helplessness" with respect to certain tasks for both sexes. Examples of learned helplessness in the workplace might include getting coffee for men and dealing with tears for men whereas for women it may be dealing with numbers and statistics. In terms used in transactional analysis this leads to parent-child interactions rather than adult-adult behavior. Some examples of the types of communication follow.

- *Father-son:* Male managers adopt a can-do approach until they make themselves physically sick rather than acknowledge vulnerability.
- *Mother-boy:* Men use female managers as mothers by telling them personal information, but not treating them as real colleagues with whom they also solve problems and perform tasks.
- *Father-girl:* Male managers become angry at female employees but protect them.
- *Mother-boy:* Male managers defer to the female managers in emotional situations in which pain is being expressed, for example, secretaries who cry, while the male managers steps aside.
- *Father-girl:* Female managers defer to male managers on policy making or budget appropriations.

Control

Men are used to being in control in mixed groups, and women are not. Habitual patterns of responding to control become critical when men and women managers work together—and when women manage men.

In order for communication to be among equals in work interactions, the following behaviors need to eliminated:

- *Girl-girl or mother-girl.* Women managers fail to share their competence with one another.
- *Father-girl and mother-boy.* Men and women managers use sex for power and control.

A parent-child interaction may feel more comfortable because it is familiar and denies the issue of sexual attraction for both the male and the female manager. These dimensions need to be explored in awareness programs for managers and skill building can be used to reeducate men and women so they can interact as adults.

Sexuality

Both actual incidents of sexual relationships that develop through work and fantasies and anxieties about them make sexuality a more pervasive issue in the workplace than many anticipated. Sexuality is always present in male-female interactions whether it takes the form of attraction or discounting. Rarely, indeed, do men and women not appraise one another sexually.

Without discussion, men and women may not understand why they are attracted to one another. Their fantasies may escalate, and they may not have a sense of choice because of the pressure of feelings. Yet we know that the reasons may include curiosity, the desire for power or control, boredom, joy and love. Talking about their motivation may defuse fantasies or at least clarify the terms of the relationship. When people are attracted to one another sexually in a way that interferes with work, the situation must be discussed for the sake of the people involved and of the organization.

Differentiated Competency Based Training Modules

Because of sex-role stereotyping and differential socialization, some men and women have acquired different abilities. Masculine competence has been valued more highly in business, government, and academe. Men and women therefore need training to recognize each other's skills, and organizations need to learn to value the skills women have that men can benefit from learning. Men and women who display skills associated with both masculine and feminine styles are described as androgynous.

To be androgynous, some women may need to learn to:

- be powerful and forthright and have a direct, visible impact on others rather than functioning behind the scenes*
- initiate and take risks, despite being so visible and vulnerable
- state their own needs and not back down even if these are not accepted immediately
- focus on a task and regard it as at least as important as the relationships of the people performing it
- build support systems with other women and share knowledge with women rather than compete with them
- analyze and generalize from experience
- behave "impersonally" more often rather than personalizing experiences
- stop turning anger, blame, and pain inward, thereby rejecting feelings of suffering and victimization
- reject feedback when it is inappropriate
- respond directly with "I" statements rather than with blaming "you" statements

*Adapted from Alice G. Sargent, *Beyond Sex Roles,* West Publishing Co., 1977

- become effective problem solvers who are analytical, systematic, and directive rather than fearful or dependent
- stop self-limiting behaviors such as allowing oneself to be interrupted or laughing after making a serious statement.

To be androgynous some men may need to learn to:

- become aware of feelings rather than avoiding or suppressing them
- regard feelings as a basic and essential part of life, rather than as impediments to achievement
- accept a share of responsiblity for "providing," but refuse total responsibility
- assert the right to work for self-fulfillment rather than only to be a "provider"
- value an identity that is not defined totally by work
- learn to accept failure at a task without feeling one has failed as a man
- accept and express the need to be nurtured when feeling hurt, afraid, vulnerable, or helpless, rather than hiding those feelings behind a mask of strength and rationality
- touch and be close to both men and women
- listen actively and be empathic without feeling responsible for problem solving
- build support systems with other men, sharing competence without competition
- personalize experience, rather than assuming that the only valid approach to life and interpersonal contact is "objective"
- accept the emotional, spontaneous, and irrational as valid parts of oneself to be explored and expressed as needed and openly express feelings of love, anger, pain, joy, loneliness, and dependency
- understand how men value women as "validators of masculinity," havens from the competitive male world, the expressive partners
- understand the impact that being male has on shaping their lives and their responses
- nurture and actively support men and women in their efforts to change

Supervisory Relationships

The most critical component for women and minorities' success is their relationship with the supervisor. This comes as no surprise given what we know about the importance of "expectation effects" in teacher-pupil relationships and intimate relationships. Expectation effects are critical to success or failure on the job, in school, and in marriage. As Robert Rosenthal (1969) reported on IQ scores, the children with higher numbers (although they were fake scores) improved more quickly because of teacher expectations. The so-called "bright" rats learned the mazes more quickly because of researcher expectations. The supervisory relationship is regarded as one of the most critical factors to women's or minorities' success.

Research on personnel interviewers by Rosen and Jerdee (1974) underscores how interview bias can determine whether women or men enter a system. Furthermore, supervisors may hold the same stereotypes as the interviewers. For example, interviewers in industry expect men to be effective because men are believed to understand financial matters, analyze situations, like science and math, accurately know how to set long-range goals, and want to get ahead. Characteristics attributed to women include enjoyment of routine, sensitivity to criticism, timidity, jealousy, too much emotionalism, sensitivity to the feelings of others, a tendency to quit more frequently than men, and a propensity to put family matters ahead of the job. In fact, women do not have more job instability than men, and they do not necessarily enjoy routine more than men. Managers who hold such stereotypes are likely to act upon them. Male supervisors report that they are more sympathetic when home life interferes with a man's work. The manager helps male employees by suggesting solutions to the problem such as different kinds of services or counseling. The supervisor probably thinks, "After all, he's the primary breadwinner." But, "I knew it was going to happen," is the common attitude among supervisors when a woman's home life interferes with her work.

To illustrate sex-linked differences in expectations of supervisors, Kay Bartol and Anthony Butterfield (1976) reversed the names of men and women in a number of case studies. They found sex-linked differences on effectiveness on two components of managerial behavior: initiating structure, considered masculine, and showing concern for others, considered feminine. Participants were asked to rate managers for effectiveness based on the three weeks they spent in a new office finding out what was happening and then developing a reorganization plan. Only the names of the managers were changed; but the behaviors remained the same. The men were rated more effective than the women who were described as autocratic, taking too much initiative, and undemocratic. Sexual prejudice cuts both ways. In contrast, the women managers were rated effective when they sought the opinions and feelings of others and got involved with employees who had problems. But a male manager who used the same approach was rated as wishy-washy and becoming overly involved.

The solution is not for men to give up their proactive organizing style or for women to become directive at the expense of feelings and concern for others. Both sexes would enhance their effectiveness by learning the attitudes and behaviors generally attributed to the other sex and developing a blend. Compensatory training can help both men and women develop qualities of so-called masculine independence and feminine nurturance.

There are similar issues in building a multicultural environment across races. The values learned from the experience could also change the nature of organizational life. The majority group subconsciously develops an arrogance that could be tempered by humility. The majority group (white people) also tends to rely too much on rationality that could be mediated by a commonsense, more natural approach of many minorities.

Upward Mobility Programs: Career Development

As management seeks effective promotion of women and minorities, it will find unclear career paths and lack of long-range human resource planning. It is essential for effectiveness and for morale that all employees have a sense of where they are going in the organization and what it takes to get there. This comes from specific information about career paths, targeted jobs, and developmental assignments that lead to specific positions.

Alternative Work Schedules

While women have widely supported alternative work opportunities, men now find them valuable too. The specific alternative work schedules that organizations have tried and found successful include flexible working hours, the compressed work week, permanent part-time work, and job sharing. The advantages to the organization of these options include increased productivity, higher morale, retaining highly competent employees who only want part-time work because of other demands in their life, reduced absenteeism, tardiness, and turnover, and a progressive image which may attract other employees. The advantages to the individual include the opportunity to be at home when children arrive home from school; two-career couples can share child care; more leisure time for education, home life and developing other sides of one's identity; commuting at different hours; opportunity to work the hours of the day one feels most effective; and opportunities for additional work.

Coalition Building Among Women and Minorities

Networks for women and minority managers help both new and old employees. Such groups also aid the organization in the recruitment, orientation, and retention of employees. Groups of minority or women managers can identify key issues of concern, ranging from promotion issues to maternity leave to part-time work.

Over a period of time, coalitions can alter the typical pattern of entry into the system for minorities and women. New female employees often try to succeed first in the white male-dominated workplace without turning to other women or minorities for friendship and support. In the process of proving themselves, many women take on necessary so-called masculine characteristics for dealing with power and conflict while shedding some of their valuable feminine behaviors of nurturance and spontaneity. As a consequence they suffer a great deal from a sense of frustration and failure.

Many women report that they avoid being branded as too seductive or nurturing by cutting down their emotional responses if they are the only women in a group. One corporate affirmative action program dealt with the problem of the lone woman by focusing on a natural work group, such as a mechanical engineering department. When a woman was about to join the group, members talked about the issues involved both before and after she joined. The group held follow-up sessions because instances of isolation developed quite quickly as they were temporarily solved. She just wasn't "one of the boys" and thus part of the informal communication network.

Women's networks offer an important way to deal with the problems of isolation, loneliness, and pressure to conform to male norms. They provide a sanctuary where feelings of frustration, anger, or loneliness can be expressed in a concerned environment. As a result of these coalitions, a number of women indicated that they felt better able to hold on to their own style and sense of self-worth rather than merely adopting the dominant male patterns.

Affirmative action efforts highlight tension and the lack of communication between women and minorities. Often, style differences create barriers. Sometimes black men and white women fear that they will be used by each other. The relationship is complicated by fantasies about power and sexual attraction. Women think black men can have power because they are men; black men think white women have access to power by asking their men for it. Both would be better off if they joined forces and acknowledged that neither of them has had much access to information or power.

Spouse Involvement

Organizations often like to keep the personal lives of their employees quite separate from their work lives, but women's entrance into the workforce joins the issue. The area of greatest concern is men and women traveling together on business trips when the norms are more relaxed and opportunities for closer contact are greater. Rather than pretending that sexual attraction and sexual harassment could never arise, organizations that have dealt directly with such issues have been able to defuse some of the fantasies and problems. Spouse involvement in affirmative action programs has altered the traditional split between work and home life and has improved morale and cooperation. In affirmative action programs spouses have also discussed mobility policy, which can help them prepare for a move. Other topics of significance are child care policies, cafeteria benefits, flex-time issues of two-career couples, and health benefits.

Affirmative Action Teams

One organization established male-female and black-white pairs for each department. The teams informed new employees about affirmative action activities. The teams also identified the development of occupational stereotyping— what became women's work in the plant. For example, quality control jobs quickly became women's work. The teams also monitored the progress of women and minorities and served as troubleshooters.

When possible, each team included the technical training director. In a manufacturing environment, one training director obtained additional technical training for women. The program was so successful that men also sought the training. Affirmative action provided everyone an opportunity and altered ineffective management training practices.

SUMMARY

In the total systems approach, affirmative action becomes a management problem. The organization views women and minorities as the experts who can solve the problem with important assistance from the Human Resources Department. The goal is for key decision makers to take on the problem and to bring their analytical and interpersonal competence to bear on its solution. All decision makers are involved so that no one feels her or his territory has been invaded.

Social and psychological research indicates that behavior changes precede attitude changes. Action may elicit a different kind of response from the habitual one. Changing the reward system can bring about further changes in both behavior and attitudes. The first phase of change is to increase awareness of and responsibility for problems. Organizations maintain momentum through incentives such as performance appraisal through developing coalitions among women and minorities and through a temporary structure within the system—a mini-affirmative action team. Organizations need at least three or five years for initial changes to occur.

This approach benefits both the white male who now holds power in the organization by increasing his life options and his work options and the women and minority persons who seek equal power and influence in the workplace. The total systems approach offers the chance to change organizational patterns of majority dominance and minority dependence and frustration.

A reallocation of power and influence occurs plus the development of new networks across more heterogeneous segments of the American population. What also occurs is a shifting of the organizational norms to encompass members of the new workforce. There seems to be a value shift slowly in America towards no longer being a melting pot but actually developing a multi-cultural environment in some parts of the United States.

References

Aries, Elizabeth, "Male-Female Interpersonal Styles in All Male, All Female and Mixed Groups" in Alice G. Sargent, *Beyond Sex Roles,* St. Paul: West Publishing, 1977.

Bartol, Kathryn M., & Butterfield, D. Anthony, "Sex Effects in Evaluating Leaders," *Journal of Applied Psychology,* vol. 61, no. 4 (1976).

Bartolome, Fernado, & Evans, Paul A. Lee, "Must Success Cost So Much?" *Harvard Business Review,* March-April 1980.

Dickens, Floyd, & Jacqueline B. Dickens. *The Black Manager Working in the Corporate World.* New York: AMACOM, 1982.

Herrmann Clark, Diane. An interview with the author, 1983.

Jackson, Bailey, "Race Identity Development Theory," *The NTL Manager's Book,* NTL Institute, Arlington, Va., 1983.

Kreps, Juanita. Speech delivered at the Department of Commerce, 1977.

Leavitt, Harold J., & Lipman-Blumen, Jean, "A Case for the Relational Manager," in *Organizational Dynamics,* pp. 27–41, 1980.

Mayo, Clara, & Henley, Nancy M., *Gender and Nonverbal Behavior* New York: Springer-Verlag, 1981.

Morley, Eileen, "Women's Thinking and Talking," Harvard Business School, Case No. 9–477–055, Harvard Case Clearing House, Boston, Mass. 02163

Rosen, Benson, & Jerdee, Thomas H., "Effects of Applicant's Sex and Difficulty of Job on Evaluations of Candidates for Managerial Positions," *Journal of Applied Psychology* August 1974, vol. 59, p. 511.

Rosenthal, Robert, & Jacobson, L., *Pygmalion in the Classroom* New York: Holt, Rinehart and Winston, 1969.

Sargent, Alice G., *Beyond Sex Roles,* St. Paul: West Publishing Co., 1977.

Sargent, Alice G., *The Androgynous Manager,* New York: AMACOM, 1981.

Wilkins, Roger, *A Man's Life: An Autobiography,* New York: Simon and Schuster, 1982.

30 Profitable Decision Making

Joseph S. Murphy

ABSTRACT

Decisions make or break us. In this article, the four components of a good decision are defined. Styles of decision making are also defined and analyzed for their strengths and weaknesses. Finally, a new style of decision making which can increase any company's profitability is presented.

AUTHOR BACKGROUND

Joseph S. Murphy, M.B.A., University of Colorado, is the president of CAM Management Consultants in Denver. His expertise lies in helping top service managers design and implement programs that maximize the talents of all employees within their organizations. He is also the co-author of *Installing Quality Circles: A Strategic Approach.*

The decision-making process is the most important activity in any business. Nothing happens until a decision is made. Surprisingly, very little has been written about this process. What constitutes a good decision? What constitutes a bad decision? How are decisions normally made? How can we improve them? These are some of the questions we will answer in this chapter.

A good decision has four components:

- Timeliness
- Correctness
- Acceptability
- Results

Each of these components must be present if a decision is to be effective. Good decisions add to the health and vitality of an organization. Bad decisions sap a business of its strength and consequently shorten its life span. The words *good* and *bad* do not necessarily connote the moral sense of *good* and *bad,* though in some cases they might. For our purpose, let us assume that a good decision maximizes all four components listed above; a bad decision does not.

EFFECT ON PROFITS

Every decision made in every organization affects profits either directly or indirectly. This is because each one has some cost associated with it. A decision by an employee to do nothing reduces productivity and profits. Conversely, a decision by an employee to spend a few minutes at the end of the day organizing a desk adds to productivity. In even a medium-sized firm there are literally millions of decisions made each day. The fact that we normally do not train employees in the decision-making process is perplexing. In the broadest sense, the profitability of any company can be determined by subtracting the cost of bad decisions from the return of good decisions.

COMPONENT DEFINITIONS

We stated above that a good decision has four components. A definition of each will be helpful to us as we try to judge the effectiveness of individual decisions and styles later in the chapter.

Timeliness

Decisions are made to affect situations encountered. We decide to eat because we are hungry. We decide to reorder supplies because we are running short. We decide to invest to maximize our return. The timeliness component refers to judging when or when not to act to maximize the outcome of the situation in the above three examples. If we decide too early we may gain weight, have excessive storage and material costs, or miss a better investment opportunity. If we decide too late, we may starve, run out of supplies, or have to settle for a lower rate of return than we could have received if we had acted in a more timely manner. So timeliness refers to making a decision at the point which maximizes our return.

Correctness

The accuracy of our decisions depends on the amount of valid information available to us and upon how we interpret this data. The more pertinent the facts at hand, the greater the chance of a correct diagnosis.

There is a direct tradeoff between timeliness and accuracy. The longer we wait, the more information we can gather. Theoretically, we could spend enough time to gather all the meaningful data available. But usually this would take so long that it would render our decision meaningless.

In our less than perfect world, we are forced to make decisions with less than perfect information. Correctness refers to how closely our final decision conforms to all of the known and unknown realities of a situation.

Acceptability

Decisions that are never implemented or that cause a large amount of expensive conflict and backlash are bad decisions. Acceptability encompasses the level of agreement that a decision has with those affected by it and those in charge of implementation. Authoritarian managers miss this component entirely and pay the price in the form of turnover, absenteeism, work slow downs, brooding employees, sabotage, conflict, defensive activities, and so on that sap a company of its resources. They also discourage the natural creativity, inventiveness, and cooperation of their employees which stymies potential growth and productivity.

Results

We stated earlier that all decisions affect profitability. This component depends on the combined results of the other three. If the decision was made in a timely manner, with all of the pertinent information available, and was accepted and implemented with the minimum amount of conflict possible, then we have maximized the results of the decision. This doesn't necessarily mean that the decision added to our profitability. It might mean that, given the situation, we lost the least amount of money possible. If this is the case, we still made a good decision.

Decision-Making Methods

Now that we have defined what constitutes a good decision, we can look at some of the more popular methods of decision making and compare them to our model. We should be able to note the strengths and weaknesses of each and then decide which one is the most profitable.

Golden rule. Some managers talk about the "golden rule" style of decision making: "Whoever has the gold sets the rules." A far cry from the biblical meaning! As long as there is only one person in the firm, this style works well. Any more than that and it becomes expensive. The timeliness portion of our model gets a plus; all the others receive negatives.

Autocratic. The autocrat uses the golden rule style with a slight substitution. Power. "Whoever has the power, sets the rules." The analysis, however, is the same. Timeliness is a plus; all of the rest are negative.

Autocratic-consultative. Managers in this category rule through power, but have learned that the input of others can increase the accuracy of their decisions. They made no bones about who has the final say. Tipoffs to this style of decision-making include a comment like "I'm paid to make decisions" or the sign "The Buck Stops Here."

Timeliness and correctness are in the plus column if the manager receives valid input. Some employees simply tell them what they want to hear out of fear. If that is the case, accuracy does not improve. Acceptability and results remain in the negative column.

The first three styles are relatively simple to judge. They are very expensive styles in any business. Not necessarily because of the cost of specific decisions, but because of the negative backlash these styles encourage. If we look simply at the direct results of a specific decision and fail to note the hard feelings and bruised egos that promote less conspicuous, but destructive, behavior we are operating in a one-dimensional managerial world.

For instance, one company has counted twenty-three identifiable costs for every turnover they experience. These costs include the decreased efficiency of a soon-to-be-leaving employee, the time this employee costs the company by talking to other employees about why they are leaving, up to and including the obvious costs for bringing a new employee up to the production level of the departed employee. These twenty-three costs consider just one turnover. When we include other profit-reducing behaviors that these three decision-making styles foster—such as theft, sabotage, work slowdowns, and so forth—it becomes apparent just how expensive they are in the day-to-day operations of any business. When we add in the lost opportunity costs that these styles bleed from a business in the form of unheard suggestions, innovations, and profitable changes, the cost of having even one manager who fits the above three categories is staggering.

Committee. Although committees are a popular form of decision making, they often make bad decisions. Voting, politics, and lack of teamwork affect the quality of their decisions. Committees are often formed by an executive who wants to avoid a potentially dangerous decision. Because committees vote, there are usually winners and losers. In fact, committees are normally composed of an odd number of members—to break ties. Often pertinent information, known to one member of the group, is withheld because that member knows that he or she will be out-voted anyway.

Let's give committees the benefit of the doubt and say they make timely decisions. That's one in the plus column. For the reasons listed above, however, committees get a negative score in each of the remaining three components—correctness, acceptability (a 5-to-4 vote does not portend strong support), and results. The only circumstance that would change our judgment is if there was a high level of teamwork on the committee. Usually the finite nature of committees and the time constraints associated with them preclude this development.

Firefighting.   Every experienced manager knows what it means to fight fires in the business sense. Emergencies crop up that need a decision *now*. Some "fires" are unavoidable—we can't predict the future with 100% accuracy. Most, however, are the result of poor planning. Many are caused by the sparks created by fighting previous fires. It can become a vicious circle that ends up "burning" the career of the firefighter. This style, except in the unavoidable situations, gets a negative score in all four columns.

Expertise.   This is a style that many companies encourage because it seems to make so much sense. Simply put, the person who is the most qualified makes the decision. Accountants make accounting decisions, salespeople make sales decisions, personnel people make personnel decisions and so on.

Specialization is the key. No one knows everything about everything. The problems associated with this style become evident when we use our model for good decisions. Timeliness and correctness are maximized, unfortunately often at the expense of acceptability and results. Problems begin when the most qualified person makes a decision that affects other people. The more complex the decision, the greater the chance of conflict. We seldom support what we don't understand. Often we fear what we don't understand. Therein lies the inherent weakness in this style of decision making. Usually the person or department that makes "expert" decisions notifies those affected by memo. They in turn, through lack of understanding or fear, begin to develop ways to "get around" the decision. Two plusses and two minuses for the expertise style.

Procrastination.   Deciding not to make a decision is a decision. Safety-oriented managers often use this style to avoid troubling situations. This method is usually accompanied by a statement like "Let's wait until more facts are in." Correctness gets a big plus, so does acceptability. Unfortunately in most cases the "chicken flies the coop before we discover we own one," so timeliness and results end up in the minus column.

Consultative.   Usually the managers who have developed this style have strong interpersonal skills. Before making an important decision, they check with as many people as possible who have pertinent information. They usually test the waters with those who will be affected by the decision to determine the acceptability of their proposed action. And, because of their knowledge of the situation, they make timely decisions. Have we hit the jackpot? Are there plusses in all four columns? Consider the following example:

> The top administrator for a medium-sized company had the responsibility for the company's fleet. A department under him was accountable for buying, selling and maintaining the cars used by hundreds of personnel—mostly field sales representatives. The company was also experiencing heavy losses. Cost had to be reduced.
> Recognizing this need, the fleet department developed a plan to moderately downgrade the types of cars used by its salesforce, while at the same time offering to split the savings, through cash bonuses, to those affected. Many field sales

representatives were consulted to determine the acceptability of the plan. All responses were positive. It seemed like a good decision in difficult times. Only people with expertise in car depreciation, insurance, maintenance, etc. could have developed the plan. The decision was approved by the president of the company, and a memo was sent to all employees involved. Annual savings were projected to be over 1.2 million dollars.

The fleet department had spent almost three months researching its recommendation. The memo sent to the sales representatives was a well-written concise explanation of the new policy. It even detailed the reasoning behind the decision. Fleet personnel had expected some negative reaction to the plan. After all "you can't please everybody." They were astounded at what did develop. It began with a trickle and ended with a tidal wave.

"What's this new fleet policy all about anyway?"
"What are the other divisions doing to cut costs?"
"Whose ideas was this?"
"Why do you always pick on the field personnel?"
"I didn't even know the company was in financial trouble."
"I've always felt like a second-class citizen out here, now I feel worse!"
"Do you know what my customers are going to say?"
"Do you know what my spouse has already said?"
"Is the president in?"
"Let me talk to him."
"I'm resigning!"
"Mr. President, can't we make one exception? Here are the reasons ——"

The plan was swept away within two weeks. It had taken thousands of dollars in time and materials to develop. It was a good plan. Many of those affected had been consulted. What went wrong?

The shell-shocked fleet department was literally incapacitated for two weeks. Gradually they began coming out of their "bombshelters" to begin to piece together what had caused the unexpectedly heavy negative response.

The bottom line came down to this: the sales department had been experiencing a serious drop in morale over the previous two years. Amazingly enough, this drop coincided with the time the sales manager had taken over his new responsibilities. He had arbitrarily raised the sales quotas, reduced allowable field expenses, and increased the reporting requirements. He had also fired several of the best-liked, most respected field managers in an effort "to get rid of the dead-wood." His managerial style and decision-making style were autocratic. The field sales force was exhibiting all of the classical symptoms, that is, low morale and high rates of turnover.

Because of a justifiable fear of reprisal, no one confronted the new sales manager. However, when the fleet department's memo was received it presented the sales representatives a safe, effective way to vent their anger, which had been building up for two years. And they took advantage of it.

The sales people that had been consulted prior to the decision had kept quiet about the situation because of their fear of reprisal. The sales manager had also been consulted. But, as is the case with most autocratic managers, he had grieviously underestimated the dissatisfaction in the field. No one had dared tell him about it. Additionally, he didn't share responsibility for the decision. It was the fleet department's. So he didn't care if it succeeded or failed.

Unfortunately for him, and fortunately for the company, once the dam sprang a leak it began seriously eroding his power base. He was replaced within six months. But the damage had already been done. The company had lost a multi-million dollar opportunity to improve its financial position.

This example vividly illustrates the potential weakness of the consultative style of decision making. Unknown forces can affect the accuracy, acceptance and hence the results of even the most carefully thought out decision. We used an actual example in this case because the consultative style is considered by many to be "the state of the art" in decision-making. If this is the case, we have to settle for a style that encompasses many potential dangers. But this isn't the case. Before we look at one more style of decision making—one that holds the most promise for the future—let us fecap the styles we have discussed so far. This is done in Figure 30.1.

None of the styles have an unqualified plus in each category. Consultative decision making comes the closest although usually a manager must possess strong interpersonal skills to even attempt this technique.

All of the methods discussed have at best a potential for minuses in the results column. But let us keep this in perspective. All we have said so far is that none of the methods described maximizes the results of a decision. An example might be helpful. Assume one of our managers makes a production decision that, when every cost is considered, saves our company five hundred thousand dollars. Good decision, right? Not necessarily. Because the manager used an autocratic style, the acceptability of the decision was poor. By using a different style, he could have saved us one million dollars. In fact, one manager was so upset with the new production rules she resigned. She went to another company

FIGURE 30.1 Style/Component Decision Matrix

Style	Component			
	Timeliness	Correctness	Acceptability	Results
Golden rule	+	−	−	−
Autocratic	+	−	−	−
Autocratic/ consultative	+	+	−	−
Committee	+	−	−	−
Firefighting	−	−	−	−
Expertise	+	+	−	−
Procrastination	−	+	+	−
Consultative	+	±	±	±

and developed an idea, which increased their profits by two million dollars. It was an idea we could have used. Our manager's style cost us two and a half million dollars. Because top management was so impressed with his five hundred thousand dollar savings, he was promoted. Now his decision making style will cost us even more money!

Contrived? Yes. Possible? Yes. Probable? More so than we think.

A Better Mousetrap

Consider this example:

Ten top managers are meeting in the boardroom of a large western company. The discussion is sometimes heated. They are trying to reach one marketing decision that will have a major impact on the company's future competitive position. They are trying to decide when and where to locate eight new distribution facilities that will place a new product closer to the perceived markets. They have been meeting for three days. Experts in various areas have been summoned to help explain difficult issues. Complex statistical reports were well read before the meeting began. However, more questions and concerns have been raised each day forcing the group to consider more and more information. Used flipchart sheets are attached to all four walls in the boardroom as a reminder of previous subjects covered. Nine of the ten (including the president who used to have sole responsibility for this type of decision) are in basic agreement as to the where and when of all the new locations. One manager is not. She is the company's top financial officer and "just can't live with the decision." She doesn't have to.

More discussion ensues. The meeting is now in its fourth day. Although the financial officer has no experience in marketing, something about one of the suggested locations has been bothering her. But she hasn't been able to put her finger on it. Not until the morning of the fourth day. Then she remembers reading about tax changes that had just been instituted in the county where this distribution center was to be placed. These changes would make that location very unprofitable. She expresses her concern. Nine sets of frustrated eyes open a little wider. They agree. The group modifies its proposal and selects another site. One by one each member states "I can live with the decision." The meeting ends after the initial assignments are made. It was a long, grueling, and ultimately very profitable meeting.

Consensus Decision Making

The meeting described was run by consensus. Simply put this means that, before a decision is reached, each person present must be in basic agreement with it. They don't have to agree 100% with the decision, but they "must be able to live with it." Any person present can stop any proposed decision.

Before we evaluate the consensus style of decision making, let us list the rules that govern its use.

Rules for Consensus

Use applicable subject matter. To use this style, the scope of the decision must be of sufficient magnitude to warrant the time and effort that will be expended. Company impact, number of people and departments affected, the long-term nature of the decision, potential negative reaction, and the number of people required for implementation should all be examined before a decision is reached to decide an issue by consensus. When in doubt, use consensus.

Absolutely no voting allowed.   We have mentioned before that voting normally produces winners and losers. Typically during implementation, winners support a decision and losers are neutral—at best. We also mentioned before that voting stifles the freeflow of information. If we know we are going to be outvoted, why even raise our concerns? Voting also impedes team development. If we know we have enough votes to carry the issue, we might decide not to explain our reasoning or listen thoroughly to "the other side."

Voting can come in many forms. Averaging, weighing, polling, a show of hands and secret ballot are all different forms of voting.

No status allowed.   Right at the heart of consensus decision making is the concept that all who have been asked to participate have equal status. If everyone is equal, there is no status. This requires the person with the highest official rank in the meeting to be willing to set aside that official power. This is easier said than done. Often underling managers will support the "power person" out of habit and/or nervousness. By speaking last, the manager can often avoid this situation and get a feel for what the others are thinking. An outside facilitator is useful when a group is first learning this process. The facilitator can spot this type of behavior and draw the group's attention to it. If the top manager is serious about the consensus style, this tendency will gradually take care of itself as the other managers realize that disagreement is not only acceptable but encouraged.

What is said in the group stays there.   This rule allows the group members to express their opinions freely and openly. Final decisions are made common knowledge, usually, as are the salient reasons behind them. However, initial differences of opinion, conflict, and the group process should remain the purview of the members.

The team wins and loses together.   Once a consensus decision is reached, everyone shares in the responsibility for its success or failure. Because everyone has said "I can live with the decision," no one person can be singled out for credit or blame. Some people say that the real test of a team is how it handles adversity. But the same is true for success. Consensus minimizes the dangers of each.

Equal time.   Everybody must be allowed to have their say without interruption. Some groups assure this process by speaking in turn and continue going around the group in this manner until a consensus is reached. Once the style is learned, this formality can be dispensed with—through a consensus decision. A third-party facilitator can also be useful in assuring equal time.

Piggybacking is O.K.   If someone in the group states an idea that spurs a thought in another member, that member is encouraged or expected to piggyback on the original thought. This is the synergistic power of teamwork in action.

Anyone can lead.   Although most groups have a formal leader responsible for keeping the group on track (content- and process-wise), the discussion leader of the group should be the person with the most knowledge in the area being discussed. This stimulates the free exchange of information and gives each member an equal responsibility for the conduct and effectiveness of the meeting.

Diversification is encouraged.   This rule satisfies the objection raised earlier about the expertise style of decision making. If only experts make a decision, there is a good chance that only experts will understand and hence support it. By encouraging an eclectic membership with the group, this danger is avoided.

The expert may be correct. But in this style, the expert must explain his or her thinking to the satisfaction of the other members. This process challenges many of the traditional givens often used by experts in any field to arrive at decisions. Sometimes these givens are no longer valid, but they have been used so often they are no longer questioned—until they are heard by experts in other fields who challenge their accuracy.

Creativity can be described as rearranging knowledge, that is, taking knowledge from one area and applying it to another. Diversification and piggybacking encourage this type of innovation, which has accounted for some of the greatest gains the human race has ever achieved.

The objective is the boss.   This rule helps the team separate partiality, power, politics, and personalities from affecting the final decision. Whatever thoughts aid in making the final decision are kept. Everything else is tossed out. Nothing is allowed to impede the group in reaching an effective decision. Keeping this rule in mind also helps the team avoid sidetracking discussions and trivial stories that add nothing to the final decision—the ultimate boss.

CONSENSUS PROS AND CONS

First the cons:

Time

It usually takes longer for a group to arrive at a decision than it does for an individual. When we consider the basic agreement necessary for a decision to be reached by the consensus style, the time required can be extended considerably. This can cause wholesale frustration in the members who are used to the other decision-making techniques. It is also very expensive. In the other styles, one person's time is required. In this style, many more people are involved.

Compromise

"A camel is a horse designed by a committee" is a statement sometimes used to describe the final output of committees. Watered-down and compromised ideas can turn excellent ideas into mediocre ones.

Accountability

"If everybody is responsible for a decision, then no one is" expresses the belief that individual responsibility is a more effective motivator than group responsibility. Members can hide within the group and surface only at safe times. This often happens in service groups, clubs, and associations where "the same few do all the work."

Difficulty

How can we expect people to change a style of behavior they have learned over many years? All the rules of consensus decision making make it difficult to remember what is appropriate and what isn't. Most people have never participated in an intense group situation. We are probably expecting too much from employees who are used to "going it alone."

Loss of Power

Superiors have worked hard for the authority and power they wield. They have put in their dues and are very reluctant to give it to people who haven't. They have proven time and time again that they can handle pressure and make good decisions. We would have to be a little crazy to upset the applecart. Why would a manager turn over his or her decision-making power to subordinates and have to live with their decisions?

Timeliness

"Our managers can't even agree on what day of the week it is much less on difficult decisions" is an often heard complaint in many companies. Asking them to come to a consensus decision would take forever. If they ever reached a decision.

Change

The fact that people hate change can be witnessed in most companies on a daily basis. Asking our managers to change would infuriate and scare them. They have learned a certain set of rules and have been successful with them. They would resist this new approach just as they resist most of the other new approaches and programs we have tried to implement in the past. This is no different.

Convenience

Our top managers are always on the road. It is almost impossible to get an hour with each of them much less expect them to meet together for days at a time. They make individual decisions now precisely because they are separated most of the time. It is impractical for them to change their management so drastically.

We have listed quite a few cons! Taken together they are an imposing group. But if even one of them is valid it would be enough to keep most companies from attempting consensus decision making. Let us see if we can respond adequately to each objection. Now the pros:

Time

It does take longer for a group to make a decision than it does for an individual. Especially considering the rules for consensus. But that is because they are considering more pertinent information than one individual alone can possess. Because of the process, the acceptability is much higher, which means implementation is easier and quicker. When the time for implementation is considered, the overall time factor is much shorter under the consensus style.

Compromise

As stated above, because consensus groups consider more pertinent information and explore different angles, they don't compromise, they maximize. In fact, individual decision makers compromise more often than groups, usually in the interests of safety or through a lack of power to go "all out." The "risky shift phenomenon" (Ziller 1957a, p. 388) was coined to point out that the decisions made by groups tended to be riskier than those by individuals.

Accountability

Because everybody must express agreement with the final decision, no one can "hide" in a consensus group. No one can say "I didn't agree, I was railroaded", or "I was outvoted." Anyone can stop the decision. Actually more responsibility for the decision is felt by consensus group members because they know they will all receive credit or blame depending on the outcome of the decision. Another occurrence is also avoided. That being the negative response some decisions receive from "jealous or ambitious" managers who don't especially want to see another manager succeed.

Difficulty

One of the advantages of teams is that no one has to remember everything; they can help each other progress. Going it alone is the difficult route. When other people are supporting us and helping us reach our goals, life becomes easier. Once managers get even a small taste of the goodwill and acceptance within consensus groups, they learn very quickly.

Loss of Power

Power has been defined as the ability to get things done. Managers who disagree with a decision the boss makes individually can usually find ways around the decision or just give it token support. Consensus greatly increases the power of the person who seemingly loses power. When everybody has had a chance to participate in a decision and gives their support to it, the common "management games" disappear. More decisions are implemented with more acceptance. That is power.

And we shouldn't forget that everybody, including the "power person," must be able to live with the decision. Therefore, the highest officially ranked person is not giving up any power in the control sense. Any decision can be stopped. However, this style guarantees that enough time is taken to ensure that each member understands and supports the final decision.

Timeliness

Many managers choose not to agree with each other (even on what day of the week it is) because they know they don't have to agree. Voting and other similar decision techniques create winners and losers. Losers have negative feelings. Consensus eliminates this state of affairs. Therefore, managers have more reason to let the objective become the boss (rule 10) and agree where agreement is warranted. It is true that the first few consensus decisions will take time. Once the process is learned, and valued, consensus meetings get to the heart of the issues quickly and make timely decisions.

Change

People love change! We would be bored to tears if nothing changed. But we only like change that we have control over. We hate feeling surprised (in a negative way) and helpless. Consensus gives everyone control. One person can stop a decision.

Convenience

Many top managers are on the road trying to make up for the poor service and production quality caused by bad decisions within the company. They are smoothing the waters and unruffling ruffled feathers. Consensus decisions would clear up many of these problems and allow them to stay at home and plan for the future. Terrific products and service entice customers to go to businesses— not the other way around.

While focusing in on the pros of consensus, let us return to the fleet department example and picture what might have happened if. . . .

A new sales manager must be hired. Because of the position, he or she will be placed on the top managerial team comprised of the president and all of the officers reporting directly to the president. The team has been using the consensus style for over one year. At first it had been difficult, but after two months they were comfortable with it. In fact, they had decided that the open sales manager position should be filled by a manager who would be compatible with the consensus style of decision making. Through a team decision, two of the team's members were asked if they would draft a list of qualifications that could be given to the personnel department to help them narrow down the field of applicants. That had been accomplished.

(The personnel department's management team also operated by consensus and included members from several of the company's divisions. They questioned the requirement that the qualified applicant be experienced in consensus decision making. They knew that this restriction would drastically narrow the choice of available candidates—some of who would possess styles that would be completely compatible with the consensus method. When they explained their reasoning to the two members of the top management team who had drafted the suggested qualifications, they met no opposition. The requirement was changed to "compatible with the consensus style of decision making." Thus the new sales manager was hired through the combined judgment of two consensus teams.)

The new sales manager met with the top management team for one month before he met with his sales management team. During that time, he learned about the consensus style by participating in the meetings. He met with the top managers individually and established relationships with each of them. Before his first meeting with the sales management team, he knew most of the company's history, its goals and objectives, and had a firm grasp of the consensus approach.

Because of his preparation, he was immediately accepted by the sales management team. It had everything to gain from his expertise and nothing to lose.

To make a long story short, over the next two years sales quotas were increased, one new field report was added, sales expenses were reduced and two incompetent managers had been replaced—much to the relief of the field sales reps. But all actions had been decided by consensus. New methods and products had also been introduced that had actually made the new requirements more palatable than the old. The decisions had met a minimum amount of resistance.

When the fleet department suggested its idea to the sales team, it was not only accepted but improved. The idea was given to the field sales teams to consider, and they improved on the idea even more. When the program was implemented, it was a sure bet. It had taken two months longer than our original example, but the company is still reaping the rewards of the decision five years later—to the tune of 1.6 million dollars a year.

This example didn't happen. But it could have happened if the company had been using the consensus style. In our final analysis we can state that consensus maximizes the timeliness, correctness, acceptability, and results of decisions.

HOW TO INSTALL CONSENSUS DECISION MAKING

The style can only be initiated by the top decision maker in an organization. Whether it's the chief executive officer or the chairman of the board or the president, only that power person can guarantee a successful implementation.

This is true because only that person's decisions are, under normal situations, untouchable. No one can rescind one of his or her decisions. For consensus to fail, all it takes is for one well-reasoned decision to be overturned by someone in greater power. That dispirits the consensus team and they decide that the results (or lack thereof) are not worth the effort. They would be right.

So our first consensus team has to be the top management team. They must set the stage and the example. The over-all style and value of consensus will be demonstrated by their success.

After the top management team is comfortable with consensus (which means they understand the rules and thoughts behind it) they can in turn go back to their staffs and begin the process. Determining when this second stage should begin should in itself be a consensus decision reached by the top management team. (We don't have to warn teams not to go ahead too quickly because that point would be raised, discussed, and used in any consensus discussion.)

The process then proceeds step-by-step throughout the organization following the same pattern. It is a slow process, but one full of fun and discovery.

Many organizations around the world are using this style already. They aren't speaking too loudly though because they don't want to give up the competitive advantage it give them. Don't be fooled by their calculated silence. Make a good decision!

Part Three

OD Research

31 Stream Analysis: A Method for Decomposing Organization Development Interventions

Jerry I. Porras
Joan Harkness
Coeleen Kiebert

ABSTRACT

In this paper, a complex organizational development intervention was conceptualized as a stream of activities flowing through time. For the purpose of analysis, this stream was then divided into a set of parallel streams each containing activities focused on altering one of four major organizational variables—technology, structure, human process, and physical environment. Linkages between actions were specified to show the relationship, or triggering effects, of one activity on another. An analysis of triggering patterns yielded some preliminary analysis into the patterns of change dynamics.

AUTHOR BACKGROUNDS

Jerry I. Porras is an associate professor of organizational behavior at the Graduate School of Business, Stanford University. His current research focuses on the development of both a process and implementation theory of planned organizational change. He has published articles on the assessment of OD interventions, methodologies in OD research and pedagogy in the teaching of OD. Professor Porras received a B.S. in electrical engineering from the University of Texas, El Paso, an M.B.A. from Cornell University, and a Ph.D. from the Graduate School of Management, U.C.L.A. He teaches courses in organization behavior, interpersonal dynamics, and organization development.

Joan Harkness has over fifteen years of experience as a health care manager specializing in the operating room environment. She has developed new organizational structures within the setting including decentralization of the nursing staff and the creation of an interfacing nonprofessional support system. She is a graduate in nursing from Northwestern University and received her M.S. in organization development from Pepperdine University. She presently serves as director of O.R. services at El Camino Hospital in Mountain View, California.

Coeleen Kiebert is owner and vice president of Sentient Systems, Inc., a human management consulting company. As an organizational development consultant and administrator of a women's counseling program, she has a long history of working primarily with health care agencies and women's organizational systems and received her M.S. in psychology from the University of California, Santa Cruz.

Complex organization development interventions, by their very nature, impact multiple sets of organizational variables. Numerous actions aimed at altering organization processes often occur at more or less the same time or, if not exactly concurrently, with a sufficient amount of overlap such that several change-related activities are typically occurring at once.

As a result of the dynamic nature of complex planned change processes, it is usually very difficult for the change practitioner to have a clear idea of where the intervention process has been, where it is now, or where it might be headed. Furthermore, once the formal intervention activities have terminated, it is also difficult to do any really rigorous Monday-morning quarterbacking to clearly analyze exactly what happened.

Change practitioners are not the only ones who suffer from an inability to really understand the events in the organization development processes. Research scholars do also. For a long time now, organization development scholars (e.g., Dunn & Swierczik 1977) have sought to develop methods for more systematic investigations of OD case studies. These efforts have focused on ways to analyze a particular case report and methods for aggregating findings derived from many different change programs. The global intent of these activities is to generate a comprehensive theory of organization development. Up to now, this intent has been thwarted by a lack of systematic methods for understanding and mapping the complex set of activities that occur in large-scale OD interventions.

The purpose of this paper is to propose an analytical approach for decomposing the complex array of actions that take place in any large-scale change program. This method, called *stream analysis,* can be used by change practitioners both during an intervention to provide clearer insights on the current state of the change process, or post hoc to analyze and better understand exactly what occurred. In addition, Organization Development theorists and researchers also can use stream analysis to analyze case descriptions of change programs and aggregate findings across different change settings.

KEY CHANGE VARIABLES

Organization development efforts are based on a systems view of the organization. As such, they must impact a wide variety of variables in order to effectively alter the functioning of the organization. Friedlander and Brown (1974) classified organization development interventions according to three major variable categories, each serving as the main focus of intervention: (1) human processual, (2) technological, and (3) structural.

More recently, a fourth major class has surfaced as an important target of organization development interventions. The internal physical setting or (4) physical environment of the organization has been found to have an important impact on organizational behavior and has become an area of concern for both change practitioners and scholars (Steele 1977).

Reviews of the OD literature indicate that few change projects actually impact all four classes of variables (Cummings 1978; Porras & Berg 1978; White & Mitchell 1977) even though one would expect that at some point in the life of any comprehensive project each of these key variables would be affected. In fact, it appears that one important reason for the lack of success of many organization development interventions is that only a subset of the key change variables are attacked (Margulies & Raia 1975). Clearly, a wide variety of reasons exists for this. It may be that the change agent often doesn't have a clear sense of when to shift from intervention activities that affect one of the variables to actions that affect another. In order to be useful, any shift in variables targeted for intervention must result in changes that reinforce those previously obtained.

Our proposed analytical approach is directed at this deficiency—an unclear sense of all the actions occurring and their interrelationship—and begins with a definition of the major variable classes that are the focus of comprehensive change interventions. As change theory evolves it may happen that new variable classes will be identified. When this occurs they can be incorporated into the framework proposed here. It possesses the flexibility necessary to include larger numbers of key variables.

STREAM THEORY

Stream theory is based on the premise that all change activities in an organization development program can be conceptualized as a stream of actions occurring over time. One physical parallel of this might be a river of water flowing across the landscape. In the case of a river, the key dimension is space while in the case of an OD process, the key dimension is time. Figure 31.1 shows an

FIGURE 31.1   Stream Representation of a Change Process

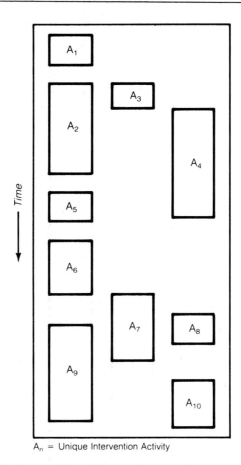

A_n = Unique Intervention Activity

example of how a change program might be pictorially represented using this stream notion. In the figure, activity 1, the first activity in the change intervention, would be shown first in the stream. It would be followed by activities 2, 3, and so on. Each block within the overall stream is drawn to begin and end at points in time corresponding to the actual beginning and ending of the intervention activity it represents.

Several characteristics of this representation should be noted. For example, two different activities might start up at the same time (A_2 and A_3) yet end at different times; one activity might start and continue on for a time with a second activity starting up somewhat later and continuing on after the first is ended (A_2 and A_4); there may be periods of time when no change activities are taking place (between A_5 and A_6); several activities may be occurring at once, each having begun at a different point in time; and so on. The result of this perspective is a pictorial representation, in correct temporal sequence, of all the activities conducted as part of a complex change program.

Although a useful analogy, this representation is not sufficient because it doesn't significantly add to current methods for understanding OD. The analysis needs to be a bit more complex and can be made so by conceptualizing several parallel streams of activities flowing over time rather than just one. This might

FIGURE 31.2　Decomposition of an OD Intervention into Its Principal Streams of Change Activity

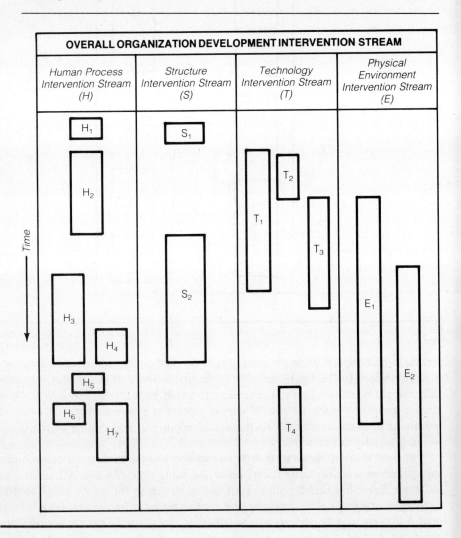

be thought of as similar to different currents flowing in a river at the same time. Each current would have its own particular characteristics but would be flowing in concert with all the other currents in the same river. In the case of the OD stream, each of a set of parallel streams could be thought of as containing all of the change activities directed at altering one of the key change variables described earlier (human process, technology, structure, or physical environment).

Figure 31.2 shows four parallel streams flowing together across time, each reflecting activities aimed at either human process, technological, structural, or environmental variables. The activities in this figure would be the same ones shown in Figure 31.1 except that now they are identified as belonging to one particular intervention stream or another. By identifying the particular focus of each change activity and placing it in its proper temporal position, we can begin to decompose a complex organization development intervention into its main parts and as a result begin to gain a better understanding of exactly what went on and when.

Although more useful than the previous representation, this depiction is still not comprehensive enough to give us the more complex view of OD intervention processes that we need. A third step therefore could be to make the appropriate interconnections between activities located in different streams. An organization development intervention is typically a building process in which one activity builds on the results of a previous activity or in which a specific activity precipitates a need for a follow-on activity. Consider a structural change that creates new work teams. This type of change might trigger the need for a human process intervention such as team building or process consultation. Neither of these human process interventions may have been necessary without the change in organizational structure. However, with the formulation of new teams, some intervention oriented toward developing more effective work relationships would probably be called for.

Figure 31.3 shows some possible interconnections between intervention activities in the four different streams. In general one could follow a single path through the intervention by proceeding down the four streams as indicated by the interconnecting arrows. Occasionally, however, as in the case of actions taken after S_1, two or more actions have been triggered by an intervention in one stream. In this case, action H_2 was precipitated by S_1, as was T_1. The action taken in S_1 required supportive actions H_2 and T_1 which were then followed by T_2. Subsequent actions would follow the same patterns and either lead to new actions, that is, make new actions possible, or trigger new actions, that is, make new actions necessary in order to bring the overall system into balance or make it consistent across its four domains.

Conceptualizing a complex organization development intervention as consisting of four parallel streams of action gives us a way of looking at change processes both from the point of view of the change agent as he or she goes through the change program, as well as from the perspective of the change researcher who is interested in understanding what went on in one change project and who might want to aggregate that understanding with knowledge gained

FIGURE 31.3 Interconnection of Change Activities Conducted in Different
Intervention Streams

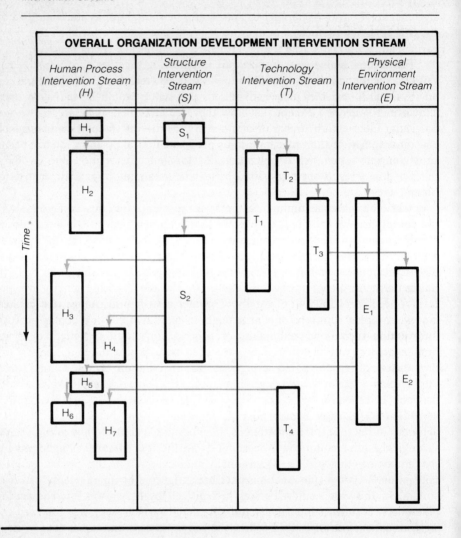

from analysis of other change processes. Stream analysis could provide a more standardized way of analyzing dissimilar change intervention programs.

The remainder of this paper will first describe a particular case in which the stream analysis approach was used on a post hoc basis to understand a nineteen-month change project conducted in a large community hospital. We will then attempt to show how one might use stream analysis to more clearly depict exactly what went on in this very complex organization development program and to highlight several interesting theoretical perspectives that grew out of having a clearer picture of the dynamics of this particular change activity.

METHODOLOGY

The methodology used in this study consisted of a series of in-depth interviews of the second and third authors, Harkness and Kiebert, conducted by the first author, Porras, who played the role of the researcher. Harkness and Kiebert therefore provided the data used for this report. Their unique roles in the change program (Kiebert was the organization development consultant; Harkness was the top manager of the target organization) provided them with somewhat different perspectives of the change process.

The interview method consisted of numerous lengthy interviews in which Porras, the researcher, asked Harkness and Kiebert about each event in the intervention process, its timing, its intent, its composition, its place in a broader theoretical framework of change, and its impact on system functioning and member behavior. Through this process, each major activity was identified and described from two perspectives, that of the client, the manager, and that of the consultant.

Initially, a flow chart, similar to one used in computer programming, was developed. It contained all of the events that had been part of the intervention process and placed these events in their proper sequence. As one might expect, the resulting diagram was extremely complex and difficult to interpret. The next step, therefore, was to categorize each activity represented in the diagram as primarily affecting one of the four key organizational variables defined above. Clearly many OD activities often impact more than one of the key variables. However, in these cases, a determination can be made about the dominant impact of the activity with a subsequent categorization into one of the four streams. Care was taken to place each activity in its proper temporal position. A box reflecting the length of the activity was used and a brief description of each action placed in the box.

Connections between activities were then made when, appropriate to distinguish those situations in which one activity led to another, or was necessitated by another from those in which subsequent activities were not truly triggered by previous actions. As noted earlier, at times, one event may have followed another because the second event was designed to provide additional reinforcement to the changes brought about by the first event. At other times, it became necessary to develop new follow-on activities because initial events may have created new needs or surfaced previously unknown problems.

Once the overall organization development effort had been charted into streams, an analysis was undertaken to determine if any clear patterns of intervention existed. We were interested in finding out if the intervention proceeded through distinguishable cycles that had some important meaning. We were also interested in determining if there were important classes of interventions that tended to systematically trigger movement into other streams. A final area of interest was to identify those points in the intervention process in which a particular activity may have been called for but was not undertaken.

ORGANIZATION DEVELOPMENT PROJECT

Site

The intervention was conducted over a nineteen-month period in the operating room of a 425-bed suburban community hospital. During the twenty years since its inception, the hospital had grown into a sophisticated medical complex serving a community population diverse in age, economic level, and racial mix. In recent years, federal and state government regulations had significantly impacted hospital operations with ever increasing demands for cost accountability, altered facilities and equipment standards, and regulation of services.

The operating room department (OR) plays a key role in the functioning of the entire hospital with 60% of all hospital patients originally coming to it for surgery. At the beginning of this research, the OR occupied a space of approximately 13,500 square feet, and handled an array of fifty patients in ten operating rooms each day with a team of thirty-five nurses, twenty to thirty doctors and thirteen nursing assistants. These fifty patients fell into any of nine different categories of surgical specialty. Since 80% of the patients were under general anesthesia during surgery, the OR team assumed complete responsibility for the total physical well-being of almost all of their patients. As a consequence, the OR team was required to provide rapid, efficient, specialty care for each patient, responding quickly to surgical needs, minimizing the anesthesia time, and maintaining sterile techniques.

HOW THE OPERATING ROOM WORKS

In order to maintain its sterile environment, the OR as a department is isolated from the rest of the hospital. Nevertheless its impact on the entire hospital is significant. The scheduling of a surgical procedure puts into motion a succession of activities that encompasses many other hospital departments. Outside of the OR a bed is reserved through the Admitting Department, diet is ordered from Food Service, the Pharmacy receives medication orders, Nursing Service is alerted to provide staffing, Housekeeping prepares the bed, Laboratory and X-Ray provide diagnostic tests, the Business Office tracks costs and billings, and Central Service, Purchasing, and Engineering provide necessary supplies and equipment.

In the OR itself, care is taken to schedule the patient for the proper amount of time needed to perform the type of surgery anticipated, reserving an operating room that is appropriately "fitted out" to accommodate the particular type of surgery. The gears of the OR then go into motion. The proper supplies are ordered, wrapped, sterilized, and gathered together into what is then referred to as a "picked case." The head nurses (HN's) coordinate equipment, sutures, instruments, and trained nurses. An anesthesiologist is assigned and his or her equipment checked and prepared. All other departments involved in the surgical procedure are notified: blood bank; x-ray; recovery room; and/or the intensive care unit. Finally, the patient's name is entered into the daily surgery schedule which is distributed throughout the hospital. Once surgery is completed and the patient sufficiently recovered, he or she is then transferred to the responsibility of the hospital staff.

Intervention

During the fifteen years prior to the planned change project described in this study, no significant improvements in the organization or management of the OR Department had taken place. Organizational structure, methods of scheduling, billing, supply handling, and personnel assignment had not substantially changed.

The change project was triggered by an increasing number of complaints from nurses and physicians about their own interrelationships as well as the work environment and managerial systems. New technology was continuously introduced into surgical procedures and physicians were demanding that nurses have expertise in the use of a growing amount of new equipment. As a consequence, systems for providing nurse training in new procedures and equipment, which had never existed, were becoming more critically important.

To compound the situation, an ever increasing workload was overwhelming all areas in the department. Supply management, instrument processing, and the physical plant itself were found inadequate to deal with growing demands. A shortage of nurses placed an added burden on the already unhappy and overworked staff.

A first attempt at systematic change occurred with the institution of a planning procedure aimed at expanding the physical facilities of the OR. This activity placed additional pressures on the existing OR director who was already stretched to the limit. At this point, an assistant OR director position was created and an external organization development consultant brought in to help identify problem areas and facilitate the actions needed to resolve them.

The consultant's initial diagnostic process included questionnaires to gather data, interviews with key managers, and observations of nursing staff at work. The initial diagnosis led to team building activities with the management group, improvements in the care and processing of instruments, minor reorganization of the management structure, and one-to-one counselling sessions with managers in an effort to improve their individual managerial skills. Two months after the beginning of the project a new organizational structure was developed and implemented.

Facilities planning continued, but now was becoming more integrated with the planned change process. Since the plans called for tripling of the floor space, it became clear that the existing systems for delivery and processing of supplies and equipment were inadequate and the development of new systems began.

The influx of new surgical technology continued to impact the functioning of the OR. Fiber optics, nitrogen-driven power tools, and LASER beam tools were only a few examples of the new equipment demanded by surgeons. Anesthesiologists were beginning to use newer anesthetic gases and needed the proper equipment to deliver them. New and more sophisticated monitoring devices were also introduced into the OR. In response to these technological demands, plans to care for all of this new equipment and to train nurses in their use were developed and implemented. Since the new equipment required specialized storage facilities, the remodeling plans had to be altered to reflect these changing needs.

In the sixth months of the project, further refinement of the organizational structure took place. Nine surgical specialties were divided into four groups called "pods" with an acting nurse manager heading each one. Each pod contained nurses who focused on a group of specialities and would be trained to deal with the ever expanding technology of those specialities. Technical training was begun immediately and carried throughout the next 12 months.

Between the third and ninth months of the OD intervention, changes were also made in the business systems of the department. Patient billing procedures were refined and updated. In addition, the scheduling office was reorganized to provide for more efficient scheduling of surgical procedures. As plans for the new facilities progressed, the need for a new system to deliver sterile supplies became apparent and work on its development begun. (This system, called the case cart system, was to eventually require two years of developmental effort.) An Anesthesia Department was created to support the anesthesiologists and their expanding technology.

In the ninth month of the project, the OR director resigned and was replaced by the assistant director who immediately redistributed the managerial functions in an effort to more effectively handle both the construction activities and case cart system design. Activities focused on clarifying new managerial roles were begun as well as efforts made to convey the managerial philosophy of the new director. Psychological tests such as the Myers-Briggs and the FIRO-B were used by the consultant to heighten managerial self-awareness and facilitate the formation of a new managerial work culture.

Ancillary areas such as the recovery room and out-patient surgery, both a part of the total department, were severely affected by the change in director. Turmoil arose in both areas resulting in the need for extensive team building efforts during the ninth months of the project. The nursing staff, having been encouraged to be more active in the operations of the department, formed an employee problem-solving group during this period. Its efforts were directed at dealing with a wide variety of issues affecting the nurses.

Approximately one year after the beginning of the intervention, renovation of the facilities began. Part of the existing facilities was torn out necessitating the movement of supplies, equipment, and offices. Construction plans called for three phases to take place over a two-year period, during which time the entire operating room suite would be torn down and rebuilt a section at a time.

By the fourteenth month, the pod organizational structure was firmly in place. The scheduling office had partially completed a system to interface with the four pods and new nursing record forms had been developed to provide a better method for billing supplies and operating room use to the patient. The billing system was also designed to be consistent with the pod organizational structure.

Formation of the middle level management team was formalized in month fifteen with the promotion of four staff nurses to the head nurse position for each pod. Team building, both across the pod head nurse team and within pods was used to further strengthen the organizational structure. For the head nurses only, one-to-one counselling and psychological testing were once again used to help develop interpersonal relation skills. Head nurses also participated in training on inventory control, budgeting, and staffing.

Although the change project continued past this point, for purposes of this research, our analysis terminated here. The overall life of the project as described was nineteen months and covered an extensive array of change activities. In the next section, the stream analytic approach will be used to decompose this complex set of interventions into a form suitable for further analysis.

Stream Analysis of the Intervention

The previous section presented only the highlights of a very complex nineteen-month planned change process. An in-depth analysis of it using the stream approach yielded a series of charts such as the one shown in Figure 31.4 which is a representative sample of the complete set of charts describing the intervention.

As shown in Figure 31.4, the intervention has been organized into the four basic streams. Each box represents an intervention activity with the beginning and ending points of the box temporally corresponding to the actual beginning and ending of the intervention activity itself. The lines connecting the various boxes reflect the relationship between activities. More specifically, they represent the need that surfaced in one activity for any subsequent activity. A brief description of this need (or "trigger") is also included to give the reader a fuller picture of the interconnection between activities.

The period shown in the chart covers from the seventh to fourteenth month of the intervention. Activities were occurring in all four streams with events triggering other events both within the same stream or across streams. A brief description of the chart may highlight some of the key characteristics of this approach.

Within the Human Process Stream, the activity H_5 is a continuation of one begun back in month two of the project. As an ongoing process of developing management planning capabilities in the organization it had earlier spawned interventions in other streams, and, in the time period shown, it triggered two

FIGURE 31.4   Stream Analysis of an Organization Development Intervention

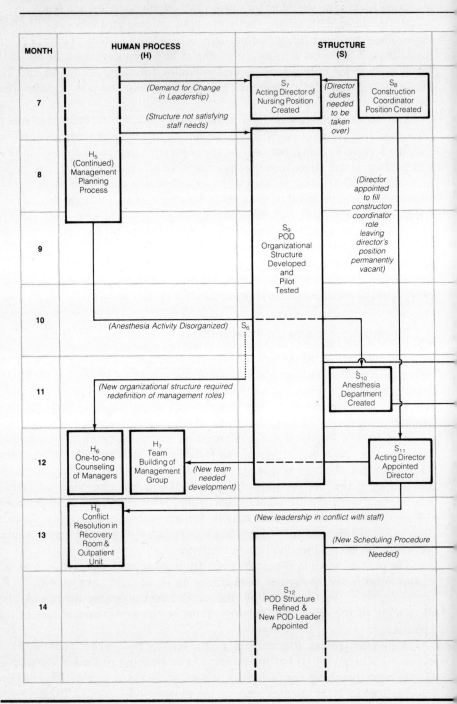

	TECHNOLOGY (T)			PHYSICAL ENVIRONMENT (E)	MONTH
					7
	T_2 (Continued) Surgical Procedures and Instruments Upgraded and Supply System Refined	T_1 (Continued) New Surgical Equipment Introduced into O.R.		E_1 (Continued) Renovation and Expansion of Facilities Planning	8
					9
					10
T_6 Scheduling Procedures Upgraded					11
(Need for technological improvement recognized)					
					12
					13
T_8 Block Scheduling Approach Developed	T_7 Case Cart System Pilot Developed and Tested				14

structural changes: S_7, the formation of an acting director's position and the appointment of the assistant director to that position; and S_8, the pilot testing of a new organizational structure called the pod system.

Pilot testing of the pod system from months eight through twelve led to a technological intervention, T_6 (upgrading of scheduling practices) and a follow-on structural intervention S_{11} (revision of the pilot pod structure and the appointment of a person to manage the experimental pod).

Activity H_6 was triggered by a structural intervention made nine months earlier. A new organizational structure had been created assigning additional responsibilities to several managers which they subsequently found themselves unable to handle. One-to-one counseling with the external consultant was instituted to help these managers diagnose themselves and plan actions to correct their deficiencies. This is an example of a change in one stream that should have been followed in a more timely fashion by a change in a second stream. In fact, the managers' situation was experienced as fairly desperate before the counseling was begun. Other pressures had drawn so much energy from the managers that the situation had to get pretty severe before this need clearly surfaced as a problem to be dealt with.

Further study of Figure 31.4 can yield many more insights into the dynamics of the intervention described. However, it is beyond our scope here to discuss it further. We present this chart only to show the analytical potential of the approach and to give the reader a flavor of what an actual segment of a complex project might look like.

Aside from a visual analysis of the events and their interrelationships, more systematic analysis is also possible. This more systematic view of the change dynamics has a potential for yielding deeper understanding of the OD process. In the next section we will present three examples of the types of information that can be generated by the stream analytic approach.

Data-Based Results

All of our examples are derived from a database generated by taking the codings of each intervention activity (e.g., S_1, H_3, E_2, etc.) and using them to list all of the triggering relationships. For example, in Figure 31.4, S_7 was triggered by H_5. This would be represented as $H_5 \rightarrow S_7$. All of these "triggered pairs" were listed in temporal order and analyzed in a variety of ways. The examples we will discuss are but three of a larger set of potential analyses that can be done.

Triggering Patterns

A frequency count performed on the trigger pairs, focused on the number of times each stream triggered a subsequent intervention (either in another stream or in the same stream). Likewise, counts were made of the number of times a stream was triggered by a previous activity. The results of this analysis are shown in Figure 31.5.

Each circle in the figure represents one of the four streams. The arrows indicate the direction of the triggering process, that is, stream A activity triggers stream B activity. In every case except three, each stream triggered activity in

FIGURE 31.5   Trigger Patterns Between and Within Intervention Streams

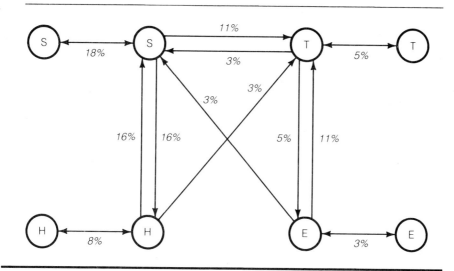

every other stream one or more times during the life of the research project. The percentages shown next to each arrow reflect the relative frequency of occurrence of that particular pattern and were calculated by dividing the number of times in which that trigger pair occurred by the total number of trigger pairs occurring during the research period. These figures therefore provide a way of comparing the various patterns that occurred.

Holes.   An analysis of this figure yields several interesting patterns. First, the intervention process never included a human process intervention leading to an environment intervention or vice versa. This situation is called a *hole* in the language of stream theory, that is, it indicates a place where some intervention was appropriate but did not, in fact, occur.

Several interventions in both the human process and environment areas warranted supporting follow-on activity in the other stream. For example, several of the key nurse managers had occupied a relatively small space in which they could easily communicate without having to leave their own desks or areas. They would simply "yell" at each other when they had a question. The reconstruction of the OR led to a large increase in the amount of space this same group occupied. No longer could they easily communicate and as a result began to be more isolated from each other and interacted less. The coordination that had resulted from the quick access previously existing began to break down. Had the physical environment change been followed by a specific human process intervention focused on establishing a new communication mechanism, this breakdown would not have occurred.

A second example highlights the reverse sequence, that is, one in which human process interventions should have been followed by a supporting environmental intervention. In this case, much effort had been expended to build up communication and problem solving between the pod leader and other nurse managers. The physical setting was such that the three pod leaders were located in a small office with only one door and in an area relatively inaccessible to the remaining staff. The result was that not enough of the desired interaction occurred. People couldn't easily circulate into the pod leader's office and, as a consequence, were reluctant to do so unless the reason was a very strong one. Here was a case where the environment needed to be altered to support the change goals of the human process activities and wasn't.

Although there were a few situations in which human process interventions did trigger technological interventions, the reverse never occurred. The same was true for environment and structure as a trigger pair. Several of the technological interventions resulted in the introduction of new equipment which tended to equalize the power relationships between doctors and nurses. The function of the nurse in the use of the equipment was such that she would, at times, tell the doctor what to do. This technological change should have been followed by a human process intervention to help both parties deal more effectively with these small shifts in power.

The relationship between environmental interventions and structural interventions had a similar one-way character; environment triggered structure, but not the other way around. This general pattern reflected another hole in the overall intervention process. The situation with the pod leaders described earlier is an example of how environmental changes could have supported structural changes. The intervention that produced the pod structure in the first place could have led to a physical design in which pod members were located adjacent to the offices of the pod leaders. Since the entire facility was being reconstructed such a design was well within the realm of possibility and would have supported the intentions of the new pod.

Centrality of structure.   Structure change appears to have played a key role in the intervention process. It was the stream most frequently triggered as well as the stream most frequently triggering. It seems that, at least for this particular change project, structure mediated many of the changes occurring in the other streams. A change in technology (for example, the introduction of new anesthetic gases and the equipment to deliver them) precipitated a change in structure (the formation of an anesthesia department) which led to an environmental change (the redesign of space to accommodate the new department) and a human process intervention (one-to-one counseling to define and clarify new roles).

Structural interventions triggered structural interventions at a greater frequency than did any other stream (18% of all trigger events were structural change triggering structural change). Next in frequency were structure triggering human process and vice versa (16% each way).

Overall, this OD intervention was characterized by the centrality of structural change and a high level of interaction between structural and human process change. It appears that a strong reinforcement exists between these two streams in the practice of planned change, a relationship long proposed and supported in the organization theory literature, but one with little empirical evidence for it in the organization development research literature.

Effect of human process interventions. Surprisingly, human process interventions did not trigger other human process interventions very frequently. This is a bit unusual for an intervention process classified as organization development. Certainly, the consultant was steeped in OD theory and tradition. Yet, as the overall project unfolded, relatively few of the human process interventions were triggered by other human process interventions. Early in the project this was not the case. All of the situations in which human process activities triggered other human process activities occurred in the first six months of the intervention. Thereafter human process activities tended to trigger primarily structural change.

On the other hand, structure change precipitated human process change fairly constantly across the entire life of the project. Since the OD consultant worked more intensely in the system during the first third of the project, this phenomenon might be best explained by her presence or absence.

Intervention Phases

A second area of interest was the possible existence of identifiable phases of intervention and the likelihood that these phases might reflect some broader cycle of change. Investigation of these questions began with a chronological listing of all the trigger pairs occurring during the 19 months of the project. In this listing, care was taken to assure that the order of triggering was temporally correct so that a true representation of the actual chronology of events could be preserved.

Analysis of the order in which the thirty-eight trigger events occurred yielded five relatively coherent and distinct phases of intervention activity. The first phase was dominated by technological change triggering both environmental and structural change. This phase is consistent with the recollections of both the consultant and manager. Technological innovation was occurring in the OR and adaptation to it was required. Early adaptation took the form of changes in both structure and physical environment as a way of coping with the new technology.

A second phase then occurred in which human process interventions and structural alterations were the sole activities occurring. An intense interaction occurred in which structural change would trigger human process change or vice versa. Structural change also triggered further structural change and human process interventions triggered more human process activities. During this phase, no other intervention stream was involved in the triggering process. Activity was completely dominated by human process and structural change.

In the third phase, physical environment and technological change began to dominate. Although some structural change occurred during this phase, the vast majority of activity was in the environmental and technological area. Environmental change tended to allow for follow-on technological change. Environment seemed to perform an enabling function, that is, changes in the physical environment made it possible for changes in technology to take place. In any case, this phase was dominated by these two streams and, in fact, no human process activity triggered or was triggered by any other stream.

The fourth phase hailed the return of structural and human process change. Although these two streams were dominant in this phase as was true in Phase II, the pattern of triggering was different. In the second phase, the majority of events were triggered by human process activities while in this phase the majority were triggered instead by structural change. So, although the two streams were once again the key ones, the process itself had a distinctive character when compared to the previous stage.

The final phase witnessed the return of technological change to the forefront, however, this time in combination with structural change rather than environmental change. Both human process and environmental activity were a part of some of the trigger pairs in this phase, yet they were a relatively infrequent occurrence. The vast majority of activity involved technology and structure.

Technology and structure played an important role in three of the five phases—technology in Phases I, II, and V and structure in Phases II, IV and V. Structure, however, was far more dominant in both the number of times it served as a trigger of subsequent actions or was triggered by prior activity. Human process, on the other hand, was only prevalent in times when structural change was also present. If a lot of environmental and/or technological change was occurring, little human process action resulted. As noted earlier, this could reflect a weakness in this particular OD project rather than a typical pattern of intervention. The study of more change processes should yield information on this point.

INTERVENTION CYCLES

Analysis of the five phases of intervention identified above yields only a few hints about possible cycles of intervention. The time period studied was not long enough nor the number of phases identified large enough to warrant much confidence in any conclusions drawn.

However, it does appear that one highly tentative observation can be made. Human process and structure change seem to cycle in and out of the overall intervention stream. Phase I was technological and was followed by human process and structure (Phase II). Phase III was environment and technology dominated and it was also followed by human process and structure (Phase IV). Phase V was technology and structure and one would expect that a sixth phase should then have been dominated by human process and structure again. (Additional research presently underway should yield data on this point.)

One way this cycle might be described more broadly is that technological and/or environmental change need to be "stabilized" by human process and structural change. Once these two latter areas are modified so that technology and physical environment alterations contribute positively to organizational performance, then additional change in technology or environment become possible. The process could be viewed as one in which technological and environmental change destabilize the organization and drive it into new ways of operating that are inconsistent with pre-existing modes, then human process and structural change must occur to get things back into equilibrium.

A second way of conceptualizing this cycle is almost the reverse of the one described above. In this view, human process and structure change could be considered enabling mechanisms which allow technological and environmental change to occur or which demand new technologies and environments. In the latter perspective, effective human processes and structures make it possible for organizational members to seek and embrace new technologies and environments rather than resist them. Using the former perspective, effective human processes and structures *allow* inevitable technological change to proceed within the system. Either way of thinking about the process could be correct. The circumstances of this research don't allow for any strong position at this time.

CONCLUSIONS

Stream analysis, as an approach to decomposing and analyzing complex OD interventions has been demonstrated here to show some promise in helping both OD practitioners and theorists better understand the planned change process. This methodology is flexible in that it can accommodate larger numbers of streams (or key variables) than the ones specified in this research. The data generated are amenable to more sophisticated quantiative analyses than the ones presented, but in the case of the project described both the time frame and number of data points were insufficient for meaningful application of more comprehensive methods.

The charts generated by this approach can provide a useful and complete view of the change process and, as such, can highlight weaknesses in past intervention practice so that future activity can be refined. They can consequently become an effective tool for learning and developing more potent intervention activity.

Stream analysis is a promising technique for both practitioners and researchers. Its application to organization development phenomena should yield more meaningful insights into the processes of planned change.

References

Cummings, T. G. Socio-technical experimentation: A review of sixteen studies. In W. A. Pasmore & J. J. Sherwood, *Socio-Technical Systems: A Source Book*. La Jolla, California: University Associates, 1978, 259–70.

Dunn, W. N., & Swierczek, F. N. Planned organizational change: Toward grounded theory. *Journal of Applied Behavioral Science*, 1977, 13 (2), 135–58.

Friedlander. F., & Brown, L. D. Organization Development. *Annual Review of Psychology*, 1974, 313–41.

Margulies, N., & Raia, A. *Conceptual Foundations of Organization Development*. New York: McGraw-Hill, 1978.

Porras, J. I., & Berg, P. O. The impact of Organization Development. *Academy of Management Review*, 1978, 3 (2), 249–66.

White, S. E. & Mitchell, T. R. Organization Development: A review of research content and research design. *Academy of Management Review*, 1976, (2), 57–73.

32 The Search for Consultant Competencies

Mel R. Spehn

ABSTRACT

This article sketches the history of the Army's adaptation of OD to OE and the training of OE consultants. It describes step by step the research into consultant competencies and the incorporation of these generic personal characteristics into a sixteen-week consultant training course. The complete comptency model is portrayed. Applications and uses of the competency model for both military and civilian consulting are explored.

AUTHOR BACKGROUNDS

Mel R. Spehn (Ph.D. in psychology) is Director of Training Developments, Organizational Effectiveness Center and School, Fort Ord, California. He cofounded a counseling/consulting firm in St. Louis, consulted with civilian and military organizations, taught graduate OD courses, presented research at APA and ASTD conferences and conducted executive effectiveness courses for the American Management Association.

In 1979 we at the U.S. Army's Organizational Effectiveness Center and School (OECS) were faced with a dilemma. We had graduated about three hundred Organizational Effectiveness Consultants (OEC's) since the first class in

Adapted from "Competency Model: Development and Uses" in *OE Communique,* vol. 5, no. 3, 1981, by Dr. Mel R. Spehn and LTC R. A. Tumelson.

July 1975. The time seemed right to evaluate how well we had done and what mistakes we had made that could be corrected in future training. In those four years we had begun to fill a longtime gnawing Army need.

CONCEPTION OF OE

In the early 1970s, driven to adapt to a new breed of soldiers who were products of both Viet Nam and the turbulent 60s, the Army sought to make greater use of the behavioral and managerial sciences. Several pilot projects (for example, survey feedback in Europe, an assessment center in Georgia, and management by objectives in Texas) and extensive research indicated that certain behavioral science and management techniques used in civilian academe and industry under the title organizational development (OD) were applicable to the Army. Those techniques that seemed to complement core Army values and leadership principles were selectively adapted for use and collectively called organizational effectiveness. (The Army's change to OE was its way to "green" OD and stop soldiers from thinking this new OD program had something to do with "olive drab," the traditional uniform color.)

In 1975 OE was officially promulgated as "the systematic military application of selected management and behavioral science skills and methods to improve the total organizational function, to accomplish assigned missions, and to increase combat readiness,"[1] OE's control center would be at Fort Ord, California, the site of one of the two-year pilot programs. But this powerful new technology needed a delivery system—the warhead needed a missile.

Approximately three hundred fifty positions were carved out of Army organizations world wide so that each division-size organization (about twenty thousand people) would have at least two OEC's available to work with its sub-units. The positions for these officers were mandated, but the use of OEC's was at the voluntary choice of sub-unit leaders. Senior noncommissioned officers and select Department of Army civilians were also assigned to serve in consultant positions especially fitted to their background and careers. A flurry of team building, goal setting, action planning, communication training, and every other form of OE effort began in small and large Army organizations from Korea to Kansas, from Panama to the Pentagon.

CONSULTANT COURSE

From the very beginning the sixteen-week Organizational Effectiveness Consultant Course (OECC) was not the usual Army classroom training. With few models to go by, the OECC of necessity became eclectic and experimentally based. Psychology, management, operations research, sociology, and other disciplines fed into the content of the course. Since the students were all seasoned people with many years' experience in managing people and resources, we at OECS drew upon their experience for much of the learning. The core of the first faculty group was a group of civilian consultants and trainers, some of whom had worked with the Navy in its OE-like Human Resource Management program.[2] The course tended from the beginning to have a practical how-to-do-it approach to consulting, with the last four weeks being a practicum for teams of students sent out with a faculty mentor to try their new skills in a real Army organization.

It seemed as if we were doing something right, for in 1978 the American Council on Education awarded the OECC sixteen graduate semester credit hours, commenting that we were "on the cutting edge of the discipline." Also at that time the Chief of Staff of the Army, General Bernard Rogers, said of the OE program:

> As all of you know, I have for some time been interested in organizational effectiveness (OE) as a technology and capability for strengthening and improving the Army in the broadest sense. The results obtained from pioneering efforts with OE during the past 4 years have been illuminating, but they are only the tip of the iceberg. Collectively, these early initiatives in line and staff units signal a significant, long-term contribution to the Army.[3]

But then General Rogers had been the "godfather" of the OE program since its inception, so he could be considered to be prejudiced.

THE SEARCH

The question still remained; how did we know we were training consultants in those skills they *really* needed to be high performers? The dilemma was that while this question had to be answered, the way to answer it was not at all evident.

Unfortunately, civilian consultant training didn't seem to offer us much guidance, although we have always strongly felt that Army consulting is basically the same as civilian consulting. The OEC may salute and call the client "General" or "Colonel" rather than "President" or "Vice President," but from then on the same skills seem to be called for. In fact, many OEC's have left the Army and made smooth transitions to civilian consulting. Glenn Varney wrote,

> Even though several university degree programs exist to develop professionals (Pepperdine, Bowling Green State, Case Western Reserve, Brigham Young) as well as nonacademic programs (University Associates, NTL Institute), and professional societies (OD Network, OD Division of the Academy of Management), there is little discussion or agreement as to what skills the OD professional needs and how these are learned.[4]

We had already tried the traditional job/task analysis. With clipboard in hand, we had shadowed some OEC's, making careful notes on the things they did. We tallied the number of phone calls made and received, interviews conducted, reports written, and so on. Yet, we knew this laundry list of tasks did not reflect the things that really made an effective consultant.

There had to be a better way to examine consultants because their success seemed to rely more on the kind of people they *were* than on the tasks they actually *did*. Consultants performing the same tasks produce vastly different results. In short, what consultants *do* to a great extent is what they *are*. But how could OECS evaluate *that*?

A SOLUTION

We were excited about solving this dilemma when the Army Research Institute (ARI) arranged a contract for OECS with McBer and Company of Boston, Massachusetts, experts at studying occupants to find out the characteristics of the individual that underlie effective work performance.[5] They even claimed the ability to distinguish the competencies of superior performers from those of ordinary performers in a particular job. They had done such research for the State Department, the Navy, banks, sales firms, and the American Management Association.

The model-building methods McBer used were thorough.[6] First came a complete search of literature concerning consultants, their roles, characteristics, interventions, and methodologies. They then searched for ideas directly concerning the competencies themselves, namely those personal trait characteristics and skills explicitly related to job performance. They discovered little of value from all these studies, beyond showing that consultants do make a difference in organizational improvement efforts (as opposed to video tapes or survey data alone).

The kind of consultant that makes a difference would have to be shown through empirical studies by going into the field and finding what successful, as opposed to unsuccessful, consultants actually do on the job. There were five stages in the process of creating a complete competency model based on real-job needs.

STAGES OF MODEL BUILDING

Stage 1. The first stage, taken in July 1979, was to assemble two "expert panels," one composed of OECS staff and faculty and the other made up of twelve practicing OE consultants, to brainstorm a list of knowledge, skills, abilities, or individual characteristics thought to be related to outstanding performance in the OE consultant's job. The combined output of the two expert panels produced 115 performance characteristics.

Stage 2. Three hundred practicing OE consultants were then sent this list and asked to rate these characteristics regarding their importance for success on the job. This second model-building stage refined the data, but the characteristics were still only "expert" hypotheses. They would have to be validated by identifying a group of individuals considered outstanding practitioners and by discovering what knowledge, skills, abilities, or other characteristics do indeed distinguish the group from their less effective counterparts.

Stage 3.   In the third stage, top performing consultants were sought through a variety of techniques: self-evaluation, OECS faculty nominations, and peer nominations. Calculations were made to eliminate any biased effects that high visibility and high rank might have in the selection process. Eventually, thirty OE consultants representing both ends of the performance spectrum were identified.

Stage 4.   In the fourth stage, all thirty OE consultants were interviewed by a team of ten McBer professionals and two specially trained OECS staff. The method used is called the *behavioral event interview*. During these two- to three-hour individual sessions, the interviewees were guided to recall very specific descriptions of high and low points in their consulting careers: What were some successes? Some failures? What did you really say? What did you actually do? An entire consulting situation would be walked through in detail. Without over-guiding the responses, the interviewer in behavioral event interviewing presses to discover *actual behavior* performed on the job.

Stage 5.   These job behaviors are called *performance indicators,* and the analysis of them to find out their correlations and overlap is what happened during the last stage of the model building. This analysis was done by teams of experts using data from the expert panels and surveys as starting points from which to look at all the interview data. Raters separately coded the interviews and then came together frequently to ensure that there was cross-coder reliability in all cases. The 115 hypothetical characteristics became 130 field-verified behaviors.

The performance indicators coalesced into natural groups called *competencies* (with three to eight indicators per competency). The competencies themselves showed similarities that allowed them to be clustered into larger categories. In the case of OE Consultants there were 130 performance indicators, 33 competencies, and 9 *competency clusters* (see Figure 32.1 for complete categories).

Some competencies were found in high-performing consultants and not as frequently or intensely in lower performers. For instance, "results orientation" seems to be a key discriminator. High performers constantly press for a difference or a change in the client system. They have a "bottom line" mentality in their work. This orientation will be balanced by other competencies (for example, "exercises restraint") so that eventually high performers are seen to be those who might not possess all competencies, but do have a high number of them.

USES OF COMPETENCY MODEL

The uses of the competency model are many, but necessarily moderated by the goals and nature of the OE Consultant program in the Army. Ideally if we know the characteristics and abilities of an effective consultant, we would select the appropriate people for training. Army personnel policy has not yet attained

FIGURE 32.1 Performance Indicators Grouped in Nine Competency Clusters

---

Competency Cluster I

Functional Knowledge
    Defined: Knowledge of OE theory and demonstrated ability to relate to that theory to organizations.

Competency I-A   Knowledge of OE Theory
    1. Uses theoretical concepts.
    2. Mentions specific theoretical references.
    3. Seeks new theories and concepts for application.

Competency I-B   Knowledge of the User Organization as a System
    4. Identifies key environmental impacts on user organizations.
    5. Identifies user organizations's subsystems and describes their interrelatedness.
    6. Mentions formal and informal organization hierarchy of user.
    7. States functions or operations of user organization.
    8. Identifies people who are functionally responsible for handling key issues.
    9. Uses formal and informal organization in the consulting process.
  10. Actively collects information on potential user organizations.

Competency Cluster II

Strong Self Concept
    Defined: Trusts self, training, and ability to take action; hears another's point of view and puts aside own agenda. Has low fear of rejection, exercises restraint and accepts responsibility for failure.

Competency II-A   Self-Confidence
  11. Accurately and honestly assesses and understands own strengths and weaknesses.
  12. Compares self favorably to others.
  13. Describes self as an expert.
  14. Sees self as a catalyst for change and innovation.
  15. Interacts with superiors comfortably; rank and position are not inhibitors.
  16. Uses knowledge to gain personal power and make things happen.

Competency II-B   Low Fear of Rejection
  17. Confronts conflict between self and others.
  18. Demonstrates more concern for being effective versus being liked.
  19. Establishes ground rules for own/other involvement.
  20. Does not personalize negative judgment by others.
  21. Explicitly disagrees with superior/user on significant issues.

Competency II-C   Perceptual Objectivity
  22. Explicitly articulates both sides of an issue.
  23. Acknowledges legitimacy of viewpoints opposite to own.
  24. Doesn't force own agenda on others.

Competency II-D   Exercises Restraint
  25. Controls impulsive behavior or remarks.
  26. Controls anger.
  27. Decides not to become involved when OE outcomes/results are questionable/marginal.
  28. Says "NO" to nonconsultive roles/responsibilities within user organization.

Competency II-E   Accepts Responsibility for Failure
  29. Critically evaluates own consultant role behavior in a failure.
  30. Explicitly accepts responsibility for failure.
  31. Mentions own possible role in a failure.
  32. Talks openly about mistakes.

Competency Cluster III

Professional Self-Image
  Defined: Presents self to others as expert resource, has a realistic sense of what an OE Consultant can/cannot do, draws on other resources and works to develop others.

Competency III-A   Recognizes, Understands and Works to Overcome the Limits of Own Expertise
  33. Recognizes limits of own expertise.
  34. Calls in colleagues/professionals for assistance, augmentation or critique.
  35. Develops and uses an informal support network within organizations.

Competency III-B   Sees Self as Substantive Expert.
  36. Presents self to others as a resource.
  37. Encourages being consulted by others.
  38. Makes substantive as well as process recommendations/observations.
  39. Devises and tests OE technologies.
  40. Clarifies role of OE Consultant.
  41. Solicits and reinforces feedback from program managers, users and/or chain-of-command.
  42. Writes cases, reports, articles, etc.
  43. Publishes and disseminates OE technologies.

Competency III-C   Develops Others Through Skill Transfer and Behavior Modeling
  44. Works to develop and transfer knowledge and skills in user organizations.
  45. Coaches others in specific OE skills and behaviors.
  46. Selectively trains others in specialized consulting roles.
  47. Acts as consultant to other OE Consultants.
  48. Demonstrates OE knowledge and skills thru own behaviors.

Competency Cluster IV

Develops Common Understanding
  Defined: Seeks clarity among user, user system and self regarding the issues, environment and OE process.

Competency IV-A   Establishes Professional Rapport
  49. Uses OE capabilities with a blend of social skills and military/professional courtesy.
  50. Establishes climate to discuss serious/sensitive issues.
  51. Focuses on relevant organizational/environmental issues.
  52. Assists user in discussing and clarifying serious/sensitive issues.
  53. Gains user commitment and support.

Competency IV-B   Concern for Clarity
  54. States expectations for own/other's performance or role.
  55. Emphasizes need for specificity and concrete documentation.
  56. Asks questions to clarify issues.
  57. Transcends symptom description to get to systemic core problems/issues.
  58. Addresses other's perception of consultant as a catalyst or initiator for organizational change.
  59. Causes organizational members to take responsibility for initiating change.
  60. Ensures user role clarity throughout entire action research process.
  61. Uses Memorandum of Understanding to document and clarify OE process.

Competency IV-C   Values User Input
  62. Considers user wants and needs.
  63. Matches OE Consultant effort/capabilities with user's commitment to time, personnel, and resources.
  64. Involves user actively in design and leadership of intervention activities.
  65. Consults user before taking action.
  66. Willingly renegotiates contract to meet organizational needs.

Competency IV-D   Identifies Key Concerns and Issues Not Identified by User
  67. Raises and discusses sensitive/tough problem areas with user.
  68. Monitors contract agreements and questions deviations from initial OE Consultant/user contract.

Competency Cluster V

Personal Influence
  Defined: Uses appropriate influence strategies to gain acceptance of an idea, plan or activity while being sensitive to own interpersonal style and opportunities for high personal impact.

Competency V-A Creates Positive Image
  69. Projects a positive self-image.
  70. Recognizes and exploits opportunities to create a positive image.
  71. Demonstrates concern to others for how they feel about consultant's presence in their organization.
  72. Documents and publicizes success.
  73. Uses success and publicity as keys to gain access to organizations and to get points across.

Competency V-B Uses Interpersonal Influence Strategies
  74. Plans influence strategy in advance; rehearses when appropriate.
  75. Demonstrates awareness of people's attitudes and motives and appeals to them.
  76. Uses strategies with great care to avoid the label of manipulator.
  77. Co-opts others; takes action to persuade others, resulting in a desired response.
  78. Influences environment or circumstances so others behave in desired fashion.

Competency V-C Demonstrates Concern for Impact
  79. Capitalizes on opportunities having high personal impact.
  80. Makes unsolicited offers to help and assistance.
  81. Influences others to get things done.
  82. Subordinates own needs to impact on user organization.

Competency V-D Communicates Ideas Clearly, both Orally and in Writing
  83. Speaks in a crisp, unhesitant, articulate manner.
  84. Writes clear, understandable reports and briefings.
  85. Uses graphics, colors, models and diagrams to enhance communications.

Competency V-E Understands, Addresses and Clarifies Own Impact on Others
  86. Addresses organizational member's expectations as a perceived catalyst for organizational change.
  87. Demonstrates sensitivity to how own actions, attitudes and behavior are perceived and when and how to enhance or soften their impact.

Competency V-F Uses Unilateral Power to Manage and Control OE Consultant Resources
  88. Makes decisions, sets goals and develops plans (while managing and controlling own OE resources).
  89. Manages subordinates, controls tasks and keeps the focus on outcomes (while managing and controlling own OE resources).
  90. Uses one-way influence: tells and directs (while managing and controlling own OE resources).
  91. Takes control of meetings and insists upon following design and/or initial objectives (while managing and controlling own OE resources.)

Competency Cluster VI

Diagnostic Skills
  Defined: Collects and organizes information gathered from different organizational sources; analyzes and provides that data to the user in a meaningful manner.

Competency VI-A Recognizes and Obtains Multiple Perspective on Situations/Problems
  92. Collects information from different levels within the organization and from its environment.
  93. Seeks additional perspective and advice from colleagues or other professionals.

Competency VI-B Uses Theories and Concepts to Develop and Articulate Diagnosis
  94. Constantly clusters small events into larger ones to identify trends, themes and root causes.
  95. Uses a variety of theories and concepts to understand and explain a situation.
  96. Uses several systems models to determine and illustrate interrelationships among data.

Competency VI-C   Demonstrates Rapid Pattern Recognition in an On-going Situation
97. Quickly senses emerging trends, problems or opportunities.
98. Rapidly classifies information into immediately usable concepts.

Competency VI-D   Effectively Uses Metaphors and Analogies
99. Uses concrete metaphors and analogies to enter another's frame of reference.
100. Facilitates understanding of a situation by presenting it as similar to another situation which is more easily understood.
101. Sets people at ease by reducing use of OE jargon.

Competency Cluster VII

Problem-Solving Skills
   Defined: Recognizes root causes of problems and recommends or helps user identify solutions; understands, identifies and uses the formal and informal power and influence structure of the organization.

Competency VII-A   Demonstrates Cause and Effect Thinking
102. Thinks in terms of why things happens as they do.
103. Analyzes events in terms of cause and effect.
104. Develops a series of inferential "if X, then Y" statements; anticipates consequences.
105. Develops contingency plans and alternative courses of action for anticipated consequences.

Competency VII-B   Identifies Key Themes in Data
106. Analyzes and distills data; identifies key components of a situation while isolating issues/groups and/or people causing the problems.
107. Has clear idea of what key themes mean and specifically addresses those meanings in feedback.
108. Uses tangible data to support and provide focus for key themes.

Competency VII-C   Identifies and Uses Influence Patterns
109. Attunes to the formal and informal patterns of influences; continually refines perceptions.
110. Identifies influential others and gains their support.
111. Understands political implication of others' behavior or action.

Competency Cluster VIII

Tactical Flexibility
   Defined: Recognizes and uses alternate courses of action to overcome barriers and achieve desired outcomes.

Competency VIII-A   Recognizes and Conforms to User Expectations and Organizational Norms
112. Matches own behavior and modes of communication (verbal, nonverbal, symbolic and written) with user expectations and organizational norms.

Competency VIII-B   Uses Problem-Focused Adaptation of Techniques and Procedures
113. Designs/adapts techniques or procedures to respond to user's desired outcomes.
114. Modifies operational design to meet emergent needs or expectations of others.
115. Makes on-line adaptation and generates alternatives.
116. Understands limits of redesigning an activity to avoid its multilation.

Competency VIII-C   Assumes and Differentiates Among Multiple Roles
117. Adopts multiple/separate roles for different situational demands and employs partner/user in complementary role when necessary.
118. Establishes multiple roles for two or more consultants.
119. Changes roles without seeming odd or manipulative.

Competency VIII-D   Takes Advantage of Opportunities
120. Responds selectively and rapidly to ongoing or upcoming activities which are opportunities for OE.
121. Links OE to organizational mission or internally/externally imposed demands.
122. Displays tactical flexibility by taking advantage of opportunities thru linking one OE operation to another.
123. Takes risk even with the possibility of failure.

Competency Cluster IX

Results Orientation
   Defined: Conducts OE operations to achieve timely, concrete, measurable outcomes.
Competency IX-A   Demonstrates Concern For Measurable Outcomes
124. Emphasizes outcomes based on specific tangible measurements.
125. Works with user to develop outcomes in terms of concrete performance
   measurements.
126. Establishes specific milestones to assess progress.
127. Determines, documents and evaluates net results of operations.
Competency IX-B   Heightened Sense of Time as a Resource
128. Uses effective time management techniques.
129. Allocates time for maximum payoff.
130. Discusses time as a cost with user.

that kind of sensitivity in selection. Therefore, it is in the area of training and development that the competency model is of greatest and primary utility.

Even within the training and development function, however, not all competencies can or should be trained. For instance, though "self-confidence" is an important competency, the trainability of such a personal characteristic in a sixteen-week course is very doubtful. Hence, 18 of the 33 competencies were selected as the "core" of the trainable OE consultant model.

Throughout 1981, the development of measurable training standards and procedures for the trainable competencies was undertaken. (See Figure 32.2.) How much "results orientation" was needed? When and how was a student able to demonstrate "tactical flexibility?" Once these types of questions were answered, the current course was looked at to see where and how the competencies were being taught. Adjustments were made to the course because of the competency model. Two major blocks of instruction were radically redesigned because of a lack of "fit" between the competencies needed and the ones being emphasized. Resequencing of some course material was needed because some competencies are prerequisites to others (e.g., "knowledge of the user organization as a system" precedes the "conformity to organizational norms").

OECS trainers had to be made aware of competencies in planning their instruction, evaluating student performance, and coaching for competency development. The summer of 1982 saw an interactive video course being developed for instructors. Consulting situations taken from the McBer study were acted out, filmed on video tape, and coded for the presence of competencies. The "discovery mode" of the tape allows the user to stop the video presentation at any point, test for recognition of a competency and ask questions about what he or she had just seen.

A forced-choice instrument is being developed to isolate competencies and get a better idea as to which ones seem to preclude the presence of others and which ones depend on the presence of others. This research will permit a more holistic and balanced competency profile than a mere taxonomy allows.

In summary, the Army's purely intuitive approach in developing the OEC course worked in the main. But knowing more explicitly what competencies are needed will allow a more systematic and purposeful approach to future adjust-

FIGURE 32.2   Sequence of Competency Based Training

1. Presentation of Overview of the objectives of the module (with reference to the terminal and intermediate learning objectives).
2. Introduction of the classroom-specific performance indicators, or proficiency criteria, which will be used to observe whether students have demonstrated the competency and to what extent.
3. The Recognition component, usually a case study to compare the presence of a competency in a given situation with a situation in which the competency was absent.
4. The Understanding component, usually a lecture presenting a model and background information about the competency.
5. The Self-assessment component, usually some form of self-rating to enable students to determine whether, or to what extent, they possess the competency.
6. The Skill Development component, usually a practice exercise and a debriefing, in which students can experiment with the new behavior, "get the feel of it," and otherwise apply it to their own use, measured against proficiency criteria.
7. The Job Application component, usually a simulation, role play, or direct performance or job-related activity, in which students apply the newly learned skill to an actual job situation, measured against proficiency criteria.
8. Follow up activities, usually including a review of the individual's performance during the module (video-taped or otherwise), goal setting and action planning, in which the student assesses the learning and makes a plan to improve upon it.

ments. It was as if throwing together the ingredients that seemed right produced a very edible cake, but now that we have a recipe, we can adjust it to different tastes. Since the "taste" for OE is now to use it in the largest of Army organizations and with the highest level clients, we can ask and now have a model to answer the questions, does a complex systems consultant need different competencies? And, if so, which ones? Also, the taste for OE is felt today on the battlefield. The Israeli Army has experimented successfully with battlefield consultants.[7] What special competencies are needed for consulting under fire?

Other uses—military and civilian—for the competency model can be: a guideline for continued professional development/continuing training of OE consultants, a baseline target for assessment center exercises, a philosophy for competency-based management courses, and a model for competency-based training of other occupations. This last aspect is quite appropriate in the Army since perhaps 80 to 85% of the competencies could be common to many leadership roles. For example, tactical flexibility is an important trait in commanders, military police, inspectors general, and dozens of other Army occupations.

CONCLUSION

The things a consultant must learn, the content of his or her profession, will continue to develop at a rapid pace. The present Army Chief of Staff General Edward Meyer wrote in 1981:

The organizational effectiveness concept is going to be important as we design the Army of the future. As our Army has fewer people in it, the ability to relate to subordinates, the ability to get the maximum out of every individual and every piece of equipment will become more and more important.[8]

And for now OECS has a good handle on the kind of person it will take to be a high-performing consultant in this Army of the future.

References

1. Headquarters, U.S. Department of the Army, Army Regulation No. 5-15, Effective 1 March 1982, Glossary 1.
2. Ferrier, Steve, Ph.D., Army Organizational Effectiveness and Navy Organizational Development: A Comparison and Contrast. *OE Communique,* Vol. 1-81, pp. 15-20.
3. Rogers, Bernard, U.S. Army, General, U.S. Army Command and General Staff College, Reference Book 12-2, Organizational Effectiveness, January 1978, p. 22.
4. Varney, Glenn H., *Exchange: The Organization Behavior Teaching Journal.* Published by the OB Teaching Association, 1978, vol. 3, no. 4, pp. 3-7.
5. Goleman, Daniel, The New Competency Tests: Matching the Right People to the Right Jobs. *Psychology Today,* 1981, 15, pp. 35-46.
6. Cullen, Bernard J., Klemp, George O. Jr., and Rossini, Lawrence A., *Competencies of Organizational Effectiveness Consultants in the U.S. Army.* Boston: McBer and Company, U.S. Army Research Institute, February 1981.
7. Burns, Frank, Major, U.S. Army, OE in the Israeli Army: An Interview with LTC S. Yoram Yair, Israeli Army. *OE Communique,* vol. 1-77, pp. 64-66.
8. Meyer, Edward C., General, U.S. Army, *OE Communique,* vol. 2-80, pp. 3-4.

33 Building on Competence: The Effective Use of Managerial Talent

Richard E. Boyatzis

ABSTRACT

Managerial talent is as valuable an asset for an organization as its patented processes, markets, plants, and cash. It is a long-term investment in the people that determine, lead, or guide the effective and efficient use of the other assets of the organization. This article reviews results from an empirical study of over two thousand practicing managers from twelve different organizations. It summarizes the findings as to which competencies are characteristic of superior performers and effective managers as compared with their less effective counterparts. The article describes how these competencies relate to the tasks and functions of management jobs and elements of the organizational environment, and outlines implications for many of the components of human resource management.

AUTHOR BACKGROUND

Dr. Richard E. Boyatzis is president and chief executive officer of McBer and Company. He has conducted research and consulted in the areas of organization and management development for a variety of industrial and government organizations, such as Monsanto, SCM, Owens-Illinois, Mattel, Twentieth Century-Fox, Cementos Anahuac, and the U.S. Navy. His recent research activities have included a generic competency model for managers, which is being used by the American Management Associations as a basis for a graduate degree program in management,

This article was adapted from *The Competent Manager: A Model for Effective Performance.* New York: John Wiley & Sons, 1982.

as well as for the design of other numerous development programs. Dr. Boyatzis has written numerous articles on human motivation, self-directed behavior change, and leadership that have appeared in scientific journals and magazines, and he is the author of *The Competent Manager.* He received both his Ph.D. and M.A. in social psychology from Harvard University, and his B.S. in Aeronautics and Astronautics from the Massachusetts Institute of Technology.

The efficient and effective use of most of an organization's resources depends on the decisions, actions, and thoughts of its managers. The managers are resources that are as vital to organizational performance as its patented products and processes, capital, or plant. Understanding the manager as a resource (that is, managerial talent) is a prerequisite to organizational improvement efforts whether the focus of these efforts is on strategy, structure, systems, culture, procedures, or whatever. This chapter opens with a description of an empirically derived competency model of managers and a model of effective performance. It then examines how these models and the concept of competence can be used as skeletal structure for an integrated human resource system within an organization.

EFFECTIVE PERFORMANCE

Effective performance of a job is the attainment of specific results (that is, outcomes) required by the job through specific actions while maintaining or being consistent with policies, procedures, and conditions of the organizational environment.

A Competency Model

A job competency is "an underlying characteristic of a person which results in effective and/or superior performance in a job" (Klemp 1980). An aggregate sample of over two thousand managers who were in forty-one different management jobs in twelve organizations was used to determine the competencies of managers that were common to those who were effective in their jobs and not to those who were less effective. Of the twenty-one characteristics initially hypothesized to relate to managerial effectiveness, thirteen were found to be competencies, as summarized in Table 33.1. They were: efficiency orientation, proactivity, diagnostic use of concepts, concern with impact, self-confidence, use of oral presentations, conceptualization (for middle and executive level managers only), use of socialized power, managing group process (for middle and executive

TABLE 33.1   Summary of Competency Results

Cluster	Competency	Threshold Competency	No Support Found
Goal and action management cluster	■ Efficiency orientation (skill, motive, social role)[1] ■ Proactivity (skill, trait, social role) ■ Diagnostic use of concepts (skill, social role) ■ Concern with impact (skill, motive)		
Leadership cluster	■ Self-confidence (skill, social role) ■ Use of oral presentations (skill, social role) ■ Conceptualization[2] (skill)	■ Logical thought (skill, social role)	
Human resources management cluster	■ Use of socialized power (skill, social role) ■ Managing group process[2] (skill, social role)	■ Accurate self-assessment (skill) ■ Positive regard[3] (skill)	
Directing subordinates cluster	■ Developing others (skill, social role)	■ Spontaneity (skill) ■ Use of unilateral power (skill, social role)	
Focus on others cluster	■ Perceptual objectivity (skill) ■ Self-control[4] (trait) ■ Stamina and adaptability (trait)		■ Concern with close relationships (skill, motive, social role) ■ Self-control (skill) ■ Stamina and adapatability (skill)
Specialized knowledge		■ Specialized knowledge (social role)	

[1]Items in parentheses indicate levels of competency for which empirical support was found.

[2]Supported as a competency at middle and executive level management jobs only.

[3]Supported as a competency at middle level management jobs only.

[4]Supported as a competency at entry level management jobs only.

level managers only), developing others, perceptual objectivity, self-control (at the trait level only), and stamina and adaptability (at the trait level only).

Six of the characteristics were found to be threshold competencies. They were: use of unilateral power, accurate self-assessment, positive regard (for middle level managers only), spontaneity, logical thought, and specialized knowledge.

For two of the characteristics, and at the skill levels of two of the other characteristics, either no support was found or the results suggested an inverse relationship to managerial effectiveness. They were: concern with close relationships, (at all levels of the characteristic), memory, self-control (at the skill level), and stamina and adaptability (at the skill level).

The competencies and threshold competencies were found to relate to each other at the skill level in a manner that yielded five clusters. These clusters were: the goal and action management cluster, which included efficiency orientation, proactivity, diagnostic use of concepts, and concern with impact; the leadership cluster, which included self-confidence, use of oral presentations, logical thought, and conceptualization; the human resource management cluster, which included use of socialized power, managing group process, accurate self-assessment, and positive regard; the directing subordinates cluster, which included developing others, use of unilateral power, and spontaneity; and the focus on others cluster, which included perceptual objectivity, self-control, stamina and adaptability, and concern with close relationships. The relationships within each cluster and between the clusters were thought to represent primary and secondary relationships, respectively, among the competencies. Although not at the skill level, the sixth cluster, specialized knowledge, is also an integral part of the model.

Differences were found in the degree to which one aspect of the environment in which managers operate demanded, required, or stimulated these competencies, in terms of whether the organizations were located in the public or the private sectors. Differences were also found in the degree to which one aspect of the managers' jobs demanded, required, or stimulated these competencies, in terms of entry, middle, or executive level management jobs.

Analysis of the combined effect of the set of competencies at the skill level was conducted to determine the degree of accuracy they would show in predicting the performance group (that is, poor, average, or superior performers) of the managers. The results indicated that the competencies correctly classified 51% of the managers, as compared to a random prediction that would have correctly classified only 33% of them.

A word of caution is in order regarding the summary and potential application of the findings from this study. First, the study was an initial attempt to determine what a generic competency model of management should include. A precise determination of causality would require additional research through longitudinal studies, as well as replication in other sets of organizations. Since the selection of organizations and jobs included in the study was not random, generalizing from these findings beyond a certain point may not be appropriate. Second, development of a comprehensive model of management would require that a similar effort be completed regarding additional job and environment variables not examined in this study.

Linking Competencies and Job Demands

The demands, or requirements, made on a person in a management job can be considered functional requirements of the particular job, situational demands, or specific demands emerging from day-to-day events on the job. Although it would be difficult to propose a framework for the varying day-to-day demands of a management job, the functional requirements of management jobs can be described in terms of five basic functions, which are: (1) planning; (2) organizing; (3) controlling; (4) motivating; and (5) coordinating. Each one of these functions can be further examined in terms of the various activities or tasks that constitute the function.

In performing the planning function, the manager is determining the goals and plans for the organization and communicating them to others. The type of planning may vary from management job to management job. An executive may be responsible for determining the strategic direction of the organization. He or she would be determining how the organization will respond to the marketplace and competitive environment in the years ahead. An entry level manager may be responsible for determining the performance goals of individual contributors (that is, salespeople, bookkeepers, engineers, production workers) and work units.

Although the specific types of goals and plans for which the manager is responsible may vary, every manager has some degree of responsibility for establishing goals and developing plans for achieving those goals. For some managers, the overall goal may be handed to them and they must establish the activity plan to achieve it. It is the competencies in the goal and action management cluster that will enable a manager to perform these tasks effectively, regardless of whether he or she is determining the goals and plans or working with others to develop them.

The degree to which the manager must communicate the goals and plans and the rationale for the goals and plans to his or her subordinates will also vary from job to job. When this is required of the manager, it is the competencies in the leadership cluster that will enable him or her to communicate this to others most effectively. Through the use of these competencies, the manager is communicating to others in the organization the direction of the organization's efforts and basic expectations as to the level of organizational performance.

In performing the organizing function, the manager is determining what human and other resources are needed and how they should be structured to accomplish the plan and achieve the goals. He or she is also establishing standards of performance for individuals and groups. Since all managers must be prepared to explain the organization of people, other resources, and activities to their subordinates, all managers should at least understand the basis for the organization of resources. Often, it is this understanding that is the basis for day-to-day decisions which the manager must make regarding the use of resources in addressing priorities and changes in priorities.

It is the competencies in the goal and action management cluster that enable the manager to determine effectively what resources are needed, how they should be structured, and what the standards of performance should be. These competencies are needed whether the manager is performing these tasks himself or herself or working with others to perform these tasks. It is the competencies in the leadership cluster that enable a manager to determine how the resources should be structured or organized, what the standards of performance should be, and communicate the rationale for the organization of resources to others. It is the competencies in the human resource management cluster that enable a manager to communicate the rationale and importance for the particular organization of resources to his or her subordinates as well as to other groups in the organization.

In performing the controlling function, a manager is monitoring the performance of individuals and groups, providing feedback on their performance, and rewarding and disciplining them based on their performance. Every manager has some degree of responsibility for monitoring performance of others or an organizational unit, providing feedback to others, and taking appropriate actions (that is, rewarding or disciplining others).

It is the competencies in the goal and action management cluster which enable a manager to effectively perform all of these tasks. Without these competencies, the manager cannot provide the *context* within which others' performance is being monitored, nor provide a basis for the rewards given nor disciplinary actions taken. It is the competencies in the directing subordinates cluster and the human resource management cluster that enable a manager to effectively provide performance feedback to others and dispense rewards and punishments.

As with the other functions, the way in which the tasks in the controlling function are performed will vary at different levels of management. For example, it is expected that at executive levels, managers will perform the monitoring and feedback tasks more through the use of management information systems than through personal interactions. As the methods of performing these tasks vary, so will the competencies needed by the manager to perform them. At the executive level, where personal performance monitoring and feedback is probably less frequent and possibly less relevant, the competencies in the directing subordinates cluster would be less relevant.

In performing the motivating function, a manager must build commitment, identity, pride, and spirit in the organization. He or she must also stimulate an interest in work and develop capability in his or her subordinates. Building the commitment, identity, and pride of others is a responsibility for the executive which is focused on the organization as a whole. For the middle level manager, the focus is more on the work group, or groups, reporting to him or her rather than on the organization as a whole. It is the competencies in the human resource management cluster and the leadership cluster that enable to manager to effectively perform these tasks. It is the competencies in the directing subordinates cluster that enable a manager to develop his or her subordinates' capability.

In performing the coordinating function, a manager must stimulate cooperation among departments, divisions, and other work groups. He or she must also negotiate resolution of conflicts or differences that emerge. It is the competencies in the human resource management cluster and the focus-on-others cluster that enable a manager to effectively perform these tasks.

As part of this function, managers are often expected to "represent" the organization and its products to various groups within the organization, but also to groups external to the organization (that is, the community, the financial community, professional associations, government agencies, consumers, etc.). This responsibility is particularly important to managers at executive levels. It is the competencies in the leadership cluster that enable a manager to effectively represent the organization and its products to others.

These relationships are summarized in Table 33.2. Certain activities, such as communicating and decision making, are essential tasks involved in the performance of each of the five basic functions of management. The competencies within a particular cluster will vary in their importance and relevance to effective performance of the tasks according to both the centrality of the function to the manager's job and the level of management job.

Links to the Organizational Environment

To complete the integrated model of management, links between the job demands, competencies, and aspects of the organizational environment must be established. It should be noted that when people think about the organizational environment, they usually consider aspects of the environment in which the organization exists (for example, the marketplace, culture, industry). These are aspects of the environment *external* to the organization. In a model of management rather than a model of organizations, the external environment should be addressed through elements in the organization's *internal* environment. These are the environmental demands over which managers have the most control. They should, and often do, reflect the external conditions. For example, the strategic condition of the industry of which an organization is a part and its position in the industry should be reflected in the organization's strategic plan. The comparability of the wages and benefits offered by an organization and its competitors, or other organizations, should be reflected in the organization's compensation and benefits system. Throughout this section, therefore, organizational environment or environment will refer to the *internal* organizational environment.

There are two elements in the organizational environment that appear most related to the performance of the planning function: (1) the strategic planning process; and (2) the business planning process. The strategic planning process requires assessment of the competitive position of the organization, anticipated changes in the marketplace and environment external to the organization (for example, changes in technology or consumer preferences), and the relative capability of the organization to respond to those changes. The business planning process includes the articulation of specific goals and objectives and can be considered the identification of the tactics associated with the overall strategy chosen. Business planning processes include operational planning (that is, day-to-day or week-to-week establishment of goals and planning of activities).

There is an additional aspect of the organizational environment linked to the planning function that is the organizational climate, or organizational culture. This was not listed above because it is not really a separate element in the organizational environment, but reflects the way in which people in the organi-

TABLE 33.2 The Relationship between Management Functions and Competency Clusters

Tasks	Relevant Competency Clusters
1. Planning function ■ Determining the goals of the organization ■ Establishing plans of action for achieving those goals ■ Determining how the plan should be accomplished ■ Communicating this to others	■ Competencies in the Goal and Action Management Cluster ■ Competencies in the Leadership Cluster
2. Organizing function ■ Determining what people and resources are needed to accomplish the plan ■ Determining how these people and resources should be structured to do it ■ Establishing the standards of performance ■ Communicating this to others	■ Competencies in the Goal and Action Management Cluster ■ Competencies in the Leadership Cluster ■ Competencies in the Human Resource Management Cluster
3. Controlling function ■ Monitoring performance of individuals and groups ■ Providing feedback to individuals and groups ■ Rewarding or disciplining based on performance	■ Competencies in the Goal and Action Management Cluster ■ Competencies in the Directing Subordinates Cluster and Human Resource Management Cluster
4. Motivating function ■ Building commitment, identity, price, and spirit in the organization ■ Stimulating an interest in work ■ Developing capability in subordinates	■ Competencies in the Human Resource Management Cluster and the Leadership Cluster ■ Competencies in the Directing Subordinates Cluster
5. Coordinating function ■ Stimulating cooperation among departments, divisions, and other work groups ■ Negotiating resolution of conflicts and differences ■ Representing the organization to outside groups	■ Competencies in the Human Resource Management Cluster and the Focus on Others Cluster ■ Competencies in the Leadership Cluster

zation perceive and react to the elements listed above. Aspects of the organizational climate should be considered indicators of how the people in the organization are responding to elements in the internal environment related to each of the managerial functions. With respect to the planning function, clarity and standards are particularly important aspects of the climate. The clarity aspect of climate refers to the degree to which people know what is expected of them (that is, performance goals) and why it is expected of them (that is, the rationale for those goals and how they correspond to the corporate objectives) (Klemp 1975). The standards aspect of climate refers to the degree to which challenging but attainable goals (that is, performance expectations) are established and the degree of emphasis placed on continually improving performance (Klemp 1975).

A manager's ability to effectively address these elements in the organizational environment through performance of the planning function will be a result of: (1) the planning tasks that are a part of his or her job, and (2) the degree to which he or she possesses the corresponding competencies in the goal and action management cluster and the leadership cluster.

There are seven elements in the organizational environment that appear most related to the performance of the organizing function:

- organization design
- job design
- the personnel planning process
- the selection and promotion system
- the succession planning and career pathing system
- the job evaluation system
- the financial resource allocation process

The organization design (that is, organization structure) should reflect appropriate flow of goods and information from one organizational unit to another, and the transformation of raw materials from suppliers to the products made available to customers. The design of jobs addresses the issues of whether the set of demands that constitute each job is meaningful to the job occupant, can be performed by a person, and correspond to the organization design.

The personnel planning process, formerly called the manpower planning process, is essential in determining the number and type of human resources needed to work toward the organization's goals. The selection and promotion system addresses the appropriate placement of personnel into jobs. The succession planning and career pathing system addresses the efficient placement of people into jobs in response to current needs and in anticipation of future needs. The job evaluation system provides the organization with a vehicle for assessing the value of the performance of each job to the accomplishment of its objectives (that is, the relative value of the contribution from people performing each of the jobs). The job evaluation system is most often used for establishing salary scales.

The financial resource allocation process includes allocating the financial and other resources to accomplish the organization's goals. This element is closely linked to the strategic and business planning processes, especially in addressing the formation and use of capital, cash flow, debt management, and similar considerations.

Another aspect of the environment linked to the organizing function is the organizational climate, in particular the responsibility, clarity, and standards aspects of climate. The responsibility aspect of climate refers to the degree and appropriateness of the delegation of decision-making authority to various jobs in the organization and the degree of risk taking encouraged (Klemp 1975).

A manager's ability to effectively address these elements of the organizational environment through performance of the organizing function will be a result of: (1) the organizing tasks that are part of his or her job; and (2) the degree to which he or she possess the competencies in the goal and action management cluster, the human resource management cluster, and the leadership cluster.

There are four elements in the organizational environment that appear most related to the performance of the controlling function:

■ product and business unit performance review process
■ individual performance review process
■ management information system
■ compensation and benefits system

The product and business unit performance review process and the individual performance review process provide management with an assessment of the performance of products, business units, and individuals toward the corporate objectives. They also provide managers and individual contributors with information as to how their own performance is contributing to corporate performance. Through these review processes and the management information system, managers are able to monitor and supervise others and the flow of work.

The compensation and benefits system is associated with performance of the controlling function as a system of rewards and punishments. This would work effectively only if the operation of the compensation and benefits system was directly related to job performance. To the extent that it is related to seniority, tenure, favoritism, or other forms of nonperformance-based discrimination, the compensation and benefits system would not be associated with effective performance of the controlling function.

An additional aspect of the organizational environment linked to the controlling function is the organization climate, in particular the rewards, clarity, and conformity aspects of the climate. The rewards aspect of the climate refers to the degree to which people feel that effective performance is recognized in an equitable manner and that rewards are used more often than punishments and threats (Klemp 1975). The conformity aspect of climate refers to the amount of rules and regulations that are thought to be unnecessary and the degree to which people are told how to perform their jobs (Klemp 1975).

A manager's ability to effectively address these elements in the organizational environment through performance of the controlling function will be a result of: (1) the controlling tasks which are part of his or her job, and (2) the degree to which he or she possesses the competencies in the goal and action management cluster, the human resource management cluster, and the directing subordinates cluster.

There are four elements in the organizational environment that appear most related to the performance of the motivating function: (1) the training and development system, (2) the compensation and benefits system, (3) the career planning process, and (4) the management information system. The training and development system includes developmental assessment of people's ability, mentoring or guidance, and training programs. All of these activities are oriented toward helping people improve their abilities. The compensation and benefits system is associated with the motivating function to the extent that it operates as an incentive system. The career planning process helps individuals make personal decisions about developmental activities and job changes in the context of long-term personal objectives and organizational needs. The management information system can be an element of the organizational environment related to the motivating function if it provides subordinates with performance information directly (that is, not requiring the personal interpretation of the manager). Of course, the management information system would only be effective in this context if individuals had clear and meaningful performance goals.

An additional aspect of the organizational environment associated with performance of the motivating function is the organizational climate, in particular the team spirit and rewards aspects of climate. The team spirit aspect of climate refers to the degree to which people feel proud to belong to the organization and they have a sense of relationships being warm, friendly, or trusting (Klemp 1975).

A manager's ability to effectively address these elements in the organizational environment through performance of the motivating function will be a result of: (1) the motivating tasks that are part of his or her job, and (2) the degree to which he or she possesses competencies in the human resource management cluster, the leadership cluster, and the directing subordinates cluster.

There are three elements in the organizational environment which appear most related to the performance of the coordinating function: (1) the public relations program, (2) the grievance procedure, and (3) the cross-functional and interdepartmental coordinating process. An appropriate grievance procedure can help establish a framework and setting for resolution of conflicts, whether the conflicts are based on an interpersonal difficulty, a problem with an organizational system or policy, or among organizational units. The cross-functional and interdepartmental coordinating process may be formal or informal. This process is often established on the basis of interpersonal relationships. The process may be supported by existence of "integrating" jobs, task forces, and other similar vehicles. The process is an important element in the potential of the organization to facilitate cooperation, collaboration, and smooth functioning. The public relations program addresses the representational task in the coordinating function. Aspects of this element may be focused on internal representation, often called internal communications programs. It is usually focused on representing the organization and its products to the world outside of the organization.

An additional aspect of the organizational environment associated with the coordinating function is the organizational climate; in particular, the team spirit and clarity aspects of the climate.

A manager's ability to effectively address these elements in the organizational environment through performance of the coordinating function will be a result of: (1) the coordinating tasks that are a part of his or her job, and (2) the degree to which he or she possesses the competencies in the human resource management cluster, the focus-on-others cluster, and the leadership cluster.

The linkages between competencies, job demands as presented by managerial functions, and the internal organizational environment are summarized in Table 33.3.

DEVELOPMENT AND USE OF MANAGEMENT COMPETENCE

Management Systems Diagnosis

The integrated model of management proposed in the prior section offers guidance in determining what aspect of an organization needs attention in solving problems, in particular problems that have to do with the human resources of the organization.

If an organization is performing effectively, in terms of its various performance measures and indicators, a periodic assessment of the soundness of its human resource system is useful. It can help to confirm the effectiveness and appropriateness of current policies, practices, systems, and programs. This type of assessment may take the form of a human resource system audit. Members of an organization could take the model proposed in Table 33.3 and systematically assess the status and responsiveness of the elements in its organizational environment to organizational needs. In addition, an assessment can be made as to the performance of its managers in terms of the five basic functions of management (that is, the management job demands). The organization can also assess the degree of managerial competence possessed by its management personnel. Through such an audit, each of the three components in the overall model can be assessed and the degree of fit of the three components can be determined.

The emphasis on *systematic* assessment cannot be exaggerated. Because of the commonly held perception that human resource systems and issues are "soft" and difficult to quantify, managers often settle for assessment methods and techniques that do not satisfy the level of rigor and soundness that they apply to assessment methods used in other aspects of organizational functioning, such as financial measurement, product quality measurement, and so forth. Although the field still has a long way to go, managers need not settle for this "soft" approach. Ongoing developments in the organizational and behavioral sciences make it possible for managers to use rigorous and sound assessment methods and techniques. The users of this technology should be cautious and use the same level of thoroughness in choosing these methods as they use in choosing methods for market research, product testing, financial performance analysis, and capital investment analysis.

Beyond a confirmation of current policies, practices, systems, and programs, a periodic assessment of the human resource system can help managers prepare for future needs. This is particularly important when an organization is contem-

TABLE 33.3 Elements of an Integrated Model of Management

Competency Clusters	Elements in the Organizational Environment
1. Planning function ■ Goal and action management cluster ■ Leadership cluster	■ Strategic planning process ■ Business planning process ■ Related climate: clarity, standards
2. Organizing function ■ Goal and action management cluster ■ Leadership cluster ■ Human resource management cluster	■ Organization design ■ Job design ■ Personnel planning process ■ Selection and promotion system ■ Succession planning and career pathing systems ■ Job evaluation system ■ Financial resource allocation process ■ Related climate: responsibility, clarity, standards
3. Controlling function ■ Goal and action management cluster ■ Directing subordinates cluster ■ Human resource management cluster	■ Product and business unit performance review process ■ Individual performance review process ■ Compensation and benefits system ■ Management information system ■ Related climate: rewards, clarity, conformity
4. Motivating function ■ Human resource management cluster ■ Leadership cluster ■ Directing subordinates cluster	■ Training and development system ■ Compensation and benefits system ■ Career planning process ■ Management information system ■ Related climate: team spirit, rewards
5. Coordinating function ■ Human resource management cluster ■ Focus on others cluster ■ Leadership cluster	■ Public relations program ■ Grievance procedures ■ Crossfunctional and interdepartmental coordinating processes ■ Climate: team spirit, clarity

plating a change in strategy, implementing a change in product technology, or offering new products to the marketplace.

Most often the perceived need for such an assessment, or audit emerges from recognition of a performance problem. This may appear as a loss of market share, high costs associated with turnover of personnel, a drop in earnings, failure of a new product to meet its performance expectations, difficulty in finding personnel for a rapidly growing company, or litigation. In this situation, the organization is most vulnerable to inappropriate diagnosis of the problems in the human resource system. Due to the pressure to identify the problem and take action to solve it, managers can easily fall prey to the confusion of symptoms and problems or choosing a problem for which they understood available solutions.

Using the model proposed in Table 33.3, guidance can be offered to the manager attempting such a diagnosis. The manager must first determine the domains in which the problem or problems exist. The domain refers to the aspects of organizational functioning which are involved. The domain of the problem may be clear. For example, a Fortune 500 industrial products company had lost 20% of its middle level managers in a year. Knowing that the industry average had been 12% and realizing that there was no dramatic change in the organization's external condition (for example, it did not have a product failure, or see the emergence of a new competitor), the managers focused on this problem. Termination interviews and follow-up conversations with several managers three months after they left were conducted. They discovered that the organization had not kept up with several competitors in incentive programs. The compensation and benefits system was not functioning adequately.

Unfortunately, identifying the domain of concern is not always so easy. Often, the domain is prematurely diagnosed because of a "pet" theory, peeve, or value of top management. Executives who do not believe that people can be trained or developed to perform jobs effectively will identify the human problem as a selection or promotion problem. You might hear them say, "If we could just get the right people, this inefficiency would stop." Or they might say, "Fire the lot of them. Let's give some of the young ones a chance. Some new blood, that's what we need!"

In situations in which the domain of the problem is unclear or highly complex, or certain executives are prone to postulate their pet peeve, a simpler but more general approach should be taken. Assessment of the organizational climate may be a useful beginning for such an analysis. Merely administering surveys or having group catharsis sessions will not provide the needed information. Surveys and other forms of information collection are helpful only if they are part of a procedure where the people involved wrestle with the interpretation of the data. Specific, concrete examples of situations in which something is not working adequately or causing difficulties is essential. This makes the interpretation of the data *real,* and avoids the possibility of a data-dump with no understanding of the information.

For example, through a climate survey process a Fortune 500 consumer products company discovered that middle management personnel felt that standards were substantially lower than they should have been. Several of the executives were shocked when they heard the middle level managers contend that mediocrity was being accepted in performance. The executives knew that the company had been reaching its objectives consistently. Managers in the marketing, research and development, and manufacturing departments explained that they could be doing even better (that is, there were lost opportunities). After probing several specific incidents which occurred over the prior three months, it was determined that the strategic plan was not understood by middle level managers and even a number of the executives. The business plans for the current year were comprehensive and well integrated with the strategic plan, but no one was paying attention to them. The plans were not functioning as guides for the managers in day-to-day decision making. The problem in this organization was uncovered after several days of meetings with various groups in the company. The product, business unit, and individual performance review processes were not functioning adequately. At the business unit level, several businesses were kept, despite their lack of attainment of performance objectives. This resulted in managers questioning the credibility of the strategic plan and deciding to shelve it. At the product level, several innovations had failed in one of the business groups. Research and development funds were continually being allocated to these products and new marketing campaigns were being developed. Managers within this group interpreted this information to mean that the business plan for those products was not to be taken seriously. The products were to be given a chance, no matter what the plan stipulated as the benchmarks for continuing investment in them. At the individual level, effort and not accomplishment of results was being rewarded through salary increases.

What had started as a climate survey process to "take stock of where we are" uncovered a major problem in the internal organizational environment. The company was able to define the problem domain and began to explore various alternative methods for addressing the problem with their product, business unit, and individual performance review process. As this company found, the source of the problem may be either: (1) the implementation and use of an existing system or process which is adequately designed; or (2) the inadequate or inappropriate design of that element in the organizational environment (that is, a problem at the organization design level). The company discovered that at the product and business unit levels, the problem was implementation of the system which they had. The strategic and business planning process provided the framework and mechanism for these reviews. They were not being conducted properly and the results were not being addressed. At the individual performance review level, the company found that the system was not designed properly. The system allowed individuals to receive favorable reviews for demonstrated effort toward objectives, but did not hold people accountable for results in terms of goal attainment.

Unfortunately, such an assessment may not go far enough to establish whether the malfunction of this element of the organizational environment is a problem or merely a symptom of another problem. The problem may be found in the assessment of the performance of the management job. Are the managers performing the basic functions and tasks that are part of the demands of their jobs? If a number of elements in the organizational environment related to one particular managerial function are malfunctioning, then that particular function needs to be examined. If the difficulty appears endemic to performance on a number of managerial functions, then there may be a complex set of problems occurring. In either case, the problem may be found in: (1) the implementation and practice of the managerial functions where the jobs have been designed appropriately; or (2) the management jobs are not designed to respond to the organization's needs (that is, a problem at the job design level).

In the example discussed, an observation had been made by one of the executives that some of his peers did not understand that they were supposed to take action concerning products and businesses based on the performance reviews at these levels. He claimed that several of the executives "couldn't tell if they were alive with a stethoscope." The corporate vice president of personnel reviewed the performance of three particular executives through documents available. He did not want to arouse fears or suspicions until he had a chance to examine the data.

The corporate vice president concluded that none of these three executives were performing the controlling functions of their jobs completely. They were not providing feedback, nor taking action when the information was negative. They would let the information emerge in other forms, and their boss, the president, could take action if he wanted. As long as events proceeded smoothly and positive results were obtained, they performed the controlling function of their jobs admirably. The corporate vice president of personnel decided that he would have to confront the president with this information. He felt that there was nothing wrong with the implementation and use of the business unit and product performance review processes, but that these three particular executives were not performing an important aspect of their jobs.

Again, the inadequate or inappropriate performance of basic managerial functions may be an indication of a more fundamental problem than the design of the jobs or implementation of the existing design of the jobs. The problem may be that people who are in the jobs are not using the corresponding competencies which enable them to perform the managerial functions. This may be the result of a problem in: (1) the selection or promotion system, which means that people with the needed competencies are not being placed into the jobs; or (2) the training and development system, in that people being placed in the jobs are not prepared adequately; or (3) the design of the management jobs or elements in the organizational environment that are not utilizing the talent available in the managers (that is, the managers have the needed competencies, but the use of the competencies is not being stimulated, demanded, or supported). In the first case, the problem may be that the selection and promotion criteria are not adequate. In the second case, there may be a problem in the competency development of managerial personnel. In the third case, the problem is probably an underutilization of managerial talent available within the organization.

In the example being discussed, the problem was difficult to see. The president of the company argued with the corporate vice president of personnel about his assessment of the three executives. The president felt that they were all loyal, competent managers who had ben committed to the company for many years. After several hours, the president finally agreed that each of the three executives had made some poor decisions regarding certain products and businesses in the past two years. He added, "Their history of performance with this company, and exceptional accomplishments in their current jobs during the prior five years gives them a basis for making a few mistakes." The corporate vice president of personnel suggested that his information did not mean that they should be fired, but that the competitive pressure in their businesses had increased tremendously in the past four years and that they had not grown along with their jobs in this one aspect. He recommended some training programs.

The criteria for promoting someone into one of these three jobs had changed in the past four years. Without recognition of this change in the competencies needed by executives in these jobs over this period, the company had not taken steps to help the executives grow and develop, nor to change the people in the jobs. Even if the three executives took early retirement or left for other companies, without altering the selection criteria, the president might find himself with the same problem next year.

In assessing the human resource system through such an "audit trail," there may be one or more of four basic types of problems uncovered.

- adequately designed organizational systems, procedures, processes, or programs are not being utilized
- elements in the internal organizational environment or management jobs are not designed appropriately
- placement of personnel (i.e., selection and promotion) is not being conducted with appropriate criteria
- development of personnel is not being adequately addressed (i.e., the quantity of activity is not adequate, the types of activities are not appropriate, or the objectives and criteria for design of the development activities are inappropriate)

Each one of these problems may also be symptoms of one of the other types of problems.

An Integrated Human Resource System

Attempts to address any of the types of problems mentioned above may be only temporarily effective or merely remove the problem from sight if they are not conducted as part of an integrated human resource system. Although some companies, government institutions, and other organizations are making advances toward this objective, most still suffer from fractionated, piecemeal, or ad hoc components and, therefore, lack an integrated human resource system (Kotter & Boyatzis 1979).

The lack of a model or paradigm on which to base such a system inhibits progress. The management model proposed and the concept of competence, specifically job competency, can be used as the basis for developing and operating an integrated human resource system. It will not be easy. A great deal more research, development, and testing will be needed before all of the specifications for such a system can be determined. The following sections of this chapter attempt to describe what a number of the components in such a system may require. They are presented as possibilities, not definitive answers.

An overall context of the discussion of specific topics is human resource system planning. A human resource system or human resource development plan should become a part of the strategic and business plans generated by organizations. The plan would encourage recognition of the importance of the human resources, or assets, of the organization, and would provide a process in which to examine the adequacy of the organization's systems, policies, procedures, and programs. It would help organizations to determine the desired and expected return on human assets. It would also aid organizations in preparing for changes in human resources available in the future (i.e., changes in work force values, number of people available, preparation of the work force prior to entering the organization, and so on) in the same way that organizations prepare for changes in product technology and market demand.

Development of Competency Models

Prior to application within a human resource system, the competencies needed must be identified and empirically determined. Because the competencies are related to effective performance of a particular job within a specific organizational environment, models must be developed and tested on many, and eventually all, of the jobs and job families (that is, sets of jobs with similar job demands) within an organization. Identification of tasks and functions (that is, job demands) is needed, but is not sufficient.

Research designs must incorporate methods that allow for an inductive identification of competencies and not merely test a priori models. The validated competencies in a model must also be related to the functional and task demands of jobs and to aspects of the organizational environment to be of the most utility. The methods must include a number of operant techniques to avoid method-bound or culturally specific results. The results must be cross-validated if applications to certain human resource systems are desired, such as selection, promotion, or performance appraisal systems, to conform to legal and ethical guidelines.

Job Design

Management jobs can be designed to allow managers to utilize the competencies they have (Hackman & Oldham 1980). Of course, in order to change the functions and tasks involved in a management job, those which currently exist must be identified and clarified. Such changes would utilize these competencies of the managers and have the effect of reducing some of the work load of other managers. It would also communicate, through job requirements, to managers in various jobs that they should have or develop these competencies.

Selection and Promotion System

The most critical implication of the findings and model for selection and promotion systems is that there *are* competencies that are directly related to effectiveness in management jobs. Assessment of these competencies can be incorporated into selection systems, but probably require different assessment technology than many organizations are using. Testing job applicants for specialized knowledge or assessing their ability to perform job functions does not provide an opportunity to assess competencies (Klemp 1980). Even assessment centers, as they are often designed, currently do not assess competencies as much as they assess performance of job functions (Williamson & Schaalman 1980). By tapping generic characteristics, rather than specific manifestations of them (that is, specific behaviors), new groups of people in the work force can be identified who have the capability to perform management jobs effectively. A person who has developed and demonstrated these competencies, but who for various reasons has not had the opportunity to do so in a job directly related to an opening, may be overlooked during a typical screening process, but would be identified through an approach based on these competencies.

Promotion procedures can be developed to assess a person's possession and demonstration of the competencies. Again, such procedures would require an assesssment technology somewhat different from that currently used in most organizations. Some organizations have designed their assessment centers and selection techniques to assess competencies by methods such as coding semi-structured interviews, simulations, and operant tests (Williamson & Schaalman 1980; Boyatzis & Williamson 1980). Basing such systems on competencies would require that organizations be prepared to replace seniority-based systems with competency-based systems. Such systems would highlight the "competencies" that people need in order to perform certain management jobs, and would avoid the often costly mistake of promoting the most effective individual contributor into a management job (for example, promoting the best salesperson to sales manager). When such procedures fail, it is probably because the competencies that enabled the person to be effective as an individual contributor are not the same competencies needed to perform effectively as a manager.

Performance Appraisal

Ideally, a performance appraisal process should include two components: (1) assessment of recent performance; and (2) assessment of development needs. The assessment of recent performance, which can be considered the performance assessment component, is the determination of whether the individual has met output objectives or task accomplishment objectives. The assessment of development, which can be considered the competency assessment component, is the documentation and recognition of competencies that the individual has demonstrated in the recent performance period and identification of competencies that should be addressed during the next performance period. To conduct the latter component of the performance appraisal, the competencies related to effective performance in the job would have to be identified. In addition, methods for documenting the demonstration of the competencies would have to be developed. These may take the form of behaviorally anchored scales or a review of specific incidents or events that occurred during the performance period. With such methods, both the manager and the person being reviewed can state their perceptions and test the accuracy of these perceptions against the other's perceptions.

Succession Planning and Career Pathing

The findings and model have implications for succession planning and the development of a career pathing system. In such a system, people can be offered a variety of options that would facilitate development of the competencies needed to perform effectively in current and future jobs. Instead of leaving the development of the generic characteristics to chance, a career pathing system in an organization can facilitate and recognize the development of such characteristics. It will also help ensure that the organization has a sufficient number of qualified people for their managerial jobs. For example, if an organization knows that a certain person would like to hold an executive management position a number of years in the future, the organization can assist this person in preparing for the promotion, and for becoming effective in the job once it is obtained, by a sequence of middle level management jobs. These jobs can be chosen so that the person can develop the generic characteristics that are known to be needed for effective performance of an executive management job.

Career Planning

The findings and model have implications for the individual's counterpart (that is, career planning) to the succession planning and career pathing system that primarily addresses the organization's needs. Through the same type of framework and assessment methods used in the selection, promotion, or performance appraisal systems, the individual can determine what type of job for which he or she is best prepared in terms of competencies. The individual would be able to identify a sequence of jobs in an organization that would satisfy future needs. These jobs could be identified in terms of development of competencies needed for the subsequent jobs. A career planning process based on competencies would also help the individual identify developmental activities that would be the most efficient and appropriate preparation for the desired career progression.

Training

One option an organization has available is to provide special training programs for its managers. The findings and model have implications for the choice of training programs and the design of the training. To be effective in competency development, the training must involve far more than teaching participants about the functions of management.

Evidence indicates that these and other generic characteristics can be developed through specific training and education programs (McClelland 1978; McClelland & Winter 1969; Winter, McClelland, & Stewart 1981; Miron & McClelland 1979; Boyatzis 1976; McClelland & Burnham 1976). There are a variety of ways to design such training and education programs. To maximize the probability that training will result in the development of competencies, there are six stages of adult competency development that should be incorporated in the training design (McClelland 1965; Knowles 1970; Kolb & Fry 1975; Kolb

& Boyatzis 1970). The six stages, called the competency acquisition process, (Spencer 1979) are:

- recognition of the competency
- understanding of the competency and how it relates to managerial effectiveness
- self-assessment or instrumented feedback on the competency
- experimentation with demonstrating the competency, or demonstrating it at a higher level of effectiveness
- practice using the competency
- application of the competency in job situations and in the context of other characteristics

People must learn how to recognize the competency and understand how it relates to performance. Material covered in activities in these stages provides people with specificity as to which competencies and behaviors are being addressed. The competencies demonstrated by superior-performing managers become the actual training or educational objectives. The various assessment methods used in the competency research studies provide specific, behavioral descriptions of how superior-performing managers think and act. They also provide case study material of people using the competencies in specific situations and events that occur on the job. People are not left wondering what relevance the training or education program has following these first two stages.

Once the image of how a superior-performing manager should think and act has been developed through the first two stages (that is, an image of the ideal), people can determine where they stand on each competency through the use of self-assessment or assessment instruments specifically chosen to measure the competency (McClelland & Boyatzis 1980). Without this third stage, people are left wondering whether they have the competency or to what degree they possess the competency.

The integration of the information on how superior-performing managers think and act (that is, the ideal) and how the potential manager stands on these competencies (that is, the real) forms the beginning of a process of self-directed change that has been shown to result effectively in behavioral change (Kolb & Boyatzis 1970). It is through the realization of personal discrepancies between the ideal and the real on such competencies that people can perceive and feel a need for change.

The fourth stage is experimentation, allowing people to try new behaviors. During this stage, people explore how the generic characteristic may be developed. In some situations, this means experimenting with ways of thinking and acting that are different from those used previously. In other situations, this means expanding the repertoire of ways of thinking and acting related to the competency.

During the fifth and sixth stages of the process, practice and application, people refine and continue to develop ways of thinking and acting that relate to the competency. They engage in activities in which they must apply these competencies to specific situations and problems encountered in their jobs. Without the last two stages, people may not be prepared to utilize the new or different competencies in real settings.

Training or education programs designed to develop competencies in managers must utilize methods of experiential learning and self-directed change as part of an adult education experience (Kolb & Boyatzis 1970; Knowles 1970). Missing any of the stages will result in only partial development of the competency.

Often training that is directed at "teaching people about the job" involves transmitting a great deal of specialized knowledge to the job incumbent. Programs designed to teach someone about their job are really attempting to develop a person's social role level of the competencies needed for the job. Therefore, whether the training objectives are to improve a person's competencies, or to help them understand the responsibilities and demands of their job, experiential learning will be more effective than mere communication of facts and concepts.

An individual who wants to develop managerial competencies may choose to attend a formal educational program. A number of colleges and universities have begun to utilize competencies as guides to and objectives for their educational programs (Winter, McClelland, & Stewart 1981).

Other Developmental Activities

The findings and model have implications for two other types of developmental activities: (1) developmental assessment; and (2) mentoring or guidance. Developmental assessment of competencies can help individuals and their managers choose appropriate training programs that the individual may attend. It may also help to provide benchmarks for the individual in terms of his or her career plan, or for the organization in terms of the timing of promotion decisions. It can provide recognition of competencies developed and, therefore, contribute to the competency assessment component of the performance appraisal process.

The concept of competence and results from job competency studies can provide the framework for the oldest management development practice used, providing guidance for subordinates. Although this has been termed many things over the years (for example, apprenticeship, mentoring, coaching, and so on) the competency framework can help managers increase the effectiveness of their day-to-day advising of subordinates as to development and performance improvement.

Compensation and Benefits

The findings and model have implications for assessing the utility of the compensation and benefits system. Does the dispensation of compensation and benefits correspond to the demonstration of needed competencies? Does the system provide incentives for performance improvement and competency development?

Other Human Resource System Components

There are a number of components of an integrated human resource system that are not directly affected, but may be indirectly affected by the findings and the model. Although a personnel planning process would not be directly altered through application of these findings or concepts, an organization's ability to identify, hire, and keep personnel with the desired competencies would result in more efficient use of human resources. This may reduce the number of people needed, or make human resources available for work on other activities.

Although a job evaluation system must be based on the relative contribution of a person in each job to the organization's overall performance, understanding the competencies needed to perform each job effectively may help in establishing comparability to wages paid by other organizations for people performing similar work. Also the development of a selection and promotion system based on competencies would contribute information to the job evaluation system as to the relative ease of obtaining and retaining people with the needed competencies.

The findings and model can even make a contribution to the effectiveness of a grievance procedure. Through the use of the model, an organization can make appropriate diagnoses as to what may be causing or stimulating the grievances, and determine what steps should be taken to address the grievance and preclude its occurrence, if possible, in the future.

CONCLUDING COMMENTS

If you are a part of the scientific management tradition, you may view competencies as the specifications for the human machinery desired to provide maximum organizational efficiency and effectiveness. If you are part of the humanistic management tradition, you may view competencies as the key that unlocks the door to individuals in realizing their maximum potential, developing ethical organizational systems, and providing maximum growth opportunities for personnel. If you are one of the people who work in organizations or one of the people who studies, thinks about, and tries to help organizations utilize their human resources effectively, this model and these findings and model should provide a needed relief from the eclectic cynicism or parochial optimism concerning management that many of us have developed.

References

Boyatzis, R. E. Power motivation training: A new treatment modality. In F. Seixas & S. Eggleston (eds.), *Work in progress on alcoholism: Annals of the New York Academy of Sciences,* 1976, *273,* 525–32.

Boyatzis, R. E., & Williamson, S. A. *Designing, selecting, and using assessment methods in human resource development.* Paper presented at the National American Society of Training and Development Convention, Anaheim, CA, April 1980.

Hackman, J. R., & Oldham, G. R. *Work redesign.* Reading, MA: Addison-Wesley, 1980.

Klemp, G. O., Jr. *Technical manual for the organization climate survey questionnaire.* Boston: McBer and Company, 1975.

Klemp, G. O., Jr. (ed.). *The assessment of occupational competence.* Report to the National Institute of Education, Washington, DC, 1980.

Knowles, M. S. *The modern practice of adult education: Androgogy versus pedagogy.* New York: Association Press, 1970.

Kolb, D. A., & Boyatzis, R. E. Goal-setting and self-directed behavior change. *Human Relations,* 1970, *23*(5), 439–57.

Kolb, D. A., & Fry, R. Toward an applied theory of experimental learning. In C. Cooper (ed.), *Theories of group processes.* London: John Wiley & Sons, 1975.

Kotter, J. P., & Boyatzis, R. E. *Human resource management: The challenge of the 1980s.* Unpublished paper, 1979.

McClelland, D. C. Toward a theory of motive acquisition. *American Psychologist,* 1965a, *20*(2), 321–33. (a)

McClelland, D. C. Achievement motivation can be developed. *Harvard Business Review,* 1965b *43*(6), 6–24, 1978. (b)

McClelland, D. C. Managing motivation to expand human freedom. *American Psychologist,* 1978, *33*(3), 201–10.

McClelland, D. C., & Boyatzis, R. E. New directions for counselors from the competency assessment movement. *Journal of Personnel and Guidance,* 1980, pp. 368–72.

McClelland, D. C., & Burnham, D. H. Power is the great motivator. *Harvard Business Review,* 1976, *54*(2), 100–11.

McClelland, D. C., & Winter, D. G. *Motivating economic achievement.* New York: The Free Press, 1969.

Spencer, L. M., Jr. *Identifying, measuring, and training soft skill competencies which predict performance in professional managerial, and human service jobs.* Paper presented at the Soft Skill Analysis Symposium, Department of the Army Training Development Institute, Fort Monroe, VA, August, 1979.

Williamson, S. A., & Schaalman, M. L. Assessment centers: Theory, practice, and implications for education. In G. O. Klemp, Jr., (ed.), *The assessment of occupational competence.* Report to the National Institute of Education, Washington, DC, 1980.

Winter, D. G., McClelland, D. C., & Stewart, A. J. *A new case for the liberal arts.* San Francisco: Jossey-Bass, Inc., Publishers, 1981.

34 Organization Inquiry: Towards a New Model of the Action Research Process

Abraham B. Shani
William A. Pasmore

ABSTRACT

Action research is one approach that has been identified as a potent method for bringing about change in organizations and advancing scientific knowledge. Through in-depth, inductive study of an action research effort in one organization, three elements crucial to achieving the intended outcomes of action research emerged: (1) contextual factors, (2) quality of relationships, and (3) the quality of the action research model itself. Within these three elements, concepts, variables, and processes were inductively derived and linked together to form a model of the action research process in organizations.

AUTHOR BACKGROUND

Abraham B. Shani is associate professor of management at the California Polytechnic State University. He received his Ph.D. in organizational behavior from Case Western Reserve University in 1981. Professor Shani has published several articles dealing with sociotechnical system design, parallel organizations, expectancy and leadership, and action research methodology. As an action researcher, he has worked with diverse organizations such as Israeli Defense Forces, Israeli Institute for Productivity, Blue Cross, Babcock and Wilcox, EPA, and the U.S. Army in Europe. His current interests are in the areas of durability of planned change efforts, development of methodologies for producing useful organizational knowledge, and organizational learning.

This study was undertaken as part of the first author's doctoral dissertation. The authors greatly appreciate the help of Frank Friedlander, David Kolb and Paul Gerhart during their research.

William A. Pasmore is associate professor of organizational behavior at the Weatherhood School of Management, Case Western Reserve University. As an educator, he has taught courses in work design, organizational behavior, organizational theory, and organizational development. As a certified consultant, he has contributed to the sociotechnical design and organization development of both industrial and nonindustrial firms. His research has appeared in a number of journals, including *Human Relations, Administrative Science Quarterly,* and *The Journal of Applied Behavioral Science.* He is coauthor of *Sociotechnical Systems: A Sourcebook.* Professor Pasmore is a graduate of Purdue University, where he received both his B.S. in industrial management and his Ph.D. in administrative sciences.

Action research (AR) may be defined as an emergent inquiry process in which behavioral science knowledge is integrated with existing organizational knowledge and applied to solve real organizational problems. It is simultaneously concerned with bringing about change in organizations, in developing self-help competencies in organizational members, and in adding to scientific knowledge. Finally, it is an evolving change process that is undertaken in a spirit of collaboration and co-inquiry.

ACTION RESEARCH FEATURES

Action research occurs in a natural setting, addresses specific issues, involves collaboration and inquiry, involves the action researcher firsthand, involves mutual education, involves the creation of a parallel structure, develops self-help competencies, strives for systems development, lays the foundation of a learning system, and generates valid knowledge.

AR occurs in a natural setting. Unlike laboratory research in which situations are artificially created to study the relationships between independent variables, or survey research that is detached from respondents, AR takes place in a natural setting.

AR addresses specific issues. Because AR is conducted in part to assist the social system under study in resolving critical dilemmas or finding solutions to significant problems, it must address itself to these issues directly rather than to take a global approach to organizational improvement. The final test of the success of an AR effort, therefore, is always measured in part by the impact it has on problems stated by members of the target system, not the researcher.

AR involves collaboration and co-inquiry. Since the members of the system under study are the ones with knowledge of the problems facing the system and are also the ones who must eventually live with the changes that are made, it is important that they be an integral part of the effort. A complete utilization of organizational internal resources, integrated with external resources, is likely to lead to a higher quality outcome for the AR effort.

AR involves the action researcher first hand.   Rather than maintaining the aloof role traditionally occupied by organizational researchers, the action researcher allows himself/herself to become immersed in the system under study. Full understanding of the system prior to and after the intervention activity requires that the action researcher be intimately acquainted with the system and how it functions, and have strong and open relationships with system members. Further, with intimate first hand knowledge, the action researcher can make suggestions that are more appropriate for the organization, and understand more fully the findings of his/her evaluation.

AR involves mutual education.   In order to build mutually satisfactory relationships of a collaborative nature, the action researcher must spend time educating the client in theories of organizational behavior, methods of organizational research, and techniques of organization development. At the same time, the action researcher must himself/herself be educated by the client in the important aspects of the system, its environment, and its people.

AR involves the creation of a parallel structure.   At its most basic level, AR involves unlocking data which are trapped in the minds of organizational members generating shared understanding of the data and applying them effectively toward organizational improvement. The parallel structure or the *AR system* (as labeled by the authors), makes the above happen. Moreover, the purpose of the AR system is to provide a permanent, institutionalized framework for a cross-section of representative organizational members to jointly inquire into an organizational phenomenon, using the variety of available resources. It is a parallel structure because it functions outside of the normal chain of command and serves as an open pipeline through which ideas and organizational knowledge within and outside the boundaries of the organization can be collected, shared, and acted upon.

AR develops self-help competencies.   Because action researchers are usually not permanent members of the social systems they interact with, and because the solutions that are found to problems are static while conditions faced by the system are dynamic, it is important to build into the system the capacity to study itself and detect areas where change is needed. Hence, the action researcher does not play the role of expert consultant, who graces the organization for a short time with his or her presence and then leaves the organization wondering what it was that he or she did. Instead, the action researcher endeavors to transfer his skills to members of the organization through training and by allowing them to struggle with issues even when he or she might have a clear idea of what solutions would probably work. Rather than breeding dependency, the action researcher attempts to increase the independence of the organization in recognizing and dealing with new problems as they arise.

AR strives for systems development.   Rather than focusing on a narrow aspect of organizational design, or simply trying to improve human processes without regard to the structure within which they must unfold, the AR approach emphasizes the consideration of organizations as holistic entities consisting of many interdependent parts. Effective change in this view requires working on more than one element of the organization at a time. Often this means that quick change in one or two areas is postponed until changes in other areas can be made as well; finding slack resources for change is not easy under any circumstances, so it is important that the resources that are available be channeled toward the accomplishment of objectives that have the greatest potential for the long range improvement of the overall organization.

AR lays the foundation of a learning system.   Beyond understanding the system being investigated, AR creates a climate that encourages learning about organizations in general. Furthermore, AR helps the organization develop its capacity to improve itself. By creating the AR system, which represents both the knowledge and resources that reside within the organization, and by focusing (among other things) on the learning process, the AR effort sets in motion the creation of a learning system.

AR generates valid knowledge.   Although AR has been called nonscientific by some because it lacks the rigor of other methods, there can be no doubt that the development of open, collaborative, and mutually satisfying relationships between the action researcher and members of the organization allow data to be collected that reflect more closely the true state of people's attitudes and emotions. Under these conditions, the potential for artifacts such as demand characteristics and evaluation apprehensions (Rosenthal & Rosnow 1969) are minimized as subjects become investigators and vice versa. Furthermore, the ongoing involvement of the action researcher provides opportunities to collect rich data through observation of the system in action under both good and bad conditions. Perhaps no other methodology is so well suited to studying the process of change in organizations, since change itself is a continuous and unpredictable happening. While the data produced by AR methods may not take the form of neat, numerical tables, they nevertheless contribute rich insights that add to the stock of applied behavioral science knowledge.

While the benefits of AR outlined above are attractive, attaining them is not easy and certainly never guaranteed. The complexity of the AR process has long been recognized (Corey 1953; Shepard 1960; Rapaport 1970; Foster 1972; Brown 1972; Cherns 1976; Susman & Evered 1978; Cunningham 1978; Margulies & Raia 1978; Holman 1979; Sanford 1981). Nevertheless, this complexity has not been given sufficient attention (Brown & Kaplan 1981; Shani 1981; Pasmore & Friedlander 1981; Agrawal et al. 1981). These oversights have produced a lack of emphasis on understanding the factors and their interrelations that might enhance or inhibit the AR process and its outcomes. This study attempts to propose a complete model of the AR process. Such a model is needed if AR is to research the goals intended by its creators, and fulfill the objectives it has promised.

THE MODEL OF THE ACTION RESEARCH PROCESS: AN OVERVIEW

This section presents an overview of the model generated through this study. The famework presented in Figure 34.1 identified the main factors influencing the evolutionary process and outcomes of the AR effort. The formulation envisions four major sets of interrelated factors/processes with a number of variables that affect the AR process: (1) contextual factors; (2) quality of relationships; (3) quality of the AR process; and (4) outcomes of the AR effort.

The Contextual Factors

The first set of factors includes four kinds of contextual factors. This set of factors is seen as contextual to the AR effort because they set the stage of the formation of relationships. The importance of understanding the characteristics of the parties involved in an organizational change effort in order to improve its quality is discussed by Argyris (1970) and Alderfer and Brown (1976).

Each of the variables can have a positive or negative effect on AR outcomes. For example, diffuse goals for the AR effort held by different individuals make it difficult to set an overall direction for the activity or to gain cooperation, whereas shared goals enhance collaboration and risk taking. Similarly, the participation of opinion leaders and occupants of powerful positions in the AR process signals that the activity is important, while reticence on their part to become involved clearly marks the AR effort as a low priority activity.

Organizational factors also influenced AR outcomes. Here, an organization with a flat structure, a climate of openness and participation at all levels, and moderate stability is thought to be a more receptive site for AR than one with a hierarchical structure, poor climate, and extremely high or low stability.

Environmental factors afffecting AR outcomes included the culture and political climate of the larger context in which the organization operated and the perceived demands of the environment for changes in organizational structure, procedures, or goals. Openly manipulative environments place little value on human development versus goal accomplishment, and call for either immediate change or no change at all make poor settings for AR. Finally, whether the researchers work to establish a learning climate and model co-inquiry skills, or instead remain aloof and mysterious will also have effects on AR outcomes.

The Quality of Relationships

If there is a single variable that differentiates AR from other research methodologies, and has the most significant impact on the outcomes eventually attained through AR, it would be the quality of the relationships between the researchers and the members of the organization. The context in which the AR effort takes place does much to determine the quality of relationships that will eventually evolve; but the management of relationships is equally important and depends on the state of several relationships between specific factors.

First, the level of trust inherent in the relationship between the researchers and organizational members will determine the level of openness and risk taking place during the inquiry and change process (Gibb 1964; Simendinger 1980). Secondly, the demonstrated concern for the other, as indicated by the levels of empathy, respect, and acceptance inherent in the relationships will either create a climate conducive to mutual exploration or one of shallow participation. Throughout the course of the AR effort, as decisions are made that shape the destiny of the effort and that of those taking part in it, an equality of influence must be reached. Power between the researchers and organizational members should be balanced, and conflict, when it occurs, should be constructively resolved rather than avoided. Finally, over time, a shared language should develop which allows participants to share in the researcher's theory development and vice versa. In this way, common understandings can be hammered out concerning different perceptions of the same events or circumstances thereby leading to mutually satisfying outcomes of the AR effort (Freire 1973).

The Action Research Process

The quality of the AR process is measured by two main components. These processes are influenced by, and, at the same time influence, the quality of the relationships among the actors involved in the effort. Furthermore, since the quality of the relationships is constantly changing throughout the evolution of the effort, the clear distinction of what variables influence what other variables is very difficult, if even possible.

The inquiry process, or more precisely the co-inquiry process, is seen as a key feature of the AR process. As its name implies, it is a joint process of the people involved to study a phenomenon. In co-inquiry, not only are organizational members involved in the venture, but it is recognized that they hold a variety of resources, knowledge, and skills that are needed to make inquiry successful. The inquiry process itself—where people are involved in the effort, information is available, people collaborate in the process of gathering valid knowledge, generate shared understanding of the organization, and people experiment with the knowledge being generated—leads to significant changes and influences the quality of outcomes of the AR effort.

The implementation process is the second main component of this set (see Figure 34.1). As experimentation continues to take place, and ideally becomes an integral routine of organizational life, ideas for change are enhanced and reformulated. This leads to implementation and systematic diffusion of changes through the system. The diffusion process is influenced by the quality of the relationships that developed and transformed through the course of the effort. At the same time, the quality of the implementation process has a direct influence on the outcomes of the AR effort.

Outcomes of the Action Research Effort

Last, Figure 34.1 focuses our attention on the outcomes of the AR effort. The authors have identified four main clusters of factors that seem central in assessing the effectiveness of AR efforts: (1) the degree of organizational improvement in terms of helping the organization to better accomplish its goals and missions; (2) the degree of improvement of the quality of worklife; (3) the

FIGURE 34.1　The Complete Theory of the Action Research Process

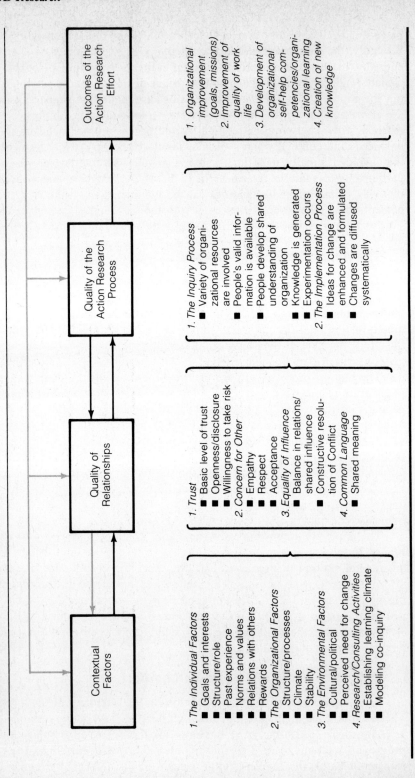

degree of development of the self-help competencies of the organization, or the degree to which the organization is able to learn about itself and act on this learning, i.e., organizational learning, and (4) the generation of new knowledge.

These outcome factors and their quality are a result of the complex interactions and activities that occur throughout the course of the AR effort. As Figure 34.1 indicates, outcomes are influenced by the quality of the AR process, which, in turn, is influenced by the quality of the relationships which are themselves influenced by contextual factors. To add to this complexity, the literature suggests that outcomes later influence the quality of the relationships that are developed, and at times, even the contextual factors. While the theory presented in Figure 34.1 helps explain and predict more precisely the reasons for the variety of approaches and outcomes associated with AR efforts, even it is too simplistic to capture the overall complexity and dynamics of AR. The next section of this paper poses some of the questions that still remain.

THE COMPLEXITY OF THE AR PROCESS: AN ILLUSTRATION

The following seven propositions serve as examples of the complexity of the AR process. Their discussion will demonstrate both the complexity and the need for further investigation of the AR process.

- *Proposition 1.* The greater the organizational need for change, the more willing participants will be to participate in the change process.
- *Proposition 2.* The greater the organizational need for change, the more difficult it is to foster relationships that are conducive to change.

Organizational members, being aware that there is a threat to organizational survival, are likely to be willing to participate in an effort to improve conditions. Furthermore, they will be more likely to work together to confront organizational issues and contribute their knowledge to solve problems. However, both the relationships between the actors involved and the impact of the contextual factors on them are more complex than the proposition above indicates.

Under conditions where the need for change is the greatest, organizational members are most likely to experience apprehension, anxiety, and uncertainty, which make relationship building difficult and resistance to change likely. Hence, when the need for organizational change is the greatest, organizational members will be most willing and least able to participate in action research.

- *Proposition 3.* To the extent that organizational members are involved in the action research effort, it is more likely that the effort will lead to organizational improvements.
- *Proposition 4.* The greater variety of resources represented in the action research system, the more difficulty there will be in arriving at shared solutions to common problems.

■ *Proposition 5*. The more the ideas for change cross organizational boundaries, the more difficult it will be for the action research system to generate a shared understanding and recommend agreed-upon solutions.

The involvement of organizational members in the AR effort is crucial to its success. The more people involved in the study, the lower the resistance to change and the higher the probability that the recommendations conceived will lead to practical organizational improvements.

In the ideal, we would like to have maximum variety of organizational resources which not only represent all parts of the organization, but also represent the variety of perceptions different people have about the organization. At the same time, however, the greater the variety of resources that are represented in the action research system, the more difficult it is to arrive at shared understandings, let alone shared solutions to problems. The more points of view, the more difficult it is to reach a common perception of the situation.

Moreover, people from different parts of the organization are likely to have more difficulty in seeing common problems; they are also likely to have more difficulty in understanding these problems that are not in their part of the organization. One can argue that a person needs to experience a problem that might look like a major one for one person can be perceived as minor to another. Hence, the more change needed in the total organization versus its parts, the more involvement will be required; but the greater the involvement, the lower the changes are that agreed-upon solutions can be found. Again, organizations most in need of change through AR are least able to use AR effectively.

■ *Proposition 6*. To the extent that the quality of the relationships within the action research system and the organization is high, the quality of the implementation process will likely be high.
■ *Proposition 7*. The more that ideas for change hold high potential for change, the more likely that their diffusion throughout the organization will be difficult.

The important role that the quality of relationships plays throughout the action research effort has already been discussed. The implementation process is just another place where their importance becomes evident. Furthermore, since the implementation of the changes is one of the most difficult steps in the action research effort, it is here where relationships are most important in overcoming the natural roadblocks to change.

As the implementation process unfolds, ideas for additional improvements are likely to emerge. Often, because the AR system is more mature, these ideas are likely to hold even greater potential for change than those originally conceived. At the same time, these ideas, because of their potential to change the system, will create the most anxiety. People are sometimes afraid to support them because of their potential to alter existing relationships and rewards; at other times, people will tire of the change process, and seek stability rather than compounded and continual experimentation with new ways of doing things. As a result, the resistance to their diffusion throughout the organization is likely to be high. Hence, those ideas that take the longest to develop and hold the greatest potential for organizational improvement are least likely to be implemented. In a sense, the more successful the AR process is initially, the more likely it is to ultimately fail.

SUMMARY

Action research was defined as an inquiry process to study phenomena in organizations in ways acceptable to both organizational members and the scientific community. Appreciating the complexity of the AR effort helps us understand why many organizations as well as organizational scientists want to avoid doing it, or have different versions of it. If anything, this study points toward the variety of things that AR can do, the difficulty in doing them, the even greater difficulty in doing them well, and recognizes that there are few, if any, shortcuts.

At the same time, the payoffs from being engaged in an AR effort for both the organizational members and the action researcher are invaluable. If the process is managed well, the results will be better than the ones that would have been achieved in either "consulting" or "research," both in terms of bringing about change in organizations and advancing scientific knowledge.

References

Agrawal, B. C. et al., "An Experiment in Action Anthropology: Yanadi Action Research Project in India," *Human Organization,* 1981, 40, pp. 87–90.

Aldefer, C. P., & Brown, D. L., *Learning from Changing.* California: Sage Publications, 1976.

Argyris, C., *Intervention Theory and Methods.* Boston: Addison-Wesley, 1970.

Brown, L. D., "Research Action: Organizational Feedback, Understanding and Change," *Journal of Applied Behavioral Science,* E, 6, 1972, pp. 687–713.

Brown, L. D., & Kaplan, E. R., "Participative Research in a Factory," in Reason and Towan (eds.) *Human Inquiry.* New York: John Wiley & Sons, 1981.

Clark, A. W., (ed.) *Experimenting with Organizational Life: The Action Research Approach.* New York: Plenum Press, 1976.

Clark, P. A., *Action Research and Organizational Change.* London: Harper and Row, 1972.

Corey, S. M., *Action Research to Improve School Practices.* New York Teachers College: Columbia University, 1953.

Cunningham, B., "Action Research: Toward a Procedural Model," *Human Relations,* 29, 3, 1976, 215–38.

Foster, M., "The Theory and Practice of Action Research in Work Organizations," *Human Relations,* 25, 1972, pp. 529–56.

Freire, P., *Pedagogy of the Oppressed.* New York: Harper and Row, 1968.

Friedlander, F., "Alternative Modes of Inquiry," presented at APA Conference, San Francisco, 1977.

Lewin, K., "Action Research and Minority Problems," *Journal of Social Issues,* 2, 1946, pp. 34–36.

Pasmore, W. A., Shani, A., & Mietus, J., "Technological Change and Work Organization," presented at the NATO Conference: Work, Organizations and Technical Change, Garmisch: West Germany, 1981.

Shani, A. B., "Understanding the Process of Action Research in Organizations: A Theoretical Perspective," unpublished doctoral dissertation, Case Western Reserve University, 1981.

Shepard, H. A., "An Action Research Model," in *An Action Research Program for Organization Improvement.* Ann Arbor: The University of Michigan Press, 1960.

Susman, G. I., & Evered, R. D., "An Assessment of the Scientific Merit of Action Research." *Administrative Science Quarterly,* 23, 1978, pp. 583–603.

35 Coping with Organizational Stress

Cary L. Cooper

ABSTRACT

This article attempts to highlight the sources of organizational stress. It also attempts to provide a framework that would help organization development practitioners, personnel consultants, and occupational medics with some suggestions as to how one should cope with stress in organizations. This article is based on seven years of research carried out by Professor Cooper and his team at the University of Manchester Institute of Science and Technology.

AUTHOR BACKGROUND

Cary L. Cooper received his B.S. and M.B.A. degrees from the University of California, Los Angeles, his Ph.D. from the University of of Leeds (U.K.), and an honorary M.Sc. from the University of Manchester (U.K.). He is the only American to hold a chair in a British University in the field of management and is currently Professor of Organizational Psychology and Head of the Department of Management Sciences, University of Manchester, Institute of Science and Technology. Professor Cooper is past chairman of the Management Education and Development Division of the American Academy of Management (the first time a U.K.-based academic has been elected to this post). He was also elected as a fellow of the British Psychological Society. Professor Cooper is currently the editor of the international quarterly journal, *Journal of Occupational Behaviour*. He is

This is a shortened and edited version of a paper which appeared in the Journal of Occupational Medicine, 1978, Vol 20 (6), 420–27. We should like to thank the Journal for permission to publish.

also on the editorial board of a number of other scholarly journals, including *Group and Organization Studies* and *Leadership and Organization Development Journal*. He has published twenty-eight books and is also the author of over one-hundred fifty scholarly articles in academic journals and a frequent contributor to *The (Manchester) Guardian* and the *The London Times* newspapers on topics of managerial and organizational behavior. He has been invited to give major addresses in universities abroad including Free University of Berlin and the University of Bergen, and to government bodies all over the world; including Japan, Norway, West Germany, Israel, Holland, Sweden, and Portugal.

There is considerable evidence from studies in the workplace[1] to suggest that occupational stressors are contributory factors in coronary heart disease (CHD) and other stress-related illnesses. Occupational stress is here defined as negative environmental factors or stressors (e.g., work overload, role conflict/ambiguity, poor working conditions) associated with a particular job. Inherent in the concept of occupational stress is the interaction of the person with his or her environment, giving rise to coping or maladaptive behavior, and ultimately, to stress-related disease.[2] Lofquist and Dawis[3] have labelled this interaction the *person environment fit*. Therefore, it is important to identify those factors within the occupational environment that impinge on the individual, creating conditions for stress-related illness and potential CHD.

A number of studies have identified factors *intrinsic to the job* that have been found to be stressors linked to CHD. Marcson[4] and Shepard[5] found, for example, that physical health is adversely affected by repetitive and dehumanizing environments (e.g., paced assembly lines). In addition, Kritsikis, Heinemann, and Eitner,[6] in a study of 150 men with angina pectoris in a population of over 4000 industrial workers in Berlin, reported that more of these workers came from work environments employing conveyor-line systems than any other work technology.

Other work has given attention to quantitative and qualitative *work overload* as a source of stress. In a study of 100 young coronary patients, Russek and Zohman[7] found that 25% had been working at two jobs and an additional 45% had worked at jobs which required (due to work overload) 60 or more hours per week. They add that although prolonged emotional strain preceded the attack in 91% of the cases, similar stress was only observed in 20% of the controls. Breslow and Buell[8] have also reported findings that support a relationship between hours of work and death from coronary heart disease. In an investigation of mortality rates of men in California, they observed that workers in light industry under the age of 45, who are on the job more than 48 hours a week, have twice the risk of death from CHD compared with similar workers working

40 or under hours a week. There is also some evidence that (for some occupations) qualitative overload is a source of stress. French, Tupper, and Mueller[9] looked at qualitative and quantitative work overload in a large university. They used questionnaires, interviews and medical examinations to obtain data on risk factors associated with CHD for 122 university administrators and professors. They found that one symptom of stress, low self-esteem, was related to work overload, but that this was different for the two occupational groupings. Qualitative overload was not significantly linked to low self-esteem among the administrators but was significantly correlated for the professors. The greater the "quality" of work expected of the professor, the lower the self-esteem. They also found that qualitative and quantitative overload were correlated to achievement orientation. And more interestingly, in a follow-up study, achievement orientation correlated very strongly with serum uric acid.[10] Several other studies have reported an association of qualitative work overload with cholesterol level: a tax deadline for accountants,[11] medical students performing a medical examination under observation,[12] etc. French and Caplan[13] summarize this research by suggesting that both qualitative and quantitative overload produce at least nine different symptoms of psychological and physical strain: job dissatisfaction, job tension, lower self-esteem, threat, embarrassment, high cholesterol levels, increased heart rate, skin resistance, and more smoking.

Another potential source of occupational stress is associated with a person's *role* at work. In particular, he or she may experience role conflict, which exists when an individual in a work role is torn by conflicting job demands, or doing things he or she really does not want to do or does not think is part of the job specification. The most frequent manifestation of this is when a person is caught between two groups of people who demand different kinds of behavior or expect that the job should entail different kinds of behavior or functions. Shirom et al[14] collected data on 762 male kibbutz members aged 30 and above, drawn from 13 kibbutzim throughout Israel. They examined the relationships between CHD (myocardial infarction, angina pectoris, and coronary insufficiency), abnormal electrocardiographic readings, CHD risk factors (systolic blood pressure, pulse rate, serum cholesterol levels, etc.) and potential sources of occupational stress (work overload, role ambiguity, role conflict, lack of physical activity). Their data was broken down by occupational groups: agricultural workers, factory groups, craftsmen, and white collar workers. It was found that there was a significant relationship between role conflict and CHD (specifically, abnormal electrocardiograph readings), but for the white collar workers only. In fact, as we moved down the ladder from occupations requiring great physical exertions (e.g., agriculture) to least (e.g., white collar), the greater was the relationship between role ambiguity/conflict and abnormal electrocardiograph findings. Role conflict was also significantly related to an index of ponderosity (excessive weight for age and height). It was also found that as we go from occupations involving excessive physical activities to those with less activity, CHD increased significantly. The inference is that as we move toward clerical, managerial, and professional occupations, we may be increasing the likelihood of occupational stress due to identity and other interpersonal dynamics and less to the physical conditions of work.

There are a number of studies that relate occupational level to CHD and mental ill health (MIH), of which Marks[15] provides an excellent review. The majority of these studies support the proposition that risk of CHD rises with occupational level.[16] Substantial national analyses of both British and American mortality data lend support to these studies. Not all researchers, however, are in agreement. Pell and D'Alonzo,[17] in a highly self-consistent longitudinal study of Dupont employees, found that incidence of myocardial infarction was inversely related to salary roll level. Stamler, Kjelsberg, and Hall[18] and Bainton and Peterson[19] also came up with contradictory results. A further group of researchers have added confusion by finding no relationship between CHD and occupation: Berkson[20] for blue versus white collar Negroes; Spain[21] for Jewish salesmen versus other occupational groupings; and Paul[22] for different job levels at the Western Electric Company.

Another important potential stressor associated with one's organizational role is *responsibility for people*. One can differentiate here between *responsibility for people* and *responsibility for things* (equipment, budgets, etc.). Wardwell et al[23] found that responsibility for people was significantly more likely to lead to CHD than responsibility for things. Increased responsibility for people frequently means that one has to spend more time interacting with others, attending meetings, working alone, and, in consequence, as in the Goddard study,[24] more time in trying to meet deadline pressures and schedules. Pincherle[25] also found this in a UK study of 2000 executives attending a medical center for a medical check-up. Of the 1200 managers sent by their companies for their annual examination, there was evidence of physical stress being linked to age and level of responsibility; the older and more responsible the executive, the greater the probability of the presence of CHD risk factors or symptoms.

Other research[26] has also established this link. The relationship between age and stress-related illness could be explained, however, by the fact that as the executive gets older the executive may be troubled by stressors other than increased responsibility, for example, as Eaton[27] suggests, by (1) a recognition that further advancement is unlikely, (2) increasing isolation and narrowing of interests, and (3) an awareness of approaching retirement. Nevertheless, the finding by French and Caplan[24] in the Goddard study does indicate that responsibility for people must play some part in the process of stress, particularly for clerical, managerial, and professional workers. They found that responsibility for people was significantly related to heavy smoking, diastolic blood pressure, and serum cholesterol levels—the more the individual had responsibility for things as opposed to people, the lower were each of these CHD risk factors.

COPING WITH STRESS

The evidence in the foregoing discussion suggests that certain occupational stressors may be major contributors to coronary risk. However, the task of removing harmful stress from the workplace is not as easy as it first appears. In the majority of cases occupational stressors and the experience of stress are directly linked to job satisfaction; hence the paradox that a factor that is a major source of satisfaction can, at the same time, increase the individual's risk of CHD. Therefore, the task of coping strategies is to prevent the deleterious effects of stress, while not eliminating it as a source of satisfaction. Selye[28] emphasizes that "we must not suppress stress in all its forms, but diminish distress and facilitate eustress" which he defines as "the satisfactory feeling that comes from the accomplishment of tasks we consider worthwhile."

There is evidence that different people are able to sustain stress with differing degrees of effectiveness; it has been found that people with certain types of behavior patterns are more likely to be at coronary risk than others.[29] The "subjective" nature of stress means that levels of stress will differ between people according to their circumstances; similarly different coping techniques will be more or less effective according to the individual.[30]

A number of possible methods have been studied under laboratory conditions and in the workplace, which may help us understand and cope with stress. First, there are the *cognitive coping strategies* open to the individual for stress reduction. Second, there are the tension-reducing or relaxation techniques. And finally, there is the social support one can get from one's work and family group.

Cognitive Coping with Stress

Lazarus[31] suggests that in a stressful situation the individual uses an active coping strategy which he or she believes will counter the threat. If active coping strategies fail, then cognitive coping is induced in the form of "situation redefinition" or "denial". This has been interpreted in another way by identifying response categories in terms of behavioral, cognitive, or decisional control over the impending stressor.[32] Behavioral control is the availability of a response that may directly influence or modify the objective characteristics of a threatening event, whereas cognitive control is the way in which an event is interpreted or appraised. Decisional control is the opportunity to choose among various courses of action. Sells[33] believes that the lack of control over a stressful stimulus is a *necessary* if not *sufficient* condition for stress. Therefore, if personal control of the objective conditions is lost, it can be regained in subjective terms by incorporating a potentially threatening event into a cognitive plan, thereby reducing anxiety.[34]

A number of potential environmental stressors have been used in experiments to test the effectiveness of cognitive coping.[35] It was found that denial and intellectualization reduced stress, as measured by physiological reactions. This work was criticized for its methodological weaknesses by Holmes and Houston[36] who tested the nature and effectiveness of more specific cognitive strategies for handling stress. They employed two strategies of redefinition and affective isolation, with the hypothesis that these would evidence less response to stress than subjects not instructed in the use of these strategies. The experimental results revealed that the cognitive coping subjects were more effective in reducing stress than the control subjects.

Houston[37] using groups of high trait and low trait denial subjects, found that in stressful situations high trait denial subjects had significantly less physiological arousal, less affective disturbance, and significantly better performance than low trait denial subjects. Therefore, characteristic users of denial found it served as an effective way to cope with threat in stressful situations. This conclusion is further supported in another study by Houston[38] where he found that low trait denial subjects were less effective copers in a situation involving threat to self-esteem. In addition, anticipatory cognitive defense mechanisms have been found to decrease levels of arousal under conditions of uncertainty.[32]

There is sufficient evidence to suggest that cognitive coping can be effective in reducing stress conditions; however, as yet, this work has largely been (experimentally) confined to laboratory conditions, with little effort to develop a practical strategy for implementing such approaches under real-life conditions.[36]

Relaxation Techniques Coping with Stress

Very often stress is an unavoidable part of the person's occupation; for example, managers and air traffic controllers, who are under stress for different reasons, but at the same time derive a great deal of satisfaction from this jobs. Recently, there has been a growing interest in individual relaxation techniques that reduce the tension of a stressful lifestyle, through techniques such as yoga, meditation, and biofeedback. These purport to help the individual "wind down" after a stressful day, and as such, may help to reduce the deleterious effects of occupational life on physical health.

Meditation involves restricting awareness to concentrate on one single source or "mantra,"[39] an activity that is repeated twice a day for approximately 20 minutes. Transcendental meditation (TM) has been reported to help work adjustment through the reduction of tension.[40] TM is not only limited to the easing of stress, but also may have other beneficial effects, as Kuna[41] reviews. It has been found to increase productivity in businessmen, improve attention, increase discriminatory capacity, alertness, and reaction time. Frew[42] concludes that meditators demonstrate increased job satisfaction and performance, less anxiety about promotion, faster work rates, and more organizational authority and responsibility. However, effectiveness of TM largely depends on the orientation and motivation of the individual. Goleman[43] identifies the importance of meditation in its capacity to break up the threat-arousal-threat spiral, so that after the individual has experienced a stressful event he or she can relax himself or herself. He adds that meditators recover more quickly from stress than nonmeditators, and are better equipped to deal with stress in their lifestyle.

Other techniques involve making the individual aware of the body's reaction to stress, whether it be physiological or psychological. Two techniques have been found to help individuals with stressful behavior reduce their life stress—through *anxiety management training* and *visuo-motor behavior rehearsal.*[44] The individual learns the cues which signal the onset of stress, such as tightening of the muscles or increase in heart rate, and he is then taught to reduce this stress through training in muscle relaxation. This has been reported by Suinn[44] to be effective in lowering stress in people faced with a variety of different personal and occupational problems.

A similar technique, using yoga and biofeedback, has been used with reasonable success in a preliminary study by Patel.[45] Individuals were taught how to relax and meditate while having continuous information about their progress from a biofeedback instrument, which served to reinforce their responses.

Social Support and Coping with Stress

A large number of studies have produced evidence indicating the importance of the social group to the individual as a source of job satisfaction.[46] In brief, the human relations approach to the workplace emphasizes the role of social relationships in achieving a satisfying and rewarding environment. There is now evidence that the individual's work group and social group may provide effective social support which offsets the effects of stress and CHD.[47] In particular, a study of social stress in Japan reveals marked differences in rates of CHD compared to the U.S., which appears to be related to certain features of Japanese lifestyle.[48] In 1962 the ratio of death rate from CHD to the total death rate was reported to be 33.2 for U.S. whites and 8.7 for the Japanese.[49] Matsumoto[48] reports that two major factors seem to be increasingly implicated in the development of CHD, namely high fat diet and emotional stress. The diet hypothesis is strongly supported by the fact that the diet in Japan derives less than 16% of its calories from fat as compared to 40% in the American diet. Also, by the findings relative to the difference between Japanese living on different diets,[50] social stress has been found to be related to CHD and is associated with the elevation of serum cholesterol. Matsumoto reports these findings from other studies on medical students during exams,[12] accountants during tax preparation deadlines,[11] and patients undergoing surgery. Matsumoto hypothesizes that the in-group work community of the individual in Japan, with its institutional stress-reducing strategies, plays an important role in decreasing the frequency of disease—"the deleterious circumstances of life need not be expressed in malfunctioning of the physiologic or psychologic systems if a meaningful social group is available through which the individual can derive emotional support and understanding." Indeed, Japan has a cultural norm towards strong group dependence and, although it has a highly structured society, it is able to counterbalance deleterious stress through effective social support.

PREVENTATIVE APPROACHES TO HEALTH-RELATED BEHAVIORS AND CHD

As we have seen, certain health-related behaviors and specific types of behavior patterns give rise to CHD risk. Therefore, in order to reduce the risk engendered by these behaviors, we need to adopt a preventative approach based on behavior modification. Ball and Turner,[51] referring to CHD, say that "since it is largely caused by man's way of life, it is only be behavioral change that the number of deaths can be reduced." However, Henderson and Enelow[52] point out that changes in behavior "must be viewed in relationship to the social structures in which they operate." Preventative measures in this area have been characterized by two main approaches—first, through the modification of single risk factors based on an individual counseling approach, and second, through the modification of one or more risk factors based on a mass education approach.

Recommendations made by the Joint Working Party[53] refer to dietary changes by reducing the present amount of fat in the diet from over 40% of total calories down to 35%. This could be achieved through a general reduction of saturated fat intake by partially substituting polyunsaturated fats, fruit, and fresh vegetables. The modification of eating habits could be achieved through education via the family doctor or clinic staff, possibly in conjunction with food and diet questionnaires to monitor eating habits.[54]

While diet may be more readily modified, smoking presents more of a problem to people who have become addicted. Although there is no doubt about the role of smoking as a CHD risk factor, there does not appear to be an effective way of inducing cessation of smoking. The Joint Working Party[53] recommends the "advice of a doctor to his patient" as one of the more effective methods of persuasion. Blackburn[54] also advocates this approach in conjunction with audiovisual aids, group meetings, aversive conditioning, and relaxation techniques. The hypothesis that smoking is necessarily a contributor to CHD does not go unchallenged and Seltzer[55] points to several studies which have found no association between smoking and CHD.[55, 56, 57, 58] Seltzer[59] claims that many other factors have to be taken into account, in particular the "constitutional" hypothesis—that coronary-prone individuals "self-select" themselves into smoking. Also, in studies where people have given up smoking, a number of habits may have been modified at the same time which have independent effects on CHD incidence.

The evidence regarding physical exercise is rather more sparse. An extensive review of the literature concerning the role of physical activity in the prevention and therapy of CHD concludes that different manifestations of CHD have varying associations with physical activity; however, it finds sufficient support for the opinion that increased physical activity should be propogated.[22] Physical exercise is recommended elsewhere[53, 54, 60]—first, as a protective measure against a sedentary lifestyle, and second, as a therapeutic measure.

The second approach based on mass education has involved a number of multifactorial studies that have been carried out with the aim of controlling one or more risk factors and measuring the effects over time to determine whether there has been any significant reduction in CHD risk as a result of screening and intervention. WHO[61] trials were, first, set up to estimate the extent to which the main risk factors of CHD can be modified in industrial workers using primarily a health education approach and a realistic level of resources; and second, to estimate the effect of such changes on CHD incidence, and the consistency of results between different countries. The study has been set up in four countries with screening and intervention in the form of treatment and advice on choles-terol-lowering diet, cessation of smoking, daily physical exercise, weight reduction, and hypotensive drug therapy. Certain drawbacks have been identified that can be generally applied to the multifactorial approach:

- In a very large study with limited resources, adherence to advice tends to be poorer than in a small intensively staffed pilot study.
- This particular study has only been going on for a short time, and it remains to be seen whether enthusiasm can be maintained over a period of years.
- The design is such that the effect of the program can only be assessed in the intervention community taken as a whole with an inevitable dilution of results.

Ball and Turner[51] also express scepticism as to the success of multifactorial approaches, saying that where several risk factors are present, trials attempting to alter any one factor are likely to give inconclusive results. Criticism has been made about the massive expenditures on the large-scale intervention trials to the comparative exclusion of further research in the etiology of CHD.[50] Furthermore, they claim that even if the intervention programs are successful, CHD will still remain a "major killer of epidemic proportions" and they conclude that funds ought to be diverted toward further research into the determinants of CHD. Several large-scale intervention studies have been carried out with varying degrees of success and their prospects are reviewed by Stamler and Berkson[62] who emphasize the need for "second generation trials" based on earlier studies.

CONCLUSION

Those of us interested in the health of people at work, in identifying, coping with, and preventing occupational ill health, cannot strongly enough support Kornhauser's[63] sentiments about the condition that organizations today should be concerned about:

mental health is not so much a freedom from specific frustrations as it is an overall balanced relationship to the world which permits a person to maintain realistic, positive belief in himself and his purposeful activities. Insofar as his entire job and life situation facilitate and support such feelings of adequacy, inner security, and meaningfulness of his existence, it can be presumed that his mental health will tend to be good. What is important in a negative way is not any single characteristic of his situation but everything that deprives the person of purpose and zest, that leaves him with negative feelings about himself, with anxieties, tensions, a sense of lostness, emptiness, and futility.

References

1. Margolis, B. L., Kroes, W. H., & Quinn, R. P. An unlisted occupational hazard. *Journal of Occupational Medicine,* 16:654–61, 1974.

2. Cooper, C. L., & Marshall, J. Occupational sources of stress: A review of the literature relating to coronary heart disease and mental ill health. *Journal of Occupational Psychology,* 49:11–28, 1976.

3. Lofquist, L. H., & Dawis, R. V. *Adjustment to Work.* New York: Appleton Century Crofts, 1969.

4. Marcson, S. *Automation, Alienation and Anomie.* New York: Harper and Row, 1970.

5. Shepard, J. M. *Automation and Alienation.* Cambridge, Mass.: MIT Press, 1971.

6. Kritsikis, S. P., Heinemann, A. L., & Eitner, S. Die angina pectoris im aspekt ihrer korrelation mit biologischer disposition psychologischen und soziologischen emflussfaktoren. *Dtsch Gesundheit,* 23:1878–85, 1968.

7. Russek, H. I., & Zohman, B. L. Relative significance of hereditary diet and occupational stress in CHD of young adults. *American Journal of Medical Science,* 235:266–75, 1958.

8. Breslow, L., & Buell, P. Mortality from coronary heart disease and physical activity of work in California. *Journal of Chronic Diseases,* 11:615–26, 1960.

9. French, J. R. P., Tupper, C. J., & Mueller, E. F. Workload of university professors. Unpublished research report. Ann Arbor, Mich.: University of Michigan, 1965.

10. Brooks, G. W., & Mueller, E. F. Serum urate concentrations among university professors. JAMA, 195:415–18, 1966.

11. Friedman, M., Rosenman, R. H., & Carroll, V. Changes in serum cholesterol and blood clotting time in men subjected to cyclic variations of occupational stress. *Circulation,* 17:852–61, 1958.

12. Dreyfuss, F., & Czackes, J. W. Blood cholesterol and uric acid of health medical students under stress of examinations. Arch Intern Med, 103:708, 1959.

13. French, J. R. P., & Caplan, R. D. Organizational stress and individual strain, the failure of success. A J Marrow (ed.) New York: AMACOM, 30–66, 1973.

14. Shirom, A., Eden, D., Wilberwasser, S., & Kellerman, J. J. Job stress and risk factors in coronary heart disease among occupational categories in Kibbutzim. *Soc Sci Med,* 7:875–92, 1973.

15. Marks, R. U. Social stress and cardiovascular disease. *Milbank Mem Fund Q,* 65:51–107, 1967.

16. Syme, S. L., Hyman, M. M., & Enterline, P. E. Some social and cultural factors associated with the occurrence of coronary heart disease, *Journal of Chronic Diseases,* 17:277–89, 1964.

17. Pell, S., & D'Alonzo, C. A. Myocardial infarction in a one year industrial study. *JAMA,* 166:332–37, 1958.

18. Stamler, J., Kjelsberg, M., & Hall, Y. Epidemiologic studies of cardiovascular-renal diseases. I. Analysis of mortality by age-race-sex-occupation. *Journal of Chronic Diseases,* 12:440–55, 1960.

19. Bainton, C. R., & Peterson, D. R. Deaths from coronary heart disease in persons fifty years of age and younger: A community-wide study. *N. Engl J Med,* 268:569–74, 1963.

20. Berkson, D. Socioeconomic correlates of atherosclerotic and hypertensive heart disease in culture, society and health. *Ann NY Acad Sci,* 84:835–50, 1960.

21. Spain, D. M. Problems in the study of coronary atherosclerosis in population groups of culture, society, and health. *Ann NY Acad Sci,* 84:816–34, 1960.

22. Paul, O. A longitudinal study of coronary heart disease. *Circulation,* 28:20–31, 1963.
23. Wardwell, W. I., Hyman, M. M., & Bahnson, C. B. Stress and coronary disease in three field studies. *Journal of Chronic Diseases,* 17:73–84, 1964.
24. French, J. R. P., & Caplan, R. D. Psychosocial factors in coronary heart disease. *Ind Med,* 39:383–97, 1970.
25. Pincherle, G: Fitness for work. *Proc R Soc Med,* 65:321–24, 1972.
26. Tethune, W. B. Emotional problems of executives in time. *Ind Med Surg,* 32:1–67, 1963.
27. Eaton, M. T. The mental health of the older executive. *Geriatrics,* 24:126–34, 1969.
28. Selye, H. Forty years of stress research: Principal remaining problems and misconceptions. *Can Med Assoc J,* 115:1976.
29. Friedman, M., & Rosenman, R. H. *Type A Behavior and Your Heart.* New Haven, Conn: Fawcett Publications, 1974.
30. Welford, A. T. Stress and performance, in Man Under Stress. London: Francis and Taylor, 1974.
31. Lazarus, R. Psychological Stress and the Coping Process. New York: McGraw-Hill, 1967.
32. Averill, J. R. Personal contact over aversive stimuli and its relationship to stress. *Psychol Bull,* 80:286–303, 1973.
33. Sells, S. B. On the nature of stress, in Social and Psychological Factors in Stress, J E McGrath (ed). New York: Holt, Rinehart and Winston, 1970.
34. Mandler, G., & Watson, D. L. Anxiety and the interruption of behavior, in Anxiety and Behavior, CD Spielberger (ed.). New York: Academic Press, 1966.
35. Lazarus, R., Opton, E., Nomikos, M., & Rankin, N. The principle of short circuiting of threat: Further evidence. *J Pers,* 33:622–35, 1965.
36. Holmes, D. S., & Houston, B. K. Effectiveness of situation redefinition and affective isolation in coping with stress. *J Pers Soc Psychol,* 29: 212–18, 1974.
37. Houston, B. K. Viability of coping strategies, denial and response to stress. *J Pers,* 41:50–58, 1973.
38. Houston, B. K. Trait and situational denial and performance in stress. *J Pers Soc Psychol,* 18:289–93, 1971.
39. Ornstein, R. E. The Psychology of Consciousness. New York: Viking Press, 1972.
40. Robbins, J., & Fisher, D. *Tranquility Without Pills,* New York: Peter H. Wyder, 1972.
41. Kuna, D. J. *Meditation and work. Voc Guid Q,* 2:70–78, 1975.
42. Frew, D. R. Transcendental meditation. *Acad Mgt J,* 17:362–68, 1974.
43. Goleman, D. Medication helps break the stress spiral. *Psychol Today,* 1976.
44. Suinn, R. M. How to break the vicious cycle of stress. *Psychol Today,* 1976.
45. Patel, C. Yoga and biofeedback on the management of hypertension. J Psychosom Res, 19, 1975.
46. Cooper, C. L. *Theories of Group Processes,* New York and London: John Wiley & Sons, 1975.
47. Cooper, C. L., & Marshall, J. Understanding Executive Stress. London: Macmillan, 1977.
48. Matsumoto, Y. S. Social stress and coronary heart disease in Japan. *Millbank Mem Fund Q,* 48, 1970.

49. Luisada, A. A. Introduction of symposium on the epidemiology of heart disease. *Am J Cardiol,* 10:316, 1962.

50. Marmot, M., & Winkelstein, W. J. Epidemiologic observations on intervention trials for prevention of coronary heart disease. *Am J Epidemiol,* 101, 1975.

51. Ball, K. P., & Turner, R. Realism in the prevention of CHD. *Prev Med,* 4:390–97, 1975.

52. Henderson, J. B., & Enelow, A. J. The coronary risk factor problem: A behavioural perspective. *Prev Med,* 5:128–48, 1976.

53. Report of the Joint Working Party of the Royal College of Physicians of London and the British Cardiac Society. *J R Coll Physicians Lond,* 10, 1976.

54. Blackburn, H. Coronary risk factors: How to evaluate and manage them. *Eur J Cardiol,* 2/3: 249–83, 1975.

55. Seltzer, C. C. The effect of smoking on coronary heart disease. *JAMA,* 203: 193, 1968.

56. Keys, A. Coronary heart disease in seven countries. *Circulation,* 41, 1970.

57. Kozarevic, D., Pirc, B., Dawber, T. R. et al: Prevalence and incidence of coronary disease in a population study, the Yugoslavia cardiovascular disease study. *J Chronic Dis,* 24:495, 1971.

58. The Framingham Study: An epidemiological investigation of cardiovascular disease, Sections 26, 27. W. B. Karrel, & T. Gordon (eds.). U.S. Public Health Service, 1970, 1971.

59. Seltzer, C. C. Smoking and cardiovascular disease. *Am Heart J,* 90, 1975.

60. Stamler, J., & Epstein, E. Coronary heart diseaes: Risk factors as guides to preventative action. *Prev Med,* 1:27–48, 1972.

61. WHO European Collaborative Group: An international controlled trial in the multifactorial prevention of coronary heart disease. *Int J Epidemiol,* 3, 1974.

62. Stamler, J., & Berkson, D. M. Prospects and multifactorial approaches emphasizing improvement in lifestyle. *Adv Exp Med Biol,* 26:213–44, 1972.

63. Kornhauser, A. *Mental Health of the Industrial Worker.* New York: John Wiley & Sons, 1965.

36 Measuring Program Implementation, Adoption, and Intermediate Goal Attainment: Missing Links in OD Program Evaluations

Philip H. Mirvis

ABSTRACT

This article looks at missing links in evaluations of organization development programs. The process of change is conceived of as including program implementation, where the work of change agents and introduction of changes must be considered; adoption of changes by work units, where the attitudes of adopters and conditions in adopting units must be assess; and intermediate goal attainment, where initial changes in conditions of work need to be observed. Measurements of these phases of the process of change complements evaluations of program results and can help explain why programs succeed or fail. Original research showing measurement of these phases of the change process is presented. Recommendations are also advanced for the use of such measurements by program personnel in planning and monitoring change programs.

AUTHOR BACKGROUND

Philip E. Mirvis is associate professor of behavioral science, Boston University, and is interested in the study of organizational change efforts. He is coeditor with Stanley Seashore, Edward Lawler, and Cortland Cammann of *Assessing Organizational Change,* and coeditor with David Berg of *Failures in Organization Development and Change.* His recent research and consultation addresses corporate acquisitions and mergers.

Adapted from chapter 14 of *Assessing Organizational Change* (New York: John Wiley, 1983), edited by Stanley Seashore, Edward Lawler, Philip Mirvis, and Cortland Cammann. Copyright © 1983. Reprinted by permission of John Wiley & Sons, Inc.

Many directors of organizational development and change programs have aspirations of evaluating these efforts under controlled experimental conditions. This involves the identification of experimental and control units within an organization, randomization or pre- and post-experimental measurement, and insulation of the participants from the context of other changes occurring in the organization. Frequently this proves incompatible with the realities of organization life—including promotions and transfers that deplete and alter the study population, social and economic changes that commingle with experimental conditions, and feelings of special treatment and inequity that create Hawthorne-like effects and their backlash. Moreover, there are methodological questions about experimentation in organizations. It is not clear whether persons or units are to be randomly selected for experiments and whether post measurements of organizational conditions can be meaningfully compared with pre measurements. Finally, the vagaries of project purpose (multiple), change components (often unknown in advance), and field conditions (seldom fully under control) make it plain that classic canons for interpreting outcomes will not apply. Accordingly, this paper proposes that program directors (as well as researchers) need not only to conduct a broad evaluation of net outcomes—whether the intended and expected goals were achieved—but need as well to reach some understanding of the processes of change and the conditions that have aided or impeded goal achievement and lead to anticipated results.

The rationale for measurement of the processes of change is straightforward. In the usual case of an organizational change program, there is no single intervention that is undertaken nor any single outcome that is changed, nor is there a simple theory connecting the two that can be tested. Instead, there are likely to be many interventions, including some that no one, least of all the director, identified at the start. There are also likely to be many goals achieved, including some that no one intended. Finally, there may be several potential paths leading from the actions to the results.[1,2]

To fully appraise such change programs, it is essential to monitor the introduction and implementation of the program, observe the work of change agents and program participants, and evaluate both the program's intermediate and final results. The questions are innumerable: Did some lines of intended action fail to be activated? or, if activated, fail to be accepted by the organization? or, if accepted, fail to have the desired effect? What are the conditions and causes that explain such results? Are they due to the change agent, members of the organization, incompatible elements in the program, or the theory underlying the program itself? Taking steps, at the start of an evaluation, to gather the data needed to answer these questions enables the assessor to interpret the findings and adjudge their generalizability and the program participants to identify problems and redirect their change efforts.

CONCEPTUALIZING THE CHANGE PROCESS

The illustration to be provided are drawn from a series of experiments organized and monitored by the Institute for Social Research (ISR) of the University of Michigan in which representatives from management and employees (or their union) form a joint committee and introduce changes in the workplace. These committees, aided by a consultant, are charged with diagnosing problems, identifying change opportunities, and introducing changes in the organization that are intended to improve its effectiveness and the quality of work life of its members. In these experiments, we distinguish several program phases between the formation of the committee and the achievement of effectiveness and quality of work life goals. These phases—program implementation, adoption, and intermediate goal attainment—present somewhat different tasks for the researcher concerned with understanding the processes of change that are involved.

The initial stage consists of the participants reaching agreement and commitment to start the program and form a joint committee.[3] At this point, the researcher is forming relationships with the committee and other interests in the organization, negotiating roles, developing assessment plans, and formulating agreements that provide for the protection of the participants' and researcher's rights in accordance with ethical standards governing organizational research.[4] This stage is followed by the actual operation of the committee and the *implementation* of specific agreed-upon interventions in the organization. Here the researcher assesses the work of the committee and the consultants and identifies the interventions that are being introduced into the organization.

These interventions, however, may be more or less effectively introduced. Similarly, they may be more or less enthusiastically received by experimental units in the organization. The next stage of the change process, then, involves the *adoption* of the program by work units. Here the researcher assesses the characteristics of the program, adopter's attitudes toward it, and environmental factors, such as time pressures and resource limitations, that may influence its reception in the organization. The actual assessment of the degree to which the program is adopted is equivalent to laboratory tests that determine whether a treatment "takes." In the field, this is called a measure of *program activation* and serves the important function of insuring against the negative appraisal of nonevents—interventions that were not actually carried out.[5]

Once adopted, it is expected that the interventions will induce changes toward the achievement of desired goals or states, and that progress toward such states will be signalled by the achievement of *intermediate goals*. Here the researcher operationalizes a model of the internal processes of the organization that might link the intervention with its intended goals.[6] Then these intervening variables are assessed to measure intermediate goal attainment. For example, some interventions, such as job enrichment, are directed toward the work environment and should have a measurable impact on job attributes. Others, such as team building, are directed toward work relationships and should have a measurable impact on cooperation. Both should eventually improve the effectiveness of the organization and the quality of work life of its members. But tracing these sequential changes tests the theory behind the interventions and helps determine how and why they succeeded or failed.

As this progression suggests, merely introducing changes into an organization does not automatically lead to changes in its effectiveness or in its quality of working life. A program may fail because of inadequate implementation and adoption; or it may fail because it did not produce the anticipated or desired outcomes.[7] The implication for a change program is clear: both a valid theory and an effective intervention are essential if successful results are to be achieved. The implication for evaluation is equally clear: successful evaluation requires an assessment of both the theory behind the intervention and its degree of implementation and adoption by the organization.

The following illustrations of approaches to assessing the processes by which programs fail or succeed treat, successively, the assessment of intervention implementation, the degree of adoption of an intervention by some parts of an organization, and the mid-program assessment of goal attainment.

ASSESSING IMPLEMENTATION

The implementation of a change program follows the diagnosis of problems and formulation of action plans. In union-management programs, as in most change efforts, the quality of the diagnosis and planning depends upon the effectiveness of the parties in gathering complete and valid information, fully digesting and openly evaluating its implications, and identifying appropriate and feasible solutions. A committee dominated by one party or another may be unable to gather unbiased data or agree upon solutions to problems. Implementation, in turn, depends upon communicating ideas to experimental units and involving them in the activation of specific interventions. Even a harmonious committee may have difficulty implementing plans if it lacks acceptance and influence in the organization. The successful implementation of a change program also depends upon the quality of technical advice and facilitation offered by consultants, the clarity and desirability of the interventions, and the time and resources available and expended in the implementation itself.

At one experimental site, the ISR assessment team* developed questionnaire measures to assess organization members' views of the working committee, the consultants, and the overall change program. The organization, an automotive assembly and supplier plant, had started a quality of work life program three years prior to this measurement. The program in the plant was directed by a committee composed of equal numbers of management and union members, and was guided by a project staff of three consultants, two of whom worked daily in the plant and took residence in the community.

Table 36.1 lists the indices used and their reliability (coefficient alpha). Measure of the working committee included the respondent's appraisal of the committee's partisan domination, and the committee's effectiveness. Measure of the project staff tapped the respondent's assessment of their effectiveness, including their working processes and helpfulness, and the problems engendered by the staff's role in the organization. Measures of the work improvement program

---

*Barry Macy, Gerry Ledford, Edward Lawler, and Aaron Nurick.

TABLE 36.1 Questionnaire Indices Used to Assess Member Views of the Implementation of a Change Program in an Auto Parts Supply Firm

I. *Working committee*
1. *Working committee domination.*   A three-item index ($\alpha = .64$) measuring the extent to which the working committee is dominated by management, the union, or the consultants. Sample item: "The working committee is dominated by management."
2. *Working committee effectiveness.*   A mean of three indices: working processes, influence in the organization and personal contact with employees. Working processes ($\alpha = .81$) was measured by four items, e.g., "The working committee is doing a good job"; personal contact ($\alpha = .71$) by two items, e.g., "I have a say in the decisions the working committee makes." Influence was a single item "How much influence does the working committee have within the plant?" The reliability of the working committee effectiveness index was .60.
3. *Working committee participation.*   A Guttman scale measuring employees' participation in the work committee. A score of 4 meant the respondent was currently a member of the committee; 3 indicated the respondent had been a member; 2 that the respondent had attended a working committee meeting; 1 that the respondent had not participated in the committee in any way.

II. *Project staff*
1. *Project staff effectiveness.*   A mean of two indices: working processes and helpfulness to the employees. Working processes ($\alpha = .89$) was measured by four items, e.g., "The project staff listens to the employees' point of view"; helpfulness ($\alpha = .86$) by two items, e.g., "The project staff helps core groups with problems." The reliability of the project staff of effectiveness index was .83.
2. *Project staff role problems.*   A two-item index ($\alpha = .62$) measuring respondents' reactions to the staff role. Sample item: "The project staff pushes too hard for changes around here."

III. *Work improvement program*
1. *Clarity of the program.*   A two-item index ($\alpha = .53$) measuring the respondents' understanding of changes introduced by the program. Sample item: "I don't know what changes the work improvement program has made in the plant."
2. *Fairness of the program.*   A two-item index ($\alpha = .52$) measuring the fairness of the program. Sample item: "The work improvement program has been beneficial to only a few employees."
3. *Desirability of the program.*   A four-item index ($\alpha = .82$) measuring overall reactions to the program. Sample item: "The work improvement program has made a lot of good changes."
4. *Program overload.*   A two-item index ($\alpha = .53$) measuring the overload caused by the program. Sample item: "There are too many changes going on around here."
5. *Overall impact.*   A four-item index ($\alpha = .82$) measuring the impact of the program on such factors as trust and communication in the organization. Sample item: "The work improvement program has increased the amount of trust between employees and the company."

Note: α = coefficient ALPHA measure of reliability.

reflected its clarity to employees, its fairness, its desirability, the overload it caused, and its overall impact on trust and communication in the organization.

Table 36.2 reports the correlations between measures of characteristics of the work committee and project staff on the one hand, with measures assessing

TABLE 36.2   Correlations between Measures of Working Committee Staff Characteristics with Member Appraisals of a Change Program
(N = 190)

	Working Committee Dominance	Working Committee Effec- tiveness	Working Committee Partici- pation	Project Staff Effec- tiveness	Project Staff Role Problems
Clarity of the program	−.42**	.29**	.21**	.22**	−.42**
Fairness of the program	−.28**	.41**	.07	.39**	−.36**
Desirability of the program	−.16	.52**	.14	.59**	−.33**
Program overload	.36**	−.32**	−.17*	−.40**	.46**
Overall program impact	−.23**	.53**	.19**	.61**	−.31**

*p < .05
**p < .01

the implementation of the work improvement program. It shows that the effectiveness of the committee and the consultants was positively related to appraisals of the fairness, clarity, and desirability of the change program and of its overall impact on trust and communication in the organization. Respondents who felt the committee was dominated by labor, management, or the consultants or who saw the consultant's role as unnecessary or problematic, gave the program a negative appraisal. Participation in the working committee was only slightly related to its positive assessment. While there is a good amount of "halo" in these correlations, the results proved helpful, when used with other information, in forming conclusions about the process of change at this site. For example, the figures show that the characteristics of the project staff were as influential as the characteristics of the committee itself in inducing supportive views and feelings; a finding that suggests consultants play an important role in introducing change when working with a committee composed of conflicting interests.[8] Surprisingly, actual participation in the work of the committee had a lesser relationship to participants' views of the program.

The researchers identified three major interventions introduced into the organization by the committee: (1) an earned idle time program in which employees, upon achieving their production standards for a day, could earn idle time and leave the plant or remain and earn a bonus; (2) an educational program consisting of voluntary courses in job skills, reading, language, and arts taught by and attended by the employees; and (3) the formation of core groups, that is, voluntary small problem-solving groups in the plant, to analyze working conditions and introduce changes of their own choosing. Analysis showed respondent's assessment of the working committee, the project staff, and the work improvement program to have a small but significant relationship with their actual participation in these interventions and a strong and significant relationship with their evaluation of these interventions. This provides evidence of the link between effective implementation and program success.

ASSESSING CONDITIONS FOR TRIAL AND SUSTAINED ADOPTION OF CHANGES

In some situations, an organizational change program may involve the implementation of certain activities whose adoption depended upon personal and environmental factors unique to each part of the organization. That is, the implementation is not and perhaps cannot be imposed on work units, but is voluntary to some degree. Accordingly, one can expect that there will be some organizational units that reject the intervention while others give it a perfunctory try; still others would be expected to adopt the intervention and sustain it over some time.

A key factor in adoption is then readiness to change. In some fashion, the risks, costs, and potential benefits come to be evaluated by a unit head and unit members. What are the risks of being noncooperative in a company-wide program? What are our priority problems, and is the proposed action likely to ameliorate them? Do we have the resources of time, energy, and competence to carry out the activity? Is the proposed activity intrinsically compatible with our values and purposes? Can we try it without committing ourselves to a permanent change that may prove irreversible? The questions are many, but all get appraised as adoption decisions are made.[9] In another research site, data were sought specifically to help assess the variations among units in adoption of a proposed change, and some of the sources of these variations. The proposed new activity involved the adoption and use of an information feedback system by branches of a metropolitan bank.[10]

The feedback system itself was designed with a task force of bank employees from all levels for implementation in the branches. Managers and supervisors in the branches were expected to hold regular feedback meetings with their staffs to review the measures of branch performance and work attitudes, participatively solve problems, and set future goals. Table 36.3 lists the measures of degree of adoption and measures of predictors of adoption gathered from branch leaders and personnel. Their reliabilities are Spearman-Brown estimates. The measures of adoption, taken six months and again one year after implementation, asked branch employees to report the number of feedback meetings held in the branch that month and the quality of the meetings, including the interest shown in the program by branch leaders and their use of the data to participatively solve problems and set goals. The predictors of adoption assessed the leader's and staff member's perceptions of problems in the branch at the start of the program, their attitudes about the feedback system, and the benefits they anticipated from its use. Leaders were interviewed regarding their need to change, their knowledge of the philosophy and goals behind the intervention, and their recognition of the

---

TABLE 36.3   Measures of Program Adoption and Predictors of Adoption

---

I. *Measures of adoption*

1. *Number of meetings.*   A three-item index (r = .66) measuring the number of feedback meetings held in a branch in a given month. Sample item: "How many meetings are held each month for working with the feedback?"

2. *Quality of meetings.*   An eight-item index (r = .90) measuring the respondent's feelings that branch leaders were interested in the feedback system and used it for participative problem solving and goal setting. Sample item: "Employees are encouraged to participate in the discussion during feedback meetings."

II. *Predictors of adoption*

1. *Perception of problem.*   Two separate two-item indices measuring the *leader's* (r = .73) and the *staff's* (r = .73) appraisal of cooperation and teller effectiveness. Sample item: "In general, how would you rate cooperation among employees in this branch?"

2. *Leader's need for change.*   A single measure appraising the leader's need for change; asked during interview: "Did you feel some changes needed to be made in the branch?" Scored positively when needed changes were consistent with changes offered by feedback system.

3. *Attitudes toward program.*   Two separate indices: a six-item index measuring the *leader's* (r = .77), and a three-item index measuring the *staff's* (r = .82) attitude toward the feedback system. Sample item: "I looked forward to receiving the first few feedback reports."

4. *Expectations of benefits.*   Two separate indices: a three-item index measuring the *leader's* (r = .62), and a two-item index measuring the *staff's* (r = .89) expectations of benefits from the feedback system. Sample item: "I thought the feedback system would help the branch work more effectively."

5. *Leader's knowledge of the program.*   A three-item index (r = .60) measuring the leader's familiarity with the feedback system and role in using it. Sample item: "I was unsure how I could most effectively use the feedback report."

6. *Leader's recognition of the program.*   A two-item index (r = .62) measuring the leader's perception of the uniqueness of the program. Sample item: "It was just another project from Branch Administration."

7. *Leader's time pressures.*   A two-item index (r = .62) measuring time pressures facing branch leaders. Sample item: "I never seem to have enough time to get things done."

8. *Leader's problems in adoption.*   A two-item index (r = .76) measuring leader's problems in adopting the feedback system. Sample item: "Sometimes I feel pressured into using the system."

9. *Leader's first experiences.*   A semantic differential scale measuring leader's reactions to the first use of the program (r = .66). A sample item asked leaders to rate the first reactions as encouraged—discouraged.

10. *Leader's time and energy given to the program.*   A four-item index (r = .79) measuring leader's time and energy given to using the feedback system. Sample item: "How much time and effort did you put into planning for feedback meeting?"

Note: r = Spearman-Brown corrections to Kudar-Richardson reliability estimates.

---

feedback system as not "just another program in the bank." Once they adopted the system, leaders were asked to report on time pressures and problems they encountered that hampered its use. They were also asked to appraise their first experiences in feedback meetings and the time and energy they devoted to the program.

Table 36.4 reports the correlations of these predictors with the trial (six months) and sustained (twelve months) adoption of the feedback system in the branches. Both the leader's and staff member's perceptions of problems in their branches and their expectations of benefits from the program correlated positively with the number of meetings held in the branches. Staff attitudes toward and expectations for the feedback system correlated positively with the number

TABLE 36.4 Correlations between Measures of Program Adoption and Predictors of Adoption

(N = 26 Branches)

	Trial Adoption		Sustained Adoption	
	Number of Meetings	*Quality of Meetings*	*Number of Meetings*	*Quality of Meetings*
Leader's perception of problems	.52**	.22	.48**	.33**
Staff's perception of problems	.43**	.14	.37*	.25
Leader's need for change	.25	.00	.11	.24
Leader's attitudes toward program	.20	−.13	.09	.23
Staff's attitudes toward program	.62**	.31*	.52**	.50**
Leader's expectation of benefits	.46**	.07	.28	.27
Staff's expectation of benefits	.62**	.00	.60**	.40*
Leader's knowledge of program	.11	.00	.13	.30
Leader's recognition of program	.10	−.01	−.07	.23
Leader's time pressures	−.31	−.14	−.24	−.26
Leader's problems in adoption	−.38*	−.49*	−.40*	−.54**
Leader's first experiences	.36*	−.09	.25	.28
Leader's time and energy given to program	.48**	−.02	.46**	.44*

*p < .05
**p < .01

and quality of meetings held, particularly in the second measurement. The leaders' reports of time pressures and problems in adoption correlated negatively with the quality and number of meetings. One leader commented upon the time pressures:

> The first priority is that we've got to be able to deal with the customer that's at the door . . . give them the service they're paying for. . . . It was hard to find the time to take another hour on a Thursday evening, before a twelve-hour Friday, and talk about a great new project we were going to learn something from.

Another reported a notable, but unavoidable, problem in the use of the system: "All of a sudden it seemed to kind of take the management of the branch a little bit out of our hands!"

In branches where the program was successfully adopted and sustained, teller performance improved, turnover decreased, and satisfaction and cooperation increased relative to a control group of branches. In branches where the feedback system was not adopted, by contrast morale plummeted, turnover increased, and teller performance was unchanged. This provides evidence of the link between sustained adoption and program success.

As in the preceding example, it should be noted that although the quantitative data obtained to help understand the dynamics of adoption or nonadoption are useful in their own right, their main utility in analysis and interpretation comes from their capacity to confirm or disconfirm ideas tentatively raised by collateral assessment information. As an example of such use, consider the connection between the bank's reward system for branch managers, and the branch adoption of the new activity. The appraisal and reward system for branch managers was oriented almost solely to branch profitability. By agreement, the feedback data from branches were not reported to top management and performance gains other than profitability could not be used in branch performance appraisals. Thus, as conditions at the site suggest, and the findings in the table support, those managers in already profitable branches did not adopt the change program except in those instances where the program had evident intrinsic appeal to them and to their staff members.

ASSESSING INTERMEDIATE GOAL ATTAINMENT

If one is to reach a confirmation or disconfirmation of some theory about organizational change, it is necessary to examine cases in which the theory has been given a fair test. A "fair" test is, at minimum, one in which the program has been activated to the point where the theoretical conditions necessary for assessing its action implications are achieved. It is in this sense that one can speak of intermediate goals in an organizational change program—the goals of introducing the desired conditions—quite apart from the longer-range goals that are expected to flow from these desired experimental or demonstration conditions. When a change assessment attends only to the ultimate criteria, there is a risk of rejecting a valid theory.

An illustration is provided from still another research site in which a team of organizational consultants set out to establish in a newly forming organization the properties of a "participative" system. The program assessors* faced the usual problem of discerning a clear and concise set of intermediate program goals; conferences with the consultants and the program participants, however, led to agreement on a list of twenty criteria that, if satisfied, would constitute evidence of a successful introduction of "participation."

Intermediate goals attainment was assessed in part by a questionnaire survey administered to all nonmanagement members of the organization about nine months after the goals had been agreed upon and formalized. Other methods of assessment were used as well, but only the questionnaire results will be discussed here.

Figure 36.1 shows the survey results with respect to the twenty implementation criteria. In the questionnaire, the criteria were stated and defined, and the respondent indicated the extent to which these objectives had been achieved. The results are shown separately for each of two main units of the organization—production and quality assurance—as well as for the whole of the organization. The figure shows that in general the intermediate objectives were considered to be achieved only "moderately," that is, halfway between "not at all" and "to a very great extent." Except for certain "feedback" and "periodic review" items, the quality assurance department shows the greater goal attainment, a finding that confirmed the observers' reports that the consultants worked more effectively in that department, and that the initial and continuing acceptance of the program objectives was greater there.

The impact of the intervention on the achievement of participative management goals was assessed directly by questions to respondents regarding the extent to which the program activities (meetings, consultations, individual counseling, role-model demonstrations) contributed to the achievement of stated goals. Figure 36.2 indicates that the program made only a slight positive contribution to the specific goals of participation by employees. The contribution was greater in the quality assurance department than in the production department.

Such measures of goal attainment and program contribution, however, assess only the intended effects of the program. Of equal interest are the unintended consequences. In this site, as an example, the consultants had not sufficiently prepared the organization for the adoption of participation. Consequently, in the first four months, countless hours were wasted in trivial group decisions. At the same time, legitimate sources of expertise were ignored in the spirit of full participation. The evaluators attributed this to the failure of the interventionists to introduce a contingency approach to decision making in the organization that specifies when participative decisions are most appropriate.[11] In addition, the evaluators found that despite the partial achievement of participative management goals, employees reported that there occurred no increase in personal influence, influence with their superiors, or influence over work deci-

---

*Dennis Perkins, Veronica Nieva, and Edward Lawler.

FIGURE 36.1   Attainment of Goals Related to Participation

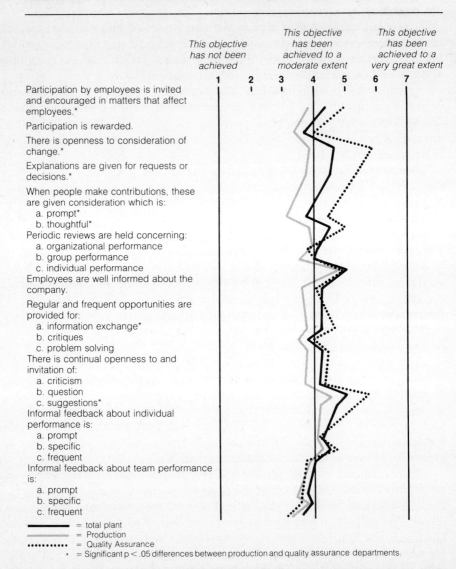

total plant

Production

Quality Assurance

* = Significant p < .05 differences between production and quality assurance departments.

sions between the start and termination of the program. Measures of general work satisfaction and involvement in the organization actually declined. The evaluators attributed this to the shift from participative to consultative management in the organization over the course of the project and the accompanying feelings of guilt by leaders and betrayal by plant employees. They noted, moreover, that the technology in the plant and the time pressures facing employees

FIGURE 36.2 Program Contribution to the Achievement of Participative Management Goals

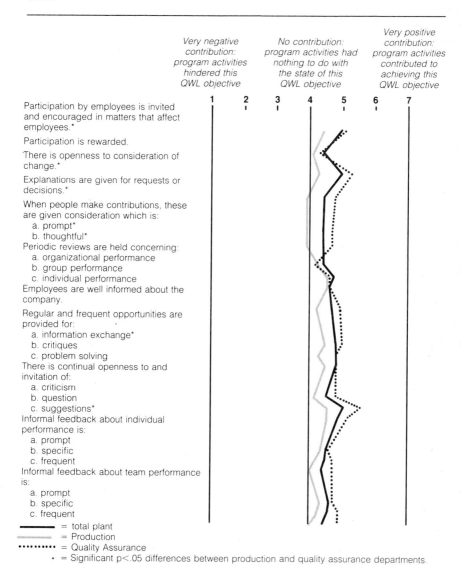

	Very negative contribution: program activities hindered this QWL objective	No contribution: program activities had nothing to do with the state of this QWL objective	Very positive contribution: program activities contributed to achieving this QWL objective

Participation by employees is invited and encouraged in matters that affect employees.*

Participation is rewarded.

There is openness to consideration of change.*

Explanations are given for requests or decisions.*

When people make contributions, these are given consideration which is:
  a. prompt*
  b. thoughtful*

Periodic reviews are held concerning:
  a. organizational performance
  b. group performance
  c. individual performance

Employees are well informed about the company.

Regular and frequent opportunities are provided for:
  a. information exchange*
  b. critiques
  c. problem solving

There is continual openness to and invitation of:
  a. criticism
  b. question
  c. suggestions*

Informal feedback about individual performance is:
  a. prompt
  b. specific
  c. frequent

Informal feedback about team performance is:
  a. prompt
  b. specific
  c. frequent

———— = total plant
———— = Production
•••••••• = Quality Assurance
  * = Significant p<.05 differences between production and quality assurance departments.

during the first production runs both made the general use of participative decision making questionable.

One can with some confidence conclude that the "participative" system of management was not, in this instance, given a trial at all, much less a fair trial. In the data shown, and the collateral information, it seems clear that because the consultants and firm members failed to fully activate the program, the theory of participation was not tested. However, this study does show how the failure to reach intermediate goals is linked with program failure.

USE OF PROCESS MEASUREMENTS
BY PROGRAM PERSONNEL

Since these measures of program implementation, adoption, and intermediate goal attainment are taken as the program begins, as change is introduced, and as first order goals are (or are not) achieved, they can be useful to program personnel. To serve this purpose, however, requires that the measurements be taken in the context of particular research designs, organizational climates, and research relationships.

It should be recognized that these process measures are interventions for program personnel: focusing their attention and energy toward achieving desired results in measured areas and arousing their apprehension and frustration if the results are not achieved. If they are to be useful to them, then, they must be taken in the context of a formative research design in which the findings inform the intervention.[12] This need not preclude a summative research design that includes pre- and post-measurements assessing the impact of the change program on the organization. Instead a summative measurement becomes an evaluation of not simply the change program, but the change program guided by evaluative data.

For these process measurements to be useful to program personnel they must also be taken in the context of a supportive organizational climate. Unfortunately, many change programs are undertaken with an attitude of omniscience and omnipotence: participants and consultants believe that with their know-how and change technology, program goals will inevitably be achieved. Moreover, this attitude is sustained by an environment in which the benefits of success and costs of failure dictate that goals must be achieved.[13] In this context, evaluation becomes like a report card and these process measurements, if unfavorable, are discounted or discredited and, if favorable, become subordinate to the final evaluative data.

An alternative approach is for the program participants and consultants to adopt a learning posture that is both receptive and responsive to these process measurements. This necessitates, first, an attitude that recognizes the limits of human knowledge and technology to create change and that acknowledges that errors and unanticipated consequences will inevitably result. Second, it requires that the development of norms that support the discovery, disclosure, and critical examination of errors and misdirections as the program is implemented and adopted and as it influences the organization.[14] In that context, these process measurements become benchmarks of the change program's progress and early warning signals if the program has gone awry.

Finally, the effective use of these measurements implies the development of new norms in research relationships. Just as the assessor intervenes in the change program, so also must the program personnel and consultants participate in the evaluation. To accomplish this researchers will have to educate them in these new methods of evaluation and invite their involvement in the formulation of the research design, development of the measures, and interpretation of the data. This will acknowledge that measurement, however concealed, affects change programs; so instead of devising covert measurements that program participants cannot decipher or discern, researchers will work with them to develop overt measurements that can be employed throughout the change effort and used by all parties to guide and direct their activities.

In the context of these research designs, organizational climates, and research relationships, these process measurements can contribute to both the accuracy of the evaluation and the effectiveness of the change program.

THE PLACE OF PROCESS MEASUREMENTS IN EVALUATION RESEARCH

The function of these measurements in evaluation research can be illustrated by a photographic analogy. At one extreme is the motion picture camera. With it in hand, the skilled master can become immersed in the drama, confident that the camera will record events. There can be no assurance, however, that the recording will be objective, for by focusing on certain aspects of the setting, the master risks becoming fixated on certain themes and interpretations. The film *Roshomon* is the model: several engaged observers produced dramatically different and incompatible pictures of the same events, with no possibility for discerning whose imagery was more or less "valid." There is a role for such observation, that is, for the trained observer's as opposed to the camera's eye, in assessing change programs. On-site observation provides a rich and passionate portrayal of an organization and its people in change. But also assessing a program with the methods described here provides a check against bias, fixation, and prejudice.

At the other extreme of the analogy is the still photograph. Taken after dramatic events, it can show vividly the effects of a stinging rebuke, of a lost love, of a murder—or when replaced by measurement—of an organization that has changed. When compared with earlier measures, it can also capture the drama, however singular, of changing events. But unless complemented by the assessment methods described here, not enough is shown of the intervening processes to explain the differences and, further, the chosen subject matter, pre-selected, may not reflect the crucial differences themselves.

The process assessments and measures described here can be likened to a photographic essay. They add depth to the film (observation) and breadth to the snapshot (pre- and post-measurement); like a "stop action" film they provide a way in which significant events may be examined, reviewed, and evaluated. Students of photography study films, photos, and stop action segments. When assessors of organizations use observations, experiments, and process measurements, they more thoughtfully examine a change program and more thoroughly evaluate its effects.

References

1. Deutscher, I. "Toward Avoiding the Goal Trap in Evaluation Research." In F. G. Caro (ed.), *Readings in Evaluation Resources.* New York: Russell Sage, 1977.

2. Angrist, S. S. "Evaluation Research: Possibilities and Limitations." *Journal of Applied Behavioral Science,* 1975, 11, 75–91.

3. Lawler, E. E., & Drexler, J. A. Dynamics of establishing cooperative quality of work life projects. *Monthly Labor Review,* (March 1978): 23–28.

4. Mirvis, P. H., & Seashore, S. E. "Being Ethical in Organizational Research." *American Psychologist,* 1979, 34, 766–80.

5. Charters, W. E., & Jones, J. E. "On the Risk of Appraising Non-Events in Program Evaluation." *Evaluation Researcher,* 1973, 11, 5–7.

6. Schulberg, H. C., & Baker F. "Program Evaluation Models and the Implementation of Research Findings." In F. G. Caro (ed.) *Readings in Evaluation Research.* New York: Russell Sage Foundation, 1971.

7. Weiss, C. H. *Evaluation Research: Methods for Assessing Program Effectiveness.* Englewood Cliffs, New Jersey: Prentice-Hall, 1972.

8. Nadler, D. A. "Consulting with Labor and Management: Some Learning from Quality of Work Life Projects." In W. Burke (ed.) *The Cutting Edge.* La Jolla, California: University Associates, 1979.

9. Zaltman, G., & Duncan, R. *Strategies for Planned Change.* New York: Wiley-Interscience, 1977.

10. Nadler, D. A., Mirvis, P. H., & Cammann, C. "The Ongoing Feedback System: Experimenting with a New Managerial Tool." *Organizational Dynamics,* 1976, 4, 63–80.

11. Vroom, V., & Yetton, P. *Leadership and Decision Making.* Pittsburgh: University of Pittsburgh Press, 1973.

12. Scriven, M. "The Methodology of Evaluation." In C. Weiss (ed.) *Evaluating Action Programs: Readings in Social Actions and Education.* Boston: Allyn & Bacon, 1972.

13. Mirvis, P. H., & Berg, D. N. *Failures in Organization Development and Change.* New York: Wiley Interscience, 1977.

14. Michael, D. N., & Mirvis, P. H. "Changing, Erring, and Learning." In P. Mirvis and D. Berg (eds.) *Failures in Organization Development and Change.* New York: Wiley Interscience, 1977.

37 Expectation Effects: Implications for Organization Development Interventions

Richard W. Woodman
Paul D. Tolchinsky

ABSTRACT

Evidence for the existence of expectation effects is reviewed with an emphasis on (1) expectations as predictors of organizational outcomes, and (2) discrepancy effects when expectations fail to match actual outcomes. Several controlled studies are reviewed that have attempted to assess the relationships between participants' expectations and other variables in OD interventions. The implications of participant expectations for organizational change programs are also discussed.

AUTHOR BACKGROUNDS

Richard W. Woodman received a B.S. in industrial engineering, an M.B.A. from Oklahoma State University, and a Ph.D. in organizational behavior from Purdue University. His work experience includes service as vice-president of a savings and loan association. Dr. Woodman's research and consulting focuses on organizational diagnosis, team development, and evaluation of OD programs.

    Paul D. Tolchinsky received a B.S. in psychology from Bowling Green State University and a Ph.D. in organizational behavior from Purdue University. His previous experience includes management positions with Detroit Bank and Trust,

This paper was presented at the National Academy of Management meeting in New York City in 1982.

Babcock and Wilcox, and General Foods Corporation. He is currently president of Creative Work-Life Systems in Cleveland, Ohio, and previously was a faculty member at Florida State University and the University of Akron. His firm specializes in QWL and sociotechnical change programs.

You see, really and truly, apart from the things anyone can pick up (the dressing) and the proper way of speaking, and so on, the difference between a lady and a flower girl is not how she behaves, but how she's treated. I shall always be a flower girl to Professor Higgins, because he always treats me as a flower girl, and always will; but I know I can be a lady to you, because you always treat me as a lady and always will.

(George Bernard Shaw, *Pygmalion*)

The possibility that merely expecting an event or outcome to occur increases the likelihood that it *does* occur is an idea that has long intrigued social scientists. In organizations, the expectations held by one person or group about the behavior of other persons or groups may serve as an important, albeit partial, determinant of behavior. People often do what others expect of them in the same sense that Eliza's behavior was affected by the expectations of Professor Higgins and those around him.

Research on expectations, as a general construct, is abundant. Expectations have been dealt with in a wide variety of disciplines and fields—education, marketing, organizational behavior, organization development, medicine, psychotherapy, sociology, and psychology—to name a few. In particular, psychologists have used Merton's concept of the self-fulfilling prophecy[1] to explain a variety of phenomena.[2]

Psychologists have defined expectations in three ways. First, there is a definition that focuses upon the expectation that a specific behavior (or act) will be followed by the attainment or nonattainment of a particular outcome. Expectations are thus defined as an individual's subjective probability that an act will be followed by a particular outcome. This concept of expectation is central to "expectancy" theories of motivation.[3]

A second definition is not limited to expectations about the consequences of one's own behavior, but is defined by the individual's subjective probability that a given state either does or will exist. Expectations about the nature of some stimulus object, the social situation, or some state of the individual have been considered as (or part of) an individual's comparison level,[4] adaptation level,[5] or frame of reference.[6]

In a third definition, expectations refer to one person's belief that another individual will behave in a certain way. It has been suggested by various theorists[7] that such expectations may contribute to the determination of what that behavior actually will be.

In a somewhat more general sense, organizational research has tended to focus on two particular aspects of expectations: (1) their ability to predict outcomes (for example, success, behavior change, greater productivity, higher satisfaction, and so on) and (2) their moderating effects on individual affect when discrepancies between expectations and actual outcomes occur. This paper will look at expectations in both perspectives. The focus will be on organizational change efforts and the effects managers' and employees' expectations may have on the success or failure of such endeavors.

EXPECTATIONS AND OUTCOMES

Does knowing the expectations of individuals allow researchers or consultants to predict specific organizational outcomes? There is considerable evidence for the operation of interpersonal self-fulfilling prophecies in the literatures of the healing professions, education, psychology, and organizational behavior.

For example, Rosenthal and Jacobson[8] have shown that pupils whose teachers expected them to "bloom" intellectually over the course of the academic year, did indeed achieve significant IQ gains over their "nonblooming" classmates, and that these gains appear to be permanent. Despite considerable controversy surrounding the initial research on teacher expectations, "subsequent experimental investigations have confirmed that teacher expectations affect student achievement."[9] Similar affects on performance have been found in other settings. Burnham demonstrated that randomly selected chidren who were learning to swim showed greater improvement when their instructors thought the children had "high" potential.[10] Similar results have been found in training disadvantaged workers,[11] in the assignment of new managers,[12] and in a variety of laboratory and field settings.[13] More recently, Eden and Shani[14] demonstrated that the expectations of Israeli Army instructors significantly affected the performance of trainees in a combat command course.

In addition, researchers in the area of psychotherapy have hypothesized that patients' expectations of outcomes affect the course of most, if not all, treatments. While the results of much research are equivocal, there is at least some support for the idea that a patient's "initial therapeutic expectancies" may play an important role in behavior change following treatment.[15]

Because of their potential impact on outcomes, expectations have been viewed as a serious confound in research with human subjects. There is considerable evidence that expectations of the experimenter may bias the behavior of subjects in a research study, primarily, as one might expect, in the direction of hypothesis confirmation.[16]

Finally, expectations have often played a central role in theories of work motivation in organizational psychology and organizational behavior. Specifically, expectancy "attitudes" are hypothesized to be related to job behavior and performance. The central concept of expectancy theories of motivation is that the force (motivation) of an individual to exert a specific amount of effort is a function of (1) the expectation that the effort will result in a specific outcome, and (2) the sum of the valences (personal utilities or satisfactions) that the individual expects to derive from the outcomes. Thus, according to the theory, individuals choose the behaviors in which they engage and the level of effort they assert on the basis of their expectations concerning the relationships among effort, the level of performance stemming from that effort, and the level of outcomes stemming from that performance.

Expectancy theory (and, by extension, employees' expectations) has been proposed to predict the following outcomes in organizational settings: job effort, job performance, job satisfaction, leadership behavior, and leadership effectiveness.[17] While a review of the empirical support for these assertions is beyond the scope of this paper, and there is still disagreement concerning much expectancy theory research,[18] there is, at least, widespread acceptance of the idea that expectations are a useful and important component in predicting organizational outcomes.

In addition, what the literature on teacher and experimenter expectancies suggests, in an organizational sense, is that managers who believe that nothing will improve the performance or morale of their employees may find their expectations confirmed, not because the program failed, but because the behavior patterns of individuals were controlled by their expectations. The same outcome may also be developed from the perspective of the individual employee. Workers develop expectancies regarding the behavior of their supervisors. Expectations that management will do nothing to improve the quality of working life may be confirmed. Because of such expectations, employees do little to assist, passively watch from the sidelines, and when in fact nothing happens say, "See, we told you so! "

DISCREPANCY EFFECTS OF EXPECTATIONS

A problem with the manipulation of expectations by the consultant, manager, leader, or researcher is that it is difficult to perfectly match expectations and outcomes; discrepancies are likely to occur. Is it better to understate, overstate, or attempt to accurately predict outcomes? At least three psychological theories suggest answers to this question:

■ cognitive dissonance or assimilation theory[19]
■ contrast theory[20]
■ assimilation-contrast theory[21]

Dissonance or assimilation theory posits that any discrepancy between expectations and actual events will be minimized or assimilated by the individuals adjusting their own perceptions of the event to be more consistent (less dissonant) with expectations. The theory suggests that an individual has cognitive elements (or "knowledges") about past behaviors, beliefs and attitudes, and environments.[22] Employees continually receive various kinds of information from their own experiences, peers, superiors, and the environment in general. These bits of information are cognitions which the individual likes to have consistent with one another. When an individual receives ideas that are psychologically dissonant, he or she attempts to reduce this mental discomfort by changing or distorting one or both of the cognitions to make them more consonant. Finally, the theory posits that the more cognitive dissonance, the more motivated the individual becomes to reduce dissonance by changing the cognitive element.

As applied to organizational improvement efforts, this theory suggests that if there is a disparity between expectations for outcomes and the objective outcomes of the intervention, the individual is stimulated to reduce the psychological tension by changing perceptions of the objective outcomes to bring them more into line with initial expectations. Therefore, if this proposition is true, the consultant should substantially lead expectations above objective outcomes to obtain a higher organizational evaluation or perception of the improvement effort. It is important to note that considerable controversy and dissatisfaction with this theory have developed in recent years due to an increasing amount of contradictory evidence.

Contrast theory assumes that the individual will magnify the difference between the actual event and expectations; that is, if the event fails to meet expectations the individual will evaluate the outcome less favorably than if that person had no prior expectations for it. When people expect a pleasant event to occur, they begin to anticipate the actual event and the pleasantness it will bring. They may do this either by fantasizing or contemplating the event's consequences or by telling others about it. If the event then fails to materialize, it may be more disvalued than if it had not been expected in the first place, perhaps due to the heightened contrast between the anticipated success and the failure that results.

The contrast explanation suggests that a slight understatement of the outcomes of organizational interventions might lead to higher organizational satisfaction with the interventions. Obviously, the expectations could not so understate the potential outcomes that the organization would decide not to participate at all.

Assimilation-contrast theory posits that performance differing only slightly from one's expectations tends to result in displacement of perceptions toward expectations (assimilation), while large variances between one's expectations and actuality tend to be exaggerated (contrast). The assimilation-contrast approach maintains that there are zones or latitudes of acceptance and rejection in perceptions. If the disparity between expectations and performance is sufficiently small to fall into the individual's latitude of acceptance, the difference between expectations and reality will be assimilated more in line with expectations than objective reality would justify. If however, the discrepancy is so large that it falls into the zone of rejection, then a contrast effect comes into being and the individual magnifies the perceived disparity. According to McClelland et al, the direction of the deviation is unimportant. Discrepancies of equal magnitude should have comparable effects with the smaller deviations both toward or away from hope producing positive affect and with larger discrepancies producing negative affect.

Assimilation-contrast theory suggests that the expectations of employees and managers regarding the outcomes of an organizational improvement effort should be as high as possible without creating a level of disparity that falls outside the individual's range of acceptance.

While a review of research on these theories is beyond the scope of this paper, it is worth noting that each has received only limited support. However, on balance, we conclude that it is probably advantageous to establish reasonably high expectations regarding the outcomes of interventions. These expectations should be such that any discrepancy that does occur is positive. In addition, it would appear that the discrepancy should not be too large. While evidence here is equivocal, researchers[23] have found that affective reactions tend to assimilate in the direction of expectations. Because the results of studies are contradictory, any conclusions regarding the magnitude of disparity must be undertaken with great caution. It is important to remember also that violations of expectations in themselves establish expectations about the reliability of the source of expectations. Once the organization begins to doubt the source of their expectations (for example, the consultant) it may be difficult to establish any expectations that differ from past behavior.

EXPECTATIONS AND ORGANIZATIONAL CHANGE

The measurement of expectations in organization development programs is not common. In this section of the paper we will review several studies, including some of our own research (see studies 1 and 2 below), which have explicitly attempted to assess the relationships between participant expectations and other variables in OD interventions.

King[24] is one of the few studies that has specifically manipulated expectations during a change effort. King focused on the expectations of managers and employees in two job design interventions, for example, job enlargement and job rotation. Managers in one job enlargement and one job rotation plant (plants 1 and 3) were told that they could expect "higher levels of output." Managers in the other two plants (plants 2 and 4) were told that the aim of management was to improve relations with employees and that "increased output was not expected to occur."

Controlling for initial differences in the average daily performance of the four plants, King found that significant performance differences did occur as a result of expectations. There were no significant interactions and no effect for treatments. Managers who were led to expect higher performance as a result of these interventions increased their plant output during the experimental period.

It was hypothesized that plants led to expect significant improvements in relations with employees would significantly reduce absenteeism in comparison to plants led to only expect performance improvements. No differences were found on measures of lost person days. Actual absences were, however, in the predicted direction. Plants 2 and 4 had fewer absences than plants 1 and 3.

Unfortunately, the manipulation of expectations may be confounded with what actually occurred during the experimental period. King does not provide a check of his manipulations until twelve months after expectations were manipulated. Because of this, it is not clear whether expectations prior to the program affected productivity or whether productivity changes during the program caused the reported higher expectations.

While the results must be viewed with caution, the research suggests that expectations played a role in the improvement of organizational performance. Managers who had higher expectations of performance also had higher levels of performance. Similar managerial "Pygmalion effects" have been suggested by Livingston[25] and Berlew and Hall.[26]

Expectations were also manipulated by Crawford, Thomas, and Fink[27] who conducted an OD intervention designed to improve the performance of "problem" sailors on both work performance and disciplinary indices in relation to two comparison groups of sailors: (1) low performing sailors on other ships, and (2) other nonsupervisory personnel on the experimental ship.

While it is plausible that expectations played a role in the improved performance of the subjects, no direct measure of expectations was reported and it is thus not possible to know if expectations were effectively manipulated nor to separate the main effect of expectations from other aspects of the intervention, that is, supervisory training, workshops, and so on.

Study 1

A one-year survey feedback project was conducted with employees of a Department of Defense military installation in the midwest.[28] Some forty-nine work groups were randomly assigned to one of three treatment or two control conditions. A major thrust of the research was to compare two varieties of survey feedback ("top down" and "bottom up") with a "data handback" condition wherein work groups received survey data, but did not participate in the formal action-planning process characteristic of survey feedback interventions.

Individuals in the two survey feedback conditions perceived their organization to be more effective and had more positive affect toward their jobs than individuals in the data handback or control conditions. However, there were no clear indications that one variety of survey feedback was superior to the other in terms of productivity indices or any measured perceptions of the work environment.

While this research did not manipulate expectations directly as was done in the King study, the moderating effect of expectations on employee perceptions was measured. Expectations were found to significantly moderate the effects of the treatments on internal work motivation. The observed interaction effect was, in large part, attributable to the data handback condition. Results suggested that, for the data handback groups, as expectations went up, internal work motivation declined. This result may be plausibly regarded as a discrepancy effect. Initially, the data handback groups had expectations similar to the survey feedback groups (that is, all believed that the potential existed for management to utilize the survey data). When these expectations were not met, these data suggest, one outcome was reduced motivation to perform work.

Study 2

Sixty-seven work groups from an engineering surveying course were utilized for a field experiment designed to measure the effects of a team development intervention.[29] These groups were randomly assigned to one of three conditions: team development groups, placebo (observation) groups, or control groups. The placebo treatment was designed (and, in fact, served to) eliminate a Hawthorne effect as a rival explanation for change.

The work groups experiencing team development did not perform better following the intervention than control groups; however, individuals in these groups perceived their groups as being more effective and reported greater participation and involvement than did members of control groups.

Information was gathered from the team development participants that allowed a comparison of early expectations to a later evaluation of the intervention. In general, evaluations following the intervention, while basically favorable, were significantly more negative than earlier expectations with regard to positive improvements in the work group. As a result, it was concluded that there was no "main effect" of expectations in the sense that expectations could plausibly explain the positive impact found on affective reactions following the team development. Rather, a discrepancy effect seemed to exist similar to that found in the Tolchinsky study. For example, an expectations measure was negatively correlated with the perceived effectiveness of the work group ($r = -.30$, $p < .05$).

In addition, a later reexamination of these same data was undertaken to explore differences in the evaluation received by the five group facilitators who conducted the intervention.[30] An interesting finding was that while there had been no differences among consultants immediately following the intervention, over time statistically significant differences in evaluation developed along several dimensions. This, too, seemed to be a kind of "discrepancy" effect. That is, it was concluded that participants' expectations of positive outcomes following the team development experience perhaps favorably and uniformly biased their initial evaluations of the consultant and the intervention. Later, as expectations were unmet, or perhaps differentially fulfilled across groups, differences in evaluations among consultants appeared.

CONCLUDING COMMENTS

When programs of change or treatment are instituted, expectations for their effectiveness are very likely to be involved. First, there is the expectation of those whose behavior or well-being is to be affected by the institution of the new program. These include the workers, the patients, the pupils, or the research subjects who, by knowing that a new procedure is being tried out, "know" that the procedure may well have some effect on them, or it would not be worth anyone's time or effort. Second, there are the expectations of those who institute the program of change or treatment. These expectations can affect the response of those whose behavior is the target of change.

A major goal in the field of organization development is to improve organizational functioning—to implement interventions that favorably impact the ultimate input/output ratio of the organization. Pragmatically, there are neither the resources nor the time to attempt to change all ineffective behaviors. Rather, it becomes paramount to identify some limited number of behaviors that, if changed, will cause change in others. One should first change the behaviors that will cause the greatest positive change in the processes and states of the organization, thereby leading to the greatest improvements in output.[31] If expectations are a predictor of successful outcomes of an intervention, it may be appropriate for the consultant or facilitator to manipulate these probability beliefs in such a way as to maximize outcomes. However, recognizing that it is improbable that outcomes would exactly match expectations, the issue of discrepancy effects must be considered. The literature suggests that the consultant might prefer to establish high, but reasonably attainable, expectations among participants of a change program.

Success in an OD effort may be dependent upon the expectation that participation in such a program will lead to the goal of improving the organization and the relationship between achieving such a goal and rewards for the individual. In organizations characterized by poor climates, defensive behaviors and/or poor worker-management relations, employees may have low expectations about the ability of management to change in any positive, meaningful way. Such expectancy evaluations may make it difficult for the organization to change. If this is the case, and the research literature indicates some support for the possibility, then it seems critical for the consultant to spend a significant amount of time manipulating expectations upward to increase the probability of any success at all.

Information regarding the effect of participants' expectations on programs involving organizational change is of great importance to researchers and consultants. Determining the role of expectations in the process of improving organizations should be a major research objective. To meet this objective, we need (1) more use of expectation measures in our published research on organization development, and (2) more controlled research in both laboratory and field settings wherein expectations are explicitly manipulated.

Notes

1. Merton, R. K. "The Self-Fulfilling Prophecy." *Antioch Review,* 1948, vol. 8, pp. 193–210; *Social Theory and Social Structure,* New York: Free Press, 1957.
2. Darley, J. M., & Fazio, R. H. Expectancy Confirmation Processes Arising in the Social Interaction Sequence. *American Psychologist,* 1980, vol. 35, pp. 867–81.
3. Porter, L. W., & Lawler, E. E. *Managerial Attitudes and Performance.* Homewood, Ill.: Irwin, 1968; Tolman, E. C. *Purposive Behavior in Animals and Men.* New York: Century, 1932; Vroom, V. H. *Work and Motivation.* New York: Wiley, 1964.
4. Thibaut, J. W., & Kelley, H. H. *The Social Psychology of Groups.* New York: Wiley, 1959.

5. Helson, H. Adaptation-Level Theory. In S. Koch (ed.), *Psychology: A Study of a Science,* vol. 1. New York: McGraw-Hill, 1959.
6. Smith, P. C., Kendall, L. M., & Hulin, C. L. *The Measurement of Satisfaction in Work and Retirement.* Chicago: Rand McNally, 1969.
7. Allport, G. The Role Expectancy. In H. Cantril (ed.), *Tensions That Cause Wars.* Urbana, Ill.: University of Illinois, 1950, pp. 43–78; Jones, R. A. *Self-Fulfilling Prophecies: Social, Psychological, and Physiological Effects of Expectancies.* Hillsdale, N.J.: Erlbaum, 1977; Rosenthal, R., & Jacobson, L. *Pygmalion in the Classroom.* New York: Holt, Rinehart, & Winston, 1968; Rosenthal, R. & Rosnow, R. L. (eds.). *Artifact in Behavioral Research.* New York: Academic Press, 1969.
8. Rosenthal, R., & Jacobson, L. *Pygmalion in the Classroom.* New York: Holt, Rinehart, & Winston, 1968.
9. Darley, J. M., & Fazio, R. H. Expectancy Confirmation Processes Arising in the Social Interaction Sequence. *American Psychologist,* 1980, vol. 35, p. 867.
10. Burnham, J. R. *Effects of Experimenter's Expectancies on Children's Ability to Learn to Swim.* Unpublished Master's Thesis, Purdue University, 1968.
11. King, A. S. Self-Fulfilling Prophecies in Training the Hard Core: Supervisors' Expectations and the Underprivileged Workers' Performance. *Social Scientist Quarterly,* 1971, vol. 52, pp. 369–78.
12. Berlew, D. C., & Hall, D. T. The Socialization of Managers: Effects of Expectations on Performance. *Administrative Science Quarterly,* 1966, vol. 11, pp. 207–23.
13. Korman, A. Expectations as a Determinant of Performance. *Journal of Applied Psychology,* 1971, vol. 55, pp. 218–22.
14. Eden, D., & Shani, A. B. Pygmalion Goes to Boot Camp: Expectancy, Leadership, and Trainee Performance. Paper presented at the 87th Annual Convention of the American Psychological Association, New York, Sept. 1–5, 1979.
15. Borkovec, T. D. The Role of Expectancy and Physiological Feedback on Fear Research: A Review with Special Reference to Subject Characteristics. *Behavior Therapy,* 1973, vol. 4, pp. 491–505; Rosen, G. M. Subjects' Initial Therapeutic Expectancies and Subjects' Awareness of Therapeutic Goals in Systematic Desensitization: A Review. *Behavior Therapy,* 1976, vol. 7, pp. 14–27; Wilkins, W. Expectancy of Therapeutic Gain: An Empirical and Conceptual Critique. *Journal of Consulting and Clinical Psychology,* 1973, vol. 40, pp. 69–77.
16. Rosenthal, R. *Experimenter Effects in Behavioral Research.* New York: Irvington, 1976; Rosenthal, R. & Rosnow, R. L. (eds.). *Artifact in Behavioral Research.* New York: Academic Press, 1969.
17. Campbell, J. P., & Pritchard, R. D. Motivation Theory in Industrial and Organizational Psychology. In M. D. Dunnette (ed.), *Handbook of Industrial and Organizational Psychology.* Chicago: Rand McNally, 1976, pp. 63–130; Graen, G. Instrumentality Theory of Work Motivation: Some Experimental Results and Suggested Modifications. *Journal of Applied Psychology Monograph,* 1969, vol. 53, pp. 1–25; House, R. J. A Path-Goal Theory of Leader Effectiveness. *Administrative Science Quarterly,* 1971, vol. 16, pp. 321–38; Mitchell, T. R. Expectancy Models of Job Satisfaction, Occupational Preference and Effort: A Theoretical, Methodological, and Empirical Appraisal. *Psychological Bulletin,* 1974, vol. 81, pp. 1053–77.
18. Schwab, D. P., Olian-Gottlieb, J. D., & Heneman, H. G. Between-Subjects Expectancy Theory Research: A Statistical Review of Studies Predicting Effort and Performance. *Psychological Bulletin,* 1979, vol. 86, pp. 139–47.

19. Festinger, L. *A Theory of Cognitive Dissonance.* Evanston, Ill.: Row, Peterson, 1957; Aronson, E., & Carlsmith, J. M. Performance Expectancy as a Determinant of Actual Performance. *Administrative Science Quarterly,* 1966, vol. 11, pp. 207–23.

20. Cardozo, R. N. An Experimental Study of Consumer Effort, Expectation, and Satisfaction. *Journal of Marketing Research,* 1965, vol. 2, pp. 244–49.

21. McClelland, D. C., Atkinson, J. W., Clark, R. A., & Lowell, E. L. *The Achievement Motive.* New York: Appleton-Century-Crofts, 1953.

22. Festinger, L. *A Theory of Cognitive Dissonance.* Evanston, Ill.: Row, Peterson, 1957.

23. Anderson, R. E. Consumer Dissatisfaction: The Effect of Disconfirmed Expectancy on Perceived Product Performance. *Journal of Marketing Research,* 1973, vol. 10, pp. 38–44; Oliver, R. L. Effects of Expectation and Disconfirmation on Post-Exposure Product Evaluations: An Alternative Interpretation. *Journal of Applied Psychology,* 1977, vol. 62, pp. 480–87.

24. King, A. S. Expectation Effects in Organization Change. *Administrative Science Quarterly,* 1974, vol. 19, pp. 221–30.

25. Livingston, J. S. Pygmalion in Management. *Harvard Business Review,* 1969, vol. 47, pp. 81–89.

26. Berlew, D. C., & Hall, D. T. The Socialization of Managers: Effects of Expectation on Performance. *Administrative Science Quarterly,* 1966, vol. 11, pp. 207–23.

27. Crawford, K. S., Thomas, E. D., & Fink, J. J. Pygmalion at Sea: Improving the Work Effectiveness of Low Performers. *Journal of Applied Behavioral Science,* 1980, vol. 16, pp. 482–505.

28. Tolchinsky, P. D. *The Effects of Survey Feedback Interventions on Employee Attitudes, Expectations, and Performance: A Longitudinal Field Study.* Unpublished Doctoral Dissertation, Purdue University, 1978.

29. Woodman, R. W., & Sherwood, J. J. Effects of Team Development Intervention: A Field Experiment. *Journal of Applied Behavioral Science,* 1980, vol. 16, pp. 211–27.

30. Woodman, R. W. A Longitudinal Investigation of Consistency in Treatment Across Consultants. Paper presented at the Southern Management Association Annual Meeting, New Orleans, Nov. 19–22, 1980. (pp. 67–69 in the *Proceedings*).

31. Bowers, D. G., Franklin, J. L., & Pecorella, P. A. Matching Problems, Precursors, and Interventions in OD: A Systematic Approach. *Journal of Applied Behavioral Science,* 1975, vol. 11, pp. 391–409.

Index

Abilene Paradox, 100, 258
Absenteeism, 367
Academy of Management, 264, 276, 278, 404
Ackoff, R., 29, 32, 33
Action research, 7, 19, 21–23, 213–17, 267, 310, 340, 438–48
  definition of, 21, 439
  features of, 439–42
  model of, 442–46
  process complexities in, 446–48
  sociotechnical and socioclinical parallels of, 23, 24
  theory of, 444
  types of, 21
Action research system, 440
Adams, J. D., 263, 289–307, 292, 303
Affirmative action, 254, 262, 350–63
  alternative work schedules for, 361
  awareness workshops for, 356–68
  career development in, 361
  climate survey for, 355
  coalition building in, 361–62
  competence and, 356–57
  control of, 357–58
  differentiated competency based training modules for, 358–59
  model for total systems change in, 352–56
  performance appraisal and, 355–56
  recruitment programs in, 355
  sexuality and, 358
  spouse involvement in, 362
  supervisory relationships in, 355–60
  teams, 362
  top management task force, 354–55
  training programs, 356
Agrawal, B. C., 441
Ahmedabad, 273
Aires, E., 363
Aldeg, 271
Alderfer, C. P., 79, 442
Aldrich, H., 58
Allen, R. F., 162, 257
Allport, G., 478, 480
Alternative work schedules, 361
American Council on Education, 404
American Management Association (AMA), 172, 405

American Society for Training and Development (ASTD), 171, 172, 219, 278
Anderson, R. E., 482, 487
Angrist, S. S., 462, 476
Angyar, A., 23
Anxiety management training, 454
Aquarian Conspiracy, The, 251
Arden House, 21
Argyris, C., 7, 15, 18, 21, 81, 82, 115, 116, 117, 160, 442
Army Research Institute (ARI), 405
Aronson, E., 480, 487
Ashkenas, R. N., 218–30
Assertiveness training, 261
Assimilation-contrast theory, 481–82
Atkinson, J. W., 480, 481, 487
Atlas Steel, 228
Atomism, 34–35
AT&T, 309
Attitudes, employee, 44
Automation, 321
Averill, J. R., 453, 454, 459
Awareness workshops, 356–68

Bahnson, C. B., 452
Bainton, C. R., 452
Baker, E. L., 160
Baker, F., 463, 476
Balans chair, 317
Bales, R. F., 171
Ball, K. P., 455, 457
Balsch, D., 18
Bamforth, K. W., 233, 272
Barber, B., 33
Barnard, C. I., 154
Bartol, K. M., 360
Bartolome, F., 148, 363
Baumgartel, H., 20
Beck, A. C., Jr., 268
Beckhard, R., 15, 18, 21, 36, 43, 77, 115, 116, 206, 328
Beer, M., 77, 80, 81, 117
Behavioral event interviews, 406
Behavior modification, 455
Bell Canada, 228
Bell, C. H., Jr., 22, 43, 77, 116, 206, 234

Benne, K. D., 14, 21, 61, 170, 200–1, 267, 274, 275
Bennis, W. G., 9, 15, 24, 43, 61, 77, 82, 115, 170, 206
Berg, D. N., 79, 81, 83, 222, 474, 476
Berg, I., 222
Berg, P. O., 384
Berger, P. L., 32
Berlew, D. C., 479, 483, 486
Berkson, D., 452, 457
Berne, E., 172
Bernstein, J. E., 290, 298
Bethlehem Steel Corporation, 5, 7
Beyond Sex Roles, 358
Bigelow, T., 210, 273
Biofeedback, 454, 455
Bion, W. R., 17, 23, 24
Blackburn, H., 456
Blake, R. R., 15, 16, 17, 18, 19, 21, 24, 29, 116, 266, 268, 281–88, 285
Blansfield, M., 16
Block, P., 149, 150
Bloom, B. S., 169
Blumberg, A., 100, 104, 110, 172
Boje, D., 58
Bolles, R. N., 256
Borkovec, T. D., 479, 486
Boss, W., 99, 103
Bounded rationality, 153
Bowers, D. G., 22, 46, 104, 109, 268, 485, 487
Bowlby, J., 17
Bowling Green State University, 404
Boyatzis, R. E., 143, 145, 414–37, 430, 432, 433, 434, 435
Bradford, L., 14, 18, 21, 170, 267
Brandeis, L., 6
Braverman, H., 5
Breslow, L., 450
Brigham Young University, 404
Brooks, G. W., 451, 458
Brower, M., 83
Brown, L. D., 44, 45, 210, 273, 384, 441, 442
Brown-Radcliffe, A. R., 32
Buchanan, P., 16
Buell, P., 450
Burck, G., 15, 19
Burke, W. W., 18, 19, 43, 143, 145, 263, 274
Burnham, D. H., 433
Burnham, J. R., 479, 486
Burns, F., 412
Business planning process, 420
Buskirk, R. H., 256
Butler, A., 154
Butterfield, D. A., 360
Byrd, R. E., 132

Cammann, C., 467, 476
Campbell, D. T., 317
Campbell, J. P., 181, 480, 486
Cantor, N., 167
Capital investment analysis, 425
Caplan, R. D., 451, 452
Capra, F., 251
Cardozo, R. N., 480, 487
Career and life planning, 253–62, 306, 351, 361, 424, 433
  in OD interventions, 254, 258, 262
  program concepts and resources and, 256–57
  program critiques, 258–61
  two-day program design, 257–58, 259
Career development. *See* Career and life planning
Career management. *See* Career and life planning
Career pathing system, 422, 433
Carlsmith, J. M., 480, 487
Carroll, V., 451, 458
Cartwright, D., 14, 21
Case Institute of Technology, 15
Case Western Reserve University, 404
Cassens, F., 16
Catalyst, 126, 127–28
Cat in the Hat, The, 3–11
Center for Disease Control, 293, 295
Centrality of structure, 398
Certified Consultants International (CCI), 51
Change,
  definition of, 61
  interpersonal strategies for organizational, 132–36
  in transorganizational systems, 61
  normative character of, 31–32
  politics of, 87–88
  resistance to, 22
  strategic, 117, 189–91
  strategies of, 131–32
  use of power to, 86–97
  whole-system, 33, 58, 352–56
Change agent, 402–12
  relationship with client, 129–130, 389. *See also* Internal change agent *and* External change agent
Change programs,
  conceptualization, 462–64
  conditions for trial and sustained adoption of change, 467–70
  implementation of, 464–67
  intermediate goal attainment, 470–74
  measurement of, 462–75
  measures of program adoption and predictors of adoption, 468

member assessment questionnaire, 465
process measurements by program
 personnel in, 474–75
process measurements in evaluation
 research in, 475–76
Changing environment
 characteristics of, 58
Charters, W. E., 463, 476
Chein, I., 21
Chemical plant maintenance, 226
Chemical plant operations, 226
Cherns, A. B., 309, 441
Chicago and Northern Railroad, 206
Chin, R., 14, 61, 274, 275
Cholesterol level, 451, 455
Churchman, C. W., 153, 155
Cinderella Complex, 357
Claire, S., 329–39
Clapp, N., 149, 150
Clark, A. W., 448
Clark, P. A., 448
Clark, R. A., 480, 481, 487
Clarkson, W., 82
Climate survey, 355, 427, 428
Coaching, 181
Coch, L., 22, 45
Cockpit crises, 281–88
Cognitive dissonance/assimilation theory,
 480–81
Cole, R. E., 46, 83
Colflesh, L., 231–52
Collier, J., 22
Compensation and benefits system, 423, 424,
 435
Competency acquisition process, 434
Competency based training program, 412
Competency clusters, 406, 407–11
Compressed work week, 361
Computer-aided design and manufacturing
 (CAD/CAM), 233
 implementation of, 238–39
 weaknesses of, 235–36
Computer manufacturer, 226
Concession bargaining, 254
Conflict episodes, 274
Conflict management
 intergroup, 17, 266
 interpersonal, 266
Connecticut Interracial Commission, 13
Contingency theory, 267–72
 application, 274–76
 diffusion, 276–78
 integrative mechanisms of, 271
Contingencies,
 human need, 72
 technological, 70–71

Contracting, 349
Contrast theory, 481
Controlling, 418, 419, 423
Cook, S., 21
Cooke, R., 65
Cooper, C. L., 449–60, 450, 455, 459
Cooper, G. E., 282
Coordinating, 418, 419, 424–25
"Coping with Managerial Stress," 291, 292
Core group. *See* Task force
Corey, K., 61
Corey, S. M., 22, 23, 441
Corporate social responsibility, 351
Cramer, A., 10
Crawford, K. S., 483
Cross-functional coordinating process, 424
Crump, R. S., 286
CSC/Pacific, Inc., 169
Culbert, S. A., 132
Cullen, B. J., 405
Culture management. *See* Organizational
 culture
Cummings, T. G., 69–75, 70, 74, 220, 210,
 214, 273, 384
Cunningham, B., 441
Cyert, R. M., 95
Czackes, J. W., 451, 455, 458

D'Alonzo, C. A., 452
Darley, J. M., 479, 485, 486
Davis, L. E., 309
Davis, S., 18, 37, 82
Davis, S. M., 153, 161, 163
Dawber, T. R., 456, 460
Dawis, R. V., 450
Dayal, I., 116
DeBoard, R., 23
Decentralization, 8, 9
Deception, 94–96
Decision making,
 components, 365, 366–67
 consensus decision making, 372–79
  how to install, 378–79
  pros and cons of, 374–78
  rules of, 372–74
 effects on profit, 366
 good vs. bad, 366
 methods, 367–74
DeMeuse, K. P., 99, 109
Democracy,
 merger with techology, 4–11
Department of Defense, 483
Department of the Army, 403
Department of the Navy, 291
Detroit Edison Company, 20
Deutscher, I., 462, 476

Developmental assessment, 435
Developmental management programs,
  action plan for implementing, 182–93
  assessing management training needs for,
    184–86
  assessing organizational change needs for,
    186–89
  assessing organizational needs for, 184–89
  evaluation and follow-up for, 193
  implementing change strategies in, 189–92
  instructional program planning in, 189–91
  organizational and improvement planning
    in, 191–92
  redirecting management development goals
    in, 182–84
  versus management development
    programs, 181
Dewey, J., 14, 167
Diagnosis, 237
  data collection, 29
Dickens, F., 363
Dickens, J. B., 363
Dicks, H. V., 23
Dickson, W. J., 15
Directed thinking, 132
Discrepancy evaluation, 347
Division of labor, 4
Donnelly, J. H., Jr., 154
Drexler, J. A., 463, 476
Dreyfuss, F., 451, 455, 458
Driscoll, J. W., 46
Droege, E., 341
Drucker, P., 5, 6, 328
Duncan, R., 467, 476
Dunn, W. N., 383
Dunnette, M. D., 181
Dutton, J. M., 266, 271
Dweck, C. S., 132
Dyer, W. G., 99, 100, 103, 116, 117

Eaton, M. T., 452
Eden, D., 451, 458, 479
EEO, 351, 352
Egan, G., 171, 172
Eitner, S., 450
Emery Air Freight Company, 46
Emery, F. E., 214, 252, 272
Employee satisfaction. *See* Quality of work
  life
Encounter groups, 174, 261
Enelow, A. J., 455
Enterline, P. E., 452, 458
Epstein, E., 456, 460
Equal employment opportunity, 186–254, 262
Equilibrium, quasi-stationary, 35
Ergonomics, 5

Esso Standard Oil (Exxon), 15, 16, 19
EST, 261
Eustress, 453
Evans, P., 148, 363
Evered, R. D., 441
Executive profile, 340–49
Executive seminars, 181
Expectation effects, 359–60, 478–85
  assimilation-contrast theory of, 481–82
  cognitive dissonance/assimilation theory
    of, 480–81
  contrast theory of, 481
  definition of, 478
  discrepancy effects and, 480–82
  organizational change and, 482–83
  organization research focus of, 479
  outcomes of, 479–80
  theory of, 479–80
Experience and Learning, 167
Experiential learning, 7, 181
  cases in, 174
  definition of, 167
  exercises in, 174
  first wave: discovery and learning and, 170,
    171–72
  fundamental types of, 168–69
  generalist school of, 176
  objectives of, 169
  professionalism in, 175–76
  roots of, 167
  second wave: proliferation and elaboration
    and, 170, 172–75
  simulations of, 174
  specifics school of, 176
  third wave: segmentation and specification
    and, 171, 175–77
Experiential Learning and Change, 168, 176
Expository Model of Science (ExpM), 29–40
  characteristics of, 30
  definition of, 30
External change agent, 124, 220
Ezriel, H., 17

Facilitation, 176
Fazio, R. H., 478, 479, 485
Feaver, D. B., 286
Ferguson, M., 251, 252
Ferrier, S., 404
Festinger, L., 14, 21, 480, 487
File Fast Office Products Company, 220–21
Filley, A., 103
Financial performance analysis, 425
Financial resource allocation process, 422
Fink, J. J., 483
FIRO-B, 342
Fischer-Quigley, E., 289–307

Fisher, D., 454, 459
Flexibility, 176
Flexible working hours, 361
Flow chart, 389
Follett, M. P., 5, 14
Foltz, J., 29
Ford, G. A., 255–57
Ford, R., 309
Fordyce, J. K., 100, 116
Fort Ord, 403
Fortune 500, 341, 427
Foster, M., 441
Foushee, H. C., 282
Framingham Study, 456, 460
Francis, C., 208, 273
Franklin, J. L., 268
Freedman, M., 222
Freire, P., 443
French, J. R. P., 17, 21, 22, 45, 89, 451, 452
French, W. L., 12–27, 15, 22, 43, 77, 116, 206, 234
Freud, S., 167
Frew, D. R., 454
Friedlander, F., 44, 45, 210, 273, 384, 438, 441, 448
Friedman, M., 451, 453, 458, 459
Frohman, M. A., 267, 276
Fromm, E., 79
Fry, R. E., 115, 176, 433

Galbraith, J., 153
Gatekeeping, 136
General Mills, 18, 19
General Motors, 77, 82, 83
Geosource, Inc., 330, 331, 337
Gerhart, P., 438
Gestalt, 174
Gherman, E. M., 290
Gibb, J. R., 15, 170, 171, 267
Gibson, J. L., 154
Glaser, B., 38
Glaser, E., 219, 220
Glen, R., 220
Global matrix, 155
Goal setting, 198, 255, 274
Goleman, D., 405, 454
Golembiewski, R. T., 43, 99, 100, 103, 104, 108, 109, 110, 116, 172
Goodstein, L. D., 44, 263
Graen, G., 480, 486
Graphic Controls Corporation, 81, 82
Gricar, B., 64
Grid organization development, 261, 268, 281–88
Grid structure, 155
Grievance procedure, 424, 436

Griffin, R. W., 308–19
Group dynamics, 24, 201–2, 274
GrouP.S., 336
Guest, R., 220, 229
Gunther, B., 172
Guskin, A. E., 276
Gutting, G., 29

Hackman, J. R., 73, 105, 309, 311, 313, 315, 317, 323, 324, 431
Hagberg, J., 256
Haire, M., 15
Haldeman, J., 208, 273
Hall, D. T., 256, 479, 483, 486
Hall, Y., 452
Halo effect, 466
Hamilton, E. L., 22
Handbook of Industrial and Organizational Psychology, 77
Hanlon, M., 220
Harding, J., 21
Harkness, J., 382–401, 389
Harriman House, 17
Harris, R. T., 99, 109
Harrison, R., 103, 116
Harvard Business School, 356
Harvey, J. B., 29, 100, 103, 109, 257, 258
Harwood Manufacturing Corporation, 22, 246
Havelock, M., 276
Havelock, R. G., 124, 126, 129, 132, 276
Hayakawa, S. I., 33
Hegelian Inquiring System, 156–57. *See also* Matrix
Heinemann, A. L., 450
Helson, H., 478, 486
Henderson, J. B., 455
Heneman, H. G., 480, 486
Henley, N. M., 356
Herberg, F., 256, 309
Herbst, P. G., 273
Herman, S., 116
Herrmann Clark, D., 351
Hicks, C., 15
Hill, M., 276
Hillmar, E. D., 268
Holes, 396–97
Holman, M. G., 441
Holmes, D. S., 453, 454
Homans, G., 171, 268
Horizontal ambition, 10
Hornstein, H. A., 274
Horst, L. A., 276
Horwitz, M., 16
Hospital emergency room, 226
House, R. J., 480, 486

Houston, B. K., 453, 454
Howe, M., 44
Howe, R. J., 44
Huasser, D. L., 104
Huber, J., 276
Hulin, C. L., 478, 486
Human needs,
    optimizing, 72–73
Human process intervention stream, 383–400
Human Relations, 24
Human resource management, 404
Human resource system, 430–31
Human resource system audit, 425–30
Human Resources Information Systems, 325
Human subsystem, 234
Humble Oil and Refinery, 16
Human, M. M., 452, 458
Hunsaker, P. L., 123–37
Huse, E. F., 52, 116, 264, 309
Hypothesis confirmation, 479

ICAM Program (Integrated Computer-Aided
    Manufacturing), 233, 238, 239, 246
Idiographics, 36–37
Idle time program, 466
Industrial engineering, 4
Industrial Revolution, 44, 45
Information systems, 210
In-house training programs, 181
Inside change agent. *See* internal change
    agent
Institute for Social Research (ISR, University
    of Michigan), 7, 21, 124, 462, 464
Instrumented laboratory, 16
Insurance claims processing, 226
Interdepartmental coordinating process, 424
Intergroup concepts
    relations in, 16, 266
    research in, 17
Intermediate goals, 463, 470–74
Internal change agents, 19, 123–36, 190
    advantages and disadvantages of, 124–25
    definition of roles of, 124, 126–29
    success guidelines for, 125–26
International Associations of Quality Circles,
    219
Interpersonal conflict, 266
    diagnostic model, 268–69
Interpersonal skills, 16, 142
Interventions, 382–401, 477–85. *See also*
    Stream analysis
    categories of, 384
    cycles of, 399–400
    key change variables and, 384
    phases of, 398–99
    reasons for lack of success in, 384

Interviewing, 193, 269, 349
Intrinsic job factors, 450
Inventurers, 256
IRS, 292, 296
Ivancevich, J. M., 154
Izroeli, D. N., 96

Jackson, B., 363
Jackson, S. E., 104, 105
Jacobson, L., 359, 478, 479, 480
James, W., 167
Janis, I., 100
Japanese management, 10, 46, 81, 139, 207,
    233
Jaques, E., 17, 23
Jelinek, M., 256
Jerdee, T. H., 360
Jick, T. D., 218–30, 220, 222
Job analysis, 321–28, 404, 422, 436
    applications of, 325–26
    maintaining an OD perspective during,
        326–27
    process of, 323–26
    purpose of, 322–23
Job competency, 415
Job data base, 325
Job Descriptive Index (JDI), 105
Job design. *See* Work design
Job Diagnostic Survey (JDS), 105, 311, 324
Job enlargement, 309
Job enrichment, 309, 463
Job evaluation system. *See* job analysis
Job performance, 480
Job rotation, 309
Job satisfaction, 452–53, 455, 480
Job sharing, 361
Job Tension Scale, 105
Joint optimization, 7
Joint Working Party of the Royal College of
    Physicians of London and the British
    Cardiac Society, 456
Jones, J. E., 171, 463, 476
Jones, J. P., 15, 18, 19
Jones, R. A., 478, 486

Kahn, R. L., 104, 105, 234, 309
Kanter, R., 222, 223, 228
Kaplan, E. R., 441
Katz, D., 234
Katz, E., 276
Katz, R. L., 143
Kaufman, S., 309, 313
Kavanagh, M. J., 267
Kellerman, J. J., 451, 458
Kelley, G., 91
Kelley, H. H., 478, 485
Kellogg, M. S., 257

Kelly, J., 116
Kendall, L. M., 478, 480
Keys, A., 456, 460
Kiebert, C., 382–401, 389
Kiepper, A., 99
Kilmann, R. H., 31, 153
King, A. S., 479, 482, 483, 486
King, D., 209
Kingdom, D. R., 153
Kirn, A. G., 256
Kirn, M., 256
Kirshenbaum, H., 257
Kjelsberg, M., 452
Klemp, G. O., Jr., 405, 415, 422, 423, 424, 432
Knight, K., 152
Knowles, M. S., 433, 435
Kolb, D. A., 176, 433, 434, 435, 438
Kolb, H. D., 19
Kolodny, H. F., 153
Koontz, H., 181
Korenich, M., 116
Korman, A., 479, 486
Kornhauser, A., 457
Kotter, J. P., 430
Kozarevic, D., 456, 460
Krathwohl, D. R., 169
Kreitner, R., 46
Kreps, J., 351
Kritsikis, S. P., 450
Kroes, W. H., 450
Kubler-Ross, E., 256
Kudar-Richardson reliability estimates, 468
Kuhn, T., 29
Kuna, D. J., 454

Laboratory training, 13–19, 267
  survey feedback, 21
Landon, D., 82
Langer, E. J., 132
Lauber, J. K., 282
Lawler, E. E., 81, 82, 181, 220, 309, 313, 317, 463, 476, 478, 485
Law of the situation, 4
Lawrence, P. R., 153, 155, 161, 162, 163, 267, 270, 271
Lazarus, R., 453, 459
Leadership, 143–45
  considerations in effective, 284, 480
Leahy, S., 20
Learning Styles Inventory, 342
Leavitt, H. J., 266, 263
Leider, R., 256
Lewin, K., 7, 13, 14, 15, 21, 22, 23, 24, 35, 170, 171, 275, 448
Lewis, J. W., 116

L-groups, 171
Liberman, M. A., 175
Liebowitz, S. J., 99, 109
Life planning. *See* career and life planning
Likert, R., 5, 7, 15, 18, 19, 20, 21, 24, 82, 201–2, 212
Likert Scale, 20
Linkage mechanisms, 92
Lipman-Blumen, J., 363
Lippitt, G. L., 21, 38, 43, 116, 196–203, 201–2, 255, 256, 257
Lippitt, R., 14, 18, 21, 22, 23
Livingston, J. S., 141, 142, 483, 487
Locke, E. A., 5
Lockean Inquiring System, 156. *See also* Matrix
Lofquist, L. H., 450
Lorentz, E., 37
Lorsch, J. W., 153, 162, 267, 270, 271
Lowell, E. L., 480, 481, 487
Luckman, T., 32
Luft, J., 256
Luisada, A. A., 455, 460
Lundberg, C. C., 114–22
Luthans, F., 46

McBer and Company, 143, 145, 405, 406, 411
McCann, J., 65
McClelland, D. C., 433, 434, 435, 480, 481, 487
McGregor, D., 14, 15, 18, 19, 21, 81, 115, 212, 201–2
McKersie, R. B., 266
McLaughlin, J., 29
Maccoby, M., 205
Machiavelli, N., 87
Macy, B. A., 81
Maier, A. A., 170
Maier, N. R., 170, 171
Mainstreaming, 140
Malden Mills, 83
Malloy, E., 220
Malott, 21
Management,
  definition of, 141
  functions of, 418
  integrated model of, 426
Management and the Worker, 15
Management by objectives (MBO), 254, 258, 268, 356, 403
Management development program
  characteristics of, 182
  purpose of, 181
  versus developmental management
    programs, 181
  weaknesses of, 181

Management information system, 423, 424
Management subsystem, 234
Management systems diagnosis, 425–30
Management theory jungle, 181
Management Values Inventory (MVI), 44
Managerial competencies, 138–51, 185
    androgynous model of, 148–51
    Burke model of, 143, 145, 146–47
    Katz model of, 143
    McBer (Boyatzis) model of, 143–44, 145
    methodology for building models of,
        145–48
    organization development model of,
        145–46
Managerial Grid, 16, 17, 261
Managerial talent, 415–36
    competency clusters and, 416–17, 421
    competency model of, 415–17
    development and use of management
        competence and, 425–26
    effective performance and, 415–25
    linking competencies and job demands to,
        417–20
    links to the organizational environment
        with, 420–25
    management functions of, 418–20
Mandler, G., 453, 459
Mann, F. C., 7, 20, 267
Manpower planning process. *See* Personnel
    planning process
Mao Tse-tung, 275
March, J. G., 95
Marcson, S., 450
Marcus, L., 229
Margolis, B. L., 450
Margulies, N., 52, 115, 116, 231–52, 235, 252,
    384, 441
Market research, 425
Market strategy, 206
Marks, R. U., 452
Marks, S. E., 166–79, 168, 176
Marmot, M., 455, 457, 460
Marrow, A. J., 7, 14, 21, 22
Marshall, J., 450, 455, 459
Maselko, J., 7
Masia, B. B., 169
Maslach, C., 104, 105, 108, 109
Maslach Burnout Inventory (MBI), 105, 106,
    107, 108
Maslow, A. H., 5, 29, 37, 140, 256
Mason, B., Jr., 15
Matrix, 143, 152–65, 197
    culture and system support, 160–61
    definition, 154–55
    essence, 158–61

Hegelian Inquiring System, 153, 156–57,
    158, 160
inquiring systems for problem solving
    within, 155–58
Lockean Inquiring system, 153, 156, 157,
    158, 159, 160
Lockean IS vs. Hegelian IS, 157–61
reward systems, 160–61
simple vs. complex organizational
    problems in, 153–55
steps in moving from Lockean IS to
    Hegelian IS, 161–64
use of an ongoing dialectic, 155
Matsumoto, Y. S., 455
Mayer, M., 9
Mayo, E., 81
MBO. *See* Management by objectives
McDermott, L. C., 320–28
Measure of program activation, 463
Mechanism, assumption of, 34–35
Meditation, 454
Megatrends, 149
Melcher, R. D., 116
Mentoring, 435
Menzel, H., 176
Merton, R. K., 478
Meyer, E. C., 412
Michael, D. N., 81
Mietus, J., 448
Miles, M. B., 175
Miles, R., 64, 211
Miller, J., 32
Mills, T., 77, 79, 80, 81, 82, 222, 229, 234
Mindell, M., 44
Mintzberg, H., 142, 185, 312
Mintzberg, J., 96
Mirvis, P. H., 76–85, 81, 82, 83, 222, 461–76,
    463, 467, 474, 476
Mission statement, 198
MIT, 18, 46
Mitchell, T. R., 384, 480, 486
Mitroff, I. I., 153
Molloy, E. S., 70
Moreno, J. L., 171, 172
Morley, E., 356
Morris, W. C., 276
Motamedi, K., 57–68
Motivation, 206, 207, 418, 419, 423–24, 479
Mouton, J. S., 16, 17, 18, 19, 29, 116, 266,
    268, 281–88, 285
Mueller, E. F., 451, 458
Multicultural work environment, 351
Multidimensional structure, 155
Munzenrider, R., 108
Murphy, J. S., 365–80
Murray, G., 18

Muse, W. V., 309
Myers, 234

Nadler, D., 220, 406, 467, 476
NASA, 143, 145, 282
NTL Institute for Applied Behavioral
    Science, 7, 14, 404. *See also* National
    Training Laboratory
Naisbitt, J., 8, 149
National Commission for Productivity and
    Quality of Work Life, 79
National Institute of Health, 291, 292, 296, 298
National Training Laboratory (NTL), 14, 15,
    17, 21, 23, 171, 172, 176. *See also* NTL
    Institute for Applied Behavioral Science
Naval Air Systems Command, 291
Naval Aviation Executive Institute (NAEI),
    291, 292, 296
Naval Ships Research and Development
    Center, 296
Neurolinguistic programming, 35
New Britain Workshops (1946), 13, 14
New Rules, 140
Nomikos, M., 453, 459
Northfield Experiment, 23
Notion of purposiveness in man, 17
Notz, W., 210, 273

Objectives, 199. *See also* Mission statement
    and Goal setting
Occupational stress, 450–57. *See also* stress
    management
    coping with stress, 452–55
        cognitive coping strategies, 453–54
        social support groups, 453, 455
        tension-reducing/relaxation
            techniques, 453, 454–55
    coronary heart disease (CHD), 450–52,
        455, 456
    definition, 450
    preventative approaches to health-related
        behaviors and CHD, 455–57
OD Network, 278, 404
Oldham, G. R., 73, 105, 313, 315, 323, 431
Olian-Gottlieb, J. D., 480, 486
Oliver, R. L., 482, 487
Olson, R., 333
Opton, E., 453, 459
O'Reilly, C. A., III, 105
Organizational awareness, 185
Organizational climate. *See* organizational
    culture
Organizational climate appraisal, 187
Organizational culture, 117, 153, 160–64, 186,
    188, 257, 331, 420–22, 422–23, 423, 424,
    427, 474

Organizational design. *See* organizational
    structure
Organizational Development Systems, Inc.,
    331
Organizational effectiveness, 402–12, 463
    competency based model, 405–12
        stages of, 405–6
        uses of, 406–12
    competency based training program, 412
    conception of, 403
    consultant characteristics of, 405
    consultant course in, 403–4
    consultant success of, 404–5
    organization development and, 403
Organizational Effectiveness Center and
    School (OECS), 402, 405, 406, 411
Organizational Effectiveness Consultant
    Course (OECC), 403–4
Organizational Effectiveness Consultants
    (OEC's), 402, 403, 413
Organizational environment, 420–25
    controlling function elements of, 423
    coordinating function elements of, 424–25
    external, 420
    internal, 420
    motivating function elements of, 423–24
    organizing function elements of, 422–23
    planning function elements of, 420–22
Organizational rating assessment, 186, 188–89
Organizational structure, 206, 210, 422
Organization Development. *See also* Change
    approaches to, 266–78
    as an applied science, 32–33, 45, 50
    as an artificial system, 32–33
    as a scientific revolution, 29
    as a social science, 33–34
    definition of, 4, 43, 77, 206, 326
    development group, 18
    differences from QWL, 80–83
    Expository Model of Science, 38
    first uses of the term, 18–19
    future of, 10
    history of, 6, 13–24
    in crisis situations, 281–88
    interventions, 383–89
    methodology, 36–37
    on-the-job application of, 16
    organizational effectiveness of, 403
    phases of, 198
    professionalism in, 50, 52, 53
    program evaluation, 461–75
    relationship to ExpM, 29–40
    role in the paradigm shift, 29
    role of personnel and industrial relations,
        19
    technological change, 248–51, 317–18

Organization Development *continued*
  top management involvement in, 16, 190,
    273, 379
  values, 42–47
  with reference to QWL, 77–84, 205–6, 214
Organization development competencies, 3,
  51, 52, 53–55
Organization performance,
  definition of, 184
"Organizations as Phrog Farms," 257, 258
Organization theory, 67
Organizing, 418, 419, 422–23
Ornstein, R. E., 454
Outside change agent. *See* External change
  agent

Participative management, 4, 10, 15, 18, 46,
  47, 115, 283, 471–74
Partin, J. J., 52
Pasmore, W. A., 204–17, 208, 209, 238–48,
  249, 264–80, 267, 273, 274, 441, 448
Passages: Predictable Crises of Adult Life,
  257
Patel, C., 453
Patient service, 226
Patten, T. H., Jr., 36, 115, 116, 253–63
Paul, O. A., 452
Pecorella, P. A., 485, 487
Pell, S., 452
Pepperdine University, 404
Percept language, 35
Performance appraisal, 355–56, 432
  business unit review process, 423
  individual, 423
  product unit review process, 423
Performance indicators, 406, 407–11
Performance review. *See* performance
  appraisal
Perls, F., 172
Permanent part-time work, 361
Personal Assessment Development System
  (PADS), 341–49
  consultant guidelines, 348–49
  consultant observations, 349
  executive profile interview content in, 345
  hypothesis, 341
  process, 341–48
Personal growth, 169–70
Person-environment fit, 450
Personnel planning process, 422, 436
Personnel specialists, 321
PERT, 316
Peter, H., 15
Peterson, D. R., 452
Pettigrew, A. M., 87, 89, 90, 92
Pfeiffer, J. W., 51, 171

Phody, L. R., 31
Physical environment intervention stream,
  386
Pincherle, G., 452
Pines, A., 108
Pines, M., 295
Pirc, B., 456, 460
Planned change. *See* Change
Plovnick, M. S., 115
Policy science, 67
Porras, J. I., 99, 109, 382–401, 384, 389
Porter, L. W., 11, 317, 478, 485
Power, 87–97, 275, 367
  bases, 88–91
  related behaviors, 94–95
  role of deception, 94–96
  strategies, 88, 91–94
Pratchen, M., 105
Pritchard, R. D., 480, 486
Problem solving, 6, 171
Process, 22
Process helper, 127, 129
Process consultation, 267, 349
Productivity, 4, 45, 46, 47, 70, 74, 139, 208,
  209, 210, 213, 219, 223, 224, 232, 233–34,
  235, 297, 320, 321, 324, 327, 329, 330,
  366
Product life cycle, 239–40
Product testing, 425
Proehl, C. W., Jr., 99
Professor Higgins, 478
Program for Specialists in Organization
  Training and Development (PSOTD), 18
Program management, 155
Programmed instruction, 181
Project management, 155, 197
Project teams, 270
Psychodrama, 14
Psychotherapy, 479
Public relations program, 424
Pygmalion, 478
Pygmalion effects, 483

Quality circles, 4, 143, 222, 227, 329–39. *See
  also* Task force
  benefits on an OD approach to, 337–39
  definition of, 330
  design of, 334–37
  steering committees, 325
  why they fail, 331–34
Quality of work life (QWL), 10, 18, 70, 74,
  75, 76, 205–17, 226, 219, 254, 273, 351,
  443, 463, 470, 472
  action research model, 213–17
  avoiding pitfalls of employee involvement
    in, 225–29

definition of, 77, 205–6
differences from OD, 80–83
focus of, 208–9
from a manager's perspective, 220–29
measurement of, 83
movement in, 6
need of worker collaboration in, 209,
    211–12, 212–13, 226, 227
pitfalls of employee involvement in, 220–25
principles of, 206–12
program of core group, 213–14, 215–16
successful programs, 206, 220
with reference to OD, 77–84, 205–6, 214
Quinn, R. P., 450

Radke, M., 14, 23
Raia, A. P., 3, 115, 116, 235, 252, 384, 441
RAMCO, 221, 224–25
Randall, L., 82
Rankin, N., 453, 459
Rapaport, R. N., 441
Rational-empirical support base, 275
Raven, B. H., 89, 100
Recruitment programs, 355
Reed, T. W., 333
Republic Aviation, 16
Research Center for Group Dynamics (MIT),
    13, 14, 20, 21, 22, 23, 24
Research projects, 93
Resource linker, 127, 128
Retreats, 16
Review of Empirical and Conceptual
    Literature on Implementation of
    Computer Technology, 233
Reward system, 4, 210
Rice, A. K., 233, 272, 273
Richards, R. A., 35
Richetto, G., 341
Richman, T., 8
Rickman, J., 23
Right brain theory, 35
Ringness, T. A., 169
Risky shift phenomenon, 376
Robbins, S. P., 96
Roberts, K., 105
Robins, J., 219, 229, 454, 459
Roethlisberger, F. J., 15, 115
Rogers, B., 404
Rogers, C., 15, 171, 172
Rokeach, M., 43
Role ambiguity, 450
Role conflict, 450, 451
Role playing, 171
Romac Industries, 317
Rosen, B., 360
Rosen, G. M., 479, 486

Rosenman, R. H., 451, 453, 458, 459
Rosenthal, R., 359, 441, 478, 479, 486
Roshomon, 475
Rosnow, R. L., 441, 478, 479, 486
Rosow, J. M., 44
Rossini, L. A., 405
Rotational assignments, 181
Rubin, I., 115
Ruh, R.H., 105
Russek, H. I., 450

Saab-Scania, 234
Sabotage, 367, 368
Salipante, P., 210, 273
Sanford, E., 441
Sargent, A. G., 138–51, 149, 358, 350–64, 364
Sashkin, M., 23, 24, 267, 276
Scanlon, J., 46
Scanlon Plan. *See* Scanlon System
Scanlon System, 46
Schaalman, M. L., 432
Schaffer, R., 228
Schein, E., 116, 170, 267
Schein, V. E., 86–97, 93, 94
Schlesinger, L., 220, 227
Schmidt, W. H., 32, 43
Schmithorst, J., 289–307
Schmuck, R. A., 43
Schneier, C., 356
Schulberg, H. C., 463, 476
Schutz, W. C., 171, 172
Schwab, D. P., 480, 486
Schwab, R., 20
Scientific management, 6
Scientific Methods, Inc., 282
Scriven, M., 474, 476
Seashore, S. E., 22, 463, 476
Selection and promotion system, 422, 436,
    430–32
Self-confrontation exercises, 255
Self-fulfilling prophecy, 478
Sells, S. B., 453
Seltzer, C. C., 456, 460
Selye, H., 453
Senge, P. M., 144
Sensitivity training, 174, 261
Serum uric acid, 451
Seuss, Dr., 3–11
Shani, A., 208, 273, 438–48, 441, 448, 479
Shaw, George Bernard, 478
Sheehy, G., 256
Shepard, H., 15, 16, 17, 18, 19, 21, 23, 52,
    253, 255, 256, 257, 266, 441
Shepard, J. M., 450
Shepard, K. O., 3
Sherif, C., 16

Sherif, M., 16, 17
Sherwood, J. J., 116, 249, 267, 484, 487
Shirom, A., 451
Silverweig, S., 162
Simon, H. A., 32, 39, 153
Simpson, E. J., 169
Simulations, 174
Sink, D., 99
Situation redefinition, 453
Skinnerian psychology, 38
Situational management, 139
Slevin, D. P., 31
Sloan School of Management (MIT), 14
Smith, F., 77, 78, 84
Smith, P. B., 14
Smith, P. C., 478, 486
Sociodrama, 17
Sociotechnical approach, 23, 24
Sociotechnical systems, 74, 209, 210, 232–51,
    272–74
  application of, 274–76
  data/diagnosis process in, 237
  definition of, 234–35
  diffusion of, 276–78
  fit of, 272, 274
  history of, 234
  implementation guidelines for, 246–48
  implementation with computer technology,
    238–39
  integration with systems development
    planning model, 241–45
  management role in, 235
  model of, 237–38
  skills needed to facilitate, 215
  strength of, 234
  team approach to, 245–46
  theory of, 236–37
Sofer, C., 23
Solem, A. R., 170
Solution giver, 127, 128
Spain, D. M., 452
Spearman-Brown corrections, 467, 468
Spehn, M. R., 402–13
Spencer, L. M., Jr., 452, 457, 456, 460
Srivastva, S., 74, 210, 214, 273
Stamler, J., 452, 456, 457, 460
Stanley, J. C., 317
State Department, 405
Steel-collar worker, 254
Steele, F., 18
Steering committees, 325
Stein, B., 222, 223, 228
Stewart, A. J., 433, 435
Stock ownership, 317
Storey, R., 271
Strategic planning, 67, 420

Strauss, A., 38
Strauss, G., 96
Stream analysis, 383, 384–400
  case study, 389–99
  centrality of structure, 397–98
  holes, 396–97
  stream theory, 384–89
Strength Development Inventory, 342
Stress management, 289–307. *See also*
    Occupational stress
  consequences of work-related stress, 290
  criteria for choosing a program consultant,
    305–6
  experience of stress, 294
  health and risk coordinates, 293, 295
  individual techniques, 293
  measuring change in the individual,
    298–304
  organizational stress, 295–96
  program benefits, 303–4
  program design, 292–96
  program evaluation, 296–97
  program implications for training and
    development staffs, 304–7
  program objectives, 296–97
  programs in federal agencies, 289–307
Structure interventions stream, 383–400
Structured interview, 186
Succession planning, 422, 433
Suinn, R. M., 454, 459
Support groups, 136
Survey feedback, 7, 13, 19–21, 65, 104,
    186–89, 193, 199, 209, 212, 216, 237, 267,
    403, 467, 471. *See also* Action research
  link with laboratory training, 21
Survey-guided development, 268
Survey Research Center (SRC, University of
    Michigan), 19, 20, 21, 23
Susman, G. I., 441
Swartz, B., 20
Swierczek, F. N., 383
Syme, S. L., 452, 458
System 1, 212
System 4, 7, 212, 268
Systematic assessment, 425
Systems,
  change, 35
  closed, 6
  dynamic, 95, 96
  open, 6, 8, 58
  static, 95
Systems development planning model, 239–41
  integration with sociotechnical systems,
    241–45
Systems theory
  link with organization development, 17

Taber, T., 65
Tannenbaum, R., 37, 82
Target group, 129
Task expertise, 176
Task force, 191, 197–203, 270, 466
  chairperson for, 200
  characteristics of, 197–98, 203
  facilitator in, 200
  goals of, 198
  ideal size of, 198
  members of, 200
  mission statement of, 198
  objectives of, 199
  organization of, 199–201
  productivity of, 201
  problems of, 202
  reasons for, 197
  recorder/reporter in, 200
  resource person in, 200
  responsibilities of, 198–99
  team building in, 201–2
  unproductive, 201–2
Task redesign, 308–18, 327. *See also* Work
  redesign
  cost/benefit analysis of proposed change,
    313–15
  definition of, 309
  development of the implementation
    strategy of, 315–16
  diagnosis of the work system and context
    of, 311–13
  evaluation of the intervention of, 316–17
  go/no-go decisions in, 315
  implementation of, 316
  integrative framework for implementation
    of, 310–17
  organization development and, 317–18
  recognizing the need for change in, 310–11
  selection of the intervention for, 311
  supplements to the intervention for, 316
Tavistock Institute, 6, 13, 17, 23, 24, 234, 272
Tavistock Clinic. *See* Tavistock Institute
Taylor, F., 4–10
Taylor, J. C., 273, 309
Teaching-Learning Process, The, 167
Team building, 176, 201–2, 261, 393, 463
  approaches to, 116
  commonalities in approaches to, 116
  conditions of disagreement vs. agreement in
    small groups in, 100–4
  critique of contemporary, 116–17
  designs, 98–111
  diagnosis, 100, 104, 109, 110
  diagnostic interviews, 100, 102
  differences in psychological burnout by
    team members in, 104–8

  history of, 115–16
  instrumentation for diagnosis for, 100, 102,
    108–11
  microinterventions and, 114, 117–21
Team development. *See* Team building
Technical interdependence, 70
Technical uncertainty, 70
"Technique for the Measurement of
    Attitudes," 20
Technological change, 232–51
  organization development and, 248–51
  team approach and, 245–46
Technological determinism, 236
Techological subsystem, 234
Technology,
  optimizing, 71
Technology intervention stream, 383–400
Tethune, W. B., 452, 459
Textile manufacturer 226
T-groups, 7, 13–15, 115, 171, 174
Theory of intervention, 7
Theory X and Theory Y, 212
Therapy, 170
Third party consultation, 266–70
  application of, 274–76
  diffusion of, 276–78
Thibaut, J. W., 478, 485
Third party feedback system, 340
Third Wave, The, 249, 323, 320
Thomas, E. D., 483
Thomas, J. M., 116
Thompson, J. D., 252, 272
Thompson, J. T., 340–49
Thorsrud, E., 234
Threat-arousal-threat spiral, 454
Toffler, A., 170, 249, 323
Tolchinsky, P. D., 477–88, 483, 484, 487
Toombs, F., 15
Torbert, W., 38, 176
Tosi, H., 271
Traditional teaching method, 167
Training and development system, 169,
    423–24, 433–34
Transactional analysis (TA), 255, 261
Transcendental meditation (TM), 454
Transorganizational development, 58
  definition of, 62
  processes in, 63–66
  purposes of, 62–63
Transorganizational systems, 58–61
  definition of, 58
  dimensions of, 59
  types of, 59–61
Tremont Hotel, 22
Trends, 7, 139, 209, 210, 224, 261–62, 278,
    317–18, 320, 321, 328

androgyny, 148–51, 358–59
high tech development, 8, 233, 249–51, 254
information-based society, 8
management issues for the 1980s, 140
value shifts, 140–45
Trist, E., 6, 16, 23, 24, 65, 214, 233, 252, 267, 272, 273
Truskie, S. D., 180–94
TUF-RUB, 221–22, 225, 228
Tupper, C. J., 451
Turner, R., 455, 457
Turning Point, The, 251
Turnover, 367, 368, 426, 470

Unfreezing,
    model of, 35
Union Carbide, 15, 18, 19
University Associates, 171, 174, 404
University of Michigan Institute of Social Research, 44
University of Southern California, 227

Vaill, P. B., 28–41, 31, 36, 51
Value clarification, 257, 258
Values,
    definition of, 43
    freedom vs. constraint of, 42–43, 44
Value systems,
    definition of, 43
van Beinum, H., 80
Varney, G. H., 49–56, 404
Van de Ven, A., 64
Vertical/horizontal integration, 206
Visuo-motor behavior rehearsal, 454
Volvo, 234
von Bertalanffy, 23
Vroom, V., 471, 476

Walker, J. L., 256
Wallace, J., 52
Walsh, J., 65
Walter, G. A., 166–79, 168, 176
Walton, R. E., 82, 205, 211, 219, 220, 222, 223, 227, 229, 266, 267, 268, 269, 271, 273
Walters, J., 273
Wardell, W. I., 452
Watson, D. L., 453, 459
Weick, K. E., 181
Weil, R., 100, 116
Weiler, N. W., 255, 256
Weir, John, 35
Weir, Joyce, 35
Weisbord, M. R., 2–11, 36, 44, 45, 78

Weiss, C. H., 464, 476
Weldon Manufacturing Company, 22
Welford, A. T., 453, 459
Western Training Laboratory (UCLA), 14
West Germany, 223
Westley, W., 79, 230
Wexler, J., 329–39
Whetten, D. A., 58
White, J. D., 295
White, J. K., 105
White, M. D., 282, 285
White, S. E., 384
WHO European Collaborative Group, 456, 460
Whyte, W. F., 22, 37, 115
Wilberwasser, S., 451, 458
Wiley, M., 37
Wilkins, A., 99, 109
Wilkins, R., 362
Wilkins, W., 479, 486
Williams, T., 63, 64
Williamson, S. A., 432
Wilson, E. A., 32
Winkelstein, W. J., 455, 460
Winter, D. G., 435, 437
Woodman, R. W., 116, 308–19, 309, 484, 489
Woodward, J., 252
Work design, 4, 23, 24, 209, 212, 213, 266, 308–18, 422, 431
    compromise in, 75
    contingencies affecting, 70–73
    overdesigned, 72
    roadblocks in, 211, 212
    types of, 71–73
    underdesigned, 72
Work groups,
    self-regulating, 72
Work overload, 450–451
Work redesign. *See* work design
Work Redesign, 323
Work-related stress, 290
Work simplification, 309
Work slowdowns, 367, 368

Yalom, I. D., 175
Yankelovich, D., 140
Yetton, P., 471, 476
Yoga, 454

Zaltman, G., 467, 476
Zautra, A., 309
Zawacki, R. A., 234
Zohman, B. L., 450
Zwerman, W. L., 252